THE
HISTORY OF ENGLAND,

FROM THE ACCESSION OF JAMES II.

BY

THOMAS BABINGTON MACAULAY.

IN FIVE VOLUMES.

VOLUME III.

A. L. BURT COMPANY, Publishers
52-58 Duane Street, New York

CONTENTS OF VOL. III.

CHAPTER XI.

	PAGE
William and Mary proclaimed in London	1
Rejoicings throughout England; Rejoicings in Holland	2
Discontent of the Clergy and of the Army	3
Reaction of Public Feeling	4
Temper of the Tories	5
Temper of the Whigs	8
Ministerial Arrangements	10
William his own Minister for Foreign Affairs	11
Danby	12
Halifax	13
Nottingham	14
Shrewsbury; The Board of Admiralty	15
The Board of Treasury; The Great Seal	16
The Judges	17
The Household	18
Subordinate Appointments	20
The Convention turned into a Parliament	21
The Members of the two Houses required to take the Oaths	25
Questions relating to the Revenue	26
Abolition of the Hearth Money	28
Repayment of the Expenses of the United Provinces; Mutiny at Ipswich	29
The first Mutiny Bill	35
Suspension of the Habeas Corpus Act	37
Unpopularity of William	38
Popularity of Mary	41
The Court Removed from Whitehall to Hampton Court	43
The Court at Kensington	45
William's foreign Favorites	46
General Maladministration	49
Dissensions Among Men in Office	49
Department of Foreign Affairs	54
Religious Disputes	55
The High Church Party	56
The Low Church Party	57
William's Views concerning Ecclesiastical Polity; Burnet, Bishop of Salisbury	59
Nottingham's Views concerning Ecclesiastical Polity	62
The Toleration Bill	64
The Comprehension Bill	70
The Bill for settling the Oaths of Allegiance and Supremacy	78
The Bill for settling the Coronation Oath	91
The Coronation	93
Promotions	95
The Coalition against France; The Devastation of the Palatinate	96
War declared against France	100

CHAPTER XII.

State of Ireland at the Time of the Revolution; the Civil Power in the hands of the Roman Catholics	102
The Military Power in the hands of the Roman Catholics	103

CONTENTS.

	PAGE.
Mutual Enmity between the Englishry and the Irishry	104
Panic among the Englishry	105
History of the town of Kenmare	106
Enniskillen	110
Londonderry	111
Closing of the Gates of Londonderry	113
Mountjoy sent to pacify Ulster	115
William opens a Negotiation with Tyrconnel	117
The Temples consulted	118
Richard Hamilton sent to Ireland on his Parole	119
Tyrconnel sends Mountjoy and Rice to France; Tyrconnel calls the Irish People to arms	121
Devastation of the Country	122
The Protestants in the South unable to resist	126
Enniskillen and Londonderry hold out; Richard Hamilton marches into Ulster with an Army	127
James determines to go to Ireland	128
Assistance furnished by Lewis to James	129
Choice of a French Ambassador to accompany James; The Count of Avaux	131
James lands at Kinsale; James enters Cork	133
Journey of James from Cork to Dublin	135
Discontent in England	137
Factions at Dublin Castle	138
James determines to go to Ulster; Journey of James to Ulster	143
The Fall of Londonderry expected	147
Succors arrive from England; Treachery of Lundy; The Inhabitants of Londonderry resolve to defend themselves	148
Their Character	150
Londonderry besieged	154
The Siege turned into a Blockade	156
Naval Skirmish in Bantry Bay	157
A Parliament summoned by James sits at Dublin	158
A Toleration Act passed	163
Acts passed for the Confiscation of the Property of Protestants	163
Issue of Base Money	168
The Great Act of Attainder	169
James prorogues his Parliament	172
Persecution of the Protestants in Ireland	173
Effect produced in England by the News from Ireland	175
Actions of the Enniskilleners	178
Distress of Londonderry	179
Expedition under Kirke arrives in Lough Foyle; Cruelty of Rosen	180
The Famine in Londonderry extreme	182
Attack on the Boom	185
The Siege of Londonderry raised	186
Operations against the Enniskilleners	189
Battle of Newton Butler	191
Consternation of the Irish	192

CHAPTER XIII.

The Revolution more violent in Scotland than in England	193
Election for the Convention; Rabbling of the Episcopal Clergy	194
State of Edinburgh	198
The Question of an Union between England and Scotland raised	199
Wish of the English Low Churchmen to preserve Episcopacy in Scotland	203
Opinions of William about Church Government in Scotland	203
Comparative Strength of Religious Parties in Scotland	205
Letter from William to the Scotch Convention; William's Instructions to his Agents in Scotland	206
The Dalrymples	207
Melville	209
James's Agents in Scotland; Dundee; Balcarras	210
Meeting of the Convention	212
Hamilton elected President	214
Committee of Elections; Edinburgh Castle summoned	215
Dundee threatened by the Convenanters	216
Letter from James to the Convention	217

CONTENTS.

	PAGE
Effect of James's Letter	219
Flight of Dundee	220
Tumultuous Sitting of the Convention	221
A Committee appointed to frame a Plan of Government	222
Resolutions proposed by the Committee	224
William and Mary proclaimed; The Claim of Right; Abolition of the Episcopacy	225
Torture	227
William and Mary accept the Crown of Scotland	227
Discontent of the Convenanters	229
Ministerial Arrangements in Scotland; Hamilton; Crawford	230
The Dalrymples; Lockhart; Montgomery; Melville	231
Carstairs; The Club formed; Annandale; Ross	232
Hume; Fletcher of Saltoun	233
War breaks out in the Highlands; State of the Highlands	234
Peculiar nature of Jacobitism in the Highlands	236
Jealousy of the Ascendency of the Campbells	246
The Stewarts and Macnaghtens; The Macleans	247
The Camerons, Lochiel	250
The Macdonalds	251
Feud between the Macdonalds and Mackintoshes; Inverness	253
Inverness threatened by Macdonald of Keppoch	254
Dundee appears in Keppoch's Camp	256
Insurrection of the Clans hostile to the Campbells	258
Tarbet's Advice to the Government	259
Indecisive Campaign in the Highlands	261
Military Character of the Highlanders	262
Quarrels in the Highland Army	263
Dundee applies to James for assistance; The War in the Highlands suspended	265
Scruples of the Covenanters about taking Arms for King William	269
The Cameronian Regiment raised	269
Edinburgh Castle surrenders	270
Session of Parliament at Edinburgh; Ascendency of the Club	272
Troubles in Athol	273
The war breaks out again in the Highlands	276
Death of Dundee	278
Retreat of Mackay	285
Effect of the battle of Killiecrankie; The Scottish Parliament adjourned	285
The Highland Army reinforced	287
Skirmish at Saint Johnston's	290
Disorders in the Highland Army	292
Mackay's Advice disregarded by the Scotch Ministers; The Cameronians stationed at Dunkeld	292
The Highlanders attack the Cameronians and are repulsed	293
Dissolution of the Highland Army	295
Intrigues of the Club; State of the Lowlands	296
	297

CHAPTER XIV.

Disputes in the English Parliament; The Attainder of Russell reversed	298
Other Attainders reversed; Case of Samuel Johnson	300
Case of Devonshire; Case of Oates	301
Bill of Rights	309
Disputes about a Bill of Indemnity	313
Last Days of Jeffreys	314
The Whigs dissatisfied with the King	317
Intemperance of Howe; Attack on Caermarthen	319
Attack on Halifax	320
Preparations for a Campaign in Ireland	323
Schomberg	324
Recess of the Parliament; State of Ireland; Advice of Avaux	326
Dismission of Melfort; Schomberg lands in Ulster	330
Carrickfergus taken; Schomberg advances into Leinster	331
The English and Irish Armies encamp near each other; Schomberg declines a Battle	333
Frauds of the English Commissariat	334
Conspiracy among the French Troops in the English Service	335
Pestilence in the English Army	335
The English and Irish Armies go into Winter Quarters	337
Various Opinions about Schomberg's Conduct	338
Maritime Affairs	339

CONTENTS.

	PAGE
Maladministration of Torrington	340
Continental Affairs	341
Skirmish at Walcourt; Imputations thrown on Marlborough	343
Pope Innocent XI. succeeded by Alexander VIII.	345
The High Church Clergy divided on the Subject of the Oaths	346
Arguments for taking the Oaths	347
Arguments against taking the Oaths	349
A great Majority of the Clergy take the Oaths	354
The Nonjurors: Ken	356
Leslie; Sherlock	358
Hickes	359
Collier	360
Dodwell	361
Kettlewell; Fitzwilliam; General Character of the Nonjuring Clergy	363
The Plan of Comprehension; Tillotson	367
An Ecclesiastical Commission issued	368
Proceedings of the Commission	369
The Convocation of the Province of Canterbury summoned: Temper of the Clergy	373
The Clergy ill-affected towards the King	374
The Clergy exasperated against the Dissenters by the Proceedings of the Scotch Presbyterians	378
Constitution of the Convocation	379
Election of Members of Convocation	379
Ecclesiastical Preferments bestowed	380
Compton discontented	381
The Convocation meets	382
The High Churchmen a Majority of the Lower House of Convocation	383
Difference between the Two Houses of Convocation	384
The Lower House of Convocation proves unmanageable	385
The Convocation prorogued	386

CHAPTER XV.

The Parliament meets; Retirement of Halifax	388
Supplies voted; the Bill of Rights passed	389
Inquiry into Naval Abuses	391
Inquiry into the Conduct of the Irish War	392
Reception of Walker in England	393
Edmund Ludlow	394
Violence of the Whigs	397
Impeachments	398
Committee of Murder	399
Malevolence of John Hampden	400
1690. The Corporation Bill	403
Debates on the Indemnity Bill	407
Case of Sir Robert Sawyer	408
The King purposes to retire to Holland	412
He is induced to change his intention; the Whigs oppose his going to Ireland; He prorogues the Parliament	414
Joy of the Tories	415
Dissolution and General Election	416
Changes in the Executive Departments	418
Caermarthen then Chief Minister	419
Sir John Lowther	420
Rise and Progress of Parliamentary Corruption in England	421
Sir John Trevor	426
Godolphin retires	427
Changes at the Admiralty	427
Changes in the Commissions of Lieutenancy	428
Temper of the Whigs; Dealings of some Whigs with Saint Germains; Shrewsbury, Ferguson	430
Hopes of the Jacobites	431
Meeting of the New Parliament; Settlement of the Revenue	432
Provision for the Princess of Denmark	435
Bill declaring the Acts of the Preceding Parliament valid	440
Debate on the Changes in the Lieutenancy of London	442
Abjuration Bill	443
Act of Grace	445

CONTENTS.

	PAGE
The Parliament prorogued; Preparations for the First War	449
Administration of James at Dublin	450
An Auxiliary Force sent from France to Ireland	452
Plan of the English Jacobites; Clarendon, Aylesbury, Dartmouth	454
Penn	455
Preston	456
The Jacobites betrayed by Fuller	457
Crone arrested	458
Difficulties of William	459
Conduct of Shrewsbury	460
The Council of Nine	462
Conduct of Clarendon; Penn held to bail	463
Interview between William and Burnet; William sets out for Ireland	464
Trial of Crone	465
Danger of Invasion and Insurrection; Tourville's Fleet in the Channel	467
Arrests of suspected Persons	468
Torrington ordered to give Battle to Tourville	469
Battle of Beachy Head	470
Alarm in London; Battle of Fleurus; Spirit of the Nation	471
Conduct of Shrewsbury	**472**

HISTORY OF ENGLAND.

CHAPTER XI.—(1689.)

THE Revolution had been accomplished. The decrees of the Convention were everywhere received with submission. London, true during fifty eventful years to the cause of civil freedom and of the reformed religion, was foremost in professing loyalty to the new Sovereigns. Garter King at Arms, after making proclamation under the windows of Whitehall, rode in state along the Strand to Temple Bar. He was followed by the maces of the two Houses, by the two Speakers, Halifax and Powle, and by a long train of coaches filled with noblemen and gentlemen. The magistrates of the City threw open their gates and joined the procession. Four regiments of militia lined the way up Ludgate Hill, round Saint Paul's Cathedral, and along Cheapside. The streets, the balconies, and the very housetops were crowded with gazers. All the steeples from the Abbey to the Tower sent forth a joyous din. The proclamation was repeated with sound of trumpet, in front of the Royal Exchange, amidst the shouts of the citizens.

In the evening every window from Whitechapel to Piccadilly was lighted up. The state rooms of the palace were thrown open, and were filled by a gorgeous company of courtiers desirous to kiss the hands of the King and Queen. The Whigs assembled there, flushed with victory and prosperity. There were among them some who might be pardoned if a vindictive feeling mingled with their joy. The most deeply injured of all who had survived the evil times was absent. Lady Russell, while her friends were crowding the galleries of Whitehall, remained in her retreat, thinking of one who, if he had been still living, would have held no undistinguished place in the ceremonies of that great day. But her daughter who had a few months before become the wife of Lord Cavendish, was presented to the royal pair by his mother the Countess of Devonshire. A letter is still extant in which the young lady described with great vivacity the roar of the populace, the blaze in the streets, the throng in the presence chamber, the beauty of Mary, and the expression which ennobled and softened the harsh features of William. But the most interesting passage is that in which the orphan girl avowed the stern delight with which she had witnessed the tardy punishment of her father's murderer.*

The example of London was followed by the provincial towns. During three weeks the Gazettes were filled with accounts of the solemnities by which the public joy manifested itself, cavalcades of gentlemen and yeomen, processions of sheriffs and bailiffs in scarlet gowns, musters of zealous Protestants with orange flags and ribbons, salutes, bonfires, illuminations, music, balls, dinners, gutters running with ale, and conduits spouting claret.†

Still more cordial was the rejoicing among the Dutch, when they learned that the first minister of their Commonwealth had been raised to a throne. On the very day of his accession he had written to assure the States General that the change in his situation had made no change in the affection which he bore to his native land, and that his new dignity would, he hoped, enable him to discharge his old duties more efficiently than ever. That oligarchical party, which had always been hostile to the doctrines of Calvin and to the House of Orange, muttered faintly that His Majesty ought to resign the Stadtholdership. But all such mutterings were drowned by the acclamations of a people proud of the genius and success of their great countryman. A day of thanksgiving was appointed. In all the cities of the Seven Provinces the public joy manifested itself by festivities of which the expense was chiefly defrayed by voluntary gifts. Every class assisted. The poorest laborer could help to set up an arch of triumph, or to bring sedge to a bonfire. Even the ruined Huguenots of France could contribute the aid of their ingenuity. One art which they had carried with them into banishment was the art of making fireworks; and they now, in honor of the victorious champion of their faith, lighted up the canals of Amsterdam with showers of splendid constellations.‡

* Letter from Lady Cavendish to Sylvia. Lady Cavendish, like most of the clever girls of that generation, had Scudery's romances in her head. She is Dorinda: her correspondent, supposed to be her cousin Jane Allington, is Sylvia: William is Ormanzor, and Mary Phenixana. London Gazette, Feb. 14, 1688-9; Luttrell's Diary.
† See the London Gazettes of February and March 1688-9, and Luttrell's Diary.
‡ Wagenaar, lxi. He quotes the proceedings of the States of the 2nd of March, 1689. London Gazette, April 11, 1689; Monthly Mercury for April, 1689.

To superficial observers it might well seem that William was, at this time, one of the most enviable of human beings. He was in truth one of the most anxious and unhappy. He well knew that the difficulties of his task were only beginning. Already that dawn which had lately been so bright was overcast; and many signs portended a dark and stormy day.

It was observed that two important classes took little or no part in the festivities by which, all over England, the inauguration of the new government was celebrated. Very seldom could either a priest or a soldier be seen in the assemblages which gathered round the market crosses where the King and Queen were proclaimed. The professional pride both of the clergy and of the army had been deeply wounded. The doctrine of non-resistance had been dear to the Anglican divines. It was their distinguishing badge. It was their favorite theme. If we are to judge by that portion of their oratory which has come down to us, they had preached about the duty of passive obedience at least as often and as zealously as about the Trinity or the Atonement.* Their attachment to their political creed had indeed been severely tried, and had, during a short time, wavered. But with the tyranny of James the bitter feeling which that tyranny had excited among them had passed away. The parson of a parish was naturally unwilling to join in what was really a triumph over those principles which, during twenty-eight years, his flock had heard him proclaim on every anniversary of the Martyrdom and on every anniversary of the Restoration.

The soldiers, too, were discontented. They hated Popery indeed; and they had not loved the banished King. But they keenly felt that, in the short campaign which had decided the fate of their country, theirs had been an inglorious part. A regular army such as had never before marched to battle under the royal standard of England, had retreated precipitately before an invader, and had then, without a struggle, submitted to him. That great force had been absolutely of no acccount in the late change, had done nothing towards keeping William out, and had done nothing towards bringing him in. The clowns, who, armed with pitchforks and mounted on carthorses, had straggled

---

* "I may be positive," says a writer who had been educated at Westminster School, "where I heard one sermon of repentance, faith, and the renewing of the Holy Ghost, I heard three of the other; and 'tis hard to say whether Jesus Christ or King Charles the First were oftener mentioned and magnified."—Bisset's Modern Fanatic, 1710.

in the train of Lovelace or Delamere, had borne a greater part in the Revolution than those splendid household troops, whose plumed hats, embroidered coats, and curvetting chargers the Londoners had so often seen with admiration in Hyde Park. The mortification of the army was increased by the taunts of the foreigners, taunts which neither orders nor punishments could entirely restrain.* At several places the anger which a brave and high spirited body of men might, in such circumstances, be expected to feel, showed itself in an alarming manner. A battalion which lay at Cirencester put out the bonfires, huzzaed for King James, and drank confusion to his daughter and his nephew. The garrison of Plymouth disturbed the rejoicings of the County of Cornwall: blows were exchanged; and a man was killed in the fray.†

The ill humor of the clergy and of the army could not but be noticed by the most heedless; for the clergy and the army were distinguished from other classes by obvious peculiarities of garb. "Black coats and red coats," said a vehement Whig in the House of Commons, "are the curses of the nation."‡ But the discontent was not confined to the black coats and the red coats. The enthusiasm with which men of all classes had welcomed William to London at Christmas had greatly abated before the close of February. The new King had, at the very moment at which his fame and fortune reached the highest point, predicted the coming reaction. That reaction might, indeed, have been predicted by a less sagacious observer of human affairs. For it is to be chiefly ascribed to a law as certain as the laws which regulate the succession of the seasons and the course of the trade winds. It is the nature of man to overrate present evil, and to underrate present good; to long for what he has not, and to be dissatisfied with what he has. This propensity, as it appears in individuals, has often been noticed both by laughing and by weeping philosophers. It was a favorite theme of Horace and of Pascal, of Voltaire and of Johnson. To its influence on the fate of great communities may be ascribed most of the revolutions and counter-revolutions recorded in history. A hundred generations have passed away since the first great na-

---

* Paris Gazette, $\frac{\text{Jan. 26.}}{\text{Feb. 5,}}$ 1689; Orange Gazette, London, Jan. 10, 1688-9.
† Grey's Debates, Howe's Speech, Feb. 26, 1688-9; Boscawen's Speech, March 1; Luttrell's Diary, Feb. 23-27.
‡ Grey's Debates, Feb. 26, 1688-9.

tional emancipation, of which an account has come down to us. We read in the most ancient of books that a people bowed to the dust under a cruel yoke, scourged to toil by hard taskmasters, not supplied with straw, yet compelled to furnish the daily tale of bricks, became sick of life, and raised such a cry of misery as pierced the heavens. The slaves were wonderfully set free: at the moment of their liberation they raised a song of gratitude and triumph: but, in a few hours, they began to regret their slavery, and to reproach the leader who had decoyed them away from the savory fare of the house of bondage to the dreary waste which still separated them from the land flowing with milk and honey. Since that time the history of every great deliverer has been the history of Moses retold. Down to the present hour rejoicings like those on the shore of the Red Sea have ever been speedily followed by murmurings like those at the Waters of Strife.* The most just and salutary revolution must produce much suffering. The most just and salutary revolution cannot preduce all the good that had been expected from it by men of uninstructed minds and sanguine tempers. Even the wisest cannot, while it is still recent, weigh quite fairly the evils which it has caused against the evils which it has removed. For the evils which it has caused are felt; and the evils which it has removed are felt no longer.

Thus it was now in England. The public was, as it always is during the cold fits which follow its hot fits, sullen, hard to please, dissatisfied with itself, dissatisfied with those who had lately been its favorites. The truce between the two great parties was at an end. Separated by the memory of all that had been done and suffered during a conflict of half a century, they had been, during a few months, united by a common danger. But the danger was over: the union was dissolved; and the old animosity broke forth again in all its strength.

James had, during the last year of his reign, been even more hated by the Tories than by the Whigs; and not without cause: for to the Whigs he was only an enemy; and to the Tories he had been a faithless and thankless friend. But the old Royalist feeling, which had seemed to be extinct in the time of his lawlesss domination, had been partially revived

* This illustration is repeated to satiety in sermons and pamphlets of the time of William the Third. There is a poor imitation of Absalom and Ahitophel entitled the Murmurers. William is Moses; Corah, Dathan, and Abiram, nonjuring Bishops; Balaam, I think, Dryden; and Phinehas Shrewsbury.

by his misfortunes. Many lords and gentlemen who had, in December, taken arms for the Prince of Orange and a Free Parliament, muttered two months later, that they had been drawn in; that they had trusted too much to His Highness's Declaration; that they had given him credit for a disinterestedness which it now appeared was not in his nature. They had meant to put on King James, for his own good, some gentle force, to punish the Jesuits and renegades who had misled him, to obtain from him some guarantee for the safety of the civil and ecclesiastical institutions of the realm, but not to uncrown and banish him. For his maladministration, gross as it had been, excuses were found. Was it strange that, driven from his native land, while still a boy, by rebels who were a disgrace to the Protestant name, and forced to pass his youth in countries where the Roman Catholic religion was established, he should have been captivated by that most attractive of all superstitions? Was it strange that, persecuted and calumniated as he had been by an implacable faction, his disposition should have become sterner and more severe than it had once been thought, and that, when those who had tried to blast his honor and to rob him of his birthright were at length in his power, he should not have sufficiently tempered justice with mercy? As to the worst charge which had been brought against him, the charge of trying to cheat his daughters out of their inheritance by fathering a supposititious child, on what grounds did it rest? Merely on slight circumstances, such as might well be imputed to accident, or to that imprudence which was but too much in harmony with his character. Did ever the most stupid country justice put a boy in the stocks without requiring stronger evidence than that on which the English people had pronounced their King guilty of the basest and most odious of all frauds? Some great faults he had doubtless committed: nothing could be more just or constitutional than that for those faults his advisers and tools should be called to a severe reckoning; nor did any of those advisers and tools more richly deserve punishment than the Roundhead sectaries whose adulation had encouraged him to persist in the fatal exercise of the dispensing power. It was a fundamental principle of law that the King could do no wrong, and that, if wrong were done by his authority, his counsellors and agents were responsible. That great rule, essential to our polity, was now inverted. The sycophants, who were legally punishable, enjoyed impunity: the King, who was not legally punishable, was punished with merciless severity. Was it possible for the Cavaliers of England, the sons of the warriors who had fought under Rupert, not to feel bitter sorrow and indignation when they reflected on the fate of their rightful liege lord, the heir of a long line of princes, lately enthroned in splendor at Whitehall, now an exile, a suppliant, a mendicant? His calamities had been greater than even those of the Blessed Martyr from whom he sprang. The father had been slain by avowed and deadly foes: the ruin of the son had been the work of his own children. Surely the punishment, even if deserved, should have been inflicted by other hands. And was it altogether deserved? Had not the unhappy man been rather weak and rash than wicked? Had he not some of the qualities of an excellent prince? His abilities were certainly not of a high order: but he was diligent: he was thrifty: he had fought bravely: he had been his own minister for maritime affairs, and had, in that capacity acquitted himself respectably: he had, till spiritual guides obtained a fatal ascendency over his mind, been regarded as a man of strict justice; and, to the last, when he was not misled by them, he generally spoke truth and dealt fairly. With so many virtues he might, if he had been a Protestant, nay, if he had been a moderate Roman Catholic, have had a prosperous and glorious reign. Perhaps it might not be too late for him to retrieve his errors. It was difficult to believe that he could be so dull and perverse as not to have profited by the terrible discipline which he had recently undergone; and, if that discipline had produced the effects which might reasonably be expected from it, England might still enjoy, under her legitimate ruler, a larger measure of happiness and tranquillity than she could expect from the administration of the best and ablest usurper.

We should do great injustice to those who held this language, if we suppose that they had, as a body, ceased to regard Popery and despotism with abhorrence. Some zealots might indeed be found who could not bear the thought of imposing conditions on their King, and who were ready to recall him without the smallest assurance that the Declaration of Indulgence should not be instantly republished, that the High Commission should not be instantly revived, that Petre should not be again seated at the Council Board, and that the Fellows of Magdalene should not again be ejected. But the number of these men was small. On the other hand, the number of those Royalists, who, if James would have acknowledged his mistakes and promised to observe the laws, were ready to rally round him, was very large. It is a remarkable fact that two able and experienced statesmen, who had borne a chief part in the Revolution, frankly acknowledged, a few days after the Revolution had been accomplished, their apprehension that a Restoration was close at hand. " If King James were a Protestant," said Halifax to Reresby, "we could not keep him out four months." "If King James," said Danby to Reresby about the same time, "would but give the country some satisfaction about religion, which he might easily do, it would be very hard to make head against him." * Happily for England, James was, as usual, his own worst enemy. No word indicating that he took blame to himself on account of the past, or that he intended to govern constitutionally for the future, could be extracted from him. Every letter, every rumor, that found its way from Saint Germains to England made men of sense fear that, if, in his present temper, he should be restored to power, the second tyranny would be worse than the first. Thus the Tories, as a body, were forced to admit, very unwillingly, that there was, at that moment, no choice but between William and public ruin. They therefore, without altogether relinquishing the hope that he who was King by right might at some future time be disposed to listen to reason, and without feeling anything like loyalty towards him who was King in possession, discontentedly endured the new government.

It may be doubted whether that government was not, during the first months of its existence, in more danger from the affection of the Whigs than from the disaffection of the Tories. Enmity can hardly be more annoying than querulous, jealous, exacting fondness; and such was the fondness which the Whigs felt for the Sovereign of their choice. They were loud in his praise. They were ready to support him with purse and sword against foreign and domestic foes. But their attachment to him was of a peculiar kind. Loyalty such as had animated the gallant gentlemen who had fought for Charles the First, loyalty such as had rescued Charles the Second from the fearful dangers and difficulties caused by twenty years of malad-

---
* Reresby's Memoirs.

ministration, was not a sentiment to which the doctrines of Milton and Sidney were favorable; nor was it a sentiment which a prince, just raised to power by a rebellion, could hope to inspire. The Whig theory of government is that kings exist for the people, and not the people for kings; that the right of a king is divine in no other sense than that in which the right of a member of parliament, of a judge, of a juryman, of a mayor, of a headborough, is divine; that while the chief magistrate governs according to law, he ought to be obeyed and reverenced; that, when he violates the law he ought to be withstood; and that, when he violates the law, grossly, systematically, and pertinaciously, he ought to be deposed. On the truth of these principles depended the justice of William's title to the throne. It is obvious that the relation between subjects who held these principles, and a ruler whose accession had been the triumph of these principles, must have been altogether different from the relation which had subsisted between the Stuarts and the Cavaliers. The Whigs loved William indeed: but they loved him, not as a king, but as a party leader; and it was not difficult to foresee that their enthusiasm would cool fast if he should refuse to be the mere leader of their party, and should attempt to be king of the whole nation. What they expected from him in return for their devotion to his cause was that he should be one of themselves, a staunch and ardent Whig; that he should show favor to none but Whigs; that he should make all the old grudges of the Whigs his own; and there was but too much reason to apprehend that, if he disappointed this expectation, the only section of the community which was zealous in his cause would be estranged from him.*

Such were the difficulties by which at the moment of his elevation, he found himself beset. Where there was a good path he had seldom failed to choose it. But now he had only a choice among paths every one of which seemed likely to lead to destruction. From one faction he could hope for no cordial support. The cordial support of the other faction he could retain only by becoming the most factious man in his kingdom, a Shaftesbury on the throne.

* Here, and in many other places, I abstain from citing authorities, because my authorities are too numerous to cite. My notions of the temper and relative position of political and religious parties in the reign of William the Third, have been derived, not from any single work, but from thousands of forgotten tracts, sermons, and satires; in fact, from a whole literature which is mouldering in old libraries.

If he persecuted the Tories, their sulkiness would infallibly be turned into fury. If he showed favor to the Tories, it was by no means certain that he would gain their goodwill; and it was but too probable that he might lose his hold on the hearts of the Whigs. Something however he must do: something he must risk: a Privy Council must be sworn in: all the great offices, political and judicial, must be filled. It was impossible to make an arrangement that would please everybody, and difficult to make an arrangement that would please anybody: but an arrangement must be made.

What is now called a ministry he did not think of forming. Indeed what is now called a ministry was never known in England till he had been some years on the throne. Under the Plantagenets, the Tudors, and the Stuarts, there had been ministers: but there had been no ministry. The servants of the Crown were not, as now, bound in frankpledge for each other. They were not expected to be of the same opinion, even on questions of the gravest importance. Often they were politically and personally hostile to each other, and made no secret of their hostility. It was not yet felt to be inconvenient or unseemly that they should accuse each other of high crimes, and demand each other's heads. No man had been more active in the impeachment of the Lord Chancellor Clarendon than Coventry, who was a Commissioner of the Treasury. No man had been more active in the impeachment of the Lord Treasurer Danby than Winnington, who was Solicitor General. Among the members of the Government there was only one point of union, their common head, the Sovereign. The nation considered him as the proper chief of the administration, and blamed him severely if he delegated his high functions to any subject. Clarendon has told us that nothing was so hateful to the Englishmen of his time as a Prime Minister. They would rather, he said, be subject to an usurper like Oliver, who was first magistrate in fact as well as in name, than to a legitimate King who referred them to a Grand Vizier. One of the chief accusations which the country party had brought against Charles the Second was that he was too indolent and too fond of pleasure to examine with care the balance sheets of public accountants and the inventories of military stores. James, when he came to the crown, had determined to appoint no Lord High Admiral or Board of

Admiralty, and to keep the entire direction of maritime affairs in his own hands; and this arrangement, which would now be thought by men of all parties unconstitutional and pernicious in the highest degree, was then generally applauded even by people who were not inclined to see his conduct in a favorable light. How completely the relation in which the King stood to his Parliament and to his ministers had been altered by the Revolution was not at first understood even by the most enlightened statesmen. It was universally supposed that the government would, as in time past, be conducted by functionaries independent of each other, and that William would exercise a general superintendence over them all. It was also fully expected that a prince of William's capacity and experience would transact much important business without having recourse to any adviser.

There were therefore no complaints when it was understood that he had reserved to himself the direction of foreign affairs. This was indeed scarcely matter of choice: for, with the single exception of Sir William Temple, whom nothing would induce to quit his retreat for public life, there was no Englishman who had proved himself capable of conducting an important negotiation with foreign powers to a successful and honorable issue. Many years had elapsed since England had interfered with weight and dignity in the affairs of the great commonwealth of nations. The attention of the ablest English politicians had long been almost exclusively occupied by disputes concerning the civil and ecclesiastical constitution of their own country. The contests about the Popish Plot and the Exclusion Bill, the Habeas Corpus Act and the Test Act, had produced an abundance, indeed a glut, of those talents which raise men to eminence in societies torn by internal factions. All the continent could not show such skillful and wary leaders of parties, such dexterous parliamentary tacticians, such ready and eloquent debaters, as were assembled at Westminster. But a very different training was necessary to form a great minister for foreign affairs; and the Revolution had on a sudden placed England in a situation in which the services of a great minister for foreign affairs were indispensable to her.

William was admirably qualified to supply that in which the most accomplished statesmen of his kingdom were deficient. He had long been pre-eminently distinguished as a negotiator He was the author and the soul of the European coalition against the French ascendency. The clue, without which it was perilous to enter the vast and intricate maze of Continental politics, was in his hands. His English counsellors, therefore, however able and active, seldom, during his reign, ventured to meddle with that part of the public business which he had taken as his peculiar province.*

The internal government of England could be carried on only by the advice and agency of English ministers. Those ministers William selected in such a manner as showed that he was determined not to proscribe any set of men who were willing to support his throne. On the day after the crown had been presented to him in the Banqueting House the Privy Council was sworn in. Most of the Councillors were Whigs: but the names of several eminent Tories appeared in the list.† The four highest offices in the state were assigned to four noblemen, the representatives of four classes of politicians.

In practical ability and official experience Danby had no superior among his contemporaries. To the gratitude of the new Sovereigns he had a strong claim; for it was by his dexterity that their marriage had been brought about in spite of difficulties which had seemed insuperable. The enmity which he had always borne to France was a scarcely less powerful recommendation. He had signed the invitation of the thirtieth of June, had excited and directed the Northern Insurrection, and had, in the Convention, exerted all his influence and eloquence in opposition to the scheme of Regency. Yet the Whigs regarded him with unconquerable distrust and aversion. They could not forget that he had, in evil days, been the first minister of the state, the head of the Cavaliers, the champion of prerogative, the persecutor of dissenters. Even in becoming a rebel, he had not ceased to be a Tory. If he had drawn the sword against the crown, he had drawn it only in defence of the Church. If he had, in the Convention, done good by opposing the scheme of Regency, he had done harm by obstinately maintaining that the throne was not vacant, and that the Estates had no right

---

* The following passage in a tract of that time expresses the general opinion. "He has better knowledge of foreign affairs than we have; but in English business it is no dishonor to him to be told his relation to us, the nature of it, and what is fit for him to do."—An Honest Commoner's Speech.

† London Gazette. Feb. 18, 1688-9.

to determine who should fill it. The Whigs were therefore of opinion that he ought to think himself amply rewarded for his recent merits by being suffered to escape the punishment of those offences for which he had been impeached ten years before. He, on the other hand, estimated his own abilities and services, which were doubtless considerable, at their full value, and thought himself entitled to the great place of Lord High Treasurer, which he had formerly held. But he was disappointed. William, on principle, thought it desirable to divide the power and patronage of the Treasury among several Commissioners. He was the first English King who never, from the beginning to the end of his reign, trusted the white staff in the hands of a single subject. Danby was offered his choice between the Presidency of the Council and a Secretaryship of State. He sullenly accepted the Presidency, and while the Whigs murmured at seeing him placed so high, hardly attempted to conceal his anger at not having been placed higher.*

Halifax, the most illustrious man of that small party which boasted that it kept the balance even between Whigs and Tories, took charge of the Privy Seal, and continued to be Speaker of the House of Lords.† He had been foremost in strictly legal opposition to the late Government, and had spoken and written with great ability against the dispensing power: but he had refused to know anything about the design of invasion: he had labored, even when the Dutch were in full march towards London, to effect a reconciliation; and he had never deserted James till James had deserted the throne. But, from the moment of that shameful flight, the sagacious Trimmer, convinced that compromise was thenceforth impossible, had taken a decided part. He had distinguished himself pre-eminently in the Convention; nor was it without a peculiar propriety that he had been appointed to the honorable office of tendering the crown, in the name of all the Estates of England, to the Prince and Princess of Orange: for our Revolution, as far as it can be said to bear the character of any single mind, assuredly bears the character of the large yet cautious mind of Halifax. The Whigs, however, were not in a temper to accept a recent service as an atonement for an old offence; and the offence of Halifax had been grave

---
* London Gazette, Feb. 18. 1688-9; Sir J. Reresby's Memoirs
† London Gazette, Feb. 18, 1688-9; Lords' Journals.

indeed. He had long before been conspicuous in their front rank during a hard fight for liberty. When they were at length victorious, when it seemed that Whitehall was at their mercy, when they had a near prospect of dominion and revenge, he had changed sides; and fortune had changed sides with him. In the great debate on the Exclusion Bill, his eloquence had struck the opposition dumb, and had put new life into the inert and desponding party of the Court. It was true, that, though he had left his old friends in the day of their insolent prosperity, he had returned to them in the day of their distress. But, now that their distress was over, they forgot that he had returned to them, and remembered only that he had left them.*

The vexation with which they saw Danby presiding in the Council, and Halifax bearing the Privy Seal, was not diminished by the news that Nottingham was appointed Secretary of State. Some of those zealous churchmen who had never ceased to profess the doctrine of non-resistance, who thought the Revolution unjustifiable, who had voted for a Regency, and who had to the last maintained that the English throne could never be one moment vacant, yet conceived it to be their duty to submit to the decision of the Convention. They had not, they said, rebelled against James. They had not elected William. But, now that they saw on the throne a Sovereign whom they never would have placed there, they were of opinion that no law, divine, or human, bound them to carry the contest further. They thought that they found, both in the Bible and in the Statute Book, directions which could not be misunderstood. The Bible enjoins obedience to the powers that be. The Statute Book contains an Act providing that no subject shall be deemed a wrong-doer for adhering to the King in possession. On these grounds many, who had not concurred in setting up the new government, believed that they might give it their support without offence to God or man. One of the most eminent politicians of this school was Nottingham. At his instance the Convention had, before the throne was filled, made such changes in the oath of allegiance as enabled him, and those who agreed with him, to take that oath without scruple. "My principles," he said, "do not permit me to bear any part in making a king. But when a king

---
* Burnet, ii. 4.

has been made, my principles bind me to pay him an obedience more strict than he can expect from those who have made him." He now, to the surprise of some of those who most esteemed him, consented to sit in the council, and to accept the seals of Secretary. William doubtless hoped that this appointment would be considered by the clergy and the Tory country gentlemen as a sufficient guarantee that no evil was meditated against the Church. Even Burnet, who at a later period felt a strong antipathy to Nottingham, owned, in some memoirs written soon after the Revolution, that the King had judged well, and that the influence of the Tory Secretary, honestly exerted in support of the new Sovereigns, had saved England from great calamities.*

The other secretary was Shrewsbury.† No man so young had within living memory occupied so high a post in the government. He had but just completed his twenty-eighth year. Nobody, however, except the solemn formalists at the Spanish embassy, thought his youth an objection to his promotion.‡ He had already secured for himself a place in history by the conspicuous part which he had taken in the deliverance of his country. His talents, his accomplishments, his graceful manners, his bland temper, made him generally popular. By the Whigs especially he was almost adored. None suspected that, with many great and many amiable qualities, he had such faults both of head and of heart as would make the rest of a life which had opened under the fairest auspices burdensome to himself and almost useless to his country.

The naval administration and the financial administration were confided to Boards. Herbert was First Commissioner of the Admiralty. He had in the late reign given up wealth and dignities when he had found that he

---

* These memoirs will be found in a manuscript volume, which is part of the Harleian Collection, and is numbered 6584. They are in fact, the first outlines of a great part of Burnet's History of His Own Times. The dates at which the different portions of this most curious and interesting book were composed are marked. Almost the whole was written before the death of Mary. Burnet did not begin to prepare his History of William's Reign for the press till ten years later. By that time his opinions, both of men and of things, had undergone considerable changes. The value of the rough draught is therefore very great: for it contains some facts which he afterwards thought it advisable to suppress, and some judgments which he afterwards saw cause to alter. I must own that I generally like his first thoughts best. Whenever his History is reprinted, it ought to be carefully collated with this volume.

When I refer to the Burnet MS. Harl. 6584, I wish the reader to understand that the MS. contains something which is not to be found in the History.

As to Nottingham's appointment, see Burnet, ii. 8; the London Gazette of March 7, 1688-9; and Clarendon's Diary of Feb. 15.

† London Gazette, Feb. 18, 1688-9.

‡ Don Pedro de Ronquillo makes this objection.

could not retain them with honor and with a good conscience. He had carried the memorable invitation to the Hague. He had commanded the Dutch fleet during the voyage from Helvoetsluys to Torbay. His character for courage and professional skill stood high. That he had had his follies and vices was well known. But his recent conduct in the time of severe trial had atoned for all, and seemed to warrant the hope that his future career would be glorious. Among the commissioners who sate with him at the Admiralty were two distinguished members of the House of Commons, William Sacheverell, a veteran Whig, who had great authority in his party, and Sir John Lowther, an honest and very moderate Tory, who in fortune and parliamentary interest was among the first of the English gentry.*

Mordaunt, one of the most vehement of the Whigs, was placed at the head of the Treasury; why, it is difficult to say. His romantic courage, his flighty wit, his eccentric invention, his love of desperate risks and startling effects, were not qualities likely to be of much use to him in financial calculations and negotiations. Delamere, a more vehement Whig, if possible, than Mordaunt, sate second at the board, and was Chancellor of the Exchequer. Two Whig members of the House of Commons were in the Commission, Sir Henry Capel, brother of the Earl of Essex who died by his own hand in the Tower, and Richard Hampden, son of the great leader of the Long Parliament. But the Commissioner on whom the chief weight of business lay was Godolphin. This man, taciturn, clear-minded, laborious, inoffensive, zealous for no government, and useful to every government, had gradually become an almost indispensable part of the machinery of the state. Though a churchman, he had prospered in a Court governed by Jesuits. Though he had voted for a Regency, he was the real head of a Treasury filled with Whigs. His abilities and knowledge, which had in the late reign supplied the deficiencies of Bellasyse and Dover, were now needed to supply the deficiencies of Mordaunt and Delamere.†

There were some difficulties in disposing of the Great Seal. The King at first wished to confide it to Nottingham, whose father had borne it during several years with high reputation.‡ Nottingham, however, declined the

---
* London Gazette, March 11, 1688-9.   † Ibid.
‡ I have followed what seems to me the most probable story. But it has been doubted

trust; and it was offered to Halifax, but was again declined. Both these lords doubtless felt that it was a trust which they could not discharge with honor to themselves or with advantage to the public. In old times, indeed, the Seal had been generally held by persons who were not lawyers. Even in the seventeenth century it had been confided to two eminent men who had never studied at any Inn of Court. Williams had been Lord Keeper to James the First. Shaftesbury had been Lord Chancellor to Charles the Second. But such appointments could no longer be made without serious inconvenience. Equity had been gradually shaping itself into a refined science, which no human faculties could master without long and intense application. Even Shaftesbury, vigorous as was his intellect, had painfully felt his want of technical knowledge;* and during the fifteen years which had elapsed since Shaftesbury had resigned the Seal, technical knowledge had constantly been becoming more and more necessary to his successors. Neither Nottingham, therefore, though he had a stock of legal learning such as is rarely found in any person who had not received a legal education, nor Halifax, though in the judicial sittings of the House of Lords, the quickness of his apprehension, and the subtlety of his reasoning had often astonished the bar, ventured to accept the highest office which an English layman can fill. After some delay the Seal was confided to a commission of eminent lawyers, with Maynard at their head.†

The choice of judges did honor to the new government. Every privy councillor was directed to bring a list. The lists were compared; and twelve men of conspicuous merit were selected.‡ The professional attainments and Whig principles of Pollexfen gave him pretensions to the highest place. But it was remembered that he had held briefs for the crown, in the Western counties, at the assizes which followed the battle of Sedgemoor. It seems indeed from the reports of the trials, that he did as little as he could do if he held the briefs at all, and that he left to the judges the business of browbeating witnesses and prisoners. Nevertheless his name was inseparably associated in the

---

whether Nottingham was invited to be Chancellor, or only to be First Commissioner of the Great Seal. Compare Burnett, ii. 3, and Boyer's History of William, 1702. Narcissus Luttrell repeatedly, and even as late as the close of 1692, speaks of Nottingham as likely to be Chancellor.

* Roger North relates an amusing story about Shaftesbury's embarrasment.
† London Gazette, March 4, 1688-9.   ‡ Burnet, ii, 5.

public mind with the Bloody Circuit. He, therefore, could not with propriety be put at the head of the first criminal court in the realm.* After acting during a few weeks as Attorney General, he was made Chief Justice of the Common Pleas. Sir John Holt, a young man, but distinguished by learning, integrity, and courage, became Chief Justice of the King's Bench. Sir Robert Atkyns, an eminent lawyer, who had passed some years in rural retirement, but whose reputation was still great in Westminster Hall, was appointed Chief Baron. Powell, who had been disgraced on account of his honest declaration in favor of the bishops, again took his seat among the judges. Treby succeeded Pollexfen as Attorney General; and Somers was made Solicitor.†

Two of the chief places in the royal household were filled by two English noblemen eminently qualified to adorn a court. The high-spirited and accomplished Devonshire was named Lord Steward. No man had done more or risked more for England during the crisis of her fate. In retrieving her liberties he had retrieved also the fortunes of his own house. His bond for thirty thousand pounds was found among the papers which James had left at Whitehall, and was cancelled by William.‡

Dorset became Lord Chamberlain, and employed the influence and patronage annexed to his functions, as he had long employed his private means, in encouraging genius and in alleviating misfortune. One of the first acts which he was under the necessity of performing must have been painful to a man of so generous a nature, and of so keen a relish for whatever was excellent in arts and letters. Dryden could no longer remain Poet Laureate. The public would not have borne to see any Papist among the servants of Their Majesties; and Dryden was not only a Papist, but an apostate. He had moreover aggravated the guilt of his apostasy by calumniating and ridiculing the church which he had deserted. He had, it was facetiously said, treated her as the Pagan persecutors of old treated her children. He had dressed her up in the skin of a wild beast, and then baited her for the public amusement.§ He was removed; but he received from the private bounty of

---

* The Protestant Mask taken off from the Jesuited Englishman, 1692.
† These appointments were not announced in the Gazette till the 6th of May; but some of them were made earlier.
‡ Kennet's Funeral Sermon on the first Duke of Devonshire, and Memoirs of the family of Cavendish, 1708.
§ See a poem entitled, A Votive Tablet to the King and Queen.

the magnificent Chamberlain a pension equal to the salary which had been withdrawn. The deposed Laureate, however, as poor of spirit as rich in intellectual gifts, continued to complain piteously, year after year, of the losses which he had not suffered, till at length his wailings drew forth expressions of well merited contempt from brave and honest Jacobites, who had sacrificed everything to their principles without deigning to utter one word of deprecation or lamentation.*

In the royal household were placed some of those Dutch nobles who stood highest in the favor of the King. Bentinck had the great office of Groom of the Stole, with a salary of five thousand pounds a year. Zulestein took charge of the robes. The Master of the Horse was Auverquerque, a gallant soldier, who united the blood of Nassau to the blood of Horn, and who wore with just pride a costly sword presented to him by the States General in acknowledgment of the courage with which he had, on the bloody day of Saint Dennis, saved the life of William.

The place of Vice Chamberlain to the Queen was given to a man who had just become conspicuous in public life, and whose name will frequently recur in the history of this reign. John Howe, or, as he was more commonly called, Jack Howe, had been sent up to the Convention by the borough of Cirencester. His appearance was that of a man whose body was worn by the constant workings of a restless and acrid mind. He was tall, lean, pale, with a haggard, eager look, expressive at once of flightiness and of shrewdness. He had been known, during several years, as a small poet; and some of the most savage lampoons which were handed about the coffee-houses were imputed to him. But it was in the House of Commons that both

---

* See Prior's Dedication of his Poems to Dorset's son and successor, and Dryden's Essay on Satire prefixed to the translations from Juvenal. There is a bitter sneer on Dryden's effeminate querulousness in Collier's Short View of the State. In Blackmore's Prince Arthur, a poem, which, worthless as it is, contains some curious allusions to contemporary men and events, are the following lines:

"The poets' nation did obsequious wait
For the kind dole divided at his gate.
Laurus among the meagre crowd appeared,
An old, revolted, unbelieving bard,
Who thronged, and shoved, and pressed, and would be heard.
Sakil's high roof, the Muses' palace, rung
With endless cries, and endless songs he sung.
To bless good Sakil Laurus would be first;
But Sakil's prince and Sakil's God he curst.
Sakil without distinction, threw his bread,
Despised the flatterer, but the poet fed."

I need not say that Sakil is Sackville, or that Laurus is a translation of the famous nickname Bayes.

his parts and his ill-nature were most signally displayed. Before he had been a member three weeks, his volubility, his asperity, and his pertinacity had made him conspicuous. Quickness, energy, and audacity, united, soon raised him to the rank of a privileged man. His enemies,— and he had many enemies,—said that he consulted his personal safety even in his most petulant moods, and that he treated soldiers with a civility which he never showed to ladies or to bishops. But no man had in larger measure that evil courage which braves and even courts disgust and hatred. No decencies restrained him; his spite was implacable: his skill in finding out the vulnerable parts of strong minds was consummate. All his great contemporaries felt his sting in their turns. Once it inflicted a wound which deranged even the stern composure of William, and constrained him to utter a wish that he were a private gentleman, and could invite Mr. Howe to a short interview behind Montague House. As yet, however, Howe was reckoned among the most strenuous supporters of the new government, and directed all his sarcasms and invectives against the malcontents.*

The subordinate places in every public office were divided between the two parties; but the Whigs had the larger share. Some persons, indeed, who did little honor to the Whig name, were largely recompensed for services which no good man would have performed. Wildman was made Postmaster General. A lucrative sinecure in the Excise was bestowed on Ferguson. The duties of the Solicitor of the Treasury were very important and very invidious. It was the business of that officer to conduct political prosecutions, to collect the evidence, to instruct the counsel for the Crown, to see that the prisoners were not liberated on insufficient bail, to see that the juries were not composed of persons hostile to the government. In the days of Charles and James, the Solicitor of the Treasury had been, with too much reason, accused of employing all the vilest artifices of chicanery against men obnoxious to the Court. The new government ought to have made a

---

* Scarcely any man of that age is more frequently mentioned in pamphlets and satires than Howe. In the famous Petition of Legion, he is designated as "that impudent scandal of Parliament." Mackay's account of him is curious. In a poem written in 1690, which I have never seen except in manuscript, are the following lines:

"First for Jack Howe with his terrible talent,
Happy the female that scapes his lampoon;
Against the ladies excessively valiant,
But very respectful to a Dragoon."

choice which was above all suspicion. Unfortunately Mordaunt and Delamere pitched upon Aaron Smith, an acrimonious and unprincipled politician, who had been the legal adviser of Titus Oates in the days of the Popish Plot, and who had been deeply implicated in the Rye House Plot. Richard Hampden, a man of decided opinions, but of moderate temper, objected to this appointment. His objections however were overruled. The Jacobites, who hated Smith and had reason to hate him, affirmed that he had obtained his place by bullying the Lords of the Treasury, and particularly by threatening that, if his just claims were disregarded, he would be the death of Hampden.*

Some weeks elapsed before all the arrangements which have been mentioned were publicly announced: and meanwhile many important events had taken place. As soon as the new Privy Councillors had been sworn in, it was necessary to submit to them a grave and pressing question. Could the Convention now assembled be turned into a Parliament? The Whigs, who had a decided majority in the Lower House, were all for the affirmative. The Tories, who knew that, within the last month, the public feeling had undergone a considerable change, and who hoped that a general election would add to their strength, were for the negative. They maintained that to the existence of a Parliament royal writs were indispensably necessary. The Convention had not been summoned by such writs: the original defect could not now be supplied: the Houses were therefore mere clubs of private men, and ought instantly to disperse.

It was answered that the royal writ was mere matter of form, and that to expose the substance of our laws and liberties to serious hazard for the sake of a form would be the most senseless superstition. Wherever the Sovereign, the Peers spiritual and temporal, and the Representatives freely chosen by the constituent bodies of the realm were met together, there was the essence of a Parliament. Such a Parliament was now in being; and what could be more absurd than to dissolve it at a conjuncture when every hour was precious, when numerous important subjects required immediate legislation, and when dangers, only to be averted by the combined efforts of King, Lords, and Commons, menaced the state? A Jacobite indeed might

---

* Sprat's True Account; North's Examen; Letter to Chief Justice Holt, 1694; Letter to Secretary Trenchard, 1694.

consistently refuse to recognize the Convention as a Parliament. For he held that it had from the beginning been an unlawful assembly, that all its resolutions were nullities, and that the Sovereigns whom it had set up were usurpers. But with what consistency could any man, who maintained that a new Parliament ought to be immediately called by writs under the great seal of William and Mary, question the authority which had placed William and Mary on the throne? Those who held that William was rightful King must necessarily hold that the body from which he derived his right was itself a rightful Great Council of the Realm. Those who, though not holding him to be rightful King, conceived that they might lawfully swear allegiance to him as King in fact, might surely, on the same principle, acknowledge the Convention as a Parliament in fact. It was plain that the Convention was the fountain-head from which the authority of all future Parliaments must be derived, and that on the validity of the votes of the Convention must depend the validity of every future statute. And how could the stream rise higher than the source? Was it not absurd to say that the Convention was supreme in the state, and yet a nullity; a legislature for the highest of all purposes, and yet no legislature for the humblest purposes; competent to declare the throne vacant, to change the succession, to fix the landmarks of the constitution, and yet not competent to pass the most trivial Act for the repairing of a pier or the building of a parish church?

These arguments would have had considerable weight, even if every precedent had been on the other side. But in truth our history afforded only one precedent which was at all in point; and that precedent was decisive in favor of the doctrine that royal writs are not indispensably necessary to the existence of a Parliament. No royal writ had summoned the Convention which recalled Charles the Second. Yet that Convention had, after his Restoration, continued to sit and to Legislate, had settled the revenue, had passed an Act of amnesty, had abolished the feudal tenures. These proceedings had been sanctioned by authority of which no party in the state could speak without reverence. Hale, a jurist held in honor by every Whig, had borne a considerable share in them, and had always maintained that they were strictly legal. Clarendon, a statesman whose memory was respected by the great body of Tories, little as he was inclined to favor any doctrine derogatory to the rights of the Crown, or to the dignity of that seal of which he was keeper, had declared that, since God had, at a most critical conjuncture, given the nation a good Parliament, it would be the height of folly to look for technical flaws in the instrument by which that Parliament was called together. Would it be pretended that the Convention of 1660 had a more respectable origin than the Convention of 1689? Was not a letter written by the first Prince of the Blood, at the request of the whole peerage, and of hundreds of gentlemen who had represented counties and towns, at least as good a warrant as a vote of the Rump?

Weaker reasons than these would have satisfied the Whigs who formed the majority of the Privy Council. The King, therefore, on the fifth day after he had been proclaimed, went with royal state to the House of Lords, and took his seat on the throne. The Commons were called in; and he, with many gracious expressions, reminded his hearers of the perilous situation of the country, and exhorted them to take such steps as might prevent unnecessary delay in the transaction of public business. His speech was received by the gentlemen who crowded the bar with the deep hum by which our ancestors were wont to indicate approbation, and which was often heard in places more sacred than the Chamber of the Peers.* As soon as he had retired, a Bill declaring the Convention a Parliament was laid on the table of the Lords, and rapidly passed by them. In the Commons the debates were warm. The house resolved itself into a Committee; and so great was the excitement that, when the authority of the Speaker was withdrawn, it was hardly possible to preserve order. Sharp personalities were exchanged. The phrase, "Hear him," a phrase which had originally been used only to silence irregular noises, and to remind members of the duty of attending to the discussion, had, during some years, been gradually becoming what it now is; that is to say, a cry indicative, according to the tone, of admiration, acquiescence, indignation, or derision. On this occasion, the Whigs vociferated "Hear, hear," so tumultuously that the Tories complained of unfair usage. Seymour, the leader of the minority, declared that there could be no freedom of debate while such clam-

---

* Van Citters, $\frac{\text{Feb. 19.}}{\text{March 1,}}$ 1688-9.

or was tolerated. Some old Whig members were provoked into reminding him that the same clamor had occasionally been heard when he presided, and had not then been repressed. Yet, eager and angry as both sides were, the speeches on both sides indicated that profound reverence for law and prescription which has long been characteristic of Englishmen, and which, though it sometimes runs into pedantry and sometimes into superstition, is not without its advantages. Even at that momentous crisis, when the nation was still in the ferment of a revolution, our public men talked long and seriously about all the circumstances of the deposition of Edward the Second, and of the deposition of Richard the Second, and anxiously inquired whether the assembly which, with Archbishop Lanfranc at its head, set aside Robert of Normandy, and put William Rufus on the throne, did or did not afterwards continue to act as the legislature of the realm. Much was said about the history of writs; much about the etymology of the word Parliament. It is remarkable, that the orator who took the most statesmanlike view of the subject was old Maynard. In the civil conflicts of fifty eventful years he had learned that questions affecting the highest interests of the commonwealth were not to be decided by verbal cavils and by scraps of Law French and Law Latin; and, being by universal acknowledgment the most subtle and the most learned of English jurists, he could express what he felt without the risk of being accused of ignorance and presumption. He scornfully thrust aside as frivolous and out of place all that black-letter learning, which some men, far less versed in such matters than himself, had introduced into the discussion. "We are," he said, "at this moment out of the beaten path. If therefore we are determined to move only in that path, we cannot move at all. A man in a revolution resolving to do nothing which is not strictly according to established form resembles a man who has lost himself in the wilderness, and who stands crying 'Where is the king's highway? I will walk nowhere but on the king's highway.' In a wilderness a man should take the track which will carry him home. In a revolution we must have recourse to the highest law, the safety of the state." Another veteran Roundhead, Colonel Birch, took the same side, and argued with great force and keenness from the precedent of 1660. Seymour and his supporters were beaten in the Committee, and did not venture to divide the House on the report. The Bill passed rapidly, and received the royal assent on the tenth day after the accession of William and Mary.*

The law which turned the Convention into a Parliament contained a clause providing that no person should, after the first of March, sit or vote in either House without taking the oaths to the new King and Queen. This enactment produced great agitation throughout society. The adherents of the exiled dynasty hoped and confidently predicted that the recusants would be numerous. The minority in both Houses, it was said, would be true to the cause of hereditary monarchy. There might be here and there a traitor; but the great body of those who had voted for a Regency would be firm. Only two bishops at most would recognize the usurpers. Seymour would retire from public life rather than abjure his principles. Grafton had determined to fly to France and throw himself at the feet of his uncle. With such rumors as these all the coffee-houses of London were filled during the latter part of February. So intense was the public anxiety that, if any man of rank was missed, two days running, at his usual haunts, it was immediately whispered that he had stolen away to Saint Germains.†

The second of March arrived; and the event quieted the fears of one party, and confounded the hopes of the other. The Primate indeed and several of his suffragans stood obstinately aloof: but three bishops and seventy-three temporal peers took the oaths. At the next meeting of the Upper House several more prelates came in. Within a week about a hundred Lords had qualified themselves to sit. Others, who were prevented by illness from appearing, sent excuses and professions of attachment to their Majesties. Grafton refuted all the stories which had been circulated about him by coming to be sworn on the first day. Two members of the Ecclesiastical Commission, Mulgrave and Sprat, hastened to make atonement for their fault by plighting their faith to William. Beaufort, who had long been considered as the type of a royalist of the old school, submitted after a very short hesitation. Ayles-

---

* Stat. 1 W. & M. sess. i. c. 1. See the Journals of the two Houses, and Grey's Debates. The argument in favor of the bill is well stated in the Paris Gazettes of March 5, and 12, 1689.
† Both Van Citters and Ronquillo mention the anxiety which was felt in London till the result was known.

bury and Dartmouth had as little scruple about taking the oath of allegiance as they afterwards had about breaking it.* The Hydes took different paths. Rochester complied with the law; but Clarendon proved refractory. Many thought it strange that the brother who had adhered to James till James absconded should be less sturdy than the brother who had been in the Dutch camp. The explanation perhaps is that Rochester would have sacrificed much more than Clarendon by refusing to take the oaths. Clarendon's income did not depend on the pleasure of the Government: but Rochester had a pension of four thousand a year, which he could not hope to retain if he refused to acknowledge the new Sovereigns. Indeed, he had so many enemies that, during some months, it seemed doubtful whether he would, on any terms, be suffered to retain the splendid reward which he had earned by persecuting the Whigs and by sitting in the High Commission. He was saved from what would have been a fatal blow to his fortunes by the intercession of Burnet, who had been deeply injured by him, and who revenged himself as became a Christian divine.†

In the Lower House four hundred members were sworn in on the second of March; and among them was Seymour. The spirit of the Jacobites was broken by his defection; and the minority, with very few exceptions, followed his example.‡

Before the day fixed for the taking of the oaths, the Commons had begun to discuss a momentous question which admitted of no delay. During the interregnum, William had, as provisional chief of the administration, collected the taxes and applied them to the public service; nor could the propriety of this course be questioned by any person who approved of the Revolution. But the Revolution was now over: the vacancy of the throne had been supplied: the Houses were sitting: the law was in full force; and it became necessary immediately to decide to what revenue the Government was entitled.

It was not denied that all the lands and hereditaments of the Crown had passed with the Crown to the new Sovereigns. It was not denied that all duties which had been granted to the Crown for a fixed term of years might be

---
* Lords' Journals, March, 1688-9.
† See the letters of Rochester and of Lady Ranelagh to Burnet on this occasion.
‡ Journals of the Commons, March 2, 1688-9. Ronquillo wrote as follows: "Es de gran consideracion que Seimor haya tomado el juramento; porque es el arrengador y el director principal, en la casa de los Comunes, de los Anglicanos."—March 8-18, 1688-9.

constitutionally exacted till that term should expire. But large revenues had been settled by Parliament on James for life; and whether what had been settled on James for life could, while he lived, be claimed by William and Mary, was a question about which opinions were divided.

Holt, Treby, Pollexfen, indeed all the eminent Whig lawyers, Somers excepted, held that these revenues had been granted to the late King, in his political capacity, but for his natural life, and ought therefore, as long as he continued to drag on his existence in a strange land, to be paid to William and Mary. It appears from a very concise and unconnected report of the debate that Somers dissented from this doctrine. His opinion was that, if the Act of Parliament which had imposed the duties in question was to be construed according to the spirit, the word life must be understood to mean reign, and that therefore the term for which the grant had been made had expired. This was surely the sound opinion: for it was plainly irrational to treat the interest of James in this grant as at once a thing annexed to his person and a thing annexed to his office; to say in the same breath that the merchants of London and Bristol must pay money because he was in one sense alive, and that his successors must receive that money because he was in another sense defunct. The House was decidedly with Somers. The members generally were bent on effecting a great reform, without which it was felt that the Declaration of Rights would be but an imperfect guarantee for public liberty. During the conflict which fifteen successive Parliaments had maintained against four successive kings, the chief weapon of the Commons had been the power of the purse; nor had the representatives of the people ever been induced to surrender that weapon without having speedy cause to repent of their too credulous loyalty. In the season of tumultuous joy which followed the Restoration, a large revenue for life had been almost by acclamation granted to Charles the Second. A few months later there was scarcely a respectable Cavalier in the kingdom who did not own that the stewards of the nation would have acted more wisely if they had kept in their hands the means of checking the abuses which disgraced every department of the government. James the Second had obtained from his submissive Parliament, without a dissentient voice, an income amply sufficient to defray the ordinary expenses of the state during his life; and, before he had enjoyed that income half a year, the great majority of those who had dealt thus liberally with him blamed themselves severely for their liberality. If experience was to be trusted, a long and painful experience, there could be no effectual security against maladministration, unless the Sovereign were under the necessity of recurring frequently to his Great Council for pecuniary aid. Almost all honest and enlightened men were therefore agreed in thinking that a part at least of the supplies ought to be granted only for a short term. And what time could be fitter for the introduction of this new practice than the year 1689, the commencement of a new reign, of a new dynasty, of a new era of constitutional government? The feeling on this subject was so strong and general that the dissentient minority gave way. No formal resolution was passed: but the House proceeded to act on the supposition that the grants which had been made to James for life had been annulled by his abdication.*

It was impossible to make a new settlement of the revenue without inquiry and deliberation. The Exchequer was ordered to furnish such returns as might enable the House to form estimates of the public expenditure and income. In the meantime, liberal provision was made for the immediate exigencies of the state. An extraordinary aid, to be raised by direct monthly assessment, was voted to the King. An Act was passed indemnifying all who had, since his landing, collected by his authority the duties settled on James; and those duties which had expired were continued for some months.

Along William's whole line of march, from Torbay to London, he had been importuned by the common people to relieve them from the intolerable burden of the hearth money. In truth, that tax seems to have united all the worst evils which can be imputed to any tax. It was unequal, and unequal in the most pernicious way: for it pressed heavily on the poor and lightly on the rich. A peasant, all whose property was not worth twenty pounds, had to pay several shillings, while the mansion of an oppulent nobleman in Lincoln's Inn Fields or St. James's Square was seldom assessed at two guineas. The collectors were empowered to examine the interior of every house in the realm, to disturb families at meals, to force the doors of bedrooms, and, if the sum demanded was not punctually

---

* Grey's Debates, Feb. 25, 26, and 27, 1688-9.

paid, to sell the trencher on which the barley loaf was divided among the poor children, and the pillow from under the head of the lying-in woman. Nor could the Treasury effectually restrain the chimney-man from using his powers with harshness; for the tax was farmed; and the Government was consequently forced to connive at outrages and exactions such as have, in every age, made the name of publican a proverb for all that is most hateful.

William had been so much moved by what he had heard of these grievances that, at one of the earliest sittings of the Privy Council, he introduced the subject. He sent a message requesting the House of Commons to consider whether better regulations would effectually prevent the abuses which had excited so much discontent. He added that he would willingly consent to the entire abolition of the tax if it should appear that the tax and the abuses were inseparable.* This communication was received with loud applause. There were indeed some financiers of the old school who muttered that tenderness for the poor was a fine thing, but that no part of the revenue of the state came in so exactly to the day as the hearth money; that the goldsmiths of the City could not always be induced to lend on the security of the next quarter's customs or excise, but that on an assignment of hearth money there was no difficulty in obtaining advances. In the House of Commons, those who thought thus did not venture to raise their voices in opposition to the general feeling. But in the Lords there was a conflict of which the event for a time seemed doubtful. At length the influence of the Court strenuously exerted, carried an Act by which the chimney tax was declared a badge of slavery, and was, with many expressions of gratitude to the King, abolished forever.†

The Commons granted, with little dispute, and without a division, six hundred thousand pounds for the purpose of repaying to the United Provinces the charges of the expedition which had delivered England. The facility with which this large sum was voted to a shrewd, diligent, and thrifty people, our allies, indeed, politically, but commercially our most formidable rivals, excited some murmurs out of doors, and was, during many years, a favorite subject of sarcasm with Tory pamphleteers.‡ The liberality

---
* Commons' Journals, and Grey's Debates, March 1, 1688-9.
† 1 W. & M. sess. i. c. 10; Burnet, ii. 13.
‡ Commons' Journals, March 15, 1688-9. So late as 1713, Arbuthnot, in the fifth part

of the House admits however of an easy explanation. On the very day on which the subject was under consideration, alarming news arrived at Westminster, and convinced many, who would at another time have been disposed to scrutinize severely any account sent in by the Dutch, that our country could not yet dispense with the services of the foreign troops.

France had declared war against the States General, and the States General had consequently demanded from the King of England those succors which he was bound by the treaty of Nimeguen to furnish.* He had ordered some battalions to march to Harwich, that they might be in readiness to cross to the Continent. The old soldiers of James were generally in a very bad temper, and this order did not produce a soothing effect. The discontent was greatest in the regiment which now ranks as the first of the line. Though borne on the English establishment, that regiment, from the time when it first fought under the great Gustavus, had been almost exclusively composed of Scotchmen; and Scotchmen have never, in any region to which their adventurous and aspiring temper has led them, failed to note and to resent every slight offered to Scotland. Officers and men muttered that a vote of a foreign assembly was nothing to them. If they could be absolved from their allegiance to King James the Seventh, it must be by the Estates at Edinburgh, and not by the Convention at Westminster. Their ill humor increased when they heard that Schomberg had been appointed their colonel. They ought perhaps to have thought it an honor to be called by the name of the greatest soldier in Europe. But, brave and skillful as he was, he was not their countryman; and their regiment, during the fifty-six years which had elapsed since it gained its first honorable distinctions in Germany, had never been commanded but by a Hepburn or a Douglas. While they were in this angry and punctilious mood, they were ordered to join the forces which were assembling at Harwich. There was much murmuring; but there was no outbreak till the regiment arrived at Ipswich. There the signal of revolt was given by two captains who were zealous for the exiled King. The market place was soon filled with pikemen and musketeers running to and fro. Gunshots were wildly fired in all directions. Those

of John Bull, alluded to this transaction with much pleasantry. "As to your Venire Facias," says John to Nick Frog, "I have paid you for one already."

* Wagenaar, lxi.

officers who attempted to restrain the rioters were overpowered and disarmed. At length the chiefs of the insurrection established some order, and marched out of Ipswich at the head of their adherents. The little army consisted of about eight hundred men. They had seized four pieces of cannon, and had taken possession of the military chest, which contained a considerable sum of money. At the distance of half a mile from the town a halt was called: a general consultation was held; and the mutineers resolved that they would hasten back to their native country, and would live and die with their rightful King. They instantly proceeded northward by forced marches.*

When the news reached London the dismay was great. It was rumored that alarming symptons had appeared in other regiments, and particularly that a body of fusileers which lay at Harwich was likely to imitate the example set at Ipswich. "If these Scots," said Halifax to Reresby, "are unsupported, they are lost. But if they are acting in concert with others, the danger is serious indeed."† The truth seems to be that there was a conspiracy which had ramifications in many parts of the army, but that the conspirators were awed by the firmness of the Government and of the Parliament. A committee of the Privy Council was sitting when the tidings of the mutiny arrived in London. William Harbord, who represented the borough of Launceston, was at the board. His colleagues entreated him to go down instantly to the House of Commons, and to relate what had happened. He went, rose in his place, and told his story. The spirit of the assembly rose to the occasion. Howe was the first to call for vigorous action. "Address the King," he said, "to send his Dutch troops after these men. I know not who else can be trusted." "This is no jesting matter," said old Birch, who had been a colonel in the service of the Parliament, and had seen the most powerful and renowned House of Commons that ever sate twice purged and twice expelled by its own soldiers; "if you let this evil spread, you will have an army upon you in a few days. Address the King to send horse and foot instantly, his own men, men whom he can trust, and to put these people down at once." The men of the long robe caught the flame. "It is not the learning of my profession that is needed here," said Treby. "What is now to be done is to meet force with force, and to main-

---
* Commons' Journals, March 15, 1688-9. † Reresby's Memoirs.

tain in the field what we have done in the senate." "Write to the sheriffs," said Colonel Mildmay, member for Essex. "Raise the militia. There are a hundred and fifty thousand of them: they are good Englishmen: they will not fail you." It was resolved that all members of the House who held commissions in the army should be dispensed from parliamentary attendance, in order that they might repair instantly to their military posts. An address was unanimously voted requesting the King to take effectual steps for the suppression of the rebellion, and to put forth a proclamation denouncing public vengeance on the rebels. One gentleman hinted that it might be well to advise His Majesty to offer a pardon to those who should peaceably submit: but the House wisely rejected the suggestion. "This is no time," it was well said, "for anything that looks like fear." The address was instantly sent up to the Lords. The Lords concurred in it. Two peers, two knights of shires, and two burgesses were sent with it to Court. William received them graciously, and informed them that he had already given the necessary orders. In fact, several regiments of horse and dragoons had been sent northwards under the command of Ginkell, one of the bravest and ablest officers of the Dutch army.*

Meanwhile the mutineers were hastening across the country which lies between Cambridge and the Wash. Their way lay through a vast and desolate fen, saturated with the moisture of thirteen counties, and overhung during the greater part of the year by a low grey mist, high above which rose, visible many miles, the magnificent tower of Ely. In that dreary region, covered by vast flights of wild fowl, a half savage population, known by the name of the Breedlings, then led an amphibious life, sometimes wading, and sometimes rowing, from one islet of firm ground to another.† The roads were among the worst in the island, and as soon as rumor announced the approach of the rebels, were studiously made worse by the country people. Bridges were broken down. Trees were laid across the highways to obstruct the progress of the cannon. Nevertheless the Scotch veterans not only pushed forward with great speed, but succeeded in carrying their

---

* Commons' Journals, and Grey's Debates, March 15, 1688-9; London Gazette, March 18.
† As to the state of this region in the latter part of the seventeenth and the earlier part or the eighteenth century, see Pepys's Diary, Sept. 18, 1663, and the Tour through the whole Island of Great Britain, 1724.

artillery with them. They entered Lincolnshire, and were not far from Sleaford, when they learned that Ginkell with an irresistible force was close on their track. Victory and escape were equally out of the question. The bravest warriors could not contend against fourfold odds. The most active infantry could not outrun horsemen. Yet the leaders, probably despairing of pardon, urged the men to try the chance of battle. In that region, a spot almost surrounded by swamps and pools was without difficulty found. Here the insurgents were drawn up; and the cannon were planted at the only point which was thought not to be sufficiently protected by natural defences. Ginkell ordered the attack to be made at a place which was out of the range of the guns; and his dragoons dashed gallantly into the water, though it was so deep that their horses were forced to swim. Then the mutineers lost heart. They beat a parley, surrendered at discretion, and were brought up to London under a strong guard. Their lives were forfeit; for they had been guilty, not merely of mutiny, which was then not a legal crime, but of levying war against the King. William, however, with politic clemency, abstained from shedding the blood even of the most culpable. A few of the ringleaders were brought to trial at the next Bury assizes, and were convicted of high treason; but their lives were spared. The rest were merely ordered to return to their duty. The regiment, lately so refractory, went submissively to the Continent, and there, through many hard campaigns, distinguished itself by fidelity, by discipline, and by valor.*

This event facilitated an important change in our polity, a change which, it is true, could not have been long delayed, but which would not have been easily accomplished except at a moment of extreme danger. The time had at length arrived at which it was necessary to make a legal distinction between the soldier and the citizen. Under the Plantagenets and the Tudors there had been no standing army. The standing army which had existed under the last kings of the House of Stuart had been regarded by every party in the state with strong and not unreasonable aversion. The common law gave the Sovereign no

* London Gazette, March 25, 1689; Van Citters to the States General, $\frac{\text{March 22,}}{\text{April 1,}}$ Letters of Nottingham in the State Paper Office, dated July 23, and August 9, 1689; Historical Record of the first Regiment of Foot, printed by authority. See also a curious digression in the Compleat History of the Life and Military Actions of Richard, Earl of Tyrconnel, 1689.

power to control his troops. The Parliament, regarding them as mere tools of tyranny, had not been disposed to give such power by statute. James, indeed, had induced his corrupt and servile judges to put on some obsolete laws a construction which enabled them to punish desertion capitally. But this construction was considered by all respectable jurists as unsound, and, had it been sound, would have been far from effecting all that was necessary for the purpose of maintaining military discipline. Even James did not venture to inflict death by sentence of a court martial. The deserter was treated as an ordinary felon, was tried at the assizes by a petty jury on a bill found by a grand jury, and was at liberty to avail himself of any technical flaw which might be discovered in the indictment.

The Revolution, by altering the relative position of the Sovereign and the Parliament, had altered also the relative position of the army and the nation. The King and the Commons were now at unity; and both were alike menaced by the greatest military power which had existed in Europe since the downfall of the Roman empire. In a few weeks thirty thousand veterans, accustomed to conquer, and led by able and experienced captains, might cross from the ports of Normandy and Brittany to our shores. That such a force would with little difficulty scatter three times that number of militia, no man well acquainted with war could doubt. There must, then, be regular soldiers; and, if there were to be regular soldiers, it must be indispensable, both to their efficiency, and to the security of every other class, that they should be kept under a strict discipline. An ill-disciplined army has ever been a more costly and a more licentious militia, impotent against a foreign enemy, and formidable only to the country which it is paid to defend. A strong line of demarcation must therefore be drawn between the soldiers and the rest of the community. For the sake of public freedom, they must, in the midst of freedom, be placed under a despotic rule. They must be subject to a sharper penal code, and to a more stringent code of procedure, than are administered by the ordinary tribunals. Some acts which in the citizen are innocent must in the soldier be crimes. Some acts which in the citizen are punished with fine or imprisonment must in the soldier be punished with death. The machinery by which courts of law ascertain the guilt or innocence of an accused citizen is too slow and too intricate to be applied to an accused soldier. For, of all the maladies incident to the body politic, military insubordination is that which requires the most prompt and drastic remedies. If the evil be not stopped as soon as it appears, it is certain to spread; and it cannot spread far without danger to the very vitals of the commonwealth. For the general safety, therefore, a summary jurisdiction of terrible extent must, in camps, be entrusted to rude tribunals composed of men of the sword.

But, though it was certain that the country could not, at that moment, be secure without professional soldiers, and equally certain that professional soldiers must be worse than useless unless they were placed under a rule more arbitrary and severe than that to which other men were subject, it was not without great misgivings that a House of Commons could venture to recognize the existence and to make provision for the government of a standing army. There was scarcely a public man of note who had not often avowed his conviction that our polity and a standing army could not exist together. The Whigs had been in the constant habit of repeating that standing armies had destroyed the free institutions of the neighboring nations. The Tories had repeated as constantly that, in our own island, a standing army had subverted the Church, oppressed the gentry, and murdered the King. No leader of either party could, without laying himself open to the charge of gross inconsistency, propose that such an army should henceforth be one of the permanent establishments of the realm. The mutiny at Ipswich, and the panic which that mutiny produced, made the first step in the right direction easy; and by that step the whole course of our subsequent legislation was determined. A short bill was brought in which began by declaring, in explicit terms, that standing armies and courts martial were unknown to the law of England. It was then enacted that, on account of the extreme perils impending at that moment over the state, no man mustered on pay in the service of the Crown should, on pain of death, or of such lighter punishment as a court martial should deem sufficient, desert his colors or mutiny against his commanding officers. This statute was to be in force only six months; and many of those who voted for it probably believed that it would, at the close of that period, be suffered to expire. The bill passed rapidly and easily. Not a single division was taken upon it in the House of Commons. A mitigating clause, indeed, which illustrates somewhat curiously the manners of that age, was added by way of rider after the third reading. This clause provided that no court martial should pass sentence of death except between the hours of six in the morning and one in the afternoon. The dinner hour was then early; and it was but too probable that a gentleman who had dined would be in a state in which he could not safely be trusted with the lives of his fellow creatures. With this amendment, the first and most concise of our many Mutiny Bills was sent up to the Lords; and was, in a few hours, hurried by them through all its stages and passed by the King.*

Thus began, without one dissentient voice in Parliament, without one murmur in the nation, a change which had become necessary to the safety of the state, yet which every party in the state then regarded with extreme dread and aversion. Six months passed; and still the public danger continued. The power necessary to the maintenance of military discipline was a second time entrusted to the Crown for a short term. The trust again expired, and was again renewed. By slow degrees familiarity reconciled the public mind to the names, once so odious, of standing army and court martial. It was proved by experience that, in a well constituted society, professional soldiers may be terrible to a foreign enemy, and yet submissive to the civil power. What had been at first tolerated as the exception began to be considered as the rule. Not a session passed without a Mutiny Bill. During two generations, indeed, an annual clamor against the new system was raised by some factious men desirous to weaken the hands of the government, and by some respectable men who felt an honest but injudicious reverence for every old constitutional tradition, and who were unable to understand that what at one stage in the progress of society is pernicious may, at another stage, be indispensable. But this clamor, as years rolled on, became fainter and fainter. The debate which recurred every spring on the Mutiny Bill came to be regarded merely as an occasion on which hopeful young orators, fresh from Christchurch, were to deliver maiden speeches, setting forth how the guards of

---

* Stat. 1 W. & M. sess. 1. c. 5; Commons' Journals, March 28, 1689.

Pisistratus seized the citadel of Athens, and how the Prætorian cohorts sold the Roman empire to Didius. At length these declamations became too ridiculous to be repeated. The most old-fashioned, the most eccentric politician could hardly, in the reign of George the Third, contend that there ought to be no regular soldiers, or that the ordinary law, administered by the ordinary courts, would effectually maintain discipline among such soldiers. All parties being agreed as to the general principle, a long succession of Mutiny Bills passed without any discussion, except when some particular article of the military code appeared to require amendment. It is perhaps because the army became thus gradually, and almost imperceptibly, one of the institutions of England, that it has acted in such perfect harmony with all her other institutions, has never once during a hundred and sixty years, been untrue to the throne, or disobedient to the law, has never once defied the tribunals or overawed the constituent bodies. To this day, however, the Estates of the Realm continue to set up periodically, with laudable jealousy, a landmark on the frontier which was traced at the time of the Revolution. They solemnly reassert every year the doctrine laid down in the Declaration of Rights; and they then grant to the Sovereign an extraordinary power to govern a certain number of soldiers according to certain rules during twelve months more.

In the same week in which the first Mutiny Bill was laid on the table of the Commons, another temporary law, made necessary by the unsettled state of the kingdom, was passed. Since the flight of James many persons who were believed to have been deeply implicated in his unlawful acts, or to be engaged in plots for his restoration, had been arrested and confined. During the vacancy of the throne, these men could derive no benefit from the Habeas Corpus Act. For the machinery by which alone that Act could be carried into execution had ceased to exist; and, through the whole of Hilary term, all the courts in Westminster Hall had remained closed. Now that the ordinary tribunals were about to resume their functions, it was apprehended that those prisoners whom it was not convenient to bring instantly to trial would demand and obtain their liberty. A bill was therefore brought in which empowered the King to detain in custody during a few weeks such persons as he should suspect of evil designs against his government. This bill passed the two Houses with little or no opposition.* But the malcontents out of doors did not fail to remark that, in the late reign, the Habeas Corpus Act had not been one day suspended. It was the fashion to call James a tyrant, and William a deliverer. Yet, before the deliverer had been a month on the throne, he had deprived Englishmen of a precious right which the tyrant had respected.† This is a kind of reproach which a government sprung from a popular revolution almost inevitably incurs. From such a government men naturally think themselves entitled to demand a more gentle and liberal administration than is expected from old and deeply rooted power. Yet such a government, having, as it always has, many active enemies, and not having the strength derived from legitimacy and prescription, can at first maintain itself only by a vigilance and a severity of which old and deeply rooted power stands in no need. Extraordinary and irregular vindications of public liberty are sometimes necessary: yet, however necessary, they are almost always followed by some temporary abridgments of that very liberty; and every such abridgment is a fertile and plausible theme for sarcasm and invective.

Unhappily sarcasm and invective directed against William were but too likely to find favorable audience. Each of the two great parties had its own reasons for being dissatisfied with him; and there were some complaints in which both parties joined. His manners gave almost universal offence. He was in truth far better qualified to save a nation than to adorn a court. In the highest parts of statesmanship, he had no equal among his contemporaries. He had formed plans not inferior in grandeur and boldness to those of Richelieu, and had carried them into effect with a tact and wariness worthy of Mazarin. Two countries, the seats of civil liberty and of the Reformed Faith, had been preserved by his wisdom and courage from extreme perils. Holland he had delivered from foreign, and England from domestic foes. Obstacles apparently insurmountable had been interposed between him and the ends on which he was intent; and those obstacles his genius had turned into stepping stones. Under his dexterous management the hereditary enemies of his house had helped him to mount a throne; and the persecutors of his religion had helped him to rescue his religion from persecution. Fleets

---

* Stat. 1 W. & M. sess. 1. c. 2.   † Ronquillo, March 8-18, 1689.

and armies, collected to withstand him, had, without a struggle, submitted to his orders. Factions and sects, divided by mortal antipathies, had recognized him as their common head. Without carnage, without devastation, he had won a victory compared with which all the victories of Gustavus and Turenne were insignificant. In a few weeks he had changed the relative position of all the states in Europe, and had restored the equilibrium which the preponderance of one power had destroyed. Foreign nations did ample justice to his great qualities. In every Continental country where Protestant congregations met, fervent thanks were offered to God, who, from among the progeny of His servants, Maurice, the deliverer of Germany, and William, the deliverer of Holland, had raised up a third deliverer, the wisest and mightiest of all. At Vienna, at Madrid, nay, at Rome, the valiant and sagacious heretic was held in honor as the chief of the great confederacy against the House of Bourbon; and even at Versailles the hatred which he inspired was largely mingled with admiration.

Here he was less favorably judged. In truth, our ancestors saw him in the worst of all lights. By the French, the Germans, and the Italians, he was contemplated at such a distance that only what was great could be discerned, and that small blemishes were invisible. To the Dutch he was brought close: but he was himself a Dutchman. In his intercourse with them he was seen to the best advantage: he was perfectly at his ease with them; and from among them he had chosen his earliest and dearest friends. But to the English he appeared in a most unfortunate point of view. He was at once too near to them and too far from them. He lived among them, so that the smallest peculiarity of temper or manner could not escape their notice. Yet he lived apart from them, and was to the last a foreigner in speech, tastes, and habits.

One of the chief functions of our Sovereigns had long been to preside over the society of the capital. That function Charles the Second had performed with immense success. His easy bow, his good stories, his style of dancing and playing tennis, the sound of his cordial laugh, were familiar to all London. One day he was seen among the elms of Saint James's Park chatting with Dryden about poetry.* Another day his arm was on Tom Durfey's

---

* See the account given in Spence's Anecdotes of the Origin of Dryden's Medal.

shoulder; and His Majesty was taking a second, while his companion sang "Phillida, Phillida," or "To horse, brave boys, to Newmarket, to horse."* James, with much less vivacity and good nature, was accessible, and, to people who did not cross him, civil. But of this sociableness William was entirely destitute. He seldom came forth from his closet; and when he appeared in the public rooms, he stood among the crowd of courtiers and ladies, stern and abstracted, making no jest and smiling at none. His freezing look, his silence, the dry and concise answers which he uttered when he could keep silence no longer, disgusted noblemen and gentlemen who had been accustomed to be slapped on the back by their royal masters, called Jack or Harry, congratulated about race cups or rallied about actresses. The women missed the homage due to their sex. They observed that the King spoke in a somewhat imperious tone even to the wife to whom he owed so much, and whom he sincerely loved and esteemed.† They were amused and shocked to see him, when the Princess Anne dined with him, and when the first green peas of the year were put on the table, devour the whole dish without offering a spoonful to Her Royal Highness: and they pronounced that this great soldier and politician was no better than a Low Dutch bear.‡

One misfortune, which was imputed to him as a crime, was his bad English. He spoke our language, but not well. His accent was foreign; his diction was inelegant; and his vocabulary seems to have been no larger than was necessary for the transaction of business. To the difficulty which he felt in expressing himself, and to his consciousness that his pronuciation was bad, must be partly ascribed the taciturnity and the short answers which gave so much offence. Our literature he was incapable of enjoying or of understanding. He never once, during his

---

* Guardian, No. 67.
† There is abundant proof that William, though a very affectionate, was not always a polite husband. But no credit is due to the story contained in the letter which Dalrymple was foolish enough to publish as Nottingham's in 1773, and wise enough to omit in the edition of 1790. How any person who knew anything of the history of those times could be so strangely deceived, it is not easy to understand, particularly as the handwriting bears no resemblance to Nottingkam's, with which Dalrymple was familiar. The letter is evidently a common newsletter, written by a scribbler, who had never seen the King and Queen except at some public place, and whose anecdotes of their private life rested on no better authority than coffee-house gossip.

‡ Ronquillo; Burnet, ii. 2; Duchess of Marlborough's Vindication. In a pastoral dialogue between Philander and Palæmon, published in 1691, the dislike with which women of fashion regarded William is mentioned. Philander says:—

"But man methinks his reason should recall,
Nor let frail woman work his second fall."

whole reign, showed himself at the theater.* The poets
who wrote Pindaric verses in his praise, complained that
their flights of sublimity were beyond his comprehension.†
Those who are acquainted with the panegyrical odes of
that age will perhaps be of opinion that he did not lose
much by his ignorance.

It is true that his wife did her best to supply what was
wanting, and that she was excellently well qualified to be
the head of the Court. She was English by birth, and
English also in her tastes and feelings. Her face was
handsome, her port majestic, her temper sweet and lively,
her manners affable and graceful. Her understanding,
though very imperfectly cultivated, was quick. There
was no want of feminine wit and shrewdness in her conversation; and her letters were so well expressed that they
deserved to be well spelt. She took much pleasure in the
lighter kinds of literature, and did something towards
bringing books into fashion among ladies of quality. The
stainless purity of her private life and the strict attention
which she paid to her religious duties were the more respectable, because she was singularly free from censoriousness, and discouraged scandal as much as vice. In dislike
of backbiting indeed she and her husband cordially agreed:
but they showed that dislike in different and in very characteristic ways. William preserved profound silence, and
gave the talebearer a look, which, as was said by a person
who had once encountered it, and who took good care
never to encounter it again, made your story go back down
your throat.‡ Mary had a way of interrupting tattle
about elopements, duels, and play-debts, by asking the
tattlers, very quietly yet significantly, whether they had
ever read her favorite sermon, Dr. Tillotson's on Evil
Speaking. Her charities were munificent and judicious;

* Tuchin's Observator of November 16, 1706.

† Prior, who was treated by William with much kindness, and who was very grateful
for it, informs us that the King did not understand poetical eulogy. The passage is in
a highly curious manuscript, the property of Lord Lansdowne.

‡ Mémoires Originaux sur le Règne et la Cour de Frédéric I., Roi de Prusse, écrits
par Christophe Comte de Dohna. Berlin, 1833. It is strange that this interesting volume should be almost unknown in England. The only copy that I have ever seen of
it was kindly given to me by Sir Robert Adair. "Le Roi," Dohna says, "avoit
une autre qualité très estimable, qui est celle de n'aimer point qu'on rendit de mauvais
offices à personne par des railleries." The Marquis de la Forêt tried to entertain His
Majesty at the expense of an English nobleman. "Ce prince," says Dohna, "prit son
air sévère, et, le regardant sans mot dire, lui fit rentrer les paroles dans le ventre. Le
Marquis m'en fit ses plaintes quelques heures après. ' J'ai mal pris ma bisque,' dit-il;
' j'ai cru faire l'agréable sur le chapitre de Milord. . . mais j'ai trouvé à qui parler,
et j'ai attrapé un regard du roi qui m'a fait passer l'envie de rire.' " Dohna supposed
that William might be less sensitive about the character of a Frenchman, and tried
the experiment. But, says he, " J'eus à peu près le même sort que M. de la Forêt."

and, though she made no ostentatious display of them, it was known that she retrenched from her own state in order to relieve Protestants whom persecution had driven from France and Ireland, and who were starving in the garrets of London. So amiable was her conduct, that she was generally spoken of with esteem and tenderness by the most respectable of those who disapproved of the manner in which she had been raised to the throne, and even of those who refused to acknowledge her as Queen. In the Jacobite lampoons of that time, lampoons which, in virulence and malignity, far exceed anything that our age has produced, she was not often mentioned with severity. Indeed she sometimes expressed her surprise at finding that libellers who respected nothing else respected her name. God, she said, knew where her weakness lay. She was too sensitive to abuse and calumny: He had mercifully spared her a trial which was beyond her strength; and the best return which she could make to Him was to discountenance all malicious reflections on the characters of others. Assured that she possessed her husband's entire confidence and affection, she turned the edge of his sharp speeches sometimes by soft and sometimes by playful answers, and employed all the influence which she derived from her many pleasing qualities to gain the hearts of the people for him.*

If she had long continued to assemble round her the best society of London, it is probable that her kindness and courtesy would have done much to efface the unfavorable impression made by his stern and frigid demeanor. Unhappily his physical infirmities made it impossible for him to reside at Whitehall. The air of Westminster, mingled

* Compare the account of Mary by the Whig Burnet with the mention of her by the Tory Evelyn in his Diary, March 8, 1694-5, and with what is said of her by the Nonjuror who wrote the Letter to Archbishop Tenison on her death in 1695. The impression which the bluntness and reserve of William and the grace and gentleness of Mary had made on the populace may be traced in the remains of the street poetry of that time. The following conjugal dialogue may still be seen on the original broadside:

"Then bespoke Mary, our most royal Queen,
'My gracious King William where are you going?'
He answered her quickly, 'I count him no man
That telleth his secret unto a woman.'
The Queen with a modest behaviour replied,
'I wish that kind Providence may be thy guide,
To keep thee from danger, my sovereign Lord,
The which will the greatest of comfort afford.'"

These lines are in an excellent collection formed by Mr. Richard Heber, and now the property of Mr. Broderip, by whom it was kindly lent to me. In one of the most savage Jacobite pasquinades of 1689, William is described as

"A churle to his wife which she makes but a jest."

with the fog of the river, which in spring tides overflowed
the courts of his palace, with the smoke of seacoal from
two hundred thousand chimneys, and with the fumes of all
the filth which was then suffered to accumulate in the
streets, was insupportable to him; for his lungs were weak,
and his sense of smell exquisitely keen. His constitutional
asthma made rapid progress. His physicians pronounced
it impossible that he could live to the end of the year. His
face was so ghastly that he could hardly be recognized.
Those who had to transact business with him were shocked
to hear him gasping for breath, and coughing till the tears
ran down his cheeks.* His mind, strong as it was, sympathized with his body. His judgment was indeed as clear
as ever. But there was, during some months, a perceptible relaxation of that energy by which he had been distinguished. Even his Dutch friends whispered that he was
not the man that he had been at the Hague.† It was absolutely necessary that he should quit London. He accordingly took up his residence in the purer air of Hampton
Court. That mansion, begun by the magnificent Wolsey,
was a fine specimen of the architecture which flourished in
England under the first Tudors: but the apartments were
not, according to the notions of the seventeenth century,
well fitted for purposes of state. Our princes therefore
had, since the Restoration, repaired thither seldom, and
only when they wished to live for a time in retirement. As
William proposed to make the deserted edifice his chief
palace, it was necessary for him to build and to plant; nor
was the necessity disagreeable to him. For he had, like
most of his countrymen, a pleasure in decorating a country
house; and next to hunting, though at a great interval, his
favorite amusements were architecture and gardening.
He had already created on a sandy heath in Guelders a
paradise, which attracted multitudes of the curious from
Holland and Westphalia. Mary had laid the first stone of
the house. Bentinck had superintended the digging of
the fishponds. There were cascades and grottoes, a spacious orangery, and an aviary which furnished Honde-

---

* Burnet, ii. 2; Burnet, MS. Harl. 6584. But Ronquillo's account is much more cir-
cumstantial. "Nada se ha visto mas desfigurado; y, quantas veces he estado con el, le he
visto toser tanto que se le saltaban las lagrimas, y se ponia moxado y arrancando; y con-
fiesan los medicos que es una asma incurable." Mar. 8-18, 1689. Avaux wrote to the
same effect from Ireland. "La santé de l'usurpateur est fort mauvaise. L'on ne croit
pas qu'il vive un an." April 8-18.

† "Hasta decir los mismos Hollandeses que lo desconozcan," says Ronquillo. "Il est
absolument mal propre pour le rôle qu'il a à jouer à l'heure qu'il est," says Avaux.
"Slothful and sickly," says Evelyn, March 29, 1689.

koeter with numerous specimens of many colored plumage.*
The King, in his splendid banishment, pined for this favorite seat, and found some consolation in creating another Loo on the banks of the Thames. Soon a wide extent of ground was laid out in formal walks and parterres. Much idle ingenuity was employed in forming that intricate labyrinth of verdure which has puzzled and amused five generations of holiday visitors from London. Limes thirty years old were transplanted from neighboring woods to shade the alleys. Artificial fountains spouted among the flower-beds. A new court, not designed with the purest taste, but stately, spacious, and commodious, rose under the direction of Wren. The wainscots were adorned with the rich and delicate carvings of Gibbons. The staircases were in a blaze with the glaring frescoes of Verrio. In every corner of the mansion appeared a profusion of gewgaws, not yet familiar to English eyes. Mary had acquired at the Hague a taste for the porcelain of China, and amused herself by forming at Hampton a vast collection of hideous images, and of vases on which houses, trees, bridges, and mandarins, were depicted in outrageous defiance of all the laws of perspective. The fashion, a frivolous and inelegant fashion it must be owned, which was thus set by the amiable Queen, spread fast and wide. In a few years almost every great house in the kingdom contained a museum of these grotesque baubles. Even statesmen and generals were not ashamed to be renowned as judges of teapots and dragons; and satirists long continued to repeat that a fine lady valued her mottled green pottery quite as much as she valued her monkey, and much more than she valued her husband.†

But the new palace was embellished with works of art of a very different kind. A gallery was erected for the cartoons of Raphael. Those great pictures, then and still the finest on our side of the Alps, had been preserved by Cromwell from the fate which befell most of the other masterpieces in the collection of Charles the First, but had been suffered to lie during many years nailed up in deal boxes. Peter, raising the cripple at the Beautiful Gate, and Paul proclaiming the Unknown God to the philoso-

---

* See Harris's description of Loo, 1699.
† Every person who is well acquainted with Pope and Addison will remember their sarcasms on this taste. Lady Mary Wortley Montague took the other side. "Old China," she says, "is below nobody's taste, since it has been the Duke of Argyle's, whose understanding has never been doubted either by his friends or enemies."

phers of Athens, were now brought forth from obscurity
to be contemplated by artists with admiration and despair.
The expense of the works at Hampton was the subject of
bitter complaint to many Tories, who had very gently
blamed the boundless profusion with which Charles the
Second had built and rebuilt, furnished and refurnished,
the dwelling of the Duchess of Portsmouth.* The expense, however, was not the chief cause of the discontent
which William's change of residence excited. There was
no longer a Court at Westminster. Whitehall, once the
daily resort of the noble and the powerful, the beautiful
and the gay, the place to which fops came to show their
new peruques, men of gallantry to exchange glances with
fine ladies; politicians to push their fortunes, loungers to
hear the news, country gentlemen to see the royal family,
was now, in the busiest season of the year, when London
was full, when Parliament was sitting, left desolate. A
solitary sentinel paced the grass-grown pavement before
that door which had once been too narrow for the opposite streams of entering and departing courtiers. The services which the metropolis had rendered to the King were
great and recent; and it was thought that he might have
requited those services better than by treating it as Lewis
had treated Paris. Halifax ventured to hint this, but was
silenced by a few words which admitted of no reply.
"Do you wish," said William peevishly, "to see me dead?" †

In a short time it was found that Hampton Court was
too far from the Houses of Lords and Commons, and from
the public offices, to be the ordinary abode of the Sovereign. Instead, however, of returning to Whitehall, William determined to have another dwelling, near enough to
his capital for the transaction of business, but not near
enough to be within that atmosphere in which he could
not pass a night without risk of suffocation. At one time
he thought of Holland House,‡ the villa of the noble family

---

* As to the works at Hampton Court see Evelyn's Diary, July 16, 1689; the Tour through Great Britain, 1724; the British Apelles; Horace Walpole on Modern Gardening; Burnet ii. 2, 3.
When Evelyn was at Hampton Court, in 1662, the cartoons were not to be seen. The triumphs of Andra Mantegna were then supposed to be the finest pictures in the palace.
† Burnet, ii. 2; Reresby's Memoirs. Ronquillo wrote repeatedly to the same effect. For example: "Bien quisiera que el Rey fuese mas comunicable, y se acomodase un poco mas al humor sociable de los Ingleses, y que estubiera en Londres: pero es cierto que sus achaques no se lo permiten." July 8–18, 1689. Avaux, about the same time, wrote this to Croissy from Ireland: "Le Prince d'Orange est toujours à Hampton Court, et jamais à la ville; et le peuple est fort mal satisfait de cette manière bizarre et retirée."
‡ Several of his letters to Heinsius are dated from Holland House.

of Rich; and he actually resided there some weeks. But he at length fixed his choice on Kensington House, the suburban residence of the Earl of Nottingham. The purchase was made for eighteen thousand guineas, and was followed by more building, more planting, more expense, and more discontent.* At present Kensington House is considered as a part of London. It was then a rural mansion, and could not, in those days of highwaymen and scourers, of roads deep in mire and nights without lamps, be the rallying point of fashionable society. It was well known that the King, who treated the English nobility and gentry so ungraciously, could, in a small circle of his own countrymen, be easy, friendly, even jovial, could pour out his feelings garrulously, could fill his glass, perhaps too often; and this was, in the view of our forefathers, an aggravation of his offences. Yet our forefathers should have had the sense and the justice to acknowledge that the patriotism, which they considered as a virtue in themselves, could not be a fault in him. It was unjust to blame him for not at once transferring to our island the love which he bore to the country of his birth. If, in essentials, he did his duty towards England, he might well be suffered to feel at heart an affectionate preference for Holland. Nor is it a reproach to him that he did not, in the season of his greatness, discard companions who had played with him in his childhood, who had stood by him firmly through all the vicissitudes of his youth and manhood, who had, in defiance of the most loathsome and deadly forms of infection, kept watch by his sick bed, who had, in the thickest of the battle, thrust themselves between him and the French swords, and whose attachment was, not to the Stadtholder or to the King, but to plain William of Nassau. It may be added that his old friends could not but rise in his estimation by comparison with his new courtiers. To the end of his life all his Dutch comrades, without exception, continued to deserve his confidence. They could be out of humor with him, it is true; and, when out of humor, they could be sullen and rude; but never did they, even when most angry and unreasonable, fail to keep his secrets and to watch over his interests with gentleman-like and soldier-like fidelity. Among his English counsellors such fidelity was rare. It is painful, but it is no more than just, to acknowledge that

---

* Luttrell's Diary; Evelyn's Diary, Feb. 25, 1689, 1690.

he had but too good reason for thinking meanly of our national character.* That character was indeed, in essentials, what it has always been. Veracity, uprightness, and manly boldness were then, as now, qualities eminently English. But those qualities, though widely diffused among the great body of the people, were seldom to be found in the class with which William was best acquainted. The standard of honor and virtue among our public men was, during his reign, at the very lowest point. His predecessors had bequeathed to him a court foul with all the vices of the Restoration, a court swarming with sycophants, who were ready, on the first turn of fortune, to abandon him as they had abandoned his uncle. Here and there, lost in that ignoble crowd, was to be found a man of true integrity and public spirit. Yet even such a man could not long live in such society without much risk that the strictness of his principles would be relaxed, and the delicacy of his sense of right and wrong impaired. It was surely unjust to blame a prince surrounded by flatterers and traitors for wishing to keep near him four or five servants whom he knew by proof to be faithful even to death.

Nor was this the only instance in which our ancestors were unjust to him. They had expected that, as soon as so distinguished a soldier and statesman was placed at the head of affairs, he would give some signal proof, they scarcely knew what, of genius and vigor. Unhappily, during the first months of his reign, almost everything went wrong. His subjects, bitterly disappointed, threw the blame on him, and began to doubt whether he merited that reputation which he had won at his first entrance into public life, and which the splendid success of his last great enterprise had raised to the highest point. Had they been in a temper to judge fairly, they would have perceived that for the maladministration of which they with good reason complained he was not responsible. He could as yet work only with the machinery which he had found;

---

* De Foe makes this excuse for William:

"We blame the King that he relies too much
On strangers, Germans, Huguenots, and Dutch,
And seldom does his great affairs of state
To English counsellors communicate.
The fact might very well be answered thus:
He has too often been betrayed by us.
He must have been a madman to rely
On English gentlemen's fidelity.
The Foreigners have faithfully obeyed him,
And none but Englishmen have e'er betrayed him."
The True Born Englishman, Part II.

and the machinery which he had found was all rust and rottenness. From the time of the Restoration to the time of the Revolution, neglect and fraud had been almost constantly impairing the efficiency of every department of the government. Honors and public trusts, peerages, baronetcies, regiments, frigates, embassies, governments, commissionerships, leases of crown lands, contracts for clothing, for provisions, for ammunition, pardons for murder, for robbery, for arson, were sold at Whitehall scarcely less openly than asparagus at Covent Garden or herrings at Billingsgate. Brokers had been incessantly plying for custom in the purlieus of the court; and of these brokers the most successful had been, in the days of Charles, the harlots, and in the days of James, the priests. From the palace, which was the chief seat of this pestilence, the taint had diffused itself through every office, and through every rank in every office, and had everywhere produced feebleness and disorganization. So rapid was the progress of the decay, that within eight years after the time when Oliver had been the umpire of Europe, the roar of the guns of De Ruyter was heard in the Tower of London. The vices which had brought that great humiliation on the country had ever since been rooting themselves deeper and spreading themselves wider. James had, to do him justice, corrected a few of the gross abuses which disgraced the naval administration. Yet the naval administration, in spite of his attempts to reform it, moved the contempt of men who were acquainted with the dockyards of France and Holland. The military administration was still worse. The courtiers took bribes from the colonels: the colonels cheated the soldiers: the commissaries sent in long bills for what had never been furnished: the keepers of the magazines sold the public stores and pocketed the price. But these evils, though they had sprung into existence and grown to maturity under the government of Charles and James, first made themselves severely felt under the government of William. For Charles and James were content to be the vassals and pensioners of a powerful and ambitious neighbor: they submitted to his ascendency: they shunned with pusillanimous caution whatever could give him offence: and thus, at the cost of the independence and dignity of that ancient and glorious crown which they unworthily wore, they avoided a conflict which would instantly have shown how helpless, under their misrule, their once formidable kingdom had become. Their ignominious policy it was neither in William's power nor in his nature to follow. It was only by arms that the liberty and religion of England could be protected against the mightiest enemy that had threatened our island since the Hebrides were strown with the wrecks of the Armada. The body politic, which, while it remained in repose, had presented a superficial appearance of health and vigor, was now under the necessity of straining every nerve in a wrestle for life or death, and was immediately found to be unequal to the exertion. The first efforts showed an utter relaxation of fiber, an utter want of training. Those efforts were, with scarcely an exception, failures; and every failure was popularly imputed, not to the rulers whose mismanagement had produced the infirmities of the state, but to the ruler in whose time the infirmities of the state became visible.

William might indeed, if he had been as absolute as Lewis, have used such sharp remedies as would speedily have restored to the English administration that firm tone which had been wanting since the death of Oliver. But the instantaneous reform of inveterate abuses was a task far beyond the powers of a prince strictly restrained by law, and restrained still more strictly by the difficulties of his situation.*

Some of the most serious difficulties of his situation were caused by the conduct of the ministers on whom, new as he was to the details of English affairs, he was forced to rely for information about men and things. There was indeed no want of ability among his chief counsellors: but one half of their ability was employed in counteracting the other half. Between the Lord President and the Lord Privy Seal there was an inveterate enemity.† It had begun twelve years before, when Danby was Lord High Treasurer, a persecutor of non-conformists, an uncompromising defender of prerogative, and when Halifax was rising to distinction as one of the most eloquent leaders of the country party. In the reign of James, the two statesmen had found themselves in opposition together; and

---
* Ronquillo had the good sense and justice to make allowances which the English did not make. After describing, in a despatch dated March 1-11, 1689, the lamentabl. state of the military and naval establishments, he says, "De esto no tiene culpa el Principe de Oranges; porque pensar que se han de poder volver en dos meses tres Reynos de abaxo arriba es una extravagancia." Lord President Stair, in a letter written from London about a month later, says that the delays of the English administration had lowered the King's reputation, "though without his fault."

† Burnet, ii. 4; Reresby.

their common hostility to France and to Rome, to the High Commission and to the dispensing power, had produced an apparent reconciliation; but as soon as they were in office together the old antipathy revived. The hatred which the Whig party felt towards them both ought, it should seem, to have produced a close alliance between them: but in fact each of them saw with complacency the danger which threatened the other. Danby exerted himself to rally round him a strong phalanx of Tories. Under the plea of ill health, he withdrew from court, seldom came to the Council over which it was his duty to preside, passed much time in the country, and took scarcely any part in public affairs except by grumbling and sneering at all the acts of the government, and by doing jobs and getting places for his personal retainers.* In consequence of this defection, Halifax became Prime Minister, as far as any minister could, in that reign, be called Prime Minister. An immense load of business fell on him; and that load he was unable to sustain. In wit and eloquence, in amplitude of comprehension and subtlety of disquisition, he had no equal among the statesmen of his time. But that very fertility, that very acuteness, which gave a singular charm to his conversation, to his oratory, and to his writings, unfitted him for the work of promptly deciding practical questions. He was slow from very quickness. For he saw so many arguments for and against every possible course, that he was longer in making up his mind than a dull man would have been. Instead of acquiescing in his first thoughts, he replied on himself, rejoined on himself, and sur-rejoined on himself. Those who heard him talk owned that he talked like an angel: but too often, when he had exhausted all that could be said, and came to act, the time for action was over.

Meanwhile the two Secretaries of State were constantly laboring to draw their master in diametrically opposite directions. Every scheme, every person, recommended by one of them was reprobated by the other. Nottingham was never weary of repeating that the old Roundhead party, the party which had taken the life of Charles the First and had plotted against the life of Charles the Second, was in principle republican, and that the Tories were the only true friends of monarchy. Shrewsbury replied that the Tories might be friends of monarchy, but

---

* Reresby's Memoirs; Burnet MS. Harl. 6584.

that they regarded James as their monarch. Nottingham was always bringing to the closet intelligence of the wild day-dreams in which a few old eaters of calf's head, the remains of the once formidable party of Bradshaw and Ireton, still indulged at taverns in the City. Shrewsbury produced ferocious lampoons which the Jacobites dropped every day in the coffee-houses. "Every Whig," said the Tory Secretary, "is an enemy of Your Majesty's prerogative." "Every Tory," said the Whig Secretary, "is an enemy of Your Majesty's title."*

At the Treasury there was a complication of jealousies and quarrels.† Both the First Commissioner, Mordaunt, and the Chancellor of the Exchequer, Delamere, were zealous Whigs: but though they held the same political creed, their tempers differed widely. Mordaunt was volatile, dissipated, and generous. The wits of that time laughed at the way in which he flew about from Hampton Court to the Royal Exchange, and from the Royal Exchange back to Hampton Court. How he found time for dress, politics, love-making, and ballad-making was a wonder.‡ Delamere was gloomy and acrimonious, austere in his private morals, and punctual in his devotions, but greedy of ignoble gain. The two principal ministers of finance, therefore, became enemies, and agreed only in hating their colleague Godolphin. What business had he at Whitehall in these days of Protestant ascendency, he who had sate at the same board with Papists, he who had never scrupled to attend Mary of Modena to the idolatrous worship of the Mass? The most provoking circumstance was that Godolphin, though his name stood only third in the commission, was really first Lord. For in financial knowledge and in habits of business Mordaunt and Delamere were mere children when compared with him; and this William soon discovered.§

Similar feuds raged at other great boards and through all the subordinate ranks of public functionaries. In every custom-house, in every arsenal, were a Shrewsbury and a Nottingham, a Delamere and a Godolphin. The Whigs complained that there was no department in which crea-

---

* Burnet, ii. 3, 4, 15. † Burnet, ii. 5.
‡ " How does he do to distribute his hours,
  Some to the Court and some to the City,
Some to the State, and some to Love's powers,
  Some to be vain and some to be witty!"
            The Modern Lampooners, a poem of 1690.

§ Burnet, ii. 4.

tures of the fallen tyranny were not to be found. It was idle to allege that these men were versed in the details of business, that they were the depositaries of official traditions, and that the friends of liberty, having been, during many years, excluded from public employment, must necessarily be incompetent to take on themselves at once the whole management of affairs. Experience doubtless had its value: but surely the first of all the qualifications of a servant was fidelity; and no Tory could be a really faithful servant of the new government. If King William were wise, he would rather trust novices zealous for his interest and honor than veterans, who might indeed possess ability and knowledge, but who would use that ability and that knowledge to effect his ruin.

The Tories, on the other hand, complained that their share of power bore no proportion to their number, or to their weight in the country, and that everywhere old and useful public servants were, for the crime of being friends to monarchy and to the Church, turned out of their posts to make way for Rye House plotters and haunters of conventicles. These upstarts, adepts in the art of factious agitation, but ignorant of all that belonged to their new calling, would be just beginning to learn their business when they had undone the nation by their blunders. To be a rebel and a schismatic was surely not all that ought to be required of a man in high employment. What would become of the finances, what of the marine, if Whigs who could not understand the plainest balance sheet were to manage the revenue, and Whigs who had never walked over a dockyard to fit out the fleet? *

The truth is that the charges which the two parties brought against each other were, to a great extent, well founded, but that the blame which both threw on William was unjust. Official experience was to be found almost exclusively among the Tories, hearty attachment to the new settlement almost exclusively among the Whigs. It was not the fault of the King that the knowledge and the zeal, which, combined, make a valuable servant of the state, must at that time be had separately or not at all. If he employed men of one party, there was great risk of

* Ronquillo calls the Whig functionaries "Gente que no tienen pratica ni experiencia." He adds, "Y de esto procede el pasarse un mes y un otro, sin executarse nada." June 24, 1689. In one of the innumerable Dialogues which appeared at that time, the Tory interlocutor puts the question: "Do you think the government would be better served by strangers to business?" The Whig answers, "Better ignorant friends than understanding enemies,"

mistakes. If he employed men of the other party, there was great risk of treachery. If he employed men of both parties, there was still some risk of mistakes; there was still some risk of treachery; and to these risks was added the certainty of dissension. He might join Whigs and Tories: but it was beyond his power to mix them. In the same office, at the same desk, they were still enemies, and agreed only in murmuring at the Prince who tried to mediate between them. It was inevitable that, in such circumstances, the administration, fiscal, military, naval, should be feeble and unsteady; that nothing should be done in quite the right way or at quite the right time: that the distractions from which scarcely any public office was exempt should produce disasters, and that every disaster should increase the distractions from which it had sprung.

There was indeed one department of which the business was well conducted; and that was the department of Foreign Affairs. There William directed everything, and, on important occasions, neither asked the advice nor employed the agency of any English politician. One invaluable assistant he had, Anthony Heinsius, who, a few weeks after the Revolution had been accomplished, became Pensionary of Holland. Heinsius had entered public life as a member of that party which was jealous of the power of the House of Orange, and desirous to be on friendly terms with France. But he had been sent in 1681 on a diplomatic mission to Versailles; and a short residence there had produced a complete change in his views. On a near acquaintance, he was alarmed by the power and provoked by the insolence of that Court of which, while he contemplated it only at a distance, he had formed a favorable opinion. He found that his country was despised. He saw his religion persecuted. His official character did not save him from some personal affronts which, to the latest day of his long career, he never forgot. He went home a devoted adherent of William and a mortal enemy of Lewis.*

The office of Pensionary, always important, was peculiarly important when the Stadtholder was absent from the Hague. Had the politics of Heinsius been still what they once were, all the great designs of William might have been frustrated. But happily there was between these two eminent men a perfect friendship, which, till death

---
* Négociations de M. Le Comte d'Avaux, 4 Mars 1683; Torcy's Memoirs.

dissolved it, appears never to have been interrupted for one moment by suspicion or ill-humor. On all large questions of European policy they cordially agreed. They corresponded assiduously and most unreservedly. For, though William was slow to give his confidence, yet, when he gave it, he gave it entire. The correspondence is still extant, and is most honorable to both. The King's letters would alone suffice to prove that he was one of the greatest statesmen whom Europe has produced. While he lived, the Pensionary was content to be the most obedient, the most trusty, and the most discreet of servants. But, after the death of the master, the servant proved himself capable of supplying with eminent ability the master's place, and was renowned throughout Europe as one of the great Triumvirate which humbled the pride of Lewis the Fourteenth.*

The foreign policy of England, directed immediately by William in close concert with Heinsius, was, at this time, eminently skillful and successful. But in every other part of the administration the evils arising from the mutual animosity of factions were but too plainly discernible. Nor was this all. To the evils arising from the mutual animosity of factions were added other evils arising from the mutual animosity of sects.

The year 1689 is not a less important epoch in the ecclesiastical than in the civil history of England. In that year was granted the first legal indulgence to Dissenters. In that year was made the last serious attempt to bring the Presbyterians within the pale of the Church of England. From that year dates a new schism made in defiance of ancient precedents, by men who had always professed to regard schism with peculiar abhorrence, and ancient precedents with peculiar veneration. In that year began the long struggle between two great parties of conformists. Those parties indeed had, under various forms, existed within the Anglican communion ever since the Reformation; but till after the Revolution they did not appear marshalled in regular and permanent order of battle against each other, and were therefore not known by established names. Some time after the accession of William they

---

* The original correspondence of William and Heinsius is in Dutch. A French translation of all William's letters, and an English translation of a few of Heinsius's letters, are among the Mackintosh MSS. The Baron Sirtema de Grovestins, who has had access to the originals, frequently quotes passages in his "Histoire des iuttes et rivalités entre les puissances maritimes et la France." There is very little difference in substance, though much in phraseology, between his version and that which I have used.

began to be called the High Church party and the Low Church party; and, long before the end of his reign, these appellations were in common use.*

In the summer of 1688 the breaches which had long divided the great body of English Protestants had seemed to be almost closed. Disputes about Bishops and Synods, written prayers and extemporaneous prayers, white gowns and black gowns, sprinkling and dipping, kneeling and sitting, had been for a short space intermitted. The serried array which was then drawn up against Popery measured the whole of the vast interval which separated Sancroft from Bunyan. Prelates recently conspicuous as persecutors, now declared themselves friends of religious liberty, and exhorted their clergy to live in a constant interchange of hospitality and of kind offices with the Separatists. Separatists, on the other hand, who had recently considered mitres and lawn sleeves as the livery of Antichrist, were putting candles in windows and throwing fagots on bonfires in honor of the prelates.

These feelings continued to grow till they attained their greatest height on the memorable day on which the common oppressor finally quitted Whitehall, and on which an innumerable multitude, tricked out in orange ribbons, welcomed the common deliverer to St. James's. When the clergy of London came, headed by Compton, to express their gratitude to him by whose instrumentality God had wrought salvation for the Church and the State, the procession was swollen by some eminent non-conformist divines. It was delightful to many good men to hear that pious and learned Presbyterian ministers had walked in the train of a bishop, had been greeted by him with fraternal kindness, and had been announced by him in the presence chamber as his dear and respected friends, separated from him indeed by some differences of opinion on minor points, but united to him by Christian charity and by common zeal for the essentials of the reformed faith. There had never before been such a day in England; and there has never since been such a day. The tide of feeling was already on the turn; and the ebb was even more rapid than the flow had been. In a very few hours the High Churchman began to feel tenderness for the enemy whose tyranny was now no longer feared, and dislike of the

---
* Though these very convenient names are not, as far as I know, to be found in any book printed during the earlier years of William's reign, I shall use them without scruple, as others have done, in writing about the transactions of those years.

allies whose services were now no longer needed. It was easy to gratify both feelings by imputing to the Dissenters the misgovernment of the exiled King. His Majesty,— such was now the language of too many Anglican divines,— would have been an excellent sovereign had he not been too confiding, too forgiving. He had put his trust in a class of men who hated his office, his family, his person, with implacable hatred. He had ruined himself in the vain attempt to conciliate them. He had relieved them, in defiance of law and of the unanimous sense of the old royalist party, from the pressure of the penal code; had allowed them to worship God publicly after their own mean and tasteless fashion; had admitted them to the bench of justice and to the Privy Council; had gratified them with fur robes, gold chains, salaries, and pensions. In return for his liberality, these people, once so uncouth in demeanor, once so savage in opposition even to legitimate authority, had become the most abject of flatterers. They had continued to applaud and encourage him when the most devoted friends of his family had retired in shame and sorrow from his palace. Who had more foully sold the religion and liberty of England than Titus? Who had been more zealous for the dispensing power than Alsop. Who had urged on the persecution of the seven Bishops more fiercely than Lobb? What chaplain impatient for a deanery had ever, even when preaching in the royal presence on the thirtieth of January or the twenty-ninth of May, uttered adulation more gross than might easily be found in those addresses by which dissenting congregations had testified their gratitude for the illegal Declaration of Indulgence? Was it strange that a prince who had never studied law books should have believed that he was only exercising his rightful prerogative, when he was thus encouraged by a faction which had always ostentatiously professed hatred of arbitrary power? Misled by such guidance he had gone further and further in the wrong path: he had at length estranged from him hearts which would once have poured forth their best blood in his defence: he had left himself no supporters except his old foes; and, when the day of peril came, he had found that the feeling of his old foes towards him was still what it had been when they had attempted to rob him of his inheritance, and when they had plotted against his life. Every man of sense had long known that the sectaries bore no love to monarchy. It had now been found that they bore as little love to freedom. To trust them with power would be an error not less fatal to the nation than to the throne. If, in order to redeem pledges somewhat rashly given it should be thought necessary to grant them relief, every concession ought to be accompanied by limitations and precautions. Above all, no man who was an enemy to the ecclesiastical constitution of the realm ought to be permitted to bear any part in the civil government.

Between the non-conformists and the rigid conformists stood the Low Church party. That party contained, as it still contains, two very different elements, a Puritan element and a Latitudinarian element. On almost every question, however, relating either to ecclesiastical polity or to the ceremonial of public worship, the Puritan Low Churchman and the Latitudinarian Low Churchman were perfectly agreed. They saw in the existing polity and in the existing ceremonial no defect, no blemish, which could make it their duty to become Dissenters. Nevertheless they held that both the polity and the ceremonial were means and not ends, and that the essential spirit of Christianity might exist without episcopal orders and without a Book of Common Prayer. They had, while James was on the throne, been mainly instrumental in forming the great Protestant coalition against Popery and tyranny; and they continued in 1689 to hold the same conciliatory language which they had held in 1688. They gently blamed the scruples of the non-conformists. It was undoubtedly a great weakness to imagine that there could be any sin in wearing a white robe, in tracing a cross, in kneeling at the rails of an altar. But the highest authority had given the plainest directions as to the manner in which such weakness was to be treated. The weak brother was not to be judged: he was not to be despised: believers who had stronger minds were commanded to soothe him by large compliances, and carefully to remove out of his path every stumbling-block which could cause him to offend. An apostle had declared that, though he had himself no misgivings about the use of animal food or of wine, he would eat herbs and drink water rather than give scandal to the feeblest of his flock. What would he have thought of ecclesiastical rulers who, for the sake of a vestment, a gesture, a posture, had not only torn the Church asunder, but had filled all the gaols of England with men of orthodox faith

and saintly life? The reflections thrown by the High
Churchmen on the recent conduct of the dissenting body
the Low Churchmen pronounced to be grossly unjust.
The wonder was, not that a few non-conformists should
have accepted with thanks an indulgence which, illegal as
it was, had opened the doors of their prisons and given
security to their hearths, but that the non-conformists generally should have been true to the cause of a constitution
from the benefits of which they had been long excluded.
It was most unfair to impute to a great party the faults
of a few individuals. Even among the bishops of the
established Church James had found tools and sycophants.
The conduct of Cartwright and Parker had been much
more inexcusable than that of Alsop and Lobb. Yet those
who held the Dissenters answerable for the errors of Alsop
and Lobb would doubtless think it most unreasonable to
hold the Church answerable for the far deeper guilt of
Cartwright and Parker.

The Low Church clergymen were a minority, and not a
large minority, of their profession: but their weight was
much more than proportioned to their numbers: for they
mustered strong in the capital; they had great influence
there; and the average of intellect and knowledge was
higher among them than among their order generally. We
should probably overrate their numerical strength, if we
were to estimate them at a tenth part of the priesthood.
Yet it will scarcely be denied that there were among them
as many men of distinguished eloquence and learning as
could be found in the other nine-tenths. Among the laity
who conformed to the established religion the parties were
not unevenly balanced. Indeed the line which separated
them deviated very little from the line which separated the
Whigs and the Tories. In the House of Commons, which
had been elected when the Whigs were triumphant, the
Low Church party greatly preponderated. In the Lords
there was an almost exact equipoise; and very slight circumstances sufficed to turn the scale.

The head of the Low Church party was the King. He
had been bred a Presbyterian: he was, from rational conviction, a Latitudinarian; and personal ambition, as well
as higher motives, prompted him to act as mediator among
Protestant sects. He was bent on effecting three great
reforms in the laws touching ecclesiastical matters. His
first object was to obtain for dissenters permission to cele-

brate their worship in freedom and security. His second object was to make such changes in the Anglican ritual and polity as, without offending those to whom that ritual and that polity were dear, might conciliate the moderate non-conformists. His third object was to throw open civil offices to Protestants without distinction of sect. All his three objects were good: but the first only was at that time attainable. He came too late for the second, and too early for the third.

A few days after his accession, he took a step which indicated, in a manner not to be mistaken, his sentiments touching ecclesiastical polity and public worship. He found only one see unprovided with a bishop. Seth Ward, who had, during many years, had charge of the diocese of Salisbury, and who had been honorably distinguished as one of the founders of the Royal Society, having long survived his faculties, died while the country was agitated by the elections for the Convention, without knowing that great events, of which not the least important had passed under his own roof, had saved his Church and his country from ruin. The choice of a successor was no light matter. That choice would inevitably be considered by the country as a prognostic of the highest import. The King too might well be perplexed by the number of divines whose erudition, eloquence, courage, and uprightness had been conspicuously displayed during the contentions of the last three years. The preference was given to Burnet. His claims were doubtless great. Yet William might have had a more tranquil reign if he had postponed for a time the well-earned promotion of his chaplain, and had bestowed the first great spiritual preferment, which, after the Revolution, fell to the disposal of the Crown, on some eminent theologian, attached to the new settlement, yet not generally hated by the clergy. Unhappily the name of Burnet was odious to the great majority of the Anglican priesthood. Though, as respected doctrine, he by no means belonged to the extreme section of the Latitudinarian party, he was popularly regarded as the personification of the Latitudinarian spirit. This distinction he owed to the prominent place which he held in literature and politics, to the readiness of his tongue and of his pen, and above all to the frankness and boldness of his nature, frankness which could keep no secret, and boldness which flinched from no danger. He had formed but a low estimate of the character of his clerical brethren considered as a body; and with his usual indiscretion, he frequently suffered his opinion to escape him. They hated him in return with a hatred which has descended to their successors, and which, after the lapse of a century and a half, does not appear to languish.

As soon as the King's decision was known, the question was everywhere asked, What will the Archbishop do? Sancroft had absented himself from the Convention: he had refused to sit in the Privy Council: he had ceased to confirm, to ordain, and to institute; and he was seldom seen beyond the walls of his palace at Lambeth. He, on all occasions, professed to think himself still bound by his old oath of allegiance. Burnet he regarded as a scandal to the priesthood, a Presbyterian in a surplice. The prelate who should lay hands on that unworthy head would commit more than one great sin. He would, in a sacred place, and before a great congregation of the faithful, at once acknowledge an usurper as a King, and confer on a schismatic the character of a Bishop. During some time Sancroft positively declared that he would not obey the precept of William. Lloyd of Saint Asaph, who was the common friend of the Archbishop and of the Bishop elect, entreated and expostulated in vain. Nottingham, who, of all the laymen connected with the new government, stood best with the clergy, tried his influence, but to no better purpose. The Jacobites said everywhere that they were sure of the good old Primate; that he had the spirit of a martyr; that he was determined to brave, in the cause of the Monarchy and of the Church, the utmost rigor of those laws with which the obsequious parliaments of the sixteenth century had fenced the Royal Supremacy. He did in truth hold out long. But at the last moment his heart failed him, and he looked round him for some mode of escape. Fortunately, as childish scruples often disturbed his conscience, childish expedients often quieted it. A more childish expedient than that to which he now resorted is not to be found in all the tomes of the casuists. He would not himself bear a part in the service. He would not publicly pray for the Prince and Princess as King and Queen. He would not call for their mandate, order it to be read, and then proceed to obey it. But he issued a commission empowering any three of his suffragans to commit in his name, and as his delegates, the sins which he did not choose to commit in person. The reproaches of all parties soon made him ashamed of himself. He then tried to suppress the evidence of his fault by means more discreditable than the fault itself. He abstracted from among the public records of which he was the guardian the instrument by which he had authorized his brethren to act for him, and was with difficulty induced to give it up.*

Burnet however had, under the authority of this instrument, been consecrated. When he next waited on Mary, she reminded him of the conversations which they had held at the Hague about the high duties and grave responsibility of Bishops. "I hope," she said, "that you will put your notions in practice." Her hope was not disappointed. Whatever may be thought of Burnet's opinions touching civil and ecclesiastical polity, or of the temper and judgment which he showed in defending those opinions, the utmost malevolence of faction could not venture to deny that he tended his flock with a zeal, diligence, and disinterestedness worthy of the purest ages of the Church. His jurisdiction extended over Wiltshire and Berkshire. These counties he divided into districts which he sedulously visited. About two months of every summer he passed in preaching, catechising, and confirming daily from church to church. When he died there was no corner of his diocese in which the people had not had seven or eight opportunities of receiving his instructions and of asking his advice. The worst weather, the worst roads, did not prevent him from discharging these duties. On one occasion, when the floods were out, he exposed his life to imminent risk rather than disappoint a rural congregation which was in expectation of a discourse from the Bishop. The poverty of the inferior clergy was a constant cause of uneasiness to his kind and generous heart. He was indefatigable and at length successful in his attempts to obtain for them from the Crown that grant which is known by the name of Queen Anne's Bounty.† He was especially careful, when he traveled through his diocese, to lay no burden on them. Instead of requiring them to entertain him, he entertained them. He always fixed his

---
* Burnet, ii. 8; Birch's Life of Tillotson; Life of Kettlewell, part iii. section 62.
† Swift, writing under the name of Gregory Misosarum, most malignantly and dishonestly represents Burnet as grudging this grant to the Church. Swift cannot have been ignorant that the Church was indebted for the grant chiefly to Burnet's persevering exertions.

headquarters at a market town, kept a table there, and, by his decent hospitality and munificent charities, tried to conciliate those who were prejudiced against his doctrines. When he bestowed a poor benefice,—and he had many such to bestow,—his practice was to add out of his own purse twenty pounds a year to the income. Ten promising young men, to each of whom he allowed thirty pounds a year, studied divinity under his own eye in the close of Salisbury. He had several children: but he did not think himself justified in hoarding for them. Their mother had brought him a good fortune. With that fortune, he always said, they must be content. He would not, for their sakes, be guilty of the crime of raising an estate out of revenues sacred to piety and charity. Such merits as these will, in the judgment of wise and candid men, appear fully to atone for every offence which can be justly imputed to him.*

When he took his seat in the House of Lords, he found that assembly busied in ecclesiastical legislation. A statesman who was well known to be devoted to the Church had undertaken to plead the cause of the dissenters. No subject in the realm occupied so important and commanding a position with reference to religious parties as Nottingham. To the influence derived from rank, from wealth, and from office, he added the higher influence which belongs to knowledge, to eloquence, and to integrity. The orthodoxy of his creed, the regularity of his devotions, and the purity of his morals gave a peculiar weight to his opinions on questions in which the interests of Christianity were concerned. Of all the ministers of the new Sovereigns, he had the largest share of the confidence of the clergy. Shrewsbury was certainly a Whig, and probably a freethinker: he had lost one religion; and it did not very clearly appear that he had found another. Halifax had been during many years accused of scepticism, deism, atheism. Danby's attachment to episcopacy and the liturgy was rather political than religious. But Nottingham was such a son as the Church was proud to own. Propositions therefore, which, if made by his colleagues,

---

* See the life of Burnet, at the end of the second volume of his history, his manuscript memoirs, Harl. 6584, his memorials touching the First Fruits and Tenths, and Somers's letter to him on that subject. See also what Dr. King, Jacobite as he was, had the justice to say in his Anecdotes. A most honorable testimony to Burnet's virtues, given by another Jacobite who had attacked him fiercely, and whom he had treated generously, the learned and upright Thomas Baker, will be found in the Gentleman's Magazine for August and September, 1791,

would infallibly produce a violent panic among the clergy, might, if made by him, find a favorable reception even in universities and chapter houses. The friends of religious liberty were with good reason desirous to obtain his co-operation; and, up to a certain point, he was not unwilling to co-operate with them. He was decidedly for a toleration. He was even for what was then called a comprehension: that is to say, he was desirous to make some alterations in the Anglican discipline and ritual for the purpose of removing the scruples of the moderate Presbyterians. But he was not prepared to give up the Test Act. The only fault which he found with that Act was that it was not sufficiently stringent, and that it left loopholes through which schismatics sometimes crept into civil employments. In truth it was because he was not disposed to part with the Test that he was willing to consent to some changes in the Liturgy. He conceived that, if the entrance of the Church were but a very little widened, great numbers who had hitherto lingered near the threshold would press in. Those who still remained without would then not be sufficiently numerous or powerful to extort any further concession, and would be glad to compound for a bare toleration.*

The opinion of the Low Churchmen concerning the Test Act differed widely from his. But many of them thought that it was of the highest importance to have his support on the great questions of Toleration and Comprehension. From the scattered fragments of information which have come down to us, it appears that a compromise was made. It is quite certain that Nottingham undertook to bring in a Toleration Bill and a Comprehension Bill, and to use his best endeavors to carry both bills through the House of Lords. It is highly probable that, in return for this great service, some of the leading Whigs consented to let the Test Act remain for the present unaltered.

There was no difficulty in framing either the Toleration Bill or the Comprehension Bill. The situation of the dissenters had been much discussed nine or ten years before, when the kingdom was distracted by the fear of a Popish plot, and when there was among Protestants a general disposition to unite against the common enemy. The government had then been willing to make large concessions

* Oldmixon would have us believe that Nottingham was not, at this time, unwilling to give up the Test Act. But Oldmixon's assertion, unsupported by evidence, is of no weight whatever; and all the evidence which he produces makes against his assertion.

to the Whig party, on condition that the crown should be suffered to descend according to the regular course. A draught of a law authorizing the public worship of the non-conformists, and a draught of a law making some alterations in the public worship of the Established Church, had been prepared, and would probably have been passed by both Houses without difficulty, had not Shaftesbury and his coadjutors refused to listen to any terms, and, by grasping at what was beyond their reach, missed advantages which might easily have been secured. In the framing of these draughts, Nottingham, then an active member of the House of Commons, had borne a considerable part. He now brought them forth from the obscurity in which they had remained since the dissolution of the Oxford Parliament, and laid them, with some slight alterations, on the table of the Lords.*

The Toleration Bill passed both Houses with little debate. This celebrated statute, long considered as the Great Charter of religious liberty, has since been extensively modified, and is hardly known to the present generation except by name. The name, however, is still pronounced with respect by many who will perhaps learn with surprise and disappointment the real nature of the law which they have been accustomed to hold in honor.

Several statutes which had been passed between the accession of Queen Elizabeth and the Revolution required all people under severe penalties to attend the services of the Church of England, and to abstain from attending conventicles. The Toleration Act did not repeal any of these statutes, but merely provided that they should not be construed to extend to any person who should testify his loyalty by taking the Oaths of Allegiance and Supremacy, and his Protestantism by subscribing the Declaration against Transubstantiation.

The relief thus granted was common between the dissenting laity and the dissenting clergy. But the dissenting clergy had some peculiar grievances. The Act of Uniformity had laid a mulct of a hundred pounds on every person who, not having received episcopal ordination, should presume to administer the Eucharist. The Five Mile Act had driven many pious and learned ministers from

---

* Burnet, ii. 6; Van Citters to the States General, March 1-11, 1689; King William's Toleration, being an explanation of that liberty of conscience which may be expected from His Majesty's Declaration, with a Bill for Comprehension and Indulgence, drawn up in order to an Act of Parliament, licensed March 25, 1689.

their houses and their friends, to live among rustics in obscure villages of which the name was not to be seen on the map. The Conventicle Act had imposed heavy fines on divines who should preach in any meeting of separatists; and, in direct opposition to the humane spirit of our law, the courts were enjoined to construe this act largely and beneficially for the suppressing of dissent and for the encouraging of informers. These severe statutes were not repealed, but were, with many conditions and precautions, relaxed. It was provided that every dissenting minister should, before he exercised his function, profess under his hand his belief in the Articles of the Church of England, with a few exceptions. The propositions to which he was not required to assent were these; that the Church has power to regulate ceremonies; that the doctrines set forth in the Book of Homilies are sound; and that there is nothing superstitious or idolatrous in the ordination service. If he declared himself a Baptist, he was also excused from affirming that the baptism of infants is a laudable practice. But, unless his conscience suffered him to subscribe thirty-four of the thirty-nine Articles, and the greater part of two other Articles, he could not preach without incurring all the punishments which the Cavaliers, in the day of their power and their vengeance, had devised for the tormenting and ruining of schismatical teachers.

The situation of the Quaker differed from that of other dissenters, and differed for the worse. The Presbyterian, the Independent, and the Baptist had no scruple about the Oath of Supremacy. But the Quaker refused to take it, not because he objected to the proposition that foreign sovereigns and prelates have no jurisdiction in England, but because his conscience would not suffer him to swear to any proposition whatever. He was therefore exposed to the severity of part of that penal code which, long before Quakerism existed, had been enacted against Roman Catholics by the Parliaments of Elizabeth. Soon after the Restoration, a severe law, distinct from the general law which applied to all conventicles, had been passed against meetings of Quakers. The Toleration Act permitted the members of this harmless sect to hold their assemblies in peace, on condition of signing three documents, a declaration against Transubstantiation, a promise of fidelity to the government, and a confession of Christian belief. The objections which the Quaker had to the Athanasian phraseology had brought on him the imputation of Socinianism: and the strong language in which he sometimes asserted that he derived his knowledge of spiritual things directly from above had raised a suspicion that he thought lightly of the authority of Scripture. He was therefore required to profess his faith in the divinity of the Son and of the Holy Ghost, and in the inspiration of the Old and New Testaments.

Such were the terms on which the Protestant dissenters of England were, for the first time, permitted by law to worship God according to their own conscience. They were very properly forbidden to assemble with barred doors, but were protected against hostile intrusion by a clause which made it penal to enter a meeting-house for the purpose of molesting the congregation.

As if the numerous limitations and precautions which have been mentioned were insufficient, it was emphatically declared that the legislature did not intend to grant the smallest indulgence to any Papist, or to any person who denied the doctrine of the Trinity as that doctrine is set forth in the formularies of the Church of England.

Of all the Acts that have ever been passed by Parliament, the Toleration Act is perhaps that which most strikingly illustrates the peculiar vices and the peculiar excellences of English legislation. The science of Politics bears in one respect a close analogy to the science of Mechanics. The mathematician can easily demonstrate that a certain power, applied by means of a certain lever or of a certain system of pulleys, will suffice to raise a certain weight. But his demonstration proceeds on the supposition that the machinery is such as no load will bend or break. If the engineer, who has to lift a great mass of real granite by the instrumentality of real timber and real hemp, should absolutely rely on the propositions which he finds in treatises on Dynamics, and should make no allowance for the imperfection of his materials, his whole apparatus of beams, wheels, and ropes would soon come down in ruin, and, with all his geometrical skill, he would be found a far inferior builder to those painted barbarians who, though they never heard of the parallelogram of forces, managed to pile up Stonehenge. What the engineer is to the mathematician, the active statesman is to the contemplative statesman. It is indeed most important that legislators and administrators should be versed in the philosophy of government, as it is most important that the architect, who has to fix an obelisk on its pedestal, or to hang a tubular bridge over an estuary, should be versed in the philosophy of equilibrium and motion. But, as he who has actually to build must bear in mind many things never noticed by D'Alembert and Euler, so must he who has actually to govern be perpetually guided by considerations to which no allusion can be found in the writings of Adam Smith or Jeremy Bentham. The perfect lawgiver is a just temper between the mere man of theory, who can see nothing but general principles, and the mere man of business, who can see nothing but particular circumstances. Of lawgivers in whom the speculative element has prevailed to the exclusion of the practical, the world has during the last eighty years been singularly fruitful. To their wisdom Europe and America have owed scores of abortive constitutions, scores of constitutions which have lived just long enough to make a miserable noise, and have then gone off in convulsions. But in English legislation the practical element has always predominated, and not seldom unduly predominated, over the speculative. To think nothing of symmetry and much of convenience; never to remove an anomoly merely because it is an anomoly; never to innovate except when some grievance is felt; never to innovate except so far as to get rid of the grievance; never to lay down any proposition of wider extent than the particular case for which it is necessary to provide; these are the rules which have from the age of John to the age of Victoria, generally guided the deliberations of our two hundred and fifty Parliaments. Our national distaste for whatever is abstract in political science amounts undoubtedly to a fault. Yet it is, perhaps, a fault on the right side. That we have been far too slow to improve our laws must be admitted. But, though in other countries there may have occasionally been more rapid progress, it would not be easy to name any other country in which there has been so little retrogression.

The Toleration Act approaches very near to the idea of a great English law. To a jurist, versed in the theory of legislation, but not intimately acquainted with the temper of the sects and parties into which the nation was divided at the time of the Revolution, that Act would seem to be a mere chaos of absurdities and contradictions. It will not bear to be tried by sound general principles. Nay, it will not bear to be tried by any principle, sound or unsound. The sound principle undoubtedly is, that mere theological error ought not to be punished by the civil magistrate. This principle the Toleration Act not only does not recognize, but positively disclaims. Not a single one of the cruel laws enacted against non-conformists by the Tudors or the Stuarts is repealed. Persecution continues to be the general rule. Toleration is the exception. Nor is this all. The freedom which is given to conscience is given in the most capricious manner. A Quaker, by making a declaration of faith in general terms, obtains the full benefit of the Act without signing one of the thirty-nine Articles. An Independent minister, who is perfectly willing to make the declaration required from the Quaker, but who has doubts about six or seven of the Articles, remains still subject to the penal laws. Howe is liable to punishment if he preaches before he has solemnly declared his assent to the Anglican doctrine touching the Eucharist. Penn, who altogether rejects the Eucharist, is at perfect liberty to preach without making any declaration whatever on the subject.

These are some of the obvious faults which must strike every person who examines the Toleration Act by that standard of just reason which is the same in all countries and in all ages. But these very faults may perhaps appear to be merits, when we take into consideration the passions and prejudices of those for whom the Toleration Act was framed. This law, abounding with contradictions which every smatterer in political philosophy can detect, did what a law framed by the utmost skill of the greatest masters of political philosophy might have failed to do. That the provisions which have been recapitulated are cumbrous, puerile, inconsistent with each other, inconsistent with the true theory of religious liberty, must be acknowledged. All that can be said in their defence is this; that they removed a vast mass of evil without shocking a vast mass of prejudice; that they put an end, at once and forever, without one division in either House of Parliament, without one riot in the streets, with scarcely one audible murmur even from the classes most deeply tainted with bigotry, to a persecution which raged during four generations, which had broken innumerable hearts, which had made innumerable firesides desolate, which had filled the prisons with men of whom the world was not worthy, which had driven thousands of those honest, diligent, and god-fearing yeomen and artisans, who are the true strength of a nation, to seek a refuge beyond the ocean among the wigwams of red Indians and the lairs of panthers. Such a defence, however weak it may appear to some shallow speculators, will probably be thought complete by statesmen.

The English, in 1689, were by no means disposed to admit the doctrine that religious error ought to be left unpunished. That doctrine was just then more unpopular than it had ever been. For it had, only a few months before, been hypocritically put forward as a pretext for persecuting the Established Church, for trampling on the fundamental laws of the realm, for confiscating freeholds, for treating as a crime the modest exercise of the right of petition. If a bill had then been drawn up granting entire freedom of conscience to all Protestants, it may be confidently affirmed that Nottingham would never have introduced such a bill; that all the bishops, Burnet included, would have voted against it; that it would have been denounced Sunday after Sunday, from ten thousand pulpits, as an insult to God and to all Christian men, and as a license to the worst heretics and blasphemers; that it would have been condemned almost as vehemently by Bates and Baxter as by Ken and Sherlock; that it would have been burned by the mob in half the market places of England; that it would never have become the law of the land, and that it would have made the very name of toleration odious during many years to the great majority of the people. And yet, if such a bill had been passed, what would it have effected beyond what was effected by the Toleration Act?

It is true that the Toleration Act recognized persecution as the rule, and granted liberty of conscience only as the exception. But it is equally true that the rule remained in force only against a few hundreds of Protestant dissenters, and that the benefit of the exceptions extended to hundreds of thousands.

It is true that it was in theory absurd to make Howe sign thirty-four or thirty-five of the Anglican Articles before he could preach, and to let Penn preach without signing one of those Articles. But it is equally true that under this arrangement both Howe and Penn got as entire liberty to preach as they could have had under the most philosophical code that Beccaria or Jefferson could have framed.

The progress of the bill was easy. Only one amendment of grave importance was proposed. Some zealous churchmen in the Commons suggested that it might be desirable to grant the toleration only for a term of seven years, and thus to bind over the non-conformists to good behavior. But this suggestion was so unfavorably received that those who made it did not venture to divide the House.*

The King gave his consent with hearty satisfaction: the bill became law; and the Puritan divines thronged to the Quarter Sessions of every county to swear and sign. Many of them probably professed their assent to the Articles with some tacit reservations. But the tender conscience of Baxter would not suffer him to qualify, till he had put on record an explanation of the sense in which he understood every proposition which seemed to him to admit of misconstruction. The instrument delivered by him to the court before which he took the oaths is still extant, and contains two passages of peculiar interest. He declared that his approbation of the Athanasian Creed was confined to that part which was properly a Creed, and that he did not mean to express any assent to the damnatory clauses. He also declared that he did not, by signing the article which anathematizes all who maintain that there is any other salvation than through Christ, mean to condemn those who entertain a hope that sincere and virtuous unbelievers may be admitted to partake in the benefits of Redemption. Many of the dissenting clergy of London expressed their concurrence in these charitable sentiments.†

The history of the Comprehension Bill presents a remarkable contrast to the history of the Toleration Bill. The two bills had a common origin, and, to a great extent, a common object. They were framed at the same time, and laid aside at the same time: they sank together into oblivion, and they were, after the lapse of several years, again brought together before the world. Both were laid by the same peer on the table of the Upper House; and both were referred to the same select committee. But it soon began to appear that they would have widely different fates. The Comprehension Bill was indeed a neater specimen of legislative workmanship than the Toleration Bill, but was not, like the Toleration Bill, adapted to the wants, the feelings, and the prejudi-

---
* Common's Journals, May 17, 1689.
† Sense of the subscribed articles by the Ministers of London, 1690; Calamy's Historical Additions to Baxter's Life.

ces of the existing generation. Accordingly while the Toleration Bill found support in all quarters, the Comprehension Bill was attacked from all quarters, and was at last coldly and languidly defended even by those who had introduced it. About the same time at which the Toleration Bill became law with the general concurrence of public men, the Comprehension Bill was, with a concurrence not less general, suffered to drop. The Toleration Bill still ranks among those great statutes which are epochs in our constitutional history. The Comprehension Bill is forgotten. No collector of antiquities has thought it worth preserving. A single copy, the same which Nottingham presented to the Peers, is still among our parliamentary records, but has been seen by only two or three persons now living. It is a fortunate circumstance that, in this copy, almost the whole history of the Bill can be read. In spite of cancellations and interlineations, the original words can easily be distinguished from those which were inserted in the committee or on the report.*

The first clause, as it stood when the bill was introduced, dispensed all the ministers of the Established Church from the necessity of subscribing the Thirty-nine Articles. For the Articles was substituted a Declaration which ran thus: "I do approve of the doctrine and worship and government of the Church of England by law established, as containing all things necessary to salvation; and I promise, in the exercise of my ministry, to preach and practice according thereunto." Another clause granted similar indulgence to the members of the two universities.

Then it was provided that any minister who had been ordained after the Presbyterian fashion might, without reordination, acquire all the privileges of a priest of the Established Church. He must, however, be admitted to his new functions by the imposition of the hands of a bishop, who was to pronounce the following form of words: "Take thou authority to preach the word of God, and administer the sacraments, and to perform all other ministerial offices in the Church of England." The person thus admitted was to be capable of holding any rectory or vicarage in the kingdom.

---

* The bill will be found among the Archives of the House of Lords. It is strange that this vast collection of important documents should have been altogether neglected, even by our most exact and diligent historians. It was opened to me by one of the most valued of my friends, Sir John Lefevre; and my researches were greatly assisted by the kindness of Mr. Thoms.

Then followed clauses providing that a clergyman might, except in a few churches of peculiar dignity, wear the surplice or not as he thought fit, that the sign of the cross might be omitted in baptism, that children might be christened, if such were the wish of their parents, without godfathers or godmothers, and that persons who had a scruple about receiving the Eucharist kneeling might receive it sitting.

The concluding clause was drawn in the form of a petition. It was proposed that the two Houses should request the King and Queen to issue a commission empowering thirty divines of the Established Church to revise the liturgy, the canons, and the constitution of the ecclesiastical courts, and to recommend such alterations as might on inquiry appear to be desirable.

The bill went smoothly through the first stages. Compton, who, since Sancroft had shut himself up at Lambeth, was virtually Primate, supported Nottingham with ardor.* In the committee, however, it appeared that there was a strong body of churchmen, who were as obstinately determined not to give up a single word or form as if they had thought that prayers were no prayers if read without the surplice, that a babe could be no Christian if not marked with the cross, that bread and wine could be no memorials of redemption or vehicles of grace if not received on bended knee. Why, those persons asked, was the docile and affectionate son of the Church to be disgusted by seeing the irreverent practices of a conventicle introduced into her majestic choirs? Why should his feelings, his prejudices, if prejudices they were, be less considered than the whims of schismatics? If, as Burnet and men like Burnet were never weary of repeating, indulgence was due to a weak brother, was it less due to the brother whose weakness consisted in the excess of his love for an ancient, a decent, a beautiful ritual, associated in his imagination from childhood with all that is most sublime and endearing, than to him whose morose and litigious mind was always devising frivolous objections to innocent and salutary usages? But in truth, the scrupulosity of the Puritan was not that sort of scrupu-

* Among the Tanner MSS. in the Bodleian Library is a very curious letter from Compton to Sancroft, about the Toleration Bill and the Comprehension Bill. "These," says Compton, "are two great works in which the being of our Church is concerned; and I hope you will send to the House for copies. For though we are under a conquest, God has given us favor in the eyes of our rulers; and we may keep our Church if we will." Sancroft seems to have returned no answer.

losity which the Apostle had commanded believers to respect. It sprang, not from morbid tenderness of conscience, but from censoriousness and spiritual pride; and none who had studied the New Testament could have failed to observe that, while we are charged carefully to avoid whatever may give scandal to the feeble, we are taught by divine precept and example to make no concession to the supercilious and uncharitable Pharisee. Was everything which was not of the essence of religion to be given up as soon as it became unpleasing to a knot of zealots whose heads had been turned by conceit and the love of novelty? Painted glass, music, holidays, fast days, were not of the essence of religion. Were the windows of King's College chapel to be broken at the demand of one set of fanatics? Was the organ of Exeter to be silenced to please another? Were all the village bells to be mute because Tribulation Wholesome and Deacon Ananias thought them profane? Was Christmas no longer to be a day of rejoicing? Was Passion week no longer to be a season of humiliation? These changes, it is true, were not yet proposed. But if,—so the High Churchmen reasoned,—we once admit that what is harmless and edifying is to be given up because it offends some narrow understandings and some gloomy tempers, where are we to stop? And is it not probable that, by thus attempting to heal one schism, we may cause another? All those things which the Puritans regard as the blemishes of the Church are by a large part of the population reckoned among her attractions. May she not, in ceasing to give scandal to a few sour precisians, cease also to influence the hearts of many who now delight in her ordinances? Is it not to be apprehended that, for every proselyte whom she allures from the meeting-house, ten of her old disciples may turn away from her maimed rites and dismantled temples, and that these new separatists may either form themselves into a sect far more formidable than the sect which we are now seeking to conciliate, or may, in the violence of their disgust at a cold and ignoble worship, be tempted to join in the solemn and gorgeous idolatry of Rome?

It is remarkable that those who held this language were by no means disposed to contend for the doctrinal Articles of the Church. The truth is that, from the time of James the First, that great party which has been peculiarly zealous for the Anglican polity and the Anglican ritual has always leaned strongly towards Arminianism, and has therefore never been much attached to a confession of faith framed by reformers who, on questions of metaphysical divinity, generally agreed with Calvin. One of the characteristic marks of that party is the disposition which it has always shown to appeal, on points of dogmatic theology, rather to the Liturgy, which was derived from Rome, than to the Articles, and Homilies, which were derived from Geneva. The Calvinistic members of the Church, on the other hand, have always maintained that her deliberate judgment on such points is much more likely to be found in an Article or a Homily than in an ejaculation of penitence or hymn of thanksgiving. It does not appear that, in the debates on the Comprehension Bill, a single High Churchman raised his voice against the clause which relieved the clergy from the necessity of subscribing the Articles, and of declaring the doctrine contained in the Homilies to be sound. Nay, the Declaration, which, in the original draught, was substituted for the Articles, was much softened down on the report. As the clause finally stood, the ministers of the Church were required, not to profess that they approved of her doctrine, but merely to acknowledge, what probably few Baptists, Quakers, or Unitarians would deny, that her doctrine contained all things necessary to salvation. Had the bill become law, the only people in the kingdom who would have been under the necessity of signing the Articles would have been the dissenting preachers.*

The easy manner in which the zealous friends of the Church gave up her confession of faith presents a striking contrast to the spirit with which they struggled for her polity and her ritual. The clause which admitted Presbyterian ministers to hold benefices without episcopal ordination was rejected. The clause which permitted scrupulous persons to communicate sitting, very narrowly escaped the same fate. In the Committee it was struck out, and, on the report, was with great difficulty restored. The majority of peers in the House was against the proposed indulgence, and the scale was but just turned by the proxies.

But by this time it began to appear that the bill which the High Churchmen were so keenly assailing was menaced by

* The distaste of the High Churchmen for the Articles is the subject of a curious pamphlet published in 1689, and entitled a Dialogue between Timothy and Titus.

dangers from a very different quarter. The same considerations which had induced Nottingham to support a comprehension made comprehension an object of dread and aversion to a large body of dissenters. The truth is that the time for such a scheme had gone by. If, a hundred years earlier, when the division in the Protestant body was recent, Elizabeth had been so wise as to abstain from requiring the observance of a few forms which a large part of her subjects considered as Popish, she might perhaps have averted those fearful calamities which, forty years after her death, afflicted the Church. But the general tendency of schism is to widen. Had Leo the Tenth, when the exactions and impostures of the Pardoners first roused the indignation of Saxony, corrected those evil practices with a vigorous hand, it is not improbable that Luther would have died in the bosom of the Church of Rome. But the opportunity was suffered to escape; and, when, a few years later, the Vatican would gladly have purchased peace by yielding the original subject of quarrel, the original subject of quarrel was almost forgotten. The inquiring spirit which had been roused by a single abuse had discovered or imagined a thousand: controversies engendered controversies: every attempt that was made to accommodate one dispute ended by producing another; and at length the General Council, which, during the earlier stages of the distemper, had been supposed to be an infallible remedy, made the case utterly hopeless. In this respect, as in many others, the history of Puritanism in England bears a close analogy to the history of Protestantism in Europe. The Parliament of 1689 could no more put an end to non-conformity by tolerating a garb or a posture than the Doctors of Trent could have reconciled the Teutonic nations to the Papacy by regulating the sale of indulgences. In the sixteenth century Quakerism was unknown; and there was not in the whole realm a single congregation of Independents or Baptists. At the time of the Revolution, the Independents, Baptists, and Quakers were probably a majority of the dissenting body; and these sects could not be gained over on any terms which the lowest of Low Churchmen would have been willing to offer. The Independent held that a national Church, governed by any central authority whatever, Pope, Patriarch, King, Bishop or Synod, was an unscriptural institution, and that every congregation of believers was, under Christ, a sovereign society. The Baptist was even more irreclaimable than the Independent, and the Quaker even more irreclaimable than the Baptist. Concessions, therefore, which would once have extinguished non-conformity, would not now satisfy even one half of the non-conformists; and it was the obvious interest of every non-conformist whom no concession would satisfy that none of his brethren should be satisfied. The more liberal the terms of comprehension, the greater was the alarm of every separatist who knew that he could, in no case, be comprehended. There was but slender hope that the dissenters, unbroken and acting as one man, would be able to obtain from the legislature full admission to civil privileges; and all hope of obtaining such admission must be relinquished if Nottingham should, by the help of some well-meaning but short-sighted friends of religious liberty, be enabled to accomplish his design. If his bill passed, there would doubtless be a considerable defection from the dissenting body; and every defection must be severely felt by a class already outnumbered, depressed, and struggling against powerful enemies. Every proselyte too must be reckoned twice over, as a loss to the party which was even now too weak, and as a gain to the party which was even now too strong. The Church was but too well able to hold her own against all the sects in the kingdom; and, if those sects were to be thinned by a large desertion, and the Church strengthened by a large reinforcement, it was plain that all chance of obtaining any relaxation of the Test Act would be at an end; and it was but too probable that the Toleration Act might not long remain unrepealed.

Even those Presbyterian ministers whose scruples the Comprehension Bill was especially intended to remove were by no means unanimous in wishing it to pass. The ablest and most eloquent preachers among them had, since the Declaration of Indulgence had appeared, been very agreeably settled in the capital and in other large towns, and were now about to enjoy, under the sure guarantee of an Act of Parliament, that toleration which, under the Declaration of Indulgence, had been illicit and precarious. The situation of these men was such as the great majority of the divines of the Established Church might well envy. Few indeed of the parochial clergy were so abundantly supplied with comforts as the favorite orator of a great assembly of non-conformists in the City. The voluntary contributions of his wealthy hearers, Aldermen and Deputies, West India merchants and Turkey merchants, Wardens of the Company of Fishmongers and Wardens of the Company of Goldsmiths, enabled him to become a land-owner or a mortgagee. The best broadcloth from Blackwell Hall, and the best poultry from Leadenhall Market, were frequently left at his door. His influence over his flock was immense. Scarcely any member of a congregation of separatists entered into a partnership, married a daughter, put a son out as apprentice, or gave his vote at an election, without consulting his spiritual guide. On all political and literary questions the minister was the oracle of his own circle. It was popularly remarked, during many years, that an eminent dissenting minister had only to determine whether he would make his son an attorney or a physician; for that the attorney was sure to have clients and the physician to have patients. While a waiting-woman was generally considered as a help-meet for a chaplain in holy orders of the Established Church, the widows and daughters of opulent citizens were supposed to belong in a peculiar manner to non-conformist pastors. One of the great Presbyterian Rabbies, therefore, might well doubt whether, in a worldly view, he should be a gainer by a comprehension. He might indeed hold a rectory or a vicarage, when he could get one. But in the meantime he would be destitute: his meeting-house would be closed: his congregation would be dispersed among the parish churches: if a benefice were bestowed on him, it would probably be a very slender compensation for the income which he had lost. Nor could he hope to have, as a minister of the Anglican Church, the authority and dignity which he had hitherto enjoyed. He would always, by a large portion of the members of that Church, be regarded as a deserter. He might, therefore, on the whole, very naturally wish to be left where he was.*

---

* Tom Brown says, in his scurrilous way, of the Presbyterian divines of that time, that their preaching "brings in money, and money buys land; and land is an amusement they all desire, in spite of their hypocritical cant. If it were not for the quarterly contributions, there would be no longer schism or separation." He asks how it can be imagined that, while "they are maintained like gentlemen by the breach, they will ever preach up healing doctrines?"—Brown's Amusements, Serious and Comical. Some curious instances of the influence exercised by the chief dissenting ministers may be found in Hawkin's Life of Johnson. In the Journal of the retired citizen (Spectator, 317.) Addison has indulged in some exquisite pleasantry on this subject. The Mr. Nisby whose opinions about the peace, the Grand Vizier, and laced coffee, are quoted with so much respect, and who is so well regaled with marrow bones, ox cheek, and a bottle of Brooks and Hellier, was John Nesbit, a highly popular preacher, who, about the time of the Revolution, became pastor of a dissenting congregation in Hare Court, Aldersgate street. In Wilson's History and Antiquities of Dissenting Churches and Meeting Houses in London, Westminister, and Southwark, will be found several instances of non-

There was consequently a division in the Whig party. One section of that party was for relieving the dissenters from the Test Act, and giving up the Comprehension Bill. Another section was for pushing forward the Comprehension Bill, and postponing to a more convenient time the consideration of the Test Act. The effect of this division among the friends of religious liberty was that the High Churchmen, though a minority in the House of Commons and not a majority in the House of Lords, were able to oppose with success both the reforms which they dreaded. The Comprehension Bill was not passed; and the Test Act was not repealed.

Just at the moment when the question of the Test and the question of the Comprehension became complicated together in a manner which might well perplex an enlightened and honest politician, both questions became complicated with a third question of great importance.

The ancient oaths of allegiance and supremacy contained some expressions which had always been disliked by the Whigs, and other expressions which Tories, honestly attached to the new settlement, thought inapplicable to princes who had not the hereditary right. The Convention had therefore, while the throne was still vacant, framed those oaths of allegiance and supremacy by which we still testify our loyalty to our Sovereign. By the Act which turned the Convention into a Parliament, the members of both Houses were required to take the new oaths. As to other persons in public trust, it was hard to say how the law stood. One form of words was enjoined by statutes, regularly passed, and not yet regularly abrogated. A different form was enjoined by the Declaration of Rights, an instrument which was indeed revolutionary and irregular, but which might well be thought equal in authority to any statute. The practice was in as much confusion as the law. It was therefore felt to be necessary, that the legislature should, without delay, pass an Act abolishing the old oaths, and determining when and by whom the new oaths should be taken.

The bill which settled this important question originated in the Upper House. As to most of the provisions there was little room for dispute. It was unanimously agreed that no person should, at any future time, be ad-

---

conformist preachers who, about this time, made handsome fortunes, generally, it should seem. by marriage.

mitted to any office, civil, military, ecclesiastical, or academical, without taking the oaths to William and Mary. It was also unanimously agreed that every person who already held any civil or military office should be ejected from it, unless he took the oaths on or before the first of August, 1689. But the strongest passions of both parties were excited by the question whether persons who already possessed ecclesiastical or academical offices should be required to swear fealty to the King and Queen on pain of deprivation. None could say what might be the effect of a law enjoining all the members of a great, a powerful, a sacred profession to make, under the most solemn sanction of religion, a declaration which might be plausibly represented as a formal recantation of all that they had been writing and preaching during many years. The Primate and some of the most eminent bishops had already absented themselves from Parliament, and would doubtless relinquish their palaces and revenues, rather than acknowledge the new Sovereigns. The example of these great prelates might perhaps be followed by a multitude of divines of humbler rank, by hundreds of canons, prebendaries, and fellows of colleges, by thousands of parish priests. To such an event no Tory, however clear his own conviction that he might lawfully swear allegiance to the King who was in possession, could look forward without the most painful emotions of compassion for the sufferers, and of anxiety for the Church.

There were some persons who went so far as to deny that the Parliament was competent to pass a law requiring a bishop to swear on pain of deprivation. No earthly power, they said, could break the tie which bound the successor of the apostles to his diocese. What God had joined no man could sunder. Kings and senates might scrawl words on parchments or impress figures on wax; but those words and figures could no more change the course of the spiritual than the course of the physical world. As the Author of the universe had appointed a certain order according to which it was His pleasure to send winter and summer, seedtime and harvest, so he had appointed a certain order, according to which He communicated His grace to His Catholic Church; and the latter order was, like the former, independent of the powers and principalities of the world. A legislature might alter the names of the months, might call June December, and December June; but in spite of the legislature, the snow would fall when the sun was in Capricorn, and the flowers would bloom when he was in Cancer. And so the legislature might enact that Ferguson or Muggleton should live in the palace at Lambeth, should sit on the throne of Augustin, should be called Your Grace, and should walk in processions before the Premier Duke: but, in spite of the legislature, Sancroft would, while Sancroft lived, be the only true Archbishop of Canterbury: and the person who should presume to usurp the archiepiscopal functions would be a schismatic. This doctrine was proved by reasons drawn from the budding of Aaron's rod, and from a certain plate which Saint James the Less, according to a legend of the fourth century, used to wear on his forehead. A Greek manuscript, relating to the deprivation of bishops, was discovered, about this time, in the Bodleian Library, and became the subject of a furious controversy. One party held that God had wonderfully brought this precious volume to light, for the guidance of His Church at a most critical moment. The other party wondered that any importance could be attached to the nonsense of a nameless scribbler of the thirteenth century. Much was written about the deprivations of Chrysostom and Photius, of Nicolaus Mysticus and Cosmas Atticus. But the case of Abiathar, whom Solomon put out of the sacerdotal office for treason, was discussed with peculiar eagerness. No small quantity of learning and ingenuity was expended in the attempt to prove that Abiathar, though he wore the ephod and answered by Urim, was not really High Priest, that he ministered only when his superior Zadoc was incapacitated by sickness or by some ceremonial pollution, and that therefore the act of Solomon was not a precedent which would warrant King William in deposing a real bishop.*

But such reasoning as this, though backed by copious citations from the Misna and Maimonides, was not generally satisfactory even to zealous churchmen. For it admitted of one answer, short, but perfectly intelligible to a plain man who knew nothing about Greek fathers or Levitical genealogies. There might be some doubt whether King Solomon had ejected a high priest: but

---

* See, among many other tracts, Dodwell's Cautionary Discourses, his Vindication of the Deprived Bishops, his Defence of the Vindication, and his Paraenesis; and Bisby's Unity of Priesthood, printed in 1692. See also Hody's tracts on the other side, the Baroccian MS., and Solomon and Abiathar, a Dialogue between Eucheres and Dyscheres.

there could be no doubt at all that Queen Elizabeth had ejected the bishops of more than half the sees in England. It was notorious that fourteen prelates had, without any proceeding in any spiritual court, been deprived by Act of Parliament for refusing to acknowledge her supremacy. Had that deprivation been null? Had Bonner continued to be, to the end of his life, the only true Bishop of London? Had his successor been an usurper? Had Parker and Jewel been schismatics? Had the Convocation of 1562, that Convocation which had finally settled the doctrine of the Church of England, been itself out of the pale of the Church of Christ? Nothing could be more ludicrous than the distress of those controversialists who had to invent a plea for Elizabeth which should not be also a plea for William. Some zealots, indeed, gave up the vain attempt to distinguish between two cases which every man of common sense perceived to be undistinguishable, and frankly owned that the deprivations of 1559 could not be justified. But no person, it was said, ought to be troubled in mind on that account; for, though the Church of England might once have been schismatical, she had become Catholic when the last of the bishops deprived by Elizabeth ceased to live.* The Tories, however, were not generally disposed to admit that the religious society to which they were fondly attached had originated in an unlawful breach of unity. They therefore took ground lower and more tenable. They argued the question as a question of humanity and of expediency. They spoke much of the debt of gratitude which the nation owed to the priesthood; of the courage and fidelity with which the order, from the primate down to the youngest deacon, had recently defended the civil and ecclesiastical constitution of the realm; of the memorable Sunday when, in all the hundred churches of the capital, scarcely one slave could be found to read the Declaration of Indulgence; of the black Friday when, amidst the blessings and the loud weeping of a mighty population, the barge of the seven prelates passed through the watergate of the Tower. The firmness with which the clergy had lately, in defiance of menace and of seduction, done what they conscientiously believed to be right, had saved the liberty and religion of England. Was

---

* Burnet, ii. 135. Of all attempts to distinguish between the deprivations of 1559 and the deprivations of 1689, the most absurd was made by Dodwell. See his Doctrine of the Church of England concerning the Independency of the Clergy on the lay Power, 1697.

no indulgence to be granted to them if they now refused to do what they conscientiously apprehended to be wrong? And where, it was said, is the danger of treating them with tenderness? Nobody is so absurd as to propose that they shall be permitted to plot against the goverment, or to stir up the multitude to insurrection. They are amenable to the law, like other men. If they are guilty of treason, let them be hanged. If they are guilty of sedition, let them be fined and imprisoned. If they omit, in their public ministrations, to pray for King William, for Queen Mary, and for the Parliament assembled under those most religious sovereigns, let the penal clauses of the Act of Uniformity be put in force. If this be not enough, let His Majesty be empowered to tender the oaths to any clergyman; and, if the oaths so tendered are refused, let deprivation follow. In this way any nonjuring bishop or rector who may be suspected, though he cannot be legally convicted, of intriguing, of writing, of talking, against the present settlement, may be at once removed from his office. But why insist on ejecting a pious and laborious minister of religion, who never lifts a finger or utters a word against the government, and who, as often as he performs morning or evening service, prays from his heart for a blessing on the rulers set over him by Providence, but who will not take an oath which seems to him to imply a right in the people to depose a sovereign? Surely we do all that is necessary if we leave men of this sort at the mercy of the very prince to whom they refuse to swear fidelity. If he is willing to bear with their scrupulosity, if he considers them, notwithstanding their prejudices, as innocent and useful members of society, who else can be entitled to complain?

The Whigs were vehement on the other side. They scrutinized, with ingenuity sharpened by hatred, the claims of the clergy to the public gratitude, and sometimes went so far as altogether to deny that the order had in the preceding year deserved well of the nation. It was true that bishops and priests had stood up against the tyranny of the late King: but it was equally true that, but for the obstinacy with which they had opposed the Exclusion Bill, he never would have been King, and that, but for their adulation and their doctrine of passive obedience, he would never have ventured to be guilty of such tyranny. Their chief business, during a quarter of a century, had been to teach the people to cringe and the prince to domineer. They were guilty of the blood of Russell, of Sidney, of every brave and honest Englishman who had been put to death for attempting to save the realm from Popery and despotism. Never had they breathed a whisper against arbitrary power till arbitrary power began to menace their own property and dignity. Then, no doubt, forgetting all their old common-places about submitting to Nero, they had made haste to save themselves. Grant,—such was the cry of these eager disputants,—grant that, in saving themselves, they saved the constitution. Are we therefore to forget that they had previously endangered it? And are we to reward them by now permitting them to destroy it? Here is a class of men closely connected with the state. A large part of the produce of the soil has been assigned to them for their maintenance. Their chiefs have seats in the legislature, wide domains, stately palaces. By this privileged body the great mass of the population is lectured every week from the chair of authority. To this privileged body has been committed the supreme direction of liberal education. Oxford and Cambridge, Westminster, Winchester, and Eton, are under priestly government. By the priesthood will to a great extent be formed the character of the nobility and gentry of the next generation. Of the higher clergy some have in their gift numerous and valuable benefices; others have the privilege of appointing judges who decide grave questions affecting the liberty, the property, the reputation of Their Majesties' subjects. And is an order thus favored by the state to give no guarantee to the state? On what principle can it be contended that it is unnecessary to ask from an Archbishop of Canterbury or from a Bishop of Durham that promise of fidelity to the government which all allow that it is necessary to demand from every layman who serves the Crown in the humblest office? Every exciseman, every collector of the customs, who refuses to swear, is to be deprived of his bread. For these humble martyrs of passive obedience and hereditary right nobody has a word to say. Yet an ecclesiastical magnate who refuses to swear is to be suffered to retain emoluments, patronage, power, equal to those of a great minister of state. It is said that it is superfluous to impose the oaths on a clergyman, because he may be punished if he breaks the law. Why is not the same argument urged in favor of the layman? And why, if the clergyman really means to observe the laws, does he scruple to take the oaths? The law commands him to designate William and Mary as King and Queen, to do this in the most sacred place, to do this in the administration of the most solemn of all the rites of religion. The law commands him to pray that the illustrious pair may be defended by a special providence, that they may be victorious over every enemy, and that their Parliament may by divine guidance be led to take such a course as may promote their safety, honor and welfare. Can we believe that his conscience will suffer him to do all this, and yet will not suffer him to promise that he will be a faithful subject to them?

To the proposition that the nonjuring clergy should be left to the mercy of the King, the Whigs, with some justice, replied that no scheme could be devised more unjust to His Majesty. The matter, they said, is one of public concern, one in which every Englishman who is unwilling to be the slave of France and of Rome has a deep interest. In such a case it would be unworthy of the Estates of the Realm to shrink from the responsibility of providing for the common safety, to try to obtain for themselves the praise of tenderness and liberality, and to leave to the Sovereign the odious task of proscription. A law requiring all public functionaries, civil, military, ecclesiastical, without distinction of persons, to take the oaths is at least equal. It excludes all suspicion of partiality, of personal malignity, of secret spying and tale-bearing. But, if an arbitrary discretion is left to the government, if one nonjuring priest is suffered to keep a lucrative benefice while another is turned with his wife and children into the street, every ejection will be considered as an act of cruelty, and will be imputed as a crime to the sovereign and his ministers.*

Thus the Parliament had to decide, at the same moment, what quantity of relief should be granted to the consciences of non-conformists and what quantity of pressure should be applied to the consciences of the clergy of the Established Church. The King conceived a hope that it might be in his power to effect a compromise agreeable to all parties. He flattered himself that the Tories might be induced to make some concession to the dissenters, on

---

* As to this controversy, see Burnet, ii. 7, 8, 9; Grey's Debates, April 19 and 22, 1689; Commons' Journals of April 20 and 22; Lords' Journals, April 21.

condition that the Whigs would be lenient to the Jacobites. He determined to try what his personal intervention would effect. It chanced that, a few hours after the Lords had read the Comprehension Bill a second time and the Bill touching the Oaths a first time, he had occasion to go down to Parliament for the purpose of giving his assent to a law. From the throne he addressed both Houses, and expressed an earnest wish that they would consent to modify the existing laws in such a manner that all Protestants might be admitted to public employment.* It was well understood that he was willing, if the legislature would comply with his request, to let clergymen who were already beneficed, continue to hold their benefices without swearing allegiance to him. His conduct on this occasion deserves undoubtedly the praise of disinterestedness. It is honorable to him that he attempted to purchase liberty of conscience for his subjects by giving up a safeguard of his own crown. But it must be acknowledged that he showed less wisdom than virtue. The only Englishman in his Privy Council whom he had consulted, if Burnet was correctly informed, was Richard Hampden; † and Richard Hampden, though a highly respectable man, was so far from being able to answer for the Whig party that he could not answer even for his own son John, whose temper, naturally vindictive, had been exasperated into ferocity by the stings of remorse and shame. The King soon found that there was in the hatred of the two great factions an energy which was wanting to their love. The Whigs, though they were almost unanimous in thinking that the sacramental test ought to be abolished, were by no means unanimous in thinking that moment well chosen for the abolition; and even those Whigs who were most desirous to see the non-conformists relieved without delay from civil disabilities, were fully determined not to forego the opportunity of humbling and punishing the class to whose instrumentality chiefly was to be ascribed that tremendous reflux of public feeling which had followed the dissolution of the Oxford Parliament. To put the Janes, the Souths, the Sherlocks into such a situation that they must either starve, or recant, publicly, and with the Gospel at their lips, all the ostentatious professions of many years was a revenge too delicious to be relinquished.

* Lords' Journals, March 16, 1689.
† Burnet, ii. 7, 8.

The Tory, on the other hand, sincerely respected and pitied those clergymen who felt scruples about the oaths. But the Test was, in his view, essential to the safety of the established religion, and must not be surrendered for the purpose of saving any man however eminent from any hardship however serious. It would be a sad day doubtless for the Church when the episcopal bench, the chapter houses of cathedrals, the halls of colleges, would miss some men renowned for piety and learning. But it would be a still sadder day for the Church when an Independent should bear the white staff, or a Baptist sit on the woolsack. Each party tried to serve those for whom it was interested: but neither party would consent to grant favorable terms to its enemies. The result was that the noncomformists remained excluded from office in the State, and the nonjurors were ejected from office in the Church.

In the House of Commons, no member thought it expedient to propose the repeal of the Test Act. But leave was given to bring in a bill repealing the Corporation Act, which had been passed by the Cavalier Parliament soon after the Restoration, and which contained a clause requiring all municipal magistrates to receive the sacrament according to the forms of the Church of England. When this bill was about to be committed, it was moved by the Tories that the committee should be instructed to make no alteration in the law touching the sacrament. Those Whigs who were zealous for the Comprehension must have been placed by this motion in an embarrassing position. To vote for the instruction would have been inconsistent with their principles. To vote against it would have been to break with Nottingham. A middle course was found. The adjournment of the debate was moved and carried by a hundred and sixteen votes to a hundred and fourteen; and the subject was not revived.* In the House of Lords a motion was made for the abolition of the sacramental test, but was rejected by a large majority. Many of those who thought the motion right in principle thought it ill-timed. A protest was entered; but it was signed only by a few peers of no great authority. It is a remarkable fact that two great chiefs of the Whig party,

---

* Burnet says (ii. 8), that the proposition to abolish the sacramental test was rejected by a great majority in both Houses. But his memory deceived him; for the only division on the subject in the House of Commons was that mentioned in the text. It is remarkable that Gwyn and Rowe, who were tellers for the majority, were two of the strongest Whigs in the House.

who were in general very attentive to their parliamentary duty, Devonshire and Shrewsbury, absented themselves on this occasion.*

The debate on the Test in the Upper House was speedily followed by a debate on the last clause of the Comprehension Bill. By that clause it was provided that thirty bishops and priests should be commissioned to revise the liturgy and canons, and to suggest amendments. On this subject the Whig peers were almost all of one mind. They mustered strong and spoke warmly. Why, they asked, were none but members of the sacerdotal order to be entrusted with this duty? Were the laity no part of the Church of England? When the Commission should have made its report, laymen would have to decide on the recommendations contained in that report. Not a line of the Book of Common Prayer could be altered but by the authority of King, Lords, and Commons. The King was a layman. Five-sixths of the Lords were laymen. All the members of the House of Commons were laymen. Was it not absurd to say that laymen were incompetent to examine into a matter which it was acknowledged that laymen must in the last resort determine? And could anything be more opposite to the whole spirit of Protestantism than the notion that a certain preternatural power of judging in spiritual cases was vouchsafed to a particular caste, and to that caste alone; that such men as Selden, as Hale, as Boyle, were less competent to give an opinion on a collect or a creed than the youngest and silliest chaplain who, in a remote manor house, passed his life in drinking ale and playing at shovelboard? What God had instituted no earthly power, lay or clerical, could alter; and of things instituted by human beings a layman was surely as competent as a clergyman to judge. That the Anglican liturgy and canons were of purely human institution the Parliament acknowledged by referring them to a Commission for revision and correction. How could it then be maintained that in such a Commission the laity, so vast a majority of the population, the laity, whose edification was the main end of all ecclesiastical regulations, and whose innocent tastes ought to be carefully consulted in the framing of the public services of religion, ought not to have a single representative? Precedent was directly opposed to this odious distinction. Repeatedly, since the

---

* Lord's Journals. March 21, 1689.

light of reformation had dawned on England, Commissioners had been empowered by law to revise the canons; and on every one of those occasions some of the Commissioners had been laymen. In the present case the proposed arrangement was peculiarly objectionable. For the object of issuing the commission was the conciliating of dissenters; and it was therefore most desirable that the Commissioners should be men in whose fairness and moderation dissenters could confide. Would thirty such men be easily found in the higher ranks of the clerical profession? The duty of the legislature was to arbitrate between two contending parties, the Non-conformist divines and the Anglican divines, and it would be the grossest injustice to commit to one of those parties the office of umpire.

On these grounds the Whigs proposed an amendment to the effect, that laymen should be joined with clergymen in the Commission. The contest was sharp. Burnet, who had just taken his seat among the peers and who seems to have been bent on winning at almost any price the good will of his brethren, argued with all his constitutional warmth for the clause as it stood. The numbers on the division proved to be exactly equal. The consequence was that, according to the rules of the House, the amendment was lost.*

At length the Comprehension Bill was sent down to the Commons. There it would easily have been carried by two to one, if it had been supported by all the friends of religious liberty. But on this subject the High Churchmen could count on the support of a large body of Low Churchmen. Those members who wished well to Nottingham's plan saw that they were outnumbered, and, despairing of a victory, began to meditate a retreat. Just at this time a suggestion was thrown out which united all suffrages. The ancient usage was that a Convocation should be summoned together with a Parliament ; and it might well be argued that, if ever the advice of a Convocation could be needed, it must be when changes in the ritual and discipline of the Church were under consideration. But, in consequence of the irregular manner in which the Estates of the Realm had been brought together during the vacancy of the throne, there was no Convocation. It was proposed that the House should ad-

---

* Lords' Journals, April 5, 1689; Burnet, ii, 10.

vise the King to take measures for supplying this defect, and that the fate of the Comprehension Bill should not be decided till the clergy had had an opportunity of declaring their opinion through the ancient and legitimate organ.

This proposition was received with general acclamation. The Tories were well pleased to see such honor done to the priesthood. Those Whigs who were against the Comprehension Bill were well pleased to see it laid aside, certainly for a year, probably forever. Those Whigs who were for the Comprehension Bill were well pleased to escape without a defeat. Some of them indeed were not without hopes that mild and liberal counsels might prevail in the ecclesiastical senate.

An address requesting William to summon the Convocation was voted without a division: the concurrence of the Lords was asked: the Lords concurred: the address was carried up to the throne by both Houses: the King promised that he would, at a convenient season, do what his Parliament desired; and Nottingham's bill was not again mentioned.

Many writers, imperfectly acquainted with the history of that age, have inferred from these proceedings that the House of Commons was an assembly of High Churchmen: but nothing is more certain than that two-thirds of the members were either Low Churchmen or not Churchmen at all. A very few days before this time an occurrence had taken place, unimportant in itself, but highly significant as an indication of the temper of the majority. It had been suggested that the House ought, in conformity with ancient usage, to adjourn over the Easter holidays. The Puritans and Latitudinarians objected: there was a sharp debate: the High Churchmen did not venture to divide; and to the great scandal of many grave persons, the Speaker took the chair at nine o'clock on Easter Monday; and there was a long and busy sitting.*

This however was by no means the strongest proof which

---

* Commons' Journals, March 28, April 1, 1689; Paris Gazette, April 23. Part of the passage in the Paris Gazette is worth quoting. "Il y eut, ce jour là (March 28), une grande contestation dans la Chambre Basse, sur la proposition qui fut faite de remettre les seances après les fêtes de Pasques observées toujours par l'Eglise Anglicane. Les Protestans conformistes furent de cet avis; et les Presbytériens emportèrent à la pluralité des voix que les séances recommenceroient le Lundy, seconde feste de Pasques." The Low Churchmen are frequently designated as Presbyterians by the French and Dutch writers of that age. There were not twenty Presbyterians, properly so called, in the House of Commons. See A. Smith and Cutler's plain Dialogue about Whig and Tory, 1690.

the Commons gave that they were far indeed from feeling extreme reverence or tenderness for the Anglican hierarchy. The bill for settling the oaths had just come down from the Lords framed in a manner favorable to the clergy. All lay functionaries were required to swear fealty to the King and Queen on pain of expulsion from office. But it was provided that every divine who already held a benefice might continue to hold it without swearing, unless the Government should see reason to call on him specially for an assurance of his loyalty. Burnet had, partly, no doubt, from the good-nature and generosity which belonged to his character, and partly from a desire to conciliate his brethren, supported this arrangement in the Upper House with great energy. But in the Lower House the feeling against the Jacobite priests was irresistibly strong. On the very day on which that House voted, without a division, the address requesting the King to summon the Convocation, a clause was proposed and carried which required every person who held any ecclesiastical or academical preferment to take the oaths by the first of August 1689, on pain of suspension. Six months, to be reckoned from that day, were allowed to the nonjuror for reconsideration. If, on the first of February 1690, he still continued obstinate, he was to be finally deprived.

The bill, thus amended, was sent back to the Lords. The Lords adhered to their original resolution. Conference after conference was held. Compromise after compromise was suggested. From the imperfect reports which have come down to us it appears that every argument in favor of lenity was forcibly urged by Burnet. But the Commons were firm: time pressed: the unsettled state of the law caused inconvenience in every department of the public service; and the Peers very reluctantly gave way. They at the same time added a clause, empowering the King to bestow pecuniary allowances out of the forfeited benefices on a nonjuring clergymen. The number of clergymen thus favored was not to exceed twelve. The allowance was not to exceed one-third of the income forfeited. Some zealous Whigs were unwilling to grant even this indulgence: but the Commons were content with the victory which they had won, and justly thought that it would be ungracious to refuse so slight a concession.*

---

* Accounts of what passed at the Conferences will be found in the Journals of the Houses, and deserve to be read.

These debates were interrupted, during a short time, by the solemnities and festivities of the coronation. When the day fixed for that great ceremony drew near, the House of Commons resolved itself into a committee for the purpose of settling the form of words in which our Sovereigns were thenceforward to enter into covenent with the nation. All parties were agreed as to the propriety of requiring the King to swear that, in temporal matters, he would govern according to law, and would execute justice in mercy. But about the terms of the oath which related to the spiritual institutions of the realm there was much debate. Should the chief magistrate promise simply to maintain the Protestant religion established by law, or should he promise to maintain that religion as it should be hereafter established by law? The majority preferred the former phrase. The latter phrase was preferred by those Whigs who were for a Comprehension. But it was admitted that the two phrases really meant the same thing, and that the oath, however it might be worded, would bind the Sovereign in his executive capacity only. This was indeed evident from the very nature of the transaction. Any compact may be annulled by the free consent of the party who alone is entitled to claim the performance. It was never doubted by the most rigid casuist that a debtor, who has bound himself under the most awful imprecations to pay a debt, may lawfully withhold payment if the creditor is willing to cancel the obligation. And it is equally clear that no assurance, exacted from a King by the Estates of his kingdom, can bind him to refuse compliance with what may at a future time be the wish of those Estates.

A bill was drawn up in conformity with the resolutions of the committee, and was rapidly passed through every stage. After the third reading, a foolish man stood up to propose a rider, declaring that the oath was not meant to restrain the Sovereign from consenting to any change in the ceremonial of the Church, provided always that episcopacy and a written form of prayer were retained. The gross absurdity of this motion was exposed by several eminent members. Such a clause, they justly remarked, would bind the King under pretence of setting him free. The coronation oath, they said, was never intended to trammel him in his legislative capacity. Leave that oath as it is now drawn, and no prince can misunderstand it. No prince can seriously imagine that the two Houses mean to exact from him a promise that he will put a veto on laws which they may hereafter think necessary to the well-being of the country. Or if any prince should so strangely misapprehend the nature of the contract between him and his subjects, any divine, any lawyer, to whose advice he may have recourse, will set his mind at ease. But if this rider should pass, it will be impossible to deny that the coronation oath is meant to prevent the King from giving his assent to bills which may be presented to him by the Lords and Commons; and the most serious inconveniences may follow. These arguments were felt to be unanswerable, and the proviso was rejected without a division.*

Every person who has read these debates must be fully convinced that the statesmen who framed the coronation oath did not mean to bind the King in his legislative capacity.† Unhappily, more than a hundred years later, a scruple, which those statesmen thought too absurd to be seriously entertained by any human being, found its way into a mind, honest, indeed, and religious, but narrow and obstinate by nature, and at once debilitated and excited by disease. Seldom, indeed, have the ambition and perfidy of tyrants produced evils greater than those which were brought on our country by that fatal conscientiousness. A conjuncture singularly auspicious, a conjuncture at which wisdom and justice might perhaps have reconciled races and sects long hostile, and might have made the British Islands one truly United Kingdom, was suffered to pass away. The opportunity, once lost, returned no more. Two generations of public men have since labored with imperfect success to repair the error which was then committed; nor is it improbable that some of the penalties of that error may continue to afflict a remote posterity.

The bill by which the oath was settled passed the Upper House without amendment. All the preparations

---

* Journals March 28, 1689; Grey's Debates.
† I will quote some expressions which have been preserved in the concise reports of these debates. Those expressions are quite decisive as to the sense in which the oath was understood by the legislators who framed it. Musgrave said, "There is no occasion for this proviso. It cannot be imagined that any bill from hence will ever destroy the legislative power." Finch said, "The words, 'established by law,' hinder not the king from passing any bill for the relief of Dissenters. The proviso makes the scruple, and gives the occasion for it." Sawyer said, "This is the first proviso of this nature that ever was in any bill. It seems to strike at the legislative power." Sir Robert Cotton said, "Though the proviso looks well and healing, yet it seems to imply a defect. Not able to alter laws as occasion requires! This, instead of one scruple, raises more, as if you were so bound up to the ecclesiastical government that you cannot make any new laws without such a proviso." Sir Thomas Lee said, "It will, I fear, creep in that other laws cannot be made without such a proviso; therefore I would lay it aside."

were complete; and, on the 11th of April, the coronation
took place. In some things it differed from ordinary cor-
onations. The representatives of the people attended the
ceremony in a body, and were sumptuously feasted in the
Exchequer Chamber. Mary, being not merely Queen
Consort, but also Queen Regent, was inaugurated in all
things like a King, was girt with a sword, lifted up into
the throne, and presented with the Bible, the spurs, and
the orb. Of the temporal grandees of the realm, and of
their wives and daughters, the muster was great and splendid. None could be surprised that the Whig aristocracy
should swell the triumph of Whig principles. But the
Jacobites saw, with concern, that many Lords who had
voted for a Regency bore a conspicuous part in the ceremonial. The King's crown was carried by Grafton, the
Queen's by Somerset. The pointed sword, emblematical
of temporal justice, was borne by Pembroke. Ormond
was Lord High Constable for the day, and rode up the
hall on the right hand of the hereditary champion, who
thrice flung down his glove on the pavement, and thrice
defied to mortal combat the false traitor who should gain-
say the title of William and Mary. Among the noble
damsels who supported the gorgeous train of the Queen
was her beautiful and gentle cousin, the Lady Henrietta
Hyde, whose father, Rochester, had to the last contended
against the resolution which declared the throne vacant.*
The show of Bishops, indeed, was scanty. The Primate
did not make his appearance and his place was supplied by
Compton. On one side of Compton, the paten was carried by Lloyd, Bishop of Saint Asaph, eminent among the
seven confessors of the preceding year. On the other side,
Sprat, Bishop of Rochester, lately a member of the High
Commission, had charge of the chalice. Burnet, the junior
prelate, preached with all his wonted ability, and more
than his wonted taste and judgment. His grave and eloquent discourse was polluted neither by flattery nor by malignity. He is said to have been greatly applauded; and it
may well be believed that the animated peroration in which
he implored heaven to bless the royal pair with long life
and mutual love, with obedient subjects, wise counsellors,
and faithful allies, with gallant fleets and armies, with victory, with peace, and finally with crowns more glorious

---

* Lady Henrietta, whom her uncle Clarendon calls "pretty little Lady Henrietta," and
"the best child in the world" (Diary, Jan. 1687-8), was soon after married to the Earl of
Dalkeith, eldest son of the unfortunate Duke of Monmouth.

and more durable than those which then glittered on the altar of the Abbey, drew forth the loudest hums of the Commons.*

On the whole the ceremony went off well, and produced something like a revival, faint, indeed, and transient, of the enthusiasm of the preceding December. The day was, in London, and in many other places, a day of general rejoicing. The churches were filled in the morning: the afternoon was spent in sport and carousing; and at night bonfires were kindled, rockets discharged, and windows lighted up. The Jacobites, however, contrived to discover or to invent abundant matter for scurrility and sarcasm. They complained bitterly that the way from the hall to the western door of the Abbey had been lined by Dutch soldiers. Was it seemly that an English king should enter into the most solemn of engagements with the English nation behind a tripple hedge of foreign swords and bayonets? Little affrays, such as, at every great pageant, almost inevitably take place between those who are eager to see the show and those whose business it is to keep the communications clear, were exaggerated with all the artifices of rhetoric. One of the alien mercenaries had backed his horse against an honest citizen who pressed forward to catch a glimpse of the royal canopy. Another had rudely pushed back a woman with the butt end of his musket. On such grounds as these the strangers were compared to those Lord Danes whose insolence, in the old time, had provoked the Anglo Saxon population to insurrection and massacre. But there was no more fertile theme for censure than the coronation medal, which really was absurd in design and mean in execution. A chariot appeared conspicuous on the reverse; and plain people were at a loss to understand what this emblem had to do with William and Mary. The disaffected wits solved the difficulty by suggesting that the artist meant to allude to that chariot which a Roman princess, lost to all filial affection, and blindly devoted to the interests of an ambitious husband, drove over the still warm remains of her father.†

---

* The sermon deserves to be read. See the London Gazette of April 14, 1689; Evelyn's Diary; Luttrell's Diary; and the Despatch of the Dutch Ambassadors to the States General.

† A specimen of the prose which the Jacobites wrote on this subject will be found among the Somers Tracts. The Jacobite verses were generally too loathsome to be quoted. I select some of the most decent lines from a very rare lampoon:

"The eleventh of April has come about,
To Westminster went the rabble rout,

Honors were, as usual, liberally bestowed at this festive season. Three garters, which happened to be at the disposal of the Crown, were given to Devonshire, Ormond and Schomberg. Prince George was created Duke of Cumberland. Several eminent men took new appellations by which they must henceforth be designated. Danby became Marquess of Caermarthen, Churchill Earl of Marlborough, and Bentinck Earl of Portland. Mordaunt was made Earl of Monmouth, not without some murmuring on the part of old exclusionists, who still remembered with fondness their Protestant Duke, and who had hoped that his attainder would be reversed, and that his title would be borne by his descendants. It was remarked that the name of Halifax did not appear in the list of promotions. None could doubt that he might easily have obtained either a blue ribbon or a ducal coronet; and, though he was honorably distinguished from most of his contemporaries by his scorn of illicit gain, it was well known that he desired honorary distinctions with a greediness of which he was himself ashamed, and which was unworthy of his fine understanding. The truth is that his ambition was at this time chilled by his fears. To those whom he trusted he hinted his apprehensions that evil times were at hand. The King's life was not worth a year's purchase: the government was disjointed, the clergy and the army disaffected, the parliament torn by factions: civil war was already raging in one part of the empire: foreign war was impending. At such a moment a minister, whether Whig or Tory, might well be

---

In order to crown a bundle of clouts,
A dainty fine king indeed.

" Descended he is from the Orange tree;
But, if I can read his destiny,
He'll once more descend from another tree,
A dainty fine king indeed.

" He has gotten part of the shape of a man,
But more of a monkey, deny it who can;
He has the head of a goose, but the legs of a crane,
A dainty fine king indeed."

A Frenchman named Le Noble, who had been banished from his own country for his crimes, but by the connivance of the police, lurked in Paris, and earned a precarious livelihood as a bookseller's hack, published on this occasion two pasquinades, now extremely scarce, "Le Couronnement de Guillemot et de Guillemette, avec le Sermon du grand Docteur Burnet," and "Le Festin de Guillemot." In wit, taste, and good sense, Le Noble's writings are not inferior to the English poem which I have quoted. He tells us that the Archbishop of York and the Bishop of London had a boxing match in the Abbey; that the champion rode up the Hall on an ass, which turned restive and kicked over the royal table with all the plate; and that the banquet ended in a fight between the peers armed with stools and benches, and the cooks armed with spits. This sort of pleasantry, strange to say, found readers; and the writer's portrait was pompously engraved with the motto, "Latrantes ride: te tua fama manet."

uneasy: but neither Whig nor Tory had so much to fear as the Trimmer, who might not improbably find himself the common mark at which both parties would take aim. For these reasons Halifax determined to avoid all ostentation of power and influence, to disarm envy by a studied show of moderation, and to attach to himself by civilities and benefits persons whose gratitude might be useful in the event of a counter-revolution. The next three months, he said, would be the time of trial. If the government got safe through the summer it would probably stand.*

Meanwhile questions of external policy were every day becoming more and more important. The work at which William had toiled indefatigably during many gloomy and anxious years was at length accomplished. The great coalition was formed. It was plain that a desperate conflict was at hand. The oppressor of Europe would have to defend himself against England allied with Charles the Second King of Spain, with the Emperor Leopold, and with the Germanic and Batavian federations, and was likely to have no ally except the Sultan, who was waging war against the House of Austria on the Danube.

Lewis had, towards the close of the preceding year, taken his enemies at a disadvantage, and had struck the first blow before they were prepared to parry it. But that blow, though heavy, was not aimed at the part where it might have been mortal. Had hostilities been commenced on the Batavian frontier, William and his army would probably have been detained on the Continent, and James might have continued to govern England. Happily, Lewis, under an infatuation which many pious Protestants confidently ascribed to the righteous judgment of God, had neglected the point on which the fate of the whole civilized world depended, and had made a great display of power, promptitude, and energy, in a quarter where the most splendid achievemeuts could produce nothing more than an illumination and a Te Deum. A French army under the command of Marshal Duras had invaded the Palatinate and some of the neighboring principalities. But this expedition, though it had been completely successful, and though the skill and vigor with which it had been conducted had excited general admiration, could not perceptibly affect the event of the tremendous struggle which was

---

* Reresby's Memoirs.

approaching. France would soon be attacked on every
side. It would be impossible for Duras long to retain possession of the provinces which he had surprised and over-
run. An atrocious thought rose in the mind of Louvois,
who, in military affairs, had the chief sway at Versailles.
He was a man distinguished by zeal for what he thought
the public interests, by capacity, and by knowledge of all
that related to the administration of war, but of a savage
and obdurate nature. If the cities of the Palatinate could
not be retained, they might be destroyed. If the soil of
the Palatinate was not to furnish supplies to the French,
it might be so wasted that it would at least furnish no
supplies to the Germans. The iron-hearted statesman submitted his plan, probably with much management and
with some disguise, to Lewis; and Lewis, in an evil hour
for his fame, assented. Duras received orders to turn one
of the fairest regions of Europe into a wilderness. Fifteen
years had elapsed since Turenne had ravaged part of that
fine country. But the ravages committed by Turenne,
though they have left a deep stain on his glory, were
mere sport in comparison with the horrors of this second
devastation. The French commander announced to near
half a million of human beings that he granted them three
days of grace, and that, within that time, they must shift
for themselves. Soon the roads and fields, which then lay
deep in snow, were blackened by innumerable multitudes
of men, women, and children flying from their homes.
Many died of cold and hunger: but enough survived to
fill the streets of all the cities of Europe with lean and
squalid beggars, who had once been thriving farmers and
shopkeepers. Meanwhile the work of destruction began.
The flames went up from every market-place, every hamlet,
every parish church, every country seat, within the devoted
provinces. The fields where the corn had been sown were
ploughed up. The orchards were hewn down. No promise of a harvest was left on the fertile plains near what had
once been Frankenthal. Not a vine, not an almond tree,
was to be seen on the slopes of the sunny hills round what
had once been Heidelberg. No respect was shown to
palaces, to temples, to monasteries, to infirmaries, to beau-
ful works of art, to monuments of the illustrious dead.
The far famed castle of the Elector Palatine was turned
into a heap of ruins. The adjoining hospital was sacked.
The provisions, the medicines, the pallets on which the

sick lay were destroyed. The very stones of which Manheim had been built were flung into the Rhine. The magnificent Cathedral of Spires perished, and with it the marble sepulchres of eight Cæsars. The coffins were broken open. The ashes were scattered to the winds.* Treves with its fair bridge, its Roman baths and amphitheater, its venerable churches, convents, and colleges, was doomed to the same fate. But, before this last crime had been perpetrated, Lewis was recalled to a better mind by the execrations of all the neighboring nations, by the silence and confusion of his flatterers, and by the expostulations of his wife. He had been more than two years secretly married to Frances de Maintenon, the governess of his natural children. It would be hard to name any woman who, with so little romance in her temper, has had so much in her life. Her early years had been passed in poverty and obscurity. Her first husband had supported himself by writing burlesque farces and poems. When she attracted the notice of her sovereign, she could no longer boast of youth or beauty: but she possessed in an extraordinary degree those more lasting charms, which men of sense, whose passions age has tamed, and whose life is a life of business and care, prize most highly in a female companion. Her character was such as has been well compared to that soft green on which the eye, wearied by warm tints and glaring lights, reposes with pleasure. A just understanding; an inexhaustible yet never redundant flow of rational, gentle, and sprightly conversation; a temper of which the serenity was never for a moment ruffled; a tact which surpassed the tact of her sex as much as the tact of her sex surpasses the tact of ours; such were the qualities which made the widow of a buffoon first the confidential friend, and then the spouse, of the proudest and most powerful of European kings. It was said that Lewis had been with difficulty prevented by the arguments and vehement entreaties of Louvois from declaring her Queen of France. It is certain that she regarded Louvois as her enemy. Her hatred of him, co-operating perhaps with better feelings, induced her to plead the cause of the unhappy people of the Rhine. She appealed to those sen-

---

* For the history of the devastation of the Palatinate, see the Memoirs of La Fare, Dangeau, Madame de la Fayette, Villars, and St. Simon, and the Monthly Mercuries for March and April 1689. The pamphlets and broadsides are too numerous to quote. One broadside, entitled "A true account of the barbarous Cruelties committed by the French in the Palatinate in Ianuary and February last," is perhaps the most remarkable.

timents of compassion which, though weakened by many
corrupting influences, were not altogether extinct in her
husband's mind, and to those sentiments of religion which
had too often impelled him to cruelty, but which, on the
present occasion, were on the side of humanity.   He re-
lented; and Treves was spared.*   In truth he could hardly
fail to perceive that he had committed a great error.   The
devastation of the Palatinate, while it had not in any sensible degree lessened the power of his enemies, had inflamed
their animosity, and had furnished them with inexhaustible matter for invective.   The cry of vengeance rose on
every side.   Whatever scruple either branch of the House
of Austria might have felt about coalescing with Protestants was completely removed.   It was in vain that Lewis
accused the Emperor and the Catholic King of having betrayed the cause of the Church; of having allied themselves
with an usurper who was the avowed champion of the
great schism; of having been accessory to the foul wrong
done to a lawful sovereign who was guilty of no crime but
zeal for the true religion.   It was in vain that James sent
to Vienna and Madrid piteous letters, in which he re-
counted his misfortunes, and implored the assistance of
his brother kings, his brethren also in the faith, against
the unnatural children and the rebellious subjects who had
driven him into exile.   There was little difficulty in framing a plausible answer both to the reproaches of Lewis and
to the supplications of James.   Leopold and Charles
declared that they had not, even for purposes of just self-
defence, leagued themselves with heretics, till their enemy
had, for purposes of unjust aggression, leagued himself
with Mahometans.   Nor was this the worst.   The French
King, not content with assisting the Moslem against the
Christians, was himself treating Christians with a barbarity
which would have shocked the very Moslem.   His infidel
allies, to do them justice, had not perpetrated on the Danube such outrages against the edifices and the members of
the Holy Catholic Church as he who called himself the
eldest son of that Church was perpetrating on the Rhine.
On these grounds, the princes to whom James had appealed
replied by appealing, with many professions of good wil
and compassion, to himself.   He was surely too just to
blame them for thinking that it was their first duty to
defend their own people against such outrages as had

* Memoirs of St. Simon.

turned the Palatinate into a desert, or for calling in the
aid of Protestants against an enemy who had not scrupled
to call in the aid of Turks.*

During the winter and the earlier part of the spring, the
powers hostile to France were gathering their strength for
a great effort, and were in constant communication with
one another. As the season for military operations approached, the solemn appeals of injured nations to the
God of battles came forth in rapid succession. The manifesto of the Germanic body appeared in February; that of
the States General in March; that of the House of Brandenburg in April; and that of Spain in May.†

Here, as soon as the ceremony of the coronation was
over, the House of Commons determined to take into consideration the late proceedings of the French King.‡ In
the debate, that hatred of the powerful, unscrupulous, and
imperious Lewis, which had, during twenty years of vassalage, been festering in the hearts of Englishmen, broke violently forth. He was called the most Christian Turk, the
most Christian ravager of Christendom, the most Christian
barbarian who had perpetrated on Christians outrages of
which his infidel allies would have been ashamed.§ A committee, consisting chiefly of ardent Whigs, was appointed
to prepare an address. John Hampden, the most ardent
Whig among them, was put into the chair; and he produced a composition too long, too rhetorical, and too vituperative, to suit the lips of the Speaker or the ears of the
King. Invectives against Lewis might, perhaps, in the
temper in which the House then was, have passed without
censure, if they had not been accompanied by severe reflections on the character and administration of Charles
the Second, whose memory, in spite of all his faults, was

---

* I will quote a few lines from Leopold's letter to James: "Nunc autem quo loco res nostræ sint, ut Serenitati vestræ auxilium præstari possit a nobis, qui non Turcico tantum bello impliciti, sed insuper etiam crudelissimo et iniquissimo a Gallis, rerum suarum, ut putabant, in Anglia securis, contra datam fidem impediti sumus, ipsimet Serenitati vestræ judicandum relinquimus. . . . Galli non tantum in nostrum et totius Christianæ orbis perniciem fœdifraga arma cum juratis Sanctæ Crucis hostibus sociare fas sibi ducunt; sed etiam in imperio, perfidiam perfidia cumulando, urbes deditione occupatas contra datam fidem immensis tributis exhaurire, exhaustas diripere, direptas funditus exscindere aut flammis delere, Palatia Principum ab omni antiquitate inter sævissima bellorum incendia intacta servata exurere, templa spoliare, dedititios in servitutem more apud barbaros usitato abducere, denique passim, imprimis vero etiam in Catholicorum ditionibus, alia horrenda, et ipsam Turcorum tyrannidem superantia immanitatis et sævitiæ exempla edere pro ludo habent."

† See the London Gazettes of Feb. 25, March 11, April 22, May 2, and the Monthly Mercuries. Some of the Declarations will be found in Dumont's Corps Universel Diplomatique.

‡ Commons' Journals, April 15, 16, 1689.

§ Oldmixon.

affectionately cherished by the Tories. There were some very intelligible allusions to Charles's dealings with the Court at Versailles, and to the foreign woman whom that Court had sent to lie like a snake in his bosom. The House was with good reason dissatisfied. The address was recommitted, and, having been made more concise, and less declamatory and acrimonious, was approved and presented.* William's attention was called to the wrongs which France had done to him and to his kingdom; and he was assured that, whenever he should resort to arms for the redress of those wrongs, he should be heartily supported by his people. He thanked the Commons warmly. Ambition, he said, should never induce him to draw the sword: but he had no choice: France had already attacked England; and it was necessary to exercise the right of self-defence. A few days later war was proclaimed.†

Of the grounds of quarrel alleged by the Commons in their address, and by the King in his manifesto, the most serious was the interference of Lewis in the affairs of Ireland. In that country great events had, during several months, followed one another in rapid succession. Of those events it is now time to relate the histoy, a history dark with crime and sorrow, yet full of interest and instruction.

CHAPTER XII.—(1689.)

WILLIAM had assumed, together with the title of King of England, the title of King of Ireland. For all our jurists then regarded Ireland as a mere colony, more important indeed than Massachusetts, Virginia, or Jamaica, but, like Massachusetts, Virginia, and Jamaica, dependent on the mother country, and bound to pay allegiance to the Sovereign whom the mother country had called to the throne.‡

In fact, however, the Revolution found Ireland emancipated from the dominion of the English colony. As early as the year 1686, James had determined to make that island a place of arms which might overawe Great Britain, and a place of refuge where, if any disaster happened in Great

---

* Commons' Journals, April 19, 24, 26, 1689.
† The declaration is dated on the 7th of May, but was not published in the London Gazette till the 13th.

‡ The general opinion of the English on this subject is clearly expressed in a little tract entitled "Aphorisms relating to the Kingdom of Ireland," which appeared during the vacancy of the throne.

Britain, the members of his Church might find refuge. With this view he had exerted all his power for the purpose of inverting the relation between the conquerors and the aboriginal population. The execution of his design he had entrusted, in spite of the remonstrances of his English counsellors, to the Lord Deputy Tyrconnel. In the autumn of 1688, the process was complete. The highest offices in the state, in the army, and in the Courts of Justice, were, with scarcely an exception, filled by Papists. A pettifogger named Alexander Fitton, who had been detected in forgery, who had been fined for misconduct by the House of Lords at Westminster, who had been many years in prison, and who was equally deficient in legal knowledge and in the natural good sense and acuteness by which the want of legal knowledge has sometimes been supplied, was Lord Chancellor. His single merit was that he had apostatised from the Protestant religion; and this merit was thought sufficient to wash out even the stain of his Saxon extraction. He soon proved himself worthy of the confidence of his patrons. On the bench of justice he declared that there was not one heretic in forty thousand who was not a villain. He often, after hearing a cause in which the interests of his Church were concerned, postponed his decision, for the purpose, as he avowed, of consulting his spiritual director, a Spanish priest, well read doubtless in Escobar.* Thomas Nugent, a Roman Catholic who had never distinguished himself at the bar except by his brogue and his blunders, was Chief Justice of the King's Bench.† Stephen Rice, a Roman Catholic, whose abilities and learning were not disputed even by the enemies of his nation and religion, but whose known hostility to the Act of Settlement excited the most painful apprehensions in the minds of all who held property under that Act, was Chief Baron of the Exchequer.‡ Richard Nagle, an acute and well read lawyer, who had been educated in a Jesuit college, and whose prejudices were such as might have been expected from his education, was Attorney General.§

Keating, a highly respectable Protestant, was still Chief

---

* King's State of the Protestants of Ireland, ii. 6, and iii. 3.
† King, iii. 3. Clarendon in a letter to Rochester (June 1, 1686), calls Nugent "a very troublesome, impertinent creature."
‡ King, iii. 3.
§ King. ii. 6, iii. 3, Clarendon in a letter to Ormond (Sept. 28, 1686), speaks highly of Nagle's knowledge and ability, but in the Diary (Jan. 31, 1686-7), calls him "a covetous, ambitious man."

Justice of the Common Pleas: but two Roman Catholic Judges sate with him. It ought to be added that one of those judges, Daly, was a man of sense, moderation, and integrity. The matters however which came before the Court of Common Pleas were not of great moment. Even the King's Bench was at this time almost deserted. The Court of Exchequer overflowed with business; for it was the only court at Dublin from which no writ of error lay to England, and consequently the only court in which the English could be oppressed and pillaged without hope of redress. Rice, it was said, had declared that they should have from him exactly what the law, construed with the utmost strictness, gave them, and nothing more. What, in his opinion, the law, strictly construed, gave them, they could easily infer from a saying which, before he became a judge, was often in his mouth. "I will drive," he used to say, "a coach and six through the Act of Settlement." He now carried his threat daily into execution. The cry of all Protestants was that it mattered not what evidence they produced before him; that, when their titles were to be set aside, the rankest forgeries, the most infamous witnesses, were sure to have his countenance. To his court his countrymen came in multitudes with writs of ejectment and writs of trespass. In his court the government attacked at once the charters of all the cities and boroughs in Ireland; and he easily found pretexts for pronouncing all those charters forfeited. The municipal corporations, about a hundred in number, had been instituted to be the strongholds of the reformed religion and of the English interest, and had consequently been regarded by the Irish Roman Catholics with an aversion which cannot be thought unnatural or unreasonable. Had those bodies been remodelled in a judicious and impartial manner, the irregularity of the proceedings by which so desirable a result had been attained might have been pardoned. But it soon appeared that one exclusive system had been swept away only to make room for another. The boroughs were subjected to the absolute authority of the Crown. Towns in which almost every householder was an English Protestant were placed under the government of Irish Roman Catholics. Many of the new aldermen had never even seen the places over which they were appointed to bear rule. At the same time the sheriffs, to whom belonged the execution of writs and the nomination of juries, were selected in almost every instance from the caste which had till very recently been excluded from all public trust. It was affirmed that some of these important functionaries had been burned in the hand for theft. Others had been servants to Protestants; and the Protestants added, with bitter scorn, that it was fortunate for the country when this was the case; for that a menial who had cleaned the plate and rubbed down the horse of an English gentleman might pass for a civilized being, when compared with many of the native aristocracy whose lives had been spent in coshering or marauding. To such sheriffs no colonist, even if he had been so strangely fortunate as to obtain a judgment, dared to entrust an execution.*

Thus the civil power had, in the space of a few months, been transferred from the Saxon to the Celtic population. The transfer of the military power had been not less complete. The army, which under the command of Ormond, had been the chief safeguard of the English ascendency, had ceased to exist. Whole regiments had been dissolved and reconstructed. Six thousand Protestant veterans, deprived of their bread, were brooding in retirement over their wrongs, or had crossed the sea and joined the standard of William. Their place was supplied by men who had long suffered oppression, and who, finding themselves suddenly transformed from slaves into masters, were impatient to pay back, with accumulated usury, the heavy debt of injuries and insults. The new soldiers, it was said, never passed an Englishman without cursing him and calling him by some foul name. They were the terror of every Protestant inn-keeper; for, from the moment when they came under his roof, they ate and drank everything: they paid for nothing; and by their rude swaggering they scared more respectable guests from his door.†

Such was the state of Ireland when the Prince of Orange landed at Torbay. From that time every packet

---

* King, ii. 5. 1, iii. 3, 5; A Short View of the Methods made use of in Ireland for the Supervision and Destruction of the Protestant Religion and Interests, by a Clergyman lately escaped from thence, licensed October 17, 1689.

† King, iii. 2. I cannot find that Charles Leslie, who was zealous on the other side, has, in his answer to King, contradicted any of these facts. Indeed Leslie gives up Tyrconnel's administration. "I desire to obviate one objection which I know will be made, as if I were about wholly to vindicate all that the Lord Tyrconnel and other of King James's ministers have done in Ireland, especially before this revolution began, and which most of anything brought it on. No; I am far from it. I am sensible that their carriage in many particulars gave greater occasion to King James's enemies than all the other maladministrations which were charged upon his government."—Leslie's Answer to King, 1692.

which arrived at Dublin brought tidings, such as could not but increase the mutual fear and loathing of the hostile races. The colonist, who, after long enjoying and abusing power, had now tasted for a moment the bitterness of servitude, the native, who having drunk to the dregs all the bitterness of servitude, had at length for a moment enjoyed and abused power, were alike sensible that a great crisis, a crisis like that of 1641, was at hand. The majority impatiently expected Phelim O'Neil to revive in Tyrconnel. The minority saw in William a second Oliver.

On which side the first blow was struck was a question which Williamites and Jacobites afterwards debated with much asperity. But no question could be more idle. History must do to both parties the justice which neither has ever done to the other, and must admit that both had fair pleas and cruel provocations. Both had been placed, by a fate for which neither was answerable, in such a situation that, human nature being what it is, they could not but regard each other with enmity. A king, who perhaps might have reconciled them, had, year after year, systematically employed his whole power for the purpose of inflaming their enmity to madness. It was now impossible to establish in Ireland a just and beneficent government, a government which should know no distinction of race or of sect, a government which, while strictly respecting the rights guaranteed by law to the new land-owners, should alleviate, by a judicious liberality, the misfortunes of the ancient gentry. The opportunity had passed away; compromise had become impossible: the two infuriated castes were alike convinced that it was necessary to oppress or to be oppressed, and that there could be no safety but in victory, vengeance, and dominion. They agreed only in spurning out of the way every mediator who sought to reconcile them.

During some weeks there were outrages, insults, evil reports, violent panics, the natural preludes of the terrible conflict which was at hand. A rumor spread over the whole island that, on the ninth of December, there would be a general massacre of the Englishry. Tyrconnel sent for the chief Protestants of Dublin to the Castle, and, with his usual energy of diction, invoked on himself all the veageance of heaven, if the report was not a cursed, a blasted, a confounded lie. It was said that, in his rage at finding his oaths ineffectual, he pulled off his hat and wig, and flung them into the fire.* But lying Dick Talbot was so well known that his imprecations and gesticulations only strengthened the apprehension which they were meant to allay. Ever since the recall of Clarendon there had been a large emigration of timid and quiet people from the Irish ports to England. That emigration now went on faster than ever. It was not easy to obtain a passage on board of a well-built or commodious vessel But many persons, made bold by excess of fear, and choosing rather to trust the winds and waves than the exasperated Irishry, ventured to encounter all the dangers of St. George's Channel and of the Welsh coast in open boats and in the depth of winter. The English who remained began, in almost every county, to draw close together. Every large country house became a fortress. Every visitor who arrived after nightfall was challenged from a loophole or from a barricaded window; and if he attempted to enter without passwords and explanations, a blunderbus was presented to him. On the dreaded night of the ninth of December, there was scarcely one Protestant mansion from the Giant's Causeway to Bantry Bay in which armed men were not watching and lights burning from the early sunset to the late sunrise.†

A minute account of what passed in one district at this time has come down to us, and well illustrates the general state of the kingdom. The south-western part of Kerry is now well known as the most beautiful tract in the British Isles. The mountains, the glens, the capes stretching far into the Atlantic, the crags on which the eagles build, the rivulets brawling down rocky passes, the lakes overhung by groves in which the wild deer find covert, attract every summer crowds of wanderers sated with the business and the pleasures of great cities. The beauties of that country are indeed too often hidden in the mist and rain which the west wind brings up from a boundless ocean. But, on the rare days when the sun shines out in all his glory, the landscape has a freshness and a warmth of coloring seldom found in our latitude. The myrtle loves the soil. The arbutus thrives better than even on the sunny shore of Calabria.‡ The turf is of livelier hue than else-

---
* A True and Impartial Account of the most material Passages in Ireland since December, 1688, by a gentleman who was an Eye-witness; licensed July 22, 1689.
† A True and Impartial Account, 1689; Leslie's Answer to King, 1692.
‡ There have been in the neighborhood of Killarney specimens of the arbutus thirty feet high and four feet and a half round. See the Philosophical Transactions, 227.

where: the hills glow with a richer purple: the varnish of the holly and ivy is more glossy; and berries of a brighter red peep through foliage of a brighter green. But during the greater part of the seventeenth century this paradise was as little known to the civilized world as Spitzbergen or Greenland. If ever it was mentioned, it was mentioned as a horrible desert, a chaos of bogs, thickets, and precipices, where the she-wolf still littered, and where some half-naked savages, who could not speak a word of English, made themselves burrows in the mud, and lived on roots and sour milk.*

At length, in the year 1670, the benevolent and enlightened Sir William Petty determined to form an English settlement in this wild district. He possessed a large domain there, which has descended to a posterity worthy of such an ancestor. On the improvement of that domain he expended, it was said, not less than ten thousand pounds. The little town which he founded, named from the bay of Kenmare, stood at the head of that bay under a mountain ridge, on the summit of which travellers now stop to gaze upon the loveliest of the three lakes of Killarney. Scarcely any village, built by an enterprising band of New Englanders, far from the dwellings of their countrymen, in the midst of the hunting grounds of the Red Indians, was more completely out of the pale of civilization than Kenmare. Between Petty's settlement and the nearest English habitation, the journey by land was of two days through a wild and dangerous country. Yet the place prospered. Forty-two houses were erected. The population amounted to a hundred and eighty. The land round the town was well cultivated. The cattle were numerous. Two small barks were employed in fishing and trading along the coast. The supply of herrings, pilchards, mackerel, and salmon was plentiful, and would have been still more plentiful, had not the beach been, in the finest part of the

---

* In a very full account of the British isles published at Nuremberg in 1690, Kerry is described as "an vielen Orten unwegsam und voller Wälder und Gebürge." Wolves still infested Ireland. "Kein schädlich Thier ist da, ausserhalb Wölff und Füches." So late as the year 1710 money was levied on presentments of the Grand Jury of Kerry for the destruction of wolves in that county. See Smith's Ancient and Modern State of the County of Kerry, 1756. I do not know that I have ever met with a better book of the kind and of the size. In a poem published as late as 1719, and entitled Macdermot, or the Irish Fortune Hunter, in six cantos, wolf-hunting and wolf-spearing are represented as common sports in Munster. In William's reign Ireland was sometimes called by the nickname of Wolfland. Thus in a poem on the battle of La Hogue, called Advice to a Painter, the terror of the Irish army is thus described:

"A chilling damp
And Wolfland howl runs thro' the rising camp."

year, covered by multitudes of seals, which preyed on the fish of the bay. Yet the seal was not an unwelcome visitor: his fur was valuable, and his oil supplied light through the long nights of winter. An attempt was made with great success to set up iron works. It was not yet the practice to employ coal for the purpose of smelting; and the manufacturers of Kent and Sussex had much difficulty in procuring timber at a reasonable price. The neighborhood of Kenmare was then richly wooded; and Petty found it a gainful speculation to send ore thither. The lovers of the picturesque still regret the woods of oak and arbutus which were cut down to feed his furnaces. Another scheme had occurred to his active and intelligent mind. Some of the neighboring islands abounded with variegated marble, red and white, purple and green. Petty well knew at what cost the ancient Romans had decorated their baths and temples with many colored columns hewn from Laconian and African quarries; and he seems to have indulged the hope that the rocks of his wild domain in Kerry might furnish embellishments to the mansions of Saint James's Square, and to the choir of Saint Paul's Cathedral.*

From the first, the settlers had found that they must be prepared to exercise the right of self-defence to an extent which would have been unnecessary and unjustifiable in a well governed country. The law was altogether without force in the highlands which lie on the south of the vale of Tralee. No officer of justice willingly ventured into those parts. One pursuivant, who in 1680 attempted to execute a warrant there, was murdered. The people of Kenmare seem however to have been sufficiently secured by their union, their intelligence, and their spirit, till the close of the year 1688. Then at length the effects of the policy of Tyrconnel began to be felt even in that remote corner of Ireland. In the eyes of the peasantry of Munster the colonists were aliens and heretics. The buildings, the boats, the machines, the granaries, the dairies, the furnaces, were doubtless contemplated by the native race with that mingled envy and contempt with which the ignorant naturally regard the triumphs of knowledge. Nor is it at all improbable that the emigrants had been guilty of those faults from which civilized men who settle among an uncivilized people are rarely free. The power derived from

---
* Smith's Ancient and Modern State of Kerry.

superior intelligence had, we may easily believe, been sometimes displayed with insolence, and sometimes exerted with injustice. Now, therefore, when the news spread from altar to altar, and from cabin to cabin, that the strangers were to be driven out, and that their houses and lands were to be given as a booty to the children of the soil, a predatory war commenced. Plunderers, thirty, forty, seventy in a troop, prowled round the town, some with firearms, some with pikes. The barns were robbed. The horses were stolen. In one foray a hundred and forty cattle were swept away and driven off through the ravines of Glengariff. In one night six dwellings were broken open and pillaged. At last the colonists, driven to extremity, resolved to die like men rather than be murdered in their beds. The house built by Petty for his agent was the largest in the place. It stood on a rocky peninsula round which the waves of the bay broke. Here the whole population assembled, seventy-five fighting men, with about a hundred women and children. They had among them sixty firelocks, and as many pikes and swords. Round the agent's house they threw up with great speed a wall of turf fourteen feet in height and twelve in thickness. The space enclosed was about half an acre. Within this rampart all the arms, the ammunition, and the provisions of the settlement were collected, and several huts of thin plank were built. When these preparations were completed, the men of Kenmare began to make vigorous reprisals on their Irish neighbors, seized robbers, recovered stolen property, and continued during some weeks to act in all things as an independent commonwealth. The government was carried on by elective officers to whom every member of the society swore fidelity on the Holy Gospels.*

While the people of the small town of Kenmare were thus bestirring themselves, similar preparations for defence were made by larger communities on a larger scale. Great numbers of gentlemen and yeomen quitted the open country, and repaired to those towns which had been founded and incorporated for the purpose of bridling the native population, and which, though recently placed under the government of Roman Catholic magistrates, were still inhabited chiefly by Protestants. A considerable body of armed colonists mustered at Sligo, another at Charleville,

* Exact Relation of the Persecutions, Robberies and Losses sustained by the Protestants of Kilmare in Ireland, 1689; Smith's Ancient and Modern State of Kerry, 1756.

a third at Mallow, a fourth still more formidable at Bandon.* But the principal strongholds of the Englishry during this evil time were Enniskillen and Londonderry.

Enniskillen, though the capital of the county of Fermanagh, was then merely a village. It was built on an island surrounded by the river which joins the two beautiful sheets of water known by the common name of Lough Erne. The stream and both the lakes were overhung on every side by natural forests. Enniskillen consisted of about eighty dwellings clustering round an ancient castle. The inhabitants were, with scarcely an exception, Protestants, and boasted that their town had been true to the Protestant cause through the terrible rebellion which broke out in 1641. Early in December they received from Dublin an intimation that two companies of Popish infantry were to be immediately quartered on them. The alarm of the little community was great, and the greater because it was known that a preaching friar had been exerting himself to inflame the Irish population of the neighborhood against the heretics. A daring resolution was taken Come what might, the troops should not be admitted. Yet the means of defence were slender. Not ten pounds of powder, not twenty firelocks fit for use, could be collected within the walls. Messengers were sent with pressing letters to summon the Protestant gentry of the vicinage to the rescue: and the summons was gallantly obeyed. In a few hours two hundred foot and a hundred and fifty horse had assembled. Tyrconnel's soldiers were already at hand. They brought with them a considerable supply of arms to be distributed among the peasantry. The peasantry greeted the royal standard with delight, and accompanied the march in great numbers. The townsmen and their allies, instead of waiting to be attacked, came boldly forth to encounter the intruders. The officers of James had expected no resistance. They were confounded when they saw confronting them a column of foot, flanked by a large body of mounted gentlemen and yeomen. The crowd of camp followers ran away in terror. The soldiers made a retreat so precipitate that it might be called a flight, and scarcely halted till they were thirty miles off at Cavan.†

---

* Ireland's Lamentation, licensed May 18, 1689.
† A True Relation of the Actions of the Inniskilling men, by Andrew Hamilton, Rector of Kilskerrie, and one of the Prebends of the Diocese of Clogher, an Eye-witness thereof and Actor therein, licensed Jan. 15, 1689-90; A Further Impartial Account of the Actions of the Inniskilling men, by Captain William MacCormick, one of the first that took up Arms, 1691.

The Protestants, elated by this easy victory, proceeded to make arrangements for the government and defence of Enniskillen and of the surrounding country. Gustavus Hamilton, a gentleman who had served in the army, but who had recently been deprived of his commission by Tyrconnel, and had since been living on an estate in Fermanagh, was appointed Governor, and took up his residence in the castle. Trusty men were enlisted and armed with great expedition. As there was a scarcity of swords and pikes, smiths were employed to make weapons by fastening scythes on poles. All the country houses round Lough Erne were turned into garrisons. No Papist was suffered to be at large in the town; and the friar who was accused of exerting his eloquence against the Englishry was thrown into prison.*

The other great fastness of Protestantism was a place of more importance. Eighty years before, during the troubles caused by the last struggle of the houses of O'Neil and O'Donnell against the authority of James the First, the ancient city of Derry had been surprised by one of the native chiefs: the inhabitants had been slaughtered, and the houses reduced to ashes. The insurgents were speedily put down and punished: the government resolved to restore the ruined town: the Lord Mayor, Aldermen, and Common Council of London were invited to assist in the work; and King James the First made over to them in their corporate capacity the ground covered by the ruins of the old Derry, and about six thousand acres in the neighborhood.†

This country, then uncultivated and uninhabited, is now enriched by industry, embellished by taste, and pleasing even to eyes accustomed to the well-tilled fields and stately manor houses of England. A new city soon arose which, on account of its connection with the capital of the empire, was called Londonderry. The buildings covered the summit and slope of a hill which overlooked the broad stream of the Foyle, then whitened by vast flocks of wild swan.‡ On the highest ground stood the cathedral, a church which, though erected when the secret of Gothic architecture was lost, and though ill-qualified to sustain a comparison with the awful temples of the middle ages, is

---

* Hamilton's True Relation; Mac Cormick's Further Impartial Account.
† Concise View of the Irish Society, 1822; Mr. Heath's interesting Account of the Worshipful Company of Grocers, Appendix 17.
‡ The Interest of England in the Preservation of Ireland, licensed July 17, 1689.

not without grace and dignity. Near the cathedral rose the palace of the bishop, whose see was one of the most valuable in Ireland. The city was in form nearly an ellipse; and the principal streets formed a cross, the arms of which met in a square called the Diamond. The original houses have been either rebuilt or so much repaired that their ancient character can no longer be traced; but many of them were standing within living memory. They were in general two stories in height; and some of them had stone staircases on the outside. The dwellings were encompassed by a wall of which the whole circumference was little less than a mile. On the bastion were planted culverins and sakers presented by the wealthy guilds of London to the colony. On some of these ancient guns, which have done memorable service to a great cause, the devices of the Fishmongers' Company, of the Vintners' Company, and of the Merchant Tailors' Company are still discernible.*

The inhabitants were Protestants of Anglo-Saxon blood. They were indeed not all of one country or of one church; but Englishmen and Scotchmen, Episcopalians and Presbyterians, seem to have generally lived together in friendship, a friendship which is sufficiently explained by their common antipathy to the Irish race and to the Popish religion. During the rebellion of 1641, Londonderry had resolutely held out against the native chieftains and had been repeatedly besieged in vain.† Since the Restoration the city had prospered. The Foyle, when the tide was high, brought up ships of large burden to the quay. The fisheries throve greatly. The nets, it was said, were sometimes so full that it was necessary to fling back multitudes of fish into the waves. The quantity of salmon caught annually was estimated at eleven hundred thousand pounds' weight.‡

The people of Londonderry shared in the alarm which, towards the close of the year 1688, was general among the Protestants settled in Ireland. It was known that the aboriginal peasantry of the neighborhood were laying in pikes and knives. Priests had been haranguing in a style of which, it must be owned, the Puritan part of the Anglo-Saxon colony had little right to complain, about the slaughter of the Amalekites, and the judgments which Saul had

---
* These things I observed or learned on the spot.
† The best account that I have seen of what passed in Londonderry during the war which began in 1641 is in Dr. Reid's History of the Presbyterian Church in Ireland.
‡ The Interest of England in the Preservation of Ireland; 1689.

brought on himself by sparing one of the proscribed race. Rumors from various quarters and anonymous letters in various hands agreed in naming the ninth of December as the day fixed for the extirpation of the strangers. While the minds of the citizens were agitated by these reports, news came that a regiment of twelve hundred Papists, commanded by a Papist, Alexander Macdonnell, Earl of Antrim, had received orders from the Lord Deputy to occupy Londonderry, and was already on the march from Coleraine. The consternation was extreme. Some were for closing the gates and resisting; some for submitting; some for temporizing. The corporation had, like the other corporations of Ireland, been remodelled. The magistrates were men of low station and character. Among them was only one person of Anglo-Saxon extraction; and he had turned Papist. In such rulers the inhabitants could place no confidence.* The Bishop, Ezekiel Hopkins, resolutely adhered to the political doctrines which he had preached during many years, and exhorted his flock to go patiently to the slaughter, rather than incur the guilt of disobeying the Lord's Annointed.† Antrim was meanwhile drawing nearer and nearer. At length the citizens saw from the walls his troops arrayed on the opposite shore of the Foyle. There was then no bridge; but there was a ferry which kept up a constant communication between the two banks of the river; and by this ferry a detachment from Antrim's regiment crossed. The officers presented themselves at the gate, produced a warrant directed to the Mayor and Sheriffs, and demanded admittance and quarters for His Majesty's soldiers.

Just at this moment thirteen young apprentices, most of whom appear, from their names, to have been of Scottish

---

* My authority for this unfavorable account of the corporation is an epic poem entitled the Londeriad. This extraordinary work must have been written very soon after the events to which it relates; for it is dedicated to Robert Rochfort, Speaker of the House of Commons; and Rochfort was Speaker from 1695 to 1699. The poet had no invention; he had evidently a minute knowledge of the city which he celebrated; and his doggerel is consequently not without historical value. He says:

> "For burgesses and freeman they had chose
> Brogue-makers, butchers, raps, and such as those:
> In all the corporation not a man
> Of British parents, except Buchanan."

This Buchanan is afterwards described:

> "A knave all o'er:
> For he had learned to tell his beads before."

† See a sermon preached by him at Dublin on Jan. 31, 1669. The text is, "Submit yourselves to every ordinance of man for the Lord's sake."

birth or descent, flew to the guard-room, armed themselves, seized the keys of the city, rushed to the Ferry Gate, closed it in the face of the King's officers, and let down the portcullis. James Morison, a citizen more advanced in years, addressed the intruders from the top of the wall and advised them to be gone. They stood in consultation before the gate till they heard him cry, "Bring a great gun this way." They then thought it time to get beyond the range of shot. They retreated, re-embarked, and rejoined their comrades on the other side of the river. The flame had already spread. The whole city was up. The other gates were secured. Sentinels paced the ramparts everywhere. The magazines were opened. Muskets and gunpowder were distributed. Messengers were sent, under cover of the following night, to the Protestant gentlemen of the neighboring counties. The bishop expostulated in vain. It is indeed probable that the vehement and daring young Scotchmen who had taken the lead on this occasion had little respect for his office. One of them broke in on a discourse with which he interrupted the military preparations by exclaiming, "A good sermon, my lord; a very good sermon: but we have not time to hear it just now."*

The Protestants of the neighborhood promptly obeyed the summons of Londonderry. Within forty-eight hours, hundreds of horse and foot came by various roads to the city. Antrim, not thinking himself strong enough to risk an attack, or not disposed to take on himself the responsibility of commencing a civil war without further orders, retired with his troops to Coleraine.

It might have been expected that the resistance of Enniskillen and Londonderry would have irritated Tyrconnel into taking some desperate step. And in truth his savage and imperious temper was at first inflamed by the news almost to madness. But, after wreaking his rage, as usual, on his wig, he became somewhat calmer. Tidings of a very sobering nature had just reached him. The Prince of Orange was marching unopposed to London. Almost every county and every great town in England had declared for him. James, deserted by his ablest captains, and by his nearest relatives, had sent commissioners to

---

* Walker's Account of the Siege of Derry, 1689; Mackenzie's Narrative of the Siege of Londonderry, 1689; An Apology for the failures charged on the Reverend Mr. Walker's Account of the late Siege of Derry, 1689; A Light to the Blind. This last work, a manuscript in the possession of Lord Fingal, is the work of a zealous Roman Catholic and a mortal enemy of England. Large extracts from it are among the Mackintosh MSS. The date in the title-page is 1711.

treat with the invaders, and had issued writs convoking a Parliament. While the result of the negotiations which were pending in England was uncertain, the Viceroy could not venture to take a bloody revenge on the refractory Protestants of Ireland. He therefore thought it expedient to affect a clemency and moderation which were by no means congenial to his disposition. The task of quieting the Englishry of Ulster was entrusted to William Stewart, Viscount Monntjoy. Mountjoy, a brave soldier, an accomplished scholar, a zealous Protestant, and yet a zealous Tory, was one of the very few members of the Established Church who still held office in Ireland. He was Master of the Ordnance in that kingdom, and was colonel of a regiment in which an uncommonly large proportion of the Englisry had been suffered to remain. At Dublin he was the center of a small circle of learned and ingenious men who had, under his presidency, formed themselves into a Royal society, the image, on a small scale, of the Royal Society of London. In Ulster, with which he was peculiarly connected, his name was held in high honor by the colonists.*
He hastened with his regiment to Londonderry and was well received there. For it was known that though he was firmly attached to hereditary monarchy he was not less firmly attached to the reformed religion. The citizens readily permitted him to leave within their walls a small garrison exclusively composed of Protestants, under the command of his lieutenant-colonel, Robert Lundy, who took the title of Governor.†

The news of Mountjoy's visit to Ulster was highly gratifying to the defenders of Enniskillen. Some gentlemen, deputed by that town, waited on him to request his good offices, but were disappointed by the reception which they found. "My advice to you is," he said, "to submit to the King's authority." "What, my Lord?" said one of the deputies; "Are we to sit still and let ourselves be butchered?" "The King," said Mountjoy, "will protect you." "If all that we hear be true," said the deputy, "His Majesty will find it hard enough to protect himself." The conference ended in this unsatisfactory manner. Enniskillen still kept its attitude of defiance; and Mountjoy returned to Dublin.‡

* As to Mountjoy's character and position, see Clarendon's letters from Ireland, particularly that to Lord Dartmouth of Feb. 8, and that to Evelyn of Feb. 14, 1685-6. "Bon officier, et homme d'esprit," says Avaux.
† Walker's Account; Light to the Blind.
‡ MacCormick's Further Impartial Account.

By this time it had indeed become evident that James could not protect himself. It was known in Ireland that he had fled; that he had been stopped; that he had fled again; that the Prince of Orange had arrived at Westminster in triumph, had taken on himself the administration of the realm, and had issued letters summoning a Convention.

Those lords and gentlemen at whose request the Prince had assumed the government, had earnestly entreated him to take the state of Ireland into his immediate consideration; and he had, in reply, assured them that he would do his best to maintain the Protestant religion and the English interest in that kingdom. His enemies afterwards accused him of utterly disregarding this promise; nay, they alleged, that he purposely suffered Ireland to sink deeper and deeper in calamity. Halifax, they said, had, with cruel and perfidious ingenuity, devised this mode of placing the Convention under a species of duress; and the trick had succeeded but too well. The vote which called William to the throne would not have passed so easily but for the extreme dangers which threatened the state; and it was in consequence of his own dishonest inactivity that those dangers had become extreme.* As this accusation rests on no proof, those who repeat it are at least bound to show that some course clearly better than the course which William took was open to him; and this they will find a difficult task. If indeed he could, within a few weeks after his arrival in London, have sent a great expedition to Ireland, that kingdom might perhaps, after a short struggle, or without a struggle, have submitted to his authority; and a long series of crimes and calamities might have been averted. But the factious orators and pamphleteers, who, much at their ease, reproached him for not sending such an expedition, would have been perplexed if they had been required to find the men, the ships, and the funds. The English army had lately been arrayed against him: part of it was still ill-disposed towards him; and the whole was utterly disorganized. Of the army which he had brought from Holland, not a regiment could be spared. He had found the treasury empty and the pay of the navy in arrear. He had no power to hypothecate any part of the public revenue. Those who lent him money lent it on

* Burnet, i. 807; and the notes by Swift and Dartmouth. Tutchin, in the Observator, repeats this idle calumny.

no other security than his bare word. It was only by the patriotic liberality of the merchants of London that he was enabled to defray the ordinary charges of government till the meeting of the Convention. It is surely unjust to blame him for not instantly fitting out, in such circumstances, an armament sufficient to conquer a kingdom.

Perceiving that, till the government of England was settled, it would not be in his power to interfere effectually by arms in the affairs of Ireland, he determined to try what effect negotiation would produce. Those who judged after the event pronounced that he had not, on this occasion, shown his usual sagacity. He ought, they said, to have known that it was absurd to expect submission from Tyrconnel. Such, however, was not, at the time, the opinion of men who had the best means of information, and whose interest was a sufficient pledge for their sincerity. A great meeting of noblemen and gentlemen who had property in Ireland was held, during the interregnum, at the house of the Duke of Ormond in St. James's Square. They advised the Prince to try whether the Lord Deputy might not be induced to capitulate on honorable and advantageous terms.* In truth there is strong reason to believe that Tyrconnel really wavered. For, fierce as were his passions, they never made him forgetful of his interest; and he might well doubt whether it were not for his interest, in declining years and health, to retire from business with full indemnity for all past offences, with high rank, and with an ample fortune, rather than to stake his life and property on the event of a war against the whole power of England. It is certain that he professed himself willing to yield. He opened a communication with the Prince of Orange, and affected to take counsel with Mountjoy, and with others who, though they had not thrown off their allegiance to James, were yet firmly attached to the Established Church and to the English connection.

In one quarter, a quarter from which William was justified in expecting the most judicious counsel, there was a strong conviction that the professions of Tyrconnel were sincere. No British statesman had then so high a reputation throughout Europe as Sir William Temple. His diplomatic skill had, twenty years before, arrested the progress of the French power. He had been a steady and a useful friend to the United Provinces and to the House

* The Orange Gazette, Jan. 10, 1689.

of Nassau. He had long been on terms of friendly confidence with the Prince of Orange, and had negotiated that marriage to which England owed her recent deliverance. With the affairs of Ireland Temple was supposed to be peculiarly well acquainted. His family had considerable property there: he had himself resided there during several years: he had represented the county of Carlow in Parliament; and a large part of his income was derived from a lucrative Irish office. There was no height of power, of rank, or of opulence to which he might not have risen, if he would have consented to quit his retreat, and to lend his assistance and the weight of his name to the new government. But power, rank and opulence had less attraction for his epicurean temper than ease and security. He rejected the most tempting invitations, and continued to amuse himself with his books, his tulips, and his pineapples, in rural seclusion. With some hesitation, however, he consented to let his eldest son, John, enter into the service of William. During the vacancy of the throne, John Temple was employed in business of high importance; and on subjects connected with Ireland, his opinion, which might reasonably be supposed to agree with his father's, had great weight. The young politician flattered himself that he had secured the services of an agent eminently qualified to bring the negotiation with Tyrconnel to a prosperous issue.

This agent was one of a remarkable family which had sprung from a noble Scottish stock, but which had long been settled in Ireland and which professed the Roman Catholic religion. In the gay crowd which thronged Whitehall, during those scandalous years of jubilee which immediately followed the Restoration, the Hamiltons were pre-eminently conspicuous. The long fair ringlets, the radiant bloom, and the languishing blue eyes of the lovely Elizabeth still charm us on the canvas of Lely. She had the glory of achieving no vulgar conquest. It was reserved for her voluptuous beauty and for her flippant wit to overcome the aversion which the cold-hearted and scoffing Grammont felt for the indissoluble tie. One of her brothers, Anthony, became the chronicler of that brilliant and dissolute society of which he had been not the least brilliant nor the least dissolute member. He deserves the high praise of having, though not a Frenchman, written the book which is, of all books, the most exquisitely French, both in spirit and in manner. Another brother, named Richard, had, in foreign service, gained some military experience. His wit and politeness had distinguished him even in the splendid circle of Versailles. It was whispered that he had dared to lift his eyes to an exalted lady, the natural daughter of the Great King, the wife of a legitimate prince of the House of Bourbon, and that she had not seemed to be displeased by the attentions of her presumptuous admirer.* Richard had subsequently returned to his native country, had been appointed brigadier-general in the Irish army, and had been sworn of the Irish Privy Council. When the Dutch invasion was expected, he came across Saint George's channel with the troops which Tyrconnel sent to reinforce the royal army. After the flight of James, those troops submitted to the Prince of Orange. Richard Hamilton not only made his own peace with what was now the ruling power, but declared himself confident that, if he were sent to Dublin, he could conduct the negotiation which had been opened there to a happy close. If he failed, he pledged his word to return to London in three weeks. His influence in Ireland was known to be great: his honor had never been questioned; and he was highly esteemed by John Temple. The young statesman declared that he would answer for his friend Richard as for himself. This guarantee was thought sufficient; and Hamilton set out for Ireland, proclaiming everywhere that he should soon bring Tyrconnel to reason. The offers which he was authorized to make to the Roman Catholics and personally to the Lord Deputy were most liberal.†

It is not impossible that Hamilton may have really meant to keep his promise. But when he arrived at Dublin he found that he had undertaken a task which he could not perform. The hesitation of Tyrconnel, whether genuine or feigned, was at an end. He had found that he had no longer a choice. He had with little difficulty stimulated the ignorant and susceptible Irish to fury. To calm them was beyond his skill. Rumors were abroad that the Viceroy was corresponding with the English; and those rumors had set the nation on fire. The cry of the common people was that, if he dared to sell them for wealth and honors, they would burn the Castle and him in it, and

---
* Mémoires de Madame de la Fayette.
† Burnet, i. 808; Life of James, ii. 320; Commons' Journals, July 29, 1689.

would put themselves under the protection of France.*
It was necessary for him to protest, truly or falsely, that
he had never harbored any thought of submission, and
that he had pretended to negotiate only for the purpose
of gaining time. Yet before he openly declared against
the English settlers, and against England herself, what
must be a war to the death, he wished to rid himself of
Mountjoy, who had hitherto been true to the cause of
James, but who, it was well known, would never consent
to be a party to the spoliation and oppression of the colonists. Hypocritical professions of friendship and of pacific
intentions were not spared. It was a sacred duty, Tyrconnel said, to avert the calamities which seemed to be impending. King James himself, if he understood the whole
case, would not wish his Irish friends to engage at that
moment in an enterprise which must be fatal to them and
useless to him. He would permit them, he would command them, to submit to necessity, and to reserve themselves for better times. If any man of weight, any man loyal,
able, and well informed, would repair to Saint Germains
and explain the state of things, His Majesty would easily
be convinced. Would Mountjoy undertake this most honorable and important mission? Mountjoy hesitated, and
suggested that some person more likely to be acceptable
to the King should be the messenger. Tyrconnel swore,
ranted, declared that, unless King James were well advised, Ireland would sink to the pit of hell, and insisted
that Mountjoy should go as the representative of the loyal
members of the Established Church, and should be accompanied by Chief Baron Rice, a Roman Catholic high
in the royal favor. Mountjoy yielded. The two ambassadors departed together, but with very different commissions. Rice was charged to tell James that Mountjoy was
a traitor at heart, and had been sent to France only that
the Protestants of Ireland might be deprived of a favorite
leader. The King was to be assured that he was impatiently expected in Ireland, and that, if he would show
himself there with a French force, he might speedily retrieve his fallen fortunes.† The Chief Baron carried with
him other instructions which were probably kept secret

---

* Avaux to Lewis, $\frac{\text{March 25,}}{\text{April 4.}}$ 1689.

† Clarke's Life of James, ii. 331; Mountjoy's Circular Letter, dated Jan. 10, 1688-9; King, iv. 8. In Light to the Blind, Tyrconnel's "wise dissimulation" is commended.

even from the Court of Saint Germains. If James should be unwilling to put himself at the head of the native population of Ireland, Rice was directed to request a private audience of Lewis, and to offer to make the island a province of France.*

As soon as the two envoys had departed, Tyrconnel set himself to prepare for the conflict which had become inevitable; and he was strenuously assisted by the faithless Hamilton. The Irish nation was called to arms; and the call was obeyed with strange promptitude and enthusiasm. The flag on the Castle of Dublin was embroidered with the words, "Now or never! Now and forever!" Those words resounded through the whole island.† Never in modern Europe has there been such a rising up of a whole people. The habits of the Celtic peasant were such that he made no sacrifice in quitting his potato ground for the camp. He loved excitement and adventure. He feared work far more than danger. His national and religious feelings had, during three years, been exasperated by the constant application of stimulants. At every fair and market he had heard that a good time was at hand, that the tyrants who spoke Saxon and lived in slated houses were about to be swept away, and that the land would again belong to its own children. By the peat fires of a hundred thousand cabins had nightly been sung rude ballads which predicted the deliverance of the oppressed race. The priests, most of whom belonged to those old families which the Act of Settlement had ruined, but which were still revered by the native population, had, from a thousand altars, charged every Catholic to show his zeal for the true Church by providing weapons against the day when it might be necessary to try the chances of battle in her cause.‡ The army, which, under Ormond, had consisted of only eight regiments, was now increased to forty-eight: and the ranks were soon full to overflowing. It was impossible to find at short notice one tenth of the number of good officers which was required. Commissions were scattered profusely among idle cosherers who claimed to

---

* Avaux to Lewis, April 13-23, 1689.
† Printed Letter from Dublin, Feb. 25, 1689; Mephibosheth and Ziba, 1689.
‡ The connection of the priests with the old Irish families is mentioned in Petty's Political Anatomy of Ireland. See the short view by a Clergyman lately escaped, 1689; Ireland's Lamentation, by an English Protestant that lately narrowly escaped with life from thence, 1689; A True Account of the State of Ireland, by a person who with Great Difficulty left Dublin, 1689; King, ii. 7. Avaux confirms all that these writers say about

be descended from good Irish families. Yet even thus the supply of captains and lieutenants fell short of the demand; and many companies were commanded by cobblers, tailors, and footmen.

The pay of the soldiers was very small. The private had no more than three pence a day. One half only of this pittance was ever given him in money; and that half was often in arrear. But a far more seductive bait than his miserable stipend was the prospect of boundless license. If the government allowed him less than sufficed for his wants, it was not extreme to mark the means by which he supplied the deficiency. Though four-fifths of the population of Ireland were Celtic and Roman Catholic, more than four-fifths of the property of Ireland belonged to the Protestant Englishry. The garners, the cellars, above all the flocks and herds of the minority, were abandoned to the majority. Whatever the regular troops spared was devoured by bands of marauders who overran almost every barony in the island. For the arming was now universal. No man dared to present himself at mass without some weapon, a pike, a long knife called a skean, or, at the very least, a strong ashen stake, pointed and hardened in the fire. The very women were exhorted by their spiritual directors to carry skeans. Every smith, every carpenter, every cutler, was at constant work on guns and blades. It was scarcely possible to get a horse shod. If any Protestant artisan refused to assist in the manufacture of implements which were to be used against his nation and his religion, he was flung into prison. It seems probable that, at the end of February, at least a hundred thousand Irishmen were in arms. Near fifty thousand of them were soldiers.* The rest were banditti, whose violence and licentiousness the government affected to disapprove, but did not really exert itself to suppress. The Protestants not only were not protected, but were not suffered to protect themselves. It was determined that they should be left unarmed in the midst of an armed and hostile population.

---

* At the French War Office is a report on the State of Ireland in February, 1689. In that report it is said that the Irish who had enlisted as soldiers were forty-five thousand, and that the number would have been a hundred thousand if all who volunteered had been admitted. See the Sad and Lamentable Condition of the Protestants in Ireland, 1689; Hamilton's True Relation, 1690; The State of Papist and Protestant Properties in the Kingdom of Ireland, 1689; A True Representation to the King and People of England, how Matters were carried on all along in Ireland, licensed Aug. 16, 1689; Letter from Dublin, 1689; Ireland's Lamentation, 1689; Compleat History of the Life and Military Actions of Richard, Earl of Tyrconnel, Generalissimo of all the Irish forces now in arms, 1689.

A day was fixed on which they were to bring all their swords and firelocks to the parish churches; and it was notified that every Protestant house in which, after that day, a weapon should be found should be given up to be sacked by the soldiers. Bitter complaints were made that any knave might, by hiding a spearhead or an old gunbarrel in a corner of a mansion, bring utter ruin on the owner.

Chief Justice Keating, himself a Protestant, and almost the only Protestant who still held a great place in Ireland, struggled courageously in the cause of justice and order against the united strength of the government and the populace. At the Wicklow Assizes of that spring, he, from the seat of judgment, set forth with great strength of language the miserable state of the country. Whole counties, he said, were devastated by a rabble resembling the vultures and ravens which follow the march of an army. Most of these wretches were not soldiers. They acted under no authority known to the law. Yet it was, he owned, but too evident that they were encouraged and screened by some who were in high command. How else could it be that a market overt for plunder should be held within a short distance of the capital? The stories which travellers told of the savage Hottentots near the Cape of Good Hope were realized in Leinster. Nothing was more common than for an honest man to lie down rich in flocks and herds acquired by the industry of a long life, and to wake a beggar. It was, however, to small purpose that Keating attempted, in the midst of that fearful anarchy, to uphold the supremacy of the law. Priests and military chiefs appeared on the bench for the purpose of overawing the judge and countenancing the robbers. One ruffian escaped because no prosecutor dared to appear. Another declared that he had armed himself in conformity to the orders of his spiritual guide, and to the example of many persons of higher station than himself, whom he saw at that moment in court. Two only of the Merry Boys, as they were called, were convicted: the worst criminals escaped; and the Chief Justice indignantly told the jurymen that the guilt of the public ruin lay at their door.*

When such disorder prevailed in Wicklow, it is easy to imagine what must have been the state of districts more barbarous and more remote from the seat of government.

---
* See the Proceedings in the State Trials.

Keating appears to have been the only magistrate who strenuously exerted himself to put the law in force. Indeed Nugent, the Chief Justice of the highest criminal court of the realm, declared on the bench of Cork that, without violence and spoliation, the intentions of the government could not be carried into effect, and that robbery must, at that conjuncture, be tolerated as a necessary evil.*

The destruction of property which took place within a few weeks would be incredible, if it were not attested by witnesses unconnected with each other and attached to very different interests. There is a close, and sometimes almost a verbal, agreement between the descriptions given by Protestants, who, during that reign of terror, escaped, at the hazard of their lives, to England, and the descriptions given by the envoys, commissaries, and captains of Lewis. All agreed in declaring that it would take many years to repair the waste which had been wrought in a few weeks by the armed peasantry.† Some of the Saxon aristocracy had mansions richly furnished, and sideboards gorgeous with silver bowls and chargers. All this wealth disappeared. One house, in which there had been three thousand pounds' worth of plate, was left without a spoon.‡ But the chief riches of Ireland consisted in cattle. Innumerable flocks and herds covered that vast expanse of emerald meadow, saturated with the moisture of the Atlantic. More than one gentleman possessed twenty thousand sheep and four thousand oxen. The freebooters who now overspread the country belonged to a class which was accustomed to live on potatoes and sour whey, and which had always regarded meat as a luxury reserved for the rich. These men at first revelled in beef and mutton, as the savage invaders, who of old poured down from the forests of the north on Italy, revelled in Massic and Falernian wines. The Protestants described with contemptuous disgust the strange gluttony of their newly liberated slaves. Carcasses, half raw and half burned to cinders, sometimes still bleeding, sometimes in a state of loathsome decay, were torn to pieces, and swallowed without salt, bread, or herbs. Those marauders who preferred boiled meat, being often in want of kettles, contrived to cook the steer in his

---
* King, iii. 10.
† Ten years, says the French Ambassador; twenty years, says a Protestant fugitive.
‡ Animadversions on the proposal for sending back the nobility and gentry of Ireland, 1689-90.

own skin. An absurd tragi-comedy is still extant, which was acted, in this and the following year, at some low theater, for the amusement of the English populace. A crowd of half-naked savages appeared on the stage, howling a Celtic song and dancing round an ox. They then proceeded to cut steaks out of the animal while still alive, and to fling the bleeding flesh on the coals. In truth the barbarity and filthiness of the banquets of the Rapparees was such as the dramatists of Grub Street could scarcely caricature. When Lent began, the plunderers generally ceased to devour, but continued to destroy. A peasant would kill a cow merely in order to get a pair of brogues. Often a whole flock of sheep, often a herd of fifty or sixty kine, were slaughtered; the beasts were flayed; the fleeces and hides were carried away; and the bodies were left to poison the air. The French ambassador reported to his master that, in six weeks, fifty thousand horned cattle had been slain in this manner, and were rotting on the ground all over the country. The number of sheep that were butchered during the same time was popularly said to have been three or four hundred thousand.*

Any estimate which can now be framed of the value of the property destroyed during this fearful conflict of races must necessarily be very inexact. We are not however absolutely without materials for such an estimate. The Quakers were neither a very numerous nor a very opulent class. We can hardly suppose that they were more than a fiftieth part of the Protestant population of Ireland, or that they possessed more than a fiftieth part of the Protestant wealth of Ireland. They were undoubtedly better treated than any other Protestant sect. James had always been partial to them; they own that Tyrconnel did his best to

---

* King, iii. 10; The Sad Estate and Condition of Ireland, as represented in a Letter from a worthy Person who was in Dublin on Friday last, March 4, 1689; Short View by a Clergyman, 1689; Lamentation of Ireland, 1689; Compleat History of the Life and Actions of Richard, Earl of Tyrconnel, 1689; The Royal Voyage, acted in 1689 and 1690. This drama, which, I believe, was performed at Bartholomew Fair, is one of the most curious of a curious class of compositions, utterly destitute of literary merit, but valuable as showing what were then the most successful claptraps for an audience composed of the common people. "The end of this play," says the author in his preface, "is chiefly to expose the perfidious, base, cowardly, and bloody nature of the Irish." The account which the fugitive Protestants give of the wanton destruction of cattle is confirmed by Avaux in a letter to Lewis, dated April 13-23, 1689, and by Desgrigny in a letter to Louvois, dated May 17-27, 1690. Most of the despatches written by Avaux during his mission to Ireland are contained in a volume of which a very few copies were printed some years ago at the English Foreign Office. Of many I have also copies made at the French Foreign Office. The letters of Desgrigny, who was employed in the Commissariat, I found in the Library of the French War Office. I cannot too strongly express my sense of the liberality and courtesy with which the immense and admirably arranged storehouses of curious information at Paris were thrown open to me.

protect them: and they seem to have found favor even in the sight of the Rapparees.* Yet the Quakers computed their pecuniary losses at a hundred thousand pounds.†

In Leinster, Munster, and Connaught, it was utterly impossible for the English settlers, few as they were and dispersed, to offer any effectual resistance to this terrible outbreak of the aboriginal population. Charleville, Mallow, Sligow, fell into the hands of the natives. Bandon, where the Protestants had mustered in considerable force, was reduced by Lieutenant General Macarthy, an Irish officer who was descended from one of the most illustrious Celtic houses, and who had long served, under a feigned name, in the French army.‡ The people of Kenmare held out in their little fastness till they were attacked by three thousand regular soldiers, and till it was known that several pieces of ordnance were coming to batter down the turf wall which surrounded the agent's house. Then at length a capitulation was concluded. The colonists were suffered to embark in a small vessel scantily supplied with food and water. They had no experienced navigator on board: but after a voyage of a fortnight, during which they were crowded together like slaves in a Guinea ship, and suffered the extremity of thirst and hunger, they reached Bristol in safety§ When such was the fate of the towns, it was evident that the country seats which the Protestant landowners had recently fortified in the three southern provinces could no longer be defended. Many families submitted, delivered up their arms, and thought themselves happy in escaping with life. But many resolute and high-spirited gentlemen and yeomen were determined to perish rather than yield. They packed up such valuable property as could easily be carried away, burned whatever they could not remove, and, well armed and mounted, set out for those spots in Ulster which were the strongholds of their race and of their faith. The flower of the Protestant population of Munster and Connaught found shelter at Enniskillen. Whatever was bravest and

---

* "A remarkable thing never to be forgotten was that they that were in government then"—at the end of 1688—"seemed to favour us and endeavour to preserve Friends." —History of the Rise and Progress of the People called Quakers in Ireland, by Wight and Rutty, Dublin, 1751. King indeed (iii. 17) reproaches the Quakers as allies and tools of the Papists.

† Wight and Rutty.

‡ Life of James, ii. 327. Orig. Mem. Macarthy and his feigned name are repeatedly mentioned by Dangeau.

§ Exact Relation of the Persecutions, Robberies and Losses sustained by the Protestants of Kilmare in Ireland, 1689.

most true-hearted in Leinster took the road to Londonderry.*

The spirit of Enniskillen and Londonderry rose higher and higher to meet the danger. At both places the tidings of what had been done by the Convention at Westminster were received with transports of joy. William and Mary were proclaimed at Enniskillen with unanimous enthusiasm, and with such pomp as the little town could furnish.† Lundy, who commanded at Londonderry, could not venture to oppose himself to the general sentiment of the citizens and of his own soldiers. He therefore gave in his adhesion to the new government, and signed a declaration by which he bound himself to stand by that government, on pain of being considered a coward and a traitor. A vessel from England soon brought a commission from William and Mary which confirmed him in his office.‡

To reduce the Protestants of Ulster to submission before aid could arrive from England was now the chief object of Tyrconnel. A great force was ordered to move northward, under the command of Richard Hamilton. This man had violated all the obligations which are held most sacred by gentlemen and soldiers, had broken faith with his most intimate friends, had forfeited his military parole, and was now not ashamed to take the field as a general against the government to which he was bound to render himself up as a prisoner. His march left on the face of the country traces which the most careless eye could not during many years fail to discern. His army was accompanied by a rabble, such as Keating had well compared to the unclean birds of prey which swarm wherever the scent of carrion is strong. The general professed himself anxious to save from ruin and outrage all Protestants who remained quietly at their homes; and he most readily gave them protections under his hand. But these protections proved of no avail; and he was forced to own that, whatever power he might be able to exercise over his soldiers, he could not keep order among the mob of camp followers. The country behind him was a wilderness; and soon the country before him became equally desolate. For, at the fame of his approach, the colonists burned their furniture,

---
* A true Representation to the King and People of England how matters were carried on all along in Ireland by the late King James, licensed Aug. 16, 1689; A True Account of the Present State of Ireland by a person that with Great Difficulty left Dublin, licensed June 8, 1689.

† Hamilton's Accounts of the Inniskilling Men, 1689.

‡ Walker's Account, 1689.

pulled down their houses, and retreated northward. Some of them attempted to make a stand at Dromore, but were broken and scattered. Then the flight became wild and tumultuous. The fugitives broke down the bridges and burned the ferry-boats. Whole towns, the seats of the Protestant population, were left in ruins without one inhabitant. The people of Omagh destroyed their own dwellings so utterly that no roof was left to shelter the enemy from the rain and wind. The people of Cavan migrated in one body to Enniskillen. The day was wet and stormy. The road was deep in mire. It was a piteous sight to see, mingled with the armed men, the women and children weeping, famished, and toiling through the mud up to their knees. All Lisburn fled to Antrim; and, as the foes drew nearer, all Lisburn and Antrim together came pouring into Londonderry. Thirty thousand Protestants, of both sexes and of every age, were crowded behind the bulwarks of the City of Refuge. There, at length, on the verge of the ocean, hunted to the last asylum, and baited into a mood in which men may be destroyed, but will not easily be subjugated, the imperial race turned desperately to bay.*

Meanwhile Mountjoy and Rice had arrived in France. Mountjoy was instantly put under arrest and thrown into the Bastile. James determined to comply with the invitation which Rice had brought, and applied to Lewis for the help of a French army. But Lewis, though he showed, as to all things which concerned the personal dignity and comfort of his royal guests, a delicacy even romantic, and a liberality approaching to profusion, was unwilling to send a large body of troops to Ireland. He saw that France would have to maintain a long war on the Continent against a formidable coalition: her expenditure must be immense; and great as were her resources, he felt it to be important that nothing should be wasted. He doubtless regarded with sincere commiseration and good will the unfortunate exiles to whom he had given so princely a welcome. Yet neither commiseration nor good will could prevent him from speedily discovering that his brother of England was the dullest and most perverse of human beings. The folly of James, his incapacity to read the char-

* Mackenzie's Narrative; Mac Cormick's Further Impartial Account; Story's Impartial History of the Affairs of Ireland, 1691; Apology for the Protestants of Ireland; Letter from Dublin of Feb. 25, 1689; Avaux to Lewis, 15-25, 1689.

acters of men and the signs of the times, his obstinacy, always most offensively displayed when wisdom enjoined concession, his vacillation, always exhibited most pitiably in emergencies which required firmness, had made him an outcast from England and might, if his counsels were blindly followed, bring great calamities on France. As a legitimate sovereign expelled by rebels, as a confessor of the true faith persecuted by heretics, as a near kinsman of the house of Bourbon, who had seated himself on the hearth of that House, he was entitled to hospitality, to tenderness, to respect. It was fit that he should have a stately palace and a spacious forest, that the household troops should salute him with the highest military honors, that he should have at his command all the hounds of the Grand Huntsman and all the hawks of the Grand Falconer. But, when a prince, who, at the head of a great fleet and army, had lost an empire without striking a blow, undertook to furnish plans for naval and military expeditions; when a prince, who had been undone by his profound ignorance of the temper of his own countrymen, of his own soldiers, of his own domestics, of his own children, undertook to answer for the zeal and fidelity of the Irish people, whose tongue he could not speak, and on whose land he had never set his foot; it was necessary to receive his suggestions with caution. Such were the sentiments of Lewis; and in these sentiments he was confirmed by his Minister of War, Louvois, who, on private as well as on public grounds, was unwilling that James should be accompanied by a large military force. Louvois hated Lauzun. Lauzun was a favorite at Saint Germains. He wore the garter, a badge of honor which has very seldom been conferred on aliens who were not sovereign princes. It was believed indeed at the French Court that, in order to distinguish him from the other knights of the most illustrious of European orders, he had been decorated with that very George which Charles the First had, on the scaffold, put into the hands of Juxon.* Lauzun had been encouraged to hope that, if French forces were sent to Ireland, he should command them; and this ambitious hope Louvois was bent on disappointing.†

An army was therefore for the present refused: but

---

* Mémoires de Madame de la Fayette; Madame de Sévigné to Madame de Grignan, February 28, 1689.
† Burnet, ii. 17; Life of James II., ii. 320, 321, 322.

everything else was granted. The Brest fleet was ordered to be in readiness to sail. Arms for ten thousand men and great quantities of ammunition were put on board. About four hundred captains, lieutenants, cadets, and gunners were selected for the important service of organizing and disciplining the Irish levies. The chief command was held by a veteran warrior, the Count of Rosen. Under him were Maumont, who held the rank of lietenant general, and a brigadier named Pusignan, Five hundred thousand crowns in gold, equivalent to about a hundred and twelve thousand pounds sterling, were sent to Brest.* For James's personal comforts provision was made with anxiety resembling that of a tender mother equipping her son for a first campaign. The cabin furniture, the camp furniture, the tents, the bedding, the plate, were luxurious and superb. Nothing which could be agreeable or useful to the exile was too costly for the munificence, or too trifling for the attention, of his gracious and splendid host. On the fifteenth of February, James paid a farewell visit to Versailles. He was conducted round the buildings and plantations with every mark of respect and kindness. The fountains played in his honor. It was the season of the Carnival: and never had the vast palace and the sumptuous gardens presented a gayer aspect. In the evening the two kings, after a long and earnest conference in private, made their appearance before a splendid circle of lords and ladies. "I hope," said Lewis, in his noblest and most winning manner, "that we are about to part, never to meet again in this world. That is the best wish I can form for you. But, if any evil chance should force you to return, be assured that you will find me to the last such as you have found me hitherto." On the seventeenth, Lewis paid in return a farewell visit to Saint Germains. At the moment of the parting embrace, he said, with his most amiable smile, "We have forgotten one thing, a cuirass for yourself. You shall have mine." The cuirass was brought, and suggested to the wits of the Court ingenious allusions to the Vulcanian panoply which Achilles lent to his feebler friend. James set out for Brest; and his wife, overcome with sickness and sorrow, shut herself up with her child to weep and pray.†

---

* Maumont's Instructions.

† Dangeau, Feb. 15-25, 17-27, 1689; Madame de Sévigné Feb. 18-28, Feb. 20, March 2. Mémoires de Madame de la Fayette.

James was accompanied or speedily followed by several of his own subjects, among whom the most distinguished were his son Berwick, Cartwright Bishop of Chester, Powis, Dover, and Melfort. Of all the retinue, none was so odious to the people of Great Britain as Melfort. He was an apostate: he was believed by many to be an insincere apostate; and the insolent, arbitrary, and menacing language of his state papers disgusted even the Jacobites. He was therefore a favorite with his master: for to James unpopularity, obstinacy, and implacability were the greatest recommendations that a minister could have.

What Frenchman should attend the King of England in the character of ambassador had been the subject of grave deliberation at Versailles. Barillon could not be passed over without a marked slight. But his self-indulgent habits, his want of energy, and, above all, the credulity with which he had listened to the professions of Sunderland, had made an unfavorable impression on the mind of Lewis. What was to be done in Ireland was not work for a trifler or a dupe. The agent of France in that kingdom must be equal to much more than the ordinary functions of an envoy. It would be his right and his duty to offer advice touching every part of the political and military administration of the country in which he would represent the most powerful and the most beneficent of allies. Barillon was therefore suffered to retire into privacy. He affected to bear his disgrace with composure. His political career, though it had brought great calamities both on the House of Stuart and on the House of Bourbon, had been by no means unprofitable to himself. He was old, he said: he was fat: he did not envy younger men the honor of living on potatoes and whiskey among the Irish bogs: he would try to console himself with partridges, with champagne, and with the society of the wittiest men and prettiest women of Paris. It was rumored, however, that he was tortured by painful emotions which he was studious to conceal: his health and spirits failed; and he tried to find consolation in religious duties. Some people were much edified by the piety of the old voluptuary: but others attributed his death, which took place not long after his retreat from public life, to shame and vexation.*

---

* Memoirs of La Fare and St. Simon; Note of Renaudot on English affairs, 1697, in the French Archives; Madame de Sévigné, $\frac{\text{Feb, 20,}}{\text{March 2.}}$ March 11-21, 1689; Letter of Madame de Coulanges to M. de Coulanges, July 23, 1691.

The Count of Avaux, whose sagacity had detected all the plans of William, and who had in vain recommended a policy which would probably have frustrated them, was the man on whom the choice of Lewis fell. In abilities Avaux had no superior among the numerous able diplomatists whom his country then possessed. His demeanor was singularly pleasing, his person handsome, his temper bland. His manners and conversation were those of a gentleman who had been bred in the most polite and magnificent of all courts, who had represented that court both in Roman Catholic and in Protestant countries, and who had acquired in his wanderings the art of catching the tone of any society into which chance might throw him. He was eminently vigilant and adroit, fertile in resources, and skillful in discovering the weak parts of a character. His own character, however, was not without its weak parts. The consciousness that he was of plebeian origin was the torment of his life. He pined for nobility with a pining at once pitiable and ludicrous. Able, experienced, and accomplished as he was, he sometimes, under the influence of this mental disease, descended to the level of Moliere's Jourdain, and entertained malicious observers with scenes almost as laughable as that in which the honest draper was made a Mamamouchi.* It would have been well if this had been the worst. But it is not too much to say that of the difference between right and wrong Avaux had no more notion than a brute. One sentiment was to him in the place of religion and morality, a superstitious and intolerant devotion to the crown which he served. This sentiment pervades all his despatches, and gives a color to all his thoughts and words. Nothing that tended to promote the interest of the French monarchy seemed to him a crime. Indeed he appears to have taken it for granted that not only Frenchmen, but all human beings, owed a natural allegiance to the House of Bourbon, and that whoever hesitated to sacrifice the happiness and freedom of his own native country to the glory of that House was a traitor. While he resided at the Hague, he always designated those Dutchmen who had sold themselves to France as the well-intentioned party. In the letters which he wrote from Ireland, the same feeling appears still more strongly. He would have been a more sagacious politician if he had

---

* See St. Simon's account of the trick by which Avaux tried to pass himself off at Stockholm as a Knight of the Order of the Holy Ghost.

sympathized more with those feelings of moral approbation and disapprobation which prevail among the vulgar. For his own indifference to all considerations of justice and mercy was such that, in his schemes, he made no allowance for the consciences and sensibilities of his neighbors. More than once he deliberately recommended wickedness so horrible that wicked men recoiled from it with indignation. But they could not succeed even in making their scruples intelligible to him. To every remonstrance he listened with a cynical sneer, wondering himself whether those who lectured him were such fools as they professed to be, or were only shamming.

Such was the man whom Lewis selected to be the companion and monitor of James. Avaux was charged to open, if possible, a communication with the malcontents in the English Parliament: and he was authorized to expend, if necessary, a hundred thousand crowns among them.

James arrived at Brest on the fifth of March, embarked there on board of a man-of-war called the Saint Michael, and sailed within forty-eight hours. He had ample time, however, before his departure, to exhibit some of the faults by which he had lost England and Scotland, and by which he was about to lose Ireland. Avaux wrote from the harbor of Brest that it would not be easy to conduct any important business in concert with the King of England. His Majesty could not keep any secret from anybody. The very foremast men of the Saint Michael had already heard him say things which ought to have been reserved for the ears of his confidential advisers.*

The voyage was safely and quietly performed; and, on the afternoon of the twelfth of March, James landed in the harbor of Kinsale. By the Roman Catholic population he was received with shouts of unfeigned transport. The few Protestants who remained in that part of the country joined in greeting him, and perhaps not insincerely. For, though an enemy of their religion, he was not an enemy of their nation; and they might reasonably hope that the worst king would show somewhat more respect for law and property than had been shown by the Merry Boys and Rapparees. The Vicar of Kinsale was among those who

---

* This letter, written to Lewis from the harbor of Brest, is in the Archives of the French Foreign Office, but is wanting in the very rare volume printed in Downing Street.

went to pay their duty: he was presented by the Bishop
of Chester, and was not ungraciously received.*

James learned that his cause was prospering. In the
three southern provinces of Ireland the Protestants were
disarmed, and were so effectually bowed down by terror
that he had nothing to apprehend from them. In the
North there was some show of resistance: but Hamilton
was marching against the malcontents; and there was
little doubt that they would easily be crushed. A day was
spent at Kinsale in putting the arms and ammunition out
of reach of danger. Horses sufficient to carry a few travellers were with some difficulty procured; and, on the fourteenth of March, James proceeded to Cork.†

We should greatly err if we imagined that the road by
which he entered that city bore any resemblance to the
stately approach which strikes the traveller of the nineteenth century with admiration. At present Cork, though
deformed by many miserable relics of a former age, holds
no mean place among the ports of the empire. The shipping is more than half what the shipping of London was
at the time of the Revolution. The customs exceed the
whole revenue which the whole kingdom of Ireland, in the
most peaceful and prosperous times, yielded to the Stuarts. The town is adorned by broad and well built streets,
by fair gardens, by a Corinthian portico which would do
honor to Palladio, and by a Gothic College worthy to
stand in the High Street of Oxford. In 1689, the city extended over about one-tenth part of the space which it
now covers, and was intersected by muddy streams, which
have long been concealed by arches and buildings. A
desolate marsh, in which the sportsman who pursued the
waterfowl sank deep in water and mire at every step, covered the area now occupied by stately buildings, the palaces of great commercial societies. There was only a single street in which two-wheeled carriages could pass each
other. From this street diverged to right and left alleys
squalid and noisome beyond the belief of those who have
formed their notions of misery from the most miserable
parts of Saint Giles's and Whitechapel. One of these
alleys, called, and, by comparison, justly called, Broad
Lane, is about ten feet wide From such places, now seats

---

* A full and true account of the Landing and Reception of the late King James at
Kinsale, in a letter from Bristol, licensed April 4, 1689; Leslie's Answer to King;
Ireland's Lamentation; Avaux, March 13-23.

† Avaux, March 13-23, 1689; Life of James, ii. 327, Orig. Mem.

of hunger and pestilence, abandoned to the most wretched of mankind, the citizens poured forth to welcome James. He was received with military honors by Macarthy, who held the chief command in Munster.

It was impossible for the King to proceed immediately to Dublin; for the southern counties had been so completely laid waste by the banditti whom the priests had called to arms that the means of locomotion were not easily to be procured. Horses had become rarities: in a large district there were only two carts; and those Avaux pronounced good for nothing. Some days elapsed before the money which had been brought from France, though no very formidable mass, could be dragged over the few miles which separated Cork from Kinsale.*

While the King and his Council were employed in trying to procure carriages and beasts, Tyrconnel arrived from Dublin. He held encouraging language. The opposition of Enniskillen he seems to have thought deserving of little consideration. Londonderry, he said, was the only important post held by the Protestants; and even Londonderry would not, in his judgment, hold out many days.

At length James was able to leave Cork for the capital. On the road, the shrewd and observant Avaux made many remarks. The first part of the journey was through wild highlands, where it was not strange that there should be few traces of art and industry. But, from Kilkenny to the gates of Dublin the path of the travellers lay over gently undulating ground, rich with natural verdure. That fertile district should have been covered with flocks and herds, orchards and cornfields; but it was an untilled and unpeopled desert. Even in the towns the artisans were very few. Manufactured articles were hardly to be found, and if found could be procured only at immense prices. The envoy at first attributed the desolation which he saw on every side to the tyranny of the English colonists. In a very short time he was forced to change his opinion.†

James received on his progress numerous marks of the good-will of the peasantry; but marks such as, to men bred in the courts of France and England, had an uncouth and ominous appearance. Though very few laborers were seen at work in the fields, the road was lined by Rapparees

---

* Avaux, March 15-25, 1689.

† Avaux, $\frac{\text{March 25,}}{\text{April 4,}}$ 1689.

armed with skeans, stakes, and half pikes, who crowded to look upon the deliverer of their race. The highway along which he travelled presented the aspect of a street in which a fair is held. Pipers came forth to play before him in a style which was not exactly that of the French opera; and the villagers danced wildly to the music. Long frieze mantles, resembling those which Spenser had, a century before, described as meet beds for rebels and apt cloaks for thieves, were spread along the path which the cavalcade was to tread; and garlands in which cabbage stalks supplied the place of laurels, were offered to the royal hand. The women insisted on kissing His Majesty; but it should seem that they bore little resemblance to their posterity; for this compliment was so distasteful to him that he ordered his retinue to keep them at a distance.*

On the twenty-fourth of March he entered Dublin. That city was then, in extent and population, the second in the British isles. It contained between six and seven thousand houses, and probably above thirty thousand inhabitants.† In wealth and beauty, however, Dublin was inferior to many English towns. Of the graceful and stately public buildings which now adorn both sides of the Liffey scarcely one had been even projected. The College, a very different edifice from that which now stands on the same site, lay quite out of the city.‡ The ground which is at present occupied by Leinster House and Charlemont House, by Sackville Street and Merrion Square, was open meadow. Most of the dwellings were built of timber, and have long given place to more substantial edifices. The Castle had in 1686 been almost uninhabitable. Clarendon had complained that he knew of no gentleman in Pall Mall who was not more conveniently and handsomely lodged than the Lord Lieutenant of Ireland. No public ceremony could be performed in a becoming manner under the Vice-regal roof. Nay, in spite of constant glazing and tiling, the rain perpetually drenched the apartments.§ Tyrconnel, since he became Lord Deputy, had erected a new building somewhat more commodious. To this building the

* A full and true Account of the Landing and Reception of the late King James; Ireland's Lamentation; Light to the Blind.
† See the calculations of Petty, King and Davenant. If the average number of inhabitants to a house was the same in Dublin as in London, the population of Dublin would have been about thirty-four thousand.
‡ John Dunton speaks of College Green near Dublin. I have seen letters of that age directed to the College, by Dublin. There are some interesting old maps of Dublin in the British Museum.
§ Clarendon to Rochester, Feb. 8, 1685-6, April 20, Aug. 12, Nov. 30, 1686

King was conducted in state through the southern part of the city. Every exertion had been made to give an air of festivity and splendor to the district which he was to traverse. The streets, which were generally deep in mud, were strewn with gravel. Boughs and flowers were scattered over the path. Tapestry and arras hung from the windows of those who could afford to exhibit such finery. The poor supplied the place of rich stuffs with blankets and coverlids. In one place was stationed a troop of friars with a cross; in another a company of forty girls dressed in white, and carrying nosegays. Pipers and harpers played "The King shall enjoy his own again." The Lord Deputy carried the sword of state before his master. The judges, the heralds, the Lord Mayor and aldermen, appeared in all the pomp of office. Soldiers were drawn up on the right and left to keep the passages clear. A procession of twenty coaches belonging to public functionaries was mustered. Before the Castle gate, the King was met by the host under a canopy borne by four bishops of his church. At the sight he fell on his knees, and passed some time in devotion. He then rose and was conducted to the chapel of his palace, once,—such are the vicissitudes of human things,—the riding-house of Henry Cromwell. A Te Deum was performed in honor of his Majesty's arrival. The next morning he held a Privy Council, discharged Chief Justice Keating from any further attendance at the Board, ordered Avaux and Bishop Cartwright to be sworn in, and issued a proclamation convoking a Parliament to meet at Dublin on the seventh of May.*

When the news that James had arrived in Ireland reached London, the sorrow and alarm were general, and were mingled with serious discontent. The multitude, not making sufficient allowance for the difficulties by which William was encompassed on every side, loudly blamed his neglect. To all the invectives of the ignorant and malicious he opposed, as was his wont, nothing but immutable gravity and the silence of profound disdain. But few minds had received from nature a temper so firm as his; and still fewer had undergone so long and so rigorous a discipline. The reproaches which had no power to shake his fortitude, tried from childhood upwards by both

---

* Life of James II., ii. 330. Full and true Account of the Landing and Reception, &c.; Ireland's Lamentation.

extremes of fortune, inflicted a deadly wound on a less resolute heart.

When all the coffee-houses were unanimously resolving that a fleet and army ought to have been long before sent to Dublin, and wondering how so renowned a politician as His Majesty could have been duped by Hamilton and Tyrconnel, a gentleman went down to the Temple Stairs, called a boat, and desired to be pulled to Greenwich. He took the cover of a letter from his pocket, scratched a few lines with a pencil, and laid the paper on the seat with some silver for his fare. As the boat passed under the dark central arch of London Bridge, he sprang into the water and disappeared. It was found that he had written these words: "My folly in undertaking what I could not execute hath done the King great prejudice which cannot be stopped—No easier way for me than this—May his undertaking prosper—May he have a blessing." There was no signature: but the body was soon found, and proved to be that of John Temple. He was young and highly accomplished: he was heir to an honorable name: he was united to an amiable woman: he was possessed of an ample fortune; and he had in prospect the greatest honors of the state. It does not appear that the public had been at all aware to what an extent he was answerable for the policy which had brought so much obloquy on the government. The King, stern as he was, had for too great a heart to treat an error as a crime. He had just appointed the unfortunate young man Secretary at War; and the commission was actually preparing. It is not improbable that the cold magnanimity of the master was the very thing which made the remorse of the servant insupportable.*

But great as were the vexations which William had to undergo, those by which the temper of his father-in-law was at this time tried were greater still. No court in Europe was distracted by more quarrels and intrigues than were to be found within the walls of Dublin Castle. The numerous petty cabals which sprang from the cupidity, the jealousy, and the malevolence of individuals scarcely deserved mention. But there was one cause of discord

---

* Clarendon's Diary; Reresby's Memoirs; Luttrell's Diary. I have followed Luttrell's version of Temple's last words. It agrees in substance with Clarendon's, but has more of the abruptness natural on such an occasion. If anything could make so tragical an event ridiculous, it would be the lamentation of the author of the Londeriad:

"The wretched youth against his friend exclaims,
And in despair drowns himself in the Thames."

which has been too little noticed, and which is the key to much that has been thought mysterious in the history of those times.

Between English Jacobitism and Irish Jacobitism there was nothing in common. The English Jacobite was animated by a strong enthusiasm for the family of Stuart; and in his zeal for the interests of that family he too often forgot the interests of the state. Victory, peace, prosperity, seemed evils to the stanch nonjuror of our island, if they tended to make usurpation popular and permanent. Defeat, bankruptcy, famine, invasion, were, in his view, public blessings, if they increased the chance of a restoration. He would rather have seen his country the last of the nations under James the Second or James the Third, than the mistress of the sea, the umpire between contending potentates, the seat of arts, the hive of industry, under a Prince of the House of Nassau or of Brunswick.

The sentiments of the Irish Jacobite were very different, and, it must in candor be acknowledged, were of a noble character. The fallen dynasty was nothing to him. He had not, like a Cheshire or Shropshire cavalier, been taught from his cradle to consider loyalty to that dynasty as the first duty of a Christian and a gentleman. All his family traditions, all the lessons taught him by his foster mother and by his priests, had been of a very different tendency. He had been brought up to regard the foreign sovereigns of his native land with the feeling with which the Jew regarded Cæsar, with which the Scot regarded Edward the First, with which the Castilian regarded Joseph Bonaparte, and with which the Pole regards the Autocrat of the Russias. It was the boast of the highborn Milesian that, from the twelfth century to the seventeenth, every generation of his family had been in arms against the English crown. His remote ancestors had contended with Fitzstephen and De Burgh. His great-grandfather had cloven down the soldiers of Elizabeth in the battle of the Blackwater. His grandfather had conspired with O'Donnel against James the First. His father had fought under Sir Phelim O'Neil against Charles the First. The confiscation of the family estate had been ratified by an Act of Charles the Second. No Puritan, who had been cited before the High Commission by Laud, who had charged by the side of Cromwell at Naseby, who had been prosecuted under the Conventicle Act, and who had been in hiding on account of the Rye House Plot, bore less affection to the House of Stuart than the O'Haras and Macmahons, on whose support the fortunes of that House now seemed to depend.

The fixed purpose of these men was to break the foreign yoke, to exterminate the Saxon colony, to sweep away the Protestant Church, and to restore the soil to its ancient proprietors. To obtain these ends they would without the smallest scruple have risen up against James; and to obtain these ends they rose up for him. The Irish Jacobites, therefore, were not at all desirous that he should again reign at Whitehall: for they were perfectly aware that a sovereign of Ireland, who was also sovereign of England, would not, and, even if he would, could not, long administer the government of the smaller and poorer kingdom in direct opposition to the feeling of the larger and richer. Their real wish was that the crowns might be completely separated, and that their island might, whether with James or without James they cared little, form a distinct state under the powerful protection of France.

While one party in the Council at Dublin regarded James merely as a tool to be employed for achieving the deliverance of Ireland, another party regarded Ireland merely as a tool to be employed for effecting the restoration of James. To the English and Scotch lords and gentlemen who had accompanied him from Brest, the island in which they now sojourned was merely a stepping-stone by which they were to reach Great Britain. They were still as much exiles as when they were at Saint Germains; and indeed they thought Saint Germains a far more pleasant place of exile than Dublin Castle. They had no sympathy with the native population of the remote and half barbarous region to which a strange chance had led them. Nay, they were bound by common extraction and by common language to that colony which it was the chief object of the native population to root out. They had indeed, like the great body of their countrymen, always regarded the aboriginal Irish with very unjust contempt, as inferior to other European nations, not only in acquired knowledge, but in natural intelligence and courage; as born Gibeonites, who had been liberally treated in being permitted to hew wood and to draw water for a wiser and mightier people. These politicians also thought,—and here they were undoubtedly in the right,—that, if their master's object was to recover the throne of England, it would be madness in him to give himself up to the guidance of the O's and the Macs who regarded England with mortal enmity. A law declaring the crown of Ireland independent, a law transferring mitres, glebes, and tithes from the Protestant to the Roman Catholic Church, a law transferring ten millions of acres from Saxons to Celts, would doubtless be loudly applauded in Clare and Tipperary. But what would be the effect of such laws at Westminster? What at Oxford? It would be poor policy to alienate such men as Clarendon and Beaufort, Ken and Sherlock, in order to obtain the applause of the Rapparees of the Bog of Allen.*

Thus the English and Irish factions in the Council at Dublin were engaged in a dispute which admitted of no compromise. Avaux meanwhile looked on that dispute from a point of view entirely his own. His object was neither the emancipation of Ireland nor the restoration of James, but the greatness of the French monarchy. In what way that object might be best attained was a very complicated problem. Undoubtedly a French statesman could not but wish for a counter-revolution in England. The effect of such a counter-revolution would be that the power which was the most formidable enemy of France would become her firmest ally, that William would sink into insignificance, and that the European coalition of which he was the chief would be dissolved. But what chance was there of such a counter-revolution? The English exiles indeed, after the fashion of exiles, confidently anticipated a speedy return to their country. James himself loudly boasted that his subjects on the other side of the water, though they had been misled for a moment by the specious names of religion, liberty, and property, were warmly attached to him, and would rally round him as soon as he appeared among them. But the wary envoy tried in vain to discover any foundation for these hopes. He could not find that they were warranted by any intelligence which had arrived from any part of Great Britain; and he was inclined to consider them as the mere daydreams of a feeble mind. He thought it unlikely that the usurper, whose ability and resolution he had, during an unintermitted conflict of ten years, learned to appreciate,

* Much light is thrown on the dispute between the English and Irish parties in James's council, by a remarkable letter of Bishop Maloney to Bishop Tyrrel, which will be found in the Appendix to King's State of the Protestants.

would easily part with the great prize which had been won by such strenuous exertions and profound combinations. It was therefore necessary to consider what arrangements would be most beneficial to France, on the supposition that it proved impossible to dislodge William from England. And it was evident that, if William could not be dislodged from England, the arrangement most beneficial to France would be that which had been contemplated eighteen months before when James had no prospect of a male heir. Ireland must be severed from the English crown, purged of the English colonists, reunited to the Church of Rome, placed under the protection of the House of Bourbon, and made, in everything but name, a French province. In war, her resources would be absolutely at the command of her Lord Paramount. She would furnish his army with recruits. She would furnish his navy with fine harbors commanding all the great western outlets of the English trade. The strong national and religious antipathy with which her aboriginal population regarded the inhabitants of the neighboring island would be a sufficient guarantee for their fidelity to that government which could alone protect her against the Saxon.

On the whole, therefore, it appeared to Avaux that, of the two parties into which the Council at Dublin was divided, the Irish party was that which it was at present for the interest of France to support. He accordingly connected himself closely with the chiefs of that party, obtained from them the fullest avowals of all that they designed, and was soon able to report to his government that neither the gentry nor the common people were at all unwilling to become French.*

The views of Louvois, incomparably the greatest statesman that France had produced since Richelieu, seem to have entirely agreed with those of Avaux. The best thing, Louvois wrote, that King James could do would be to forget that he had reigned in great Britain, and to think only of putting Ireland into a good condition, and of establishing himself firmly there. Whether this were the true interest of the House of Stuart may be doubted. But it was undoubtedly the true interest of the House of Bourbon.†

---

* Avaux, $\frac{\text{March 25,}}{\text{April 4.}}$ 1689, April 13-23. But it is less from any single letter, than from the whole tendency and spirit of the correspondence of Avaux, that I have formed my notion of his objects.

† "Il faut donc, oubliant qu'il a esté Roy d'Angleterre et d'Escosse, ne penser qu'à ce

About the Scotch and English exiles, and especially about Melfort, Avaux constantly expressed himself with an asperity hardly to have been expected from a man of so much sense and so much knowledge of the world. Melfort was in a singularly unfortunate position. He was a renegade: he was a mortal enemy of the liberties of his country: he was of a bad and tyrannical nature; and yet he was, in some sense, a patriot. The consequence was that he was more universally detested than any man of his time. For, while his apostasy and his arbitrary maxims of government made him the abhorrence of England and Scotland, his anxiety for the dignity and integrity of the empire made him the abhorrence of the Irish and of the French.

The first question to be decided was whether James should remain at Dublin, or should put himself at the head of his army in Ulster. On this question the Irish and British factions joined battle. Reasons of no great weight were adduced on both sides; for neither party ventured to speak out. The point really in issue was whether the King should be in Irish or in British hands. If he remained at Dublin, it would be scarcely possible for him to withhold his assent from any bill presented to him by the Parliament which he had summoned to meet there. He would be forced to plunder, perhaps to attaint, innocent Protestant gentlemen and clergymen by hundreds; and he would thus do irreparable mischief to his cause on the other side of Saint George's Channel. If he repaired to Ulster, he would be within a few hours' sail of Great Britain. As soon as Londonderry had fallen, and it was universally supposed that the fall of Londonderry could not be long delayed, he might cross the sea with part of his forces, and land in Scotland, where his friends were supposed to be numerous. When he was once on British ground, and in the midst of British adherents, it would no longer be in the power of the Irish to extort his consent to their schemes of spoliation and revenge.

The discussions in the Council were long and warm. Tyrconnel, who had just been created a Duke, advised his master to stay at Dublin. Melfort exhorted His Majesty to set out for Ulster. Avaux exerted all his influence in support of Tyrconnel; but James, whose personal inclinations

---

qui peut bonifier l'Irlande, et luy faciliter les moyens d'y subsister,"—Louvois to Avaux, June 3-13, 1689.

were naturally on the British side of the question, determined to follow the advice of Melfort.* Avaux was deeply mortified. In his official letters he expressed with great acrimony his contempt for the King's character and understanding. On Tyrconnel, who had said that he despaired of the fortunes of James, and that the real question was between the King of France and the Prince of Orange, the Ambassador pronounced what was meant to be a warm eulogy, but may perhaps be more properly called an invective. "If he were a born Frenchman, he could not be more zealous for the interests of France."† The conduct of Melfort, on the other hand, was the subject of an invective which much resembles eulogy: "He is neither a good Irishman nor a good Frenchman. All his affections are set on his own country."‡

Since the King was determined to go northward, Avaux did not choose to be left behind. The royal party set out, leaving Tyrconnel in charge at Dublin, and arrived at Charlemont on the thirteenth of April. The journey was a strange one. The country all along the road had been completely deserted by the industrious population, and laid waste by bands of robbers. "This," said one of the French officers, "is like travelling through the deserts of Arabia."§ Whatever effects the colonists had been able to remove were at Londonderry or Enniskillen. The rest had been stolen or destroyed. Avaux informed his court that he had not been able to get one truss of hay for his horses without sending five or six miles. No laborer dared bring anything for sale lest some marauder should lay hands on it by the way. The ambassador was put one night into a miserable tap-room full of soldiers smoking, another night into a dismantled house without windows or shutters to keep out the rain. At Charlemont, a bag of oatmeal was, with great difficulty, and as a matter of favor, procured for the French legation. There was no wheaten bread except at the table of the King, who had brought a little flour from Dublin, and to whom Avaux had lent a servant who knew how to bake. Those who were honored with an invitation to the royal table had their bread and wine measured out to them. Everybody else, however high in

---

* See the despatches written by Avaux during April 1689; Light to the Blind.
† Avaux, April 6-16, 1689. ‡ Avaux, May 8-18, 1689.
§ Pusignan to Avaux, $\frac{\text{March 30,}}{\text{April 9,}}$ 1689.

rank, ate horsecorn, and drank water or detestable beer, made with oats instead of barley, and flavored with some nameless herb as a substitute for hops.* Yet report said that the country between Charlemont and Strabane was even more desolate than the country between Dublin and Charlemont. It was impossible to carry a large stock of provisions. The roads were so bad, and the horses so weak, that the baggage wagons had all been left far behind. The chief officers of the army were consequently in want of necessaries; and the ill-humor which was the natural effect of these privations was increased by the insensibility of James, who seemed not to be aware that everybody about him was not perfectly comfortable.†

On the fourteenth of April the King and his train proceeded to Omagh. The rain fell: the wind blew: the horses could scarcely make their way through the mud, and in the face of the storm; and the road was frequently intersected by torrents which might almost be called rivers. The travellers had to pass several fords where the water was breast high. Some of the party fainted from fatigue and hunger. All around lay a frightful wilderness. In a journey of forty miles Avaux counted only three miserable cabins. Everything else was rock, bog, and moor. When at length the travellers reached Omagh, they found it in ruins. The Protestants, who were the majority of the inhabitants, had abandoned it, leaving not a wisp of straw nor a cask of liquor. The windows had been broken: the chimneys had been beaten in: the very locks and bolts of the doors had been carried away.‡

Avaux had never ceased to press the King to return to Dublin: but these expostulations had hitherto produced no effect. The obstinacy of James, however, was an obstinacy which had nothing in common with manly resolution, and which, though proof to argument, was easily shaken by caprice. He received at Omagh, early on the sixteenth of April, letters which alarmed him. He learned that a strong body of Protestants was in arms at Strabane, and that English ships of war had been seen near the mouth of Lough Foyle. In one minute three messages were sent to summon Avaux to the ruinous chamber in which the

* This lamentable account of the Irish beer is taken from a despatch which Desgrigny wrote from Cork to Louvois, and which is in the archives of the French War Office.
† Avaux, April 13-23, 1689; April 20-30.
‡ Avaux to Lewis, April 15-25, 1689, and to Louvois, of the same date.

royal bed had been prepared. There James, half dressed, and with the air of a man bewildered by some great shock, announced his resolution to hasten back instantly to Dublin. Avaux listened, wondered and approved. Melfort seemed prostrated by despair. The travellers retraced their steps, and, late in the evening got back to Charlemont. There the King received dispatches very different from those which had terrified him a few hours before. The Protestants who had assembled near Strabane had been attacked by Hamilton. Under a true-hearted leader they would doubtless have stood their ground. But Lundy, who commanded them, had told them that all was lost, had ordered them to shift for themselves, and had set them the example of flight.* They had accordingly retired in confusion to Londonderry, The King's correspondents pronounced it to be impossible that Londonderry should hold out. His Majesty had only to appear before the gates; and they would instantly fly open. James now changed his mind again, blamed himself for having been persuaded to turn his face southward, and, though it was late in the evening, called for his horses. The horses were in miserable plight; but, weary and half-starved as they were, they were saddled. Melfort, completely victorious, carried off his master to the camp. Avaux, after remonstrating to no purpose, declared that he was resolved to return to Dublin. It may be suspected that the extreme discomfort which he had undergone had something to do with this resolution. For complaints of that discomfort make up a large part of his letters; and, in truth, a life passed in the palaces of Italy, in the neat parlors and gardens of Holland, and in the luxurious pavilions which adorned the suburbs of Paris, was a bad preparation for the ruined hovels of Ulster. He gave, however, to his master a more weighty reason for refusing to proceed northward. The journey of James had been undertaken in opposition to the unanimous sense of the Irish, and had excited great alarm among them. They apprehended that he meant to quit them, and to make a descent on Scotland. They knew that once landed in Great Britain, he would have neither the will, nor the power to do those things which they most desired. Avaux, by refusing to proceed further, gave them an assurance that, whoever

---

* Commons' Journals, Aug. 12, 1689; Mackenzie's Narrative.

might betray them, France would be their constant friend.*
While Avaux was on his way to Dublin, James hastened towards Londonderry. He found his army concentrated a few miles south of the city. The French generals who had sailed with him from Brest were in his train; and two of them, Rosen and Maumont, were placed over the head of Richard Hamilton.† Rosen was a native of Livonia, who had in early youth become a soldier of fortune, who had fought his way to distinction, and who, though utterly destitute of the graces and accomplishments characteristic of the court of Versailles, was nevertheless high in favor there. His temper was savage: his manners were coarse; his language was a strange jargon compounded of various dialects of French and German. Even those who thought best of him, and who maintained that his rough exterior covered some good qualities, owned that his looks were against him, and that it would be unpleasant to meet such a figure in the dusk at the corner of a wood.‡ The little that is known of Maumont is to his honor.

In the camp it was generally expected that Londonderry would fall without a blow. Rosen confidently predicted that the mere sight of the Irish army would terrify the garrison into submission. But Richard Hamilton, who knew the temper of the colonists better, had misgivings. The assailants were sure of one important ally within the walls. Lundy, the Governor, professed the Protestant religion and had joined in proclaiming William and Mary; but he was in secret communication with the enemies of his Church and of the Sovereigns to whom he had sworn fealty. Some have suspected that he was a concealed Jacobite, and that he had affected to acquiesce in the Revolution only in order that he might be better able to assist in bringing about a Restoration, but it is probable that his conduct is rather to be attributed to faintheartedness and poverty of spirit than to zeal for any public cause. He seems to have thought resistance hopeless; and in truth, to a military eye, the defences of Londonderry appeared contemptible. The fortifications consisted of a simple wall overgrown with grass and weeds:

---

* Avaux, April 17-27, 1689. The story of these strange changes of purpose is told very disingenuously by James in his Life, ii. 330, 331, 332. Orig. Mem.
† Life of James, ii. 334, 335. Orig. Mem.
‡ Memoirs of Saint Simon. Some English writers ignorantly speak of Rosen as having been, at this time, a Marshal of France. He did not become so till 1703. He had long been a Maréchal de Camp, which is a very different thing, and had been recently promoted to the rank of Lieutenant-General,

there was no ditch even before the gates: the draw-bridges had long been neglected: the chains were rusty and could scarcely be used: the parapets and towers were built after a fashion that might well move disciples of Vauban to laughter; and these feeble defences were on almost every side commanded by heights. Indeed those who laid out the city had never meant that it should be able to stand a regular siege, and had contented themselves with throwing up works sufficient to protect the inhabitants against a tumultuary attack of the Celtic peasantry. Avaux assured Louvois that a single French battalion would easily storm such a fastness. Even if the place should, notwithstanding all disadvantages, be able to repel a large army directed by the science and experience of generals who had served under Conde and Turenne, hunger must soon bring the contest to an end. The stock of provisions was small; and the population had been swollen to seven or eight times the ordinary number by a multitude of colonists flying from the rage of the natives.*

Lundy, therefore, from the time when the Irish army entered Ulster, seems to have given up all thought of serious resistance. He talked so despondingly that the citizens and his own soldiers murmured against him. He seemed, they said, to be bent on discouraging them. Meanwhile the enemy drew daily nearer and nearer; and it was known that James himself was coming to take the command of his forces.

Just at this moment a glimpse of hope appeared. On the fourteenth of April ships from England anchored in the bay. They had on board two regiments which had been sent, under the command of a colonel named Cunningham, to reinforce the garrison. Cunningham and several of his officers went on shore and conferred with Lundy. Lundy dissuaded them from landing their men. The place, he said, could not hold out. To throw more troops into it would therefore be worse than useless: for the more numerous the garrison, the more prisoners would fall into the hands of the enemy. The best thing that the two regiments could do would be to sail back to England. He meant, he said, to withdraw himself privately; and the inhabitants must then try to make good terms for themselves.

---

* Avaux, April 4-14, 1689. Among the MSS. in the British Museum is a curious report on the defences of Londonderry, drawn up in 1705 for the Duke of Ormond by a French engineer named Thomas.

He went through the form of holding a council of war, but from this council he excluded all those officers of the garrison whose sentiments he knew to be different from his own. Some who had ordinarily been summoned on such occasions, and who now came uninvited, were thrust out of the room. Whatever the Governor said was echoed by his creatures. Cunningham and Cunningham's companions could scarcely venture to oppose their opinion to that of a person whose local knowledge was necessarily far superior to theirs, and whom they were by their instructions directed to obey. One brave soldier murmured, "Understand this," he said: "to give up Londonderry is to give up Ireland." But his objections were contemptuously overruled.* The meeting broke up. Cunningham and his officers returned to the ships, and made preparations for departing. Meanwhile Lundy privately sent a messenger to the headquarters of the enemy, with assurances that the city should be peaceably surrendered on the first summons.

But as soon as what had passed in the council of war was whispered about the streets, the spirit of the soldiers and citizens swelled up high and fierce against the dastardly and perfidious chief who had betrayed them. Many of his own officers declared that they no longer thought themselves bound to obey him. Voices were heard threatening, some that his brains should be blown out, some that he should be hanged on the walls. A deputation was sent to Cunningham imploring him to assume the command. He excused himself on the plausible ground that his orders were to take directions in all things from the Governor.† Meanwhile it was rumored that the persons most in Lundy's confidence were stealing out of the town one by one. Long after dusk on the evening of the seventeenth it was found that the gates were open and that the keys had disappeared. The officers who made the discovery took on themselves to change the passwords and to double the guards. The night, however, passed over without any assault.‡

After some anxious hours the day broke. The Irish, with James at their head, were now within four miles of the city. A tumultuous council of the chief inhabitants

---
* Commons' Journals, August 12, 1689.
† The best history of these transactions will be found in the Journals of the House of Commons, August 12, 1689. See also the narratives of Walker and Mackenzie.
‡ Mackenzie's Narrative.

was called. Some of them vehemently reproached the Governor to his face with his treachery. He had sold them, they cried, to their deadliest enemy: he had refused admission to the force which good King William had sent to defend them. While the altercation was at the height, the sentinels who paced the ramparts announced that the vanguard of the hostile army was in sight. Lundy had given orders that there should be no firing: but his authority was at an end. Two gallant soldiers, Major Henry Baker and Captain Adam Murray, called the people to arms. They were assisted by the eloquence of an aged clergyman, George Walker, rector of the parish of Donaghmore, who had, with many of his neighbors, taken refuge in Londonderry. The whole crowded city was moved by one impulse. Soldiers, gentlemen, yeomen, artisans, rushed to the walls and manned the guns. James, who, confident of success, had approached within a hundred yards of the southern gate, was received with a shout of "No surrender," and with a fire from the nearest bastion. An officer of his staff fell dead by his side. The King and his attendants made all haste to get out of reach of the cannon balls. Lundy, who was now in imminent danger of being torn limb from limb by those whom he had betrayed, hid himself in an inner chamber. There he lay during the day, and, with the generous and politic connivance of Murray and Walker, made his escape at night in the disguise of a porter.* The part of the wall from which he let himself down is still pointed out; and people still living talk of having tasted the fruit of a pear tree which assisted him in his descent. His name is, to this day, held in execration by the Protestants of the North of Ireland; and his effigy is still annually hung and burned by them with marks of abhorrence similar to those which in England are appropriated to Guy Faux.

And now Londonderry was left destitute of all military and of all civil government. No man in the town had a right to command any other: the defences were weak: the provisions were scanty: an incensed tyrant and a great army were at the gates. But within was that which has often, in desperate extremities, retrieved the fallen fortunes of nations. Betrayed, deserted, disorganized, unprovided with resources, begirt with enemies, the noble city was still no easy conquest. Whatever an engineer might think

---
* Walker and Mackenzie.

of the strength of the ramparts, all that was most intelligent, most courageous, most high-spirited among the Englishry of Leinster and of Northern Ulster was crowded behind them. The number of men capable of bearing arms within the walls was seven thousand; and the whole world could not have furnished seven thousand men better qualified to meet a terrible emergency with clear judgment, dauntless valor, and stubborn patience. They were all zealous Protestants; and the Protestantism of the majority was tinged with Puritanism. They had much in common with that sober, resolute, and God-fearing class out of which Cromwell had formed his unconquerable army. But the peculiar situation in which they had been placed had developed in them some qualities which, in the mother country, might possibly have remained latent. The English inhabitants of Ireland were an aristocratic caste, which had been enabled, by superior civilization, by close union, by sleepless vigilance, by cool intrepidity, to keep in subjection a numerous and hostile population. Almost every one of them had been in some measure trained both to military and to political functions. Almost every one was familiar with the use of arms, and was accustomed to bear a part in the administration of justice. It was remarked by contemporary writers that the colonists had something of the Castilian haughtness of manner, though none of the Castilian indolence, that they spoke English with remarkable purity and correctness, and that they were, both as militiamen and as jurymen, superior to their kindred in the mother country.* In all ages, men situated as the Anglo-Saxons in Ireland were situated have had peculiar vices and peculiar virtues, the vices and virtues of masters, as opposed to the vices and virtues of slaves. The member of a dominant race is, in his dealings with the subject race, seldom indeed fraudulent,—for fraud is the resource of the weak,—but imperious, insolent, and cruel. Towards his brethren, on the other hand, his conduct is generally just, kind, and even noble. His self-respect leads him to respect all who belong to his own order. His interest impels him to cultivate a good understanding with those whose prompt, strenuous, and courageous assistance may at any moment be necessary to preserve his property

---

* See the Character of the Protestants of Ireland, 1689, and the Interests of England in the Preservation of Ireland, 1689. The former pamphlet is the work of an enemy, the latter of a zealous friend.

and life. It is a truth ever present to his mind that his own well-being depends on the ascendency of the class to which he belongs. His very selfishness therefore is sublimed into public spirit; and this public spirit is stimulated to fierce enthusiasm by sympathy, by the desire of applause, and by the dread of infamy. For the only opinion which he values is the opinion of his fellows; and in their opinion devotion to the common cause is the most sacred of duties. The character, thus formed, has two aspects. Seen on one side, it must be regarded by every well constituted mind with disapprobation. Seen on the other, it irresistibly extorts applause. The Spartan, smiting and spurning the wretched Helot, moves our disgust. But the same Spartan, calmly dressing his hair, and uttering his concise jests, on what he well knows to be his last day, in the pass of Thermopylæ, is not to be contemplated without admiration. To a superficial observer it may seem strange that so much evil and so much good should he found together. But in truth the good and the evil, which at first sight appear almost incompatible, are closely connected, and have a common origin. It was because the Spartan had been taught to revere himself as one of a race of sovereigns, and to look down on all that was not Spartan as of an inferior species, that he had no fellow feeling for the miserable serfs who crouched before him, and that the thought of submitting to a foreign master, or of turning his back before an enemy, never, even in the last extremity, crossed his mind. Something of the same character, compounded of tyrant and hero, has been found in all nations which have domineered over more numerous nations. But it has nowhere in modern Europe shown itself so conspicuously as in Ireland. With what contempt, with what antipathy, the ruling minority in that country long regarded the subject majority may be best learned from the hateful laws which, within the memory of men still living, disgraced the Irish statute book. Those laws were at length annulled: but the spirit which had dictated them survived them, and even at this day sometimes breaks out in excesses pernicious to the commonwealth and dishonorable to the Protestant religion. Nevertheless it is impossible to deny that the English colonists have had, with too many of the faults, all the noblest virtues of a sovereign caste. The faults have, as was natural, been most offensively exhibited in times of prosperity and security: the virtues have been most resplendent in times of distress and peril; and never were those virtues more signally displayed than by the defenders of Londonderry, when their governor had abandoned them, and when the camp of their mortal enemy was pitched before their walls.

No sooner had the first burst of the rage excited by the perfidy of Lundy spent itself than those whom he had betrayed proceeded, with a gravity and prudence worthy of the most renowned senate, to provide for the order and defence of the city. Two governors were elected, Baker and Walker. Baker took the chief military command. Walker's especial business was to preserve internal tranquillity, and to dole out supplies from the magazines.* The inhabitants capable of bearing arms were distributed into eight regiments. Colonels, captains, and subordinate officers were appointed. In a few hours every man knew his post, and was ready to repair to it as soon as the beat of the drum was heard. That machinery, by which Oliver had, in the preceding generation, kept up among his soldiers so stern and so pertinacious an enthusiasm, was again employed with not less complete success. Preaching and praying occupied a large part of every day. Eighteen clergymen of the Established Church and seven or eight non-conformist ministers were within the walls. They all exerted themselves indefatigably to rouse and sustain the spirit of the people. Among themselves there was for the time entire harmony. All disputes about church government, postures, ceremonies were forgotten. The Bishop, having found that his lectures on passive obedience were derided even by the Episcopalians, had withdrawn himself first to Raphoe, and then to England, and was preaching in a chapel in London.† On the other hand, a Scotch fanatic named Hewson, who had exhorted the Presbyterians not to ally themselves with such as refused to subscribe the Covenant, had sunk under the well-merited disgust and scorn of the whole Protestant community.‡ The aspect of the Cathedral was remarkable. Cannon were

---
* There was afterwards some idle dispute about the question whether Walker was properly governor or not. To me it seems quite clear that he was so.
† Mackenzie's Narrative; Funeral sermon on Bishop Hopkins, 1690.
‡ Walker's True Account, 1689. See also the Apology for the True Account, and the Vindication of the True Account, published in the same year. I have called this man by the name by which he was known in Ireland. But his real name was Houstoun. He is frequently mentioned in the strange volume entitled Faithful Contendings Displayed.

planted on the summit of the broad tower which has since given place to a tower of different proportions. Ammunition was stored in the vaults. In the choir the liturgy of the Anglican Church was read every morning. Every afternoon the Dissenters crowded to a simpler worship.*

James had waited twenty-four hours, expecting, as it should seem, performance of Lundy's promises; and in twenty-four hours the arrangements for the defence of Londonderry were complete. On the evening of the nineteenth of April, a trumpeter came to the southern gate, and asked whether the engagements into which the governor had entered would be fulfilled. The answer was that the men who guarded these walls had nothing to do with the governor's engagements, and were determined to resist to the last.

On the following day a messenger of the higher rank was sent, Claude Hamilton, Lord Strabane, one of the few Roman Catholic peers of Ireland. Murray, who had been appointed to the command of one of the eight regiments into which the garrison was distributed, advanced from the gate to meet the flag of truce; and a short conference was held. Strabane had been authorized to make large promises. The citizens should have a free pardon for all that was past if they would submit to their sovereign. Murray himself should have a colonel's commission, and a thousand pounds in money. "The men of Londonderry," answered Murray, "have done nothing that requires a pardon, and own no Sovereign but King William and Queen Mary. It will not be safe for your lordship to stay longer, or to return on the same errand. Let me have the honor of seeing you through the lines."†

James had been assured, and had fully expected that the city would yield as soon as it was known that he was before the walls. Finding himself mistaken, he broke loose from the control of Melfort, and determined to return instantly to Dublin. Rosen accompanied the King. The direction of the siege was entrusted to Maumont. Richard Hamilton was second and Pusignan third, in command.

The operations now commenced in earnest. The besiegers began by battering the town. It was soon on fire in several places. Roofs and upper stories of houses, fell in, and crushed the inmates. During a short time the gar-

---
* A view of the Danger and Folly of being public-spirited, by William Hamill, 1721.
† See Walker's True Account and Mackenzie's Narrative.

rison, many of whom had never before seen the effect of a cannonade, seemed to be discomposed by the crash of chimneys, and by the heaps of ruin mingled with disfigured corpses. But familiarity with danger and horror produced in a few hours the natural effect. The spirit of the people rose so high that their chiefs thought it safe to act on the offensive. On the twenty-first of April a sally was made under the command of Murray. The Irish stood their ground resolutely; and a furious and bloody contest took place. Maumont, at the head of a body of cavalry, flew to the place where the fight was raging. He was struck in the head by a musket ball, and fell a corpse. The besiegers lost several other officers, and about two hundred men, before the colonists could be driven in. Murray escaped with difficulty. His horse was killed under him; and he was beset by enemies: but he was able to defend himself till some of his friends made a rush from the gate to his rescue, with old Walker at their head.*

In consequence of the death of Maumont, Richard Hamilton was once more commander of the Irish army. His exploits in that post did not raise his reputation. He was a fine gentleman and a brave soldier; but he had no pretensions to the character of a great general, and had never, in his life, seen a siege.† Pusignan had more science and energy. But Pusignan survived Maumont little more than a fortnight. At four in the morning of the sixth of May, the garrison made another sally, took several flags, and killed many of the besiegers. Pusignan, fighting gallantly, was shot through the body. The wound was one which a skillful surgeon might have cured: but there was no such surgeon in the Irish camp, and the communication with Dublin was slow and irregular. The poor Frenchman died, complaining bitterly of the barbarous ignorance and negligence which had shortened his days. A medical man, who had been sent down express from the capital, arrived

---

* Walker; Mackenzie; Avaux, $\frac{\text{April 26,}}{\text{May 6,}}$ 1689. There is a tradition among the Protestants of Ulster that Maumont fell by the sword of Murray; but on this point the report made by the French ambassador to his master is decisive. The truth is that there are almost as many mythical stories about the siege of Londonderry, as about the siege of Troy. The legend about Murray and Maumont dates from 1689. In the Royal Voyage, which was acted in that year, the combat between the heroes is described in these sonorous lines:

"They met; and Monsieur at the first encounter
Fell dead, blaspheming, on the dusty plain,
And dying, bit the ground."

† "Si c'est celuy qui est sorti de France le dernier, qui s'appelloit Richard, il n'a jamais reu de siège, ayant tousjours servi en Rousillon."—Louvois to Avaux, June 3-13, 1689.

after the funeral. James, in consequence, as it should seem, of this disaster, established a daily post between Dublin Castle and Hamilton's headquarters. Even by this conveyance letters did not travel very expeditiously: for the couriers went on foot, and, from fear probably of the Enniskilleners, took a circuitous route from military post to military post.*

May passed away: June arrived; and still Londonderry held out. There had been many sallies and skirmishes with various success: but, on the whole, the advantage had been with the garrison. Several officers of note had been carried prisoners into the city; and two French banners, torn after hard fighting from the besiegers, had been hung as trophies in the chancel of the cathedral. It seemed that the siege must be turned into a blockade. But before the hope of reducing the town by main force was relinquished, it was determined to make a great effort. The point selected for assault was an outwork called Windmill Hill, which was not far from the southern gate. Religious stimulants were employed to animate the courage of the forlorn hope. Many volunteers bound themselves by oath to make their way into the works or to perish in the attempt. Captain Butler, son of the Lord Mountgarret, undertook to lead the sworn men to the attack. On the walls the colonists were drawn up in three ranks. The office of those who were behind was to load the muskets of those who were in front. The Irish came on boldly and with a fearful uproar, but after long and hard fighting were driven back. The women of Londonderry were seen amidst the thickest fire serving out water and ammunition to their husbands and brothers. In one place, where the wall was only seven feet high, Butler and some of his sworn men succeeded in reaching the top; but they were all killed or made prisoners. At length, after four hundred of the Irish had fallen, their chiefs ordered a retreat to be sounded.†

Nothing was left but to try the effect of hunger. It was known that the stock of food in the city was but slender.

---

* Walker; Mackenzie; Avaux to Louvois, May 2-12, 4-14, 1689; James to Hamilton, May 28/June 8, in the library of the Royal Irish Academy, Louvois wrote to Avaux in great indignation. "La mauvaise conduite que l'on a tenue devant Londondery a cousté la vie à M. de Maumont et à M. de Pusignan. Il ne faut pas que sa Majesté Britannique croye qu'en faisant tuer des officiers generaux comme des soldats, on puisse ne l'en point laisser manquer. Ces sortes de gens sont rares en tout pays, et doivent estre menagez."

† Walker; Mackenzie; Avaux, June 16-26, 1689.

Indeed it was thought strange that the supplies should have held out so long. Every precaution was now taken against the introduction of provisions. All the avenues leading to the city by land were closely guarded. On the south were encamped, along the left bank of the Foyle, the horsemen who had followed Lord Galmoy from the valley of the Barrow. Their chief was, of all the Irish captains, the most dreaded and the most abhorred by the Protestants. For he had disciplined his men with rare skill and care; and many frightful stories were told of his barbarity and perfidy. Long lines of tents, occupied by the infantry of Butler and O'Neil, of Lord Slane and Lord Gormanstown, by Nugent's Westmeath men, by Eustace's Kildare men, and by Cavanagh's Kerry men, extended northward till they again approached the water side.* The river was fringed with forts and batteries, which no vessel could pass without great peril. After some time it was determined to make the security still more complete by throwing a barricade across the stream, about a mile and a half below the city. Several boats full of stones were sunk. A row of stakes was driven into the bottom of the river. Large pieces of fir-wood, strongly bound together, formed a boom which was more than a quarter of a mile in length and which was firmly fastened to both shores by cables a foot thick.† A huge stone, to which the cable on the left bank was attached, was removed many years later, for the purpose of being polished and shaped into a column. But the intention was abandoned, and the rugged mass still lies, not many yards from its original site, amidst the shades which surround a pleasant country house named Boom Hall. Hard by is a well from which the besiegers drank. A little further off is a burial ground where they laid their slain, and where even in our own time the spade of the gardener has struck upon many skulls and thighbones at a short distance beneath the turf and flowers.

While these things were passing in the North, James was holding his court at Dublin. On his return thither from Londonderry he received intelligence that the French

---

* As to the discipline of Galmoy's Horse, see the letter of Avaux to Louvois, dated September 10-20. Horrible stories of the cruelty, both of the colonel and of his men, are told in the Short View, by a Clergyman, printed in 1689, and in several other pamphlets of that year. For the distribution of the Irish forces, see the contemporary maps of the siege. A catalogue of the regiments meant, I suppose, to rival the Catalogue in the Second Book of the Iliad, will be found in the Londeriad.

† Life of Admiral Sir John Leake, by Stephen M. Leake, Clarencieux King at Arms, 1750. Of this book only fifty copies were printed.

fleet, commanded by the Count of Chateau Renaud, had anchored in Bantry Bay, and had put on shore a large quantity of military stores and a supply of money. Herbert, who had just been sent to those seas with an English squadron for the purpose of intercepting the communications between Britanny and Ireland, learned where the enemy lay, and sailed into the bay with the intention of giving battle. But the wind was unfavorable to him: his force was greatly inferior to that which was opposed to him; and, after some firing, which caused no serious loss to either side, he thought it prudent to stand out to sea, while the French retired into the recesses of the harbor. He steered for Scilly, where he expected to find reinforcements; and Chateau Renaud, content with the credit which he had acquired, and afraid of losing it if he stayed, hastened back to Brest, though earnestly entreated by James to come around to Dublin.

Both sides claimed the victory. The Commons at Westminster absurdly passed a vote of thanks to Herbert. James, not less absurdly, ordered bonfires to be lighted and a Te Deum to be sung. But these marks of joy by no means satisfied Avaux, whose national vanity was too strong even for his characteristic prudence and politeness.

He complained that James was so unjust and ungrateful as to attribute the result of the late action to the reluctance with which the English seamen fought against their rightful King and their old commander, and that His Majesty did not seem to be well pleased by being told that they were flying over the ocean pursued by the triumphant French. Dover, too, was a bad Frenchman. He seemed to take no pleasure in the defeat of his countrymen, and had been heard to say that the affair in Bantry Bay did not deserve to be called a battle.*

On the day after the Te Deum had been sung at Dublin for this indecisive skirmish, the Parliament convoked by James assembled. The number of temporal peers of Ireland, when he arrived in that kingdom, was about a hundred. Of these only fourteen obeyed his summons. Of the fourteen, ten were Roman Catholics. By the reversing of old attainders, and by new creations, seventeen

---

* Avaux, May 8-18, $\frac{\text{May } 26,}{\text{June } 5,}$ 1689; London Gazette, May 9, Life of James, ii. 370; Burchett's Naval Transactions; Commons' Journals, May 18, 21. From the Memoirs of Madame de la Fayette it appears that the paltry affair was correctly appreciated at Versailles.

more Lords, all Roman Catholics, were introduced into the Upper House. The Protestant Bishops of Meath, Ossory, Cork, and Limerick, whether from a sincere conviction that they could not lawfully withhold their obedience even from a tyrant, or from a vain hope that the heart even of a tyrant might be softened by their patience, made their appearance in the midst of their mortal enemies.

The House of Commons consisted almost exclusively of Irishmen and Papists. With the writs the returning officers had received from Tyrconnel letters naming the persons whom he wished to see elected. The largest constituent bodies in the kingdom were at this time very small. For scarcely any but Roman Catholics dared to show their faces, and the Roman Catholic freeholders were then very few, not more, it is said, in some counties, than ten or twelve. Even in cities so considerable as Cork, Limerick, and Galway, the number of persons who, under the new charters, were entitled to vote, did not exceed twenty-four. About two hundred and fifty members took their seats. Of these only six were Protestants.* The list of the names sufficiently indicates the religious and political temper of the assembly. Alone among the Irish parliaments of that age, this parliament was filled with Dermots and Geohegans, O'Neils and O'Donovans, Macmahons, Macnamaras, and Macgillicuddies. The lead was taken by a few men whose abilities had been improved by the study of the law, or by experience acquired in foreign countries. The Attorney General, Sir Richard Nagle, who represented the county of Cork, was allowed, even by Protestants, to be an acute and learned jurist. Francis Plowden, the Commissioner of Revenue who sate for Bannow, and acted as chief minister of finance, was an Englishman, and, as he had been a principal agent of the Order of Jesuits in money matters, must be supposed to have been an excellent man of business.† Colonel Henry Luttrell, member for the county of Carlow, had served long in France, and had brought back to his native Ireland a sharpened intellect and polished manners, a flattering tongue, some skill in war, and much more skill in intrigue. His elder brother, Colonel Simon Luttrell, who was member for the county

---
* King, iii. 12; Memoirs of Ireland from the Restoration, 1716. Lists of both Houses will be found in King's Appendix.

† I found proof of Plowden's connection with the Jesuits in a Treasury Letter-book, June 12, 1689.

of Dublin, and military governor of the capital, had also
resided in France, and, though inferior to Henry in parts
and activity, made a highly distinguished figure among the
adherents of James. The other member for the county of
Dublin was Colonel Patrick Sarsfield. This gallant officer
was regarded by the natives as one of themselves: for his
ancestors on the paternal side, though originally English,
were among those early colonists who were proverbially
said to have become more Irish than Irishmen. His mother
was of noble Celtic blood; and he was firmly attached to
the old religion. He had inherited an estate of about two
thousand a year, and was therefore one of the wealthiest
Roman Catholics in the kingdom. His knowledge of
courts and camps was such as few of his countrymen possessed. He had long borne a commission in the English
Life Guards, had lived much about Whitehall, and had
fought bravely under Monmouth on the Continent, and
against Monmouth at Sedgemoor. He had, Avaux wrote,
more personal influence than any man in Ireland, and was
indeed a gentlemen of eminent merit, brave, upright, honorable, careful of his men in quarters, and certain to be
always found at their head in the day of battle. His intrepidity, his frankness, his boundless good nature, his
stature, which far exceeded that of ordinary men, and the
strength which he exerted in personal conflict, gained for
him the affectionate admiration of the populace. It is remarkable that the Englishry generally respected him as a
valiant, skillful, and generous enemy, and that, even in
the most ribald farces which were performed by mounte-
banks in Smithfield, he was always excepted from the disgraceful imputations which it was then the fashion to
throw on the Irish nation.*

But men like these were rare in the House of Commons
which had met at Dublin. It is no reproach to the Irish
nation, a nation which has since furnished its full proportion of eloquent and accomplished senators, to say that, of
all the parliaments which have met in the British islands,
Barebone's parliament not excepted, the assembly convoked

---

* "Sarsfield," Avaux wrote to Louvois, Oct. 11-21, 1689, "n'est pas un homme de la naissance de mylord Galloway" (Galmoy, I suppose) "ny de Makarty: mais c'est un gentilhomme distingué par son mérite, qui a plus de crédit dans ce royaume qu'aucun homme que je connoisse. Il a de la valeur, mais surtout de l'honneur et de la probité à toute épreuve . . . homme qui sera toujours à la tête de ses troupes, et qui en aura grand soin." Leslie, in his Answer to King, says that the Irish Protestants did justice to Sarsfield's integrity and honour. Indeed, justice is done to Sarsfield even in such scurrilous pieces as the Royal Flight.

by James was the most deficient in all the qualities which a legislature should possess. The stern domination of a hostile class had blighted the faculties of the Irish gentleman. If he was so fortunate as to have lands, he had generally passed his life on them, shooting, fishing, carousing and making love among his vassals. If his estate had been confiscated, he had wandered about from bawn to bawn and from cabin to cabin, levying small contributions, and living at the expense of other men. He had never sate in the House of Commons: he had never even taken an active part at an election: he had never been a magistrate: scarcely ever had he been on a grand jury. He had therefore absolutely no experience of public affairs. The English squire of that age, though assuredly not a very profound or enlightened politician, was a statesman and a philosopher when compared with the Roman Catholic squire of Munster or Connaught.

The parliaments of Ireland had then no fixed place of assembling. Indeed they met so seldom and broke up so speedily that it would hardly have been worth while to build and furnish a palace for their special use. It was not till the Hanoverian dynasty had been long on the throne, that a senate house which sustains a comparison with the finest compositions of Inigo Jones arose between the College and the Castle. In the seventeenth century there stood, on the spot where the portico and dome of the Four Courts now overlook the Liffey, an ancient building which had once been a convent of Dominican friars, but had, since the Reformation, been appropriated to the use of the legal profession, and bore the name of the King's Inns. There accommodation had been provided for the parliament. On the seventh of May, James, dressed in royal robes and wearing a crown, took his seat on the throne in the House of Lords, and ordered the Commons to be summoned to the bar.*

He then expressed his gratitude to the natives of Ireland for having adhered to his cause when the people of his other kingdoms had deserted him. His resolution to abolish all religious disabilities in all his dominions he declared to be unalterable. He invited the Houses to take the Act of Settlement into consideration, and to redress the

---

* Journal of the Parliament in Ireland, 1689. The reader must not imagine that this Journal has an official character. It is merely a compilation made by a Protestant pamphleteer, and printed in London.

injuries of which the old proprietors of the soil had reason to complain. He concluded by acknowledging in warm terms his obligations to the King of France.*

When the royal speech had been pronounced, the Chancellor directed the Commons to repair to their chamber and to elect a Speaker. They chose the Attorney General Nagle; and the choice was approved by the King.†

The Commons next passed resolutions expressing warm gratitude both to James and to Lewis. Indeed it was proposed to send a deputation with an address to Avaux; but the Speaker pointed out the gross impropriety of such a step; and, on this occasion, his interference was successful.‡ It was seldom however that the House was disposed to listen to reason. The debates were all rant and tumult. Judge Daly, a Roman Catholic, but an honest and able man, could not refrain from lamenting the indecency and folly with which the members of his Church carried on the work of legislation. Those gentlemen, he said, were not a parliament: they were a mere rabble: they resembled nothing so much as the mob of fishermen and market gardeners, who, at Naples, yelled and threw up their caps in honor of Massaniello. It was painful to hear member after member talking wild nonsense about his own losses, and clamoring for an estate, when the lives of all and the independence of their common country were in peril. These words were spoken in private; but some tale-bearer repeated them to the Commons. A violent storm broke forth. Daly was ordered to attend at the bar; and there was little doubt that he would be severely dealt with. But, just when he was at the door, one of the members rushed in shouting, "Good news: Londonderry is taken." The whole House rose. All the hats were flung into the air. Three loud huzzas were raised. Every heart was softened by the happy tidings. Nobody would hear of punishment at such a moment. The order for Daly's attendance was discharged amidst cries of "No submission: no submission: we pardom him." In a few hours it was known that Londonderry held out as obstinately as ever. This transaction, in itself unimportant, deserves to be recorded, as showing how destitute that House of Commons was of the qualities which ought to be found in the great council of a king-

---

* Life of James, ii. 355. † Journal of the Parliament in Ireland.
‡ Avaux, $\frac{\text{May 26,}}{\text{June 5,}}$ 1689.

dom. And this assembly, without experience, without gravity, and without temper, was now to legislate on questions which would have tasked to the utmost the capacity of the greatest statesmen.*

One Act James induced them to pass which would have been most honorable to him and to them, if there were not abundant proofs that it was meant to be a dead letter. It was an Act purporting to grant entire liberty of conscience to all Christian sects. On this occasion a proclamation was put forth announcing in boastful language to the English people that their rightful King had now signally refuted those slanderers who had accused him of affecting zeal for religious liberty merely in order to serve a turn. If he were at heart inclined to persecution, would he not have persecuted the Irish Protestants? He did not want power. He did not want provocation. Yet at Dublin, where the members of his Church were the majority, as at Westminster, where they were a minority, he had firmly adhered to the principles laid down in his much maligned Declaration of Indulgence.† Unfortunately for him, the same wind which carried his fair professions to England carried thither also evidence that his professions were insincere. A single law, worthy of Turgot or of Franklin, seemed ludicrously out of place in the midst of a crowd of laws which would have disgraced Gardiner or Alva.

A necessary preliminary to the vast work of spoliation and slaughter on which the legislators of Dublin were bent, was an Act annulling the authority which the English Parliament, both as the supreme legislature and as th supreme Court of Appeal, had hitherto exercised over Ireland.‡ This Act was rapidly passed; and then followed, in quick succession, confiscations and proscriptions on a gigantic scale. The personal estates of absentees above the age of seventeen years were transferred to the King. When lay property was thus invaded, it was not likely that the endowments, which had been, in contravention of every sound principle, lavished on the Church of the minority, would be spared. To reduce those endowments,

---

* A True Account of the Present State of Ireland, by a Person that with Great Difficulty left Dublin, 1689; Letter from Dublin, dated June 12, 1689; Journal of the Parliament in Ireland.

† Life of James, ii. 361, 362, 363. In the Life it is said that the proclamation was put forth without the privity of James, but that he subsequently approved of it. See Welwood's Answer to the Declaration. 1689.

‡ Light to the Blind; An Act declaring that the Parliament of England cannot bind Ireland against Writs of Error and Appeals, printed in London, 1690.

without prejudice to existing interests, would have been a reform worthy of a good prince and of a good parliament. But no such reform would satisfy the vindictive bigots who sate at the King's Inns. By one sweeping Act the greater part of the tithe was transferred from the Protestant to the Roman Catholic clergy; and the existing incumbents were left, without one farthing of compensation, to die of hunger.* A Bill repealing the Act of Settlement and transferring many thousands of square miles from Saxon to Celtic landlords was brought in and carried by acclamation.†

Of legislation such as this it is impossible to speak too severely: but for the legislators there are excuses which it is the duty of the historian to notice. They acted unmercifully, unjustly, unwisely. But it would be absurd to expect mercy, justice, or wisdom from a class of men first abased by many years of oppression, and then maddened by the joy of a sudden deliverance, and armed with irresistible power. The representatives of the Irish nation were, with few exceptions, rude and ignorant. They had lived in a state of constant irritation. With aristocratical sentiments they had been in a servile position. With the highest pride of blood, they had been exposed to daily affronts, such as might well have roused the choler of the humblest plebeian. In sight of the fields and castles which they regarded as their own, they had been glad to be invited by a peasant to partake of his whey and his potatoes. Those violent emotions of hatred and cupidity which the situation of the native gentleman could scarcely fail to call forth appeared to him under the specious guise of patriotism and piety. For his enemies were the enemies of his nation; and the same tyranny which had robbed him of his patrimony had robbed his Church of vast wealth bestowed on her by the devotion of an earlier age. How was power likely to be used by an uneducated and inexperienced man, agitated by strong desires and resentments which he mistook for sacred duties? And, when two or three hundred such men were brought together in one assemby, what was to be expected but that the passions which each had long nursed in silence would be at once matured into fearful vigor by the influence of sympathy?

* An Act concerning Appropriate Tythes and other duties payable to Ecclesiastical Dignitaries. London, 1690.
† An act for repealing the Acts of Settlement and Explanation, and all Grants, Patents, and Certificates pursuant to them or any of them. London, 1690.

Between James and his parliament there was little in common, except hatred of the Protestant religion. He was an Englishman. Superstition had not utterly extinguished all national feeling in his mind; and he could not but be displeased by the malevolence with which his Celtic supporters regarded the race from which he sprang. The range of his intellectual vision was small. Yet it was impossible that, having reigned in England, and looking constantly forward to the day when he should reign in England once more, he should not take a wider view of politics than was taken by men who had no objects out of Ireland. The few Irish Protestants who still adhered to him and the British nobles, both Protestant and Roman Catholic, who had followed him into exile, implored him to restrain the violence of the rapacious and vindictive senate which he had convoked. They with peculiar earnestness implored him not to consent to the repeal of the Act of Settlement. On what security, they asked, could any man invest his money or give a portion to his children, if he could not rely on positive laws and on the uninterupted possession of many years? The military adventurers among whom Cromwell portioned out the soil might perhaps be regarded as wrong-doers. But how large a part of their estates had passed, by fair purchase, into other hands! How much money had proprietors borrowed on mortgage, on statute merchant, on statute staple! How many capitalists had, trusting to legislative acts and to royal promises, come over from England, and bought land in Ulster and Leinster, without the least misgiving as to the title! What a sum had those capitalists expended, during a quarter of a century, in building, draining, enclosing, planting! The terms of the compromise which Charles the Second had sanctioned might not be in all respects just. But was one injustice to be redressed by committing another injustice more monstrous still? And what effect was likely to be produced in England by the cry of thousands of innocent English families whom an English king had doomed to ruin? The complaints of such a body of sufferers might delay, might prevent, the restoration to which all loyal subjects were eagerly looking forward; and, even if His Majesty should, in spite of those complaints, be happily restored, he would to the end of his life feel the pernicious effects of the injustice which evil advisers were now urging him to commit. He would find that, in trying to quiet one set of malcontents, he had created another. As surely as he yielded to the clamor raised at Dublin for a repeal of the Act of Settlement, he would, from the day on which he returned to Westminster, be assailed by as loud and pertinacious a clamor for a repeal of that repeal. He could not but be aware that no English parliament, however loyal, would permit such laws as were now passing through the Irish parliament to stand. Had he made up his mind to take the part of Ireland against the universal sense of England? If so, to what could he look forward but another banishment and another deposition? Or would he, when he had recovered the greater kingdom, revoke the boons by which, in his distress, he had purchased the help of the smaller? It might seem an insult to him even to suggest that he could harbor the thought of such unprincely, of such unmanly, perfidy. Yet what other course would be left to him? And was it not better for him to refuse unreasonable concessions now than to retract those concessions hereafter in a manner which must bring on him reproaches insupportable to a noble mind? His situation was doubtless embarrassing. Yet in this case, as in other cases, it would be found that the path of justice was the path of wisdom.*

Though James had, in his speech at the opening of the session, declared against the Act of Settlement, he felt that these arguments were unanswerable. He held several conferences with the leading members of the House of Commons, and earnestly recommended moderation. But his exhortations irritated the passions which he wished to allay. Many of the native gentry held high and violent language. It was impudent, they said, to talk about the rights of purchasers. How could right spring out of wrong? People who chose to buy property acquired by injustice must take the consequences of their folly and cupidity. It was clear that the Lower House was altogether impracticable. James had, four years before, refused to make the smallest concession to the most obsequious parliament that has ever sat in England; and it might have been expected that the obstinacy, which he had never wanted when it was a vice, would not have failed him now when it would have been a virtue. During a short time he seemed determined to act justly. He even talked of dis-

---

* See the paper delivered to James by Chief Justice Keating, and the speech of the Bishop of Meath. Both are in King's appendix. Life of James ii. 357-361.

solving the Parliament. The chiefs of the old Celtic families on the other hand, said publicly that, if he did not give them back their inheritance, they would not fight for his. His very soldiers railed on him in the streets of Dublin. At length he determined to go down himself to the House of Peers, not in his robes and crown, but in the garb in which he had been used to attend debates at Westminster, and personally to solicit the Lords to put some check on the violence of the Commons. But just as he was getting into his coach for this purpose he was stopped by Avaux. Avaux was as zealous as any Irishman for the bills which the Commons were urging forward. It was enough for him that those bills seemed likely to make the enmity between England and Ireland irreconcileable. His remonstrances induced James to abstain from openly opposing the repeal of the Act of Settlement. Still the unfortunate Prince continued to cherish some faint hope that the law for which the Commons were so zealous would be rejected, or at least modified, by the Peers. Lord Granard, one of the few Protestant noblemen who sate in that Parliament, exerted himself strenuously on the side of public faith and sound policy. The King sent him a message of thanks. "We Protestants," said Granard to Powis, who brought the message, "are few in number. We can do little. His Majesty should try his influence with the Roman Catholics." "His Majesty," answered Powis with an oath, "dares not say what he thinks." A few days later James met Granard riding towards the parliament house. "Where are you going, my Lord?" said the King. "To enter my protest, sir," answered Granard, "against the repeal of the Act of Settlement." "You are right," said the King: "but I am fallen into the hands of people who will ram that and much more down my throat."*

James yielded to the will of the Commons: but the unfavorable impression which his short and feeble resistance had made upon them was not to be removed by his submission. They regarded him with profound distrust: they considered him as at heart an Englishman; and not a day passed without some indication of this feeling. They were in no haste to grant him a supply. One party among them planned an address urging him to dismiss Melfort as an enemy of their nation. Another party drew up a bill

---

* Leslie's Answer to King; Avaux, $\frac{\text{May 26,}}{\text{June 5.}}$ 1689; Life of James, ii. 358.

for deposing all the Protestant bishops, even the four who were then actually sitting in Parliament. It was not without difficulty that Avaux and Tyrconnel, whose influence in the Lower House far exceeded the King's, could restrain the zeal of the majority.*

It is remarkable that, while the King was losing the confidence and good will of the Irish Commons by faintly defending against them, in one quarter, the institution of property, he was himself, in another quarter, attacking that institution with a violence, if possible, more reckless than theirs. He soon found that no money came into his exchequer. The cause was sufficiently obvious. Trade was at an end. Floating capital had been withdrawn in great masses from the island. Of the fixed capital much had been destroyed, and the rest was lying idle. Thousands of those Protestants who were the most industrious and intelligent part of the population had emigrated to England. Thousands had taken refuge in the places which still held out for William and Mary. Of the Roman Catholic peasantry who were in the vigor of life the majority had enlisted in the army or had joined gangs of plunderers. The poverty of the treasury was the necessary effect of the poverty of the country: public prosperity could be restored only by the restoration of private prosperity: and private prosperity could be restored only by years of peace and security. James was absurd enough to imagine that there was a more speedy and efficacious remedy. He could, he conceived, at once extricate himself from his financial difficulties by the simple process of calling a farthing a shilling. The right of coining was undoubtedly a flower of the prerogative: and, in his view, the right of coining included the right of debasing the coin. Pots, pans, knockers of doors, pieces of ordnance which had long been past use, were carried to the mint. In a short time lumps of base metal, nominally worth near a million sterling, intrinsically worth about a sixtieth part of that sum, were in circulation. A royal edict declared these pieces to be legal tender in all cases whatever. A mortgage for a thousand pounds was cleared off by a bag of counters made out of old kettles. The creditors who complained to the Court of Chancery were told by Fitton to take their

---

* Avaux, $\frac{\text{May 28,}}{\text{June 7}}$ 1689, and $\frac{\text{June 30,}}{\text{July 10.}}$ The author of Light to the Blind strongly condemns the indulgence shown to the Protestant Bishops who adhered to James.

money and be gone. But of all classes the tradesmen of Dublin, who were generally Protestants, were the greatest losers. At first, of course, they raised their demands: but the magistrates of the city took on themselves to meet this heretical machination by putting forth a tariff regulating prices. Any man who belonged to the caste now dominant might walk into a shop, lay on the counter a bit of brass worth three pence, and carry off goods to the value of half a guinea. Legal redress was out of the question Indeed the sufferers thought themselves happy if, by the sacrifice of their stock in trade, they could redeem their limbs and their lives. There was not a baker's shop in the city round which twenty or thirty soldiers were not constantly prowling. Some persons who refused the base money were arrested by troopers and carried before the provost marshal, who curssd them, swore at them, locked them up in dark cells, and by threatening to hang them at their own doors, soon overcame their resistance. Of all the plagues of that time none made a deeper or more lasting impression on the minds of the Protestants of Dublin than the plague of the brass money.* To the recollection of the confusion and misery which had been produced by James's coin must be in part ascribed the strenuous opposition which, thirty-five years later, large classes, firmly attached to the House of Hanover, offered to the government of George the First in the affair of Wood's patent.

There can be no question that James, in thus altering, by his own authority, the terms of all the contracts in the kingdom, assumed a power which belonged only to the whole legislature. Yet the Commons did not remonstrate. There was no power, however unconstitutional, which they were not willing to concede to him, as long as he used it to crush and plunder the English population. On the other hand, they respected no prerogative, however ancient, however legitimate, however salutary, if they apprehended that he might use it to protect the race which they abhorred. They were not satisfied till they had extorted his reluctant consent to a portentous law, a law without a parallel in the history of civilized countries, the great Act of Attainder.

A list was framed containing between two and three

---

* King, iii. 11; Brief Memoirs by Haynes, Assay Master of the Mint, among the Lansdowne MSS. at the British Museum, No. 801. I have seen several specimens of this coin. The execution is surprisingly good, all circumstances considered.

thousand names. At the top was half the peerage of Ireland. Then came baronets, knights, clergymen, squires, merchants, yeomen, artisans, women, children. No investigation was made. Any member who wished to rid himself of a creditor, a rival, a private enemy, gave in the name to the clerk at the table, and it was generally inserted without discussion. The only debate of which any account has come down to us related to the Earl of Strafford. He had friends in the House who ventured to offer something in his favor. But a few words from Simon Luttrell settled the question. "I have," he said, "heard the King say some hard things of that Lord." This was thought sufficient, and the name of Strafford stands fifth in the long table of the proscribed.*

Days were fixed before which those whose names were on the list were required to surrender themselves to such justice as was then administered to English Protestants in Dublin. If a proscribed person was in Ireland, he must surrender himself by the tenth of August. If he had left Ireland since the fifth of November, 1688, he must surrender himself by the first of September. If he had left Ireland before the fifth of November, 1688, he must surrender himself by the first of October. If he failed to appear by the appointed day, he was to be hanged, drawn, and quartered without a trial, and his property was to be confiscated. It might be physically impossible for him to deliver himself up within the time fixed by the Act. He might be bedridden. He might be in the West Indies. He might be in prison. Indeed there notoriously were such cases. Among the attained Lords was Mountjoy. He had been induced, by the villainy of Tyrconnel, to trust himself at Saint Germains: he had been thrown into the Bastile: he was still lying there; and the Irish Parliament was not ashamed to enact that, unless he could, within a few weeks, make his escape from his cell, and present himself at Dublin, he should be put to death.†

As it was not even pretended that there had been any inquiry into the guilt of those who were thus proscribed, as not a single one among them had been heard in his own defence, and as it was certain that it would be physically impossible for many of them to surrender themselves in time,

---
* King, iii. 12.
† An Act for the Attainder of divers Rebels and for preserving the Interest of loyal Subjects, London, 1690.

it was clear that nothing but a large exercise of the royal prerogative of mercy could prevent the perpetration of iniquities so horrible that no precedent could be found for them even in the lamentable history of the troubles of Ireland. The Commons therefore determined that the royal prerogative of mercy should be limited. Several regulations were devised for the purpose of making the passing of pardons difficult and costly; and finally it was enacted that every pardon granted by His Majesty, after the end of November, 1689, to any of the many hundreds of persons who had been sentenced to death without a trial, should be absolutely void and of none effect. Sir Richard Nagle came in state to the bar of the Lords and presented the bill with a speech worthy of the occasion. "Many of the persons here attainted," said he, "have been proved traitors by such evidence as satisfies us. As to the rest we have followed common fame."*

With such reckless barbarity was the list framed that fanatical royalists, who were, at that very time, hazarding their property, their liberty, their lives, in the cause of James, were not secure from proscription. The most learned man of whom the Jacobite party could boast was Henry Dodwell, Camdenian Professor in the University of Oxford. In the cause of hereditary monarchy he shrank from no sacrifice and from no danger. It was about him that William uttered those memorable words: "He has set his heart on being a martyr; and I have set mine on disappointing him." But James was more cruel to friends than William to foes. Dodwell was a Protestant: he had some property in Connaught: these crimes were sufficient; and he was set down in the long roll of those who were doomed to the gallows and the quartering block.†

That James would give his assent to a bill which took from him the power of pardoning, seemed to many persons impossible. He had, four years before, quarrelled with the most loyal of parliaments rather than cede a prerogative which did not belong to him. It might, therefore, well be expected that he would now have struggled hard to retain a precious prerogative which had been enjoyed by his predecessors ever since the origin of the monarchy, and

---

* King, iii. 13.

† His name is in the first column of page 30, in that edition of the List which was licensed March 26, 1690. I should have thought that the proscribed person must have been some other Henry Dodwell. But Bishop Kennett's second letter to the Bishop of Carlisle, 1716, leaves no doubt about the matter.

which even the Whigs allowed to be a flower properly belonging to the Crown. The stern look and raised voice with which he had reprimanded the Tory gentlemen, who, in the language of profound reverence and fervent affection, implored him not to dispense with the laws, would now have been in place. He might also have seen that the right course was the wise course. Had he, on this great occasion, had the spirit to declare that he would not shed the blood of the innocent, and that, even as respected the guilty, he would not divest himself of the power of tempering judgment with mercy, he would have regained more hearts in England than he would have lost in Ireland. But it was ever his fate to resist where he should have yielded, and to yield where he should have resisted. The most wicked of all laws received his sanction; and it is but a very small extenuation of his guilt that his sanction was somewhat reluctantly given.

That nothing might be wanting to the completeness of this great crime, extreme care was taken to prevent the persons who were attainted from knowing that they were attained, till the day of grace fixed in the Act was passed. The roll of names was not published, but kept carefully locked up in Fitton's closet. Some Protestants, who still adhered to the cause of James, but who were anxious to know whether any of their friends or relations had been proscribed, tried hard to obtain a sight of the list: but solicitations, remonstrance, even bribery, proved vain. Not a single copy got abroad till it was too late for any of the thousands who had been condemned without a trial to obtain a pardon.*

Towards the close of July James prorogued the Houses. They had sate more than ten weeks: and in that space of time they had proved most fully that, great as have been the evils which Protestant ascendency has produced in Ireland, the evils produced by Popish ascendency would have been greater still. That the colonists when they had won the victory, grossly abused it, that their legislation was, during many years, unjust and tyrannical, is most true. But it is not less true that they never quite came up to the

---

* A list of most of the names of the Nobility, Gentry, and Commonalty of England and Ireland (amongst whom are several Women and Children) who are all, by an Act of a Pretended Parliament assembled in Dublin, attainted of High Treason, 1690; An Account of the Transactions of the late King James in Ireland, 1690; King, iii. 13; Memoirs of Ireland. 1716.

atrocious example set by their vanquished enemy during his short tenure of power.

Indeed, while James was loudly boasting that he had passed an Act granting entire liberty of conscience to all sects, a persecution as cruel as that of Languedoc was raging through all the provinces which owned his authority. It was said by those who wished to find an excuse for him that almost all the Protestants, who still remained in Munster, Connaught, and Leinster, were his enemies, and that it was not as schismatics, but as rebels in heart, who wanted only opportunity to become rebels in act, that he gave them up to be oppressed and despoiled; and to this excuse some weight might have been allowed if he had strenuously exerted himself to protect those few colonists, who, though firmly attached to the reformed religion, were still true to the doctrines of non-resistance and of indefeasible hereditary right. But even these devoted royalists found that their heresy was in his view a crime for which no services or sacrifices would atone. Three or four noblemen, members of the Anglican Church, who had welcomed him to Ireland, and had sate in his parliament, represented to him that, if the rule which forbade any Protestant to possess any weapon were strictly enforced, their country houses would be at the mercy of the Rapparees, and obtained from him permission to keep arms sufficient for a few servants. But Avaux remonstrated. The indulgence, he said, was grossly abused: these Protestant lords were not to be trusted: they were turning their houses into fortresses: His Majesty would soon have reason to repent his goodness. These representations prevailed; and Roman Catholic troops were quartered in the suspected dwellings.*

Still harder was the lot of those Protestant clergymen who continued to cling, with desperate fidelity, to the cause of the Lord's Anointed. Of all the Anglican divines the one who had the largest share of James's good graces seems to have been Cartwright. Whether Cartwright could long have continued to be a favorite without being an apostate may be doubted. He died a few weeks after his arrival in Ireland; and thenceforward his Church had no one to plead her cause. Nevertheless a few of her prelates and priests continued for a time to teach what they

---

* Avaux, $\frac{\text{July 27,}}{\text{Aug. 6,}}$ 1689.

had taught in the days of the Exclusion Bill. But it was at the peril of life and limb that they exercised their functions. Every wearer of a cassock was a mark for the insults and outrages of soldiers and Rapparees. In the country his house was robbed and he was fortunate if it was not burned over his head. He was hunted through the streets of Dublin with cries of "There goes the devil of a heretic." Sometimes he was knocked down; sometimes he was cudgelled.* The rulers of the University of Dublin, trained in the Anglican doctrine of passive obedience, had greeted James on his first arrival at the Castle, and had been assured by him that he would protect them in the enjoyment of their property and their privileges. They were now, without any trial, without any accusation, thrust out of their house. The communion plate of the chapel, the books in the library, the very chairs and beds of the collegians were seized. Part of the building was turned into a magazine, part into a barrack, part into a prison. Simon Luttrell, who was governor of the capital, was, with great difficulty and by powerful intercession induced to let the ejected fellows and scholars depart in safety. He at length permitted them to remain at large, with this condition, that, on pain of death, no three of them should meet together.† No Protestant divine suffered more hardships than Doctor William King, Dean of Saint Patrick's. He had been long distinguished by the fervor with which he had inculcated the duty of passively obeying even the worst rulers. At a later period, when he had published a defence of the revolution, and had accepted a mitre from the new government, he was reminded that he had invoked the divine vengeance on the usurpers, and had declared himself willing to die a hundred deaths rather than desert the cause of hereditary right. He had said that the true religion had often been strengthened by persecution, but could never be strengthened by rebellion; that it would be a glorious day for the Church of England when a whole cartload of her ministers should go to the gallows for the doctrine of non-resistance; and that his highest ambition was to be one of such a company.‡ It is not improbable that, when he spoke thus, he felt as he spoke. But his principles, though they might perhaps have held out against the severities and the promises of William, were not proof

---

* King's State of the Protestants in Ireland, iii. 19.   † Ibid, iii. 15.
‡ Leslie's Answer to King.

against the ingratitude of James. Human nature at last asserted its rights. After King had been repeatedly imprisoned by the government to which he was devotedly attached, after he had been insulted and threatened in his own choir by the soldiers, after he had been interdicted from burying in his own churchyard, and from preaching in his own pulpit, after he had narrowly escaped with life from a musket-shot fired at him in the street, he began to think the Whig theory of government less unreasonable and unchristian than it had once appeared to him, and persuaded himself that the oppressed Church might lawfully accept deliverance, if God should be pleased, by whatever means, to send it to her.

In no long time it appeared that James would have done well to hearken to those counsellors who had told him that the acts by which he was trying to make himself popular in one of his three kingdoms, would make him odious in the other. It was in some sense fortunate for England that after he had ceased to reign here, he continued during more than a year to reign in Ireland. The revolution had been followed by a reaction of public feeling in his favor. That reaction, if it had been suffered to proceed uninterrupted, might perhaps not have ceased till he was again King: but it was violently interrupted by himself. He would not suffer his people to forget: he would not suffer them to hope; while they were trying to find excuses for his past errors, and to persuade themselves that he would not repeat those errors, he forced upon them, in their own despite, the conviction that he was incorrigible, that the sharpest discipline of adversity had taught him nothing, and that, if they were weak enough to recall him, they would soon have to depose him again. It was in vain that the Jacobites put forth pamphlets about the cruelty with which he had been treated by those who were nearest to him in blood, about the imperious temper and uncourteous manners of William, about the favor shown to the Dutch, about the heavy taxes, about the suspension of the Habeas Corpus Act, about the dangers which threatened the Church from the enmity of Puritans and Latitudinarians. James refuted these pamphlets far more effectually than all the ablest and most eloquent Whig writers united could have done. Every week came the news that he had passed some new Act for robbing or murdering Protestants. Every colonist who succeeded in stealing across the sea from Leinster to Holyhead or Bristol, brought fearful reports of the tyranny under which his brethren groaned. What impression these reports made on the Protestants of our island may be easily inferred from the fact that they moved the indignation of Ronquillo, a Spaniard and a bigoted member of the Church of Rome. He informed his Court that, though the English laws against Popery might seem severe, they were so much mitigated by the prudence and humanity of the government, that they caused no annoyance to quiet people; and he took upon himself to assure the Holy See that what a Roman Catholic suffered in London was nothing when compared with what a Protestant suffered in Ireland.*

The fugitive Englishry found in England warm sympathy and munificent relief. Many were received into the houses of friends and kinsmen. Many were indebted for the means of subsistance to the liberality of strangers. Among those who bore a part in this work of mercy, none contributed more largely or less ostentatiously than the Queen. The House of Commons placed at the King's disposal fifteen thousand pounds for the relief of those refugees whose wants were most pressing, and requested him to give commissions in the army to those who were qualified for military employment.† An Act was also passed enabling beneficed clergymen who had fled from Ireland to hold preferment in England.‡ Yet the interest which the nation felt in these unfortunate guests was languid when compared with the interest excited by that portion of the Saxon colony which still maintained in Ulster a desperate conflict against overwhelming odds. On this subject scarcely one dissentient voice was to be heard in our island. Whigs, Tories, nay even the Jacobites in whom Jacobitism had not extinguished every patriotic sentiment, gloried in the glory of Enniskillen and Londonderry. The House of Commons was all of one mind. "This is no time to be counting cost," said honest Birch, who well remembered the way in which Oliver had made war on the Irish. "Are those brave fellows in Londonderry to be deserted? If we lose them will not all the world cry shame upon us? A boom across the river! Why have we not cut the boom in

---

* "En comparazion de lo que se hace in Irlanda con los Protestantes, es nada," April 29 / May 9, 1689; "Para que vea Su Santitad que aqui estan los Catolicos mas benignamente tratados que los Protestantes in Irlanda," June 19-29.

† Commons' Journals, June 15, 1689. ‡ Stat. 1 W. & M. sess., c. 29.

pieces? Are our brethren to perish almost in sight of England, within a few hours voyage of our shores?"* Howe, the most vehement man of one party, declared that the hearts of the people were set on Ireland. Seymour, the leader of the other party, declared that, though he had not taken part in setting up the new government, he should cordially support it in all that might be necessary for the preservation of Ireland.† The Commons appointed a committee to inquire into the cause of the delays and miscarriages which had been all but fatal to the Englishry of Ulster. The officers to whose treachery or cowardice the public ascribed the calamities of Londonderry were put under arrest. Lundy was sent to the Tower, Cunningham to the Gate House. The agitation of the public mind was in some degree calmed by the announcement that, before the end of summer, an army powerful enough to re-establish the English ascendency in Ireland would be sent across Saint George's Channel, and that Schomberg would be the general. In the meantime an expedition which was thought to be sufficient for the relief of Londonderry was despatched from Liverpool under the command of Kirke. The dogged obstinacy with which this man had, in spite of royal solicitations, adhered to his religion, and the part which he had taken in the Revolution, had perhaps entitled him to an amnesty for past crimes. But it is difficult to understand why the government should have selected for a post of the highest importance, an officer who was generally and justly hated, who had never shown eminent talents for war, and who, both in Africa and in England, had notoriously tolerated among his soldiers a licentiousness, not only shocking to humanity, but also incompatible with discipline.

On the sixteenth of May, Kirke's troops embarked: on the twenty-second they sailed: but contrary winds made the passage slow, and forced the armament to stop long at the Isle of Man. Meanwhile the Protestants of Ulster were defending themselves with stubborn courage against a great superiority of force. The Enniskilleners had never ceased to wage a vigorous partisan war against the native population. Early in May they marched to encounter a large body of troops from Connaught, who had made an inroad into Donegal. The Irish were speedily routed, and fled to Sligo with the loss of a hundred and twenty men killed and

* Grey's Debates, June 19, 1689.   † Grey's Debates, June 22, 1689.

sixty taken. Two small pieces of artillery and several horses fell into the hands of the conquerors. Elated by this success, the Enniskilleners soon invaded the county of Cavan, drove before them fifteen hundred of James's troops, took and destroyed the castle of Ballincarrig, reputed the strongest in that part of the kingdom, and carried off the pikes and muskets of the garrison. The next incursion was into Meath. Three thousand oxen and two thousand sheep were swept away and brought safe to the little island in Lough Erne. These daring exploits spread terror even to the gates of Dublin. Colonel Hugh Sutherland was ordered to march against Enniskillen with a regiment of dragoons and two regiments of foot. He carried with him arms for the native peasantry, and many repaired to his standard. The Enniskilleners did not wait till he came into their neighborhood, but advanced to encounter him. He declined an action, and retreated, leaving his stores at Belturbet under the care of a detachment of three hundred soldiers. The Protestants attacked Belturbet with vigor, made their way into a lofty house which overlooked the town, and thence opened such a fire that in two hours the garrison surrendered. Seven hundred muskets, a great quantity of powder, many horses, many sacks of biscuits, many barrels of meal, were taken, and were sent to Enniskillen. The boats which brought these precious spoils were joyfully welcomed. The fear of hunger was removed. While the aboriginal population had, in many counties, altogether neglected the cultivation of the earth, in the expectation, it should seem, that marauding would prove an inexhaustible resource, the colonists, true to the provident and industrious character of their race, had, in the midst of war, not omitted carefully to till the soil in the neighborhood of their strongholds. The harvest was now not far remote; and, till the harvest, the food taken from the enemy would be amply sufficient.*

Yet in the midst of success and plenty, the Enniskilleners were tortured by a cruel anxiety for Londonderry. They were bound to the defenders of that city, not only by religious and national sympathy, but by common interest. For there could be no doubt that, if Londonderry fell, the whole Irish army would instantly march in irre-

---

*Hamilton's True Relation; Mac Cormick's Further Account. Of the island generally, Avaux says, "On n'attend rien de cette recolte cy, les paysans ayant presque tous pris les armes."—Letter to Louvois, March 19-29, 1689.

sistible force upon Lough Erne. Yet what could be done? Some brave men were for making a desperate attempt to relieve the besieged city; but the odds were too great. Detachments, however, were sent which infested the rear of the blockading army, cut off supplies, and, on one occasion, carried away the horses of three entire troops of cavalry.* Still the line of posts which surrounded Londonderry by land remained unbroken. The river was still strictly closed and guarded. Within the walls the distress had become extreme. So early as the eighth of June horseflesh was almost the only meat which could be purchased; and of horseflesh the supply was scanty. It was necessary to make up the deficiency with tallow; and even tallow was doled out with a parsimonious hand.

On the fifteenth of June a gleam of hope appeared. The sentinels on the top of the cathedral saw sails nine miles off in the bay of Lough Foyle. Thirty vessels of different sizes were counted. Signals were made from the steeples and returned from the mastheads, but were imperfectly understood on both sides. At last a messenger from the fleet eluded the Irish sentinels, dived under the boom, and informed the garrison that Kirke had arrived from England with troops, arms, ammunition, and provisions, to relieve the city.†

In Londonderry expectation was at the height: but a few hours of feverish joy were followed by weeks of misery. Kirke thought it unsafe to make any attempt, either by land or by water, on the lines of the besiegers, and retired to the entrance of Lough Foyle, where, during several weeks, he lay inactive.

And now the pressure of famine became every day more severe. A strict search was made in all the recesses of all the houses of the city; and some provisions, which had been concealed in cellars by people who had since died or made their escape, were discovered and carried to the magazines. The stock of cannon balls was almost exhausted; and their place was supplied by brickbats coated with lead. Pestilence began, as usual, to make its appearance in the train of hunger. Fifteen officers died of fever in one day. The governor, Baker, was among those who sank under the disease. His place was supplied by Colonel John Mitchelburne.‡

---

*Hamilton's True Relation. † Walker.
‡ Walker; Mackenzie.

Meanwhile it was known at Dublin that Kirke and his squadron were on the coast of Ulster. The alarm was great at the Castle. Even before this news arrived, Avaux had given it as his opinion that Richard Hamilton was unequal to the difficulties of the situation. It had therefore been resolved that Rosen should take the chief command. He was now sent down with all speed.*

On the nineteenth of June he arrived at the headquarters of the besieging army. At first he attempted to undermine the walls; but his plan was discovered; and he was compelled to abandon it after a sharp fight, in which more than a hundred of his men were slain. Then his fury rose to a strange pitch. He, an old soldier, a Marshal of France in expectancy, trained in the school of the greatest generals, accustomed, during many years, to scientific war, to be baffled by a mob of country gentlemen, farmers, shopkeepers, who were protected only by a wall which any good engineer would at once have pronounced untenable! He raved, he blasphemed, in a language of his own, made up of all the dialects spoken from the Baltic to the Atlantic. He would raze the city to the ground; he would spare no living thing; no, not the young girls; not the babies at the breast. As to the leaders, death was too light a punishment for them: he would rack them; he would roast them alive. In his rage he ordered a shell to be flung into the town with a letter containing a horrible menace. He would, he said, gather into one body all the Protestants who had remained at their homes between Charlemont and the sea, old men, women, children, many of them near in blood and affection to the defenders of Londonderry. No protection, whatever might be the authority by which it had been given, should be respected. The multitude thus brought together should be driven under the walls of Londonderry, and should there be starved to death in the sight of their countrymen, their friends, their kinsmen. This was no idle threat. Parties were instantly sent out in all directions to collect victims. At dawn, on the morning of the second of July, hundreds of Protestants, who were charged with no crime, who were incapable of bearing arms, and many of whom had protections granted by James, were dragged to the gates of the city. It was imagined that the piteous sight would quell the spirit of the colonists. But the only effect was to

---
* Avaux, June 16-26, 1689.

rouse that spirit to still greater energy. An order was immediately put forth that no man should utter the word Surrender on pain of death; and no man uttered that word. Several prisoners of high rank were in the town. Hitherto they had been well treated, and had received as good rations as were measured out to the garrison. They were now closely confined. A gallows was erected on one of the bastions; and a message was conveyed to Rosen, requesting him to send a confessor instantly to prepare his friends for death. The prisoners in great dismay wrote to the savage Livonian, but received no anawer. They then addressed themselves to their countryman, Richard Hamilton. They were willing, they said, to shed their blood for their King; but they thought it hard to die the ignominious death of thieves in consequence of the barbarity of their own companions in arms. Hamilton, though a man of lax principles, was not cruel. He had been disgusted by the inhumanity of Rosen, but, being only second in command, could not venture to express publicly all that he thought. He however remonstrated strongly. Some Irish officers felt on this occasion as it was natural that brave men should feel, and declared, weeping with pity and indignation, that they should never cease to have in their ears the cries of the poor women and children who had been driven at the point of the pike to die of famine between the camp and the city. Rosen persisted during forty-eight hours. In that time many unhappy creatures perished: but Londonderry held out as resolutely as ever; and he saw that his crime was likely to produce nothing but hatred and obloquy. He at length gave way, and suffered the survivors to withdraw. The garrison then took down the gallows which had been erected on the bastion.*

When the tidings of these events reached Dublin, James, though by no means prone to compassion, was startled by an atrocity of which the civil wars of England had furnished no example, and was displeased by learning that protections, given by his authority, and guaranteed by his honor, had been publicly declared to be nullities. He complained to the French ambassador, and said, with a warmth which the occasion fully justified, that Rosen was a barbarous Muscovite. Melfort could not refrain from

---

* Walker; Mackenzie; Light to the Blind; King, iii. 13; Leslie's Answer to King; Life of James. ii. 366. I ought to say that on this occasion King is unjust to James.

adding that, if Rosen had been an Englishman, he would have been hanged. Avaux was utterly unable to understand this effeminate sensibility. In his opinion, nothing had been done that was at all reprehensible; and he had some difficulty in commanding himself when he heard the King and the secretary blame, in strong language, an act of wholesome severity.* In truth the French ambassador and the French general were well paired. There was a great difference, doubtless, in appearance and manner, between the handsome, graceful, and refined politician, whose dexterity and suavity had been renowned at the most polite courts of Europe, and the military adventurer, whose look and voice reminded all who came near him that he had been born in a half savage country, that he had risen from the ranks, and that he had once been sentenced to death for marauding. But the heart of the diplomatist was really even more callous than that of the soldier.

Rosen was recalled to Dublin; and Richard Hamilton was again left in the chief command. He tried gentler means than those which had brought so much reproach on his predecessor. No trick, no lie, which was thought likely to discourage the starving garrison was spared. One day a great shout was raised by the whole Irish camp. The defenders of Londonderry were soon informed that the army of James was rejoicing on account of the fall of Enniskillen. They were told that they had now no chance of being relieved, and were exhorted to save their lives by capitulating. They consented to negotiate. But what they asked was, that they should be permitted to depart armed and in military array, by land or by water at their choice. They demanded hostages for the exact fulfilment of these conditions, and insisted that the hostages should be sent on board of the fleet which lay in Lough Foyle. Such terms Hamilton durst not grant: the Governors would abate nothing: the treaty was broken off, and the conflict recommenced.†

By this time July was far advanced; and the state of the city was, hour by hour, becoming more frightful. The number of inhabitants had been thinned more by famine and disease than by the fire of the enemy. Yet that fire

---

* Leslie's Answer to King; Avaux, July 5-15, 1689. "Je trouvay l'expression bien forte: mais je ne voulois rien répondre, car le Roy s'estoit desja fort emporté."
† Mackenzie.

was more constant than ever. One of the gates was beaten in: one of the bastions was laid in ruins; but the breaches made by day were repaired by night with indefatigable activity. Every attack was still repelled. But the fighting men of the garrison were so much exhausted that they could scarcely keep their legs. Several of them in the act of striking at the enemy, fell down from mere weakness. A very small quantity of grain remained, and was doled out by mouthfuls. The stock of salted hides was considerable, and by gnawing them the garrison appeased the rage of hunger. Dogs, fattened on the blood of the slain who lay unburied round the town, were luxuries which few could afford to purchase. The price of a whelp's paw was five shillings and sixpence. Nine horses were still alive, and but barely alive. They were so lean that little meat was likely to be found upon them. It was, however, determined to slaughter them for food. The people perished so fast, that it was impossible for the survivors to perform the rights of sepulture. There was scarcely a cellar in which some corpse was not decaying. Such was the extremity of distress that the rats who came to feast in those hideous dens were eagerly hunted and greedily devoured. A small fish, caught in the river, was not to be purchased with money. The only price for which such a treasure could be obtained was some handfuls of oatmeal. Leprosies, such as strange and unwholsome diet engenders, made existence a constant torment. The whole city was poisoned by the stench exhaled from the bodies of the dead and of the half dead. That there should be fits of discontent and insubordination among men enduring such misery was inevitable. At one moment it was suspected that Walker had laid up somewhere a secret store of food, and was revelling in private, while he exhorted others to suffer resolutely for the good cause. His house was strictly examined; his innocence fully proved: he regained his popularity; and the garrison, with death in near prospect, thronged to the cathedral to hear him preach, drank in his earnest eloquence with delight, and went forth from the house of God with haggard faces and tottering steps, but with spirit still unsubdued. There were, indeed, some secret plottings. A very few obscure traitors opened communications with the enemy. But it was necessary that all such dealings should be carefully concealed. None dared to utter publicly any words save words of defiance and stubborn resolution. Even in that extremity the general cry was, "No surrender." And there were not wanting voices which, in low tones, added, "First the horses and hides; and then the prisoners; and then each other." It was afterwards related, half in jest, yet not without a horrible mixture of earnest, that a corpulent citizen, whose bulk presented a strange contrast to the skeletons which surrounded him, thought it expedient to conceal himself from the numerous eyes which followed him with cannibal looks whenever he appeared in the streets.*

It was no slight aggravation of the sufferings of the garrison that all this time the English ships were seen far off in Lough Foyle. Communication between the fleet and the city was almost impossible. One diver who had attempted to pass the boom was drowned. Another was hanged. The language of signals was hardly intelligible. On the thirteenth of July, however, a piece of paper sewed up in a cloth button came to Walker's hands. It was a letter from Kirke, and contained assurances of speedy relief. But more than a fortnight of intense misery had since elapsed; and the hearts of the most sanguine were sick with deferred hope. By no art could the provisions which were left be made to hold out two days more.†

Just at this time Kirke received from England a despatch, which contained positive orders that Londonderry should be relieved. He accordingly determined to make an attempt which, as far as appears, he might have made, with at least an equally fair prospect of success, six weeks earlier.‡

Among the merchant ships which had come to Lough Foyle under his convoy was one called the Mountjoy. The master, Micaiah Browning, a native of Londonderry, had brought from England a large cargo of provisions. He had, it is said, repeatedly remonstrated against the inaction of the armament. He now eagerly volunteered to

---

* Walker's Account. "The fat man in Londonderry" became a proverbial expression for a person whose prosperity excited the envy and cupidity of his less fortunate neighbors.

† This, according to Narcissus Luttrell, was the report made by Captain Withers, afterwards a highly distinguished officer, on whom Pope wrote an epitaph.

‡ The despatch, which positively commanded Kirke to attack the boom, was signed by Schomberg, who had already been appointed commander-in-chief of all the English forces in Ireland. A copy of it is among the Nairne MSS. in the Bodleian Library. Wodrow, on no better authority than the gossip of a country parish in Dumbartonshire, attributes the relief of Londonderry to the exhortations of a heroic Scotch preacher named Gordon. I am inclined to think that Kirke was more likely to be influenced by a peremptory order from Schomberg, than by the united eloquence of a whole synod of Presbyterian divines.

take the first risk of succoring his fellow citizens; and his offer was accepted. Andrew Douglas, master of the Phœnix, who had on board a great quantity of meal from Scotland, was willing to share the danger and the honor. The two merchantmen were to be escorted by the Dartmouth, a frigate of thirty-six guns, commanded by Captain John Leake, afterwards an admiral of great fame.

It was the twenty-eighth of July. The sun had just set: the evening sermon in the cathedral was over: and the heart-broken congregation had separated; when the sentinels on the tower saw the sails of three vessels coming up the Foyle. Soon there was a stir in the Irish camp. The besiegers were on the alert for miles along both shores. The ships were in extreme peril: for the river was low; and the only navigable channel ran very near to the left bank, where the headquarters of the enemy had been fixed, and where the batteries were most numerous. Leake performed his duty with a skill and spirit worthy of his noble profession, exposed his frigate to cover the merchantmen, and used his guns with great effect. At length the little squadron came to the place of peril. Then the Mountjoy took the lead, and went right at the boom. The huge barricade cracked and gave way: but the shock was such that the Mountjoy rebounded, and stuck in the mud. A yell of triumph rose from the banks: the Irish rushed to their boats, and were preparing to board: but the Dartmouth poured on them a well directed broadside which threw them into disorder. Just then the Phœnix dashed at the breach which the Mountjoy had made, and was in a moment within the fence. Meantime the tide was rising fast. The Mountjoy began to move, and soon passed safe through the broken stakes and floating spars. But her brave master was no more. A shot from one of the batteries had struck him; and he died by the most enviable of all deaths, in sight of the city which was his birthplace, which was his home, and which had just been saved by his courage and self-devotion from the most frightful form of destruction. The night had closed in before the conflict at the boom began: but the flash of the guns was seen, and the noise heard, by the lean and ghastly multitude which covered the walls of the city. When the Mountjoy grounded, and when the shout of triumph rose from the Irish on both sides of the river, the hearts of the besieged died within them. One who endured the unutterable anguish of that moment has told us that they looked fearfully livid in each other's eyes. Even after the barricade had been passed, there was a terrible half hour of suspense. It was ten o'clock before the ships arrived at the quay. The whole population was there to welcome them. A screen made of casks filled with earth was hastily thrown up to protect the landing place from the batteries on the other side of the river; and then the work of unloading began. First were rolled on shore barrels containing six thousand bushels of meal. Then came great cheeses, casks of beef, flitches of bacon, kegs of butter, sacks of pease and biscuit, ankers of brandy. Not many hours before, half a pound of tallow and three quarters of a pound of salted hide had been weighed out with niggardly care to every fighting man. The ration which each now received was three pounds of flour, two pounds of beef, and a pint of pease. It is easy to imagine with what tears grace was said over the suppers of that evening. There was little sleep on either side of the wall. The bonfires shone bright along the whole circuit of the ramparts. The Irish guns continued to roar all night; and all night the bells of the rescued city made answer to the Irish guns with a peal of joyous defiance. Through the three following days the batteries of the enemy continued to play. But, on the third night, flames were seen arising from the camp; and, when the first of August dawned, a line of smoking ruins marked the site lately occupied by the huts of the besiegers; and the citizens saw far off the long column of pikes and standards retreating up the left bank of the Foyle towards Strabane.*

So ended this great siege, the most memorable in the annals of the British isles. It had lasted a hundred and five days. The garrison had been reduced from about seven thousand effective men to about three thousand. The loss of the besiegers cannot be precisely ascertained. Walker estimated it at eight thousand men. It is certain from the despatches of Avaux that the regiments which returned from the blockade had been so much thinned that many of them were not more than two hundred strong. Of thirty-six French gunners who had superintended the cannonading, thirty-one had been killed or disabled.† The

---

* Walker; Mackenzie; Histoire de la Revolution d'Irlande, Amsterdam, 1691; London Gazette. Aug. 5, 12, 1689; Letter of Buchan among the Nairne MSS.; Life of Sir John Leake; the Londeriad; Observations on Mr. Walker's Account of the Siege of Londonderry, licensed Oct. 4, 1689.
† Avaux to Seignelay, July 18-28; to Lewis, Aug. 9-19.

means both of attack and of defence had undoubtedly been such as would have moved the great warriors of the Continent to laughter; and this is the very circumstance which gives so peculiar an interest to the history of the contest. It was a contest, not between engineers, but between nations; and the victory remained with the nation which, though inferior in number, was superior in civilization, in capacity for self-government, and in stubbornness of resolution.*

As soon as it was known that the Irish Army had retired, a deputation from the city hastened to Lough Foyle, and invited Kirke to take the command. He came accompanied by a long train of officers, and was received in state by the two governors, who delivered up to him the authority which, under the pressure of necessity, they had assumed. He remained only a few days; but he had time to show enough of the incurable vices of his character to disgust a population distinguished by austere morals and ardent public spirit. There was, however, no outbreak. The city was in the highest good humor. Such quantities of provisions had been landed from the fleet that there was in every house a plenty never before known. A few days earlier a man had been glad to obtain for twenty pence a mouthful of carrion scraped from the bones of a starved horse. A pound of good beef was now sold for three halfpence. Meanwhile all hands were busied in removing corpses which had been thinly covered with earth, in filling up the holes which the shells had ploughed in the ground, and in repairing the battered roofs of the houses. The recollection of past dangers and privations, and the consciousness of having deserved well of the English nation and of all Protestant churches, swelled the hearts of the towns-people with honest pride. That pride grew stronger when they received from William a letter, acknowledging, in the most affectionate language, the debt which he owed to the brave and trusty citizens of his good city. The whole population crowded to the Diamond to hear the royal epistle read. At the close all the guns on the ramparts sent forth a voice of joy: all the ships in the river made

---

* "You will see here, as you have all along, that the tradesmen of Londonderry had more skill in their defence than the great officers of the Irish Army in their attacks."—Light to the Blind. The author of this work is furious against the Irish gunners. The boom, he thinks, would never have been broken if they had done their duty. Were they drunk? Were they traitors? He does not determine the point. "Lord," he exclaims, "who seest the hearts of people, we leave the judgment of this affair to thy mercy. In the interim those gunners lost Ireland."

answer: barrels of ale were broken up; and the health of Their Majesties was drunk with shouts and volleys of musketry.

Five generations have since passed away; and still the wall of Londonderry is to the Protestants of Ulster what the trophy of Marathon was to the Athenians. A lofty pillar, rising from a bastion which bore during many weeks the heaviest fire of the enemy is seen far up and far down the Foyle. On the summit is the statue of Walker, such as when, in the last and most terrible emergency, his eloquence roused the fainting courage of his brethren. In one hand he grasps a Bible. The other, pointing down the river, seems to direct the eyes of his famished audience to the English topmast in the distant bay. Such a monument was well deserved: yet it was scarcely needed: for in truth the whole city is to this day a monument of the great deliverance. The wall is carefully preserved; nor would any plea of health or convenience be held by the inhabitants sufficient to justify the demolition of that sacred enclosure which, in the evil time, gave shelter to their race and their religion.* The summit of the ramparts forms a pleasant walk. The bastions have been turned into little gardens. Here and there, among the shrubs and flowers, may be seen the old culverins which scattered bricks, cased with lead, among the Irish ranks. One antique gun, the gift of the Fishmongers of London, was distinguished, during the hundred and five memorable days, by the loudness of its report, and still bears the name of Roaring Meg. The cathedral is filled with relics and trophies. In the vestibule is a huge shell, one of many hundreds of shells which were thrown into the city. Over the altar are still seen the French flag-staves, taken by the garrison in a desperate sally. The white ensigns of the House of Bourbon have long been dust: but their place has been supplied by new banners, the work of the fairest hands of Ulster. The anniversary of the day on which the gates were closed, and the anniversary of the day on which the siege was raised, have been down to our own time celebrated by salutes, processions, banquets, and sermons: Lundy has been executed in effigy; and the sword, said by tradition to be that of Maumont, has, on great occasions, been carried in triumph. There is still a Walker Club and a Murray Club.

---

*In a collection entitled "Deriana," which was published more than sixty years ago, is a curious letter on this subject.

The humble tombs of the Protestant captains have been carefully sought out, repaired, and embellished. It is impossible not to respect the sentiment which indicates itself by these tokens. It is a sentiment which belongs to the higher and purer part of human nature, and which adds not a little to the strength of states. A people which takes no pride in the noble achievements of remote ancestors will never achieve anything worthy to be remembered with pride by remote descendants. Yet it is impossible for the moralist or the statesman to look with unmixed complacency on the solemnities with which Londonderry commemorates her deliverance, and on the honors which she pays to those who saved her. Unhappily the animosities of her brave champions have descended with their glory. The faults which are ordinarily found in dominant castes and dominant sects have not seldom shown themselves without disguise at her festivities; and even with the expressions of pious gratitude which have resounded from her pulpits have too often been mingled words of wrath and defiance.

The Irish army which had retreated to Strabane remained there but a very short time. The spirit of the troops had been depressed by their recent failure, and was soon completely cowed by the news of a great disaster in another quarter.

Three weeks before this time the Duke of Berwick had gained an advantage over a detachment of the Enniskilleners, and had, by their own confession, killed or taken more than fifty of them. They were in hopes of obtaining some assistance from Kirke, to whom they had sent a deputation; and they still persisted in rejecting all terms offered by the enemy. It was therefore determined at Dublin that an attack should be made upon them from several quarters at once. Macarthy, who had been rewarded for his services in Munster with the title of Viscount Mountcashel, marched towards Lough Erne from the east with three regiments of foot, two regiments of dragoons, and some troops of cavalry. A considerable force, which lay encamped near the mouth of the river Drowes, was at the same time to advance from the west. The Duke of Berwick was to come from the north, with such horse and dragoons as could be spared from the army which was besieging Londonderry. The Enniskilleners were not fully apprised of the whole plan which had been laid for their destruction:

but they knew that Macarthy was on the road with a force exceeding any which they could bring into the field. Their anxiety was in some degree relieved by the return of the deputation which they had sent to Kirke. Kirke could spare no soldiers: but he had sent some arms, some ammunition, and some experienced officers, of whom the chief were Colonel Wolseley and Lieutenant Colonel Berry. These officers had come by sea round the coast of Donegal, and had run up the Erne. On Sunday, the twenty-ninth of July, it was known that their boat was approaching the island of Enniskillen. The whole population, male and female, came to the shore to greet them. It was with difficulty that they made their way to the Castle through the crowds which hung on them, blessing God that dear old England had not quite forgotten the Englishmen who were upholding her cause against great odds in the heart of Ireland.

Wolseley seems to have been in every respect well qualified for his post. He was a stanch Protestant, had distinguished himself among the Yorkshiremen who rose up for the Prince of Orange and a free Parliament, and had, even before the landing of the Dutch army, proved his zeal for liberty and pure religion, by causing the Mayor of Scarborough, who had made a speech in favor of King James, to be brought into the market-place and well tossed there in a blanket.* This vehement hatred of Popery was, in the estimation of the men of Enniskillen, the first of all the qualifications of a leader; and Wolseley had other and more important qualifications. Though himself regularly bred to war, he seems to have had a peculiar aptitude for the management of irregular troops. He had scarcely taken on himself the chief command when he received notice that Mountcashel had laid siege to the Castle of Crum. Crum was the frontier garrison of the Protestants of Fermanagh. The ruins of the old fortifications are now among the attractions of a beautiful pleasure-ground situated on a woody promontory which overlooks Lough Erne. Wolseley determined to raise the siege. He sent Berry forward with such troops as could be instantly put in motion, and promised to follow speedily with a larger force.

Berry, after marching some miles, encountered thirteen

---

* Bernardi's Life of Himself, 1737. Wolseley's exploit at Scarborough is mentioned in one of the letters published by Sir Henry Ellis.

companies of Macarthy's dragoons, commanded by Anthony, the most brilliant and accomplished of all who bore the name of Hamilton, but much less successful as a soldier than as a courtier, a lover, and a writer. Hamilton's dragoons ran at the first fire: he was severely wounded; and his second in command was shot dead. Macarthy soon came up to support Hamilton; and at the same time Wolseley came up to support Berry. The hostile armies were now in presence of each other. Macarthy had above five thousand men and several pieces of artillery. The Enniskilleners were under three thousand; and they had marched in such haste that they had brought only one day's provisions. It was therefore absolutely necessary for them either to fight instantly or to retreat. Wolseley determined to consult the men; and this determination, which, in ordinary circumstances, would have been most unworthy of a general, was fully justified by the peculiar composition and temper of the little army, an army made up of gentlemen and yeomen fighting, not for pay, but for their lands, their wives, their children, and their God. The ranks were drawn up under arms; and the question was put, "Advance or Retreat?" The answer was a universal shout of "Advance." Wolseley gave out the word "No Popery." It was received with loud applause. He instantly made his dispositions for an attack. As he approached, the enemy, to his great surprise, began to retire. The Enniskilleners were eager to pursue with all speed: but their commander, suspecting a snare, restrained their ardor and positively forbade them to break their ranks. Thus one army retreated and the other followed, in good order, through the little town of Newton Butler. About a mile from that town the Irish faced about, and made a stand. Their position was well chosen. They were drawn up on a hill at the foot of which lay a deep bog. A narrow paved causeway which ran across the bog was the only road by which the cavalry of the Enniskilleners could advance; for on the right and left were pools, turf pits and quagmires, which afforded no footing to horses. Macarthy placed his cannon in such a manner as to sweep this causeway.

Wolseley ordered infantry to the attack. They struggled through the bog, made their way to firm ground, and rushed on the guns. There was then a short and desperate fight. The Irish cannoneers stood gallantly to their pieces till they were cut down to a man. The Enniskillen horse, no longer in danger of being mowed down by the fire of the artillery, came fast up the causeway. The Irish dragoons who had run away in the morning were smitten with another panic, and, without striking a blow, galloped from the field. The horse followed the example. Such was the terror of the fugitives that many of them spurred hard till their beasts fell down, and then continued to fly on foot, throwing away carbines, swords, and even coats, as incumbrances. The infantry, seeing themselves deserted, flung down their pikes and muskets and ran for their lives. The conquerors now gave loose to that ferocity which has seldom failed to disgrace the civil wars of Ireland. The butchery was terrible. Near fifteen hundred of the vanquished were put to the sword. About five hundred more, in ignorance of the country, took a road which led to Lough Erne. The lake was before them; the enemy behind: they plunged into the waters and perished there. Macarthy, abandoned by his troops, rushed into the midst of the pursuers, and very nearly found the death which he sought. He was wounded in several places: he was struck to the ground; and in another moment his brains would have been knocked out with the butt end of a musket, when he was recognized and saved. The colonists lost only twenty men killed and fifty wounded. They took four hundred prisoners, seven pieces of cannon, fourteen barrels of powder, all the drums and all the colors of the vanquished enemy.*

The battle of Newton Butler was won on the third day after the boom thrown over the Foyle was broken. At Strabane the news met the Celtic army which was retreating from Londonderry. All was terror and confusion: the tents were struck: the military stores were flung by wagon loads into the waters of the Mourne; and the dismayed Irish, leaving many sick and wounded to the mercy of the victorious Protestants, fled to Omagh, and thence to

---

* Hamilton's True Relation; Mac Cormick's Further Account; London Gazette, Aug. 22, 1689; Life of James, ii. 368, 369; Avaux to Lewis, Aug. 4-14, and to Louvois of the same date. Story mentions a report that the panic among the Irish was caused by the mistake of an officer who called out "Right about face" instead of "Right face." Neither Avaux nor James had heard anything about this mistake. Indeed the dragoons who set the example of flight were not in the habit of waiting for orders to turn their backs on an enemy. They had run away once before on that very day. Avaux gives a very simple account of the defeat: "Ces mesmes dragons qui avoient fuy le matin laschèrent le pied avec tout le reste de la cavalerie, sans tirer un coup de pistolet; et ils s'enfuirent tous avec une telle épouvante qu'ils jettèrent mousquetons, pistolets, et espées; et la plupart d'eux, ayant crevè leurs chevaux, se dèshabillèrent pour aller plus viste à pied."

Charlemont. Sarsfield, who commanded at Sligo, found it necessary to abandon that town, which was instantly occupied by a detachment of Kirke's troops.* Dublin was in consternation. James dropped words which indicated an intention of flying to the Continent. Evil tidings indeed came fast upon him. Almost at the same time at which he learned that one of his armies had raised the siege of Londonderry, and that another had been routed at Newton Butler, he received intelligence scarcely less disheartening from Scotland.

It is now necessary to trace the progress of those events, to which Scotland owes her political and her religious liberty, her prosperity, and her civilization.

CHAPTER XIII.—(1689-'90.)

THE violence of revolutions is generally proportioned to the degree of the maladministration which has produced them. It is therefore not strange that the government of Scotland, having been during many years far more oppressive and corrupt than the government of England, should have fallen with a far heavier ruin. The movement against the last king of the House of Stuart was in England conservative, in Scotland destructive. The English complained, not of the law, but of the violation of the law. They rose up against the first magistrate merely in order to assert the supremacy of the law. They were for the most part strongly attached to the Church established by law. Even in applying that extraordinary remedy to which an extraordinary emergency compelled them to have recourse, they deviated as little as possible from the ordinary methods prescribed by the law. The convention which met at Westminster, though summoned by irregular writs, was constituted on the exact model of a regular Great Council of the Realm. No man was invited to the Upper House whose right to sit there was not clear. The knights and burgesses of the Lower House were chosen by those electors who would have been entitled to send members to a Parliament called under the great zeal. The franchises of the forty shilling freeholder, of the house-

---

* Hamilton's True Relation.

holder paying scot and lot, of the burgage tenant, of the liveryman of London, of the Master of Arts of Oxford, were respected. The sense of the constituent bodies was taken with as little violence on the part of mobs, with as little trickery on the part of returning officers, as at any general election of that age. When at length the Estates met, their deliberations were carried on with perfect freedom and in strict accordance with ancient forms. There was indeed, after the first flight of James, an alarming anarchy in London and in some parts of the country. But that anarchy nowhere lasted longer than forty-eight hours. From the day on which William reached Saint James's, not even the most unpopular agents of the fallen government, not even the ministers of the Roman Catholic Church, had anything to fear from the fury of the populace.

In Scotland the course of events was very different. There the law itself was a grievance; and James had perhaps incurred more unpopularity by enforcing it than by violating it. The Church established by law was the most odious institution in the realm. The tribunals had pronounced some sentences so flagitious, the Parliament had passed some Acts so oppressive, that, unless those sentences and those Acts were treated as nullities, it would be impossible to bring together a convention commanding the public respect and expressing the public opinion. It was hardly to be expected, for example, that the Whigs, in this day of their power, would endure to see their hereditary leader, the son of a martyr, the grandson of a martyr, excluded from the Parliament House in which nine of his ancestors had sate as Earls of Argyle, and excluded by a judgment on which the whole kingdom cried shame. Still less was it to be expected that they would suffer the election of members for counties and towns to be conducted according to the provisions of the existing law. For under the existing law no elector could vote without swearing that he renounced the covenant, and that he acknowledged the royal supremacy in matters ecclesiastical.* Such an oath no rigid Presbyterian could take. If such an oath had been exacted, the constituent bodies would have been merely small knots of prelatists: the business of devising securities against oppression would have been left to the oppressors; and the great party which had been

---
* Act Parl. Scot., Aug. 31, 1681.

most active in effecting the revolution would, in an assembly sprung from the revolution, have had not a single representative.*

William saw that he must not think of paying to the laws of Scotland that scrupulous respect which he had wisely and righteously paid to the laws of England. It was absolutely necessary that he should determine by his own authority how that Convention which was to meet at Edinburgh should be chosen, and that he should assume the power of annulling some judgments and some statutes. He accordingly summoned to the Parliament House several Lords who had been deprived of their honors by sentences which the general voice loudly condemned as unjust; and he took on himself to dispense with the Act which deprived Presbyterians of the elective franchise.

The consequence was that the choice of almost all the shires and burghs fell on Whig candidates. The defeated party complained loudly of foul play, of the rudeness of the populace, and of the partiality of the presiding magistrates; and these complaints were in many cases well founded. It is not under such rulers as Lauderdale and Dundee that nations learn justice and moderation.†

Nor was it only at the elections that the popular feeling so long and so severely compressed, exploded with violence. The heads and the hands of the martyred Whigs were taken down from the gates of Edinburgh, carried in procession by great multitudes to the cemeteries, and laid in the earth with solemn respect.‡ It would have been well if the public enthusiasm had manifested itself in no less praiseworthy form. Unhappily, throughout a large part of Scotland the clergy of the Established Church were, to use the phrase then common, rabbled. The morning of Christmas day was fixed for the commencement of these outrages. For nothing disgusted the rigid Covenanter more than the reverence paid by the prelatist to the ancient holidays of the Church. That such reverence may be carried to an absurd extreme is true. But a philosopher may perhaps be inclined to think the opposite extreme not less absurd, and may ask why religion should reject the aid of associations which exist in every nation

---

* Balcarras's Memoirs; Short History of the Revolution in Scotland in a letter from a Scotch gentleman in Amsterdam to his friend in London, 1712.
† Balcarras's Memoirs; Life of James, ii. 341.
‡ A Memorial for His Highness the Prince of Orange in Relation to the Affairs of Scotland, by two Persons of Quality, 1689.

sufficiently civilized to have a calendar, and which are found by experience to have a powerful and often a salutary effect. The Puritan, who was, in general, but too ready to follow precedents and analogies drawn from the history and jurisprudence of the Jews, might have found in the Old Testament quite as clear warrant for keeping festivals in honor of great events as for assassinating bishops and refusing quarter to captives. He certainly did not learn from his master, Calvin, to hold such festivals in abhorrence; for it was in consequence of the strenuous exertions of Calvin that Christmas was, after an interval of some years, again observed by the citizens of Geneva.* But there had arisen in Scotland Calvinists who were to Calvin what Calvin was to Laud. To these austere fanatics a holiday was an object of positive disgust and hatred. They long continued in their solemn manifestoes to reckon it among the sins which would one day bring down some fearful judgment on the land that the Court of Session took a vacation in the last week of December.†

On Christmas day, therefore, the Covenanters held armed musters by concert in many parts of the western shires. Each band marched to the nearest manse, and sacked the cellar and larder of the minister which at that season were probably better stocked than usual. The priest of Baal was reviled and insulted, sometimes beaten, sometimes ducked. His furniture was thrown out of the windows; his wife and children turned out of doors in the snow. He was then carried to the market-place, and exposed during some time as a malefactor. His gown was torn to shreds over his head; if he had a prayer book in his pocket it was burned; and he was dismissed with a charge, never, as he valued his life, to officiate in the parish again. The work of reformation having been thus completed, the reformers locked up the church and departed

---

* See Calvin's Letter to Haller, iv. Non. Jan. 1551: "Priusquam urbem unquam ingrederer, nullæ prorsus erant feriæ præter diem Dominicum. Ex quo sum revocatus hoc temperamentum quæsivi, ut Christi natalis celebraretur."

† In the Act, Declaration, and Testimony of the Seceders, dated in December, 1736, it is said that "countenance is given by authority of Parliament to the observation of Holidays in Scotland, by the vacation of our most considerable Courts of Justice in the latter end of December." This is declared to be a national sin, and a ground of the Lord's indignation. In March, 1758, the Associate Synod addressed a Solemn Warning to the nation, in which the same complaint was repeated. A poor crazy creature, whose nonsense has been thought worthy of being reprinted even in our own time, says: "I leave my testimony against the abominable Act of the pretended Queen Anne and her pretended British, really Brutish Parliament, for enacting the observance of that which is called the Yule Vacancy."—The Dying Testimony of William Wilson, sometime Schoolmaster in Park, in the Parish of Douglas, aged 68, who died in 1757.

with the keys. In fairness to these men it must be owned that they had suffered such oppression as may excuse, though it cannot justify, their violence; and that, though they were rude even to brutality, they do not appear to have been guilty of any intentional injury to life or limb.*

The disorder spread fast. In Ayrshire, Clydesdale, Nithisdale, Annandale, every parish was visited by these turbulent zealots. About two hundred curates,—so the episcopal parish priests were called,—were expelled. The graver Covenanters, while they applauded the fervor of their riotous brethren, were apprehensive that proceedings so irregular might give scandal, and learned, with especial concern, that here and there an Achan had disgraced the good cause by stooping to plunder the Canaanites whom he ought only to have smitten. A general meeting of ministers and elders was called for the purpose of preventing such discreditable excesses. In this meeting it was determined that, for the future, the ejection of the established clergy should be performed in a more ceremonious manner. A form of notice was drawn up and served on every curate in the Western Lowlands who had not yet been rabbled. This notice was simply a threatening letter commanding him to quit his parish peaceably, on pain of being turned out by force.†

The Scottish bishops, in great dismay, sent the Dean of Glasgow to plead the cause of their persecuted Church at Westminster. The outrages committed by the Covenanters were in the highest degree offensive to William, who had, in the south of the island, protected even Benedictines and Franciscans from insult and spoliation. But, though he had at the request of a large number of the noblemen and gentlemen of Scotland, taken on himself provisionally the executive administration of that kingdom, the means of maintaining order there were not at his command. He had not a single regiment north of the Tweed, or indeed within many miles of that river. It was vain to hope that mere words would quiet a nation which had not, in any age, been very amenable to control, and which was now agitated by hopes and resentments, such as great revolutions, following great oppressions, naturally engender.

---

* An Account of the Present Persecution of the Church in Scotland, in several Letters, 1690; The Case of the afflicted Clergy in Scotland, truly represented, 1690; Faithful Contendings Displayed. Burnet, i. 805.

† The form of notice will be found in the book entitled Faithful Contendings Displayed.

A proclamation was however put forth, directing that all people should lay down their arms, and that, till the Convention should have settled the government, the clergy of the Established Church should be suffered to reside on their cures without molestation. But this proclamation, not being supported by troops, was little regarded. On the very day after it was published at Glasgow, the venerable cathedral of that city, almost the only fine church of the middle ages which stands uninjured in Scotland, was attacked by a crowd of Presbyterians from the meeting houses, with whom were mingled many of their fiercer brethren from the hills. It was a Sunday: but to rabble a congregation of prelatists was held to be a work of necessity and mercy. The worshippers were dispersed, beaten, and pelted with snowballs. It was indeed asserted that some wounds were inflicted with much more formidable weapons.*

Edinburgh, the seat of government, was in a state of anarchy. The Castle, which commanded the whole city, was still held for James by the Duke of Gordon. The common people were generally Whigs. The College of Justice, a great forensic society composed of judges, advocates, writers to the signet, and solicitors, was the stronghold of Toryism: for a rigid test had during some years excluded Presbyterians from all the departments of the legal profession. The lawyers, some hundreds in number, formed themselves into a battalion of infantry, and for a time effectually kept down the multitude. They paid, however, so much respect to William's authority as to disband themselves when his proclamation was published. But the example of obedience which they had set was not imitated. Scarcely had they laid down their weapons when Covenanters from the west, who had done all that was to be done in the way of pelting and hustling the curates of their own neighborhood, came dropping into Edinburgh, by tens and twenties, for the purpose of protecting, or, if need should be, of overawing the Convention. Glasgow alone sent four hundred of these men. It could hardly be doubted that they were directed by some leader of great weight. They showed themselves little in any public place: but it was known that every cellar was filled

---

* Account of the Present Persecution, 1690. Case of the afflicted Clergy, 1690; A true Account of that Interruption that was made of the service of God on Sunday last, being the 17th of February, 1689, signed by James Gibson, Acting for the Lord Provost of Glasgow.

witn them: and it might well be apprehended that, at the first signal, they would pour forth from their caverns, and appear armed around the Parliament House.*

It might have been expected that every patriotic and enlightened Scotchman would have earnestly desired to see the agitation appeased, and some government established which might be able to protect property and to enforce the law. An imperfect settlement which could be speedily made might well appear to such a man preferable to a perfect settlement which must be the work of time. Just at this moment, however, a party, strong both in numbers and abilities, raised a new and most important question, which seemed not unlikely to prolong the interregnum till the autumn. This party maintained that the Estates ought not immediately to declare William and Mary King and Queen, but to propose to England a treaty of union, and to keep the throne vacant till such a treaty should be concluded on terms advantageous to Scotland.†

It may seem strange that a large portion of a people, whose patriotism, exhibited, often in a heroic, and sometimes in a comic form, has long been proverbial, should have been willing, nay impatient, to surrender an independence which had been, through many ages, dearly prized and manfully defended. The truth is that the stubborn spirit which the arms of the Plantagenets and Tudors had been unable to subdue had begun to yield to a very different kind of force. Custom-houses and tariffs were rapidly doing what the carnage of Falkirk and Halidon, of Flodden, and of Pinkie, had failed to do. Scotland had some experience of the effects of a union. She had, near forty years before, been united to England on such terms as England, flushed with conquest, chose to dictate. That union was inseparably associated in the minds of the vanquishsd people with defeat and humiliation. And yet even that union, cruelly as it had wounded the pride of the Scots, had promoted their prosperity. Cromwell, with wisdom and liberality rare in his age, had established the most complete freedom of trade between the dominant and the subject country. While he governed, no prohibition, no duty, impeded the transit of commodities from any part of the island to any other. His navigation laws imposed no restraint on the trade of Scotland. A Scotch vessel was at liberty to carry a Scotch cargo to Barbadoes,

---

* Balcarras's Memoirs; Mackay's Memoirs. † Burnet, ii. 21.

and to bring the sugars of Barbadoes into the port of London.* The rule of the Protector, therefore, had been propitious to the industry and to the physical well-being of the Scottish people. Hating him and cursing him, they could not help thriving under him, and often, during the administration of their legitimate princes, looked back with regret to the golden days of the usurper.†

The Restoration came, and changed everything. The Scots regained their independence, and soon began to find that independence had its discomfort as well as its dignity. The English Parliament treated them as aliens and as rivals. A new Navigation Act put them on almost the same footing with the Dutch. High duties, and in some case prohibitory duties, were imposed on the products of Scottish industry. It is not wonderful that a nation eminently industrious, shrewd, and enterprising, a nation which, having been long kept back by a sterile soil and a severe climate, was just beginning to prosper in spite of these disadvantages, and which found its progress suddenly stopped, should think itself cruelly treated. Yet there was no help. Complaint was vain. Retaliation was impossible. The sovereign, even if he had the wish, had not the power, to bear himself evenly between his large and his small kingdom, between the kingdom from which he drew an annual revenue of a million and a half and the kingdom from which he drew an annual revenue of little more than sixty thousand pounds. He dared neither to refuse his assent to any English law injurious to the trade of Scotland, nor to give his assent to any Scotch law injurious to the trade of England.

The complaints of the Scotch, however, were so loud that Charles, in 1667, appointed commissioners to arrange

---

* Scobel, 1654, cap. 9; and Oliver's Ordinance in Council of the 12th of April in the same year.

† Burnet and Fletcher of Saltoun mention the prosperity of Scotland under the Protector, but ascribe it to a cause quite inadequate to the production of such an effect. "There was," says Burnet, "a considerable force of about seven or eight thousand men kept in Scotland. The pay of the army brought so much money into the Kingdom that it continued all that while in a very flourishing state. . . . . . We always reckon those eight years of usurpation a time of great peace and prosperity." "During the time of the usurper Cromwell," says Fletcher, "we imagined ourselves to be in a tolerable condition with respect to the last particular (trade and money) by reason of that expense which was made in the realm by those forces that kept us in subjection." The true explanation of the phenomenon about which Burnet and Fletcher blundered so grossly will be found in a pamphlet entitled, "Some seasonable and modest Thoughts partly occasioned by and partly concerning the Scotch East India Company," Edinburgh, 1696. See the proceedings of the Wednesday Club in Friday Street upon the subject of a Union with Scotland, December 1705. See also the seventh Chapter of Mr. Burton's valuable History of Scotland.

the terms of a commercial treaty between the two British kingdoms. The conferences were soon broken off; and all that passed while they continued proved that there was only one way in which Scotland could obtain a share of the commercial prosperity which England at that time enjoyed.* The Scotch must become one people with the English. The parliament which had hitherto sate at Edinburgh must be incorporated with the Parliament which sate at Westminster. The sacrifice could not but be painfully felt by a brave and haughty people, who had, during twelve generations, regarded the southern domination with deadly aversion, and whose hearts still swelled at the thought of the death of Wallace and of the triumphs of Bruce. There were doubtless many punctilious patriots who would have strenuously opposed a union even if they could have foreseen that the effect of a union would be to make Glasgow a greater city than Amsterdam, and to cover the dreary Lothians with harvests and woods, neat farm-houses and stately mansions. But there was also a large class which was not disposed to throw away great and substantial advantages in order to preserve mere names and ceremonies; and the influence of this class was such that, in the year 1670, the Scotch Parliament made direct overtures to England.† The King undertook the office of mediator; and negotiators were named on both sides; but nothing was concluded.

The question, having slept during eighteen years, was suddenly revived by the Revolution. Different classes, impelled by different motives, concurred on this point. With merchants, eager to share in the advantages of the West Indian Trade, were joined active and aspiring politicians who wished to exhibit their abilities in a more conspicuous theater than the Scottish Parliament House, and to collect riches from a more copious source than the Scottish treasury. The cry for union was swelled by the voices of some artful Jacobites, who merely wished to cause discord and delay, and who hoped to attain this end by mixing up with the difficult question which it was the especial business of the Convention to settle another question more difficult still. It is probable that some who disliked the ascetic habits and rigid discipline of the Presby-

---
* See the paper in which the demands of the Scotch Commissioners are set forth. It will be found in the Appendix to De Foe's History of the Union, No. 13.
* Act, Parl. Scot., July 30, 1670

terians, wished for a union as the only mode of maintaining prelacy in the northern part of the island. In a united Parliament the English members must greatly preponderate; and in England the bishops were held in high honor by the great majority of the population. The Episcopal Church of Scotland, it was plain, rested on a narrow basis, and would fall before the first attack. The Episcopal Church of Great Britain might have a foundation broad and solid enough to withstand all assaults.

Whether, in 1689, it would have been possible to effect a civil union without a religious union may well be doubted. But there can be no doubt that a religious union would have been one of the greatest calamities that could have befallen either kingdom. The union accomplished in 1707 has indeed been a great blessing both to England and to Scotland. But it has been a blessing because, in constituting one State, it left two churches. The political interest of the contracting parties was the same: but the ecclesiastical dispute between them was one which admitted of no compromise. They could therefore preserve harmony only by agreeing to differ. Had there been an amalgamation of the hierarchies, there never would have been an amalgamation of the nations. Successive Mitchells would have fired at successive Sharpes. Five generations of Claverhouses would have butchered five generations of Camerons. Those marvellous improvements which have changed the face of Scotland would never have been effected. Plains now rich with harvests would have remained barren moors. Waterfalls which now turn the wheels of immense factories, would have resounded in a wilderness. New Lanark would still have been a sheep-walk, and Greenock a fishing hamlet. What little strength Scotland could, under such a system, have possessed, must, in an estimate of the resources of Great Britain, have been, not added, but deducted. So encumbered, our country never could have held, either in peace or in war, a place in the first rank of nations. We are unfortunately not without the means of judging of the effect which may be produced on the moral and physical state of a people by establishing, in the exclusive enjoyment of riches and dignity, a Church loved and reverenced only by the few, and regarded by the many with religious and national aversion. One such Church is quite burden enough for the energies of one empire.

But these things, which to us, who have been taught by a bitter experience, seem clear, were by no means clear in 1689, even to very tolerant and enlightened politicians. In truth the English Low Churchmen were, if possible, more anxious than the English High Churchmen to preserve Episcopacy in Scotland. It is a remarkable fact that Burnet, who was always accused of wishing to establish the Calvinistic discipline in the south of the island, incurred great unpopularity among his own countrymen by his efforts to uphold prelacy in the north. He was doubtless in error: but his error is to be attributed to a cause which does him no discredit. His favorite object, an object unattainable indeed, yet such as might well fascinate a large intellect and a benevolent heart, had long been an honorable treaty between the Anglican Church and the Nonconformists. He thought it most unfortunate that one opportunity of concluding such a treaty should have been lost at the time of the Restoration. It seemed to him that another opportunity was afforded by the Revolution. He and his friends were eagerly pushing forward Nottingham's Comprehension Bill, and were flattering themselves with vain hopes of success. But they felt that there could hardly be a Comprehension in one of the two British kingdoms, unless there were also a Comprehension in the other. Concession must be purchased by concession. If the Presbyterian pertinaciously refused to listen to any terms of compromise where he was strong, it would be almost impossible to obtain for him liberal terms of compromise where he was weak. Bishops must therefore be allowed to keep their sees in Scotland, in order that divines not ordained by bishops might be allowed to hold rectories and canonries in England.

Thus the cause of the Episcopalians in the north and the cause of the Presbyterians in the south were bound up together in a manner which might well perplex even a skillful statesman. It was happy for our country that the momentous question which excited so many strong passions, and which presented itself in so many different points of views, was to be decided by such a man as William. He listened to Episcopalians, to Latitudinarians, to Presbyterians, to the Dean of Glasgow, who pleaded for the apostolic succession, to Burnet, who represented the danger of alienating the Anglican clergy, to Carstairs who hated prelacy with the hatred of a man whose thumbs were deeply marked by the screws of prelatists. Surrounded by these eager advocates, William remained calm and impartial. He was indeed eminently qualified by his situation as well as by his personal qualities to be the umpire in that great contention. He was the King of a prelatical kingdom. He was the Prime Minister of a Presbyterian republic. His unwillingness to offend the Anglican Church of which he was the head, and his unwillingness to offend the reformed churches of the continent which regarded him as a champion divinely sent to protect them against the French tyranny, balanced each other, and kept him from leaning unduly to either side. His conscience was perfectly neutral. For it was his deliberate opinion that no form of ecclesiastical polity was of divine institution. He dissented equally from the school of Laud and from the school of Cameron, from the men who held there could not be a Christian Church without bishops, and from the men who held that there could not be a Christian Church without synods. Which form of government should be adopted was in his judgment a question of mere expediency. He would probably have preferred a temper between the two rival systems, a hierarchy in which the chief spiritual functionaries should have been something more than moderators and something less than prelates. But he was far too wise a man to think of settling such a matter according to his own personal tastes. He determined therefore that, if there was on both sides a disposition to compromise, he would act as mediator. But, if it should appear that the public mind of England and the public mind of Scotland had taken the ply strongly in opposite directions, he would not attempt to force either nation into conformity with the opinion of the other. He would suffer each to have its own church, and would content himself with restraining both churches from persecuting nonconformists, and from encroaching on the functions of the civil magistrate.

The language which he held to those Scottish Episcopalians who complained to him of their sufferings and implored his protection was well weighed and well guarded, but clear and ingenuous. He wished, he said, to preserve, if possible, the institution to which they were so much attached, and to grant, at the same time, entire liberty of conscience to that party which could not be reconciled to any deviation from the Presbyterian model. But the bishops must take care that they did not, by their own rashness and obstinacy, put it out of his power to be of any use to them. They must also distinctly understand that he was resolved not to force on Scotland by the sword a form of ecclesiastical government which she detested. If, therefore, it should be found that prelacy could be maintained only by arms, he should yield to the general sentiment, and should merely do his best to obtain for the Episcopalian minority permission to worship God in freedom and safety.*

It is not likely that, even if the Scottish bishops had, as William recommended, done all that meekness and prudence could do to conciliate their countrymen, episcopacy could, under any modification, have been maintained. It was indeed asserted by writers of that generation, and has been repeated by writers of our generation, that the Presbyterians were not, before the revolution, the majority of the people of Scotland.† But in this assertion there is an obvious fallacy. The effective strength of sects is not to be ascertained merely by counting heads. An established church, a dominant church, a church which has the exclusive possession of civil honors and emoluments, will always rank among its nominal members multitudes who have no religion at all; multitudes who, though not destitute of religion, attend little to theological disputes, and have no scruple about conforming to the mode of worship which happens to be established; and multitudes who have scruples about conforming, but whose scruples have yielded to worldly motives. On the other hand, every member of an oppressed church is a man who has a very decided preference for that church. Every person who, in the time of Diocletian, joined in celebrating the Christian mysteries might reasonably be supposed to be a firm believer in Christ. But it may well be doubted whether one single Pontiff or Augur in the Roman Senate was a firm believer in Jupiter. In Mary's reign, everybody who attended the secret meetings of the Protestants was a real Protestant: but hundreds of thousands went to mass who, as appeared before she had been dead a month, were not

---

* Burnet, ii. 23

† See, for example, a pamphlet entitled "Some questions resolved concerning Episcopal and Presbyterian government in Scotland, 1690." One of the questions is, whether Scottish presbytery be agreeable to the general inclinations of that people. The author answers the question in the negative, on the ground that the upper and middle classes had generally conformed to the Episcopal Church before the Revolution.

real Roman Catholics. If, under the kings of the House of Stuart, when a Presbyterian was excluded from political power and from the learned professions, was daily annoyed by informers, by tyrannical magistrates, by licentious dragoons, and was in danger of being hanged if he heard a sermon in the open air, the population of Scotland was not very unequally divided between Episcopalians and Presbyterians, the rational inference is that more than nineteen-twentieths of those Scotchmen whose conscience was interested in the matter were Presbyterians, and that the Scotchmen, who were decidedly and on conviction Episcopalians, were a small minority. Against such odds the bishops had but little chance; and whatever chance they had they made haste to throw away; some of them because they sincerely believed that their allegiance was still due to James; others probably because they apprehended that William would not have the power, even if he had the will, to serve them, and that nothing but a counter revolution in the State could avert a revolution in the Church.

As the new King of England could not be at Edinburgh during the sitting of the Scottish Convention, a letter from him to the Estates was prepared with great skill. In this document he professed warm attachment to the Protestant religion, but gave no opinion touching those questions about which Protestants were divided. He had observed, he said, with great satisfaction that many of the Scottish nobility and gentry with whom he had conferred in London were inclined to a union of the two British kingdoms. He was sensible how much such a union would conduce to the happiness of both; and he would do all in his power towards the accomplishing of so good a work.

It was necessary that he should allow a large discretion to his confidential agents at Edinburgh. The private instructions with which he furnished those persons could not be minute, but were highly judicious. He charged them to ascertain to the best of their power the real sense of the Convention, and to be guided by it. They must remember that the first object was to settle the government. To that object every other object, even the union, must be postponed. A treaty between two independent legislatures, distant from each other several days' journey, must necessarily be a work of time; and the throne could not safely remain vacant while the negotiations were pending. It was therefore important that His Majesty's agents should be on their guard against the arts of persons who, under pretence of promoting the union, might really be contriving only to prolong the interregnum. If the Convention should be bent on establishing the Presbyterian form of church government, William desired that his friends would do all in their power to prevent the triumphant sect from retaliting what it had suffered.*

The person by whose advice William appears to have been at this time chiefly guided as to Scotch politics was a Scotchman of great abilities and attainments, Sir James Dalrymple, of Stair, the founder of a family eminently distinguished at the bar, on the bench, in the Senate, in diplomacy, in arms, and in letters, but distinguished also by misfortunes and misdeeds which have furnished poets and novelists with materials for the darkest and most heart-rending tales. Already Sir James had been in mourning for more than one strange and terrible death. One of his sons had died by poison. One of his daughters had poniarded her bridegroom on the wedding night. One of his grandsons had in boyish sport been slain by another. Savage libellers asserted, and some of the superstitious vulgar believed, that calamities so portentous were the consequences of some connection between the unhappy race and the powers of darkness. Sir James had a wry neck; and he was reproached with this misfortune as if it had been a crime, and was told that it marked him out as a man doomed to the gallows. His wife, a woman of great ability, art, and spirit, was popularly nicknamed the Witch of Endor. It was gravely said that she had cast fearful spells on those whom she hated, and that she had been seen in the likeness of a cat seated on the cloth of state by the side of the Lord High Commissioner. The man, however, over whose roof so many curses appeared to hang, did not, as far as we can now judge, fall short of that very low standard of morality which was generally attained by politicians of his age and nation. In force of mind and extent of knowledge he was superior to them all. In his youth he had borne arms: he had then been a professor of philosophy: he had then studied law, and had become, by general ac-

---

* The instructions are in the Leven and Melville papers. They bear date March 7, 1688-9. On the first occasion on which I quote this most valuable collection, I cannot refrain from acknowledging the obligations under which I, and all who take an interest in the history of our island, lie to the gentleman who has performed so well the duty of an editor.

knowledgment, the greatest jurist that his country had
produced. In the days of the Protectorate, he had been
a judge. After the Restoration, he had made his peace
with the royal family, had sate in the Privy Council, and
had presided with unrivalled ability in the Court of Session.
He had doubtless borne a share in many unjustifiable
acts: but there were limits which he never passed.
He had a wonderful power of giving to any proposition
which it suited him to maintain a plausible aspect of legality
and even of justice; and this power he frequently
abused. But he was not, like many of those among whom
he lived, impudently and unscrupulously servile. Shame
and conscience generally restrained him from committing
any bad action for which his rare ingenuity could not
frame a specious defence; and he was seldom in his place
at the council boards when anything outrageously unjust
or cruel was to be done. His moderation at length gave
offence to the Court. He was deprived of his high office,
and found himself in so disagreeable a situation that he
retired to Holland. There he employed himself in correcting
the great work on jurisprudence which has preserved
his memory fresh down to our own time. In his
banishment he tried to gain the favor of his fellow exiles,
who naturally regarded him with suspicion. He protested,
and perhaps with truth, that his hands were pure
from the blood of the persecuted Covenanters. He made a
high profession of religion, prayed much, and observed
weekly days of fasting and humiliation. He even consented,
after much hesitation, to assist with his advice and
his credit the unfortunate enterprise of Argyle. When
that enterprise had failed, a prosecution was instituted at
Edinburgh against Dalrymple; and his estates would
doubtless have been confiscated, had they not been saved
by an artifice which subsequently became common among
the politicians of Scotland. His eldest son and heir apparent,
John, took the side of the government, supported the
dispensing power, declared against the Test, and accepted
the place of Lord Advocate, when Sir George Mackenzie,
after holding out through ten years of foul drudgery, at
length showed signs of flagging. The services of the
younger Dalrymple were rewarded by a remission of the
forfeiture which the offences of the elder had incurred.
Those services indeed were not to be despised. For Sir
John, though inferior to his father in depth and extent of

legal learning, was no common man. His knowledge was
great and various: his parts were quick; and his eloquence
was singularly ready and graceful. To sanctity he made
no pretensions. Indeed Episcopalians and Presbyterians
agreed in regarding him as little better than an atheist.
During some months Sir John at Edinburgh affected to
condemn the disloyalty of his unhappy parent, Sir James;
and Sir James, at Leyden, told his Puritan friends how
deeply he lamented the wicked compliances of his unhappy
child Sir John.

The Revolution came, and brought a large increase of
wealth and honors to the House of Stair. The son
promptly changed sides, and co-operated ably and zealously with the father. Sir James established himself in
London for the purpose of giving advice to William on
Scotch affairs. Sir John's post was in the Parliament
House at Edinburgh. He was not likely to find any equal
among the debaters there, and was prepared to exert all
his powers against the dynasty which he had lately
served.*

By the large party which was zealous for the Calvinistic
church government John Dalrymple was regarded with
incurable distrust and dislike. It was therefore necessary
that another agent should be employed to manage that
party. Such an agent was George Melville, Lord Melville,
a nobleman connected by affinity with the unfortunate
Monmouth, and with that Leslie who had, in 1640, invaded
England at the head of a Scottish army. Melville had always been accounted a Whig and a Presbyterian. Those
who speak of him most favorably have not ventured to
ascribe to him eminent intellectual endowment or exalted
public spirit. But he appears from his letters to have been
by no means deficient in that homely prudence the want
of which has often been fatal to men of brighter genius and of
purer virtue. That prudence had restrained him from going very far in opposition to the tyranny of the Stuarts:
but he had listened while his friends talked about resistance, and therefore, when the Rye House Plot was discovered, thought it expedient to retire to the continent. In

---

* As to the Dalrymples, see the Lord President's own writings, and among them his
Vindication of the Divine Perfections; Wodrow's Analecta; Douglas's Peerage; Lockhart's Memoirs; the Satyre on the Familie of Stairs; the Satyric Lines upon the long
wished for and timely Death of the Right Honourable Lady Stairs; Law's Memorials;
and the Hyndford Papers, written in 1704-5, and printed with the Letters of Carstairs.
Lockhart, though a mortal enemy of John Dalrymple, says, "There was none in the
parliament capable to take up the cudgels with him."

his absence he was accused of treason, and was convicted on evidence which would not have satisfied any impartial tribunal. He was condemned to death: his honor and lands were declared forfeit: his arms were torn with contumely out of the Heralds' Book; and his domains swelled the estate of the cruel and rapacious Perth. The fugitive, meanwhile, with characteristic wariness, lived quietly on the Continent, and discountenanced the unhappy projects of his kinsman Monmouth, but cordially approved of the enterprise of the Prince of Orange.

Illness had prevented Melville from sailing with the Dutch expedition: but he arrived in London a few hours after the new Sovereigns had been proclaimed there. William instantly sent him down to Edinburgh, in the hope, as it should seem, that the Presbyterians would be disposed to listen to moderate counsels proceeding from a man who was attached to their cause, and who had suffered for it. Melville's second son, David, who had inherited, through his mother, the title of Earl of Leven, and who had acquired some military experience in the service of the Elector of Brandenburgh, had the honor of being the bearer of a letter from the new King of England to the Scottish Convention.*

James had entrusted the conduct of his affairs in Scotland to John Graham, Viscount Dundee and Colin Lindsay, Earl of Balcarras. Dundee had commanded a body of Scottish troops which had marched into England to oppose the Dutch: but he had found, in the inglorious campaign which had been fatal to the dynasty of Stuart, no opportunity of displaying the courage and military skill which those who most detest his merciless nature allow him to have possessed. He lay with his forces not far from Watford, when he was informed that James had fled from Whitehall and that Feversham had ordered all the royal army to disband. The Scottish regiments were thus left, without pay or provisions, in the midst of a foreign and indeed a hostile nation. Dundee, it is said, wept with grief and rage. Soon, however, more cheering intelligence arrived from various quarters. William wrote a few lines to say that, if the Scots would remain quiet, he would pledge his honor for their safety; and, some hours later, it was known that James had returned

* As to Melville, see the Leven and Melville Papers, *passim*, and the preface; the Act Parl. Scot., June 16, 1685; and the Appendix, June 13, Burnet, ii. 24; and the Burnet MS. Harl. 6584

to his capital. Dundee repaired instantly to London.*
There he met his friend Balcarras, who had just arrived
from Edinburgh. Balcarras, a man distinguished by his
handsome person and by his accomplishments, had, in his
youth, affected the character of a patriot, but had deserted
the popular cause, had accepted a seat in the Privy Council, had become a tool of Perth and Melfort, and had been
one of the commissioners who were appointed to execute
the office of Treasurer, when Queensbury was disgraced
for refusing to betray the interests of the Protestant religion.†

Dundee and Balcarras went together to Whitehall, and
had the honor of accompanying James in his last walk up
and down the Mall. He told them that he intended to put
his affairs in Scotland under their management. "You, my
Lord Balcarras, must undertake the civil business: and
you, my Lord Dundee, shall have a commission from me
to command the troops." The two noblemen vowed that
they would prove themselves deserving of his confidence,
and disclaimed all thought of making their peace with the
Prince of Orange.‡

On the following day James left Whitehall forever; and
the Prince of Orange arrived at Saint James's. Both Dundee and Balcarras swelled the crowd which thronged to
greet the deliverer, and were not ungraciously received.
Both were well known to him. Dundee had served under
him on the continent;§ and the first wife of Balcarras had
been a lady of the House of Orange, and had worn on

---

* Creichton's Memoirs. † Mackay's Memoirs.
‡ Memoirs of the Lindsays.
§ About the early relation between William and Dundee, some Jacobite, many years after they were both dead, invented a story which by successive embellishments was at last improved into a romance such as it seems strange that even a child should believe to be true. The last edition runs thus: William's horse was killed under him at Seneff, and his life was in imminent danger. Dundee, then Captain Graham, mounted His Highness again. William promised to reward this service with promotion, but broke his word, and gave to another the commission which Graham had been led to expect. The injured hero went to Loo. There he met his successful competitor and gave him a box on the ear. The punishment for striking in the palace was the loss of the offending right hand; but this punishment the Prince of Orange ungraciously remitted. "You," he said, "saved my life; I spare your right hand; and now we are quits."

Those who, down to our time, have repeated this nonsense seem to have thought, first, that the Act of Henry the Eighth "for punishment of murder and malicious bloodshed within the King's Court" (Stat. 33 Hen. VIII. c. 2) was law in Guelders; and, secondly, that, in 1674, William was a King, and his house a King's Court. They were also not aware that he did not purchase Loo till long after Dundee had left the Netherlands. See Harris's Description of Loo, 1699.

This legend, of which I have not been able to discover the slightest trace in the voluminous Jacobite literature of William's reign, seems to have originated about a quarter of a century after Dundee's death, and to have attained its full absurdity in another quarter of a century.

her wedding day, a superb pair of emerald earrings, the gift of her cousin the Prince.*

The Scottish Whigs, then assembled in great uumbers at Westminster, earnestly pressed William to proscribe by name four or five men who had, during the evil times, borne a conspicuous part in the proceedings of the Privy Council at Edinburgh. Dundee and Balcarras were particularly mentioned. But the Prince had determined that, as far as his power extended, all the past should be covered with a general amnesty, and absolutely refused to make any declaration which could drive to despair even the most guilty of his uncle's servants.

Balcarras went repeatedly to Saint James's, had several audiences of William, professed deep respect for His Highness, and owned that King James had committed great errors, but would not promise to concur in a vote of deposition. William gave no signs of displeasure, but said at parting: "Take care, my Lord, that you keep within the law; for, if you break it, you must expect to be left to it."†

Dundee seems to have been less ingenuous. He employed the mediation of Burnet, opened a negotiation with Saint James's, declared himself willing to acquiesce in the new order of things, obtained from William a promise of protection, and promised in return to live peaceably. Such credit was given to his professions, that he was suffered to travel down to Scotland under the escort of a troop of cavalry. Without such an escort the man of blood, whose name was never mentioned but with a shudder at the hearth of any Presbyterian family, would, at that conjuncture, have had but a perilous journey through Berwickshire and the Lothians.‡

February was drawing to a close when Dundee and Balcarras reached Edinburgh. They had some hope that they might be at the head of a majority in the Convention. They therefore exerted themselves vigorously to consolidate and animate their party. They assured the rigid royalists, who had a scruple about sitting in an assembly convoked by an usurper, that the rightful King particularly wished no friend of hereditary monarchy to be absent. More than one waverer was kept steady by being assured, in confident terms, that a speedy restoration was inevita-

---

* Memoirs of the Lindsays. † Memoirs of the Lindsays.
‡ Burnet, ii. 22; Memoirs of the Lindsays.

able. Gordon had determined to surrender the Castle, and had begun to remove his furniture: but Dundee and Balcarras prevailed on him to hold out some time longer. They informed him that they had received from Saint Germains full powers to adjourn the Convention to Stirling, and that, if things went ill at Edinburgh, those powers would be used.*

At length the fourteenth of March, the day fixed for the meeting of the Estates, arrived, and the Parliament House was crowded. Nine prelates were in their places. When Argyle presented himself, a single lord protested against the admission of a person whom a legal sentence, passed in due form and still unreversed, had deprived of the honors of the peerage. But this objection was overruled by the general sense of the assembly. When Melville appeared, no voice was raised against his admission. The Bishop of Edinburgh officiated as chaplain, and made it one of his petitions that God would help and restore King James.† It soon appeared that the general feeling of the Convention was by no means in harmony with this prayer. The first matter to be decided was the choice of a president. The Duke of Hamilton was supported by the Whigs, the Marquess of Athol by the Jacobites. Neither candidate possessed, and neither deserved, the entire confidence of his supporters. Hamilton had been a Privy Councillor of James, had borne a part in many unjustifiable acts, and had offered but a very cautious and languid opposition to the most daring attacks on the laws and religion of Scotland. Not till the Dutch guards were at Whitehall had he ventured to speak out. Then he had joined the victorious party, and had assured the Whigs that he had pretended to be their enemy, only in order that he might, without incurring suspicion, act as their friend. Athol was still less to be trusted. His abilities were mean, his temper false, pusillanimous, and cruel. In the late reign he had gained a dishonorable notoriety by the barbarous actions of which he had been guilty in Argyleshire. He had turned with the turn of fortune, and had paid servile court to the Prince of Orange, but had been coldly received, and had now, from mere mortification, come back to the party

---

* Balcarras's Memoirs.

† Act Parl. Scot., Mar. 14, 1689; History of the late Revolution in Scotland, 1690; An Account of the Proceedings of the Estates of Scotland, fol. Lond. 1689.

which he had deserted.* Neither of the rival noblemen had chosen to stake the dignities and lands of his house on the issue of the contention between the rival kings. The eldest son of Hamilton had declared for James, and the eldest son of Athol for William, so that, in any event, both coronets and both estates were safe.

But in Scotland the fashionable notions touching political morality were lax; and the aristocratical sentiment was strong. The Whigs were therefore willing to forget that Hamilton had lately sate in the council of James. The Jacobites were equally willing to forget that Athol had lately fawned on William. In political inconsistency those two great lords were far indeed from standing by themselves: but in dignity and power they had scarcely an equal in the assembly. Their descent was eminently illustrious: their influence was immense: one of them could raise the Western Lowlands; the other could bring into the field an army of northern mountaineers. Round these chiefs therefore the hostile factions gathered.

The votes were counted; and it appeared that Hamilton had a majority of forty. The consequence was that about forty of the defeated party instantly passed over to the victors.† At Westminster such a defection would have been thought strange: but it seems to have caused little surprise at Edinburgh. It is a remarkable circumstance that the same country should have produced in the same age the most wonderful specimens of both extremes of human nature. No class of men mentioned in history has ever adhered to a principle with more inflexible pertinacity than was found among the Scotch Puritans. Fine and imprisonment, the shears and the branding iron, the boot, the thumbscrew, and the gallows could not extort from the stubborn Covenanter one evasive word on which it was possible to put a sense inconsistent with his theological system. Even in things indifferent he would hear of no compromise; and he was but too ready to consider all who recommended prudence and charity as traitors to the cause of truth. On the other hand, the Scotchmen of that generation who made a figure in the Parliament House and in the Council Chamber were the most dishonest and unblushing time-servers that the world has ever seen. The

* Balcarras's narrative exhibits both Hamilton and Athol in a most unfavorable light. See also the Life of James, ii. 338, 339.
† Act Parl. Scot., March 14th, 1688-9; Balcarras's Memoirs; History of the late Revolution in Scotland; Life of James, ii. 342.

English marvelled alike at both classes. There were many stout hearted non-conformists in the South; but scarcely any who in obstinacy, pugnacity, and hardihood could bear a comparison with the men of the school of Cameron. There were many knavish politicians in the South; but few so utterly destitute of morality, and still fewer so utterly destitute of shame, as the men of the school of Lauderdale. Perhaps it is natural that the most callous and impudent vice should be found in the near neighborhood of unreasonable and impracticable virtue. Where enthusiasts are ready to destroy or to be destroyed for trifles magnified into importance by a squeamish conscience, it is not strange that the very name of conscience should become a byword of contempt to cool and shrewd men of business.

The majority, reinforced by the crowd of deserters from the minority, proceeded to name a Committee of Elections. Ffteen persons were chosen, and it soon appeared that twelve of these were not disposed to examine severely into the regularity of any proceeding of which the result had been to send up a Whig to the Parliament House. The Duke of Hamilton is said to have been disgusted by the gross partiality of his own followers, and to have exerted himself, with but little success, to restrain their violence.*

Before the Estates proceeded to deliberate on the business for which they had met, they thought it necessary to provide for their own security. They could not be perfectly at ease while the roof under which they sate was commanded by the batteries of the Castle. A deputation was therefore sent to inform Gordon that the Convention required him to evacuate the fortress within twenty-four hours, and that if he complied, his past conduct should not be remembered against him. He asked a night for consideration. During that night his wavering mind was confirmed by the exhortations of Dundee and Balcarras. On the morrow he sent an answer drawn in respectful but evasive terms. He was very far, he declared, from meditating harm to the City of Edinburgh. Least of all could he harbor any thought of molesting an august assembly which he regarded with profound reverence. He would willingly give bond for his good behavior to the amount of twenty thousand pounds sterling. But he was in communication with the government now established in England. He was in hourly expectation of important des-

---

* Balcaras's Memoirs; History of the late Revoltion in Scotland, 1690.

patches from that government; and, till they arrived, he should not feel himself justified in resigning his command. These excuses were not admitted. Heralds and trumpeters were sent to summon the Castle in form, and to denounce the penalties of high treason against those who should continue to occupy that fortress in defiance of the authority of the Estates. Guards were at the same time posted to intercept all communication between the garrison and the city.*

Two days had been spent in these preludes, and it was expected that on the third morning the great contest would begin. Meanwhile the population of Edinburgh was in an excited state. It had been discovered that Dundee had paid visits to the Castle; and it was believed that his exhortations had induced the garrison to hold out. His own soldiers were known to be gathering round him; and it might well be apprehended that he would make some desperate attempt. He, on the other hand, had been informed that the Western Covenanters, who filled the cellars of the city, had vowed vengeance on him; and, in truth, when we consider that their temper was singularly savage and implacable, that they had been taught to regard the slaying of a persecutor as a duty, that no examples furnished by Holy Writ had been more frequently held up to their admiration than Ehud stabbing Eglon, and Samuel hewing Agag limb from limb; that they had never heard any achievement in the history of their own country more warmly praised by their favorite teachers than the butchery of Cardinal Beatoun and of Archbishop Sharpe, we may well wonder that a man who had shed the blood of the saints like water should have been able to walk the High Street in safety during a single day. The enemy whom Dundee had most reason to fear was a youth of distinguished courage and abilities named William Cleland. Cleland had, when little more than sixteen years old, borne arms in that insurrection which had been put down at Bothwell Bridge. He had since disgusted some virulent fanatics by his humanity and moderation. But with the great body of Presbyterians his name stood high. For with the strict morality and ardent zeal of a Puritan he united some accomplishments of which few Puritans could boast. His manners were polished, and his literary and

* Act Parl. Scot., March 14, and 15, 1689; Balcarras's Memoirs; London Gaz. March 25; History of the late Revolution in Scotland, 1690; Account of the Proceedings of the Estates of Scotland, 1689.

scientific attainments respectable. He was a linguist, a mathematician, and a poet. It is true that his hymns, odes, ballads, and Hudibrastic satires are of very little intrinsic value; but, when it is considered that he was a mere boy when most of them were written, it must be admitted that they show considerable vigor of mind. He was now at Edinburgh: his influence among the West Country Whigs assembled there was great: he hated Dundee with deadly hatred, and was believed to be meditating some act of violence.*

On the fifteenth of March Dundee received information that some of the Covenanters had bound themselves together to slay him and Sir George Mackenzie, whose eloquence and learning, long prostituted to the service of tyranny, had made him more odious to the Presbyterians than any other man of the gown. Dundee applied to Hamilton for protection; and Hamilton advised him to bring the matter under the consideration of the Convention at the next sitting.†

Before that sitting a person named Crane arrived from France with a letter addressed by the fugitive King to the Estates. The letter was sealed: the bearer, strange to say, was not furnished with a copy for the information of the heads of the Jacobite party; nor did he bring any message, written or verbal, to either of James's agents. Balcarras and Dundee were mortified by finding that so little confidence was reposed in them, and were harassed by painful doubts touching the contents of the document on which so much depended. They were willing, however, to hope for the best. King James could not, situated as he was, be so ill advised as to act in direct opposition to the counsel and entreaties of his friends. His letter, when opened,

---

* See Cleland's Poems, and the commendatory poems contained in the same volume, Edinburgh, 1697. It has been repeatedly asserted that this William Cleland was the father of William Cleland, the Commissioner of Taxes, who was well known twenty years later in the literary society of London, who rendered some not very reputable services to Pope, and whose son John was the author of an infamous book but too widely celebrated. This is an entire mistake. William Cleland, who fought at Bothwell Bridge, was not twenty-eight when he was killed in August 1689; and William Cleland, the Commissioner of Taxes, died at sixty-seven in September 1741. The former therefore cannot have been the father of the latter. See the Exact Narrative of the battle of Dunkeld; the Gentleman's Magazine for 1746; and Warburton's note on the Letter to the Publisher of the Dunciad, a letter signed W. Cleland, but really written by Pope. In a paper drawn up by Sir Robert Hamilton, the oracle of the extreme Covenanters, and a blood-thirsty ruffian, Cleland is mentioned as having been once leagued with those fanatics, but afterwards a great opposer of their testimony. Cleland probably did not agree with Hamilton in thinking it a sacred duty to cut the throats of prisoners of war who had been received to quarter. See Hamilton's Letter to the Societies, Dec. 7, 1685.

must be found to contain such gracious assurances as would animate the royalists and conciliate the moderate Whigs. His adherents, therefore, determined that it should be produced.

When the Convention reassembled on the morning of Saturday the sixteenth of March, it was proposed that measures should be taken for the personal security of the members. It was alleged that the life of Dundee had been threatened; that two men of sinister appearance had been watching the house where he lodged, and had been heard to say that they would use the dog as he had used them. Mackenzie complained that he too was in danger, and, with his usual copiousness and force of language, demanded the protection of the Estates. But the matter was lightly treated by the majority; and the Convention passed on to other business.*

It was then announced that Crane was at the door of the Parliament House. He was admitted. The paper of which he was in charge was laid on the table. Hamilton remarked that there was, in the hands of the Earl of Leven, a communication from the Prince by whose authority the Estates had been convoked. That communication seemed to be entitled to precedence. The Convention was of the same opinion; and the well-weighed and prudent letter of William was read.

It was then moved that the letter of James should be opened. The Whigs objected that it might possibly contain a mandate dissolving the Convention. They therefore proposed that, before the seal was broken, the Estates should resolve to continue sitting, notwithstanding any such mandate. The Jacobites, who knew no more than the Whigs what was in the letter, and were impatient to have it read, eagerly assented. A vote was passed by which the members bound themselves to consider any order which should command them to separate as a nullity, and to remain assembled till they should have accomplished the work of securing the liberty and religion of Scotland. This vote was signed by almost all the lords and gentlemen who were present. Seven out of nine bishops subscribed it. The names of Dundee and Balcarras, written by their own hands, may still be seen on

---

* Balcarras's Memoirs. But the fullest account of these proceedings is furnished by some manuscript notes which are in the library of the Faculty of Advocates. Balcarras's dates are not quite exact. He probably trusted to his memory for them. I have corrected them from the parliamentary record.

the original roll. Balcarras afterwards excused what, on his principles, was, beyond all dispute, a flagrant act of treason, by saying that he and his friends had, from zeal for their master's interest, concurred in a declaration of rebellion against their master's authority; that they had anticipated the most salutary effects from the letter; and that, if they had not made some concession to the majority, the letter would not have been opened.

In a few minutes the hopes of Balcarras were grievously disappointed. The letter from which so much had been hoped and feared was read with all the honors which Scottish Parliaments were in the habit of paying to royal communications: but every word carried despair to the hearts of the Jacobites. It was plain that adversity had taught James neither wisdom nor mercy. All was obstinacy, cruelty, insolence. A pardon was promised to those traitors who should return to their allegiance within a fortnight. Against all others unsparing vengeance was denounced. Not only was no sorrow expressed for past offences: but the letter was itself a new offence: for it was written and countersigned by the apostate Melfort, who was, by the statutes of the realm, incapable of holding the office of secretary, and who was not less abhorred by the Protestant Tories than by the Whigs. The hall was in a tumult. The enemies of James were loud and vehement. His friends, angry with him, and ashamed of him, saw that it was vain to think of continuing the struggle in the Convention. Every vote which had been doubtful when his letter was unsealed was now irrecoverably lost. The sitting closed in great agitation.*

It was Saturday afternoon. There was to be no other meeting till Monday morning. The Jacobite leaders held a consultation, and came to the conclusion that it was necessary to take a decided step. Dundee and Balcarras must use the powers with which they had been entrusted. The minority must forthwith leave Edinburgh and assemble at Stirling. Athol assented, and undertook to bring a great body of his clansmen from the Highlands to protect the deliberations of the Royalist Convention. Everything was arranged for the secession; but, in a few hours,

---

* Act. Parl. Scot., March 16, 1688-9; Balcarras's Memoirs; History of the late Revolution in Scotland, 1690; Account of the Proceedings of the Estates of Scotland, 1689; London Gaz., March 25, 1689; Life of James, ii. 342. Burnet blunders strangely about these transactions.

the tardiness of one man and the haste of another ruined the whole plan.

The Monday came. The Jacobite lords and gentlemen were actually taking horse for Stirling, when Athol asked for a delay of twenty-four hours. He had no personal reason to be in haste. By staying he ran no risk of being assassinated. By going he incurred the risks inseparable from civil war. The members of his party, unwilling to separate from him, consented to the postponement which he requested, and repaired once more to the Parliament House. Dundee alone refused to stay a moment longer. His life was in danger. The Convention had refused to protect him. He would not remain to be a mark for the pistols and daggers of murderers. Balcarras expostulated to no purpose. "By departing alone," he said, "you will give the alarm and break up the whole scheme." But Dundee was obstinate. Brave as he undoubtedly was, he seems, like many other brave men, to have been less proof against the danger of assassination than against any other form of danger. He knew what the hatred of the Covenanters was: he knew how well he had earned their hatred; and he was haunted by that consciousness of inexpiable guilt, and by that dread of a terrible retribution, which the ancient polytheists personified under the awful name of the Furies. His old troopers, the Satans and Beelzebubs, who had shared his crimes, and who now shared his perils, were ready to be the companions of his flight.

Meanwhile the Convention had assembled. Mackenzie was on his legs, and was pathetically lamenting the hard condition of the Estates, at once commanded by the guns of a fortress and menaced by a fanatical rabble, when he was interrupted by some sentinels who came running from the posts near the Castle. They had seen Dundee at the head of fifty horse on the Stirling road. That road ran close under the huge rock on which the citadel is built. Gordon had appeared on the ramparts, and had made a sign that he had something to say. Dundee had climbed high enough to hear and to be heard, and was then actually conferring with the Duke. Up to that moment the hatred with which the Presbyterian members of the assembly regarded the merciless persecutor of their brethren in the faith had been restrained by the decorous forms of parliamentary deliberation. But now the explosion was terrible. Hamilton himself, who, by the acknowledgment of his opponents, had hitherto performed the duties of president with gravity and impartiality, was the loudest and fiercest man in the hall. "It is high time," he cried, "that we should look to ourselves. The enemies of our religion and of our civil freedom are mustering all around us ; and we may well suspect that they have accomplices even here. Look at the doors. Lay the keys on the table. Let nobody go out but those lords and gentlemen whom we shall appoint to call the citizens to arms. There are some good men from the West of Edinburgh, men for whom I can answer." The assembly raised a general cry of assent. Several members of the majority boasted that they too had brought with them trusty retainers who would turn out at a moment's notice against Claverhouse and his dragoons. All that Hamilton proposed was instantly done. The Jacobites, silent and unresisting, became prisoners. Leven went forth and ordered the drums to beat. The Covenanters of Lanarkshire and Ayrshire promptly obeyed the signal. The force thus assembled had indeed no very military appearance, but was amply sufficient to overawe the adherents of the House of Stuart. From Dundee nothing was to be hoped or feared. He had already scrambled down the Castle hill, rejoined his troopers, and galloped westward. Hamilton now ordered the doors to be opened. The suspected members were at liberty to depart. Humbled and broken-spirited, yet glad that they had come off so well, they stole forth through the crowd of stern fanatics which filled the High Street. All thought of secession was at an end.*

On the following day it was resolved that the kingdom should be put into a posture of defence. The preamble of this resolution contained a severe reflection on the perfidy of the traitor who, within a few hours after he had, by an engagement subscribed with his own hand, bound himself not to quit his post in the Convention, had set the example of desertion and given the signal of civil war. All Protestants, from sixteen to sixty, were ordered to hold themselves in readiness to assemble in arms at the first summons; and, that none might pretend ignorance, it was directed that the edict should be proclaimed at all the market crosses throughtout the realm.†

---

* Balcarras's Memoirs; MS. in the library of the Faculty of Advocates.
† Act Parl. Scot., March 19, 1688–9; History of the late Revolution in Scotland, 1690.

The Estates then proceeded to send a letter of thanks to William. To this letter were attached the signatures of many noblemen and gentlemen who were in the interest of the banished king. The bishops, however, unanimously refused to subscribe their names.

It had long been the custom of the Parliaments of Scotland to entrust the preparation of Acts to a select number of members who were designated as the Lords of Articles. In conformity with this usage, the business of framing a plan for the settling of the government was now confided to a committee of twenty-four. Of the twenty-four, eight were peers, eight representatives of counties, and eight representatives of towns. The majority of the committee were Whigs; and not a single prelate had a seat.

The spirit of the Jacobites, broken by a succession of disasters, was, about this time, for a moment revived by the arrival of the Duke of Queensberry from London. His rank was high: his influence was great: his character, by comparison with the characters of those who surrounded him, was fair. When Popery was in the ascendent, he had been true to the cause of the Protestant Church; and, since Whiggism had been in the ascendent, he had been true to the cause of hereditary monarchy. Some thought that, if he had been earlier in his place, he might have been able to render important service to the House of Stuart.* Even now the stimulants which he applied to his torpid and feeble party produced some faint symptoms of returning animation. Means were found of communicating with Gordon; and he was earnestly solicited to fire on the city. The Jacobites hoped that, as soon as the cannon balls had beaten down a few chimneys, the Estates would adjourn to Glasgow. Time would thus be gained; and the royalists might be able to execute their old project of meeting in a separate convention. Gordon however positively refused to take on himself so grave a responsibility on no better warrant than the request of a small cabal.†

By this time the Estates had a guard on which they could rely more firmly than on the undisciplined and turbulent Covenanters of the West. A squadron of English men of war from the Thames had arrived in the Frith of Forth. On board were the three Scottish regiments which had accompanied William from Holland. He had, with

* Balcarras. † Ibid.

great judgment, selected them to protect the assemby which was to settle the government of their country; and, that no cause of jealousy might be given to a people exquisitely sensitive on points of national honor, he had purged the army of all Dutch soldiers, and had thus reduced the number of men to about eleven hundred. This little force was commanded by Hugh Mackay, a Highlander of noble descent, who had long served on the continent, and who was distinguished by courage of the truest temper, and by a piety such as is seldom found in soldiers of fortune. The Convention passed a resolution appointing Mackay general of their forces. When the question was put on this resolution, the Archbishop of Glasgow, unwilling doubtless to be a party to such an usurpation of powers which belonged to the King alone, begged that the prelates might be excused from voting. Divines, he said, had nothing to do with military arrangements. "The Fathers of the Church," answered a member very keenly. "have been lately favored with a new light. I have myself seen military orders signed by the most reverend person who has suddenly become so scrupulous. There was indeed one difference: those orders were for dragooning Protestants; and the resolution before us is meant to protect us from Papists." *

The arrival of Mackay's troops, and the determination of Gordon to remain inactive, quelled the spirit of the Jacobites. They had indeed one chance left. They might possibly, by joining with those Whigs who were bent on a union with England, have postponed during a considerable time the settlement of the government. A negotiation was actually opened with this view, but was speedily broken off. For it soon appeared that the party which was for James was really hostile to the union, and that the party which was for the union was really hostile to James. As these two parties had no object in common, the only effect of a coalition between them must have been that one of them would have become the tool of the other. The question of the union therefore was not raised.† Some Jacobites retired to their country seats: others, though they remained at Edinburgh, ceased to show themselves in the Parliament House: many passed over to the

---

* Act Parl. Scot.; History of the late Revolution, 1690; Memoirs of North Britain, 1715.
† Balcarras.

winning side; and, when at length the resolutions prepared by the Twenty-Four were submitted to the Convention, it appeared that the great body which on the first day of the session had rallied round Athol had dwindled away to nothing.

The resolutions had been framed, as far as possible, in conformity with the example recently set at Westminster. In one important point, however, it was absolutely necessary that the copy should deviate from the original. The Estates of England had brought two charges against James, his misgovernment and his flight, and had, by using the soft word "Abdication," evaded, with some sacrifice of verbal precision, the question whether subjects may lawfully depose a bad prince. That question the Estates of Scotland could not evade. They could not pretend that James had deserted his post. For he had never, since he came to the throne, resided in Scotland. During many years that kingdom had been ruled by sovereigns who dwelt in another land. The whole machinery of the administration had been constructed on the supposition that the king would be absent, and was therefore not necessarily deranged by that flight which had, in the south of the island, dissolved all government, and supended the ordinary course of justice. It was only by letter that the King could, when he was at Whitehall, communicate with the Council and the Parliament at Edinburgh; and by letter he could communicate with them when he was at Saint Germains or at Dublin. The Twenty-Four were therefore forced to propose to the Estates a resolution distinctly declaring that James the Seventh had by his misconduct forfeited the crown. Many writers have inferred from the language of this resolution that sound political principles had made a greater progress in Scotland than in England. But the whole history of the two countries, from the Restoration to the Union, proves this inference to be erroneous. The Scottish Estates used plain language, simply because it was impossible for them, situated as they were, to use evasive language.

The person who bore the chief part in framing the resolution, and in defending it, was Sir John Dalrymple, who had recently held the high office of Lord Advocate, and had been an accomplice in some of the misdeeds which he now arraigned with great force of reasoning and eloquence. He was strenuonsly supported by Sir James Montgomery, member for Ayrshire, a man of considerable abilities, but of loose principles, turbulent temper, insatiable cupidity, and implacable malevolence. The Archbishop of Glasgow and Sir George Mackenzie spoke on the other side: but the only effect of their oratory was to deprive their party of the advantage of being able to allege that the Estates were under duress, and that liberty of speech had been denied to the defenders of hereditary monarchy.

When the question was put, Athol, Queensberry, and some of their friends withdrew. Only five members voted against the resolution which pronounced that James had forfeited his right to the allegiance of his subjects. When it was moved that the Crown of Scotland should be settled as the Crown of England had been settled, Athol and Queensberry reappeared in the hall. They had doubted, they said, whether they could justifiably declare the throne vacant. But, since it had been declared vacant, they felt no doubt that William and Mary were the persons who ought to fill it.

The Convention then went forth in procession to the High Street. Several great nobles, attended by the Lord Provost of the capital and by the heralds, ascended the octagon tower from which rose the city cross surmounted by the unicorn of Scotland.* Hamilton read the vote of the Convention; and a King at Arms proclaimed the new Sovereigns with sound of trumpet. On the same day the Estates issued an order that the parochial clergy should, on pain of deprivation, publish from their pulpits the proclamation which had just been read at the city cross, and should pray for King William and Queen Mary.

Still the interregnum was not at an end. Though the new Sovereigns had been proclaimed, they had not yet been put into possession of the royal authority by a formal tender and a formal acceptance. At Edinburgh, as at Westminster, it was thought necessary that the instrument which settled the government should clearly define and solemnly assert those privileges of the people which the Stuarts had illegally infringed. A Claim of Right was therefore drawn up by the Twenty-Four, and adopted by the Convention. To this claim, which purported to be merely declaratory of the law as it stood, was added a supplementary paper containing a list of grievances which

---
* Every reader will remember the malediction which Sir Walter Scott, in the Fifth canto of Marmion, pronounced on the dunces who removed this interesting monument.

could be remedied only by new laws. One most important article, which we should naturally expect to find at the head of such a list, the Convention, with great practical prudence, but in defiance of notorious facts and of unanswerable arguments, placed in the Claim of Right. Nobody could deny that prelacy was established by Act of Parliament. The power exercised by the bishops might be pernicious, unscriptural, antichristian: but illegal it certainly was not; and to pronounce it illegal was to outrage common sense. The Whig leaders, however, were much more desirous to get rid of episcopacy than to prove themselves consummate publicists and logicians. If they made the abolition of episcopacy an article of the contract by which William was to hold the crown, they attained their end, though doubtless in a manner open to much criticism. If, on the other hand, they contented themselves with resolving that episcopacy was a noxious institution which at some future time the legislature would do well to abolish, they might find that their resolution, though unobjectionable in form, was barren of consequences. They knew that William by no means sympathized with their dislike of bishops, and that, even had he been much more zealous for the Calvinistic model than he was, the relation in which he stood to the Anglican Church would make it difficult and dangerous for him to declare himself hostile to a fundamental part of the constitution of that Church. If he should become King of Scotland without being fettered by any pledge on this subject, it might well be apprehended that he would hesitate about passing an Act which would be regarded with abhorrence by a large body of his subjects in the south of the island. It was therefore most desirable that the question should be settled while the throne was still vacant. In this opinion many politicians concurred, who had no dislike to rochets and mitres, but who wished that William might have a quiet and prosperous reign. The Scottish people,—so these men reasoned,—hated episcopacy. The English loved it. To leave William any voice in the matter was to put him under the necessity of deeply wounding the strongest feelings of one of the nations which he governed. It was therefore plainly for his own interest that the question, which he could not settle in any manner without incurring a fearful amount of obloquy, should be settled for him by others who were exposed to no such danger. He was not yet

Sovereign of Scotland. While the interregnum lasted, the supreme power belonged to the Estates; and for what the Estates might do the prelatists of his southern kingdom could not hold him responsible. The elder Dalrymple wrote strongly from London to this effect; and there can be little doubt that he expressed the sentiments of his master. William would have sincerely rejoiced if the Scots could have been reconciled to a modified episcopacy. But, since that could not be, it was manifestly desirable that they should themselves, while there was yet no king over them, pronounce the irrevocable doom of the institution which they abhorred.*

The Convention, therefore, with little debate as it should seem, inserted in the Claim of Right a clause declaring that prelacy was an insupportable burden to the kingdom, that it had been long odious to the body of the people, and that it ought to be abolished.

Nothing in the proceedings at Edinburgh astonishes an Englishman more than the manner in which the Estates dealt with the practice of torture. In England torture had always been illegal. In the most servile times the judges had unanimously pronounced it so. Those rulers who had occasionally resorted to it had, as far as was possible, used it in secret, had never pretended that they had acted in conformity with either statute law or common law, and had excused themselves by saying that the extraordinary peril to which the state was exposed had forced them to take on themselves the responsibility of employing extraordinary means of defence. It had therefore never been thought necessary by any English Parliament to pass any Act or resolution touching this matter. The torture was not mentioned in the Petition of Right, or in any of the statutes framed by the Long Parliament. No member of the Convention of 1689 dreamed of proposing that the instrument which called the Prince and Princess of Orange to the throne should contain a declaration against the using of racks and thumb-screws for the purpose of forcing prisoners to accuse themselves. Such a declaration would have been justly regarded as weakening rather than strengthening a rule which, as far back as the days of the Plantagenets, had been proudly

---

* "It will be neither secuir nor kynd to the King to expect it to be (by) Act of Parliament after the settlement, which will lay it at his door." Dalrymple to Melville, 5 April, 1689: Leven and Melville Papers.

declared by the most illustrious sages of Westminster Hall to be a distinguishing feature of the English jurisprudence.* In the Scottish Claim of Right, the use of torture without evidence, or in ordinary cases, was declared to be contrary to law. The use of torture, therefore, where there was strong evidence, and where the crime was extraordinary, was, by the plainest implication, declared to be according to law; nor did the Estates mention the use of torture among the grievances which required a legislative remedy. In truth, they could not condemn the use of torture without condemning themselves. It had chanced that while they were employed in settling the government, the eloquent and learned Lord President Lockhart had been foully murdered in a public street through which he was returning from church on a Sunday. The murderer was seized, and proved to be a wretch who, having treated his wife barbarously and turned her out of doors, had been compelled by a decree of the Court of Session to provide for her. A savage hatred of the judges by whom she had been protected had taken possession of his mind, and had goaded him to a horrible crime and a horrible fate. It was natural that an assassination attended by so many circumstances of aggravation should move the indignation of the members of the Convention. Yet they should have considered the gravity of the conjuncture and the importance of their own mission. They unfortunately, in the heat of passion, directed the magistrates of Edinburgh to strike the prisoner in the boots, and named a committee to superintend the operation. But for this unhappy event, it is probable that the law of Scotland concerning torture would have been immediately assimilated to the law of England.†

Having settled the Claim of Right, the Convention proceeded to revise the coronation oath. When this had been done, three members were appointed to carry the Instrument of Government to London. Argyle, though not in strictness of law, a Peer, was chosen to represent the Peers: Sir James Montgomery represented the Commissioners of Shires, and Sir John Dalrymple the Commissioners of Towns.

The Estates then adjourned for a few weeks, having first passed a vote which empowered Hamilton to take such

---

* There is a striking passage on this subject in Fortescue.
† Act Parl. Scot., April 1, 1689; Orders of Committee of Estates, May 16, 1689; London Gazette, April 11.

measures as might be necessary for the preservation of the public peace till the end of the interregnum.

The ceremony of the inauguration was distinguished from ordinary pageants by some highly interesting circumstances. On the eleventh of May the three Commissioners came to the Council Chamber at Whitehall, and thence, attended by almost all the Scotchmen of note who were then in London, proceeded to the Banqueting House. There William and Mary appeared seated under a canopy. A splendid circle of English nobles and statesmen stood round the throne: but the sword of state was committed to a Scotch Lord; and the oath of office was administered after the Scotch fashion. Argyle recited the words slowly. The royal pair, holding up their hands towards heaven, repeated after him till they came to the last clause. There William paused. That clause contained a promise that he would root out all heretics and all enemies of the true worship of God; and it was notorious that, in the opinion of many Scotchmen, not only all Roman Catholics, but all Protestant Episcopalians, all Independents, Baptists, and Quakers, all Lutherans, nay all British Presbyterians who did not hold themselves bound by the Solemn League and Covenant, were enemies of the true worship of God.* The King had apprised the Commisioners that he could not take this part of the oath without a distinct and public explanation; and they had been authorized by the Convention to give such an explanation as would satisfy him. "I will not," he now said, "lay myself under any obligation to be a persecutor." "Neither the words of this oath," said one of the Commissioners, "nor the laws of Scotland, lay any such obligation on Your Majesty." "In that sense, then, I swear," said William; "and I desire you all, my lords and gentlemen, to witness

---

* As it has lately been denied that the extreme Presbyterians entertained an unfavorable opinion of the Lutherans, I will give two decisive proofs of the truth of what I have asserted in the text. In the book entitled Faithful Contendings Displayed is a report of what passed at the General Meeting of the United Societies of Covenanters on the 24th of October, 1688. The question was propounded whether there should be an association with the Dutch. "It was concluded unanimously," says the Clerk of the Societies, "that we could not have an association with the Dutch in one body, nor come formally under their conduct, being such a promiscuous conjunction of reformed Lutheran malignants and sectaries, to join with whom were repugnant to the testimony of the Church of Scotland." In the Protestation and Testimony drawn up on the 2d of October 1707, the United Societies complain that the crown has been settled on" the Prince of Hanover, who has been bred and brought up in the Lutheran religion, which is not only different from, but even in many things contrary unto that purity in doctrine, reformation, and religion, we in these nations had attained unto, as is very well known." They add: "The admitting such a person to reign over us is not only contrary to our Solemn League and Covenant, but to the very Word of God itself, Deut. xvii."

that I do so." Even his detractors have generally admitted that on this great occasion he acted with uprightness, dignity, and wisdom.*

As King of Scotland, he soon found himself embarrassed at every step by all the difficulties which had embarrassed him as King of England, and by other difficulties which in England were happily unknown. In the north of the island, no class was more dissatisfied with the Revolution than the class which owed most to the Revolution. The manner in which the Convention had decided the question of ecclesiastical polity had not been more offensive to the bishops themselves than to those fiery Covenanters who had long, in defiance of sword and carbine, boot and gibbet, worshipped their Maker after their own fashion in caverns and on mountain tops. Was there ever, these zealots exclaimed, such a halting between two opinions, such a compromise between the Lord and Baal? The Estates ought to have said that episcopacy was an abomination in God's sight, and that, in obedience to his word, and from fear of his righteous judgment, they were determined to deal with this great national sin and scandal after the fashion of those saintly rulers who of old cut down the groves and demolished the altars of Chemosh and Astarte. Unhappily, Scotland was ruled, not by pious Josiahs, but by careless Gallios. The anti-christian hierarchy was to be abolished, not because it was an insult to heaven, but because it was felt as a burden on earth; not because it was hateful to the great Head of the Church, but because it was hateful to the people. Was public opinion, then, the test of right and wrong in religion? Was not the order which Christ had established in his own house to be held equally sacred in all countries and through all ages? And was there no reason for following that order in Scotland, except a reason which might be urged with equal force for maintaining prelacy in England, Popery in Spain, and Mahometanism in Turkey? Why, too, was nothing said of those Covenants which the nation had so generally subscribed and so generally violated? Why was it not distinctly affirmed that the promises set down in those rolls were still binding, and would to the end of time be binding, on the kingdom? Were these

* History of the late Revolution in Scotland; London Gazette, May 16, 1689. The official account of what passed was evidently drawn up with great care. See also the Royal Diary, 1702. The writer of this work professes to have derived his information from a divine who was present.

truths to be suppressed from regard for the feelings and
interests of a prince who was all things to all men, an ally
of the idolatrous Spaniard and of the Lutheran Dane, a
Presbyterian at the Hague and a prelatist at Whitehall?
He, like Jehu in ancient times, had doubtless so far done
well that he had been the scourge of the idolatrous House
of Ahab. But he, like Jehu, had not taken heed to walk in
the divine law with his whole heart, but had tolerated and
practiced impieties differing only in degree from those of
which he had declared himself the enemy. It would have
better become godly senators to remonstrate with him on
the sin which he was committing by conforming to the
Anglican ritual, and by maintaining the Anglican Church
government, than to flatter him by using a phraseology
which seemed to indicate that they were as deeply tainted
with Erastianism as himself. Many of those who held
this language refused to do any act which could be construed into a recognition of the new Sovereigns, and would
rather have been fired upon by files of musketeers, or tied
to stakes within low-water mark, than have uttered a
prayer that God would bless William and Mary.

Yet the King had less to fear from the pertinacious adherence of these men to their absurd principles than from
the ambition and avarice of another set of men who had
no principles at all. It was necessary that he should immediately name ministers to conduct the government of
Scotland; and, name whom he might, he could not fail to
disappoint and irritate a multitude of expectants. Scotland was one of the least wealthy countries in Europe; yet
no country in Europe contained a greater number of
clever and selfish politicians. The places in the gift of the
crown were not enough to satisfy one twentieth part of
the place-hunters, every one of whom thought that his
own services had been pre-eminent, and that whoever
might be passed by, he ought to be remembered. William
did his best to satisfy these innumerable and insatiable
claimants by putting many offices into commission.
There were, however, a few great posts which it was impossible to divide. Hamilton was declared Lord High
Commissioner, in the hope that immense pecuniary allowances, a residence in Holyrood Palace, and a pomp and
dignity little less than regal, would content him. The
Earl of Crawford was appointed President of the Parliament; and it was supposed that this appointment would

conciliate the rigid Presbyterians: for Crawford was what they called a professor. His letters and speeches are, to use his own phraseology, exceeding savory. Alone, or almost alone, among the prominent politicians of that time, he retained the style which had been fashionable in the preceding generation. He had a text from the Pentateuch or the Prophets ready for every occasion. He filled his despatches with allusions to Ishmael and Hagar, Hannah and Eli, Elijah, Nehemiah, and Zerubbabel, and adorned his oratory with quotations from Ezra and Haggai. It is a circumstance strikingly characteristic of the man, and of the school in which he had been trained, that, in all the mass of his writing which has come down to us, there is not a single word indicating that he had ever in his life heard of the New Testament. Even in our own time some persons of a peculiar taste have been so much delighted by the rich unction of his eloquence, that they have confidently pronounced him a saint. To those whose habit is to judge of a man rather by his actions than by his words, Crawford will appear to have been a selfish, cruel politician, who was not at all the dupe of his own cant, and whose zeal against Episcopal government was not a little whetted by his desire to obtain a grant of Episcopal domains. In excuse for his greediness, it ought to be said that he was the poorest noble of a poor nobility, and that before the Revolution he was sometimes at a loss for a meal and a suit of clothes.*

The ablest of Scottish politicians and debaters, Sir John Dalrymple, was appointed Lord Advocate. His father, Sir James, the greatest of Scottish jurists, was placed at the head of the Court of Session. Sir William Lockhart, a man whose letters prove him to have possessed considerable ability, became Solicitor General.

Sir James Montgomery had flattered himself that he should be the chief minister. He had distinguished him-

---

* See Crawford's Letters and Speeches, *passim*. His style of begging for a place was peculiar. After owning, not without reason, that his heart was deceitful and desperately wicked, he proceeded thus: "The same Omnipotent Being who hath said, when the poor and needy seek water and there is none, and their tongue faileth for thirst, He will not forsake them, notwithstanding of my present low condition, can build me a house if He think fit."—Letter to Melville of May 28, 1689. As to Crawford's poverty and his passion for Bishops' lands, see his letter to Melville of the 4th of December, 1690. As to his humanity, see his letter to Melville, Dec. 11, 1690. All these letters are among the Leven and Melville Papers. The author of An Account of the Late Establishment of Presbyterian Government says of a person who had taken a bribe of ten or twelve pounds, "Had he been as poor as my Lord Crawford, perhaps he had been the more excusable." See also the dedication of the celebrated tract entitled Scotch Presbyterian Eloquence Displayed.

self highly in the Convention. He had been one of the Commissioners who had tendered the Crown and administered the oath to the new Sovereigns. In parliamentary ability and eloquence he had no superior among his countrymen, except the new Lord Advocate. The Secretaryship was, not indeed in dignity, but in real power, the highest office in the Scottish government; and this office was the reward to which Montgomery thought himself entitled. But the Episcopalians and the moderate Presbyterians dreaded him as a man of extreme opinions and of bitter spirit. He had been a chief of the Covenanters: he had been prosecuted at one time for holding conventicles, and at another time for harboring rebels: he had been fined: he had been imprisoned: he had been almost driven to take refuge from his enemies beyond the Atlantic in the infant settlement of New Jersey. It was apprehended that, if he were now armed with the whole power of the crown he would exact a terrible retribution for what he had suffered.*
William therefore preferred Melville, who, though not a man of eminent talents, was regarded by the Presbyterians as a thorough-going friend, and yet not regarded by the Episcopalians as an implacable enemy. Melville fixed his residence at the English Court, and became the regular organ of communication between Kensington and the authorities at Edinburgh.

William had, however, one Scottish adviser who deserved and possessed more influence than any of the ostensible ministers. This was Carstairs, one of the most remarkable men of that age. He united great scholastic attainments with great aptitude for civil business, and the firm faith and ardent zeal of a martyr with the shrewdness and suppleness of a consummate politician. In courage and fidelity he resembled Burnet; but he had, what Burnet wanted, judgment, self-command, and a singular power of keeping secrets. There was no post to which he might not have aspired if he had been a layman, or a priest of the Church of England. But a Presbyterian clergyman could not hope to attain any high dignity either in the north or in the south of the island. Carstairs was forced to content himself with the substance of power, and to leave the semblance to others. He was named Chaplain to

---

* Burnet, ii. 23, 24; Fountainhall Papers, 13 Aug. 1684, 14 and 15 Oct. 1684, 3 May 1685; Montgomery to Melville, June 23, 1689, in the Leven and Melville Papers; Pretences of the French Invasion Examined, licensed May 25, 1692.

their Majesties for Scotland: but wherever the King was, in England, in Ireland, in the Netherlands, there was this most trusty and most prudent of courtiers. He obtained from the royal bounty a modest competence; and he desired no more. But it was well known that he could be as useful a friend and as formidable an enemy as any member of the cabinet; and he was designated at the public offices and in the ante-chambers of the palace by the significant nickname of the Cardinal.*

To Montgomery was offered the place of Lord Justice Clerk. But that place, though high and honorable, he thought below his merits and his capacity; and he returned from London to Scotland with a heart ulcerated by hatred of his ungrateful master and of his successful rivals. At Edinburgh a knot of Whigs, as severely disappointed as himself by the new arrangements, readily submitted to the guidance of so bold and able a leader. Under his direction these men, among whom the Earl of Annandale and Lord Ross were the most conspicuous, formed themselves into a society called the Club, appointed a clerk, and met daily at a tavern to concert plans of opposition. Round this nucleus soon gathered a great body of greedy and angry politicians.† With these dishonest malcontents, whose object was merely to annoy the government and to get places, were leagued other malcontents, who in the course of a long resistance to tyranny, had become so perverse and irritable that they were unable to live contentedly even under the mildest and most constitutional rule. Such a man was Sir Patrick Hume. He had returned from exile, as litigious, as impracticable, as morbidly jealous of all superior authority, and as fond of haranguing, as he had been four years before, and was as much bent on making a merely nominal sovereign of William as he had formerly been bent on making a merely nominal general of Argyle.‡ A man far superior morally and intellectually to Hume, Fletcher of Saltoun, belonged to the same party. Though not a member of the Convention, he was a most active

---

* See the life and correspondence of Carstairs, and the interesting memorials of him in the Caldwell Papers, printed in 1854. See also Mackay's character of him, and Swift's note. Swift's word is not to be taken against a Scotchman and a Presbyterian. I believe, however, that Carstairs, though an honest and pious man in essentials, had his full share of the wisdom of the serpent.

† Sir John Dalrymple to Lord Melville, June 18, 20, 25, 1689; Leven and Melville Papers.

‡ There is an amusing description of Sir Patrick in the Hyndford MS. written about 1704, and printed among the Carstairs Papers. "He is a lover of set speeches, and can hardly give audience to private friends without them."

member of the Club.* He hated monarchy; he hated democracy: his favorite project was to make Scotland an oligarchical republic. The King, if there must be a King, was to be a mere pageant. The lowest class of the people were to be bondsmen. The whole power, legislative and executive, was to be in the hands of the Parliament. In other words, the country was to be absolutely governed by a hereditary aristocracy, the most needy, the most haughty, and the most quarrelsome in Europe. Under such a polity there could have been neither freedom nor tranquillity. Trade, industry, science, would have languished; and Scotland would have been a smaller Poland, with a puppet sovereign, a turbulent diet, and an enslaved people. With unsuccessful candidates for office, and with honest but wrong-headed republicans, were mingled politicians whose course was determined merely by fear. Many sycophants, who were conscious that they had, in the evil time, done what deserved punishment, were desirous to make their peace with the powerful and vindictive Club, and were glad to be permitted to atone for their servility to James by their opposition to William.† The great body of Jacobites meanwhile stood aloof, saw with delight the enemies of the House of Stuart divided against one another, and indulged the hope that the confusion would end in the restoration of the banished King.‡

While Montgomery was laboring to form out of various materials a party which might, when the Convention should reassemble, be powerful enough to dictate to the throne, an enemy still more formidable than Montgomery had set up the standard of civil war in a region about which the politicians of Westminster, and indeed most of the politicians of Edinburgh, knew no more than about Abyssinia or Japan.

It is not easy for a modern Englishman, who can pass in a day from his club in St. James's Street to his shooting box among the Grampians, and who finds in his shooting box all the comforts and luxuries of his club, to believe that, in the time of his great-grandfathers, St. James's Street had as little connection with the Grampians as

---

* "No man, though not a member, busier than Saltoun."—Lockhart to Melville, July 11, 1689; Leven and Melville Papers. See Fletcher's own works, and the descriptions of him in Lockhart's and Mackay's Memoirs.

† Dalrymple says, in a letter of the 5th of June, "All the malignants, for fear, are come into the Club; and they all vote alike."

‡ Balcarras.

with the Andes. Yet so it was. In the south of our island scarcely anything was known about the Celtic part of Scotland; and what was known excited no feeling but contempt and loathing. The crags and the glens, the woods and the waters, were indeed the same that now swarm every autumn with admiring gazers and sketchers. The Trosachs wound as now between gigantic walls of rock tapestried with broom and wild roses: Foyers came headlong down through the birch wood with the same leap and the same roar with which he still rushes to Loch Ness; and, in defiance of the sun of June, the snowy scalp of Ben Cruachan rose, as it still rises, over the willowy islets of Loch Awe. Yet none of these sights had power, till a recent period, to attract a single poet or painter from more opulent and more tranquil regions. Indeed law and police, trade and industry, have done far more than people of romantic dispositions will readily admit, to develop in our minds a sense of the wilder beauties of nature. A traveller must be freed from all apprehension of being murdered or starved before he can be charmed by the bold outlines and rich tints of the hills. He is not likely to be thrown into ecstacies by the abruptness of a precipice from which he is in imminent danger of falling two thousand feet perpendicular; by the boiling waves of a torrent which suddenly whirls away his baggage and forces him to run for his life; by the gloomy grandeur of a pass where he finds a corpse which marauders have just stripped and mangled; or by the screams of those eagles whose next meal may probably be on his own eyes. About the year 1730, Captain Burt, one of the first Englishmen who caught a glimpse of the spots which now allure tourists from every part of the civilized world, wrote an account of his wanderings. He was evidently a man of a quick, an observant and a cultivated mind, and would doubtless, had he lived in our age, have looked with mingled awe and delight on the mountains of Invernesshire. But, writing with the feeling which was universal in his own age, he pronounced those mountains monstrous excrescences. Their deformity, he said, was such that the most sterile plains seemed lovely by comparison. Fine weather, he complained, only made bad worse; for, the clearer the day, the more disagreeably did those misshapen masses of gloomy brown and dirty purple affect the eye. What a contrast, he exclaimed, between these horrible prospects and the beauties of Richmond Hill!* Some persons may think that Burt was a man of vulgar and prosaical mind: but they will scarcely venture to pass a similar judgment on Oliver Goldsmith. Goldsmith was one of the very few Saxons, who, more than a century ago, ventured to explore the Highlands. He was disgusted by the hideous wilderness, and declared that he greatly preferred the charming country round Leyden, the vast expanse of verdant meadow, and the villas with their statues and grottoes, trim flower-beds, and rectilinear avenues. Yet it is difficult to believe that the author of the Traveller and of the Deserted Village was naturally inferior in taste and sensibility to the thousands of clerks and milliners who are now thrown into raptures by the sight of Loch Katrine and Loch Lomond.† His feelings may easily be explained. It was not till roads had been cut out of the rocks, till bridges had been flung over the courses of the rivulets, till inns had succeeded to dens of robbers, till there was as little danger of being slain or plundered in the wildest defile of Badenoch or Lochaber as in Cornhill, that strangers could be enchanted by the blue dimples of the lakes and by the rainbows which overhung the waterfalls, and could derive a solemn pleasure even from the clouds and tempests which lowered on the mountain tops.

The change in the feeling with which the Lowlanders regarded the Highland scenery was closely connected with a change not less remarkable in the feeling with which they regarded the Highland race. It is not strange that the Wild Scotch, as they were sometimes called, should, in the seventeenth century, have been considered by the Sax-

---

* Captain Burt's Letters from Scotland.

† "Shall I tire you with a description of this unfruitful country, where I must lead you over their hills all brown with heath, or their valleys scarce able to feed a rabbit? . . . Every part of the country presents the same dismal landscape. No grove or brook lend their music to cheer the stranger."—Goldsmith to Bryanton, Edinburgh, Sept. 26, 1753. In a letter written soon after from Leyden to the Reverend Thomas Contarine, Goldsmith says, "I was wholly taken up in observing the face of the country. Nothing can equal its beauty. Wherever I turned my eye, fine houses, elegant gardens, statues, grottos, vistas presented themselves. Scotland and this country bear the highest contrast; there, hills and rocks intercept every prospect; here it is all a continued plain." See Appendix C. to the First Volume of Mr. Forster's Life of Goldsmith. I will cite the testimony of another man of genius in support of the doctrine propounded in the text. No human being has ever had a finer sense of the beauties of nature than Gray. No prospect surpasses in grandeur and loveliness the first view of Italy from Mount Cenis. Had Gray enjoyed that view from the magnificent road constructed in this century, he would undoubtedly have been in raptures. But in his time the descent was performed with extreme inconvenience and with not a little peril. He therefore, instead of breaking forth into ejaculations of admiration and delight, says most unpoetically, "Mount Cenis, I confess, carries the permission mountains have of being frightful rather too far; and its horrors were accompanied with too much danger to give one time to reflect upon their beauties."—Gray to West, Nov. 16, 1739.

ons as mere savages. But it is surely strange that, considered as savages, they should not have been objects of interest and curiosity. The English were then abundantly inquisitive about the manners of rude nations separated from our island by great continents and oceans. Numerous books were printed describing the laws, the superstitions, the cabins, the repasts, the dresses, the marriages, the funerals of Laplanders and Hottentots, Mohawks and Malays. The plays and poems of that age are full of allusions to the usages of the black men of Africa and to the red men of America. The only barbarian about whom there was no wish to have any information was the Highlander. Five or six years after the Revolution, an indefatigible angler published an account of Scotland. He boasted that, in the course of his rambles from lake to lake, and from brook to brook, he had left scarcely a nook of the kingdom unexplored. But when we examine his narrative, we find that he had never ventured beyond the extreme skirts of the Celtic region. He tells us that even from the people who lived close to the passes he could learn little or nothing about the Gaelic population. Few Englishmen, he says, had ever seen Inverary. All beyond Inverary was chaos.* In the reign of George the First, a work was published which professed to give a most exact account of Scotland; and in this work, consisting of more than three hundred pages, two contemptuous paragraphs were thought sufficient for the Highlands and the Highlanders.† We may well doubt whether, in 1689, one in twenty of the well read gentlemen who assembled at Will's coffee-house knew that, within the four seas, and at the distance of less than five hundred miles from London, were many minature courts, in each of which a petty prince, attended by guards, by armor bearers. by musicians, by an hereditary orator, by an hereditary poet-laureate, kept a rude state, dispensed a rude justice, waged wars, and concluded treaties. While the old Gaelic institutions were in full vigor, no account of them was given by any observer, qualified to jndge of them fairly. Had such an observer studied the character of the Highlanders, he would doubtless have found in it closely intermingled the good and

---

* Northern Memoirs, by R. Franck Philanthropus, 1694. The author had caught a few glimpses of Highland scenery, and speaks of it much as Burt spoke in the following generation: "It is a part of the creation left undressed; rubbish thrown aside when the magnificent fabric of the world was created; as void of form as the natives are indifferent of morals and good manners."

† Journey through Scotland by the author of the Journey through England, 1723.

the bad qualities of an uncivilized nation. He would have found that the people had no love for their country or for their king; that they had no attachment to any commonwealth larger than the clan, or to any magistrate superior to the chief. He would have found that life was governed by a code of morality and honor widely different from that which is established in peaceful and prosperous societies. He would have learned that a stab in the back, or a shot from behind a fragment of rock, were approved modes of taking satisfaction for insults. He would have heard men relate boastfully how they or their fathers had wreaked on hereditary enemies in a neighboring valley such vengeance as would have made old soldiers of the Thirty Years' War shudder. He would have found that robbery was held to be a calling, not merely innocent, but honorable. He would have seen, wherever he turned, that dislike of steady industry, and that disposition to throw on the weaker sex the heaviest part of manual labor, which are characteristic of savages. He would have been struck by the spectacle of athletic men basking in the sun, angling for salmon, or taking aim at grouse, while their aged mothers, their pregnant wives, their tender daughters, were reaping the scanty harvest of oats. Nor did the women repine at their hard lot. In their view it was quite fit that a man, especially if he assumed the aristocratic title of Duinhe Wassel, and adorned his bonnet with the eagle's feather, should take his ease, except when he was fighting, hunting, or marauding. To mention the name of such a man in connection with commerce or with any mechanical art was an insult. Agriculture was indeed less despised. Yet a high-born warrior was much more becomingly employed in plundering the land of others than in tilling his own. The religion of the greater part of the Highlands was a rude mixture of Popery and Paganism. The symbol of redemption was associated with heathen sacrifices and incantations. Baptized men poured libations of ale to one Dæmon, and set out drink offerings of milk for another. Seers wrapped themselves up in bulls' hides, and awaited, in that vesture, the inspiration which was to reveal the future. Even among those minstrels and genealogists whose hereditary vocation was to preserve the memory of past events, an inquirer would have found very few who could read. In truth, he might easily have journeyed from sea to sea without discovering a page of Gaelic printed or written. The price which he would have had to pay for his knowledge of the country would have been heavy. He would have had to endure hardships as great as if he had sojourned among the Esquimaux or the Samoyeds. Here and there, indeed, at the castle of some great lord who had a seat in the Parliament and Privy Council, and who was accustomed to pass a large part of his life in the cities of the South, might have been found wigs and embroidered coats, plate and fine linen, lace and jewels, French dishes and French wines. But, in general, the traveller would have been forced to content himself with very different quarters. In many dwellings the furniture, the food, the clothing, nay the very hair and skin of his hosts, would have put his philosophy to the proof. His lodging would sometimes have been in a hut of which every nook would have swarmed with vermin. He would have inhaled an atmosphere thick with peat smoke, and foul with a hundred noisome exhalations. At supper grain fit only for horses would have been set before him, accompanied by a cake of blood drawn from living cows. Some of the company with which he would have feasted would have been covered with cutaneous eruptions, and others would have been smeared with tar, like sheep. His couch would have been the bare earth, dry or wet as the weather might be; and from that couch he would have risen half poisoned with stench, half blind with the reek of turf, and half mad with the itch.*

This is not an attractive picture. And yet an enlightened and dispassionate observer would have found in the character and manners of this rude people something which might well excite admiration and a good hope. Their courage was what great exploits achieved in all the four quarters of the globe have since proved it to be. Their intense attachment to their own tribe and to their own patriarch, though politically a great evil, partook of the nature of virtue. The sentiment was misdirected and ill regulated; but still it was heroic. There must be some elevation of soul in a man who loves the society of which he is a member and the leader whom he follows with a love

---

* Almost all these circumstances are taken from Burt's Letters. For the tar I am indebted to Cleland's poetry. In his verses on the "Highland Host" he says:

"The reason is, they're smeared with tar,
Which doth defend their head and neck,
Just as it doth their sheep protect."

stronger than the love of life. It was true that the Highlander had few scruples about shedding the blood of an enemy: but it was not less true that he had high notions of the duty of observing faith to allies and hospitality to guests. It was true that his predatory habits were most pernicious to the commonwealth. Yet those erred greatly who imagined that he bore any resemblance to villains who, in rich and well governed communities, live by stealing. When he drove before him the herds of Lowland farmers up the pass which led to his native glen, he no more considered himself as a thief than the Raleighs and Drakes considered themselves as thieves when they divided the cargoes of Spanish galleons. He was a warrior seizing lawful prize of war, of war never once intermitted during the thirty-five generations which had passed away since the Teutonic invaders had driven the children of the soil to the mountains. That, if he was caught robbing on such principles, he should, for the protection of peaceful industry, be punished with the utmost rigor of the law, was perfectly just. But it was not just to class him morally with the pickpockets who infested Drury Lane Theater, or the highwaymen who stopped coaches on Blackheath. His inordinate pride of birth and his contempt for labor and trade were indeed great weaknesses, and had done far more than the inclemency of the air and the sterility of the soil to keep his country poor and rude. Yet even here there was some compensation. It must in fairness be acknowledged that the patrician virtues were not less widely diffused among the population of the Highlands than the patrician vices. As there was no other part of the island where men, sordidly clothed, lodged, and fed indulged themselves to such a degree in the idle sauntering habits of an aristocracy, so there was no other part of the island where such men had in such a degree the better qualities of an aristocracy, grace and dignity of manner, self-respect, and that noble sensibility which makes dishonor more terrible than death. A gentleman of Sky or Lochaber, whose clothes were begrimed with the accumulated filth of years, and whose hovel smelt worse than an English hog-stye, would often do the honors of that hovel with a lofty courtesy worthy of the splendid circle of Versailles. Though he had as little book-learning as the most stupid plough-boys of England, it would have been a great error to put him in the same intellectual rank with such plough-boys. It is indeed only by reading that men can become profoundly acquainted with any science. But the arts of poetry and rhetoric may be carried near to absolute perfection, and may exercise a mighty influence on the public mind, in an age in which books are wholly, or almost wholly, unknown. The first great painter of life and manners has described with a vivacity which makes it impossible to doubt that he was copying from nature, the effect produced by eloquence and song on audiences ignorant of the alphabet. It is probable that, in the Highland councils, men who would not have been qualified for the duty of parish clerk sometimes argued questions of peace and war, of tribute and homage, with ability worthy of Halifax and Caermarthen, and that, at the Highland banquets, minstrels who did not know their letters sometimes poured forth rhapsodies in which a discerning critic might have found passages such as would have reminded him of the tenderness of Otway or of the vigor of Dryden.

There was therefore even then evidence sufficient to justify the belief that no natural inferiority had kept the Celt far behind the Saxon. It might safely have been predicted that, if ever an efficient police should make it impossible for the Highlander to avenge his wrongs by violence and to supply his wants by rapine, if ever his faculties should be developed by the civilizing influence of the Protestant religion and of the English language, if ever he should transfer to his country and to her lawful magistrates the affection and respect with which he had been taught to regard his own petty community and his own petty prince, the kingdom would obtain an immense accession of strength for all the purposes both of peace and of war.

Such would doubtless have been the decision of a well-informed and impartial judge. But no such judge was then to be found. The Saxons who dwelt far from the Gaelic provinces could not be well informed. The Saxons who dwelt near those provinces could not be impartial. National enmities have always been fiercest among borderers; and the enmity between the Highland borderer and the Lowland borderer along the whole frontier was the growth of ages, and was kept fresh by constant injuries. One day many square miles of pasture land were swept bare by armed plunderers from the hills. Another day a score of plaids dangled in a row on the gallows of Crieff or Stirling. Fairs were indeed held on the debatable land for the necessary interchange of commodities. But to those fairs both parties came prepared for battle; and the day often ended in bloodshed. Thus the Highlander was an object of hatred to his Saxon neighbors; and from his Saxon neighbors those Saxons who dwelt far from him learned the very little that they cared to know about his habits. When the English condescended to think of him at all,—and it was seldom that they did so,—they considered him as a filthy abject savage, a slave, a Papist, a cutthroat, and a thief.*

This contemptuous loathing lasted till the year 1745, and was then for a moment succeeded by intense fear and rage. England, thoroughly alarmed, put forth her whole strength. The Highlands were subjugated rapidly, completely, and forever. During a short time the English nation, still heated by the recent conflict, breathed nothing but vengeance. The slaughter on the field of battle and on the scaffold was not sufficient to slake the public thirst for blood. The sight of the tartan inflamed the populace of London with hatred which showed itself by unmanly outrages to defenceless captives. A political and social revolution took place through the whole Celtic region. The power of the chiefs was destroyed: the people were disarmed: the use of the old national garb was interdicted: the old pre-

---

* A striking illustration of the opinion which was entertained of the Highlander by his Lowland neighbors, and which was by them communicated to the English, will be found in a volume of Miscellanies published by Afra Behn in 1685. One of the most curious pieces in the collection is a coarse and profane Scotch poem entitled, "How the first Hielandman was made." How and of what materials he was made I shall not venture to relate. The dialogue which immediately follows his creation may be quoted, I hope, without much offence:

" Says God to the Hielandman, 'Quhair wilt thou now?'
'I will down to the Lowlands, Lord, and there steal a cow.'
'Ffy,' quod St. Peter, 'thou wilt never do weel,
'An thou, but new made, so sune gais to steal.'
'Umff,' quod the Hielandman, and swore by yon kirk,
'So long as I may geir get to steal, will I nevir work.' "

An eminent Lowland Scot, the brave Colonel Cleland, about the same time, described the Highlander in the same manner:

"For a misobliging word
She'll dirk her neighbour o'er the board,
If any ask her of her drift,
Forsooth, her nainself lives by theft."

Much to the same effect are the very few words which Franck Philanthropus (1694) spares to the Highlanders: "They live like lairds and die like loons, hating to work and no credit to borrow: they make depredations and rob their neighbours." In the History of the Revolution in Scotland, printed at Edinburgh in 1690, is the following passage: "The Highlanders of Scotland are a sort of wretches that have no other consideration of honour, friendship, obedience, or government, than as, by any alteration of affairs or revolution in the government, they can improve to themselves an opportunity of robbing or plundering their bordering neighbours.

datory habits were effectually broken; and scarcely had this change been accomplished when a strange reflux of public feeling began. Pity succeeded to aversion. The nation execrated the cruelties which had been committed on the Highlanders, and forgot that for those cruelties it was itself answerable. Those very Londoners, who, while the memory of the march to Derby was still fresh, had thronged to hoot and pelt the rebel prisoners, now fastened on the prince who had put down the rebellion the nickname of butcher. Those barbarous institutions and usages, which, while they were in full force, no Saxon had thought worthy of serious examination, or had mentioned except with contempt, had no sooner ceased to exist than they became objects of curiosity, of interest, even of admiration. Scarcely had the chiefs been turned into mere landlords, when it became the fashion to draw invidious comparisons between the rapacity of the landlord and the indulgence of the chief. Men seemed to have forgotten that the ancient Gaelic polity had been found to be incompatible with the authority of law, had obstructed the progress of civilization, had more than once brought on the empire the curse of civil war. As they had formerly seen only the odious side of that polity, they could now see only the pleasing side. The old tie, they said, had been parental: the new tie was purely commercial. What could be more lamentable than that the head of a tribe should eject, for a paltry arrear of rent, tenants who were his own flesh and blood, tenants whose forefathers had often with their bodies covered his forefathers on the field of battle? As long as there were Gaelic marauders, they had been regarded by the Saxon population as hateful vermin who ought to be exterminated without mercy. As soon as the extermination had been accomplished, as soon as cattle were as safe in the Perthshire passes as in Smithfield market, the freebooter was exalted into a hero of romance. As long as the Gaelic dress was worn, the Saxons had pronounced it hideous, ridiculous, nay, grossly indecent. Soon after it had been prohibited, they discovered that it was the most graceful drapery in Europe. The Gaelic monuments, the Gaelic usages, the Gaelic superstitions, the Gaelic verses, disdainfully neglected during many ages, began to attract the attention of the learned from the moment at which the peculiarities of the Gaelic race began to disappear. So strong was this impulse that, where the Highlands were concerned, men of sense gave ready credence to stories without evidence, and men of taste gave rapturous applause to compositions without merit. Epic poems, which any skillful and dispassionate critic would at a glance have perceived to be almost entirely modern, and which, if they had been published as modern, would have instantly found their proper place in company with Blackmore's Alfred and Wilkie's Epigoniad, were pronounced to be fifteen hundred years old, and were gravely classed with the Iliad. Writers of a very different order from the imposter who fabricated these forgeries saw how striking an effect might be produced by skillful pictures of the old Highland life. Whatever was repulsive was softened down: whatever was graceful and noble was brought prominently forward. Some of these works were executed with such admirable art that, like the historical plays of Shakespeare, they superseded history. The visions of the poet were realities to his readers. The places which he described became holy ground, and were visited by thousands of pilgrims. Soon the vulgar imagination was so completely occupied by plaids, targets, and claymores, that, by most Englishmen, Scotchman and Highlander were regarded as synonymous words. Few people seemed to be aware that, at no remote period, a Macdonald or a Macgregor in his tartan was to a citizen of Edinburgh or Glasgow what an Indian hunter in his war paint is to an inhabitant of Philadelphia or Boston. Artists and actors represented Bruce and Douglas in striped petticoats. They might as well have represented Washington brandishing a tomahawk, and girt with a string of scalps. At length this fashion reached a point beyond which it was not easy to proceed. The last British King who held a court in Holyrood thought that he could not give a more striking proof of his respect for the usages which had prevailed in Scotland before the Union, than by disguising himself in what, before the Union, was considered by nine Scotchmen out of ten as the dress of a thief.

Thus it has chanced that the old Gaelic institutions and manners have never been exhibited in the simple light of truth. Up to the middle of the last century, they were seen through one false medium: they have since been seen through another. Once they loomed dimly through an obscuring and distorting haze of prejudice; and no sooner had that fog dispersed than they appeared bright with all the richest tints of poetry. The time when a perfectly fair picture could have been painted has now passed away. The original has long disappeared: no authentic effigy exists; and all that is possible is to produce an imperfect likeness by the help of two portraits, of which one is a coarse caricature and the other a masterpiece of flattery.

Among the erroneous notions which have been commonly received concerning the history and character of the Highlanders is one which it is especially necessary to correct. During the century which commenced with the campaign of Montrose, and terminated with the campaign of the young Pretender, every great military exploit which was achieved on British ground in the cause of the House of Stuart was achieved by the valor of Gaelic tribes. The English have therefore very naturally ascribed to those tribes the feelings of English cavaliers, profound reverence for the royal office, and enthusiastic attachment to the royal family. A close inquiry however will show that the strength of these feelings among the Celtic clans has been greatly exaggerated.

In studying the history of our civil contentions, we must never forget that the same names, badges, and war-cries had very different meaning, in different parts of the British isles. We have already seen how little there was in common between the Jacobitism of Ireland and the Jacobitism of England. The Jacobitism of the Scotch Highlander was, at least in the seventeenth century, a third variety, quite distinct from the other two. The Gaelic population was far indeed from holding the doctrines of passive obedience and non-resistance. In fact disobedience and resistance made up the ordinary life of that population. Some of those very clans which it has been the fashion to describe as so enthusiastically loyal that they were prepared to stand by James to the death, even when he was in the wrong, had never, while he was on the throne, paid the smallest respect to his authority, even when he was clearly in the right. Their practice, their calling, had been to disobey and to defy him. Some of them had actually been proscribed by sound of horn for the crime of withstanding his lawful commands, and would have torn to pieces without scruple any of his officers who had dared to venture beyond the passes for the purpose of executing his warrant. The English Whigs were accused by their opponents of holding doctrines dangerously lax touching the obedience due to the chief magistrate. Yet no respectable English Whig ever defended rebellion, except as a rare and extreme remedy for rare and extreme evils. But among those Celtic chiefs whose loyalty has been the theme of so much warm eulogy were some whose whole existence from boyhood upwards had been one long rebellion. Such men, it is evident, were not likely to see the Revolution in the light in which it appeared to an Oxonian non-juror. On the other hand they were not, like the aboriginal Irish, urged to take arms by impatience of Saxon domination. To such domination the Scottish Celt had never been subjected. He occupied his own wild and sterile region, and followed his own national usages. In his dealings with the Saxons, he was rather the oppressor than the oppressed. He exacted blackmail from them: he drove away their flocks and herds; and they seldom dared to pursue him to his native wilderness. They had never portioned out among themselves his dreary region of moor and shingle. He had never seen the tower of his hereditary chieftains occupied by an usurper who could not speak Gaelic, and who looked on all who spoke it as brutes and slaves: nor had his national and religious feelings ever been outraged by the power and splendor of a church which he regarded as at once foreign and heretical.

The real explanation of the readiness with which a large part of the population of the Highlands, twice in the seventeenth century, drew the sword for the Stuarts, is to be found in the internal quarrels which divided the commonwealth of clans. For there was a commonwealth of clans, the image, on a reduced scale, of the great commonwealth of European nations. In the smaller of these two commonwealths, as in the larger, there were wars, treaties, alliances, disputes about territory and precedence, a system of public law, a balance of power. There was one inexhaustible source of discontents and quarrels. The feudal system had, some centuries before, been introduced into the hill country, but had neither destroyed the patriarchal system nor amalgamated completely with it. In general, he who was lord in the Norman polity was also chief of the Celtic polity; and, when this was the case, there was no conflict. But, when the two characters were separated, all the willing and loyal obedience was reserved for the chief. The lord had only what he could get and hold by force. If he was able, by the help of his own tribe, to keep in subjection tenants who were not of his own tribe, there was a tyranny of clan over clan, the most galling, perhaps, of all forms of tyranny. At different times different races had risen to an authority which had produced general fear and envy. The Macdonalds had once possessed, in the Hebrides and throughout the mountain country of Argyleshire and Ivernesshire, an ascendency similar to that which the House of Austria had once possessed in Christendom. But the ascendency of the Macdonalds had, like the ascendency of the House of Austria, passed away; and the Campbells, the children of Diarmid, had become in the Highlands what the Bourbons had become in Europe.* The parallel might be carried far. Imputations similar to those which it was the fashion to throw on the French government were thrown on the Campbells. A peculiar dexterity, a peculiar plausibility of address, a peculiar contempt for the obligations of plighted faith, were ascribed, with or without reason, to the dreaded race. "Fair and false like a Campbell," became a proverb. It was said that Mac Callum More after Mac Callum More had, with unwearied, unscrupulous, and unrelenting ambition, annexed mountain after mountain and island after island to the original domains of his House. Some tribes had been expelled from their territory, some compelled to pay tribute, some incorporated with the conquerors. At length the number of fighting men who bore the name of Campbell was sufficient to meet in the field of battle the combined forces of all the other western clans. It was during those civil troubles which commenced in 1638 that the power of this aspiring family reached the zenith. The Marquess of Argyle was the head of a party as well as the head of a tribe. Possessed of two different kinds of authority, he used each of them in such a way as to extend and fortify the other. The knowledge that he could bring into the field the claymores of five thousand half heathen mountaineers added to his influence among the austere Presbyterians who filled the Privy Council and the General Assembly of Edinburgh. His influence at Edinburgh added to the ter-

* Since this passage was written I was much pleased by finding that Lord Fountainhall used, in July 1676, exactly the same illustration which had occurred to me. He says that "Argyle's ambitious grasping at the mastery of the Highlands and Western Islands of Mull, Ila, &c., stirred up other clans to enter into a combination for bearing him downe, like the confederat forces of Germanie, Spain, Holland &c., against the growth of the French."

ror which he inspired among the mountains. Of all the Highland Princes whose history is well known to us he was the greatest and most dreaded. It was while his neighbors were watching the increase of his power with hatred which fear could scarcely keep down that Montrose called them to arms. The call was promptly obeyed. A powerful coalition of clans waged war, nominally for King Charles, but really against Mac Callum More. It is not easy for any person who has studied the history of that contest to doubt that, if Argyle had supported the cause of monarchy, his neighbors would have declared against it. Grave writers tell of the victory gained at Iverlochy by the royalists over the rebels. But the peasants who dwell near the spot speak more accurately. They talk of the great battle won there by the Macdonalds over the Campbells.

The feelings which had produced the coalition against the Marquess of Argyle retained their force long after his death. His son, Earl Archibald, though a man of many eminent virtues, inherited, with the ascendency of his ancestors, the unpopularity which such ascendency could scarcely fail to produce. In 1675, several warlike tribes formed a confederacy against him, but were compelled to submit to the superior force which was at his command. There was therefore great joy from sea to sea when, in 1681, he was arraigned on a futile charge, condemned to death, driven into exile, and deprived of his dignities: there was great alarm when, in 1685, he returned from banishment, and sent forth the fiery cross to summon his kinsmen to his standard; and there was again great joy when his enterprise had failed, when his army had melted away, when his head had been fixed on the Tolbooth of Edinburgh, and when those chiefs who had regarded him as an oppressor had obtained from the Crown, on easy terms, remissions of old debts and grants of new titles. While England and Scotland generally were execrating the tyranny of James, he was honored as a deliverer in Appin and Lochaber, in Glenroy and Glenmore.* The hatred excited by the power and ambition of the House of Argyle was not satisfied even when the head of that House had perished, when his children were fugitives, when strangers garrisoned

---

* In the introduction to the Memoirs of Sir Ewan Cameron is a very sensible remark: "It may appear paradoxical: but the editor cannot help hazarding the conjecture that the motives which prompted the Highlanders to support King James were substantially the same as those by which the promoters of the Revolution were actuated." The whole introduction, indeed, well deserves to be read.

the castle of Inverary, and when the whole shore of Loch Fyne had been laid waste by fire and sword. It was said that the terrible precedent which had been set in the case of the Macgregors ought to be followed, and that it ought to be made a crime to bear the odious name of Campbell.

On a sudden all was changed. The Revolution came. The heir of Argyle returned in triumph. He was, as his predecessors had been, the head, not only of a tribe, but of a party. The sentence which had deprived him of his estate and of his honors was treated by the majority of the Convention as a nullity. The doors of the Parliament House were thrown open to him: he was selected from the whole body of Scottish nobles to administer the oath of office to the new Sovereigns; and he was authorized to raise an army on his domains for the service of the Crown. He would now, doubtless, be as powerful as the most powerful of his ancestors. Backed by the strength of the Government, he would demand all the long and heavy arrears of rent and tribute which were due to him from his neighbors, and would exact revenge for all the injuries and insults which his family had suffered. There was terror and agitation in the castles of twenty petty kings. The uneasiness was great among the Stewarts of Appin, whose territory was close pressed by the sea on one side, and by the race of Diarmid on the other. The Macnaghtens were still more alarmed. Once they had been the masters of those beautiful valleys through which the Ara and the Shira flow into Loch Fyne. But the Campbells had prevailed. The Macnaghtens had been reduced to subjection, and had, generation after generation, looked up with awe and detestation to the neighboring Castle of Inverary. They had recently been promised a complete emancipation. A grant, by virtue of which their chief would have held his estate immediately from the Crown, had been prepared and was about to pass the seals, when the Revolution suddenly extinguished a hope which amounted almost to certainty.*

The Macleans remembered that, only fourteen years before, their lands had been invaded and the seat of their chief taken and garrisoned by the Campbells.† Even be-

---

* Skene's Highlanders of Scotland; Douglas's Baronage of Scotland.

† See the Memoirs of the life of Sir Ewan Cameron, and the Historical and Genealogical Account of the Clan Maclean, by a Senachie. Though this last work was published so late as 1838, the writer seems to have been inflamed by animosity as fierce as that with which the Macleans of the seventeenth century regarded the Campbells. In the

fore William and Mary had been proclaimed at Edinburgh, a Maclean, deputed doubtless by the head of his tribe, had crossed the sea to Dublin, and had assured James that, if two or three battalions from Ireland landed in Argyleshire, they would be immediately joined by four thousand four hundred claymores.*

A similar spirit animated the Camerons. Their ruler, Sir Ewan Cameron, of Lochiel, surnamed the Black, was in personal qualities unrivalled among the Celtic princes. He was a gracious master, a trusty ally, a terrible enemy. His countenance and bearing were singularly noble. Some persons who had been at Versailles, and among them the shrewd and observant Simon Lord Lovat, said that there was, in person and manner, a most striking resemblance between Lewis the Fourteenth and Lochiel; and whoever compares the portraits of the two will perceive that there really was some likeness. In stature the difference was great. Lewis, in spite of high-heeled shoes and a towering wig, hardly reached the middle size. Lochiel was tall and strongly built. In agility and skill at his weapons he had few equals among the inhabitants of the hills. He had repeatedly been victorious in single combat. He was a hunter of great fame. He made vigorous war on the wolves which, down to his time, preyed on the red deer of the Grampians; and by his hand perished the last of the ferocious breed which is known to have wandered at large in our island. Nor was Lochiel less distinguished by intellectual than by bodily vigor. He might indeed have seemed ignorant to educated and travelled Englishmen, who had studied the classics under Busby at Westminster and under Aldrich at Oxford, who had learned something about the sciences among Fellows of the Royal Society, and something about the fine arts in the galleries of Florence and Rome. But though Lochiel had very little knowledge of books, he was eminently wise in council, eloquent in debate, ready in devising expedients, and skillful in managing the minds of men. His understand-

---

short compass of one page the Marquis of Argyle is designated as "the diabolical Scotch Cromwell," "the vile vindictive persecutor," "the base traitor," and "the Argyle impostor." In another page he is "the insidious Campbell, fertile in villany," "the avaricious slave," "the coward of Argyle," and "the Scotch traitor." In the next page he is "the base and vindictive enemy of the House of Maclean," "the hypocritical Covenanter," "the incorrigible traitor," "the cowardly and malignant enemy." It is a happy thing that passions so violent can now vent themselves only in scolding.

* Letter of Avaux to Louvois, April 6-16, 1689, enclosing a paper entitled Mémoire du Chevalier Macklean.

ing preserved him from those follies into which pride and anger frequently hurried his brother chieftains. Many, therefore, who regarded his brother chieftains as mere barbarians, mentioned him with respect. Even at the Dutch Embassy in Saint James's Square he was spoken of as a man of such capacity and courage that it would not be easy to find his equal. As a patron of literature, he ranks with the magnificent Dorset. If Dorset out of his own purse allowed Dryden a pension equal to the profits of the Laureateship, Lochiel is said to have bestowed on a celebrated bard, who had been plundered by marauders, and who implored alms in a pathetic Gaelic ode, three cows, and the almost incredible sum of fifteen pounds sterling. In truth, the character of this great chief was depicted two thousand five hundred years before his birth, and depicted, —such is the power of genius,—in colors which will be fresh as many years after his death. He was the Ulysses of the Highlands.*

He held a large territory peopled by a race which reverenced no lord, no king but himself. For that territory, however, he owed homage to the House of Argyle; and he was deeply in debt to his feudal superiors for rent. This vassalage he had doubtless been early taught to consider as degrading and unjust. In his minority he had been the ward in chivalry of the politic Marquess, and had been educated at the Castle of Inverary. But at eighteen the boy broke loose from the authority of his guardian, and fought bravely both for Charles the First and for Charles the Second. He was therefore considered by the English as a Cavalier, was well received at Whitehall after the Restoration, and was knighted by the hand of James. The compliment, however, which was paid to him, on one of his appearances at the English Court, would not have seemed very flattering to a Saxon. "Take care of your pockets, my lords," cried His Majesty; "here comes the king of the thieves." The loyalty of Lochiel is

---

* See the singularly interesting Memoirs of Sir Ewan Cameron of Lochiel, printed at Edinburgh for the Abbotsford Club in 1842. The MS. must have been at least a century older. See also in the same volume the account of Sir Ewan's death, copied from the Balhadie papers. I ought to say that the author of the Memoirs of Sir Ewan, though evidently well informed about the affairs of the Highlands and the characters of the most distinguished chiefs, was grossly ignorant of English politics and history. I will quote what Van Citters wrote to the States General about Lochiel, $\frac{\text{Nov. 26.}}{\text{Dec. 6,}}$ 1689: "Sir Evan Cameron, Lord Locheale, een man,—soo ik hoor van die hem lange gekent en dagelyk hebben mede omgegaan,—van so groot verstant, courage, en beleyt, als weyniges syns gelycke syn."

almost proverbial; but it was very unlike what was called loyalty in England. In the records of the Scottish Parliament he was, in the days of Charles the Second, described as a lawless and rebellious man, who held lands masterfully and in high contempt of the royal authority.* On one occasion the Sheriff of Invernesshire was directed by King James to hold a court in Lochaber. Lochiel, jealous of this interference with his own patriarchal despotism, came to the tribunal at the head of four hundred armed Camerons. He affected great reverence for the royal commission, but he dropped three or four words which were perfectly understood by the pages and armor-bearers who watched every turn of his eye. "Is none of my lads so clever as to send this judge packing? I have seen them get up a quarrel when there was less need of one." In a moment a brawl began in the crowd, none could say how or where. Hundreds of dirks were out: cries of "Help," and "Murder," were raised on all sides: many wounds were inflicted: two men were killed: the sitting broke up in tumult; and the terrified Sheriff was forced to put himself under the protection of the chief, who, with a plausible show of respect and concern, escorted him safe home. It is amusing to think that the man who performed this feat is constantly extolled as the most faithful and dutiful of subjects by writers who blame Somers and Burnet as contemners of the legitimate authority of sovereigns. Lochiel would undoubtedly have laughed the doctrine of non-resistance to scorn. But scarcely any chief in Invernesshire had gained more than he by the downfall of the House of Argyle, or had more reason than he to dread the restoration of that House. Scarcely any chief in Invernesshire, therefore, was more alarmed and disgusted by the proceedings of the Convention.

But of all those Highlanders who looked on the recent turn of fortune with painful apprehension the fiercest and the most powerful were the Macdonalds. More than one of the magnates who bore that widespread name laid claim to the honor of being the rightful successor of those Lords of the Isles, who, as late as the fifteenth century, disputed the pre-eminence of the Kings of Scotland. This genealogical controversy, which has lasted down to our own time, caused much bickering among the competitors. But they all agreed in regretting the past splendor of their

---
* Act Parl., July 5, 1661.

dynasty, and in detesting the upstart race of Campbell. The old feud had never slumbered. It was still constantly repeated, in verse and prose, that the finest part of the domain belonging to the ancient heads of the Gaelic nation, Islay, where they had lived with the pomp of royalty, Iona, where they had been interred with the pomp of religion, the paps of Jura, the rich peninsula of Kintyre, had been transferred from the legitimate possessors to the insatiable Mac Callum More. Since the downfall of the House of Argyle, the Macdonalds, if they had not regained their ancient superiority, might at least boast that they had now no superior. Relieved from the fear of their mighty enemy in the West, they had turned their arms against weaker enemies in the East, against the clan of Mackintosh and against the town of Inverness.

The clan of Mackintosh, a branch of an ancient and renowned tribe which took its name and badge from the wild cat of the forests, had a dispute with the Macdonalds, which originated, if tradition may be believed, in those dark times when the Danish pirates wasted the coasts of Scotland. Inverness was a Saxon colony among the Celts, a hive of traders and artisans, in the midst of a population of loungers and plunderers, a solitary outpost of civilization in a region of barbarians. Though the buildings covered but a small part of the space over which they now extend; though the arrival of a brig in the port was a rare event; though the Exchange was the middle of a miry street, in which stood a market cross much resembling a broken milestone; though the sittings of the municipal council were held in a filthy den with a rough-cast wall; though the best houses were such as would now be called hovels; though the best roofs were of thatch; though the best ceilings were of bare rafters; though the best windows were, in bad weather, closed with shutters for want of glass; though the humbler dwellings were mere heaps of turf, in which barrels with the bottoms knocked out served the purpose of chimneys; yet to the mountaineer of the Grampians this city was as Babylon or as Tyre. Nowhere else had he seen four or five hundred houses, two churches, twelve maltkilns, crowded close together. Nowhere else had he been dazzled by the splendor of rows of booths, where knives, horn spoons, tin kettles, and gaudy ribbons were exposed to sale. Nowhere else had he been on board of one of those huge ships which brought sugar and wine over the sea from countries far beyond the limits of his geography.* It is not strange that the haughty and warlike Macdonalds, despising peaceful industry, yet envying the fruits of that industry, should have fastened a succession of quarrels on the people of Inverness. In the reign of Charles the Second, it had been apprehended that the town would be stormed and plundered by those rude neighbors. The terms of peace which they offered showed how little they regarded the authority of the prince and of the law. Their demand was that a heavy tribute should be paid to them, that the municipal magistrates should bind themselves by an oath to deliver up to the vengeance of the clan every burgher who should shed the blood of a Macdonald, and that every burgher who should anywhere meet a person wearing the Macdonald tartan should ground arms in token of submission. Never did Lewis the Fourteenth, not even when he was encamped between Utrecht and Amsterdam, treat the States General with such despotic insolence.† By the intervention of the Privy Council of Scotland, a compromise was effected: but the old animosity was undiminished.

Common enmities and common apprehensions produced a good understanding between the town and the clan of Mackintosh. The foe most hated and dreaded by both was Colin Macdonald of Keppoch, an excellent specimen of the genuine Highland Jacobite. Keppoch's whole life had been passed in insulting and resisting the authority of the Crown. He had been repeatedly charged on his allegiance to desist from his lawless practices, but had treated every admonition with contempt. The government, however, was not willing to resort to extremities against him; and he long continued to rule undisturbed the stormy peaks of Coryarrick, and the gigantic terraces which still mark the limits of what was once the Lake of Glenroy. He was famed for his knowledge of all the ravines and caverns of that dreary region; and such was the skill with which he could track a herd of cattle to the most secret hiding-place that he was known by the nickname of Coll

---

* See Burt's Third and Fourth Letters. In the early editions is an engraving of the market cross of Inverness, and of that part of the street where the merchants congregated.

I ought here to acknowledge my obligations to Mr. Robert Carruthers, who kindly furnished me with much curious information about Inverness, and with some extracts from the municipal records.

† I am indebted to Mr Carruthers for a copy of the demands of the Macdonalds, and of the answer of the Town Council.

of the Cows.* At length his outrageous violations of all law compelled the Privy Council to take decided steps. He was proclaimed a rebel: letters of fire and sword were issued against him, under the seal of James; and a few weeks before the Revolution, a body of royal troops, supported by the whole strength of the Mackintoshes, marched into Keppoch's territories. Keppoch gave battle to the invaders, and was victorious. The King's forces were put to flight; the King's captain was slain; and this by a hero whose loyalty to the King many writers have very complacently contrasted with the factious turbulence of the Whigs.†

If Keppoch had ever stood in any awe of the government, he was completely relieved from the feeling by the general anarchy which followed the Revolution. He wasted the lands of the Mackintoshes, advanced to Inverness, and threatened the town with destruction. The danger was extreme. The houses were surrounded only by a wall which time and weather had so loosened that it shook in every storm. Yet the inhabitants showed a bold front; and their courage was stimulated by their preachers. Sunday the twenty-eight of April was a day of alarm and confusion. The savages went round and round the small colony of Saxons like a troop of famished wolves round a sheep-fold. Keppoch threatened and blustered. He would come in with all his men. He would sack the place. The burghers meanwhile mustered in arms round the market cross to listen to the oratory of their ministers. The day closed without an assault: the Monday and the Tuesday passed away in intense anxiety; and then an unexpected mediator made his appearance.

Dundee, after his flight from Edinburgh, had retired to his country seat in that valley through which the Glamis descends to the ancient castle of Macbeth. Here he remained quiet during some time. He protested that he had no intention of opposing the new government. He declared himself ready to return to Edinburgh; if only he could be assured that he should be protected against lawless violence; and he offered to give his word of honor, or, if that were not sufficient to give bail, that he would keep the peace. Some of his old soldiers had accompanied him, and formed a garrison sufficient, to protect his house

---

* Colt's Deposition, Appendix to the Act Parl., of July 14, 1690.
† See the Life of Sir Ewan Cameron.

against the Presbyterians of the neighborhood. Here he might possibly have remained unharmed and harmless, had not an event for which he was not answerable made his enemies implacable, and made him desperate.*

An emissary of James had crossed from Ireland to Scotland with letters addressed to Dundee and Balcarras. Suspicion was excited. The messenger was arrested, interrogated, and searched; and the letters were found. Some of them proved to be from Melfort, and were worthy of him. Every line indicated those qualities which had made him the abhorrence of his country, and the favorite of his master. He announced with delight the near approach of the day of vengeance and rapine, of the day when the estates of the seditious would be divided among the loyal, and when many who had been great and prosperous would be exiles and beggars. The King, Melfort said, was determined to be severe. Experience had at length convinced His Majesty that mercy would be weakness. Even the Jacobites were disgusted by learning that a restoration would be immediately followed by a confiscation and a proscription. Some of them pretended to suspect a forgery. Others did not hesitate to say that Melfort was a villain, that he wished to ruin Dundee and Balcarras, and that, for that end, he had written these odious despatches, and had employed a messenger who had very dexterously managed to be caught. It is however quite certain that Melfort never disavowed these papers, and that, after they were published, he continued to stand as high as ever in the favor of James. It can therefore hardly be doubted that in those passages which shocked even the zealous supporters of hereditary right, the Secretary merely expressed with fidelity the feelings and intentions of his master.† Hamilton, by virtue of the powers which the Estates had, before their adjournment, confided to him, ordered Balcarras and Dundee to be arrested. Balcarras was taken, and was confined, first in his own house, and then in the Tolbooth of Edinburgh. But to seize Dundee was not so easy an enterprise. As soon as he heard that warrants were out against him, he crossed the Dee with his followers,

---

* Balcarras's Memoirs; History of the late Revolution in Scotland.
† There is among the Nairne Papers in the Bodleian Library a curious MS. entitled "Journal de ce qui s'est passé en Irlande depuis l'arrivée de Sa Majesté." In this journal there are notes and corrections in English and French; the English in the handwriting of James, the French in the handwriting of Melfort. The letters intercepted by Hamilton are mentioned, and mentioned in a way which plainly shows that they were genuine; nor is there the least sign that James disapproved of them.

and remained a short time in the wild domains of the House of Gordon. There he held some communication with the Macdonalds and Camerons about a rising. But he seems at this time to have known little and cared little about the Highlanders. For their national character he probably felt the dislike of a Saxon, for their military character the contempt of a professional soldier. He soon returned to the Lowlands, and stayed there till he learned that a considerable body of troops had been sent to apprehend him.* He then betook himself to the hill country as his last refuge, pushed northward through Strathdon and Strathbogie, crossed the Spey, and on the morning of the first of May, arrived with a small band of horsemen at the camp of Keppoch before Inverness.

The new situation in which Dundee was now placed, the new view of society which was presented to him, naturally suggested new projects to his inventive and enterprising spirit. The hundreds of athletic Celts whom he saw in their national order of battle were evidently not allies to be despised. If he could form a great coalition of clans, if he could muster under one banner ten or twelve thousand of those hardy warriors, if he could induce them to submit to the restraints of discipline, what a career might be before him!

A commission from King James, even when King James was securely seated on the throne, had never been regarded with much respect by Coll of the Cows. That chief, however, hated the Campbells with all the hatred of a Macdonald, and promptly gave in his adhesion to the cause of the House of Stuart. Dundee undertook to settle the dispute between Keppoch and Inverness. The town agreed to pay two thousand dollars, a sum which, small as it might be in the estimation of the goldsmiths of Lombard Street, probably exceeded any treasure that had ever been carried into the wilds of Coryarrick. Half the sum was raised, not without difficulty, by the inhabitants; and Dundee is said to have passed his words for the remainder.†

He next tried to reconcile the Macdonalds with the

---

* "Nor did ever," says Balcarras, addressing James, "the Viscount of Dundee think of going to the Highlands without further orders from you, till a party was sent to apprehend him."

† See the narrative sent to James in Ireland and received by him July 7, 1689. It is among the Nairne Papers. See also the Memoirs of Dundee. 1714; Memoirs of Sir Ewan Cameron; Balcarras's Memoirs; Mackay's Memoirs. These narratives do not perfectly agree with each other, or with the information which I obtained from Inverness.

Mackintoshes, and flattered himself that the two warlike tribes, lately arrayed against each other, might be willing to fight side by side under his command. But he soon found that it was no light matter to take up a Highland feud. About the rights of the contending Kings neither clan knew anything nor cared anything. The conduct of both is to be ascribed to local passions and interests. What Argyle was to Keppoch, Keppoch was to the Mackintoshes. The Mackintoshes therefore remained neutral; and their example was followed by the Macphersons, another branch of the race of the wild cat. This was not Dundee's only disappointment. The Mackenzies, the Frasers, the Grants, the Munros, the Mackays, the Macleods, dwelt at a great distance from the territory of Mac Callum More. They had no dispute with him; they owed no debt to him; and they had no reason to dread the increase of his power. They therefore did not sympathize with his alarmed and exasperated neighbors, and could not be induced to join the confederacy against him.*
Those chiefs, on the other hand, who lived nearer to Inverary, and to whom the name of Campbell had long been terrible and hateful, greeted Dundee eagerly, and promised to meet him at the head of their followers on the eighteenth of May. During the fortnight which preceded that day, he traversed Badenoch and Athol, and exhorted the inhabitants of those districts to rise in arms. He dashed into the Lowlands with his horsemen, surprised Perth, and carried off some Whig gentlemen prisoners to the mountains. Meanwhile the fiery crosses had been wandering from hamlet to hamlet over all the heaths and mountains thirty miles round Ben Nevis; and when he reached the trysting place in Lochaber he found that the gathering had begun. The head-quarters were fixed close to Lochiel's house, a large pile built entirely of fir wood, and considered, in the Highlands, as a superb palace. Lochiel, surrounded by more than six hundred broadswords, was there to receive his guests. Macnaghten of Macnaghten and Stewart of Appin were at the muster with their little clans. Macdonald of Keppoch led the warriors who had, a few months before, under his command, put to flight the musketeers of King James. Macdonald of Clanronald was of tender years: but he was brought to the camp by his uncle

---

* Memoirs of Dundee; Tarbet to Melville, 1st June 1689, in the Leven and Melville Papers.

who acted as regent during the minority. The youth was attended by a picked body guard composed of his own cousins, all comely in appearance, and good men of their hands. Macdonald of Glengarry, conspicuous by his dark brow and his lofty stature, came from that great valley where a chain of lakes, then unknown to fame, and scarcely set down in maps, is now the daily highway of steam vessels passing and repassing between the Atlantic and the German Ocean. None of the rulers of the mountains had a higher sense of his personal dignity, or was more frequently engaged in disputes with other chiefs. He generally affected in his manners and in his housekeeping a rudeness beyond that of his rude neighbors, and professed to regard the very few luxuries which had then found their way from the civilized parts of the world into the Highlands as signs of the effeminacy and degeneracy of the Gaelic race. But on this occasion he chose to imitate the splendor of Saxon warriors, and rode on horseback before his four hundred plaided clansmen in a steel cuirass and a coat embroidered with gold lace. Another Macdonald, destined to a lamentable and horrible end, led a band of hardy freebooters from the dreary pass of Glencoe. Somewhat later came the great Hebridean potentates. Macdonald of Sleat, the most opulent and powerful of all the grandees who laid claim to the lofty title of Lord of the Isles, arrived at the head of seven hundred fighting men from Sky. A fleet of long boats brought five hundred Macleans from Mull under the command of their chief, Sir John of Duart. A far more formidable array had in old times followed his forefathers to battle. But the power, though not the spirit, of the clan had been broken by the arts and arms of the Campbells. Another band of Macleans arrived under a valiant leader, who took his title from Lochbuy, which is, being interpreted, the Yellow Lake.*

It does not appear that a single chief who had not some

---

* Narrative in the Nairne Papers; Depositions of Colt, Osburne, Malcolm, and Stewart of Ballachan in the Appendix to the Act Parl. of July 14. 1690; Memoirs of Sir Ewan Cameron. A few touches I have taken from an English translation of some passages in a lost epic poem written in Latin, and called the Grameis. The writer was a zealous Jacobite named Phillipps. I have seldom made use of the Memoirs of Dundee, printed in 1714, and never without some misgiving. The writer was certainly not, as he pretends, one of Dundee's officers, but a stupid and ignorant Grub Street garreteer. He is utterly wrong both as to the place and as to the time of the most important of all the events which he relates, the battle of Killiecrankie. He says that it was fought on the banks of the Tummell, and on the 13th of June. It was fought on the banks of the Garry, and on the 27th of July. After giving such a specimen of inaccuracy as this, it would be idle to point out minor blunders.

special cause to dread and detest the House of Argyle obeyed Dundee's summons. There is indeed strong reason to believe that the chiefs who came would have remained quietly at home if the government had understood the politics of the Highlands. Those politics were thoroughly understood by one able and experienced statesman, sprung from the great Highland family of Mackenzie, the Viscount Tarbet. He at this conjuncture pointed out to Melville by letter, and to Mackay in conversation, both the cause and the remedy of the distempers which seemed likely to bring on Scotland the calamities of civil war. There was, Tarbet said, no general disposition to insurrection among the Gael. Little was to be apprehended even from those Popish clans which were under no apprehension of being subjected to the yoke of the Campbells. It was notorious that the ablest and most active of the discontented chiefs troubled themselves not at all about the questions which were in dispute between the Whigs and the Tories. Lochiel in particular, whose eminent personal qualities made him the most important man among the mountaineers, cared no more for James than for William. If the Camerons, the Macdonalds, and the Macleans could be convinced that, under the new government, their estates and their dignities would be safe, if Mac Callum More would make some concessions, if their Majesties would take on themselves the payment of some arrears of rent, Dundee might call the clans to arms: but he would call to little purpose. Five thousand pounds, Tarbet thought, would be sufficient to quiet all the Celtic magnates; and in truth, though that sum might seem ludicrously small to the politicians of Westminster, though it was not larger than the annual gains of the Groom of the Stole, or of the Paymaster of the Forces, it might well be thought immense by a barbarous potentate who, while he ruled hundreds of square miles, and could bring hundreds of warriors into the field, had perhaps never had fifty guineas at once in his coffers.*

Though Tarbet was considered by the Scottish ministers of the new Sovereigns as a very doubtful friend, his advice was not altogether neglected. It was resolved that overtures such as he recommended should be made to the

---

* From a letter of Archibald Earl of Argyle to Lauderdale, which bears date the 25th of June 1664, it appears that a hundred thousand marks Scots, little more than five thousand pounds sterling, would, at that time, have very nearly satisfied all the claims of Mac Callum More on his neighbors.

malcontents. Much depended on the choice of an agent; and unfortunately the choice showed how little the prejudices of the wild tribes of the hills were understood at Edinburgh. A Campbell was selected for the office of gaining over to the cause of King William men whose only quarrel to King William was that he countenanced the Campbells. Offers made through such a channel were naturally regarded as at once snares and insults. After this it was to no purpose that Tarbet wrote to Lochiel and Mackay to Glengarry. Lochiel returned no answer to Tarbet; and Glengarry returned to Mackay a coldly civil answer, in which the general was advised to imitate the example of Monk.*

Mackay, meanwhile, wasted some weeks in marching, in countermarching and in indecisive skirmishing. He afterward honestly admitted that the knowledge which he had acquired, during thirty years of military service on the continent, was, in the new situation in which he was placed, useless to him. It was difficult in such a country to track the enemy. It was impossible to drive him to bay. Food for an invading army was not to be found in the wilderness of heath and shingle; nor could supplies for many days be transported far over quaking bogs and up precipitous ascents. The general found that he had tired his men and their horses almost to death, and yet had effected nothing. Highland auxiliaries might have been of the greatest use to him: but he had few such auxiliaries. The chief of the Grants, indeed, who had been persecuted by the late government, and had been accused of conspiring with the unfortunate Earl of Argyle, was zealous on the side of the Revolution. Two hundred Mackays, animated probably by family feeling, came, from the northern extremity of our island, where at midsummer there is no night, to fight under a commander of their own name: but in general the clans which took no part in the insurrection awaited the event with cold indifference, and pleased themselves with the hope that they should easily make their peace with the conquerors, and be permitted to assist in plundering the conquered.

An experience of little more than a month satisfied Mackay that there was only one way in which the Highlands could be subdued. It was idle to run after the

---

* Mackay's Memoirs; Tarbet to Melville, June 1, 1689, in the Leven and Melville Papers; Dundee to Melfort, June 27, in the Nairne Papers.

mountaineers up and down their mountains. A chain of fortresses must be built in the most important situations, and must be well garrisoned. The place with which the general proposed to begin was Inverlochy, where the huge remains of an ancient castle stood and still stand. This post was close to an arm of the sea, and was in the heart of the country occupied by the discontented clans. A strong force stationed there, and supported, if necessary, by ships of war, would effectually overawe at once the Macdonalds, the Camerons and the Macleans.*

While Mackay was representing in his letters to the council at Edinburgh the necessity of adopting this plan, Dundee was contending with difficulties which all his energy and dexterity could not completely overcome.

The Highlanders, while they continued to be a nation living under a peculiar polity, were in one sense better and in another sense worse fitted for military purposes than any other nation in Europe. The individual Celt was morally and physically well qualified for war, and especially for war in so wild and rugged a country as his own. He was intrepid, strong, fleet, patient of cold, of hunger, and of fatigue. Up steep crags, and over treacherous morasses, he moved as easily as the French household troops paced along the great road from Versailles to Marli. He was accustomed to the use of weapons and to the sight of blood: he was a fencer: he was a marksman; and before he had ever stood in the ranks, he was already more than half a soldier.

As the individual Celt was easily turned into a soldier, so a tribe of Celts was easily turned into a battalion of soldiers. All that was necessary was that the military organization should be conformed to the patriarchal organization. The chief must be colonel: his uncle or his brother must be major: the tacksmen, who formed what may be called the peerage of the little community, must be the captains; the company of each captain must consist of those peasants who lived on his land, and whose names, faces, connections, and characters were perfectly known to him: the subaltern officers must be selected among the Duinhe Wassels, proud of the eagle's feather: the henchman was an excellent orderly: the hereditary piper and his sons formed the band; and the clan became at once a regiment. In such a regiment was found from

---

* See Mackay's Memoirs, and his letter to Hamilton of the 14th of June 1689.

the first moment that exact order and prompt obedience in which the strength of regular armies consists. Every man, from the highest to the lowest, was in his proper place, and knew that place perfectly. It was not necessary to impress by threats or by punishment on the newly enlisted troops the duty of regarding as their head him whom they had regarded as their head ever since they could remember anything. Every private had, from infancy, respected his corporal much and his captain more, and had almost adored his colonel. There was therefore no danger of mutiny. There was as little danger of desertion. Indeed the very feelings which most powerfully impel other soldiers to desert kept the Highlander to his standard. If he left it whither was he to go? All his kinsmen, all his friends, were arrayed round it. To separate himself from it was to separate himself forever from his family, and to incur all the misery of that very home-sickness which, in regular armies, drives so many recruits to abscond at the risk of stripes and of death. When these things are fairly considered, it will not be thought strange that the Highland clans should have occasionally achieved great martial exploits.

But those very institutions which made a tribe of Highlanders, all bearing the same name, and all subject to the same ruler, so formidable in battle, disqualified the nation for war on a large scale. Nothing was easier than to turn clans into efficient regiments: but nothing was more difficult than to combine these regiments in such a manner as to form an efficient army. From the shepherds and herdsmen who fought in the ranks up to the chiefs, all was harmony and order. Every man looked up to his immediate superior; and all looked up to the common head. But with the chief this chain of subordination ended. He knew only how to govern, and had never learned to obey. Even to royal proclamations, even to Acts of Parliament, he was accustomed to yield obedience only when they were in perfect accordance with his own inclinations. It was not to be expected that he would pay to any delegated authority a respect which he was in the habit of refusing to the supreme authority. He thought himself entitled to judge of the propriety of every order which he received. Of his brother chiefs, some were his enemies, and some his rivals. It was hardly possible to keep him from affronting them, or to convince him that they were not affronting him. All his followers sympathized with all his animosities, considered his honor as their own, and were ready at his whistle to array themselves round him in arms against the commander-in-chief. There was therefore very little chance that by any contrivance any five clans could be induced to cooperate heartily with one another during a long campaign. The best chance, however, was when they were led by a Saxon. It is remarkable that none of the great actions performed by the Highlanders during our civil wars was performed under the command of a Highlander. Some writers have mentioned it as a proof of the extraordinary genius of Montrose and Dundee that those captains, though not themselves of Gaelic race or speech, should have been able to form and direct confederacies of Gaelic tribes. But in truth it was precisely because Montrose and Dundee were not Highlanders that they were able to lead armies composed of Highland clans. Had Montrose been chief of the Camerons, the Macdonalds would never have submitted to his authority. Had Dundee been chief of Clanronald, he would never have been obeyed by Glengarry. Haughty and punctilious men, who scarcely acknowledged the King to be their superior, would not have endured the superiority of a neighbor, an equal, a competitor. They could far more easily bear the preeminence of a distinguished stranger. Yet even to such a stranger they would allow only a very limited and a very precarious authority. To bring a chief before a court-martial, to shoot him, to cashier him, to degrade him, to reprimand him publicly was impossible. Macdonald of Keppoch or Maclean of Duart would have struck dead any officer who had demanded his sword, and told him to consider himself as under arrest; and hundreds of claymores would instantly have been drawn to protect the murderer. All that was left to the commander under whom these potentates condescended to serve was to argue with them, to supplicate them, to flatter them, to bribe them; and it was only during a short time that any human skill could preserve harmony by these means. For every chief thought himself entitled to peculiar observance; and it was therefore impossible to pay marked court to any one without disobliging the rest. The general found himself merely the president of a congress of petty kings. He was perpetually called upon to hear and to compose disputes about pedigrees, about precedence, about the division of spoil. His decision, be it what it might, must offend somebody. At any moment he might hear that his right wing had fired on his center in pursuance of some quarrel two hundred years old, or that a whole battalion had marched back to its native glen, because another battalion had been put in the post of honor. A Highland bard might easily have found in the history of the year 1689 subjects very similar to those with which the war of Troy furnished the great poets of antiquity. One day Achilles is sullen, keeps his tent, and announces his intention to depart with all his men. The next day Ajax is storming about the camp, and threatening to cut the throat of Ulysses.

Hence it was that, though the Highlanders achieved some great exploits in the civil wars of the seventeenth century, those exploits left no trace which could be discerned after the lapse of a few weeks. Victories of strange and almost portentous splendor produced all the consequences of defeat. Veteran soldiers and statesmen were bewildered by these sudden turns of fortune. It was incredible that undisciplined men should have performed such feats of arms. It was incredible that such feats of arms, having been performed, should be immediately followed by the triumph of the conquered and the submission of the conquerors. Montrose, having passed rapidly from victory to victory, was, in the full career of success, suddenly abandoned by his followers. Local jealousies and local interests had brought his army together. Local jealousies and local interests dissolved it. The Gordons left him because they fancied that he neglected them for the Macdonalds. The Macdonalds left him because they wanted to plunder the Campbells. The force which had once seemed sufficient to decide the fate of a kingdom melted away in a few days; and the victories of Tippermuir and Kilsyth were followed by the disaster of Philiphaugh. Dundee did not live long enough to experience a similar reverse of fortune: but there is every reason to believe that, had his life been prolonged one fortnight, his history would have been the history of Montrose retold.

Dundee made one attempt, soon after the gathering of the clans in Lochaber, to induce them to submit to the discipline of a regular army. He called a council of war to consider this subject. His opinion was supported by all the officers who had joined him from the low country.

Distinguished among them were James Seton, Earl of Dunfermline, and James Galloway, Lord Dunkeld. The Celtic chiefs took the other side. Lochiel, the ablest among them, was their spokesman, and argued the point with much ingenuity and natural eloquence. "Our system,"—such was the substance of his reasoning,—"may not be the best: but we were bred to it from childhood: we understand it perfectly: it is suited to our peculiar institutions, feelings, and manners. Making war after our own fashion, we have the expertness and coolness of veterans. Making war in any other way, we shall be raw and awkward recruits. To turn us into soldiers like those of Cromwell and Turenne would be the business of years: and we have not even weeks to spare. We have time enough to unlearn our own discipline, but not time enough to learn yours." Dundee, with high compliments to Lochiel, declared himself convinced, and perhaps was convinced: for the reasonings of the wise old chief were by no means without weight.*

Yet some Celtic usages of war were such as Dundee could not tolerate. Cruel as he was, his cruelty always had a method and a purpose. He still hoped that he might be able to win some chiefs who remained neutral; and he carefully avoided every act which could goad them into open hostility. This was undoubtedly a policy likely to promote the interest of James: but the interest of James was nothing to the wild marauders who used his name and rallied round his banner merely for the purpose of making profitable forays and wreaking old grudges. Keppoch especially, who hated the Mackintoshes much more than he loved the Stuarts, not only plundered the territory of his enemies, but burned whatever he could not carry away. Dundee was moved to great wrath by the sight of the blazing dwellings. "I would rather," he said, "carry a musket in a respectable regiment than be captain of such a gang of thieves." Punishment was of course out of the question. Indeed it may be considered as a remarkable proof of the general's influence that Coll of the Cows deigned to apologize for conduct for which, in a well governed army, he would have been shot.†

As the Grants were in arms for King William, their property was considered as fair prize. Their territory was invaded by a party of Camerons: a skirmish took place:

---

* Memoirs of Sir Ewan Cameron. † Ibid.

some blood was shed; and many cattle were carried off to Dundee's camp, where provisions were greatly needed. This raid produced a quarrel, the history of which illustrates in the most striking manner the character of a Highland army. Among those who were slain in resisting the Camerons was a Macdonald of the Glengarry branch, who had long resided among the Grants, had become in feelings and opinions a Grant, and had absented himself from the muster of his tribe. Though he had been guilty of a high offence against the Gaelic code of honor and morality, his kinsmen remembered the sacred tie which he had forgotten. Good or bad, he was bone of their bone: he was flesh of their flesh; and he should have been reserved for their justice. The name which he bore, the blood of the Lords of the Isles, should have been his protection. Glengarry in a rage went to Dundee and demanded vengeance on Lochiel and the whole race of Cameron. Dundee replied that the unfortunate gentleman who had fallen was a traitor to the clan as well as to the King. Was it ever heard of in war that the person of an enemy, a combatant in arms, was to be held inviolable on account of his name and descent? And, even if wrong had been done, how was it to be redressed? Half the army must slaughter the other half before a finger could be laid on Lochiel. Glengarry went away raging like a madman. Since his complaints were disregarded by those who ought to right him, he would right himself: he would draw out his men, and fall sword in hand on the murderers of his cousin. During some time he would listen to no expostulation. When he was reminded that Lochiel's followers were in number nearly double of the Glengarry men, "No matter," he cried, "one Macdonald is worth two Camerons." Had Lochiel been equally irritable and boastful, it is probable that the Highland insurrection would have given little more trouble to the government, and that the rebels would have perished obscurely in the wilderness by one another's claymores. But nature had bestowed on him in large measure the qualities of a statesman, though fortune had hidden those qualities in an obscure corner of the world. He saw that this was not a time for brawling; his own character for courage had long been established; and his temper was under strict government. The fury of Glengarry, not being inflamed by any fresh provocation, rapidly abated. Indeed there were some who suspected that he had never been quite so pugnacious as he had affected to be, and that his bluster was meant only to keep up his own dignity in the eyes of his retainers. However this might be, the quarrel was composed; and the two chiefs met with the outward show of civility at the general's table.*

What Dundee saw of his Celtic allies must have made him desirous to have in his army some troops on whose obedience he could depend, and who would not, at a signal from their colonel, turn their arms against their general and their king. He accordingly, during the month of May and June, sent to Dublin a succession of letters earnestly imploring assistance. If six thousand, four thousand, three thousand, regular soldiers were now sent to Lochaber, he trusted that His Majesty would soon hold a court in Holyrood. That such a force might be spared hardly admitted of a doubt. The authority of James was at that time acknowledged in every part of Ireland, except on the shores of Lough Erne and behind the ramparts of Londonderry. He had in that kingdom an army of forty thousand men. An eighth part of such an army would scarcely be missed there, and might, united with the clans which were in insurrection, effect great things in Scotland.

Dundee received such answers to his applications as encouraged him to hope that a large and well appointed force would soon be sent from Ulster to join him. He did not wish to try the chance of battle before these succors arrived.† Mackay, on the other hand, was weary of marching to and fro in a desert. His men were exhausted and out of heart. He thought it desirable that they should withdraw from the hill country, and William was of the same opinion.

In June therefore the civil war was, as if by concert between the generals, completely suspended. Dundee remained in Lochaber, impatiently awaiting the arrival of troops and supplies from Ireland. It was impossible for him to keep his Highlanders together in a state of inactivity. A vast extent of moor and mountain was required to furnish food for so many mouths. The clans therefore went back to their own glens, having promised to reassemble on the first summons.

---

* Memoirs of Sir Ewan Cameron.
† Dundee to Melfort, June 27, 1689.

Meanwhile Mackay' soldiers, exhausted by severe exertions and privations, were taking their ease in quarters scattered over the low country from Aberdeen to Stirling. Mackay himself was at Edinburgh, and was urging the ministers there to furnish him with the means of constructing a chain of fortifications among the Grampians. The ministers had, it should seem, miscalculated their military resources. It had been expected that the Campbells would take the field in such force as would balance the whole strength of the clans which marched under Dundee. It had also been expected that the Covenanters of the West would hasten to swell the ranks of the army of King William. Both expectations were disappointed. Argyle had found his principality devastated, and his tribe disarmed and disorganized. A considerable time must elapse before his standard would be surrounded by an array such as his forefathers had led to battle. The Covenanters of the West were in general unwilling to enlist. They were assuredly not wanting in courage; and they hated Dundee with deadly hatred. In their part of the country the memory of his cruelty was still fresh. Every village had its own tale of blood. The grey-headed father was missed in one dwelling, the hopeful stripling in another. It was remembered but too well how the dragoons had stalked into the peasant's cottage, cursing and damning him, themselves, and each other at every second word, pushing from the ingle nook his grandmother of eighty, and thrusting their hands into the bosom of his daughter of sixteen; how the abjuration had been tendered to him; how he had folded his arms and said "God's will be done"; how the colonel had called for a file with loaded muskets; and how in three minutes the good man of the house had been wallowing in a pool of blood at his own door. The seat of the martyr was still vacant at the fireside; and every child could point out his grave still green amidst the heath. When the people of this region called their oppressor a servant of the devil, they were not speaking figuratively. They believed that between the bad man and the bad angel there was a close alliance on definite terms; that Dundee had bound himself to do the work of hell on earth, and that, for high purposes, hell was permitted to protect its slave till the measure of his guilt should be full. But, intensely as these men abhorred Dundee, most of them had a scruple about drawing the sword for William. A great meeting was held in the parish church of Douglas; and the question was propounded, whether, at a time when war was in the land, and when an Irish invasion was expected, it were not a duty to take arms. The debate was sharp and tumultuous. The orators on one side adjured their brethren not to incur the curse denounced against the inhabitants of Meroz, who came not to the help of the Lord against the mighty. The orators on the other side thundered against sinful associations. There were malignants in William's army: Mackay's own orthodoxy was problematical: to take military service with such comrades, and under such a general, would be a sinful association. At length after much wrangling, and amidst great confusion, a vote was taken; and the majority pronounced that to take military service would be a sinful association. There was however a large minority; and, from among the members of this minority, the Earl of Angus was able to raise a body of infantry, which is still, after the lapse of more than a hundred and sixty years, known by the name of the Cameronian Regiment. The first lieutenant colonel was Cleland, that implacable avenger of blood who had driven Dundee from the Convention. There was no small difficulty in filling the ranks; for many West country Whigs, who did not think it absolutely sinful to enlist, stood out for terms subversive of all military discipline. Some would not serve under any colonel, major, captain, sergeant, or corporal, who was not ready to sign the Covenant. Others insisted that, if it should be found absolutely necessary to appoint any officer who had taken the tests imposed in the late reign, he should at least qualify himself for command by publicly confessing his sin at the head of the regiment. Most of the enthusiasts who had proposed these conditions were induced by dexterous management to abate much of their demands. Yet the new regiment had a very peculiar character. The soldiers were all rigid Puritans. One of their first acts was to petition the Parliament that all drunkenness, licentiousness, and profaneness might be severely punished. Their own conduct must have been exemplary: for the worst crime which the most austere bigotry could impute to them was that of huzzaing on the King's birthday. It was originally intended that with the military organization of the corps should be interwoven the organization of a Presbyterian congregation. Each company was to furnish an elder; and the elders were, with the chaplain, to form an ecclesiastical court for the suppression of immorality and heresy. Elders, however, were not appointed: but a noted hill preacher, Alexander Shields, was called to the office of chaplain. It is not easy to conceive that fanaticism can be heated to a higher temperature than that which is indicated by the writings of Shields. According to him, it should seem to be the first duty of a Christian ruler, to persecute to the death every heterodox subject, and the first duty of a Christian subject to poniard a heterodox ruler. Yet there was then in Scotland an enthusiasm compared with which the enthusiasm even of this man was lukewarm. The extreme Covenanters protested against his defection as vehemently as he had protested against the Black Indulgence and the oath of supremacy, and pronounced every man who entered Angus's regiment guilty of a wicked confederacy with malignants.*

Meanwhile Edinburgh Castle had fallen, after holding out more than two months. Both the defence and the attack had been languidly conducted. The Duke of Gordon, unwilling to incur the mortal hatred of those at whose mercy his lands and life might soon be, did not choose to batter the city. The assailants, on the other hand, carried on their operations with so little energy and so little vigilance that a constant communication was kept up between the Jacobites within the citadel and the Jacobites without. Strange stories were told of the polite and facetious messages which passed between the besieged and the besiegers. On one occasion Gordon sent to inform the magistrates that he was going to fire a salute on account of some news which he had received from Ireland, but that the good town need not be alarmed, for that his guns would not be loaded with ball. On another occasion, his drums beat a parley; the white flag was hung out: a conference took place; and he gravely informed the enemy that all his cards had been thumbed to pieces, and begged to have a few more packs. His friends established a telegraph by means of which they conversed with him across the lines

---

* See Faithful Contendings Displayed, particularly the proceedings of April 29 and 30 and of May 13, and 14, 1689; the petition to Parliament drawn up by the regiment, on July 18, 1689; the protestation of Sir Robert Hamilton of November 6, 1689; and the admonitory Epistle to the Regiment, dated March 27, 1690. The Society people, as they called themselves, seem to have been especially shocked by the way in which the King's birthday had been kept. "We hope," they wrote, "ye are against observing anniversary days as well as we, and that ye will mourn for what ye have done." As to the opinions and temper of Alexander Shields, see his Hind Let Loose.

of sentinels. From a window in the top story of one of the loftiest of those gigantic houses, a few of which still darken the High Street, a white cloth was hung out when all was well, and a black cloth when things went ill. If it was necessary to give more detailed information, a board was held up inscribed with capital letters so large that they could, by the help of a telescope, be read on the ramparts of the castle. Agents laden with letters and fresh provisions managed, in various disguises and by various shifts, to cross the sheet of water which then lay on the north of the fortress, and to clamber up the precipitous ascent. The peal of a musket from a particular half moon was the signal which announced to the friends of the House of Stuart that another of their emissaries had got safe up the rock. But at length the supplies were exhausted; and it was necessary to capitulate. Favorable terms were readily granted: the garrison marched out; and the keys were delivered up amidst the acclamations of a great multitude of burghers.*

But the government had far more acrimonious and more pertinacious enemies in the Parliament House than in the Castle. When the Estates reassembled after their adjournment, the crown and scepter of Scotland were displayed with the wonted pomp in the hall as types of the absent sovereign. Hamilton rode in state from Holyrood up the High Street as Lord High Commissioner; and Crawford took the chair as President. Two Acts, one turning the Convention into a Parliament, the other recognizing William and Mary as King and Queen, were rapidly passed and touched with the scepter; and then the conflict of factions began.†

It speedily appeared that the opposition which Montgomery had organized was irresistibly strong. Though made up of many conflicting elements, Republicans, Whigs, Tories, zealous Presbyterians, bigoted Prelatists, it acted for a time as one man and drew to itself a multitude of those mean and timid politicians who naturally gravitate towards the stronger party. The friends of the government were few and disunited. Hamilton brought but half a heart to the discharge of his duties. He had always been unstable; and he was now discontented. He held in-

---

*Siege of the Castle of Edinburgh, printed for the Bannatyne Club· Lond. Gaz., June 10-20, 1689.
† Act Parl. Scot., June 5, June 17, 1689.

deed the highest place to which a subject could aspire. But he imagined that he had only the show of power while others enjoyed the substance, and was not sorry to see those of whom he was jealous thwarted and annoyed. He did not absolutely betray the prince whom he represented: but he sometimes tampered with the chiefs of the Club, and sometimes did sly ill turns to those who were joined with him in the service of the Crown.

His instructions directed him to give the royal assent to laws for the mitigating or removing of numerous grievances, and particularly to a law restricting the power and reforming the constitution of the Committee of Articles, and to a law establishing the Presbyterian Church Government.* But it mattered not what his instructions were. The chiefs of the Club were bent on finding a cause of quarrel. The propositions of the Government touching the Lords of the Articles were contemptuously rejected. Hamilton wrote to London for fresh directions; and soon a second plan, which left little more than the name of the once despotic Committee, was sent back. But the second plan, though such as would have contented judicious and temperate reformers, shared the fate of the first. Meanwhile the chiefs of the Club laid on the table a law which interdicted the King from ever employing in any public office any person who had ever borne any part in any proceeding inconsistent with the Claim of Right, or who had ever obstructed or retarded any good design of the Estates. This law, uniting, within a very short compass, almost all the faults which a law can have, was well known to be aimed at the Lord President of the Court of Session, and at his son the Lord Advocate. Their prosperity and power made them objects of envy to every disappointed candidate for office. That they were new men, the first of their race who had risen to distinction, and that nevertheless they had, by the mere force of ability, become as important in the state as the Duke of Hamilton or the Earl of Argyle, was a thought which galled the hearts of many needy and haughty patricians. To the Whigs of Scotland the Dalrymples were what Halifax and Caermarthen were to the Whigs of England. Neither the exile of Sir James, nor the zeal with which Sir John had promoted the revolution, was received as an atonement for old delinquency. They had both served the bloody and

---

* The instructions will be found among the Somers Tracts.

idolatrous House. They had both oppressed the people of God. Their late repentance might perhaps give them a fair claim to pardon, but surely gave them no right to honors and rewards.

The friends of the government in vain attempted to divert the attention of the Parliament from the business of persecuting the Dalrymple family to the important and pressing question of Church Government. They said that the old system had been abolished; that no other system had been substituted; that it was impossible to say what was the established religion of the kingdom; and that the first duty of the legislature was to put an end to an anarchy which was daily producing disasters and crimes. The leaders of the Club were not to be so drawn away from their object. It was moved and resolved that the consideration of ecclesiastical affairs should be postponed till secular affairs had been settled. The unjust and absurd Act of Incapacitation was carried by seventy-four voices to twenty-four. Another vote still more obviously aimed at the House of Stair speedily followed. The Parliament laid claim to a veto on the nomination of the judges, and assumed the power of stopping the signet, in other words, of suspending the whole administration of justice, till this claim should be allowed. It was plain from what passed in debate, that though the chiefs of the Club had begun with the Court of Session, they did not mean to end there. The arguments used by Sir Patrick Hume and others led directly to the conclusion that the King ought not to have the appointment of any great public functionary. Sir Patrick indeed avowed, both in speech and in writing, his opinion that the whole patronage of the realm ought to be transferred from the Crown to the Estates. When the place of Treasurer, of Chancellor, of Secretary, was vacant, the Parliament ought to submit two or three names to His Majesty; and one of those names His Majesty ought to be bound to select.*

All this time the Estates obstinately refused to grant any supply till their Acts should have been touched with the scepter. The Lord High Commissioner was at length so much provoked by their perverseness that, after long temporizing, he refused to touch even Acts which were in themselves unobjectionable, and to which his instructions

---
* As to Sir Patrick's views, see his letter of the 7th of June, and Lockhart's letter of the 11th of July, in the Leven and Melville Papers.

empowered him to consent. This state of things would have ended in some great convulsion, if the King of Scotland had not been also King of a much greater and more opulent kingdom. Charles the First had never found any parliament at Westminster more unmanageable than William, during this session, found the parliament at Edinburgh. But it was not in the power of the parliament at Edinburgh to put on William such a pressure as the parliament at Westminster had put on Charles. A refusal of supplies at Westminster was a serious thing, and left the Sovereign no choice except to yield, or to raise money by unconstitutional means. But a refusal of supplies at Edinburgh reduced him to no such dilemma. The largest sum that he could hope to receive from Scotland in a year was less than what he received from England every fortnight. He had therefore only to entrench himself within the limits of his undoubted prerogative, and there to remain on the defensive, till some favorable conjuncture should arrive.*

While these things were passing in the Parliament House, the civil war in the Highlands, having been during a few weeks suspended, broke forth again more violently than before. Since the splendor of the House of Argyle had been eclipsed, no Gaelic chief could vie in power with the Marquess of Athol. The district from which he took his title, and of which he might almost be called the sovereign, was in extent larger than an ordinary county, and was more fertile, more diligently cultivated, and more thickly peopled than the greater part of the Highlands. The men who followed his banner were supposed to be not less numerous than all the Macdonals and Macleans united, and were, in strength and courage, inferior to no tribe in the mountains. But the clan had been made insignificant by the insignificance of the chief. The Marquess was the falsest, the most fickle, the most pusillanimous, of mankind. Already, in the short space of six months, he had been several times a Jacobite, and several times a Williamite. Both Jacobites and Williamites regarded him with contempt and distrust, which respect for his immense power prevented them from fully expressing. After repeatedly vowing fidelity to both parties, and repeatedly betraying both, he began to think that he should best pro-

* My chief materials for the history of this session have been the Acts, the Minutes and the Leven and Melville Papers.

vide for his safety by abdicating the functions both of a peer and of a chieftain, by absenting himself both from the Parliament House at Edinburgh and from his castle in the mountains, and by quitting the country to which he was bound by every tie of duty and honor at the very crisis of her fate. While all Scotland was waiting with impatience and anxiety to see in which army his numerous retainers would be arrayed, he stole away to England, settled himself at Bath, and pretended to drink the waters.* His principality, left without a head, was divided against itself. The general leaning of the Athol men was towards King James. For they had been employed by him, only four years before, as the ministers of his vengeance against the House of Argyle. They had garrisoned Inverary: they had ravaged Lorn: they had demolished houses, cut down fruit trees, burned fishing boats, broken millstones, hanged Campbells, and were therefore not likely to be pleased by the prospects of Mac Callum More's restoration. One word from the Marquess would have sent two thousand claymores to the Jacobite side. But that word he would not speak; and the consequence was, that the conduct of his followers was as irresolute and inconsistent as his own.

While they were waiting for some indication of his wishes, they were called to arms at once by two leaders, either of whom might, with some show of reason, claim to be considered as the representative of the absent chief. Lord Murray, the Marquess's eldest son, who was married to a daughter of the Duke of Hamilton, declared for King William. Stewart of Ballenach, the Marquess's confidential agent, declared for King James. The people knew not which summons to obey. He whose authority would have been held in profound reverence had plighted faith to both sides, and had then run away for fear of being under the necessity of joining either; nor was it very easy to say whether the place which he had left vacant belonged to his steward or to his heir apparent.

The most important military post in Athol was Blair Castle. The house which now bears that name is not distinguished by any striking peculiarity from other country seats of the aristocracy. The old building was a lofty

---

* "Athol," says Dundee, contemptuously, "is gone to England, who did not know what to do."—Dundee to Melfort, June 27, 1689. See Athol's letters to Melville of the 21st of May and the 8th of June, in the Leven and Melville Papers.

tower of rude architecture which commanded a vale watered by the Garry. The walls would have offered very little resistance to a battering train, but were quite strong enough to keep the herdsmen of the Grampians in awe. About five miles south of this stronghold, the valley of the Garry contracts itself into the celebrated glen of Killiecrankie. At present a highway as smooth as any road in Middlesex ascends gently from the low country to the summit of the defile. White villas peep from the birch forest; and, on a fine summer day, there is scarcely a turn of the pass at which may not be seen some angler casting his fly on the foam of the river, some artist sketching a pinnacle of rock, or some party of pleasure banqueting on the turf in the fretwork of shade and sunshine. But, in the days of William the Third, Killiecrankie was mentioned with horror by the peaceful and industrious inhabitants of the Perthshire lowlands. It was deemed the most perilous of all those dark ravines through which the marauders of the hills were wont to sally forth. The sound, so musical to modern ears, of the river brawling round the mossy rocks and among the smooth pebbles, the masses of grey crag and dark verdure worthy of the pencil of Wilson, the fantastic peaks bathed, at sunrise and sunset, with light rich as that which glows on the canvas of Claude, suggested to our ancestors thoughts of murderous ambuscades, and of bodies stripped, gashed, and abandoned to the birds of prey. The only path was narrow and rugged: a horse could with difficulty be led up: two men could hardly walk abreast; and, in some places, the way ran so close by the precipice that the traveller had great need of a steady eye and foot. Many years later, the first Duke of Athol constructed a road up which it was just possible to drag his coach. But even that road was so steep and so straight that a handful of resolute men might have defended it against an army;* nor did any Saxon consider a visit to Killiecrankie as a pleasure, till experience had taught the English Government that the weapons by which the Celtic clans could be most effectually subdued were the pickaxe and the spade.

The country which lay just above this pass was now the theater of a war such as the Highlands had not often witnessed. Men wearing the same tartan, and attached to the same lord were arrayed against each other. The name of the

---
* Memoirs of Ewan Cameron.

absent chief was used, with some show of reason, on both sides. Ballenach, at the head of a body of vassals who considered him as the representative of the Marquess, occupied Blair Castle. Murray, with twelve hundred followers, appeared before the walls, and demanded to be admitted into the mansion of his family, the mansion which would one day be his own. The garrison refused to open the gates. Messengers were sent off by the besiegers to Edinburgh, and by the besieged to Lochaber.* In both places the tidings produced great agitation. Mackay and Dundee agreed in thinking that the crisis required prompt and strenuous exertion. On the fate of Blair Castle probably depended the fate of all Athol. On the fate of Athol might depend the fate of Scotland. Mackay hastened northward, and ordered his troops to assemble in the low country of Perthshire. Some of them were quartered at such a distance that they did not arrive in time. He soon, however, had with him the three Scotch regiments which had served in Holland, and which bore the names of their colonels, Mackay himself, Balfour, and Ramsay. There was also a gallant regiment of infantry from England, then called Hastings's, but now known as the thirteenth of the line. With these old troops were joined two regiments newly levied in the Lowlands. One of them was commanded by Lord Kenmore; the other, which had been raised on the Border, and which is still styled the King's Own Borderers, by Lord Leven. Two troops of horse, Lord Annandale's and Lord Belhaven's, probably made up the army to the number of above three thousand men. Belhaven rode at the head of his troop: but Annandale, the most factious of all Montgomery's followers, preferred the Club and the Parliament House to the field.†

Dundee, meanwhile, had summoned all the clans which acknowledged his commission to assemble for an expedition into Athol. His exertions were strenuously seconded by Lochiel. The fiery crosses were sent again in all haste through Appin and Ardnamurchan, up Glenmore, and along Loch Leven. But the call was so unexpected, and the time allowed was so short, that the muster was not a very full one. The whole number of broadswords seems to have been under three thousand. With this force, such as it was, Dundee set forth. On his march he was joined by succors which had just arrived from Ulster. They consisted

---

* Mackay's Memoirs.   † Mackay's Memoirs.

of little more than three hundred Irish foot, ill armed, ill clothed, and ill disciplined. Their commander was an officer named Cannon, who had seen service in the Netherlands, and who might perhaps have acquitted himself well in a subordinate post and in a regular army, but who was altogether unequal to the part now assigned to him.* He had already loitered among the Hebrides so long that some ships which had been sent with him, and which were laden with stores, had been taken by English cruisers. He and his soldiers had with difficulty escaped the same fate. Incompetent as he was, he bore a commission which gave him military rank in Scotland next to Dundee.

The disappointment was severe. In truth, James would have done better to withhold all assistance from the Highlanders than to mock them by sending them, instead of the well appointed army which they had asked and expected, a rabble contemptible in numbers and appearance. It was now evident that whatever was done for his cause in Scotland must be done by Scottish hands.†

While Mackay from one side, and Dundee from the other, were advancing towards Blair Castle, important events had taken place there. Murray's adherents soon began to waver in their fidelity to him. They had an old antipathy to Whigs; for they considered the name of Whig as synonymous with the name of Campbell. They saw arrayed against them a large number of their kinsmen, commanded by a gentleman who was supposed to possess the confidence of the Marquess. The besieging army therefore melted rapidly away. Many returned home on the plea that, as their neighborhood was about to be the seat of war, they must place their families and cattle in security. Others more ingenuously declared that they would not fight in such a quarrel. One large body went to a brook, filled their bonnets with water, drank a health to King James, and then dispersed.‡ Their zeal for King James, however, did not induce them to join the standard of his general. They lurked among the rocks and thickets which overhang the Garry, in the hope that there would soon be a battle, and that, whatever might be the event, there would be fugitives and corpses to plunder.

Murray was in a strait. His force had dwindled to three or four hundred men: even in those men he could put lit-

* Van Odyck to the Greffier of the States General, Aug. 2-12, 1689.
† Memoirs of Sir Ewan Cameron.   ‡ Balcarras's Memoirs.

tle trust; and the Macdonalds and Camerons were advancing fast. He therefore raised the siege of Blair Castle, and retired with a few followers into the defile of Killiecrankie. There he was soon joined by a detachment of two hundred fusileers whom Mackay had sent forward to secure the pass. The main body of the Lowland army speedily followed.*

Early in the morning of Saturday the twenty-seventh of July, Dundee arrived at Blair Castle. There he learned that Mackay's troops were already in the ravine of Killiecrankie. It was necessary to come to a prompt decision. A council of war was held The Saxon officers were generally against hazarding a battle. The Celtic chiefs were of a different opinion. Glengarry and Lochiel were now both of a mind. "Fight, my Lord," said Lochiel with his usual energy: "fight immediately, fight, if you have only one to three. Our men are in heart. Their only fear is that the enemy should escape. Give them their way; and be assured that they will either perish or gain a complete victory. But if you restrain them, if you force them to remain on the defensive, I answer for nothing. If we do not fight, we had better break up and retire to our mountains." †

Dundee's countenance brightened. "You hear, gentlemen," he said to his Lowland officers, "you hear the opinion of one who understands Highland war better than any of us." No voice was raised on the other side. It was determined to fight; and the confederated clans in high spirits set forward to encounter the enemy.

The enemy meanwhile had made his way up the pass. The ascent had been long and toilsome; for even the foot had to climb by twos and threes; and the baggage horses, twelve hundred in number, could mount only one at a time. No wheeled carriage had ever been tugged up that arduous path. The head of the column had emerged and was on the table land, while the rear-guard was still in the plain below. At length the passage was effected; and the troops found themselves in a valley of no great extent. Their right was flanked by a rising ground, their left by the Garry. Wearied with their morning's work, they threw themselves on the grass to take some rest and refreshment.

---

* Mackay's Short Relation, dated Aug. 17, 1689.
† Memoirs to Sir Ewan Cameron.

Early in the afternoon they were roused by an alarm that the Highlanders were approaching. Regiment after regiment started up and got into order. In a little while the summit of an ascent which was about a musket shot before them was covered with bonnets and plaids. Dundee rode forward for the purpose of surveying the force with which he was to contend, and then drew up his own men with as much skill as their peculiar character permitted him to exert. It was desirable to keep the clans distinct. Each tribe, large or small, formed a column separated from the next column by a wide interval. One of these battalions might contain seven hundred men, while another consisted of only a hundred and twenty. Lochiel had represented that it was impossible to mix different tribes without destroying all that constituted the peculiar strength of a Highland army.*

On the right, close to the Garry, were the Macleans. Nearest to them were Cannon and his Irish foot. Next stood the Macdonalds of Clanronald, commanded by the guardian of their young prince. On their left were other bands of Macdonalds. At the head of one large battalion towered the stately form of Glengarry, who bore in his hands the royal standard of King James the Seventh.† Still further to the left were the cavalry, a small squadron, consisting of some Jacobite gentlemen who had fled from the Lowlands to the mountains, and of about forty of Dundee's old troopers. The horses had been ill fed and ill tended among the Grampians, and looked miserably lean and feeble. Beyond them was Lochiel with his Camerons. On the extreme left, the men of Sky were marshalled by Macdonald of Sleat.‡

In the Highlands, as in all countries where war had not become a science, men thought it the most important duty of a commander to set an example of personal courage and of bodily exertion. Lochiel was especially renowned for his physical prowess. His clansmen looked big with pride when they related how he had himself broken hostile ranks and hewn down tall warriors. He probably owed quite as much of his influence to those achievements as to the high qualities which, if fortune had placed him in the English Parliament or at the French Court, would have

---

* Memoirs of Sir Ewan Cameron; Mackay's Memoirs.
† Douglas's Baronage of Scotland.
‡ Memoirs of Sir Ewan Cameron.

made him one of the foremost men of the age. He had the sense however to perceive how erroneous was the notion which his countrymen had formed. He knew that to give and to take blows was not the business of a general. He knew with how much difficulty Dundee had been able to keep together, during a few days, an army composed of several clans; and he knew that what Dundee had effected with difficulty Cannon would not be able to effect at all. The life on which so much depended must not be sacrificed to a barbarous prejudice. Lochiel therefore adjured Dundee not to run into any unnecessary danger. "Your Lordship's business," he said, "is to overlook everything, and to issue your commands. Our business is to execute those commands bravely and promptly." Dundee answered with calm magnanimity that there was much weight in what his friend Sir Ewan had urged, but that no general could effect anything great without possessing the confidence of his men. "I must establish my character for courage. Your people expect to see their leaders in the thickest of the battle; and to-day they shall see me there. I promise you, on my honor, that in future fights, I will take more care of myself."

Meanwhile a fire of musketry was kept up on both sides, but more skillfully and more steadily by the regular soldiers than by the mountaineers. The space between the armies was one cloud of smoke. Not a few Highlanders dropped; and the clans grew impatient. The sun however was low in the west before Dundee gave the order to prepare for action. His men raised a great shout. The enemy, probably exhausted by the toil of the day, returned a feeble and wavering cheer. "We shall do it now," said Lochiel: "that is not the cry of men who are going to win." He had walked through all his ranks, had addressed a few words to every Cameron, and had taken from every Cameron a promise to conquer or die.*

It was past seven o'clock. Dundee gave the word. The Highlanders dropped their plaids. The few who were so luxurious as to wear rude socks of untanned hide spurned them away. It was long remembered in Lochaber that Lochiel took off what probably was the only pair of shoes in his clan, and charged barefoot at the head of his men. The whole line advanced firing. The enemy returned the fire and did much execution. When only a

---

* Memoirs of Sir Ewan Cameron.

small space was left between the armies, the Highlanders suddenly flung away their firelocks, drew their broadswords, and rushed forward with a fearful yell. The Lowlanders prepared to receive the shock: but this was then a long and awkward process; and the soldiers were still fumbling with the muzzles of their guns and the handles of their bayonets when the whole flood of Macleans, Macdonalds, and Camerons came down. In two minutes the battle was lost and won. The ranks of Balfour's regiment broke. He was cloven down while struggling in the press. Ramsay's men turned their backs and dropped their arms. Mackay's own foot were swept away by the furious onset of the Camerons. His brother and nephew exerted themselves in vain to rally the men. The former was laid dead on the ground by a stroke from a claymore. The latter, with eight wounds in his body, made his way through the tumult and carnage to his uncle's side. Even in that extremity Mackay retained all his self-possession. He had still one hope. A charge of horse might recover the day; for of horse the bravest Highlanders were supposed to stand in awe. But he called on the horse in vain. Belhaven indeed behaved like a gallant gentleman, but his troopers, appalled by the rout of the infantry, galloped off in disorder: Annandale's men followed: all was over; and the mingled torrent of redcoats and tartans went raving down the valley to the gorge of Killiecrankie.

Mackay, accompanied by one trusty servant, spurred bravely through the thickest of the claymores and targets, and reached a point from which he had a view of the field. His whole army had disappeared with the exception of some Borderers whom Leven had kept together, and of the English regiment, which had poured a murderous fire into the Celtic ranks, and which still kept unbroken order. All the men that could be collected were only a few hundreds. The general made haste to lead them across the Garry, and, having put that river between them and the enemy, paused for a moment to meditate on his situation.

He could hardly understand how the conquerors could be so unwise as to allow him even that moment for deliberation. They might with ease have killed or taken all who were with him before the night closed in. But the energy of the Celtic warriors had spent itself in one furious rush and one short struggle. The pass was choked by the twelve hundred beasts of burden which carried the provisions and baggage of the vanquished army. Such a booty was irresistibly tempting to men who were impelled to war quite as much by the desire of rapine as by the desire of glory. It is probable that few even of the chiefs were disposed to leave so rich a prize for the sake of King James. Dundee himself might at that moment have been unable to persuade his followers to quit the heaps of spoil, and to complete the great work of the day; and Dundee was no more.

At the beginning of the action he had taken his place in front of his little band of cavalry. He bade them follow him, and rode forward. But it seemed to be decreed that, on that day, the Lowland Scotch should in both armies appear to disadvantage. The horse hesitated. Dundee turned round, stood up in his stirrups, and, waving his hat, invited them to come on. As he lifted his arm, his cuirass rose, and exposed the lower part of his left side. A musket ball struck him: his horse sprang forward and plunged into a cloud of smoke and dust, which hid from both armies the fall of the victorious general. A person named Johnstone was near him, and caught him as he sank down from the saddle. "How goes the day?" said Dundee. "Well for King James;" answered Johnstone: "but I am sorry for your Lordship." "If it is well for him," answered the dying man, "it matters the less for me." He never spoke again: but when, half an hour later, Lord Dunfermline and some other friends came to the spot, they thought that they could still discern some faint remains of life. The body, wrapped in two plaids, was carried to the Castle of Blair.*

Mackay, who was ignorant of Dundee's fate, and well acquainted with Dundee's skill and activity, expected to be instantly and hotly pursued, and had very little expectation of being able to save the scanty remains of the vanquished army. He could not retreat by the pass: for the Highlanders were already there. He therefore resolved to push across the mountains towards the valley of the Tay. He soon overtook two or three hundred of his run-

---

* As to the battle, see Mackay's Memoirs, Letters, and Short Relation; the Memoirs of Dundee; Memoirs of Sir Ewan Cameron; Nisbet and Osburne's depositions in the Appendix to the Act Parl. of July 14, 1690. See also the account of the battle in one of Burt's Letters. Macpherson printed a letter from Dundee to James dated the day after the battle. I need not say that it is as impudent a forgery as Fingal. The author of the Memoirs of Dundee says that Lord Leven was scared by the sight of the Highland weapons and set the example of flight This is a spiteful falsehood. That Leven behaved remarkably well is proved by Mackay's Letters, Memoirs, and Short Relation.

aways who had taken the same road. Most of them belonged to Ramsay's regiment, and must have seen service. But they were unarmed: they were utterly bewildered by the recent disaster; and the general could find among them no remains either of martial discipline or of martial spirit. His situation was one which must have severely tried the firmest nerves. Night had set in: he was in a desert: he had no guide: a victorious enemy was, in all human probability, on his track; and he had to provide for the safety of a crowd of men who had lost both head and heart. He had just suffered a defeat of all defeats the most painful and humiliating. His domestic feelings had been not less severely wounded than his professional feelings. One dear kinsman had just been struck dead before his eyes. Another, bleeding from many wounds, moved feebly at his side. But the unfortunate general's courage was sustained by a firm faith in God, and a high sense of duty to the state. In the midst of misery and disgrace, he still held his head nobly erect, and found fortitude, not only for himself, but for all around him. His first care was to be sure of his road. A solitary light which twinkled through the darkness guided him to a small hovel. The inmates spoke no tongue but the Gaelic, and were at first scared by the appearance of uniforms and arms. But Mackay's gentle manner removed their apprehension: their language had been familiar to him in childhood; and he retained enough of it to communicate with them. By their directions, and by the help of a pocket map, in which the routes through that wild country were roughly laid down, he was able to find his way. He marched all night. When day broke his task was more difficult than ever. Light increased the terror of his companions. Hastings's men and Leven's men indeed still behaved themselves like soldiers. But the fugitives from Ramsay's were a mere rabble They had flung away their muskets. The broadswords from which they had fled were ever in their eyes. Every fresh object caused a fresh panic. A company of herdsmen in plaids driving cattle was magnified by imagination into a host of Celtic warriors. Some of the runaways left the main body and fled to the hills, where their cowardice met with a proper punishment. They were killed for their coats and shoes; and their naked carcasses were left for a prey to the eagles of Ben Lawers. The desertion would have been much greater, had not Mackay and his officers, pistol in hand, threatened to blow out the brains of any man whom they caught attempting to steal off.

At length the weary fugitives came in sight of Weem Castle. The proprietor of the mansion was a friend to the new government, and extended to them such hospitality as was in his power. His stores of oatmeal were brought out: kine were slaughtered: and a rude and hasty meal was set before the numerous guests. Thus refreshed, they again set forth, and marched all day over bog, moor, and mountain. Thinly inhabited as the country was, they could plainly see that the report of their disaster had already spread far, and that the population was everywhere in a state of great excitement. Late at night they reached Castle Drummond, which was held for King William by a small garrison; and, on the following day, they proceeded with less difficulty to Stirling.*

The tidings of their defeat had outrun them. All Scotland was in a ferment. The disaster had indeed been great; but it was exaggerated by the wild hopes of one party and by the wild fears of the other. It was at first believed that the whole army of King William had perished; that Mackay himself had fallen; that Dundee, at the head of a great host of barbarians, flushed with victory and impatient for spoil, had already descended from the hills; that he was master of the whole country beyond the Forth; that Fife was up to join him; that in three days he would be at Stirling; that in a week he would be at Holyrood. Messengers were sent to urge a regiment which lay in Northumberland to hasten across the border. Others carried to London earnest entreaties that his Majesty would instantly send every soldier that could be spared, nay, that he would come himself to save his northern kingdom. The factions of the Parliament House, awestruck by the common danger, forgot to wrangle. Courtiers and malcontents with one voice implored the Lord High Commissioner to close the session, and to dismiss them from a place where their deliberations might soon be interrupted by the mountaineers. It was seriously considered whether it might not be expedient to abandon Edinburgh, to send the numerous state prisoners who were in the Castle and the Tolbooth on board of a man of war which lay off Leith, and to transfer the seat of government to Glasgow.

---

* Mackay's Memoirs; Life of General Hugh Mackay by J. Mackay of Rockfield.

The news of Dundee's victory was everywhere speedily followed by the news of his death; and it is a strong proof of the extent and vigor of his faculties that his death seems everywhere to have been regarded as a complete set off against his victory. Hamilton, before he adjourned the Estates, informed them that he had good tidings for them, that Dundee was certainly dead, and that therefore the rebels had on the whole sustained a defeat. In several letters written at that conjuncture by able and experienced politicians a similar opinion is expressed. The messenger who rode with the news of the battle to the English capital was fast followed by another who carried a despatch to the King, and, not finding his Majesty at St. James's galloped to Hampton Court. Nobody in the capital ventured to break the seal: but fortunately, after the letter had been closed, some friendly hand had hastily written on the outside a few words of comfort: "Dundee is killed. Mackay has got to Stirling:" and these words seem to have quieted the minds of the Londoners.*

From the pass of Killiecrankie the Highlanders had retired, proud of their victory, and laden with spoil, to the Castle of Blair. They boasted that the field of battle was covered with heaps of Saxon soldiers, and that the appearance of the corpses bore ample testimony to the power of a good Gaelic broadsword in a good Gaelic right hand. Heads were found cloven down to the throat, and skulls struck clean off just above the ears. The conquerors however had bought their victory dear. While they were advancing they had been much galled by the musketry of the enemy: and, even after the decisive charge, Hastings's Englishmen and some of Leven's Borderers had continued to keep up a steady fire. A hundred and twenty Camerons had been slain: the loss of the Macdonalds had been still greater; and several gentlemen of birth and note had fallen.†

Dundee was buried in the church of Blair Athol: but no monument was erected over his grave; and the church itself has long disappeared. A rude stone on the field of battle marks, if local tradition can be trusted, the place where he fell.‡ During the last three months of his life he

---
* Letters of the Extraordinary Ambassadors to the Greffier of the States General, August 2-12, 1689; and a letter of the same date from Van Odyck, who was at Hampton Court.
† Memoirs of Sir Ewan Cameron; Memoirs of Dundee.
‡ The tradition is certainly much more than a hundred and twenty years old. The stone was pointed out to Burt.

had approved himself a great warrior and politician; and his name is therefore mentioned with respect by that large class of persons who think that there is no excess of wickedness for which courage and ability do not atone.

It is curious that the two most remarkable battles that perhaps were ever gained by irregular over regular troops should have been fought in the same week: the battle of Killiecrankie and the battle of Newton Butler. In both battles the success of the irregular troops was singularly rapid and complete. In both battles the panic of the regular troops, in spite of the conspicuous examples of courage set by their generals, was singularly disgraceful. It ought also to be noted, that of these extrordinary victories, one was gained by Celts over Saxons, and the other by Saxons over Celts. The victory of Killiecrankie, indeed, though neither more splendid nor more important than the victory of Newton Butler, is far more widely renowned; and the reason is evident. The Anglo-Saxon and the Celt have been reconciled in Scotland, and have never been reconciled in Ireland. In Scotland all the great actions of both races are thrown into a common stock, and are considered as making up the glory which belongs to the whole country. So completely has the old antipathy been extinguished that nothing is more usual than to hear a Lowlander talk with complacency and even with pride of the most humiliating defeat that his ancestors ever underwent. It would be difficult to name any eminent man in whom national feeling and clannish feeling were stronger than in Sir Walter Scott. Yet when Sir Walter Scott mentioned Killiecrankie he seemed utterly to forget that he was a Saxon, that he was of the same blood and of the same speech with Ramsay's foot and Annandale's horse. His heart swelled with triumph when he related how his own kindred had fled like hares before a smaller number of warriors of a different breed and of a different tongue.

In Ireland the feud remains unhealed. The name of Newton Butler, insultingly repeated by a minority, is hateful to the great majority of the population. If a monument were set up on the field of battle, it would probably be defaced; if a festival were held in Cork or Waterford on the anniversary of the battle, it would probably be interrupted by violence. The most illustrious Irish poet of our time would have thought it treason to his country to sing the praises of the conquerors. One of the most learned and diligent Irish archæologists of our time has labored, not indeed very successfully, to prove that the event of the day was decided by a mere accident from which the Englishry could derive no glory. We cannot wonder that the victory of the Highlanders should be more celebrated than the victory of the Enniskilleners, when we consider that the victory of the Highlanders is matter of boast to all Scotland, and that the victory of the Enniskilleners is matter of shame to three-fourths of Ireland.

As far as the great interests of the state were concerned, it mattered not at all whether the battle of Killiecrankie were lost or won. It is very improbable that even Dundee, if he had survived the most glorious day of his life, could have surmounted those difficulties which sprang from the peculiar nature of his army, and which would have increased tenfold as soon as the war was transferred to the Lowlands. It is certain that his successor was altogether unequal to the task. During a day or two, indeed, the new general might flatter himself that all would go well. His army was rapidly swollen to near double the number of claymores that Dundee had commanded. The Stewarts of Appin, who, though full of zeal, had not been able to come up in time for the battle, were among the first who arrived. Several clans who had hitherto waited to see which side was the stronger, were now eager to descend on the Lowlands under the standard of King James the Seventh. The Grants indeed continued to bear true allegiance to William and Mary; and the Mackintoshes were kept neutral by unconquerable aversion to Keppoch. But Macphersons, Farquharsons, and Frasers came in crowds to the camp at Blair. The hesitation of the Athol men was at an end. Many of them had lurked, during the fight, among the crags and birch trees of Killiecrankie, and, as soon as the event of the day was decided, had emerged from those hiding places to strip and butcher the fugitives who tried to escape by the pass. The Robertsons, a Gaelic race, though bearing a Saxon name, gave in at this conjuncture their adhesion to the cause of the exiled King. Their chief, Alexander, who took his appellation from his lordship of Struan, was a very young man and a student at the University of St. Andrew's. He had there acquired a smattering of letters, and had been initiated much more deeply into Tory politics. He now joined the Highland army, and continued, through a long life, to be constant to the Jacobite cause. His part, however, in public affairs was so insignificant that his name would not now be remembered, if he had not left a volume of poems, always very stupid and often very profligate. Had this book been manufactured in Grub Street, it would scarcely have been honored with a quarter of a line in the Dunciad. But it attracted some notice on account of the situation of the writer. For, a hundred and twenty years ago, an eclogue or a lampoon written by a Highland chief was a literary portent.*

But, though the numerical strength of Cannon's forces was increasing, their efficiency was diminishing. Every new tribe which joined the camp brought with it some new cause of dissension. In the hour of peril, the most arrogant and mutinous spirits will often submit to the guidance of superior genius. Yet, even in the hour of peril, and even to the genius of Dundee, the Celtic chiefs had yielded but a precarious and imperfect obedience. To restrain them, when intoxicated with success and confident of their strength, would probably have been too hard a task even for him, as it had been, in the preceding generation, too hard a task for Montrose. The new general did nothing but hesitate and blunder. One of his first acts was to send a large body of men, chiefly Robertsons, down into the low country for the purpose of collecting provisions. He seems to have supposed that this detachment would without difficulty occupy Perth. But Mackay had already restored order among the remains of his army: he had assembled round him some troops which had not shared in the disgrace of the late defeat; and he was again ready for action. Cruel as his sufferings had been, he had wisely and magnanimously resolved not to punish what was past. To distinguish between degrees of guilt was not easy. To decimate the guilty would have been to commit a frightful massacre. His habitual piety too led him to consider the unexampled panic which had seized his soldiers as a proof rather of the divine displeasure than of their cowardice. He acknowledged with heroic humility that the singular firmness which he had himself displayed in the midst of the confusion and havoc was not his own, and that he might well, but for the support of a

---

* See the History prefixed to the poems of Alexander Robertson. In this history he is represented as having joined before the battle of Killiecrankie. But it appears from the evidence which is in the Appendix to the Act Parl. Scot., of July 14, 1690, that he came in on the following day.

higher power, have behaved as pusillanimously as any of the wretched runaways who had thrown away their weapons and implored quarter in vain from the barbarous marauders of Athol. His dependence on heaven did not, however, prevent him from applying himself vigorously to the work of providing, as far as human prudence could provide, against the recurrence of such a calamity as that which he had just experienced. The immediate cause of the late defeat was the difficulty of fixing bayonets. The firelock of the Highlander was quite distinct from the weapon which he used in close fight. He discharged his shot, threw away his gun, and fell on with his sword. This was the work of a moment. It took the regular musketeer two or three minutes to alter his missile weapon into a weapon with which he could encounter an enemy hand to hand; and during these two or three minutes the event of the battle of Killiecrankie had been decided. Mackay therefore ordered all his bayonets to be so formed that they might be screwed upon the barrel, without stopping it up, and that his men might be able to receive a charge at the very instant after firing.*

As soon as he learned that a detachment of the Gaelic army was advancing towards Perth, he hastened to meet them at the head of a body of dragoons who had not been in the battle, and whose spirit was therefore unbroken. On Wednesday the thirty-first of July, only four days after his defeat, he fell in with the Robertsons, attacked them, routed them, killed a hundred and twenty of them, and took thirty prisoners, with the loss of only a single soldier.† This skirmish produced an effect quite out of proportion to the number of the combatants or of the slain. The reputation of the Celtic arms went down almost as fast as it had risen. During two or three days it had been everywhere imagined that those arms were invincible. There was now a reaction. It was perceived that what had happened at Killiecrankie was an exception to ordinary rules, and that the Highlanders were not, except in very peculiar circumstances, a match for good regular troops.

Meanwhile the disorders of Cannon's camp went on increasing. He called a council of war to consider what course it would be advisable to take. But, as soon as the council had met, a preliminary question was raised. Who were entitled to be consulted? The army was almost ex-

---

* Mackay's Memoirs. † Ibid.; Memoirs of Sir Ewan Cameron.

clusively a Highland army. The recent victory had been won exclusively by Highland warriors. Great chiefs, who had brought six or seven hundred fighting men into the field, did not think it fair that they should be outvoted by gentlemen from Ireland and from the low country, who bore indeed King James's commission, and were called colonels and captains, but who were colonels without regiments and captains without companies. Lochiel spoke strongly in behalf of the class to which he belonged: but Cannon decided that the votes of the Saxon officers should be reckoned.*

It was next considered what was to be the plan of the campaign. Lochiel was for advancing, for marching towards Mackay, wherever Mackay might be, and for giving battle again. It can hardly be supposed that success had so turned the head of the wise chief of the Camerons as to make him insensible of the danger of the course which he recommended. But he probably conceived that nothing but a choice between dangers was left to him. His notion was that vigorous action was necessary to the very being of a Highland army, and that the coalition of clans would last only while they were impatiently pushing forward from battle-field to battle-field. He was again overruled. All his hopes of success were now at an end. His pride was severely wounded. He had submitted to the ascendency of a great captain: but he cared as little as any Whig for a royal commission. He had been willing to be the right hand of Dundee: but he would not be ordered about by Cannon. He quitted the camp, and retired to Lochaber. He indeed directed his clans to remain. But the clan, deprived of the leader whom it adored, and aware that he had withdrawn himself in ill humor, was no longer the same terrible column which had a few days before kept so well the vow to perish or to conquer. Macdonald of Sleat, whose forces exceeded in number those of any other of the confederate chiefs, followed Lochiel's example and returned to Sky.†

Mackay's arrangements were by this time complete; and he had little doubt that, if the rebels came down to attack him, the regular army would retrieve the honor which had been lost at Killiecrankie. His chief difficulties arose from the unwise interference of the ministers of the Crown at Edinburgh with matters which ought to have been left

---

* Memoirs of Sir Ewan Cameron.   † Memoirs of Sir Ewan Cameron.

to his direction. The truth seems to be that they, after the ordinary fashion of men who, having no military experience, sit in judgment on military operations, considered success as the only test of the ability of a commander. Whoever wins a battle is, in the estimation of such persons, a great general: whoever is beaten is a bad general; and no general had ever been more completely beaten than Mackay. William, on the other hand, continued to place entire confidence in his unfortunate lieutenant. To the disparaging remarks of critics who had never seen a skirmish, Portland replied, by his master's orders, that Mackay was perfectly trustworthy, that he was brave, that he understood war better than any other officer in Scotland, and that it was much to be regretted that any prejudice should exist against so good a man and so good a soldier.*

The unjust contempt with which the Scotch Privy Councillors regarded Mackay led them into a great error which might well have caused a great disaster. The Cameronian regiment was sent to garrison Dunkeld. Of this arrangement Mackay altogether disapproved. He knew that at Dunkeld these troops would be near the enemy; that they would be far from all assistance; that they would be in an open town; that they would be surrounded by a hostile population; that they were very imperfectly disciplined, though doubtless brave and zealous; that they were regarded by the whole Jacobite party throughout Scotland with peculiar malevolence; and that in all probability some great effort would be made to disgrace and destroy them.†

The general's opinion was disregarded; and the Cameronians occupied the post assigned to them. It soon appeared that his forebodings were just. The inhabitants of the country round Dunkeld furnished Cannon with intelligence and urged him to make a bold push. The peasantry of Athol, impatient for spoil, came in great numbers to swell his army. The regiment hourly expected to be attacked, and became discontented and turbulent. The men, intrepid, indeed, both from constitution and from enthusiasm, but not yet broken to habits of military submission, expostulated with Cleland, who commanded them. They

---

* See Portland's Letters to Melville of April 22. and May 15, 1690, in the Leven and Melville Papers.

† Mackay's Memoirs; Memoirs of Sir Ewan Cameron.

had, they imagined, been recklessly, if not perfidiously, sent to certain destruction. They were protected by no ramparts: they had a very scanty stock of ammunition: they were hemmed in by enemies. An officer might mount and gallop beyond reach of danger in an hour: but the private soldier must stay and be butchered. "Neither I," said Cleland, "nor any of my officers will, in any extremity, abandon you. Bring out my horse, all our horses; they shall be shot dead." These words produced a complete change of feeling. The men answered that the horses should not be shot, that they wanted no pledge from their brave colonel except his word, and that they would run the last hazard with him. They kept their promise well. The Puritan blood was now thoroughly up; and what that blood was when it was up had been proved on many fields of battle.

That night the regiment passed under arms. On the morning of the following day, the twenty-first of August, all the hills round Dunkeld were alive with bonnets and plaids. Cannon's army was much larger than that which Dundee had commanded, and was accompanied by more than a thousand horses laden with baggage. Both the horses and baggage were probably part of the booty of Killiecrankie. The whole number of Highlanders was estimated by those that saw them at from four to five thousand men. They came furiously on. The outposts of the Cameronians were speedily driven in. The assailants came pouring on every side into the streets. The church, however, held out obstinately. But the greater part of the regiment made its stand behind a wall which surrounded a house belonging to the Marquess of Athol. This wall, which had two or three days before been hastily repaired with timber and loose stones, the soldiers defended desperately with musket, pike, and halbert. Their bullets were soon spent; but some of the men were employed in cutting lead from the roof of the Marquess's house and shaping it into slugs. Meanwhile all the neighboring houses were crowded from top to bottom with Highlanders, who kept up a galling fire from the windows. Cleland, while encouraging his men, was shot dead. The command devolved on Major Henderson. In another minute Henderson fell pierced with three mortal wounds. His place was supplied by Captain Munro, and the contest went on with undiminished fury. A party of the Cameronians sallied farth, set fire to the houses from which the fatal shots had come, and turned the keys in the door. In one single dwelling sixteen of the enemy were burnt alive. Those who were in the fight described it as a terrible initiation for recruits. Half the town was blazing; and with the incessant roar of the guns were mingled the piercing shrieks of wretches perishing in the flames. The struggle lasted four hours. By that time the Cameronians were reduced nearly to their last flask of powder: but their spirit never flagged. "The enemy will soon carry the wall. Be it so. We will retreat into the house: we will defend it to the last; and, if they force their way into it, we will burn it over their heads and our own." But, while they were revolving these desperate projects, they observed that the fury of the assault slackened. Soon the Highlanders began to fall back: disorder visibly spread among them; and whole bands began to march off to the hills. It was in vain that their general ordered them to return to the attact. Perseverance was not one of their military virtues. The Cameronians meanwhile, with shouts of defiance, invited Amalek and Moab to come back and to try another chance with the chosen people. But these exhortations had as little effect as those of Cannon. In a short time the whole Gaelic army was in full retreat towards Blair. Then the drums struck up: the victorious Puritans threw their caps into the air, raised, with one voice, a psalm of triumph and thanksgiving, and waved their colors, colors which were on that day unfurled for the first time in the face of an enemy, but which have since been proudly borne in every quarter of the world, and which are now embellished with the Sphinx and the Dragon, emblems of brave actions achieved in Egypt and China.*

The Cameronians had good reason to be joyful and thankful; for they had finished the war. In the rebel camp all was discord and dejection. The Highlanders blamed Cannon; Cannon blamed the Highlanders; and the host which had been the terror of Scotland melted fast away. The confederate chiefs signed an association by which they declared themselves faithful subjects of King James, and bound themselves to meet again at a future time. Having

---

* Exact Narrative of the Conflict at Dunkeld between the Earl of Angus's Regiment and the Rebels, collected from several Officers of that Regiment who were Actors in or Eye-witnesses of all that's here narrated in Reference to those Actions; Letter of Lieutenant Blackader to his brother, dated Dunkeld, Aug. 21, 1689; Faithful Contendings Displayed; Minute of the Scotch Privy Council of August 28, quoted by Mr. Burton.

gone through this form,—for it was no more,—they departed, each to his home. Cannon and his Irishmen retired to the Isle of Mull. The Lowlanders who had followed Dundee to the mountains shifted for themselves as they best could. On the twenty-fourth of August, exactly four weeks after the Gaelic army had won the battle of Killiecrankie, that army ceased to exist. It ceased to exist, as the army of Montrose had, more than forty years earlier, ceased to exist, not in consequence of any great blow from without, but by a natural dissolution, the effect of internal malformation. All the fruits of victory were gathered by the vanquished. The Castle of Blair, which had been the immediate object of the contest, opened its gates to Mackay; and a chain of military posts, extending northward as far as Inverness, protected the cultivators of the plains against the predatory inroads of the mountaineers.

During the autumn the government was much more annoyed by the Whigs of the low country than by the Jacobites of the hills. The Club, which had, in the late session of Parliament, attempted to turn the kingdom into an oligarchical republic, and which had induced the Estates to refuse supplies and to stop the administration of justice, continued to sit during the recess, and harassed the ministers of the Crown by systematic agitation. The organization of this body, contemptible as it may appear to the generation which had seen the Roman Catholic Association and the League against the Corn Laws, was then thought marvellous and formidable. The leaders of the confederacy boasted that they would force the King to do them right. They got up petitions and addresses, tried to inflame the populace by means of the press and the pulpit, employed emissaries among the soldiers, and talked of bringing up a large body of Covenanters from the west to overawe the Privy Council. In spite of every artifice, however, the ferment of the public mind gradually subsided. The government, after some hesitation, ventured to open the courts of justice which the Estates had closed. The Lords of Session appointed by the King took their seats; and Sir James Dalrymple presided. The Club attempted to induce the advocates to absent themselves from the bar, and entertained some hope that the mob would pull the judges from the bench. But it speedily became clear that there was much more likely to be a scarcity of fees than of lawyers to take them: the common people of Edinburgh were well pleased to see again a tribunal associated in their imagination with the dignity and prosperity of their city; and by many signs it appeared that the false and greedy faction which had commanded a majority of the legislature did not command a majority of the nation.*

CHAPTER XIV.—(1689-90.)

TWENTY-FOUR hours before the war in Scotland was brought to a close by the discomfiture of the Celtic army at Dunkeld, the Parliament broke up at Westminster. The Houses had sate ever since January without a recess. The Commons, who were cooped up in a narrow space, had suffered severely from heat and discomfort; and the health of many members had given way. The fruit, however, had not been proportioned to the toil. The last three months of the session had been almost entirely wasted in disputes, which have left no trace in the Statute Book. The progress of salutary laws had been impeded, sometimes by bickerings between the Whigs and the Tories, and sometimes by bickerings between the Lords and the Commons.

The Revolution had scarcely been accomplished when it appeared that the supporters of the Exclusion Bill had not forgotten what they had suffered during the ascendency of their enemies, and were bent on obtaining both reparation and revenge. Even before the throne was filled, the Lords appointed a committee to examine into the truth of the frightful stories which had been circulated concerning the death of Essex. The committee, which consisted of zealous Whigs, continued its inquiries till all reasonable men were convinced that he had fallen by his own hand, and till his wife, his brother, and his most intimate friends were desirous that the investigation should be carried no further.† Atonement was made, without any opposition on the part of the Tories, to the memory and the families of

---

* The History of Scotland during this autumn will be best studied in the Leven and Melville Papers.

† See the Lords' Journals of Feb. 5, 1688-9, and of many subsequent days; Braddon' pamphlet, entitled the Earl of Essex's Memory and Honour Vindicated, 1690; and the London Gazette of July 31, and August 4, and 7, 1690, in which Lady Essex and Burne publicly contradicted Braddon.

some other victims, who were themselves beyond the reach of human power. Soon after the Convention had been turned into a Parliament, a bill for reversing the attainder of Lord Russell was presented to the peers, was speedily passed by them, was sent down to the Lower House, and was welcomed there by no common signs of emotion. Many of the members had sate in that very chamber with Russell. He had long exercised there an influence resembling the influence which, within the memory of this generation, belonged to the upright and benevolent Althorpe; an influence derived, not from superior skill in debate or in declamation, but from spotless integrity, from plain good sense, and from that frankness, that simplicity, that good nature, which are singularly graceful and winning in a man raised by birth and fortune high above his fellows. By the Whigs Russell had been honored as a chief; and his political adversaries had admitted that, when he was not misled by associates less respectable and more artful than himself, he was as honest and kind-hearted a gentleman as any in England. The manly firmness and Christian meekness with which he had met death, the desolation of his noble house, the misery of the bereaved father, the blighted prospects of the orphan children,* above all, the union of womanly tenderness and angelic patience in her who had been dearest to the brave sufferer, who had sate, with the pen in her hand, by his side at the bar, who had cheered the gloom of his cell, and who, on his last day, had shared with him the memorials of the great sacrifice, had softened the hearts of many who were little in the habit of pitying an opponent. That Russell had many good qualities, that he had meant well, that he had been hardly used, was now admitted even by courtly lawyers who had assisted in shedding his blood, and by courtly divines who had done their worst to blacken his reputation. When, therefore, the parchment which annulled his sentence was laid on the table of that assembly in which, eight years before, his face and his voice had been so well known, the excitement was great. One old Whig member tried to speak, but was overcome by his feelings. "I cannot," he

---

* Whether the attainder of Lord Russell would, if unreversed, have prevented his son from succeeding to the earldom of Bedford, is a difficult question. The old Earl collected the opinions of the greatest lawyers of the age, which may still be seen among the archives at Woburn. It is remarkable that one of these opinions is signed by Pemberton, who had presided at the trial. This circumstance seems to prove that the family did not impute to him any injustice or cruelty; and in truth he had behaved as well as any judge, before the Revolution, ever behaved on a similar occasion.

faltered out, "name my Lord Russell without disorder. It is enough to name him. I am not able to say more." Many eyes were directed towards that part of the house where Finch sate. The highly honorable manner in which he had quitted a lucrative office, as soon as he had found that he could not keep it without supporting the dispensing power, and the conspicuous part which he had borne in the defence of the bishops, had done much to atone for his faults. Yet, on this day, it could not be forgotten that he had strenuously exerted himself, as counsel for the Crown, to obtain that judgment which was now to be solemnly revoked. He rose, and attempted to defend his conduct: but neither his legal acuteness, nor that fluent and sonorous elocution which was in his family an hereditary gift, and of which none of his family had a larger share than himself, availed him on this occasion. The House was in no humor to hear him, and repeatedly interrupted him by cries of "Order." He had been treated, he was told, with great indulgence. No accusation had been brought against him. Why then should he, under pretence of vindicating himself, attempt to throw dishonorable imputations on an illustrious name, and to apologize for a judicial murder? He was forced to sit down, after declaring that he meant only to clear himself from the charge of having exceeded the limits of his professional duty, that he disclaimed all intention of attacking the memory of Lord Russell, and that he should sincerely rejoice at the reversing of the attainder. Before the House rose the bill was read a second time, and would have been instantly read a third time and passed, had not some additions and omissions been proposed, which would, it was thought, make the reparation more complete. The amendments were prepared with great expedition; the Lords agreed to them; and the King gladly gave his assent.*

This bill was soon followed by three other bills which annulled three wicked and infamous judgments, the judgment against Sidney, the judgment against Cornish, and the judgment against Alice Lisle.†

Some living Whigs obtained without difficulty redress for injuries which they had suffered in the late reign. The sentence of Samuel Johnson was taken into consideration

---

* Grey's Debates, March 1688-9.
† The Acts which reversed the attainders of Russell, Sidney, Cornish, and Alice Lisle were private Acts. Only the titles therefore are printed in the Statute Book: but the Acts will be found in Howell's Collection of State Trials.

by the House of Commons. It was resolved that the scourging which he had undergone was cruel, and that his degradation was of no legal effect. The latter proposition admitted of no dispute: for he had been degraded by the prelates who had been appointed to govern the diocese of London during Compton's suspension. Compton had been suspended by a decree of the High Commission; and the decrees of the High Commission were universally acknowledged to be nullities. Johnson had, therefore, been stripped of his robe by persons who had no jurisdiction over him. The Commons requested the king to compensate the sufferer by some ecclesiastical preferment.* William, however, found that he could not, without great inconvenience, grant this request. For Johnson, though brave, honest, and religious, had always been rash, mutinous and quarrelsome; and, since he had endured for his opinions a martyrdom more terrible than death, the infirmities of his temper and understanding had increased to such a degree that he was as offensive to Low Churchmen as to High Churchmen. Like too many other men, who are not to be turned from the path of right by pleasure, by lucre, or by danger, he mistook the impulses of his pride and resentment for the monitions of conscience, and deceived himself into a belief that in treating friends and foes with indiscriminate insolence and asperity, he was merely showing his Christian faithfulness and courage. Burnet, by exhorting him to patience and forgiveness of injuries, made him a mortal enemy. "Tell his Lordship," said the inflexible priest, "to mind his own business, and to let me look after mine."† It soon began to be whispered that Johnson was mad. He accused Burnet of being the author of the report, and avenged himself by writing libels so violent that they strongly confirmed the imputation which they were meant to refute. The King thought it better to give out of his own revenue a liberal compensation for wrongs which the Commons had brought to his notice than to place an eccentric and irritable man in a situation of dignity and public trust. Johnson was gratified with a present of a thousand pounds and a pension of three hundred a year for two lives. His son was also provided for in the public service.‡

---

* Commons' Journals, June 24, 1689.
† Johnson tells this story himself in his strange pamphlet entitled, Notes upon the Phœnix Edition of the Pastoral Letter, 1694.
‡ Some Memorials of the Reverend Samuel Johnson, prefixed to the folio edition of his works, 1710.

While the Commons were considering the case of Johnson the Lords were scrutinizing with severity the proceedings which had, in the late reign, been instituted against one of their own order, the Earl of Devonshire. The judges who had passed sentence on him were strictly interrogated; and a resolution was passed declaring that in his case the privileges of the peerage had been infringed, and that the Court of King's Bench, in punishing a hasty blow by a fine of thirty thousand pounds, had violated common justice and the Great Charter.*

In the cases which have been mentioned, all parties seem to have agreed in thinking that some public reparation was due. But the fiercest passions both of Whigs and Tories were soon roused by the noisy claims of a wretch whose sufferings, great as they might seem, had been trifling when compared with his crimes. Oates had come back, like a ghost from the place of punishment, to haunt the spots which had been polluted by his guilt. The three years and a half which followed his scourging he had passed in one of the cells of Newgate, except when on certain days, the anniversaries of his perjuries, he had been brought forth and set on the pillory. He was still, however, regarded by many fanatics as a martyr; and it was said that they were able so far to corrupt his keepers that, in spite of positive orders from the government, his sufferings were mitigated by many indulgences. While offenders, who, compared with him, were innocent, grew lean on the prison allowance, his cheer was mended by turkeys and chines, capons and sucking pigs, venison pasties and hampers of claret, the offerings of zealous Protestants.† When James had fled from Whitehall, and when London was in confusion, it was moved, in the Council of Lords which had provisionally assumed the direction of affairs, that Oates should be set at liberty. The motion was rejected:‡ but the jailers, not knowing whom to obey in that time of anarchy, and desiring to conciliate a man who had once been, and might perhaps again be, a terrible enemy, allowed their prisoner to go freely about the town.§ His uneven legs and his hideous face, made more hideous by the shearing which his ears had undergone, were

---

* Lords' Journals, May 15, 1689.
† North's Examen. 224. North's evidence is confirmed by several contemporary squibs in prose and verse. See also the εἰκὼν βροτολελλον, 1697.
‡ Halifax MS. in the British Museum.
§ Epistle dedicatory to Oates's εἰκὼν βασιλιεῇ

now again seen every day in Westminster Hall and the Court of Requests.* He fastened himself on his old patrons, and, in that drawl which he affected as a mark of gentility, gave them the history of his wrongs and of his hopes. It was impossible, he said, that now, when the good cause was triumphant, the discoverer of the plot could be overlooked. " Charles gave me nine hundred pounds a year. Sure William will give me more."†

In a few weeks he brought his sentence before the House of Lords by a writ of error. This is a species of appeal which raises no question of fact. The Lords, while sitting judicially on the writ of error, were not competent to examine whether the verdict which pronounced Oates guilty was or was not according to the evidence. All that they had to consider was whether, the verdict being supposed to be according to the evidence, the judgment was legal. But it would have been difficult even for a tribunal composed of veteran magistrates, and was almost impossible for an assembly of noblemen who were all strongly biassed on one side or on the other, and among whom there was at that time not a single person whose mind had been disciplined by the study of jurisprudence, to look steadily at the mere point of law, abstracted from the special circumstances of the case. In the view of one party, a party which even among the Whig peers was probably a small minority, the appellant was a man who had rendered inestimable service to the cause of liberty and religion, and who had been requited by long confinement, by degrading exposure, and by torture not to be thought of without a shudder. The majority of the House more justly regarded him as the falsest, the most malignant, and the most impudent being that had ever disgraced the human form. The sight of that brazen forehead, the accents of that lying tongue, deprived them of all mastery over themselves. Many of them doubtless remembered with shame and remorse that they had been his dupes, and that, on the very

---

* In a ballad of the time are the following lines :

" Come listen, ye Whigs, to my pitiful moan,
All you that have ears, when the Doctor has none

These lines must have been in Mason's head when he wrote the couplet

" Witness, ye Hills, ye Johnsons, Scots, Shebbeares ;
Hark to my call ; for some of you have ears."

† North's Examen. 224, 254. North says " six hundred a year." But I have taken the larger sum from the impudent petition which Oates addressed to the Commons, July 25 1689. See the Journals.

last occasion on which he had stood before them, he had
by perjury induced them to shed the blood of one of them
own illustrious order. It was not to be expected that a
crowd of gentlemen under the influence of feelings like
these would act with the cold impartiality of a court of
justice. Before they came to any decision on the legal
question which Titus had brought before them, they picked
a succession of quarrels with him. He had published a
paper magnifying his merits and his sufferings. The Lords
found out some pretence for calling this publication a
breach of privilege, and sent him to the Marshalsea. He
petitioned to be released: but an objection was raised to
his petition. He had described himself as a Doctor of
Divinity; and their lordships refused to acknowledge him
as such. He was brought to their bar, and asked where he
had graduated. He answered, "At the university of Salamanca." This was no new instance of his mendacity and
effrontery. His Salamanca degree had been, during many
years, a favorite theme of all the Tory satirists from Dryden
downwards: and even on the continent the Salamanca Doctor
was a nickname in ordinary use.* The Lords, in their hatred
of Oates, so far forgot their own dignity as to treat this ridiculous matter seriously. They ordered him to efface from his
petition the words "Doctor of Divinity." He replied that he
could not in conscience do it; and he was accordingly sent
back to gaol.†

These preliminary proceedings indicated, not obscurely,
what the fate of the writ of error would be. The counsel for
Oates had been heard. No counsel appeared against him. The
Judges were required to give their opinions. Nine of them
were in attendance; and among the nine were the Chiefs of
three Courts of Common Law. The unanimous answer of these
grave, learned, and upright magistrates was that the Court of
King's Bench was not competent to degrade a priest from his
sacred office, or to pass a sentence of perpetual imprisonment;
and that, therefore, the judgment against Oates was contrary to
law, and ought to be reversed. The Lords should undoubtedly
have considered themselves as bound by this opinion. That
they knew Oates to be the worst of men was nothing to
the purpose. To them, sitting as a court of justice, he
ought to have been merely a John of Style, or a John of

---

* Van Citters, in his despatches to the States General, uses this nickname quite gravely.
† Lords' Journals, May 30, 1689.

Nokes. But their indignation was violently excited. Their habits were not those which fit men for the discharge of judicial duties. The debate turned almost entirely on matters to which no allusion ought to have been made. Not a single peer ventured to affirm that the judgment was legal: but much was said about the odious character of the appellant, about the impudent accusation which he had brought against Catherine of Braganza, and about the evil consequences which might follow if so bad a man were capable of being a witness. "There is only one way," said the Lord President, "in which I can consent to reverse the fellow's sentence. He has been whipped from Aldgate to Tyburn. He ought to be whipped from Tyburn back to Aldgate." The question was put. Twenty-three peers voted for reversing the judgment; thirty-five for affirming it.*

This decision produced a great sensation, and not without reason. A question was now raised which might justly excite the anxiety of every man in the kingdom. That question was whether the highest tribunal, the tribunal on which, in the last resort, depended the most precious interests of every English subject, was at liberty to decide judicial questions on other than judicial grounds, and to withhold from a suitor what was admitted to be his legal right, on account of the depravity of his moral character. That the supreme Court of Appeal ought not to be suffered to exercise arbitrary power, under the forms of ordinary justice, was strongly felt by the ablest men in the House of Commons, and by none more strongly than by Somers. With him, and with those who reasoned like him, were, on this occasion, allied all the weak and hot-headed zealots who still regarded Oates as a public benefactor, and who imagined that to question the existence of the Popish plot was to question the truth of the Protestant religion. On the very morning after the decision of the Peers had been pronounced, keen reflections were thrown, in the House of Commons, on the justice of their lordships. Three days later, the subject was brought forward by a Whig Privy Councillor, Sir Robert Howard, member for Castle Rising. He was one of the Berkshire branch of his noble family, a branch which enjoyed, in that age, the unenviable distinction of being wonderfully fertile of bad rhymers. The

* Lords' Journals, May 31, 1689. Commons' Journals, Aug. 2; North's Examen, 234; Narcissus Luttrell's Diary.

poetry of the Berkshire Howards was the jest of three generations of satirists. The mirth began with the first representation of the Rehearsal, and continued down to the last edition of the Dunciad.* But Sir Robert, in spite of his bad verses, and of some foibles and vanities which had caused him to be brought on the stage under the name of Sir Positive Atall, had in Parliament the weight which a stanch party man, of ample fortune, of illustrious name, of ready utterance, and of resolute spirit, can scarcely fail to possess.† When he rose to call the attention of the Commons to the case of Oates, some Tories, animated by the same passions which had prevailed in the other House, received him with loud hisses. In spite of this most unparliamentary insult, he persevered; and it soon appeared that the majority was with him. Some orators extolled the patriotism and courage of Oates: others dwelt much on a prevailing rumor, that the solicitors who were employed against him on behalf of the Crown, had distributed large sums of money among the jurymen. These were topics on which there was much difference of opinion. But that the sentence was illegal was a proposition which admitted of no dispute. The most eminent lawyers in the House of Commons declared that, on this point, they entirely concurred in the opinion given by the judges in the House of Lords. Those who had hissed when the subject was introduced were so effectually cowed that they did not venture to demand a division; and a bill annulling the sentence was brought in, without any opposition.‡

The Lords were in an embarrassing situation. To retract was not pleasant. To engage in a contest with the Lower House, on a question on which that House was clearly in the right, and was backed at once by the opinions of the sages of the law, and by the passions of the populace, might be dangerous. It was thought expedient to take a middle course. An address was presented to the King, requesting him to pardon Oates.§ But this concession only

---
* Sir Robert was the original hero of the Rehearsal, and was called Bilboa. In the remodelled Dunciad, Pope inserted the Lines—

"And highborn Howard, more majestic sire,
With Fool of Quality completes the quire."

Pope's highborn Howard was Edward Howard, the author of the British Princes. Dorset ridiculed Edward Howard's poetry in a short satire, in which thought and wit are packed as close as in the finest passages of Hudibras.

† Key to the Rehearsal; Shadwell's Sullen Lovers; Pepys, May 5, 8, 1668; Evelyn, Feb. 16, 1684-5.

‡ Grey's Debates and Commons' Journals, June 4, and 11, 1689.
§ Lords' Journals, June 6, 1689.

made bad worse. Titus had, like every other human being, a right to justice: but he was not a proper object of mercy. If the judgment against him was illegal, it ought to have been reversed. If it was legal, there was no ground for remitting any portion of it. The Commons, very properly, persisted, passed their bill, and sent it up to the Peers. Of this bill the only objectionable part was the preamble, which asserted, not only that the judgment was illegal, a proposition which appeared on the face of the record to be true, but also that the verdict was corrupt, a proposition which, whether true or false, was certainly not proved.

The Lords were in a great strait. They knew that they were in the wrong. Yet they were determined not to proclaim, in their legislative capacity, that they had, in their judicial capacity, been guilty of injustice. They again tried a middle course. The preamble was softened down: a clause was added which provided that Oates should still remain incapable of being a witness; and the bill thus altered was returned to the Commons.

The Commons were not satisfied. They rejected the amendments, and demanded a free conference. Two eminent Tories, Rochester and Nottingham, took their seats in the Painted Chamber as managers for the Lords. With them was joined Burnet, whose well known hatred of Popery was likely to give weight to what he might say on such an occasion. Somers was the chief orator on the other side: and to his pen we owe a singularly lucid and interesting abstract of the debate.

The Lords frankly owned that the judgment of the Court of King's Bench could not be defended. They knew it to be illegal, and had known it to be so even when they affirmed it. But they had acted for the best. They accused Oates of bringing an impudently false accusation against Queen Catharine; they mentioned other instances of his villainy; and they asked whether such a man ought still to be capable of giving testimony in a court of justice. The only excuse which in their opinion could be made for him was, that he was insane; and in truth, the incredible insolence and absurdity of his behavior when he was last before them seemed to warrant the belief that his brain had been turned, and that he was not to be trusted with the lives of other men. The Lords could not therefore degrade themselves by expressly rescinding what they had done; nor could they consent to pronounce the verdict corrupt on no better evidence than common report.

The reply was complete and triumphant. "Oates is now the smallest part of the question. He has, Your Lordships say, falsely accused the Queen Dowager and other innocent persons. Be it so. This bill gives him no indemnity. We are quite willing, that, if he is guilty, he shall be punished. But for him, and for all Englishmen, we demand that punishment shall be regulated by law, and not by the arbitrary discretion of any tribunal. We demand that when a writ of error is before Your Lordships, you shall give judgment on it according to the known customs and statutes of the realm. We deny that you have any right, on such an occasion, to take into consideration the moral character of a plantiff or the political effect of a decision. It is acknowledged by yourselves that you have, merely because you thought ill of this man, affirmed a judgment which you knew to be illegal. Against this assumption of arbitrary power the Commons protest; and they hope that you will now redeem what you must feel to be an error. Your Lordships intimate a suspicion that Oates is mad. That a man is mad may be a very good reason for not punishing him at all. But how it can be a reason for inflicting on him a punishment which would be illegal even if he were sane, the Commons do not comprehend. Your Lordships think that you should not be justified in calling a verdict corrupt which has not been legally proved to be so. Suffer us to remind you that you have two distinct functions to perform. You are judges, and you are legislators. When you judge, your duty is strictly to follow the law. When you legislate, you may properly take facts from common fame. You invert this rule. You are lax in the wrong place, and scrupulous in the wrong place. As judges, you break through the law for the sake of a supposed convenience. As legislators, you will not admit any fact without such technical proof as it is rarely possible for legislators to obtain."*

This reasoning was not and could not be answered. The Commons were evidently flushed with their victory in the argument, and proud of the appearance which Somers had made in the Painted Chamber. They particularly charged

---

* Commons' Journals, Aug. 2, 1689; Dutch Ambassadors Extraordinary to the States General, $\frac{\text{July 3}}{\text{Aug. 9}}$.

him to see that the report which he had made of the conference was accurately entered in the journals. The Lords very wisely abstained from inserting in their records an account of the debate in which they had been so signally discomfited. But, though conscious of their faults, and ashamed of it, they could not be brought to do public penance by owning in the preamble of the Act, that they had been guilty of injustice. The minority was, however, strong. The resolution to adhere was carried by only twelve votes, of which ten were proxies.* Twenty-one Peers protested. The Bill dropped. Two Masters in Chancery were sent to announce to the Commons the final resolution of the Peers. The Commons thought this proceeding unjustifiable in substance and uncourteous in form. They determined to remonstrate; and Somers drew up an excellent manifesto, in which the vile name of Oates was scarcely mentioned, and in which the Upper House was with great earnestness and gravity exhorted to treat judicial questions judicially. and not, under pretence of administering law, to make law.† The wretched man, who had now a second time thrown the political world into confusion, received a pardon, and was set at liberty. His friends in the Lower House moved an address to the Throne, requesting that a pension sufficient for his support might be granted to him‡ He was consequently allowed about three hundred a year, a sum which he thought unworthy of his acceptance, and which he took with the savage snarl of disappointed greediness.

From the dispute about Oates sprang another dispute, which might have produced very serious consequences. The instrument which had declared William and Mary King and Queen was a revolutionary instrument. It had been drawn up by an assembly unknown to the ordinary law, and had never received the royal sanction. It was evidently desirable that this great contract between the governors and the governed, this title-deed by which the King held his throne and the people their liberties, should be put into a strictly regular form. The Declaration of Rights was therefore turned into a Bill of Rights ; and the Bill of Rights speedily passed the Commons: but in the Lords difficulties arose.

The Declaration had settled the crown, first on William

---
*Lords' Journals, July 30, 1689: Luttrell's Diary: Clarendon's Diary, July 31, 1689.
†See the Commons' Journals of July 31, and August 13, 1689.
‡Commons' Journals, Aug. 20.

and Mary jointly, then on the survivor of the two, then on Mary's posterity, then on Anne and her posterity, and, lastly, on the posterity of William by any other wife than Mary. The Bill had been drawn in exact conformity with the Declaration. Who was to succeed if Mary, Anne, and William should all die without posterity, was left in uncertainty. Yet the event for which no provision was made was far from improbable. Indeed it really came to pass. William had never had a child. Anne had repeatedly been a mother, but had no child living. It would not be very strange if, in a few months, disease, war, or treason should remove all those who stood in the entail. In what state would the country then be left? To whom would allegiance be due? The Bill indeed contained a clause which excluded Papists from the throne. But would such a clause supply the place of a clause designating the successor by name? What if the next heir should be a prince of the House of Savoy not three months old? It would be absurd to call such an infant a Papist. Was he then to be proclaimed King? Or was the crown to be in abeyance till he came to an age at which he might be capable of choosing a religion? Might not the most honest and the most intelligent men be in doubt whether they ought to regard him as their Sovereign? And to whom could they look for a solution of this doubt? Parliament there would be none: for the Parliament would expire with the prince who had convoked it. There would be mere anarchy, anarchy which might end in the destruction of the monarchy, or in the destruction of public liberty. For these weighty reasons, Burnet, at William's suggestion, proposed in the House of Lords that the crown should, failing heirs of his Majesty's body, be entailed on an undoubted Protestant, Sophia, Duchess of Brunswick Lunenburg, grand-daughter of James the First, and daughter of Elizabeth, Queen of Bohemia.

The Lords unanimously assented to this amendment: but the Commons unanimously rejected it. The cause of the rejection no contemporary writer has satisfactorily explained. One Whig historian talks of the machinations of the republicans, another of the machinations of the Jacobites.* But it is quite certain that four-fifths of the represent-

* Oldmixon accuses the Jacobites, Burnet the Republicans. Though Burnet took a prominent part in the discussion of this question, his account of what passed is grossly inaccurate. He says that the clause was warmly debated in the Commons, and that Hampden spoke strongly for it. But we learn from the Journals (June 19, 1689) that it was rejected *nemine contradicente*. The Dutch Ambassadors describe it as "een propositie 'twelck geen ingressie schynt te sullen vinden."

atives of the people were neither Jacobites nor republicans. Yet not a single voice was raised in the Lower House in favor of the clause which in the Upper House had been carried by acclamation. The most probable explanation seems to be that the gross injustice which had been committed in the case of Oates had irritated the Commons to such a degree that they were glad of an opportunity to quarrel with the Peers. A conference was held. Neither assembly would give way. While the dispute was hottest, an event took place which, it might have been thought, would have restored harmony. Anne gave birth to a son. The child was baptized at Hampton Court with great pomp, and with many signs of public joy. William was one of the sponsors. The other was the accomplished Dorset, whose roof had given shelter to the Princess in her distress. The King bestowed his own name on his godson, and announced to the splendid circle assembled round the font that the little William was henceforth to be called Duke of Gloucester.*

The birth of this child had greatly diminished the risk against which the Lords had thought it necessary to guard. They might therefore have retracted with a good grace. But their pride had been wounded by the severity with which their decision on Oates's writ of error had been censured in the Painted Chamber. They had been plainly told across the table that they were unjust judges; and the imputation was not the less irritating, because they were conscious that it was deserved. They refused to make any concession; and the Bill of Rights was suffered to drop.†

But the most exciting question of this long and stormy session was, what punishment should be inflicted on those men who had, during the interval between the dissolution of the Oxford Parliament and the Revolution, been the advisers or the tools of Charles and James. It was happy for England that, at this crisis, a prince who belonged to neither of her factions, who loved neither, who hated neither, and who, for the accomplishment of a great design, wished to make use of both, was the moderator between them.

The two parties were now in a position closely resembling that in which they had been twenty-eight years before.

---

* London Gazette, Aug. 1, 1689; Luttrell's Diary.
† The History of this Bill may be traced in the Journals of the two Houses, and in Grey's Debates.

The party indeed which had then been undermost was now uppermost: but the analogy between the situations is one of the most perfect that can be found in history. Both the Restoration and the Revolution were accomplished by coalitions. At the Restoration, those politicians who were peculiarly zealous for liberty assisted to reëstablish monarchy: at the Revolution those politicians who were peculiarly zealous for monarchy assisted to vindicate liberty. The Cavalier would, at the former conjuncture, have been able to effect nothing without the help of Puritans who had fought for the Covenant; nor would the Whig, at the latter conjuncture, have offered a successful resistance to arbitrary power, had he not been backed by men who had a very short time before condemned resistance to arbitrary power as a deadly sin. Conspicuous among those by whom, in 1660, the royal family was brought back, were Hollis, who had, in the days of the tyrrany of Charles the First, held down the Speaker in the chair by main force, while Black Rod knocked for admission in vain; Ingoldsby, whose name was subscribed to the memorable death warrant; and Prynne, whose ears Laud had cut off, and who, in return, had borne the chief part in cutting off Laud's head. Among the seven who, in 1688, signed the invitation to William, were Compton, who had long enforced the duty of obeying Nero; Danby, who had been impeached for endeavoring to establish military despotism; and Lumley, whose blood-hounds had tracked Monmouth to that last sad hiding-place among the fern. Both in 1660 and in 1688, while the fate of the nation still hung in the balance, forgiveness was exchanged between the hostile factions. On both occasions the reconciliation, which had seemed to be cordial in the hour of danger, proved false and hollow in the hour of triumph. As soon as Charles the Second was at Whitehall, the Cavalier forgot the good service recently done by the Presbyterians, and remembered only their old offences. As soon as William was King, too many of the Whigs began to demand vengeance for all that they had, in the days of the Rye House Plot, suffered at the hands of the Tories. On both occasions the Sovereign found it difficult to save the vanquished party from the fury of his triumphant supporters; and on both occasions those whom he had disappointed of their revenge murmured bitterly against the government which had been so weak and ungrateful as to protect its foes against its friends.

So early as the twenty-fifth of March, William called the attention of the Commons to the expediency of quieting the public mind by an amnesty. He expressed his hope that a bill of general pardon and oblivion would be as speedily as possible presented for his sanction, and that no exceptions would be made, except such as were absolutely necessary for the vindication of public justice and for the safety of the state. The Commons unanimously agreed to thank him for this instance of his paternal kindness: but they suffered many weeks to pass without taking any step towards the accomplishment of his wish. When at length the subject was resumed, it was resumed in such a manner as plainly showed that the majority had no real intention of putting an end to the suspense which embittered the lives of all those Tories who were conscious that, in their zeal for prerogative, they had sometimes overstepped the exact line traced by law. Twelve categories were framed, some of which were so extensive as to include tens of thousands of delinquents; and the House resolved that, under every one of these categories, some exceptions should be made. Then came the examination into the cases of individuals. Numerous culprits and witnesses were summoned to the bar; the debates were long and sharp; and it soon became evident that the work was interminable. The summer glided away: the autumn was approaching: the session could not last much longer; and of the twelve distinct inquisitions which the Commons had resolved to institute, only three had been brought to a close. It was necessary to let the bill drop for that year.*

Among the many offenders whose names were mentioned in the course of these inquiries was one who stood alone and unapproached in guilt and infamy, and whom Whigs and Tories were equally willing to leave to the extreme rigor of the law. On that terrible day which was succeeded by the Irish Night, the roar of a great city disappointed of its revenge had followed Jeffreys to the drawbridge of the Tower. His imprisonment was not strictly legal: but he at first accepted with thanks and blessings the protection which those dark walls, made famous by so many crimes and sorrows, afforded him against the fury of the multitude.† Soon, however, he became sensible that his life

---

* See Grey's debates, and the Commons' Journals from March to July. The twelve categories will be found in the Journals of the 23d and 29th of May and of the 8th of June.

† Halifax MS. in the British Museum.

was still in imminent peril. For a time he flattered himself with the hope that a writ of Habeas Corpus would liberate him from his confinement, and that he should be able to steal away to some foreign country, and to hide himself with part of his ill-gotten wealth from the detestation of mankind: but, till the government was settled, there was no court competent to grant a writ of Habeas Corpus; and, as soon as the government had been settled, the Habeas Corpus Act was suspended.* Whether the legal guilt of murder could be brought home to Jeffreys may be doubted. But he was morally guilty of so many murders that, if there had been no other way of reaching his life, a retrospective Act of Attainder would have been clamorously demanded by the whole nation. A disposition to triumph over the fallen has never been one of the besetting sins of Englishmen: but the hatred of which Jeffreys was the object was without a parellel in our history, and partook but too largely of the savageness of his own nature. The people, where he was concerned, were as cruel as himself, and exulted in his misery as he had been accustomed to exult in the misery of convicts listening to the sentence of death, and of families clad in mourning. The rabble congregated before his deserted mansion in Duke Street, and read on the door, with shouts of laughter, the bills announcing the sale of his property. Even delicate women, who had tears for highwaymen and house-breakers, breathed nothing but vengeance against him. The lampoons on him which were hawked about the town were distinguished by an atrocity rare even in those days.† Hanging would be too mild a death for him: a grave under the gibbet would be too respectable a resting-place: he ought to be whipped to death at the cart's tail: he ought to be tortured like an Indian: he ought to be devoured alive. The street poets portioned out all his joints with cannibal ferocity, and computed how many pounds of steaks might be cut from his well fattened carcass. Nay, the rage of his enemies was such that, in language seldom heard in England, they proclaimed their wish that he might go to the place of wailing and gnashing

---

* The Life and Death of George Lord Jeffreys, Finch's speech in Grey's Debates, March 1, 1688-9.

†See among many other pieces, Jeffrey's Elegy, the Letter to the Lord Chancellor exposing to him the sentiments of the people, the Elegy on Dangerfield, Dangerfield's Ghost to Jeffreys, the Humble Petition of Widows and fatherless Children in the West, the Lord Chancellor's Discovery and Confession made in the Time of his Sickness in the Tower; Hickeringill's Ceremony-monger; a broadside entitled "O rare show! O rare sight! O strange monster! The like not in Europe! To be seen near Tower Hill, a few doo— beyond the Lion's den."

of teeth, to the worm that never dies, to the fire that is never quenched. They exhorted him to hang himself in his garters, and to cut his throat with his razor. They put up horrible prayers that he might not be able to repent, that he might die the same hard-hearted, wicked Jeffreys that he had lived. His spirit, as mean in adversity as insolent and inhuman in prosperity, sank under the load of public abhorrence. His constitution, originally bad, and much impaired by intemperance, was completely broken by anxiety. He was tormented by a cruel internal disease, which the most skillful surgeons of that age were seldom able to relieve. One solace was left to him, brandy. Even when he had causes to try and councils to attend, he had seldom gone to bed sober. Now, when he had nothing to occupy his mind save terrible recollections and terrible forebodings, he abandoned himself without reserve to his favorite vice. Many believed him to be bent on shortening his life by excess. He thought it better, they said, to go off in a drunken fit than to be hacked by Ketch, or torn limb from limb by the populace.

Once he was roused from a state of abject despondency by an agreeable sensation, speedily followed by a mortifying disappointment. A parcel had been left for him at the Tower. It appeared to be a barrel of Colchester oysters, his favorite dainties. He was greatly moved: for there are moments when those who least deserve affection are pleased to think that they inspire it. "Thank God," he exclaimed, "I have still some friends left." He opened the barrel; and from among a heap of shells out tumbled a stout halter.*

It does not appear that one of the flatterers or buffoons whom he had enriched out of the plunder of his victims came to comfort him in the day of trouble. But he was not left in utter solitude. John Tutchin, whom he had sentenced to be flogged every fortnight for seven years, made his way into the Tower, and presented himself before the fallen oppressor. Poor Jeffreys, humbled to the dust, behaved with abject civility, and called for wine. "I am glad, sir," he said, "to see you." "And I am glad," answered the resentful Whig, "to see Your Lordship in this place." "I served my master," said Jeffreys: "I was bound in conscience to do so." "Where was your conscience," said Tutchin, "when you passed that sentence on

* Life and Death of George Lord Jeffreys.

me at Dorchester?" "It was set down in my instructions," answered Jeffreys, fawningly, "that I was to show no mercy to men like you, men of parts and courage. When I went back to court I was reprimanded for my lenity."* Even Tutchin, acrimonious as was his nature, and great as were his wrongs, seems to have been a little mollified by the pitiable spectacle which he had at first contemplated with vindictive pleasure. He always denied the truth of the report that he was the person who sent the Colchester barrel to the Tower.

A more benevolent man, John Sharp, the excellent Dean of Norwich, forced himself to visit the prisoner. It was a painful task: but Sharp had been treated by Jeffreys, in old times, as kindly as it was in the nature of Jeffreys to treat anybody, and had once or twice been able, by patiently waiting till the storm of curses and invectives had spent itself, and by dexterously seizing the moment of good humor, to obtain for unhappy families some mitigation of their sufferings. The prisoner was surprised and pleased. "What," he said," dare you own me now?" It was in vain, however, that the amiable divine tried to give salutary pain to that seared conscience. Jeffreys, instead of acknowledging his guilt, exclaimed vehemently against the injustice of mankind. "People call me a murderer for doing what at the time was applauded by some who are now high in public favor. They call me a drunkard because I take punch to relieve me in my agony." He would not admit that, as President of the High Commission, he had done anything that deserved reproach. His colleagues, he said, were the real criminals; and now they threw all the blame on him. He spoke with peculiar asperity of Sprat, who had undoubtedly been the most humane and moderate member of the board.

It soon became clear that the wicked judge was fast sinking under the weight of bodily and mental suffering. Doctor John Scott, prebendary of Saint Paul's, a clergyman of great sanctity, and author of the Christian Life, a treatise once widely renowned, was summoned, probably on the recommendation of his intimate friend Sharp, to the bedside of the dying man. It was in vain, however, that Scott spoke, as Sharp had already spoken, of the hideous butcheries of Dorchester and Taunton. To the last Jeffreys continued to repeat that those who thought him cruel did

---

* Tutchin himself gives this narrative in the Bloody Assizes.

not know what his orders were, that he deserved praise instead of blame, and that his clemency had drawn on him the extreme displeasure of his master.*

Disease, assisted by strong drink and by misery, did its work fast. The patient's stomach rejected all nourishment. He dwindled in a few weeks from a portly and even corpulent man to a skeleton. On the eighteenth of April he died, in the forty-first year of his age. He had been Chief Justice of the King's Bench at thirty-five, and Lord Chancellor at thirty-seven. In the whole history of the English bar there is no other instance of so rapid an elevation, or of so terrible a fall. The emaciated corpse was laid, with all privacy, next to the corpse of Monmouth in the chapel of the Tower.†

The fall of this man, once so great and so much dreaded, the horror with which he was regarded by all the respectable members of his own party, the manner in which the least respectable members of that party renounced fellowship with him in his distress, and threw on him the whole blame of crimes which they had encouraged him to commit, ought to have been a lesson to those intemperate friends of liberty who were clamoring for a new proscription. But it was a lesson which too many of them disregarded. The King had, at the very commencement of his reign, displeased them by appointing a few Tories and Trimmers to high offices; and the discontent excited by these appointments had been inflamed by his attempt to obtain a general amnesty for the vanquished. He was in truth not a man to be popular with the vindictive zealots

---

* See the Life of Archbishop Sharp, by his son. What passed between Scott and Jeffreys was related by Scott to Sir Joseph Jekyl. See Tindall's History; Eachard, iii, 932. Eachard's informant, who is not named, but who seems to have had good opportunities of knowing the truth, said that Jeffreys died, not, as the vulgar believed, of drink, but of the stone. The distinction is of little importance. It is certain that Jeffreys was grossly intemperate, and his malady was one which intemperance notoriously tends to aggravate.

† See a full and True Account of the Death of George Lord Jeffreys, licensed on the day of his death. The wretched Le Noble was never weary of repeating that Jeffreys was poisoned by the usurper. I will give a short passage as a specimen of the calumnies of which William was the object. "Il envoya," says Pasquin, " ce fin ragoût de champignons au Chancelier Jeffreys, prisonnier dans la Tour, qui les trouva du même goust, et du même assaisonnement que furent les derniers dont Agrippine regala le bonhomme Claudius son époux, et que Neron appella depuis la viande de Dieux." Marforio asks: "Le Chancelier est donc Mort dans la Tour?" Pasquin answers: "Il estoit trop fidèle à son Roi légitime, et trop habile dans les loix du royaume, pour échapper à l'Usurpateur qu'il ne vouloit point reconnoistre. Guillemot prit soin de faire publier que ce malheureux prisonnier estoit attaqué d'une fièvre maligne: mais, à parler franchement, il vivroit peut-estre encore, s'il n'avoit rien mangé que de la main de ses anciens cuisiniers."—Le Festin de Guillemot, 1689. Dangeau (May 7,) mentions a report that Jeffreys had poisoned himself. In 1693 the corpse of Jeffreys was, by the royal permission, removed from the chapel of the Tower, and laid in the Church of St. Mary Aldermary.

of any faction. For among his peculiarities was a certain ungracious humanity which rarely conciliated his foes, which often provoked his adherents, but in which he doggedly persisted, without troubling himself either about the thanklessness of those whom he had saved from destruction, or about the rage of those whom he had disappointed of their revenge. Some of the Whigs now spoke of him as bitterly as they had ever spoken of either of his uncles. He was a Stuart after all, and was not a Stuart for nothing. Like the rest of the race, he loved arbitrary power. In Holland, he had succeeded in making himself, under the forms of a republican polity, scarcely less absolute than the old hereditary Counts had been. In consequence of a strange combination of circumstances, his interest had, during a short time, coincided with the interest of the English people: but, though he had been a deliverer by accident, he was a despot by nature. He had no sympathy with the just resentments of the Whigs. He had objects in view which the Whigs would not willingly suffer any Sovereign to attain. He knew that the Tories were the only tools for his purpose. He had, therefore, from the moment at which he took his seat on the throne, favored them unduly. He was now trying to procure an indemnity for those very delinquents whom he had, a few months before, described in his Declaration as deserving of exemplary punishment. In November he had told the world that the crimes in which these men had borne a part had made it the duty of subjects to violate their oath of allegiance, of soldiers to desert their standards, of children to make war on their parents. With what consistency then could he recommend that such crimes should be covered by a general oblivion? And was there not too much reason to fear that he wished to save the agents of tyranny from the fate which they merited, in the hope that, at some future time, they might serve him as unscrupulously as they had served his father-in-law?*

Of the members of the House of Commons who were animated by these feelings, the fiercest and most audacious

* Among the numerous pieces in which the malcontent Whigs vented their anger, none is more curious than the poem entitled the Ghost of Charles the Second. Charles addresses William thus:
"Hail, my blest Nephew, whom the fates ordain
To fill the measure of the Stuart's reign,
That all the ills by our whole race designed
In thee their full accomplishment might find:
'Tis thou that art decreed this point to clear,
Which we have laboured for these four-score year."

was Howe. He went so far on one occasion as to move that an inquiry should be instituted into the proceedings of the Parliament of 1685, and that some note of infamy should be put on all who, in that Parliament, had voted with the Court. This absurd and mischievous motion was discountenanced by all the most respectable Whigs, and strongly opposed by Birch and Maynard.* Howe was forced to give way: but he was a man whom no check could abash; and he was encouraged by the applause of many hot-headed members of his party, who were far from foreseeing that he would, after having been the most rancorous and unprincipled of Whigs, become, at no distant time, the most rancorous and unprincipled of Tories.

This quick-witted, restless, and malignant politician, though himself occupying a lucrative place in the royal household, declaimed, day after day, against the manner in which the great offices of state were filled; and his declamations were echoed, in tones somewhat less sharp and vehement, by other orators. No man, they said, who had been a minister of Charles or of James ought to be a minister of William. The first attack was directed against the Lord President Caermarthen. Howe moved that an address should be presented to the King, requesting that all persons who had ever been impeached by the Commons might be dismissed from his Majesty's counsels and presence. The debate on this motion was repeatedly adjourned. While the event was doubtful, William sent Dykvelt to expostulate with Howe. Howe was obdurate. He was what is vulgarly called a disinterested man; that is to say, he valued money less than the pleasure of venting his spleen and of making a sensation. "I am doing the King a service," he said: "I am rescuing him from false friends; and, as to my place, that shall never be a gag to prevent me from speaking my mind." The motion was made, but completely failed. In truth the proposition, that mere accusation, never prosecuted to conviction, ought to be considered as a decisive proof of guilt, was shocking to natural justice. The faults of Caermarthen had doubtless been great; but they had been exaggerated by party spirit, had been expiated by severe suffering, and had been redeemed by recent and eminent services. At the time when he raised the great county of York in arms against Popery and tyranny, he had been assured by some of the most

* Grey's Debates, June 12, 1689.

eminent Whigs that all old quarrels were forgotten. Howe indeed maintained that the civilities which had passed in the moment of peril signified nothing. "When a viper is on my hand," he said, "I am very tender of him: but as soon as I have him on the ground, I set my foot on him and crush him." The Lord President, however, was so strongly supported that, after a discussion which lasted three days, his enemies did not venture to take the sense of the House on the motion against him. In the course of the debate a grave constitutional question was incidentally raised. This question was whether a pardon could be pleaded in bar of a parliamentary impeachment. The Commons resolved, without a division, that a pardon could not be so pleaded.*

The next attack was made on Halifax. He was in a much more invidious position than Caermarthen, who had, under pretence of ill health, withdrawn himself almost entirely from business. Halifax was generally regarded as the chief adviser of the Crown, and was in an especial manner held responsible for all the faults which had been committed with respect to Ireland. The evils which had brought that Kingdom to ruin might, it was said, have been averted by timely precaution, or remedied by vigorous exertion. But the government had foreseen nothing: it had done little; and that little had been done neither at the right time nor in the right way. Negotiation had been employed instead of troops, when a few troops might have sufficed. A few troops had been sent when many were needed. The troops that had been sent had been ill equipped and ill commanded. Such, the vehement Whigs exclaimed, were the natural fruits of that great error which King William had committed on the first day of his reign. He had placed in Tories and Trimmers a confidence which they did not deserve. He had, in a peculiar manner, entrusted the direction of Irish affairs to the Trimmer of Trimmers, to a man whose ability nobody disputed, but who was not firmly attached to the new government, who, indeed, was incapable of being firmly attached to any government, who had always halted between two opinions, and who, till the moment of the flight of James, had not given up the hope that the discontents of the nation might be quieted without a change of dynasty. Howe, on twenty

* See Commens' Journals, and Grey's Debates, June 1, 3 and 4, 1689: Life of William, 1704.

occasions, designated Halifax as the cause of all the calamities of the country. Monmouth held similar language in the House of Peers. Though First Lord of the Treasury, he paid no attention to financial business, for which he was altogether unfit, and of which he had very soon become weary. His whole heart was in the work of persecuting the Tories. He plainly told the King that nobody who was not a Whig ought to be employed in the public service. William's answer was cool and determined. "I have done as much for your friends as I can do without danger to the state; and I will do no more."* The only effect of this reprimand was to make Monmouth more factious than ever. Against Halifax especially he intrigued and harangued with indefatigable animosity. The other Whig Lords of the Treasury, Delamere and Capel, were scarcely less eager to drive the Lord Privy Seal from office; and personal jealousy and antipathy impelled the Lord President to conspire with his own accusers against his rival.

What foundation there may have been for the imputations thrown at this time on Halifax cannot now be fully ascertained. His enemies, though they interrogated numerous witnesses, and though they obtained William's reluctant permission to inspect the minutes of the Privy Council, could find no evidence which would support a definite charge.† But it was undeniable that the Lord Privy Seal had acted as minister for Ireland, and that Ireland was all but lost. It is unnecessary, and indeed absurd, to suppose, as many Whigs supposed, that his administration was unsuccessful because he did not wish it to be successful. The truth seems to be that the difficulties of the situation were great, and that he, with all his ingenuity and eloquence, was ill qualified to cope with those difficulties. The whole machinery of government was out of joint; and he was not the man to set it right. What was wanted was not what he had in large measure, wit, taste, amplitude of comprehension, subtlety in drawing distinctions; but what he had not, prompt decision, indefatigable energy, and stubborn resolution. His mind was at best of too soft a temper for such work as he had now to do, and had been recently made softer by severe affliction. He had lost two sons in less than twelve months. A letter is still extant, in which

---
* Burnet MS. Harl. 6584; Avaux to De Croissy, June 16-26, 1689.
† As to the minutes of the Privy Council, see the Commons' Journals of June 22 and 28, and of July 3, 5, 13, and 16.

he at this time complained to his honored friend Lady Russell of the desolation of his hearth and of the cruel ingratitude of the Whigs. We possess, also, the answer, in which she gently exhorted him to seek for consolation where she had found it under trials not less severe than his.*

The first attack on him was made in the Upper House. Some Whig Peers, among whom the wayward and petulant First Lord of the Treasury was conspicuous, proposed that the King should be requested to appoint a new Speaker. The friends of Halifax moved and carried the previous question.† About three weeks later his persecutors brought forward, in a Committee of the whole House of Commons, a resolution which imputed to him no particular crime either of omission or of commission, but which simply declared it to be advisable that he should be dismissed from the service of the Crown. The debate was warm. Moderate politicians of both parties were unwilling to put a stigma on a man, not indeed faultless, but distinguished both by his abilities and his amiable qualities. His accusers saw that they could not carry their point, and tried to escape from a decision which was certain to be adverse to them, by proposing that the Chairman should report progress. But their tactics were disconcerted by the judicious and spirited conduct of Lord Eland, now the Marquess's only son. "My father has not deserved," said the young nobleman, "to be thus trifled with. If you think him culpable, say so. He will at once submit to your verdict. Dismission from Court has no terrors for him. He is raised, by the goodness of God, above the necessity of looking to office for the means of supporting his rank." The Committee divided, and Halifax was absolved by a majority of fourteen.‡

---

*The letter of Halifax to Lady Russell, is dated on the 23d of July 1689, about a fortnight after the attack on him in the Lords, and about a week before the attack on him in the Commons.

†See the Lords' Journals of July 10, 1689, and a letter from London dated July 11-21, and transmitted by Croissy to Avaux. Don Pedro de Ronquillo mentions this attack of the Whig Lords on Halifax in a despatch of which I cannot make out the date.

‡This was on Saturday the 3d of August. As the division was in Committee, the numbers do not appear in the Journals. Clarendon, in his Diary, says that the majority was eleven. But Narcissus Luttrell, Oldmixon, and Tindal agree in putting it at fourteen. Most of the little information which I have been able to find about the debate is contained in a despatch of Don Pedro de Ronquillo. "Se rosolvio," he says, "que el sabado, en comity de toda la casa, se tratasse del estado de la nacion para representarle al Rey. Emperose por acusar al Marques de Olifax; y reconociendo sus emulos que no tenian partido bastante, quisieron remitir para otro dia esta mocion: pero el Conde de Elan, primogenito del Marques de Olifax, miembro de la casa, les dijo que su padre no era hombre para andar peloteando con el, y que se tubiesse culpa lo acabasen de castigar, que el no havia menester estar en la corte para portarse conforme á su estado, pues Dios

Had the division been postponed a few hours, the majority would probably have been much greater. The Commons voted under the impression that Londonderry had fallen, and that all Ireland was lost. Scarcely had the House risen when a courier arrived with news that the boom on the Foyle had been broken. He was speedily followed by a second who announced the raising of the siege, and by a third who brought the tidings of the battle of Newton Butler. Hope and exultation succeeded to discontent and dismay.* Ulster was safe; and it was confidently expected that Schomberg would speedily reconquer Leinster, Connaught, and Munster. He was now ready to set out. The port of Chester was the place from which he was to take his departure. The army which he was to command had assembled there; and the Dee was crowded with men of war and transports. Unfortunately almost all those English soldiers who had seen war had been sent to Flanders. The bulk of the force destined for Ireland consisted of men just taken from the plough and the threshing floor. There was, however, an excellent brigade of Dutch troops under the command of an experienced officer, the Count of Solmes. Four regiments, one of cavalry and three of infantry, had been formed out of the French refugees, many of whom had borne arms with credit. No person did more to promote the raising of these regiments than the Marquess of Ruvigny. He had been during many years an eminently faithful and useful servant of the French government. So highly was his merit appreciated at Versailles that he had been solicited to accept indulgences which scarcely any other heretic could by any solicitation obtain. Had he chosen to remain in his native country, he and his household would have been permitted to worship God privately according to their own forms. But Ruvigny rejected all offers, cast in his lot with his brethren, and, at upwards of eighty years of age, quitted Versailles, where he might still have been a favorite, for a modest dwelling at Greenwich. That dwelling was, during the last months of his life, the resort of all that was most distinguished among his fellow exiles. His abilities, his experience, and his munificent kindness, made him the undisputed chief of

---

le havia dado abundamente para poderlo hazer; con que por pluralidad de voces vencio sur partido." I suspect that Lord Eland meant to sneer at the poverty of some of his father's persecutors, and at the greediness of others.

* This change of feeling, immediately following the debate on the motion for removing Halifax, is noticed by Ronquillo.

the refugees. He was at the same time half an Englishman: for his sister had been Countess of Southampton, and he was uncle of Lady Russell. He was long past the time of action. But his two sons, both men of eminent courage, devoted their swords to the service of William. The younger son, who bore the name of Caillemote, was appointed colonel of one of the Huguenot regiments of foot. The two other regiments of foot were commanded by La Melloniere and Cambon, officers of high reputation. The regiment of horse was raised by Schomberg himself, and bore his name. Ruvigny lived just long enough to see these arrangements complete.*

The general to whom the direction of the expedition against Ireland was confided had wonderfully succeeded in obtaining the affection and esteem of the English nation. He had been made a Duke, a Knight of the Garter, and Master of the Ordnance; he was now placed at the head of an army; and yet his elevation excited none of that jealousy which showed itself as often as any mark of royal favor was bestowed on Bentinck, on Zulestein, or on Auverquerque. Schomberg's military skill was universally acknowledged. He was regarded by all Protestants as a confessor who had endured everything short of martyrdom for the truth. For his religion he had resigned a splendid income, had laid down the truncheon of a Marshal of France, and had, at near eighty years of age, begun the world again as a needy soldier of fortune. As he had no connection with the United Provinces, and had never belonged to the little Court of the Hague, the preference given to him over English captains was justly ascribed, not to national or personal partiality, but to his virtues and his abilities. His deportment differed widely from that of the other foreigners who had just been created English peers. They, with many respectable qualities, were, in tastes, manners, and predilections, Dutchmen, and could not catch the tone of the society to which they had been transferred. He was a citizen of the world, had travelled over all Europe, had commanded armies on the Meuse, on the Ebro, and on the Tagus, had shone in the splendid circle of Versailles, and had been in high favor at the Court of Berlin. He had

---

*As to Ruvigny, see Saint Simon's Memoirs of the year 1697; Burnet i. 366. There is some interesting information about Ruvigny and about the Huguenot regiments in a narrative written by a French refugee of the name of Dumont. This narrative, which is in manuscript, and which I shall occasionally quote as the Dumont MS., was kindly lent to me by Dr. Vignoles, Dean of Ossory.

often been taken by French noblemen for a French nobleman. He had passed some time in England, spoke English remarkably well, accommodated himself easily to English manners, and was often seen walking in the park with English companions. In youth his habits had been temperate; and his temperance had its proper reward, a singularly green and vigorous old age. At fourscore he retained a strong relish for innocent pleasures: he conversed with great courtesy and sprightliness: nothing could be in better taste than his equipages and his table; and every cornet of cavalry envied the grace and dignity with which the veteran appeared in Hyde Park on his charger at the head of his regiment.* The House of Commons had, with general approbation, compensated his losses and rewarded his services by a grant of a hundred thousand pounds. Before he set out for Ireland, he requested permission to express his gratitude for this magnificent present. A chair was set for him within the bar. He took his seat there with the mace at his right hand, rose, and in a few graceful words returned his thanks and took his leave. The Speaker replied that the Commons could never forget the obligation under which they already lay to his Grace, that they saw him with pleasure at the head of an English army, that they felt entire confidence in his zeal and ability, and that, at whatever distance he might be, he would always be in a peculiar manner an object of their care. The precedent set on this interesting occasion was followed with the utmost minuteness, a hundred and twenty-five years later, on an occasion more interesting still. Exactly on the same spot on which, in July 1689, Schomberg had acknowledged the liberality of the nation, a chair was set, in July 1814, for a still more illustrious warrior, who came to return thanks for a still more splendid mark of public gratitude. Few things illustrate more strikingly the peculiar character of the English government and people than the circumstance that the House of Commons, a popular assembly, should, even in a moment of joyous enthusiasm, have adhered to ancient forms with the punctilious accuracy of a College of Heralds; that the sitting and rising, the covering and the uncovering, should have been regulated by exactly the same etiquette in the nineteenth century as in the seventeenth; and that the same mace which had been held at the right

*See the Abrégé de la Vie de Frederic Duc de Schomberg by Luzancy, 1690, the Memoirs of count Dohna, and the note of Saint Simon on Dangeau's Journal, July 30, 1690.

hand of Schomberg should have been held in the same position at the right hand of Wellington.*

On the twentieth of August the Parliament, having been constantly engaged in business during seven months, broke up, by the royal command, for a short recess. The same Gazette which announced that the Houses had ceased to sit announced that Schomberg had landed in Ireland.†

During the three weeks which preceded his landing, the dismay and confusion at Dublin Castle had been extreme. Disaster had followed disaster so fast that the mind of James, never very firm, had been completely prostrated. He had learned first that Londonderry had been relieved; then that one of his armies had been beaten by the Enniskilleners; then that another of his armies was retreating, or rather flying, from Ulster, reduced in numbers and broken in spirit; then that Sligo, the key of Connaught, had been abandoned to the Englishry. He had found it impossible to subdue the colonists, even when they were left almost unaided. He might therefore well doubt whether it would be possible for him to contend against them when they were backed by an English army, under the command of the greatest general living. The unhappy prince seemed, during some days, to be sunk in despondency. On Avaux the danger produced a very different effect. Now, he thought, was the time to turn the war between the English and the Irish into a war of extirpation, and to make it impossible that the two nations could ever be united under one government. With this view, he coolly submitted to the King a proposition of almost incredible atrocity. There must be a Saint Bartholomew. A pretext would easily be found. No doubt, when Schomberg was known to be in Ireland, there would be some excitement in those southern towns of which the population was chiefly English. Any disturbance, wherever it might take place, would furnish an excuse for a general massacre of the Protestants of Leinster, Munster, and Connaught.‡ As the King did not at first express any horror at this suggestion § the envoy, a few days later, returned to the subject, and pressed his

---

*See the Commons' Journals of July 16, 1689, and of July 1, 1814.

†Journals of the Lords and Commons, Aug. 20, 1689; London Gazette, Aug. 22.

‡"J'estois d'avis qu', après que la descente seroit faite. si on apprenoit que des Protestans se fussent soulevez en quelques endroits du royaume, on fit main basse sur tous généralement."—Avaux. $\frac{\text{July, 31}}{\text{Aug. 10.}}$ 1689.

§"Le Roy d'Angleterre m'avoit écouté assez paisiblement la premièr fois que je luy avois proposé ce qu'il y avoit à faire contre les Protestans."—Avaux, Aug. 4-14.

Majesty to give the necessary orders. Then James, with a warmth which did him honor, declared that nothing should induce him to commit such a crime. "These people are my subjects; and I cannot be so cruel as to cut their throats while they live peaceably under my government." "There is nothing cruel," answered the callous diplomatist, "in what I recommend. Your Majesty ought to consider that mercy to Protestants is cruelty to Catholics." James, however, was not to be moved; and Avaux retired in very bad humor. His belief was that the King's professions of humanity were hypocritical, and that, if the orders for the butchery were not given, they were not given only because his Majesty was confident that the Catholics all over the country would fall on the Protestants without waiting for orders.* But Avaux was entirely mistaken. That he should have supposed James to be as profoundly immoral as himself is not strange. But it is strange that so able a man should have forgotten that James and himself had quite different objects in view. The object of the Ambassador's politics was to make the separation between England and Ireland eternal. The object of the King's politics was to unite England and Ireland under his own scepter; and he could not but be aware that, if there should be a general massacre of the Protestants of three provinces, and he should be suspected of having authorized it or of having connived at it, there would in a fortnight be not a Jacobite left even at Oxford.†

Just at this time the prospects of James, which had seemed hopelessly dark, began to brighten. The danger which unnerved him had roused the Irish people. They had, six months before, risen up as one man against the Saxons. The army which Tyrconnel had formed was, in proportion to the population from which it was taken, the largest that Europe had ever seen. But that army had sustained a long succession of defeats and disgraces, unredeemed by a single brilliant achievement. It was the

---

*Avaux, Aug. 4-14. He says, "Je m'imagine qu'il est persuadé que, quoiqu'il ne donne point d'ordre sur cela, la plupart des Catholiques de la campagne se jetteront sur les Protestans."

†Lewis, Aug. 27. / Sept. 6, reprimanded Avaux, though much too gently, for proposing to butcher the whole Protestant population of Leinster, Connaught, and Munster. "Je n'approuve pas cependant la proposition que vous faites de faire main basse sur tous les Protestans du Royaume, du moment qu', en quelque endroit que ce soit, ils se seront soulevez: et, outre que la punition d'une infinité d'innocens pour peu de coupables ne seroit pas juste, d'ailleurs les représailles contre les Catholiques seroient d'autant plus dangereuses, que les premiers se trouveront mieux armez et soutenus de toutes les forces d'Angleterre."

fashion, both in England and on the Continent, to ascribe those defeats and disgraces to the pusillanimity of the Irish race.* That this was a great error is sufficiently proved by the history of every war which has been carried on in any part of Christendom during five generations. The raw material out of which a good army may be formed existed in great abundance among the Irish. Avaux informed his government that they were a remarkably handsome, tall, and well made race; that they were personally brave; that they were sincerely attached to the cause for which they were in arms; that they were violently exasperated against the colonists. After extolling their strength and spirit, he proceeded to explain why it was that, with all their strength and spirit, they were constantly beaten. It was vain, he said, to imagine that bodily prowess, animal courage, or patriotic enthusiasm would, in the day of battle, supply the place of discipline. The infantry were ill armed and ill trained. They were suffered to pillage wherever they went. They had contracted all the habits of banditti. There was among them scarcely one officer capable of showing them their duty. Their colonels were generally men of good family, but men who had never seen service. The captains were butchers, tailors, shoemakers. Hardly one of them troubled himself about the comforts, the accoutrements, or the drilling of those over whom he was placed. The dragoons were little better than the infantry. But the horse were, with some exceptions, excellent. Almost all the Irish gentlemen who had any military experience held commissions in the cavalry; and by the exertions of these officers, some regiments had been raised and disciplined which Avaux pronounced equal to any that he had ever seen. It was therefore evident that the inefficiency of the foot and of the dragoons was to be ascribed to the vices, not of the Irish character, but of the Irish administration.†

---

*Ronquillo, Aug. 9-19, speaking of the Siege of Londonderry, expresses his astonishment, "que una plaza sin fortificazion y sin gentes de guerra aya hecho una defensa tan gloriosa, y que los sitiadores al contrario ayan sido tan poltrones."

†This account of the Irish army is compiled from numerous letters written by Avaux to Lewis and to Lewis's ministers. I will quote a few of the most remarkable passages. "Les plus beaux hommes," Avaux says of the Irish, "qu'on peut voir. Il n'y en a presque point au dessous de cinq pieds cinq à six pouces." It will be remembered that the French foot is longer than ours. "Ils sont très bien faits; mais il ne sont ny disciplinez ny armez, et de surplus sont de grands voleurs." "La plupart de ces régimens sont levez par des gentilshommes qui n'ont jamais esté à l'armée. Ce sont des tailleurs, des bouchers, des cordonniers, qui ont formé les compagnies et qui en sont les Capitaines." "Jamais troupes n'ont marché comme font celles-cy. Ils vont comme des bandits, et pillent tout ce qu'ils trouvent en chemin." "Quoiqu'il soit vrai que les soldats paroissent fort résolus à bien faire, et qu'ils soient fort animez contre les rebelles, néantmoins

The events which took place in the autumn of 1689 sufficiently proved that the ill-fated race, which enemies and allies generally agreed in regarding with unjust contempt, had, together with the faults inseparable from poverty, ignorance, and superstition, some fine qualities which have not always been found in more prosperous and more enlightened communities. The evil tidings which terrified and bewildered James stirred the whole population of the southern provinces like the peal of a trumpet sounding to battle. That Ulster was lost, that the English were coming, that the death grapple between the two hostile nations was at hand, was proclaimed from all the altars of three and twenty counties. One last chance was left; and, if that chance failed, nothing remained but the despotic, the merciless rule of the Saxon colony and of the heretical church. The Roman Catholic priest who had just taken possession of the glebe house and the chancel, the Roman Catholic squire who had just been carried back on the shoulders of the shouting tenantry into the hall of his fathers, would be driven forth to live on such alms as peasants, themselves oppressed and miserable, could spare. A new confiscation would complete the work of the Act of Settlement; and the followers of William would seize whatever the followers of Cromwell had spared. These apprehensions produced such an outbreak of patriotic and religious enthusiasm as deferred for a time the inevitable day of subjugation. Avaux was amazed by the energy which, in circumstances so trying, the Irish displayed. It was indeed the wild and unsteady energy of a half barbarous people: it was transient: it was often misdirected: but though transient and misdirected, it did wonders. The French ambassador was forced to own that those officers of whose incompetency and inactivity he had so often complained had suddenly shaken off their lethargy. Recruits came in by thousands. The ranks which had been thinned under the walls of Londonderry were soon again full to overflowing.* Great efforts

il ne suffit pas de cela pour combattre.... Les officiers subalternes sont mauvais, et, à la reserve d'un très petit nombre, il n'y en a point qui ayt soin des soldats, des armes, et de la discipline." "On a beaucoup plus de confiance en la cavalerie, dont la plus grande partie est assez bonne." Avaux mentions several regiments of horse with particular praise. Of two of these he says: "On ne peut voir de meilleur régiment." The correctness of the opinion which he had formed both of the infantry and of the cavalry was, after his departure from Ireland, signally proved at the Boyne.

*I will quote a passage or two from the despatches written at this time by Avaux. On September 7-17, he says: "De quelque costé qu'on se tournât on ne pouvoit rien prevoir que de désagréable. Mais dans cette extrémité chacun s'est évertué. Les officiers ont fait leurs recrues avec beaucoup de diligence." Three days later he says: "Il y a quinze were made to arm and clothe the troops; and, in the short space of a fortnight, everything presented a new and cheering aspect.

The Irish required of the King, in return for their strenuous exertions in his cause, one concession which was by no means agreeable to him. The unpopularity of Melfort had become such that his person was scarcely safe. He had no friend to speak a word in his favor. The French hated him. In every letter which arrived at Dublin from England or from Scotland, he was described as the evil genius of the House of Stuart. It was necessary for his own sake to dismiss him. An honorable pretext was found. He was ordered to repair to Versailles, to represent there the state of affairs in Ireland, and to implore the French government to send over without delay six or seven thousand veteran infantry. He laid down the seals; and they were, to the great delight of the Irish, put into the hands of an Irishman, Sir Richard Nagle, who had made himself conspicuous as Attorney General and Speaker of the House of Commons. Melfort took his departure under cover of the night: for the rage of the populace against him was such that he could not without danger show himself in the streets of Dublin by day. On the following morning James left his capital in the opposite direction to encounter Schomberg.*

Schomberg had landed in the north of Ulster. The force which he had brought with him did not exceed ten thousand men. But he expected to be joined by the armed colonists and by the regiments which were under Kirke's command. The coffee-house politicians of London fully expected that such a general with such an army would speedily reconquer the island. Unhappily it soon appeared that the means which had been furnished to him were altogether inadequate to the work which he had to perform: of the greater part of these means he was speedily deprived by a succession of unforeseen calamities; and the whole campaign was merely a long struggle maintained by his prudence and resolution against the utmost spite of fortune.

---

jours que nous n'espérions guère de pouvoir mettre les choses en si bon estat: mais my Lord Tyrconnel et tous les Irlandais ont travaillé avec tant d'empressement qu'on s'est mis en estat de deffense."

*Avaux, Aug. 20-30. Aug. 25, Sept. 4, Aug. 26, Sept. 5,; Life of James, ii. 373; Melfort's vindication of himself among the Nairne Papers. Avaux says: "Il pourra partir ce soir à la nuit: car je vois bien qu'il apprehende qu'il ne sera pas sur pour luy de partir en plein jour."

He marched first to Carrickfergus. That town was held for James by two regiments of infantry. Schomberg battered the walls; and the Irish, after holding out a week, capitulated. He promised that they should depart unharmed; but he found it no easy matter to keep his word. The people of the town and neighborhood were generally Protestants of Scottish extraction. They had suffered much during the short ascendency of the native race; and what they had suffered they were now eager to retaliate. They assembled in great multitudes, enclaiming that the capitulation was nothing to them, and that they would be revenged. They soon proceeded from words to blows. The Irish, disarmed, stripped, and hustled, clung for protection to the English officers and soldiers. Schomberg with difficulty prevented a massacre by spurring, pistol in hand, through the throng of enraged colonists.*

From Carrickfergus Schomberg proceeded to Lisbon, and thence, through towns left without an inhabitant, and over plains on which not a cow, nor a sheep, nor a stack of corn was to be seen, to Loughbrickland. Here he was joined by three regiments of Enniskilleners, whose dress, horses, and arms looked strange to eyes accustomed to the pomp of reviews, but who in natural courage were inferior to no troops in the world, and who had, during months of constant watching and skirmishing, acquired many of the essential qualities of soldiers.†

Schomberg continued to advance towards Dublin through a desert. The few Irish troops which remained in the south of Ulster retreated before him, destroying as they retreated. Newry, once a well built and thriving Protestant borough, he found a heap of smoking ashes. Carlingford too had perished. The spot where the town had once stood was marked only by the massy remains of the old Norman castle. Those who ventured to wander from the camp reported that the country, as far as they could explore it, was a wilderness. There were cabins, but no inmates: there was rich pasture, but neither flock nor herd: there were cornfields; but the harvest lay on the ground soaked with rain.‡

While Schomberg was advancing through a vast solitude, the Irish forces were rapidly assembling from every

---

* Story's Impartial History of the Wars of Ireland, 1693; Life of James, ii. 374; Avaux Sept. 7-17, 1689; Nihell's Journal, printed in 1689, and reprinted by Macpherson.
† Story's Impartial History. Ibid.

quarter. On the tenth of September the royal standard of James was unfurled on the tower of Drogheda; and beneath it were soon collected twenty thousand fighting men, the infantry generally bad, the cavalry generally good, but both infantry and cavalry full of zeal for their country and their religion.* The troops were attended as usual by a great multitude of camp followers, armed with scythes, half pikes, and skeans. By this time Schomberg had reached Dundalk. The distance between the two armies was not more than a long day's march. It was therefore generally expected that the fate of the island would speedily be decided by a pitched battle.

In both camps, all who did not understand war were eager to fight; and, in both camps, the few who had a high reputation for military science were against fighting. Neither Rosen nor Schomberg wished to put everything on a cast. Each of them knew intimately the defects of his own army; and neither of them was fully aware of the defects of the other's army. Rosen was certain that the Irish infantry were worse equipped, worse officered, and worse drilled, than any infantry that he had ever seen from the Gulf of Bothnia to the Atlantic; and he supposed that the English troops were well trained, and were, as they doubtless ought to have been, amply provided with everything necessary to their efficiency. Numbers, he rightly judged, would avail little against a great superiority of arms and discipline. He therefore advised James to fall back, and even to abandon Dublin to the enemy rather than hazard a battle the loss of which would be the loss of all. Athlone was the best place in the kingdom for a determined stand. The passage of the Shannon might be defended till the succors which Melfort had been charged to solicit came from France; and those succors would change the whole character of the war. But the Irish, with Tyrconnel at their head, were unanimous against retreating. The blood of the whole nation was up. James was pleased with the enthusiasm of his subjects, and positively declared that he would not disgrace himself by leaving his capital to the invaders without a blow.†

In a few days it became clear that Schomberg had determined not to fight. His reasons were weighty. He had

---
*Avaux, Sept. 10-20, 1689; Story's Impartial History; Life of James, ii. 377, 378, Orig. Mem. Story and James agree in estimating the Irish army at about twenty thousand men. See also Dangeau, Oct. 28, 1689.
†Life of James, ii. 377, 378, Orig. Mem.

some good Dutch and French troops. The Enniskilleners who had joined him had served a military apprenticeship, though not in a very regular manner. But the bulk of his army consisted of English peasants who had just left their cottages. His musketeers had still to learn how to load their pieces: his dragoons had still to learn how to manage their horses; and these inexperienced recruits were for the most part commanded by officers as inexperienced as themselves. His troops were therefore not generally superior in discipline to the Irish, and were in number far inferior. Nay, he found that his men were almost as ill armed, as ill lodged, and as ill clad, as the Celts to whom they were opposed. The wealth of the English nation and the liberal votes of the English parliament had entitled him to expect that he should be abundantly supplied with all the munitions of war. But he was cruelly disappointed. The administration had, ever since the death of Oliver, been constantly becoming more and more imbecile, more and more corrupt; and now the Revolution reaped what the Restoration had sown. A crowd of negligent or ravenous functionaries, formed under Charles and James, plundered, starved, and poisoned the armies and fleets of William. Of these men the most important was Henry Shales, who, in the late reign, had been Commissary General to the camp at Hounslow. It is difficult to blame the new government for continuing to employ him: for, in his own department, his experience far surpassed that of any other Englishman. Unfortunately, in the same school in which he had acquired his experience, he had learned the whole art of peculation. The beef and brandy which he furnished were so bad that the soldiers turned from them with loathing: the tents were rotten: the clothing was scanty: the muskets broke in the handling. Great numbers of shoes were set down to the account of the government: but, two months after the Treasury had paid the bill, the shoes had not arrived in Ireland. The means of transporting baggage and artillery were almost entirely wanting. An ample number of horses had been purchased in England with the public money, and had been sent to the banks of the Dee. But Shales had let them out for harvest work to the farmers of Cheshire, had pocketed the hire,* and had left the troops in Ulster to get on as they

---

*See Grey's Debates, Nov. 26, 27, 28, 1689, and the Dialogue between a Lord Lieutenant and one of his Deputies, 1692.

best might. Schomberg thought that, if he should, with an ill trained and ill appointed army, risk a battle against a superior force, he might not improbably be defeated; and he knew that a defeat might be followed by the loss of one kingdom, perhaps by the loss of three kingdoms. He therefore made up his mind to stand on the defensive till his men had been disciplined, and till reinforcements and supplies should arrive.

He entrenched himself near Dundalk in such a manner that he could not be forced to fight against his will. James, emboldened by the caution of his adversary, and disregarding the advice of Rosen advanced to Ardee, appeared at the head of the whole Irish army before the English lines, drew up horse, foot, and artillery, in order of battle, and displayed his banner. The English were impatient to fall on. But their general had made up his mind and was not to be moved by the bravadoes of the enemy, or by the murmurs of his own soldiers. During some weeks he remained secure within his defences, while the Irish lay a few miles off. He set himself assiduously to drill those new levies which formed the greater part of his army. He ordered the musketeers to be constantly exercised in firing, sometimes at marks, and sometimes by platoons; and from the way in which they at first acquitted themselves, it plainly appeared that he had judged wisely in not leading them out to battle. It was found that not one in four of the English soldiers could manage his piece at all; and whoever succeeded in discharging it, no matter in what direction, thought that he had performed a great feat.

While the Duke was thus employed, the Irish eyed his camp without daring to attack it. But within that camp soon appeared two evils more terrible than the foe, treason and pestilence. Among the best troops under his command were the French exiles. And now a grave doubt arose touching their fidelity. The real Huguenot refugees, indeed, might safely be trusted. The dislike with which the most zealous English Protestant regarded the House of Bourbon and the Church of Rome was a lukewarm feeling when compared with that inextinguishable hatred which glowed in the bosom of the persecuted, dragooned, expatriated Calvinist of Languedoc. The Irish had already remarked that the French heretic neither gave nor took quarter.* Now, however, it was found that with

---

*Nihell's Journal. A French officer, in a letter to Avaux, written soon after Schom-

those emigrants who had sacrificed everything for the reformed religion were intermingled emigrants of a very different sort, deserters who had run away from their standards in the Low Countries, and had colored their crime by pretending that they were Protestants, and that their conscience would not suffer them to fight for the persecutor of their Church. Some of these men, hoping that by a second treason they might obtain both pardon and reward, opened a correspondence with Avaux. The letters were intercepted; and a formidable plot was brought to light. It appeared that, if Schomberg had been weak enough to yield to the importunity of those who wished him to give battle, several French companies would, in the heat of the action, have fired on the English, and gone over to the enemy. Such a defection might well have produced a general panic in a better army than that which was encamped under Dundalk. It was necessary to be severe. Six of the conspirators were hanged. Two hundred of their accomplices were sent in irons to England. Even after this winnowing, the refugees were long regarded by the rest of the army with unjust out not unnatural suspicion. During some days, indeed, there was great reason to fear that the enemy would be entertained with a bloody fight between the English soldiers and their French allies.*

A few hours before the execution of the chief conspirators, a general muster of the army was held; and it was observed that the ranks of the English battalions looked thin. From the first day of the campaign, there had been much sickness among the recruits: but it was not till the time of the equinox that the mortality became alarming. The autumnal rains of Ireland are usually heavy; and this year they were heavier than usual. The whole country was deluged; and the Duke's camp became a marsh. The Enniskillen men were seasoned to the climate. The Dutch were accustomed to live in a country which, as a wit of that age said, draws fifty feet of water. They kept their huts dry and clean; and they had experienced and careful officers who did not suffer them to omit any precaution. But the peasants of Yorkshire and Derbyshire had neither constitutions prepared to resist the pernicious influence,

---

berg's landing, says: "Les Huguenots font plus de mal que les Anglois, et tuent force Catholiques pour avoir fait résistance."

*Story; Narrative transmitted by Avaux to Seignelay, $\frac{\text{Nov 26,}}{\text{Dec. 6,}}$ 1689; London Gazette, Oct. 14, 1689. It is curious that, though Dumont was in the camp before Dundalk, there is in his MS. no mention of the conspiracy among the French.

nor skill to protect themselves against it. The bad provisions furnished by the commissariat aggravated the maladies generated by the air. Remedies were almost entirely wanting. The surgeons were few. The medicine chest contained little more than lint and plasters for wounds. The English sickened and died by hundreds. Even those who were not smitten by the pestilence were unnerved and dejected, and, instead of putting forth the energy which is the heritage of our race, awaited their fate with the helpless apathy of Asiatics. It was in vain that Schomberg tried to teach them to improve their habitations, and to cover the wet earth with a thick carpet of fern. Exertion had become more dreadful to them than death. It was not to be expected that men who would not help themselves should help each other. Nobody asked and nobody showed compassion. Familiarity with ghastly spectacles produced a hard-heartedness and a desperate impiety of which an example will not easily be found even in the history of infectious diseases. The moans of the sick were drowned by the blasphemy and ribaldry of their comrades. Sometimes, seated on the body of a wretch who had died in the morning, might be seen a wretch destined to die before night, cursing, singing loose songs, and swallowing usquebaugh to the health of the devil. When the corpses were taken away to be buried the survivors grumbled. A dead man, they said, was a good screen and a good stool. Why, when there was so abundant a supply of such useful articles of furniture, were people to be exposed to the cold air and forced to crouch on the moist ground.*

Many of the sick were sent by the English vessels which lay off the coast to Belfast, where a great hospital had been prepared. But scarce half of them lived to the end of the voyage. More than one ship lay long in the bay of Carrickfergus, heaped with carcasses, and exhaling the stench of death, without a living man on board.†

The Irish army suffered much less. The kerne of Munster or Connaught was quite as well off in the camp as if he had been in his own mud cabin inhaling the vapors of his own quagmire. He naturally exulted in the distress of the Saxon heretics, and flattered himself that they would be destroyed without a blow. He heard with delight the

---
*Story s Impartial History; Dumont MS. The profaneness and dissoluteness of the camp during the sickness are mentioned in many contemporary pamphlets both in verse and prose. See particularly a Satire entitled Reformation of Manners, part ii.
†Story's Impartial History.

guns pealing all day over the graves of the English officers, till at length the funerals became too numerous to be celebrated with military pomp, and the mournful sounds were succeeded by a silence more mournful still.

The superiority of force was now so decidedly on the side of James that he could safely venture to detach five regiments from his army, and to send them into Connaught. Sarsfield commanded them. He did not, indeed, stand so high as he deserved in the royal estimation. The King, with an air of intellectual superiority which must have made Avaux and Rosen bite their lips, pronounced him a brave fellow, but very scantily supplied with brains. It was not without great difficulty that the ambassador prevailed on his Majesty to raise the best officer in the Irish army to the rank of brigadier. Sarsfield now fully vindicated the favorable opinion which his French patrons had formed of him. He dislodged the English from Sligo; and he effectually secured Galway, which had been in considerable danger.*

No attack, however, was made on the English entrenchments before Dunkalk. In the midst of difficulties and disasters hourly multiplying, the great qualities of Schomberg appeared hourly more and more conspicuous. Not in the full tide of success, not on the fields of Montes Claros, not under the walls of Maestricht, had he so well deserved the admiration of mankind. His resolution never gave way. His prudence never slept. His temper, in spite of manifold vexations and provocations, was always cheerful and serene. The effective men under his command, even if all were reckoned as effective who were not stretched on the earth by fever, did not now exceed five thousand. These were hardly equal to their ordinary duty; and yet it was necessary to harass them with double duty. Nevertheless so masterly were the old man's dispositions that with this small force he faced during several weeks twenty thousand troops who were accompanied by a multitude of armed banditti. At length, early in November, the Irish dispersed, and went to winter quarters. The Duke then broke up his camp and retired into Ulster. Just as the remains of his army were about to move, a rumor spread that the enemy was approaching in great force. Had this rumor been true, the danger would have been extreme.

‡Avaux, Oct. 11-21, Nov. 14-24, 1689; Story's Impartial History; Life of James, ii. 382, 383, Orig. Mem.; Nihell's Journal.

But the English regiments, though they had been reduced to a third part of their complement, and though the men who were in best health were hardly able to shoulder arms, showed a strange joy and alacrity at the prospect of battle, and swore that the Papists should pay for all the misery of the last month. "We English," Schomberg said, identifying himself good-humoredly with the people of the country which had adopted him, "we English have stomach enough for fighting. It is a pity that we are not as fond of some other parts of a soldier's business."

The alarm proved false. The Duke's army departed unmolested: but the highway along which he retired presented a piteous and hideous spectacle. A long train of wagons laden with the sick jolted over the rugged pavement. At every jolt some wretched man gave up the ghost. The corpse was flung out and left unburied to the foxes and crows. The whole number of those who died, in the camp at Dundalk, in the hospital at Belfast, on the road, and on the sea, amounted to above six thousand. The survivors were quartered for the winter in the towns and villages of Ulster. The general fixed his headquarters at Lisburn.*

His conduct was variously judged. Wise and candid men said that he had surpassed himself, and that there was no other captain in Europe who, with ignorant officers, with scanty stores, having to contend at once against a hostile army of greatly superior force, against a villainous commissariat, against a nest of traitors in his own camp, and against a disease more murderous than the sword, would have brought the campaign to a close without the loss of a flag or a gun. On the other hand, many of those newly commissioned majors and captains, whose helplessness had increased all his perplexities, and who had not one qualification for their post except personal courage, grumbled at the skill and patience which had saved them from destruction. Their complaints were echoed on the other side of Saint George's Channel. Some of the murmuring, though unjust, was excusable. The parents, who had sent a gallant lad, in his first uniform, to fight his way

---

*Story's Impartial History; Schomberg's Despatches; Nihell's Journal, and James's Life; Burnet, ii. 20; Dangeau's journal during this autumn; the Narrative sent by Avaux to Seignelay, and the Dumont MS. The lying of the London Gazette is monstrous. Through the whole autumn the troops are constantly said to be in good condition. In the absurd drama entitled the Royal Voyage, which was acted for the amusement of the rabble of London in 1689, the Irish are represented as attacking some of the sick English. The English put the assailants to the rout, and then drop down dead.

to glory, might be pardoned if, when they learned that he had died on a wisp of straw without medical attendance, and had been buried in a swamp without any Christian or military ceremony, their affliction made them hasty and unreasonable. But with the cry of bereaved families was mingled another cry much less respectable. All the hearers and tellers of news abused the general who furnished them with so little news to hear and to tell. For men of that sort are so greedy after excitement that they far more readily forgive a commander who loses a battle than a commander who declines one. The politicians who delivered their oracles from the thickest cloud of tobacco smoke at Garroway's, confidently asked, without knowing anything, either of war in general, or of Irish war in particular, why Schomberg did not fight. They could not venture to say that he did not understand his calling. He had, in his day, they acknowledged, been an excellent officer: but he was very old. He seemed to bear his years well: but his faculties were not what they had been: his memory was failing; and it was well known that he sometimes forgot in the afternoon what he had done in the morning. It may be doubted whether there ever existed a human being whose mind was quite as firmly toned at eighty as at forty. But that Schomberg's intellectual powers had been little impaired by years is sufficiently proved by his despatches which are still extant, and which are models of official writing, terse, perspicuous, full of important facts and weighty reasons, compressed into the smallest possible number of words. In those despatches he sometimes alluded, not angrily, but with calm disdain, to the censures thrown upon his conduct by shallow babblers, who, never having seen any military operation more important than the relieving of the guard at Whitehall, imagined that the easiest thing in the world was to gain great victories in any situation and against any odds, and by sturdy patriots who were convinced that one English carter or thresher, who had not yet learned how to load a gun or port a pike, was a match for any six musketeers of King Lewis's household.*

Unsatisfactory as had been the results of the campaign in Ireland, the results of the maritime operations of the year were more unsatisfactory still. It had been confidently expected that, on the sea, England, allied with Holland,

*See his despatches in the Appendix to Dalrymple's Memoirs.

would have been far more than a match for the power of Lewis: but everything went wrong. Herbert had, after the unimportant skirmish of Bantry Bay, returned with his squadron to Portsmouth. There he found that he had not lost the good opinion either of the public or of the government. The House of Commons thanked him for his services; and he received signal marks of the favor of the Crown. He had not been at the coronation, and had therefore missed his share of the rewards which, at the time of that solemnity, had been distributed among the chief agents in the Revolution. The omission was now repaired; and he was created Earl of Torrington. The King went down to Portsmouth, dined on board of the Admiral's flag ship, expressed the fullest confidence in the valor and loyalty of the navy, knighted two gallant captains, Cloudesley Shovel and John Ashby, and ordered a donative to be divided among the seamen.*

We cannot justly blame William for having a high opinion of Torrington. For Torrington was generally regarded as one of the bravest and most skillful officers in the navy. He had been promoted to the rank of Rear Admiral of England by James who, if he understood anything, understood maritime affairs. That place and other lucrative places Torrington had relinquished when he found that he could retain them only by submitting to be a tool of the Jesuitical cabal. No man had taken a more active, a more hazardous, or a more useful part in effecting the Revolution. It seemed, therefore, that no man had fairer pretensions to be put at the head of the naval administration. Yet no man could be more unfit for such a post. His morals had always been loose, so loose, indeed, that the firmness with which, in the late reign, he had adhered to his religion, had excited much surprise. His glorious disgrace, indeed, seemed to have produced a salutary effect on his character. In poverty and exile he rose from a voluptuary into a hero. But, as soon as prosperity returned, the hero sank again into a voluptuary; and the relapse was deep and hopeless. The nerves of his mind, which had been during a short time braced to a high tone, were now so much relaxed by vice that he was utterly incapable of self-denial or of strenuous exertion. The vulgar courage of a foremast man he still retained. But both as Admiral and as First Lord of the Admiralty he was utterly inefficient. Month after

---
*London Gazette, May 20, 1689.

month the fleet, which should have been the terror of the seas, lay in harbor while he was diverting himself in London. The sailors, punning upon his new title, gave him the name of Lord Tarry-in-town. When he came on shipboard he was accompanied by a bevy of courtesans. There was scarcely an hour of the day or of the night when he was not under the influence of claret. Being insatiable of pleasure, he necessarily became insatiable of wealth. Yet he loved flattery almost as much as either wealth or pleasure. He had long been in the habit of exacting the most abject homage from those who were under his command. His flagship was a little Versailles. He expected his captains to attend him to his cabin when he went to bed, and to assemble every morning at his levee. He even suffered them to dress him. One of them combed his flowing wig; another stood ready with the embroidered coat. Under such a chief there could be no discipline. His tars passed their time in rioting among the rabble of Portsmouth Those officers who had won his favor by servility and adulation easily obtained leave of absence, and spent weeks in London, revelling in taverns, scouring the streets, or making love to the masked ladies in the pit of the theater. The victuallers soon found out with whom they had to deal, and sent down to the fleet casks of meat which dogs would not touch, and barrels of beer which smelt worse than bilge water. Meanwhile the British Channel seemed to be abandoned to French rovers. Our merchantmen were boarded in sight of the ramparts of Plymouth. The sugar fleet from the West Indies lost seven ships. The whole value of the prizes taken by the cruisers of the enemy in the immediate neighborhood of our island, while Torrington was engaged with his bottle and his harem, was estimated at six hundred thousand pounds. So difficult was it to obtain the convoy of a man-of-war, except by giving immense bribes, that our traders were forced to hire the services of Dutch privateers, and found these foreign mercenaries much more useful and much less greedy than the officers of our own royal navy.*

The only department with which no fault could be found was the department of Foreign Affairs. There William was his own minister; and, where he was his own

---

*Commons' Journals Nov. 13, 23. 1689; Grey's Debates, Nov. 13, 14, 18, 23, 1689. See among numerous pasquinades, the Parable of the Bearbaiting, Reformation of Manners, a Satire, the Mock Mourners, a Satire. See also Pepys's Diary kept at Tangier, Oct. 15, 1683.

minister, there were no delays, no blunders, no jobs, no treasons. The difficulties with which he had to contend were indeed great. Even at the Hague he had to encounter an opposition which all his wisdom and firmness could, with the strenuous support of Heinsius, scarcely overcome. The English were not aware that, while they were murmuring at their Sovereign's partiality for the land of his birth, a strong party in Holland was murmuring at his partiality for the land of his adoption. The Dutch ambassadors at Westminster complained that the terms of alliance which he proposed were derogatory to the dignity and prejudicial to the interests of the republic; that wherever the honor of the English flag was concerned, he was punctilious and obstinate; that he peremptorily insisted on an article which interdicted all trade with France, and which could not but be grievously felt on the Exchange of Amsterdam; that when they expressed a hope that the Navigation Act would be repealed, he burst out a laughing, and told them that the thing was not to be thought of. He carried all his points; and a solemn contract was made by which England and the Batavian federation bound themselves to stand firmly by each other against France, and not to make peace except by mutual consent. But one of the Dutch plenipotentiaries declared that he was afraid of being one day held up to obloquy as a traitor for conceding so much; and the signature of another plainly appeared to have been traced by a hand shaking with emotion.*

Meanwhile, under William's skillful management, a treaty of alliance had been concluded between the States General and the Emperor. To that treaty Spain and England gave in their adhesion; and thus the four great powers, which had long been bound together by a friendly understanding, were bound together by a formal contract.†

But before that formal contract had been signed and sealed, all the contracting parties were in arms. Early in the year 1689 war was raging all over the continent from the Hæmus to the Pyrenees. France, attacked at once on every side, made on every side a vigorous defence; and her Turkish allies kept a great German force fully employed

---

*The best account of these negotiations will be found in Wagenaar, lxi. He had access to Witsen's papers, and has quoted largely from them. It was Witsen who signed in violent agitation, "zo als," he says, "myne beevende hand getuigen kan." The treaties will be found in Dumont's Corps Diplomatique. They were signed in August 1869.

†The treaty between the Emperor and the States General is dated May 12, 1689. It will be found in Dumont's Corps Diplomatique.

in Servia and Bulgaria. On the whole, the results of the military operations of the summer were not unfavorable to the confederates. Beyond the Danube, the Christians, under Prince Lewis of Baden, gained a succession of victories over the Mussulmans. In the passes of Roussillon the French troops contended without any decisive advantage against the martial peasantry of Catalonia. One German army, led by the Elector of Bavaria, occupied the Archbishopric of Cologne. Another was commanded by Charles, Duke of Lorraine, a sovereign who, driven from his own dominions by the arms of France, had turned soldier of fortune, and had, as such, obtained both distinction and revenge. He marched against the devastators of the Palatinate, forced them to retire behind the Rhine, and, after a long seige, took the important and strongly fortified city of Mentz.

Between the Sambre and the Meuse the French, commanded by Marshal Humieres, were opposed to the Dutch, commanded by the Prince of Waldeck, an officer who had long served the States General with fidelity and ability, though not always with good fortune, and who stood high in the estimation of William. Under Waldeck's orders was Marlborough, to whom William had confided an English brigade consisting of the best regiments of the old army of James. Second to Marlborough in command, and second also in professional skill, was Thomas Talmash, a brave soldier, destined to a fate never to be mentioned without shame and indignation. Between the army of Waldeck and the army of Humieres no general action took place: but in a succession of combats the advantage was on the side of the confederates. Of these combats the most important took place at Walcourt on the fifth of August. The French attacked an outpost defended by the English brigade, were vigorously repulsed, and were forced to retreat in confusion, abandoning a few field pieces to the conquerors, and leaving more than six hundred corpses on the ground. Marlborough, on this as on every similar occasion, acquitted himself like a valiant and skillful captain. The Coldstream Guards commanded by Talmash, and the regiment which is now called the sixteenth of the line, commanded by Colonel Robert Hodges, distinguished themselves highly. The Royal regiment too, which had a few months before set up the standard of rebellion at Ipswich, proved on this day that William, in freely pardoning that great fault, had acted not less wisely than generously. The testimony which Waldeck in his despatch bore to the gallant conduct of the islanders was read with delight by their countrymen. The fight, indeed, was no more than a skirmish: but it was a sharp and bloody skirmish. There had within living memory been no equally serious encounter between the English and French; and our ancestors were naturally elated by finding that many years of inaction and vassalage did not appear to have enervated the courage of the nation.*

The Jacobites, however, discovered in the events of the campaign abundant matter for invective. Marlborough was, not without reason, the object of their bitterest hatred. In his behavior on a field of battle malice itself could find little to censure: but there were other parts of his conduct which presented a fair mark for obloquy. Avarice is rarely the vice of a young man: it is rarely the vice of a great man: but Marlborough was one of the few who have, in the bloom of youth, loved lucre more than wine or women, and who have, at the height of greatness, loved lucre more than power or fame. All the precious gifts which nature had lavished on him he valued chiefly for what they would fetch. At twenty he made money of his beauty and his vigor. At sixty he made money of his genius and his glory. The applauses which were justly due to his conduct at Walcourt could not altogether drown the voices of those who muttered that, wherever a broad piece was to be saved or got, this hero was a mere Euclio, a mere Harpagon; that, though he drew a large allowance under pretence of keeping a public table, he never asked an officer to dinner; that his muster rolls were fraudulently made up; that he pocketed pay in the names of men who had long been dead, of men who had been killed in his own sight four years before at Sedgemoor; that there were twenty such names in one troop; that there were thirty-six in another. Nothing but the union of dauntless courage and commanding powers of mind with a bland temper and winning manners could have enabled him to gain and keep, in spite of faults eminently unsoldierlike, the good will of his soldiers.†

---

*See the despatch of Waldeck in the London Gazette, Aug. 26, 1689; Historical Records of the First Regiment of Foot; Dangeau, Aug. 28; Monthly Mercury, September, 1689.
†See the Dear Bargain, a Jocobite pamphlet, clandestinely printed in 1690. "I have not patience," says the writer, "after this wretch (Marlborough) to mention any other. All are innocent comparatively, even Kirke himself."

About the time at which the contending armies in every part of Europe were going into winter quaters, a new Pontiff ascended the chair of Saint Peter. Innocent the Eleventh was no more. His fate had been strange indeed. His conscientious and fervent attachment to the Church of which he was the head had induced him, at one of the most critical conjunctures in her history, to ally himself with her mortal enemies. The news of his decease was received with concern and alarm by Protestant princes and commonwealths, and with joy and hope at Versailles and Dublin. An extraordinary ambassador of high rank was instantly despatched by Lewis to Rome. The French garrison which had been placed in Avignon was withdrawn. When the votes of the Conclave had been united in favor of Peter Ottobuoni, an ancient Cardinal, who assumed the appellation of Alexander the Eighth, the representative of France assisted at the installation, bore up the cope of the new Pontiff, and put into the hands of his Holiness a letter in which the most Christian King declared that he renounced the odious privilege of protecting robbers and assassins. Alexander pressed the letter to his lips, embraced the bearer, and talked with rapture of the near prospect of reconciliation. Lewis began to entertain a hope that the influence of the Vatican might be exerted to dissolve the alliance between the House of Austria and the heretical usurper of the English throne. James was even more sanguine. He was foolish enough to expect that the new Pope would give him money, and ordered Melfort, who had now acquitted himself of his mission at Versailles, to hasten to Rome, and beg his Holiness to contribute something towards the good work of upholding pure religion in the British islands. But it soon appeared that Alexander, though he might hold language different from that of his predecessor, was determined to follow in essentials his predecessor's policy. The original cause of the quarrel between the Holy See and Lewis, was not removed. The King continued to appoint prelates: the Pope continued to refuse them institution; and the consequence was that a fourth part of the dioceses of France had bishops who were incapable of performing any episcopal function.*

---

*See the Mercuries for September, 1689, and the four following months. See also Welwood's Mercurius Reformatus of Sept. 18, Sept. 25, and Oct. 8, 1689. Melfort's Instructions, and his memorials to the Pope and the Cardinal of Este, are among the Nairne Papers; and some extracts have been printed by Macpherson.

The Anglican Church was, at this time not less distracted than the Gallican Church. The first of August had been fixed by Act of Parliament as the day before the close of which all beneficed clergymen and all persons holding academical offices must, on pain of suspension, swear allegiance to William and Mary. During the earlier part of the summer, the Jacobites had hoped that the number of nonjurors would be so considerable as seriously to alarm and embarrass the government. But this hope was disappointed. Few indeed of the clergy were Whigs. Few were Tories of that moderate school which acknowledged, reluctantly and with reserve, that extreme abuses might sometimes justify a nation in resorting to extreme remedies. The great majority of the profession still held the doctrine of passive obedience: but that majority was now divided into two sections. A question, which, before the Revolution, had been mere matter of speculation, and had therefore, though sometimes incidentally raised, been, by most persons, very superficially considered, had now become practically most important. The doctrine of passive obedience being taken for granted, to whom was that obedience due? While the hereditary right and the possession were conjoined, there was no room for doubt: but the hereditary right and the possession were now separated. One prince, raised by the Revolution, was reigning at Westminster, passing laws, appointing magistrates and prelates, sending forth armies and fleets. His judges decided causes. His sheriffs arrested debtors, and executed criminals. Justice, order, property, would cease to exist, and society would be resolved into chaos but for his Great Seal. Another prince, deposed by the Revolution, was living abroad. He could exercise none of the powers and perform none of the duties of a ruler, and could, as it seemed, be restored only by means as violent as those by which he had been displaced. To which of these two princes did Christian men owe allegiance?

To a large part of the clergy it appeared that the plain letter of Scripture required them to submit to the Sovereign who was in possession, without troubling themselves about his title. The powers which the Apostle, in the text most familiar to the Anglican divines of that age, pronounces to be ordained of God, are not the powers that can be traced back to a legitimate origin, but the powers that be. When Jesus was asked whether the chosen people might lawfully give tribute to Cæsar he replied by asking the questioners, not whether Cæsar could make out a pedigree derived from the old royal house of Judah, but whether the coin which they scrupled to pay into Cæsar's treasury came from Cæsar's mint, in other words, whether Cæsar actually possessed the authority and performed the functions of a ruler.

It is generally held, with much appearance of reason, that the most trustworthy comment on the text of the Gospels and Espistles, is to be found in the practice of the primitive Christians, when that practice can be satisfactorily ascertained; and it so happened that the times during which the Church is universally acknowledged to have been in the highest state of purity were times of frequent and violent political change. One at least of the Apostles appears to have lived to see four Emperors pulled down in little more than a year. Of the martyrs of the third century a great proportion must have been able to remember ten or twelve revolutions. Those martyrs must have had occasion often to consider what was their duty towards a prince just raised to power by a successful insurrection. That they were, one and all, deterred by the fear of punishment from doing what they thought right, is an imputation which no candid infidel would throw on them. Yet, if there be any proposition which can with perfect confidence be affirmed touching the early Christians, it is this, that they never once refused obedience to any actual ruler on account of the illegitimacy of his title. At one time, indeed, the supreme power was claimed by twenty or thirty competitors. Every province from Britain to Egypt had its own Augustus. All these pretenders could not be rightful Emperors. Yet it does not appear that, in any place, the faithful had any scruple about submitting to the person who, in that place, exercised the imperial functions. While the Christian of Rome obeyed Aurelian, the Christian of Lyons obeyed Tetricus, and the Christian of Palmyra obeyed Zenobia. "Day and night,"—such were the words which the great Cyprian, Bishop of Carthage, addressed to the representative of Valerian and Gallienus,— "day and night do we Christians pray to the one true God for the safety of our Emperors." Yet those Emperors had a few months before pulled down their predecessor Æmilianus, who had pulled down his predecessor Gallus, who had climbed to power on the ruins of the house of his predecessor Decius, who had slain his predecessor Philip, who had slain his predecessor Gordian. Was it possible to believe that a saint, who had, in the short space of thirteen or fourteen years, borne true allegiance to this series of rebels and regicides, would have made a schism in the Christian body rather than acknowledge King William and Queen Mary? A hundred times those Anglican divines who had taken the oaths challenged their more scrupulous brethren to cite a single instance in which the primitive Church had refused obedience to a successful usurper; and a hundred times the challenge was evaded. The nonjurors had little to say on this head, except that precedents were of no force when opposed to principles, a proposition which came with but a bad grace from a school which had always professed an almost superstitious reverence for the authority of the Fathers.*

To precedents drawn from later and more corrupt times, little respect was due. But, even in the history of later and more corrupt times, the nonjurors could not easily find any precedent that could serve their purpose. In our own country many Kings, who had not the hereditary right, had filled the throne: but it had never been thought inconsistent with the duty of a Christian to be a true liegeman to such Kings. The usurpation of Henry the Fourth, the more odious usurpation of Richard the Third, had produced no schism in the Church. As soon as the usurper was firm in his seat, Bishops had done homage to him for their domains: Convocations had presented addresses to him, and granted him supplies; nor had any casuist ever pronounced that such submission to a prince in possession was deadly sin.†

---

*See the Answer of a Nonjuror to the Bishop of Sarum's challenge in the Appendix to the Life of Kettlewell. Among the Tanner MSS. in the Bodleian Library is a paper which, as Sancroft thought it worth preserving, I venture to quote The writer, a strong nonjuror, after trying to evade, by many pitiable shifts, the argument drawn by a more compliant divine from the practice of the primitive Church, proceeds thus: "Suppose the primitive Christians all along, from the time of the very Apostles, had been as regardless of their oaths by former princes as he suggests, will he therefore say that their practice is to be a rule? Ill things have been done, and very generally abetted, by men of otherwise very orthodox principles." The argument from the practice of the primitive Christians is very strongly put in a tract entitled The Doctrine of Nonresistance or Passive Obedience No Way concerned in the Controversies now depending between the Williamites and the Jacobites, by a Lay Gentleman, of the Communion of the Church of England, as by Law establish'd, 1689. The author of this tract was Edmund Bohun, whom I shall have occasion to mention hereafter.

†One of the most adulatory addresses ever voted by a Convocation was to Richard the Third. It will be found in Wilkins's Concilia. Dryden, in his fine *rifacimento* of one of the finest passages in the Prologue to the Canterbury Tales, represents the Good Parson as choosing to resign his benefice rather than acknowledge the Duke of Lancaster to be King of England. For this representation no warrant can be found in Chaucer's Poem, or anywhere else. Dryden wished to write something that would gall the

With the practice of the whole Christian world the authoritative teaching of the Church of England appeared to be in strict harmony. The Homily on Willful Rebellion, a discourse which inculcates, in unmeasured terms, the duty of obeying rulers, speaks of none but actual rulers. Nay, the people are distinctly told in that Homily that they are bound to obey, not only their legitimate prince, but any usurper whom God shall in anger set over them for their sins. And surely it would be the height of absurdity to say that we must accept submissively such usurpers as God sends in anger but most pertinaciously withhold our obedience from usurpers whom He sends in mercy. Grant that it was a crime to invite the Prince of Orange over, a crime to join him, a crime to make him King; yet what was the whole history of the Jewish nation and of the Christian Church but a record of cases in which Providence had brought good out of evil? And what theologian would assert that, in such cases, we ought, from abhorrence of the evil, to reject the good?

On these grounds a large body of divines, still reasserting the doctrine that to resist the Sovereign must always be sinful, conceived that William was now the Sovereign whom it would be sinful to resist.

To these arguments the nonjurors replied that Saint Paul must have meant by the powers that be the rightful powers that be; and that to put any other interpretation on his words would be to outrage common sense, to dishonor religion, to give scandal to weak believers, to give an occasion of triumph to scoffers. The feelings of all mankind must be shocked by the proposition that, as soon as a King, however clear his title, however wise and good his administration, is expelled by traitors, all his servants are bound to abandon him, and to range themselves on the side of his enemies. In all ages and nations, fidelity to a good cause in adversity had been regarded as a virtue. In all ages and nations, the polititian whose practice was always to be on the side which was uppermost had been despised. This new Toryism was worse than Whiggism. To break through the ties of allegiance because the Sovereign was a tyrant was doubtless a very great sin: but it was a sin for which specious names and pretexts might be found, and into which a brave and generous man, not in-

clergy who had taken the oaths, and therefore attributed to a Roman Catholic priest of the fourteenth century a superstition which originated among the Anglican priests of the seventeenth century.

structed in divine truth and guarded by divine grace, might easily fall. But to break through the ties of allegiance merely because the Sovereign was unfortunate was not only wicked, but dirty. Could any unbeliever offer a greater insult to the Scriptures than by asserting that the Scriptures had enjoined on Christians as a sacred duty what the light of nature had taught heathens to regard as the last excess of baseness? In the Scriptures was to he found the history of a King of Israel, driven from his palace by an unnatural son, and compelled to fly beyond Jordan. David, like James, had the right: Absalom, like William, had the possession. Would any student of the sacred writings dare to affirm that the conduct of Shimei on that occasion was proposed as a pattern to be imitated, and that Barzillai, who loyally adhered to his fugitive master, was resisting the ordinance of God, and receiving to himself damnation? Would any true son of the Church of England seriously maintain that a man who was a strenuous royalist till after the battle of Naseby, who then went over to the Parliament, who, as soon as the Parliament had been purged became an obsequious servant of the Rump, and who, as soon as the Rump had been ejected, professed himself a faithful subject of the Protector, was more deserving of the respect of Christian men than the stout old Cavalier who bore true fealty to Charles the First in prison and to Charles the Second in exile, and who was ready to put lands, liberty, life, in peril, rather than acknowledge, by word or act, the authority of any of the upstart governments which, duiing that evil time, obtained possession of a power not legitimately theirs? And what distinction was there between that case and the case which had now arisen? That Cromwell had actually enjoyed as much power as William, nay much more power than William, was quite certain. That the power of William, as well as the power of Cromwell, had an illegitimate origin every divine who held the doctrine of non-resistance would admit. How then was it possible for such a divine to deny that obedience had been due to Cromwell and yet to affirm that it was due to William? To suppose that there could be such inconsistency without dishonesty would be, not charity, but weakness. Those who were determined to comply with the Act of Parliament would do better to speak out, and to say, what everybody knew, that they complied simply to save their benefices.

The motive was no doubt strong. That a clergyman who was a husband and a father should look forward with dread to the first of August and the First of February was natural. But he would do well to remember that, however terrible might be the day of suspension and the day of deprivation, there would assuredly come two other days more terrible still, the day of death and the day of judgment.*

The swearing clergy, as they were called, were not a little perplexed by this reasoning. Nothing embarrassed them more than the analogy which the nonjurors were never weary of pointing out between the usurpation of Cromwell and the usurpation of William. For there was in that age no High Churchman who would not have thought himself reduced to an absurdity, if he had been reduced to the necessity of saying that the Church had commanded her sons to obey Cromwell. And yet it was impossible to prove that William was more fully in possession of supreme power than Cromwell had been. The swearers therefore avoided coming to close quarters with the nonjurors on this point, as carefully as the nonjurors avoided coming to close quarters with the swearers on the question touching the practice of the primitive Church.

The truth is that the theory of government which had long been taught by the clergy was so absurd that it could lead to nothing but absurdity. Whether the priest who adhered to that theory swore or refused to swear, he was alike unable to give a rational explanation of his conduct. If he swore, he could vindicate his swearing only by laying down propositions against which every honest heart instinctively revolts, only by proclaiming that Christ had commanded the Church to desert the righteous cause as soon as that cause ceased to prosper, and to strengthen the hands of successful villainy against afflicted virtue. And yet, strong as were the objections to this doctrine, the objections to the doctrine of the nonjuror were, if possible, stronger still. According to him, a Christian nation ought always to be in a state of slavery or in a state of anarchy. Something is to be said for the man who sacrifices liberty to preserve order. Something is to be said for the man who sacrifices order to preserve liberty. For liberty and order are two of the greatest blessings which a society can

---

*See the Defence of the Profession which the Right Reverend Father in God, John Lake, Lord Bishop of Chichester, made upon his Deathbed concerning Passive Obedience and the New Oaths, 1690.

enjoy; and, when unfortunately they appear to be incompatible, much indulgence is due to those who take either side. But the nonjuror sacrificed, not liberty to order, not order to liberty, but both liberty and order to a superstition as stupid and degrading as the Egyptian worship of oats and onions. While a particular person, differing from other persons by the mere accident of birth, was on the throne, though he might be a Nero, there was to be no insubordination. When any other person was on the throne, though he might be an Alfred, there was to be no obedience. It mattered not how frantic and wicked might be the administration of the dynasty which had the hereditary title, or how wise and virtuous might be the administration of a government sprung from a revolution. Nor could any time of limitation be pleaded against the claim of the expelled family. The lapse of years, the lapse of ages, made no change. To the end of the world, Christians were to regulate their political conduct simply according to the pedigree of their ruler. The year 1800, the year 1900, might find princes who derived their title from the votes of the Convention reigning in peace and prosperity. No matter: they would still be usurpers; and, if, in the twentieth or twenty-first century, any person who could make out a better title by blood to the crown should call on a late posterity to acknowledge him as King, the call must be obeyed on peril of eternal perdition.

A Whig might well enjoy the thought that the controversies which had arisen among his adversaries had established the soundness of his own political creed. The disputants, who had long agreed in accusing him of an impious error, had now effectually vindicated him, and refuted one another. The High Churchman who took the oaths had shown by irrefragable arguments from the Gospels and the Epistles, from the uniform practice of the primitive Church, and from the explicit declarations of the Anglican Church, that Christians were not in all cases bound to pay obedience to the prince who had the hereditary title. The High Churchman who would not take the oaths had shown as satisfactorily that Christians were not in all cases bound to pay obedience to the prince who was actually reigning. It followed that, to entitle a government to the allegiance of subjects, something was necessary different from mere legitimacy, and different also from mere possession. What that something was the Whigs had no difficulty in pronouncing. In their view, the end for which all governments had been instituted was the happiness of society. While the magistrate was, on the whole, notwithstanding some faults, a minister for good, Reason taught mankind to obey him; and Religion, giving her solemn sanction to the teaching of Reason, commanded mankind to revere him as divinely commissioned. But if he proved to be a minister for evil, on what grounds was he to be considered as divinely commissioned? The Tories who swore had proved that he ought not to be so considered on account of the origin of his power: the Tories who would not swear had proved as clearly that he ought not to be so considered on account of the existence of his power.

Some violent and acrimonious Whigs triumphed ostentatiously and with merciless insolence over the perplexed and divided priesthood. The nonjuror they generally affected to regard with contemptuous pity as a dull and perverse, but sincere, bigot, whose absurd practice was in harmony with his absurd theory, and who might plead, in excuse for the infatuation which impelled him to ruin his country, that the same infatuation had impelled him to ruin himself. They reserved the sharpest taunts for those divines who, having, in the days of the Exclusion Bill and the Rye House Plot, been distinguished by zeal for the divine and indefeasible right of the hereditary Sovereign, were now ready to swear fealty to an usurper. Was this then the real sense of all those sublime phrases which had resounded during twenty-nine years from innumerable pulpits? Had the thousands of clergymen, who had so loudly boasted of the unchangeable loyalty of their order, really meant only that their loyalty would remain unchangeable till the next change of fortune? It was idle, it was impudent in them to pretend that their present conduct was consistent with their former language. If any reverend doctor had at length been convinced that he had been in the wrong, he surely ought, by an open recantation, to make all the amends now possible to the persecuted, the calumniated, the murdered defenders of liberty. If he was still convinced that his old opinions were sound, he ought manfully to cast in his lot with the nonjuror. Respect, it was said, is due to him who ingenuously confesses an error: respect is due to him who courageously suffers for an error: but it is difficult to respect a minister of religion, who, while asserting that he still adheres to the principles of the Tories, saves a benefice by taking an oath which can be honestly taken only on the principles of the Whigs.

These reproaches, though perhaps not altogether unjust, were unseasonable. The wiser and more moderate Whigs, sensible that the throne of William could not stand firm if it had not a wider basis than their own party, abstained at this conjuncture from sneers and invectives, and exerted themselves to remove the scruples and to soothe the irritated feelings of the clergy. The collective power of the rectors and vicars of England was immense; and it was much better that they should swear for the most flimsy reason which could be devised by a sophist than that they should not swear at all.

It soon became clear that the arguments for swearing, backed as they were by some of the strongest motives which can influence the human mind, had prevailed. Above twenty-nine thirtieths of the profession submitted to the law. Most of the divines of the capital, who then formed a separate class, and who were as much distinguished from the rural clergy by liberality of sentiment as by eloquence and learning, gave in their adhesion to the government early, and with every sign of cordial attachment. Eighty of them repaired together, in full term, to Westminster Hall, and were there sworn. The ceremony occupied so long a time that little else was done that day in the Courts of Chancery and King's Bench.* But in general the compliance was tardy, sad, and sullen. Many, no doubt, deliberately violated what they believed to be their duty. Conscience told them that they were committing a sin. But they had not fortitude to resign the parsonage, the garden, the glebe, and to go forth without knowing where to find a meal or a roof for themselves and their little ones. Many swore with doubts and misgivings.† Some declared, at the moment of taking the oath, that they did not mean to promise that they would not submit to James, if he should ever be in a condition to demand their allegiance.‡ Some clergymen in the North were, on the first of August, going in a company to swear, when they were met on the road by the news of the battle which had been fought,

---
*London Gazette, June 30, 1689; Luttrell's Diary. "The eminentest men," says Luttrell.
†See in Kettlewell's Life, iii. 72, the retractation drawn by him for a clergyman who had taken the oaths, and who afterwards repented of having done so.
‡See the account of Dr. Dove's conduct in Clarendon's Diary, and the account of Dr. Marsh's conduct in the Life of Kettlewell.

four days before, in the pass of Killiecrankie. They immediately turned back, and did not again leave their homes on the same errand till it was clear that Dundee's victory had made no change in the state of public affairs.* Even of those whose understandings were fully convinced that obedience was due to the existing government, very few kissed the book with the heartiness with which they had formerly plighted their faith to Charles and James. Still the thing was done. Ten thousand clergymen had solemnly called heaven to attest their promise that they would be true liegemen to William; and this promise, though it by no means warranted him in expecting that they would strenuously support him, had at least deprived them of a great part of their power to injure him. They could not, without entirely forfeiting that public respect on which their influence depended, attack, except in an indirect and timidly cautious manner, the throne of one whom they had, in the presence of God, vowed to obey as their King. Some of them, it is true, affected to read the prayers for the new Sovereigns in a peculiar tone which could not be misunderstood.† Others were guilty of still grosser indecency. Thus, one wretch, just after praying for William and Mary in the most solemn office of religion, took off a glass to their damnation. Another, after performing divine service on a fast day appointed by their authority, dined on a pigeon pie, and while he cut it up, uttered a wish that it was the usurper's heart. But such audacious wickedness was doubtless rare and was injurious rather to the Church than to the government.‡

Those clergymen and members of the Universities who incurred the penalties of the law were about four hundred in number. Foremost in rank stood the Primate and six of his suffragans, Turner of Ely, Lloyd of Norwich, Frampton of Gloucester, Lake of Chichester, White of Peterborough, and Ken of Bath and Wells. Thomas of Worcester would have made a seventh: but he died three weeks before the day of suspension. On his deathbed he adjured his clergy to be true to the cause of hereditary right, and declared that those divines who tried to make out that the oaths might be taken without any departure from the loyal doctrines of the Church of England seemed

---

*The Anatomy of a Jacobite Tory, 1690.

†Dialogue between a Whig and a Tory.

‡Luttrell's Diary, November, 1691, February, 1692.

to him to reason more Jesuitically than the Jesuits themselves.*

Ken, who, both in intellectual and in moral qualities, ranked highest among the nonjuring prelates, hesitated long. There were few clergymen who could have submitted to the new government with a better grace. For, when non-resistance and passive obedience were the favorite themes of his brethren, he had scarcely ever alluded to politics in the pulpit. He owned that the arguments in favor of swearing were very strong. He went indeed so far as to say that his scruples would be completely removed, if he could be convinced that James had entered into engagements for ceding Ireland to the French King. It is evident, therefore, that the difference between Ken and the Whigs was not a difference of principle. He thought, with them, that misgovernment, carried to a certain point, justified a transfer of allegiance, and doubted only whether the misgovernment of James had been carried quite to that point. Nay, the good Bishop actually began to prepare a pastoral letter explaining his reasons for taking the oaths. But, before it was finished, he received information which convinced him that Ireland had not been made over to France: doubts came thick upon him: he threw his unfinished letter into the fire, and implored his less scrupulous friends not to urge him further. He was sure, he said, that they had acted uprightly: he was glad that they could do with a clear conscience what he shrank from doing: he felt the force of their reasoning: he was all but persuaded; and he was afraid to listen longer lest he should be quite persuaded: for, if he should comply, and his misgivings should afterwards return, he should be the most miserable of men. Not for wealth, not for a palace, not for a peerage, would he run the smallest risk of ever feeling the torments of remorse. It is a curious fact that, of the seven nonjuring prelates, the only one whose name carries with it much weight was on the point of swearing, and was prevented from doing so, as he himself acknowledged, not by the force of reason, but by a morbid scrupulosity which he did not advise others to imitate.†

---

*Life of Kettlewell, iii. 4.

†See Turner's Letter to Sancroft, dated on Ascension Day, 1689. The original is among the Tanner MSS. in the Bodleian Library. But the letter will be found, with much other curious matter, in the Life of Ken by a Layman, lately published. See also the Life of Kettlewell, iii. 95; and Ken's Letter to Burnet, dated October 5, 1689, in Hawkin's Life of Ken. "I am sure," Lady Russell wrote to Dr. Fitzwilliam, "the Bishop of Bath and Wells excited others to comply, when he could not bring himself to

Among the priests who refused the oaths were some men eminent in the learned world, as grammarians, chronologists, canonists, and antiquaries, and a very few who were distinguished by wit and eloquence; but scarcely one can be named who was qualified to discuss any large question of morals or politics, scarcely one whose writings do not indicate either extreme feebleness or extreme flightiness of mind. Those who distrust the judgment of a Whig on this point will probably allow some weight to the opinion which was expressed, many years after the Revolution, by a philosopher of whom the Tories are justly proud. Johnson, after passing in review the celebrated divines who had thought it sinful to swear allegiance to William the Third and George the First, pronounced that, in the whole body of nonjurors, there was one, and one only, who could reason.*

The nonjuror in whose favor Johnson made this exception was Charles Leslie. Leslie had, before the Revolution, been Chancellor of the diocese of Connor in Ireland. He had been forward in opposition to Tyrconnel; had, as a justice of the peace for Monaghan, refused to acknowledge a papist as sheriff of that county; and had been so courageous as to send some officers of the Irish army to prison for marauding. But the doctrine of non-resistance, such as it had been taught by Anglican divines in the days

---

do so, but rejoiced when others did." Ken declared that he had advised nobody to take the oaths, and that his practice had been to remit those who asked his advice to their own studies and prayers. Lady Russell's assertion and Ken's denial will be found to come nearly to the same thing, when we make those allowances which ought to be made for situation and feeling, even in weighing the testimony of the most veracious witnesses. Ken, having at last determined to cast in his lot with the nonjurors, naturally tried to vindicate his consistency as far as he honestly could. Lady Russell, wishing to induce her friend to take the oaths, naturally made as much of Ken's disposition to compliance as she honestly could. She went too far in using the word "excited." On the other hand, it is clear that Ken, by remitting those who consulted him to their own studies and prayers, gave them to understand that, in his opinion, the oath was lawful to those who, after a serious inquiry, thought it lawful. If people had asked him whether they might lawfully commit perjury or adultery, he would assuredly have told them, not to consider the point maturely and to implore the divine direction, but to abstain on peril of their souls.

*See the conversation of June 9, 1784, in Boswell's Life of Johnson, and the note. Boswell, with his usual absurdity, is sure that Johnson could not have recollected "that the seven bishops, so justly celebrated for their magnanimous resistance to arbitrary power, were yet nonjurors." Only five of the seven were nonjurors; and anybody but Boswell would have known that a man may resist arbitrary power, and yet not be a good reasoner. Nay, the resistance which Sancroft and the other nonjuring bishops offered to arbitrary power, while they continued to hold the doctrine of non-resistance, is the most decisive proof that they were incapable of reasoning. It must be remembered that they were prepared to take the whole kingly power from James, and to bestow it on William, with the title of Regent. Their scruple was merely about the word King.

I am surprised that Johnson should have pronounced William Law no reasoner. Law did indeed fall into great errors; but they were errors against which logic affords no security. In mere dialectical skill he had very few superiors. That he was more than once victorious over Hoadley no candid Whig will deny. But Law did not belong to the generation with which I have now to do.

of the Rye House Plot, was immovably fixed in his mind. When the state of Ulster became such that a Protestant who remained there could hardly avoid being either a rebel or a martyr, Leslie fled to London. His abilities and his connections were such that he might easily have obtained high preferment in the Church of England. But he took his place in the front rank of the Jacobite body, and remained there steadfastly through all the dangers and vicissitudes of three and thirty troubled years. Though constantly engaged in theological controversy with Deists, Jews, Socinians, Presbyterians, Papists, and Quakers, he found time to be one of the most voluminous political writers of his age. Of all the nonjuring clergy he was the best qualified to discuss constitutional questions. For, before he had taken orders, he had resided long in the Temple, and had been studying English history and law, while most of the other chiefs of the schism had been poring over the Acts of Chalcedon, or seeking for wisdom in the Targum of Onkelos.*

In 1689, however, Leslie was almost unknown in England. Among the divines who incurred suspicion on the first of August in that year, the highest in popular estimation was without dispute Doctor William Sherlock. Perhaps no simple Presbyter of the Church of England has ever possessed a greater authority over his brethren than belonged to Sherlock at the time of the Revolution. He was not of the first rank among his contemporaries as a scholar, as a preacher, as a writer on theology, or as a writer on politics: but in all the four characters he had distinguished himself. The perspicuity and liveliness of his style have been praised by Prior and Addison. The facility and assiduity with which he wrote are sufficiently proved by the bulk and the dates of his works. There were, indeed, among the clergy men of brighter genius and men of wider attainments: but during a long period there was none who more completely represented the order, none who, on all subjects, spoke more precisely the sense of the Anglican priesthood, without any taint of Latitudinarianism, of Puritanism, or of Popery. He had, in the days of the Exclusion Bill, when the power of the dissenters was very great in Parliament and in the country, written strongly against the sin of non-conformity. When the Rye House Plot was detected, he had zealously

---

*Ware's History of the Writers of Ireland, continued by Harris.

defended by tongue and pen the doctrine of non-resistance. His services to the cause of episcopacy and monarchy were so highly valued that he was made Master of the Temple. A pension was also bestowed on him by Charles: but that pension James soon took away: for Sherlock, though he held himself bound to pay passive obedience to the civil power, held himself equally bound to combat religious errors, and was the keenest and most laborious of that host of controversialists who, in the day of peril, manfully defended the Protestant faith. In little more than two years he published sixteen treatises, some of them large books, against the high pretensions of Rome. Not content with the easy victories which he gained over such feeble antagonists as those who were quartered at Clerkenwell and the Savoy, he had the courage to measure his strength with no less a champion than Bossuet, and came out of the conflict without discredit. Nevertheless Sherlock still continued to maintain that no oppression could justify Christians in resisting the kingly authority. When the Convention was about to meet, he strongly recommended in a tract which was considered as the manifesto of a large part of the clergy, that James should be invited to return on such conditions as might secure the laws and religion of the nation.* The vote which placed William and Mary on the throne filled Sherlock with sorrow and anger. He is said to have exclaimed that if the Convention was determined on a revolution, the clergy would find forty thousand good Churchmen to effect a restoration.† Against new oaths he gave his opinion plainly and warmly. He professed himself at a loss to understand how any honest man could doubt that, by the powers that be, Saint Paul meant legitimate powers and no others. No name was, in 1689, cited by the Jacobites more proudly or more fondly than that of Sherlock. Before the end of 1690 that name excited very different feelings.

A few other nonjurors ought to be particularly noticed. High among them in rank was George Hickes, Dean of Worcester. Of all the Englishmen of his time he was the most versed in the old Teutonic languages; and his knowledge of the early Christian literature was extensive. As to his capacity for political discussions, it may be sufficient to say that his favorite argument for passive obedience was

---
*Letter to a member of the Convention, 1689.
†Johnson's Notes on the Phœnix Edition of Burnet's Pastoral Letter, 1692.

drawn from the story of the Theban legion. He was the younger brother of that unfortunate John Hickes who had been found hidden in the malthouse of Alice Lisle. James had, in spite of all solicitation, put both John Hickes and Alice Lisle to death. Persons who did not know the strength of the Dean's principles thought that he might possibly feel some resentment on this account: for he was of no gentle or forgiving temper, and could retain during many years a bitter remembrance of small injuries. But he was strong in his religious and political faith; he reflected that the sufferers were dissenters; and he submitted to the will of the Lord's Anointed, not only with patience but with complacency. He became, indeed, a more loving subject than ever from the time when his brother was hanged and his brother's benefactress beheaded. While almost all other clergymen, appalled by the Declaration of Indulgence and by the proceedings of the High Commission, were beginning to think that they had pushed the doctrine of non-resistance a little too far, he was writing a vindication of his darling legend, and trying to convince the troops at Hounslow that, if James should be pleased to massacre them all, as Maximian had massacred the Theban legion, for refusing to commit idolatry, it would be their duty to pile their arms, and meekly to receive the crown of martyrdom. To do Hickes justice, his whole conduct after the Revolution proved that his servility had sprung neither from fear nor from cupidity, but from mere bigotry.*

Jeremy Collier, who was turned out of the preachership of the Rolls, was a man of a much higher order. He is well entitled to grateful and respectful mention : for to his eloquence and courage is to be chiefly ascribed the purification of our lighter literature from that foul taint which had been contracted during the Antipuritan reaction. He was, in the full force of the words, a good man. He was also a man of eminent abilities, a great master of sarcasm, a great master of rhetoric.† His reading too, though undigested, was of immense extent. But his mind was nar-

---

* The best notion of Hickes's character will be formed from his numerous controversial writings, particularly his Jovian, written in 1684, his Thebæan Legion no Fable, written in 1687, though not published till 1714, and his Discourses upon Dr. Burnet and Dr. Tillotson, 1695. His literary fame rests on works of a very different kind.

† Collier's Tracts on the Stage are, on the whole, his best pieces. But there is much that is striking in his political pamphlets. His " Persuasive to Consideration, tendered to the Royalists, particularly those of the Church of England," seems to me one of the best productions of the Jacobite press.

row: his reasoning, even when he was so fortunate as to have a good cause to defend, was singularly futile and inconclusive; and his brain was almost turned by pride, not personal, but professional. In his view, a priest was the highest of human beings, except a bishop. Reverence and submission were due from the best and greatest of the laity to the least respectable of the clergy. However ridiculous a man in holy orders might make himself, it was impiety to laugh at him. So nervously sensitive indeed was Collier on this point that he thought it profane to throw any reflection even on the ministers of false religions. He laid it down as a rule that Muftis and Augurs ought always to be mentioned with respect. He blamed Dryden for sneering at the Hierophants of Apis. He praised Racine for giving dignity to the character of a priest of Baal. He praised Corneille for not bringing that learned and reverend divine Tiresias on the stage in the tragedy of Œdipus. The omission, Collier owned, spoiled the dramatic effect of the piece: but the holy function was much too solemn to be played with. Nay, incredible as it may seem, he thought it improper in the laity to sneer even at Presbyterian preachers. Indeed his Jacobitism was little more than one of the forms in which his zeal for the dignity of his profession manifested itself. He abhorred the Revolution less as a rising up of subjects against their King than as a rising up of the laity against the sacerdotal caste. The doctrines which had been proclaimed from the pulpit during thirty years had been treated with contempt by the Convention. A new government had been set up in opposition to the wishes of the spiritual peers in the House of Lords and of the priesthood throughout the country. A secular assembly had taken upon itself to pass a law requiring archbishops and bishops, rectors and vicars, to abjure, on pain of deprivation, what they had been teaching all their lives. Whatever meaner spirits might do, Collier was determined not to be led in triumph by the victorious enemies of his order. To the last he would confront, with the authoritative port of an ambassador of heaven, the anger of the powers and principalities of the earth.

In parts Collier was the first man among the nonjurors. In erudition the first place must be assigned to Henry Dodwell, who, for the unpardonable crime of having a small estate in Mayo, had been attainted by the Popish Parliament at Dublin. He was Camdenian Professor of

Ancient History in the University of Oxford, and had already acquired considerable celebrity by chronological and geographical researches; but though he never could be persuaded to take orders, theology was his favorite study. He was doubtless a pious and sincere man. He had perused innumerable volumes in various languages, and had indeed acquired more learning than his slender faculties were able to bear. The small intellectual spark which he possessed was put out by the fuel. Some of his books seem to have been written in a madhouse, and, though filled with proofs of his immense reading, degrade him to the level of James Naylor and Ludowick Muggleton. He began a dissertation intended to prove that the law of nations was a divine revelation made to the family which was preserved in the ark. He published a treatise in which he maintained that a marriage between a member of the Church of England and a dissenter was a nullity, and that the couple were in the sight of heaven guilty of adultery. He defended the use of instrumental music in public worship on the ground that the notes of the organ had a power to counteract the influence of devils on the spinal marrow of human beings. In his treatise on this subject he remarked that there was high authority for the opinion that the spinal marrow, when decomposed, became a serpent. Whether this opinion were or were not correct, he thought it unnecessary to decide. Perhaps, he said, the eminent men in whose works it was found had meant only to express figuratively the great truth, that the Old Serpent operates on us chiefly through the spinal marrow.* Dodwell's speculations on the state of human beings after death are, if possible, more extraordinary still. He tells us that our souls are naturally mortal. Annihilation is the fate of the greater part of mankind, of heathens, of Mahometans, of unchristened babes. The gift of immortality is conveyed in the sacrament of baptism: but to the efficacy of the sacrament it is absolutely necessary that the water be poured and the words pronounced by a minister who has been ordained by a bishop. In the natural course of things, therefore, all Presbyterians, In-

---

* See Brokesby's Life of Dodwell. The Discourse against Marriage in different Communions is known to me, I ought to say, only from Brokesby's copious abstract. That Discourse is very rare. It was originally printed as an appendage to a sermon preached by Leslie. When Leslie collected his works he omitted the Discourse, probably because he was ashamed of it. I have not been able to find it in the Library of the British Museum. The Treatise on the Lawfulness of Instrumental Music I have read; and incredibly absurd it is

dependents, Baptists, and Quakers would, like the inferior animals, cease to exist. But Dodwell was far too good a churchman to let off dissenters so easily. He informs them that, as they have had an opportunity of hearing the Gospel preached, and might, but for their own perverseness, have received episcopalian baptism, God will, by a preternatural act of power, bestow immortality on them in order that they may be tormented for ever and ever.*

No man abhorred the growing latitudinarianism of those times more than Dodwell. Yet no man had more reason to rejoice in it. For, in the earlier part of the seventeenth century, a speculator who had dared to affirm that the human soul is by its nature mortal, and does, in the great majority of cases, actually die with the body, would have been burned alive in Smithfield. Even in days which Dodwell could well remember, such heretics as himself would have been thought fortunate if they escaped with life, their backs flayed, their ears clipped, their noses slit, their tongues bored through with red hot iron, and their eyes knocked out with brickbats. With the nonjurors, however, the author of this theory was still the great Mr. Dodwell; and some who thought it culpable lenity to tolerate a Presbyterian meeting, thought it at the same time gross illiberality to blame a learned and pious Jacobite for denying a doctrine so utterly unimportant in a religious point of view as that of the immortality of the soul.†

Two other nonjurors deserve special mention, less on account of their abilities and learning, than on account of their rare integrity, and of their not less rare candor. These were John Kettlewell, Rector of Coleshill, and John Fitzwilliam, Canon of Windsor. It is remarkable that both these men had seen much of Lord Russell, and that both, though differing from him in political opinions, and strongly disapproving the part which he had taken in the Whig plot, had thought highly of his character, and had been sincere mourners for his death. He had sent to

---

* Dodwell tells us that the title of the work in which he first promulgated this theory was framed with great care and precision. I will therefore transcribe the title page: "An Epistolary Discourse proving from Scripture and the First Fathers that the Soul is naturally Mortal, Immortalized actually by the Pleasure of God to Punishment or to Reward, by its Union with the Divine Baptismal Spirit, wherein is proved that none have the Power of giving this Divine Immortalizing Spirit since the Apostles but only the Bishops. By H. Dodwell." Dr. Clarke, in a Letter to Dodwell (1706), says that this Epistolary Discourse is "a book at which all good men are sorry, and all profane men rejoice."

† See Leslie's Rehearsals, No. 286, 287.

Kettlewell an affectionate message from the scaffold in Lincoln's Inn Fields. Lady Russell, to her latest day, loved, trusted, and revered Fitzwilliam, who, when she was a girl, had been the friend of her father, the virtuous Southampton. The two clergymen agreed in refusing to swear: but they, from that moment, took different paths. Kettlewell was one of the most active members of his party: he declined no drudgery in the common cause, provided only that it were such drudgery as did not misbecome an honest man; and he defended his opinions in several tracts, which give a much higher notion of his sincerity than of his judgment or acuteness.* Fitzwilliam thought that he had done enough in quitting his pleasant dwelling and garden under the shadow of Saint George's Chapel, and in betaking himself with his books to a small lodging in an attic. He could not with a safe conscience acknowledge William and Mary: but he did not conceive that he was bound to be always stirring up sedition against them; and he passed the last years of his life, under the powerful protection of the House of Bedford, in innocent and studious repose.†

Among the less distinguished divines who forfeited their benefices, were doubtless many good men: but it is certain that the moral character of the nonjurors, as a class, did not stand high. It seems hard to impute laxity of principle to persons who undoubtedly made a great sacrifice to principle. And yet experience abundantly proves that many who are capable of making a great sacrifice, when their blood is heated by conflict, and when the public eye is fixed upon them, are not capable of persevering long in the daily practice of obscure virtues. It is by no means improbable that zealots may have given their lives for a religion which had never effectually restrained their vindictive or their licentious passions. We learn indeed from fathers of the highest authority that, even in the purest ages of the Church, some confessors, who had manfully refused to save themselves from torments and death by throwing frankincense on the altar of Jupiter afterwards brought scandal on the Christian name by gross

---

* See his works, and the highly curious life of him which was compiled from the papers of his friends Hickes and Nelson.

† See Fitzwilliam's correspondence with Lady Russell, and his evidence on the trial of Ashton, in the State Trials. The only work which Fitzwilliam, as far as I have been able to discover, ever published was a sermon on the Rye House Plot, preached a few weeks after Russell's execution. There are some sentences in this sermon which I a little wonder that the widow and the family forgave.

fraud and debauchery.* For the nonjuring divines great allowance must in fairness be made. They were doubtless in a most trying situation. In general, a schism, which divides a religious community, divides the laity as well as the clergy. The seceding pastors, therefore, carry with them a large part of their flocks, and are consequently assured of a maintenance. But the schism of 1689 scarcely extended beyond the clergy. The law required the rector to take the oaths, or to quit his living; but no oath, no acknowledgment of the title of the new King and Queen, was required from the parishioner as a qualification for attending divine service, or for receiving the Eucharist. Not one in fifty, therefore, of those laymen who disapproved of the Revolution thought himself bound to quit his pew in the old church, where the old liturgy was still read, and where the old vestments were still worn, and to follow the ejected priests to a conventicle, a conventicle, too, which was not protected by the Toleration Act. Thus the new sect was a sect of preachers without hearers; and such preachers could not make a livelihood by preaching. In London, indeed, and in some other large towns, those vehement Jacobites, whom nothing would satisfy but to hear King James and the Prince of Wales prayed for by name, were sufficiently numerous to make up a few small congregations, which met secretly and under constant fear of the constables, in rooms so mean that the meeting houses of the Puritan dissenters might by comparison be called palaces. Even Collier, who had all the qualities which attract large audiences, was reduced to be the minister of a little knot of malecontents, whose oratory was on a second floor in the city. But the nonjuring clergymen who were able to obtain even a pittance by officiating at such places, were very few. Of the rest some had independent means: some lived by literature: one or two practised physic. Thomas Wagstaffe, for example, who had been Chancellor of Litchfield, had many patients, and made himself conspicuous by always visiting them in full

* Cyprian, in one of his Epistles, addresses the confessors thus: "Quosdam audio inficere numerum vestrum, et laudem præcipui nominis prava sua conversatione destruere... Cum quanto nominis vestri pudore delinquitur quando alius aliquis temulentus et lasciviens demoratur; alius in eam patriam unde extorris est regreditur, ut deprehensus non jam quasi Christianus, sed quasi nocens pereat." He uses still stronger language in the book de Unitate Ecclesiæ; "Neque enim confessio immunem facit ab insidiis diaboli, aut contra tentationes et pericula et incursus atque impetus sæculares adhuc in sæculo positum perpetua securitate defendit; cæterum nunquam in confessoribus fraudes et stupra et adulteria postmodum videremus, quæ nunc in quibusdam videntes ingemiscimus et dolemus."

canonicals.* But these were exceptions. **Industrious** poverty is a state by no means unfavorable to virtue; but it is dangerous to be at once poor and idle; and most of the clergymen who had refused to swear found themselves thrown on the world, with nothing to eat and with nothing to do. They naturally became beggars and loungers. Considering themselves as martyrs suffering in a public cause, they were not ashamed to ask any good churchman for a guinea. Most of them passed their lives in running about from one Tory coffee-house to another, abusing the Dutch, hearing and spreading reports that within a month His Majesty would certainly be on English ground, and wondering who would have Salisbury when Burnet was hanged. During the Session of Parliament the lobbies and the Court of Requests were crowded with deprived parsons, asking who was up, and what the numbers were on the last division. Many of the ejected divines became domesticated, as chaplains, tutors, and spiritual directors, in the houses of opulent Jacobites. In a situation of this kind, a man of pure and exalted character, such a man as Ken was among the nonjurors, and Watts among the non-conformists, may preserve his dignity, and may much more than repay by his example and his instructions the benefits which he receives. But to a person whose virtue is not high-toned this way of life is full of peril. If he is of a quiet disposition, he is in danger of sinking into a servile, sensual, drowsy parasite. If he is of an active and aspiring nature, it may be feared that he will become expert in those bad arts by which more easily than by faithful service, retainers make themselves agreeable or formidable. To discover the weak side of every character, to flatter every passion and prejudice, to sow discord and jealousy where love and confidence ought to exist, to watch the moment of indiscreet openness for the purpose of extracting secrets important to the prosperity and honor of families, such are the practices by which keen and restless spirits have too often avenged themselves for the humiliation of dependence. The public voice loudly accused many nonjurors of requiting the hospitality of their benefactors with villainy as black as that of the hypocrite depicted in the masterpiece of Molière. Indeed when Cibber under-

---

* Much curious information about the nonjurors will be found in the Biographical Memoirs of William Bowyer, Printer, which forms the first volume of Nichols's Literary Anecdotes of the eighteenth century. A specimen of Wagstaffe's prescriptions is in the Bodleian Library.

took to adapt that noble comedy to the English stage, he made his Tartuffe a nonjuror; and Johnson, who cannot be supposed to have been prejudiced against the nonjurors, frankly owned that Cibber had done them no wrong.*

There can be no doubt that the schism caused by the oaths would have been far more formidable, if, at this crisis, any extensive change had been made in the government or in the ceremonial of the Established Church. It is a highly instructive fact that those enlightened and tolerant divines who most ardently desired such a change, saw reason, not long afterwards, to be thankful that their favorite project had failed.

Whigs and Tories had in the late Session combined to get rid of Nottingham's Comprehension Bill by voting an address which requested the King to refer the whole subject to the Convocation. Burnet foresaw the effect of this vote. The whole scheme, he said, was utterly ruined.† Many of his friends, however, thought differently; and among these was Tillotson. Of all the members of the Low Church party, Tillotson stood highest in general estimation. As a preacher he was thought by his contemporaries to have surpassed all rivals living or dead. Posterity has reversed this judgment. Yet Tillotson still keeps his place as a legitimate English classic. His highest flights were indeed far below those of Taylor, of Barrow, and of South; but his oratory was more correct and equable than theirs. No quaint conceits, no pedantic quotations from Talmudists and scholiasts, no mean images, buffoon stories, scurrilous invectives, ever marred the effect of his grave and temperate discourses. His reasoning was

---

* Cibber's play, as Cibber wrote it, ceased to be popular when the Jacobites ceased to be formidable, and is now known only to the curious. In 1768, Bickerstaffe altered it into the Hypocrite, and substituted Dr. Cantwell, the Methodist, for Dr. Wolfe, the Nonjuror. "I do not think," said Johnson, "the character of the Hypocrite justly applicable to the Methodist; but it was very applicable to the nonjurors." Boswell asked him if it were true that the nonjuring clergymen intrigued with the wives of their patrons. "I am afraid," said Johnson, "many of them did." This conversation took place on the 27th of March, 1775. It was not merely in careless talk that Johnson expressed an unfavorable opinion of the nonjuror. In his Life of Fenton, who was a nonjuror, are these remarkable words: "It must be remembered that he kept his name unsullied, and never suffered himself to be reduced, like too many of the same sect, to mean arts and dishonorable shifts." See the Character of a Jacobite, 1690. Even in Kettlewell's Life, compiled from the papers of his friends Hickes and Nelson, will be found admissions which show that, very soon after the schism, some of the nonjuring clergy fell into habits of idleness, dependence, and mendicancy, which lowered the character of the whole party. "Several undeserving persons, who are always the most confident, by their going up and down, did much prejudice to the truly deserving, whose modesty would not suffer them to solicit for themselves. . . . . . Mr. Kettlewell was also very sensible that some of his brethren spent too much of their time at places of concourse and news, by depending for their subsistence upon those whom they there not acquainted with."

† Heresby's Memoirs, 344.

just sufficiently profound and sufficiently refined to be followed by a popular audience with that slight degree of intellectual exertion which is a pleasure. His style is not brilliant; but it is pure, transparently clear, and equally free from the levity and from the stiffness which disfigure the sermons of some eminent divines of the seventeenth century. He is always serious: yet there is about his manner a certain graceful ease which marks him as a man who knows the world, who has lived in populous cities and in splendid courts, and who has conversed, not only with books, but with lawyers and merchants, wits and beauties, statesmen and princes. The greatest charm of his compositions, however, is derived from the benignity and candor which appear in every line, and which shone forth not less conspicuously in his life than in his writings.

As a theologian, Tillotson was certainly not less latitudinarian than Burnet. Yet many of those clergymen to whom Burnet was an object of implacable aversion, spoke of Tillotson with tenderness and respect. It is therefore not strange that the two friends should have formed different estimates of the temper of the priesthood, and should have expected different results from the meeting of the Convocation. Tillotson was not displeased with the vote of the Commons. He conceived that changes made in religious institutions by mere secular authority might disgust many churchmen, who would yet be perfectly willing to vote, in an ecclesiastical synod, for changes more extensive still; and his opinion had great weight with the King.*
It was resolved that the Convocation should meet at the beginning of the next session of Parliament, and that in the meantime a commission should issue empowering some eminent divines to examine the Liturgy, the canons, and the whole system of jurisprudence administered by the Courts Christian, and to report on the alterations which it might be desirable to make.†

Most of the Bishops who had taken the oaths were in this commission; and with them were joined twenty priests of great note. Of the twenty, Tillotson was the most important: for he was known to speak the sense both of the King and of the Queen. Among those Commissioners who looked up to Tillotson as their chief were Stillingfleet, Dean of St. Paul's, Sharp, Dean of Norwich,

---
* Birch's Life of Tillotson.
† See the Discourse concerning the Ecclesiastical Commission.

Patrick, Dean of Peterborough, Tenison, Rector of Saint Martin's, and Powler, to whose judicious firmness was chiefly to be ascribed the determination of the London clergy not to read the Declaration of Indulgence.

With such men as those who have been named were mingled some divines who belonged to the High Church party. Conspicuous among these were two of the rulers of Oxford, Aldrich, and Jane. Aldrich had recently been appointed Dean of Christchurch, in the room of the Papist Massey, whom James had, in direct violation of the laws, placed at the head of that great college. The new Dean was a polite, though not a profound scholar, and a jovial, hospitable gentleman. He was the author of some theological tracts which have long been forgotten, and of a compendium of logic which is still used: but the best works which he has bequeathed to posterity are his catches. Jane, the King's Professor of Divinity, was a graver but a less estimable man. He had borne the chief part in framing that decree by which his University ordered the works of Milton and Buchanan to be publicly burned in the schools. A few years later, irritated and alarmed by the persecution of the Bishops and by the confiscation of the revenues of Magdalene College, he had renounced the doctrine of non-resistance, had repaired to the headquarters of the Prince of Orange, and had assured His Highness that Oxford would willingly coin her plate for the support of the war against her oppressor. During a short time Jane was generally considered as a Whig, and was sharply lampooned by some of his old allies. He was so unfortunate as to have a name which was an excellent mark for the learned punsters of his University. Several epigrams were written on the doublefaced Janus, who, having got a professorship by looking one way, now hoped to get a bishopric by looking another. That he hoped to get a bishopric was perfectly true. He demanded the see of Exeter as a reward due to his services. He was refused: the refusal convinced him that the Church had as much to apprehend from Latitudinarianism as from Popery; and he speedily became a Tory again.*

Early in October the Commissioners assembled in the Jerusalem Chamber. At their first meeting they determined to propose that, in the public services of the Church, lessons taken from the canonical books of Scripture should be substituted for

---

* Birch's Life of Tillotson; Life of Prideaux; Gentleman's Magazine for June and July, 1745.

the lessons taken from the Apocrypha.* At the second meeting a strange question was raised by the very last person who ought to have raised it. Sprat, Bishop of Rochester, had, without any scruple, sate, during two years, in the unconstitutional tribunal which had, in the late reign, oppressed and pillaged the Church of which he was a ruler. But he had now become scrupulous, and was not ashamed, after acting without hesitation under King James's commission, to express a doubt whether King William's commission were legal. To a plain understanding the doubt seems to be childish. King William's commission gave power neither to make laws nor to administer laws, but simply to inquire and to report. Even without a royal commission, Tillotson, Patrick, and Stillingfleet might, with perfect propriety, have met to discuss the state and prospects of the Church, and to consider whether it would or would not be desirable to make some concession to the dissenters. And how could it be a crime for subjects to do at the request of their Sovereign that which it would have been innocent and laudable to do without any such request? Sprat, however, was seconded by Jane. There was a sharp altercation; and Lloyd, Bishop of Saint Asaph, who, with many good qualities, had an irritable temper, was provoked into saying something about spies. Sprat withdrew and came no more. His example was soon followed by Jane and Aldrich.† The Commissioners proceeded to take into consideration the question of the posture at the Eucharist. It was determined to recommend that a communicant, who after conference with his minister, should declare that he could not conscientiously receive the bread and wine kneeling, might receive them sitting. Mew, Bishop of Winchester, an honest man, but illiterate, weak even in his best days, and now fast sinking into dotage, protested against this concession, and withdrew from the assembly. The other members continued to apply themselves vigorously to their task; and no more secessions took place, though there were great differences of opinion, and though the debates were sometimes warm. The highest churchmen who still remained were Doctor William Beveridge, Archdeacon of Colchester, who many years later became Bishop of Saint Asaph, and Doctor John Scott, the same who had prayed by the deathbed of Jeffreys. The most active among the Latitudinarians appear to have been Burnet, Fowler, and Tenison.

---

* Diary of the Proceedings of the Commissioners, taken by Dr. Williams, afterwards Bishop of Chichester, one of the Commissioners, every night after he went home from the several meetings. This most curious Diary was printed by order of the House of Commons in 1554.
† Williams's Diary.

The baptismal service was repeatedly discussed. As to matter of form the Commissioners were disposed to be indulgent. They were generally willing to admit infants into the Church without sponsors and without the sign of the cross. But the majority, after much debate, steadily refused to soften down or explain away those words which, to all minds not sophisticated, appear to assert the regenerating virtue of the sacrament.*

As to the surplice, the Commissioners determined to recommend that a large discretion should be left to the Bishops. Expedients were devised by which a person who had received Presbyterian ordination might, without admitting, either expressly or by implication, the invalidity of that ordination, become a minister of the Church of England.†

The ecclesiastical calendar was carefully revised. The great festivals were retained. But it was not thought desirable that Saint Valentine, Saint Chad, Saint Swithin, Saint Edward, King of the West Saxons, Saint Dunstan, and Saint Alphage, should share the honors of Saint John and Saint Paul; or that the Church should appear to class the ridiculous fable of the discovery of the cross with facts so awfully important as the Nativity, the Passion, the Resurrection and the Ascension of her Lord.‡

The Athanasian Creed caused much perplexity. Most of the Commissioners were equally unwilling to give up the doctrinal clauses and to retain the damnatory clauses. Burnet, Fowler, and Tillotson, were desirous to strike this famous symbol out of the Liturgy altogether. Burnet brought forward one argument, which to himself probably did not appear to have much weight, but which was admirably calculated to perplex his opponents, Beveridge and Scott. The Council of Ephesus had always been reverenced by Anglican divines as a synod which had truly represented the whole body of the faithful, and which had been divinely guided in the way of truth. The voice of that Council was the voice of the Holy Catholic and Apostolic Church, not yet corrupted by superstition, or rent asunder by schism. During more than twelve centuries the world had not seen an ecclesiastical assembly which had an equal claim to the respect of believers. The Council of Ephesus had, in the plainest terms, and under the most terrible penalties, forbidden Christians to frame or to impose on their

---

* William's Diary. † Ibid.
‡ See the alterations in the Book of Common Prayer prepared by the Royal Commissioners for the revision of the Liturgy in 1689, and printed by order of the House of Commons in 1854.

brethren **any creed** other than the creed settled by the Nicene Fathers. It should seem, therefore, that, if the Council of Ephesus was really under the direction of the Holy Spirit, whoever uses the Athanasian Creed must, in the very act of uttering an anathema against his neighbors, bring down an anathema on his own head.* In spite of the authority of the Ephesian Fathers, the majority of the Commissioners determined to leave the Athanasian Creed in the Prayer-Book; but they proposed to add a rubric drawn up by Stillingfleet, which declared that the damnatory clauses were to be understood to apply only to such as obstinately denied the substance of the Christian Faith. Obstinacy is of the nature of moral pravity, and is not imputable to a candid and modest enquirer who, from some defect or malformation of the intellect, is mistaken as to the comparative weight of opposite arguments or testimonies. Orthodox believers were, therefore, permitted to hope that the heretic who had honestly and humbly sought for truth would not be everlastingly punished for having failed to find it.†

Tenison was entrusted with the business of examining the Liturgy, and of collecting all those expressions to which objections had been made, either by theological or by literary critics. It was determined to remove some obvious blemishes. And it would have been wise in the Commissioners to stop here. Unfortunately they determined to rewrite a great part of the Prayer-Book. It was a bold undertaking; for in general the style of that volume is such as cannot be improved. The English Liturgy indeed gains by being compared even with those fine ancient Liturgies from which it is to a great extent taken. The essential qualities of devotional eloquence, conciseness, majestic simplicity, pathetic earnestness of supplication, sobered by a profound reverence, are common between the translations and the originals. But in the subordinate graces of diction the originals must be allowed to be far inferior to the translations. And the reason is obvious. The technical phraseology of Christianity did not become a part of the Latin language till that language had passed the age of maturity and was sinking into barbarism. But the technical phraseology of

---

* It is difficult to conceive stronger or clearer language than that used by that Council. Τούτων τοίνυν ἀναγνωσθέντων, ὥρισεν ἡ ἁγία σύνοδος, ἑτέραν πίστιν μηδενὶ ἐξεῖναι προσφέρειν, ἤγουν συγγράφειν, ἢ συντιθέναι, παρὰ τὴν ὁρισθεῖσαν παρὰ τῶν ἁγίων πατέρων τῶν ἐν τῇ Νικαέων συνελθόντων σὺν ἁγίῳ πνεύματι· τοὺς δὲ τολμῶντας ἢ συντιθέναι πίστιν ἑτέραν, ἤγουν προκομίζειν, ἢ προσφέρειν τοῖς ἐθέλουσιν ἐπιστρέφειν εἰς ἐπίγνωσιν τῆς ἀληθείας, ἢ ἐξ Ἑλληνισμοῦ, ἢ ἐξ Ἰουδαϊσμοῦ, ἢ ἐξ αἱρέσεως οἱασδηποτοῦν, τούτους, εἰ μὲν εἶεν ἐπίσκοποι ἢ κληρικοί, ἀλλοτρίους εἶναι τοὺς ἐπισκόπους τῆς ἐπισκοπῆς, καὶ τοὺς κληρικοὺς τοῦ κλήρου, εἰ δὲ λαϊκοὶ εἶεν, ἀναθεματίζεσθαι.—Concil. Ephes. Actio VI.

† William's Diary; Alterations in the Books of Common Prayer.

Christianity was found in the Anglo-Saxon and the Norman French, long before the union of those two dialects had produced a third dialect superior to either. The Latin of the Roman Catholic services, therefore, is Latin in the last stage of decay. The English of our services is English in all the vigor and suppleness of early youth. To the great Latin writers, to Terence and Lucretius, to Cicero and Cæsar, to Tacitus and Quintilian, the noblest compositions of Ambrose and Gregory would have seemed to be, not merely bad writing, but senseless gibberish.* The diction of our Book of Common Prayer, on the other hand, has directly or indirectly contributed to form the diction of almost every great English writer, and has extorted the admiration of the most accomplished infidels and of the most accomplished nonconformists, of such men as David Hume and Robert Hall.

The style of the Liturgy, however, did not satisfy the Doctors of the Jerusalem Chamber. They voted the Collects too short and too dry; and Patrick was entrusted with the duty of expanding and ornamenting them. In one respect, at least, the choice seems to have been unexceptionable; for, if we judge by the way in which Patrick paraphrased the most sublime Hebrew poetry, we shall probably be of opinion that, whether he was or was not qualified to make the Collects better, no man that ever lived was more competent to make them longer.†

It mattered little, however, whether the recommendations of the Commissioners were good or bad. They were all doomed before they were known. The writs summoning the Convocation of the Province of Canterbury had been issued; and the clergy were everywhere in a state of violent excitement. They had just taken the oaths, and were smarting from the earnest reproofs of nonjurors, from the insolents taunts of Whigs, and

---

* It is curious to consider how those great masters of the Latin tongue who used to sup with Mæcenas and Pollio would have been perplexed by "Tibi Cherubim et Seraphim incessabili voce proclamant, Sanctus, Sanctus, Sanctus, Dominus Deus Sabaoth;" or by "Ideo cum angelis et archangelis, cum thronis et dominationibus."

† I will give two specimens of Patrick's workmanship. "He maketh me," says David, "to lie down in green pastures: he leadeth me beside the still waters." Patrick's version is as follows: "For as a good shepherd leads his sheep in the violent heat to shady places, where they may lie down and feed (not in parched, but) in fresh and green pastures, and in the evening leads them (not to muddy and troubled waters, but) to pure and quiet streams; so hath he already made a fair and plentiful provision for me, which I enjoy in peace without any disturbance."

In the Song of Solomon is an exquisitely beautiful verse. "I charge you, O daughters of Jerusalem, if ye find my beloved, that ye tell him that I am sick of love." Patrick's version runs thus: "So I turned myself to those of my neighbors and familiar acquaintance who were awakened by my cries to come and see what the matter was; and conjured them as they would answer it to God, that if they met with my beloved, they would let him know —What shall I say?—What shall I desire you to tell him but that I do not enjoy myself now that I want his company, nor can be well till I recover his love again?"

often undoubtedly from the stings of remorse. The announcement that a Convocation was to sit for the purpose of deliberating on a plan of comprehension roused all the strongest passions of the priest who had just complied with the law, and was ill satisfied or half satisfied with himself for complying. He had an opportunity of contributing to defeat a favorite scheme of that government which had exacted from him, under severe penalties, a submission not easily to be reconciled to his conscience or his pride. He had an opportunity of signalizing his zeal for that Church whose characterestic doctrines he had been accused of deserting for lucre. She was now, he conceived, threatened by a danger as great as that of the preceding year. The Latitudinarians of 1689 were not less eager to humble and to ruin her than the Jesuits of 1688 had been. The Toleration Act had done for the Dissenters quite as much as was compatible with her dignity and security; and nothing more ought to be conceded, not the hem of one of her vestments, not an epithet from the beginning to the end of her Liturgy. All the reproaches which had been thrown on the ecclesiastical commission of James were transferred to the ecclesiastical commission of William. The two commissions indeed had nothing but the name in common. But the name was associated with illegality and oppression, with the violation of dwellings and the confiscation of freeholds, and was therefore assiduously sounded with no small effect by the tongues of the spiteful in the ears of the ignorant.

The King too, it was said, was not sound. He conformed indeed to the established worship; but his was a local and occasional conformity. For some ceremonies to which High Churchmen were attached he had a distaste which he was at no pains to conceal. One of his first acts had been to give orders that in his private chapel the service should be said instead of being sung; and this arrangement, though warranted by the rubric, caused much murmuring.* It was known that he was so profane as to sneer at a practice which had been sanctioned by high ecclesiastical authority, the practice of touching for the scrofula. This ceremony had come down almost unaltered from the darkest of the dark ages to the time of Newton and Locke. The Stuarts frequently dispensed the healing influences in the Banqueting House. The days on which this miracle was to be wrought were fixed at sittings of the

---

* William's dislike to the Cathedral service is sarcastically noticed by Leslie in the Rehearsal, No. 7. See also a letter from a Member of the House of Commons to his Friend in the Country, 1689, and Bisset's Modern Fanatic, 1710.

Privy Council, and were solemnly notified by the clergy in all the parish churches of the realm.* When the appointed time came, several divines in full canonicals stood round the canopy of state. The surgeon of the royal household introduced the sick. A passage from the sixteenth chapter of the Gospel of Saint Mark was read. When the words, "They shall lay their hands on the sick, and they shall recover," had been pronounced, there was a pause; and one of the sick was brought up to the King. His Majesty stroked the ulcers and swellings, and hung round the patient's neck a white riband to which was fastened a gold coin. The other sufferers were then led up in succession; and, as each was touched, the chaplain repeated the incantation, "They shall lay their hands on the sick, and they shall recover." Then came the epistle, prayers, antiphonies, and a benediction. The service may still be found in the prayer-books of the reign of Anne. Indeed it was not till some time after the accession of George the First that the University of Oxford ceased to reprint the Office of Healing together with the Liturgy. Theologians of eminent learning, ability, and virtue gave the sanction of their authority to this mummery; † and what is stranger still, medical men of high note believed, or affected to believe, in the balsamic virtues of the royal hand. We must suppose that every surgeon who attended Charles the Second was a man of high repute for skill; and more than one of the surgeons who attended Charles the Second has left us a solemn profession of faith in the King's miraculous power. One of them is not ashamed to tell us that the gift was communicated by the unction administered at the coronation; that the cures were so numerous and sometimes so rapid that they could not be attributed to any natural cause; that the failures were to be ascribed to want of faith on the part of the patients; that Charles once handled a scrofulous Quaker and made him a healthy man and a sound Churchman in a moment; that, if those who had been healed lost or sold the piece of gold which had been hung round their necks, the ulcers broke forth again, and could be removed only by a second touch and a second talisman. We cannot wonder that, when men of science gravely repeated such nonsense, the vulgar should have believed it. Still less can we wonder that wretches tortured by a disease over which

---

* See the Order in Council of Jan. 9, 1683.
† See Collier's Desertion discussed, 1689. Thomas Carte, who was a disciple, and, at one time, an assistant of Collier, inserted, so late as the year 1747, in a bulky History of England, an exquisitely absurd note, in which he assured the world that, to his certain knowledge, the Pretender had cured the scrofula, and very gravely inferred that the healing virtue was transmitted by inheritance, and was quite independent of any unction. See Carte's History of England, vol. i. page 291.

natural remedies had no power should have eagerly drunk in tales of preternatural cures; for nothing is so credulous as misery. The crowds which repaired to the palace on the days of healing were immense. Charles the Second, in the course of his reign, touched near a hundred thousand persons. The number seems to have increased or diminished as the king's popularity rose or fell. During that Tory reaction which followed the dissolution of the Oxford Parliament, the press to get near him was terrific. In 1682, he performed the rite eight thousand five hundred times. In 1684, the throng was such that six or seven of the sick were trampled to death. James, in one of his progresses, touched eight hundred persons in the choir of the Cathedral of Chester. The expense of the ceremony was little less than ten thousand pounds a year, and would have been much greater but for the vigilance of the royal surgeons, whose business it was to examine the applicants, and to distinguish those who came for the cure from those who came for the gold.*

William had too much sense to be duped, and too much honesty to bear a part in what he knew to be an imposture. "It is a silly superstition," he exclaimed, when he heard that, at the close of Lent, his palace was besieged by a crowd of the sick: "Give the poor creatures some money, and send them away."† On one single occasion he was importuned into laying his hand on a patient. "God give you better health," he said, "and more sense." The parents of scrofulous children cried out against his cruelty: bigots lifted up their hands and eyes in horror at his impiety: Jacobites sarcastically praised him for not presuming to arrogate to himself a power which belonged only to legitimate sovereigns; and even some Whigs thought that he acted unwisely in treating with such marked contempt a superstition which had a strong hold on the vulgar mind: but William was not to be moved, and was accordingly set down by many High Churchmen as either an infidel or a puritan.‡

---

* See the Preface to a Treatise on Wounds, by Richard Wiseman, Sergeant Chirurgeon to His Majesty, 1676. But the fullest information on this curious subject will be found in the Charisma Basilicon, by John Browne, Chirurgeon in ordinary to His Majesty, 1684. See also the ceremonies used in the Time of King Henry VII. for the Healing of them that be diseased with the King's Evil, published by His Majesty's Command, 1686; Evelyn's Diary, March 28, 1684; and Bishop Cartwright's Diary, Aug. 28, 29, and 30, 1687. It is incredible that so large a proportion of the population should have been really scrofulous. No doubt many persons who had slight and transient maladies were brought to the king; and the recovery of these persons kept up the vulgar belief in the efficacy of his touch.

† Paris Gazette, April 23, 1689.

‡ See Whiston's Life of himself. Poor Whiston, who believed in everything but the Trinity, tells us gravely that the single person whom William touched was cured, notwithstanding His Majesty's want of faith. See also the Athenian Mercury of January 16, 1691.

The chief cause, however, which at this time made even the most moderate plan of comprehension hateful to the priesthood still remains to be mentioned. What Burnet had foreseen and foretold had come to pass. There was throughout the clerical profession a strong disposition to retaliate on the Presbyterians of England the wrongs of the Episcopalians of Scotland. It could not be denied that even the highest churchmen had, in the summer of 1688, generally declared themselves willing to give up many things for the sake of union. But it was said, and not without plausibility, that what was passing on the other side of the Border proved union on any reasonable terms to be impossible. With what face, it was asked, can those who will make no concession to us where we are weak, blame us for refusing to make any concession to them where we are strong? We cannot judge correctly of the principles and feelings of a sect from the professions which it makes in a time of feebleness and suffering. If we would know what the Puritan spirit really is, we must observe the Puritan when he is dominant. He was dominant here in the last generation; and his little finger was thicker than the loins of the prelates. He drove hundreds of quiet students from their cloisters, and thousands of respectable divines from their parsonages, for the crime of refusing to sign his Covenant. No tenderness was shown to learning, to genius, or to sanctity. Such men as Hall and Sanderson, Chillingworth and Hammond, were not only plundered, but flung into prisons, and exposed to all the rudeness of brutal jailers. It was made a crime to read fine psalms and prayers bequeathed to the faithful by Ambrose and Chrysostom. At length the nation became weary of the reign of the saints. The fallen dynasty and the fallen hierarchy were restored. The Puritan was in his turn subjected to disabilities and penalties; and he immediately found out that it was barbarous to punish men for entertaining conscientious scruples about a garb, about a ceremony, about the functions of ecclesiastical officers. His piteous complaints and his arguments in favor of toleration had at length imposed on many well meaning persons. Even zealous churchmen had begun to entertain a hope that the severe discipline which he had undergone had made him candid, moderate, charitable. Had this been really so, it would doubtless have been our duty to treat his scruples with extreme tenderness. But, while we were considering what we could do to meet his wishes in England, he had obtained ascendency in Scotland; and, in an instant, he was all himself again, bigoted, insolent, and cruel. Manses had been sacked; churches shut up; prayer-books burned; sacred garments torn; congregations dispersed by violence; priests hustled, pelted, pilloried, driven forth, with their wives and babes, to beg or die of hunger. That these outrages were to be imputed, not to a few lawless marauders, but to the great body of the Presbyterians of Scotland, was evident from the fact that the government had not dared either to inflict punishment on the offenders or to grant relief to the sufferers. Was it not fit then that the Church of England should take warning? Was it reasonable to ask her to mutilate her apostolical polity and her beautiful ritual for the purpose of conciliating those who wanted nothing but power to rabble her as they had rabbled her sister? Already these men had obtained a boon which they ill deserved, and which they never would have granted. They worshipped God in perfect security. Their meeting-houses were as effectually protected as the choirs of our cathedrals. While no episcopal minister could, without putting his life in jeopardy, officiate in Ayrshire or Renfrewshire, a hundred Presbyterian ministers preached unmolested every Sunday in Middlesex. The legislature had, with a generosity perhaps imprudent, granted toleration to the most intolerant of men; and with toleration it behoved them to be content.

Thus several causes conspired to inflame the parochial clergy against the scheme of comprehension. Their temper was such that, if the plan framed in the Jerusalem Chamber had been directly submitted to them, it would have been rejected by a majority of twenty to one. But in the Convocation their weight bore no proportion to their number. The Convocation has, happily for our country, been so long utterly insignificant that, till a recent period, none but curious students cared to inquire how it was constituted; and even now many persons, not generally ill informed, imagine it to be a council representing the Church of England. In truth, the Convocation so often mentioned in our ecclesiastical history is merely the synod of the Province of Canterbury, and never had a right to speak in the name of the whole clerical body. The Province of York has also its Convocation: but, till the eighteenth century was far advanced, the Province of York was generally so poor, so rude, and so thinly peopled, that, in political importance, it could hardly be considered as more than a tenth part of the kingdom. The sense of the Southern clergy was therefore popularly considered as the sense of the whole profession. When the formal concurrence of the Northern clergy was required, it seems to have been given as a matter of course. Indeed, the canons passed by the Convocation of Canterbury in 1604 were ratified by James the First, and were ordered to be strictly observed in every part of the kingdom, two years before the Convocation of York went through the form of approving them. Since these ecclesiastical councils became mere names, a great change has taken place in the relative position of the two Archbishoprics. In all the elements of power, the region beyond Trent is now at least a third part of England. When in our own time the representative system was adjusted to the altered state of the country, almost all the small boroughs which it was necessary to disfranchise were in the south. Two thirds of the new members given to great provincial towns were given to the north. If, therefore, any English government should suffer the Convocations, as now constituted, to meet for the despatch of business, two independent synods would be legislating at the same time for one Church. It is by no means impossible that one assembly might adopt canons which the other might reject, that one assembly might condemn as heretical propositions which the other might hold to be orthodox.* In the seventeenth century no such danger was apprehended. So little indeed was the Convocation of York then considered, that the two Houses of Parliament had, in their address to William, spoken only of one Convocation, which they called the Convocation of the Clergy of the Kingdom.

The body which they thus not very accurately designated is divided into two Houses. The Upper House is composed of the Bishops of the Province of Canterbury. The Lower House consisted, in 1689, of a hundred and forty-four members. Twenty-two Deans and fifty-four Archdeacons sate there in virtue of their offices. Twenty-four divines sate as proctors for twenty-four chapters. Only forty-four proctors were elected by the eight thousand parish priests of the twenty-two dioceses. These forty-four proctors, however, were almost all of one mind. The elections had in former times been conducted in the most quiet and decorous manner. But on this occasion the canvassing was eager: the contests were sharp: Clarendon, who had refused to take the oaths, and his brother Rochester, the leader of the party which in the House of Lords had opposed the Comprehension Bill, had gone to Ox-

---

* In several recent publications the apprehension that differences might arise between the Convocation of York and the Convocation of Canterbury has been contemptuously pronounced chimerical. But it is not easy to understand why two independent Convocations should be less likely to differ than two Houses of the same Convocation; and it is matter of notoriety that, in the reigns of William the Third and Anne, the two Houses of the Convocation of Canterbury scarcely ever agreed.

ford, the headquarters of that party, for the purpose of animating and organizing the opposition.* The representatives of the parochial clergy must have been men whose chief distinction was their zeal: for in the whole list can be found not a single illustrious name, and very few names which are now known even to persons well read in ecclesiastical history.† The official members of the Lower House, among whom were many distinguished scholars and preachers, seem to have been not very unequally divided.

During the summer of 1689 several high spiritual dignities became vacant, and were bestowed on divines who were sitting in the Jerusalem Chamber. It has already been mentioned that Thomas, Bishop of Worcester, died just before the day fixed for taking the oaths, Lake, Bishop of Chichester, lived just long enough to refuse them, and with his last breath declared that he would maintain even at the stake the doctrine of indefeasible hereditary right. The see of Chichester was filled by Patrick, and that of Worcester by Stillingfleet; and the deanery of Saint Paul's which Stillingfleet quitted was given to Tillotson. That Tillotson was not raised to the episcopal bench excited some surprise. But in truth it was because the government held his services in the highest estimation that he was suffered to remain a little longer a simple presbyter. The most important office in the Convocation was that of Prolocutor of the Lower House: the Prolocutor was to be chosen by the members: and it was hoped at court that they would choose Tillotson. It had in fact been already determined that he should be the next Archbishop of Canterbury. When he went to kiss hands for his new deanery he warmly thanked the King. "Your Majesty has now set me at ease for the remainder of my life." "No such thing, Doctor, I assure you," said William. He then plainly intimated that, whenever Sancroft should cease to fill the highest ecclesiastical station, Tillotson would succeed to it. Tillotson stood aghast; for his nature was quiet and unambitious; he was beginning to feel the infirmities of old age; he cared little for rank or money: the worldly advantages which he most valued were an honest fame and the general good will of mankind: those advantages he already possessed; and he could not but be aware that, if he

---

* Birch's Life of Tilotson; Life of Prideaux. From Clarendon's Diary, it appears that he and Rochester were at Oxford on the 23d of September.
† See the Roll in the Historical account of the present Convocation, appended to the second edition of Vox Cleri, 1690. The most considerable name that I perceive in the list of proctors chosen by the parochial clergy is that of Dr. John Mill, the editor of the Greek Testament.

became primate, he should incur the bitterest hatred of a powerful party, and should become a mark for obloquy, from which his gentle and sensitive nature shrank as from the rack or the wheel. William was earnest and resolute. "It is necessary," he said, "for my service; and I must lay on your conscience the responsibility of refusing me your help." Here the conversation ended. It was, indeed, not necessary that the point should be immediately decided; for several months were still to elapse before the Archbishopric would be vacant.

Tillotson bemoaned himself with unfeigned anxiety and sorrow to Lady Russell, whom, of all human beings, he most honored and trusted.* He hoped, he said, that he was not inclined to shrink from the service of the Church; but he was convinced that his present line of service was that in which he could be most useful. If he should be forced to accept so high and so invidious a post as the primacy, he should soon sink under the load of duties and anxieties too heavy for his strength. His spirits, and with his spirits his abilities, would fail him. He gently complained of Burnet, who loved and admired him with a truly generous heartiness, and who had labored to persuade both the King and Queen that there was in England only one man fit for the highest ecclesiastical dignity. "The Bishop of Salisbury," said Tillotson, "is one of the best and worst friends that I know."

Nothing that was not a secret to Burnet was likely to be long a secret to anybody. It soon began to be whispered about that the King had fixed on Tillotson to fill the place of Sancroft. The news caused cruel mortification to Compton, who, not unnaturally, conceived that his own claims were unrivalled. He had educated the Queen and her sister; and to the instruction which they had received from him might fairly be ascribed, at least in part, the firmness with which, in spite of the influence of their father, they had adhered to the established religion. Compton was, moreover, the only prelate who, during the late reign, had raised his voice in Parliament against the dispensing power, the only prelate who had been suspended by the High Commission, the only prelate who had signed the invitation to the Prince of Orange, the only prelate who had ac-

---

* The letter in which Tillotson informed Lady Russell of the King's intentions is printed in Birch's book: but the date is clearly erroneous. Indeed I feel assured that parts of two distinct letters have been by some blunder joined together. In one passage Tillotson informs his correspondent that Stillingfleet is made Bishop of Worcester, and in another that Walker is made Bishop of Derry. Now Stillingfleet was consecrated Bishop of Worcester on the 13th of October, 1689, and Walker was not made Bishop of Derry till June 1690.

tually taken arms against Popery and arbitrary power, the only prelate, save one, who had voted against a Regency. Among the ecclesiastics of the Province of Canterbury who had taken the oaths, he was highest in rank. He had therefore held, during some months, a vicarious primacy; he had crowned the new Sovereigns; he had consecrated the new Bishops: he was about to preside in the Convocation. It may be added, that he was the son of an Earl, and that no person of equally high birth then sate, or had ever sate, since the Reformation, on the episcopal bench. That the government should put over his head a priest of his own diocese, who was the son of a Yorkshire clothier, and who was distinguished only by abilities and virtues, was provoking; and Compton, though by no means a bad-hearted man, was much provoked. Perhaps his vexation was increased by the reflection that he had, for the sake of those by whom he was thus slighted, done some things which had strained his conscience and sullied his reputation, that he had at one time practised the disingenuous arts of a diplomatist, and at another time given scandal to his brethren by wearing the buffcoat and jackboots of a trooper. He could not accuse Tillotson of inordinate ambition. But, though Tillotson was most unwilling to accept the Archbishopric himself, he did not use his influence in favor of Compton, but earnestly recommended Stillingfleet as the man fittest to preside over the Church of England. The consequence was that, on the eve of the meeting of Convocation, the Bishop who was to be at the head of the Upper House became the personal enemy of the presbyter whom the government wished to see at the head of the Lower House. This quarrel added new difficulties to difficulties which little needed any addition.*

It was not till the twentieth of November that the Convocation met for the despatch of business. The place of meeting had, in former times, been Saint Paul's Cathedral. But Saint Paul's Cathedral was slowly rising from its ruins; and, though the dome already towered high above the hundred steeples of the City, the choir had not yet been opened for public worship. The assembly therefore sate at Westminster.† A table was placed in the beautiful chapel of Henry the Seventh. Compton was in the chair. On his right and left those suffragans of Canterbury who had taken the oaths were ranged

---

* Birch's Life of Tillotson. The account there given of the coldness between Compton and Tillotson was taken by Birch from the MSS. of Henry Wharton, and is confirmed by many circumstances which are known from other sources of intelligence.
† Chamberlayne's State of England, 18th edition.

in gorgeous vestments of scarlet and miniver. Below the table was assembled the crowd of presbyters. Beveridge preached a Latin sermon, in which he warmly eulogized the existing system, and yet declared himself favorable to a moderate reform. Ecclesiastical laws were, he said, of two kinds. Some laws were fundamental and eternal: they derived their authority from God; nor could any religious community abrogate them without ceasing to form a part of the universal Church. Other laws were local and temporary. They had been framed by human wisdom, and might be altered by human wisdom. They ought not indeed to be altered without grave reasons. But surely, at that moment, such reasons were not wanting. To unite a scattered flock in one fold under one shepherd, to remove stumbling blocks from the path of the weak, to reconcile hearts long estranged, to restore spiritual discipline to its primitive vigor, to place the best and purest of Christian societies on a base broad enough to stand against all the attacks of earth and hell, these were objects which might well justify some modification, not of Catholic institutions, but of national or provincial usages.*

The Lower House, having heard this discourse, proceeded to appoint a Prolocutor. Sharp, who was probably put forward by the members favorable to a comprehension as one of the highest churchmen among them, proposed Tillotson. Jane, who had refused to act under the Royal Commission, was proposed on the other side. After some animated discussion, Jane was elected by fifty-five votes to twenty-eight.†

The Prolocutor was formally presented to the Bishop of London, and made, according to ancient usage, a Latin oration. In this oration the Anglican Church was extolled as the most perfect of all institutions. There was a very intelligible intimation that no change whatever in her doctrine, her discipline, or her ritual was required: and the discourse concluded with a most significant sentence. Compton, when a few months before he exhibited himself in the somewhat unclerical character of a colonel of horse, had ordered the colors of his regiment to be embroidered with the well known words "Nolumus leges Angliæ mutari"; and with these words Jane closed his peroration.‡

Still, the Low Churchmen did not relinquish all hope. They very wisely determined to begin by proposing to substitute les-

---
* Concio ad Synodum per Gulielmum Beveregium, 1689.
† Luttrell's Diary; Historical Account of the Present Convocation.
‡ Kennet's History, iii. 552.

sons taken from the canonical books for the lessons taken from the Apocrypha. It should seem that this was a suggestion which, even if there had not been a single dissenter in the kingdom, might well have been received with favor. For the Church had, in her sixth Article, declared that the canonical books were, and that the Apocryphal books were not, entitled to be called Holy Scriptures, and to be regarded as the rule of faith. Even this reform, however, the High Churchmen were determined to oppose. They asked, in pamphlets which covered the counters of Paternoster Row and Little Britain, why country congregations should be deprived of the pleasure of hearing about the ball of pitch with which Daniel choked the dragon, and about the fish whose liver gave forth such a fume as sent the devil flying from Ecbatana to Egypt. And were there not chapters of the wisdom of the Son of Sirach far more interesting and edifying than the genealogies and muster rolls which made up a large part of the Chronicles of the Jewish Kings, and of the narrative of Nehemiah? No grave divine however would have liked to maintain, in Henry the Seventh's Chapel, that it was impossible to find, in many hundreds of pages dictated by the Holy Spirit, fifty or sixty chapters more edifying than anything which could be extracted from the works of the most respectable uninspired moralist or historian. The leaders of the majority therefore determined to shun a debate in which they must have been reduced to a disagreeable dilemma. Their plan was, not to reject the recommedations of the Commissioners, but to prevent those recommendations from being discussed; and with this view a system of tactics was adopted which proved successful.

The law, as it had been interpreted during a long course of years, prohibited the Convocation from even deliberating on any ecclesiastical ordinance without a previous warrant from the Crown. Such a warrant, sealed with the great seal, was brought in form to Henry the Seventh's Chapel by Nottingham. He at the same time delivered a message from the King. His Majesty exhorted the assembly to consider calmly and without prejudice the recommendations of the Commission, and declared that he had nothing in view but the honor and advantage of the Protestant religion in general, and of the Church of England in particular.*

The Bishops speedily agreed on an address of thanks for the royal message, and requested the concurrence of the Lower

---

* Historical Account of the Present Convocation, 1689.

House. Jane and his adherents raised objection after objection. First they claimed the privilege of presenting a separate address. When they were forced to waive this claim, they refused to agree to any expression which imported that the Church of England had any fellowship with any other Protestant community. Amendments and reasons were sent backward and forward. Conferences were held at which Burnet on one side and Jane on the other were the chief speakers. At last, with great difficulty, a compromise was made; and an address, cold and ungracious compared with that which the Bishops had framed, was presented to the King in the Banqueting House. He dissembled his vexation, returned a kind answer, and intimated a hope that the assembly would now at length proceed to consider the great question of Comprehension.*

Such however was not the intention of the leaders of the Lower House. As soon as they were again in Henry the Seventh's Chapel, one of them raised a debate about the nonjuring Bishops. In spite of the unfortunate scruple which those prelates entertained, they were learned and holy men. Their advice might, at this conjuncture, be of the greatest service to the Church. The Upper House was hardly an Upper House in the absence of the Primate and of many of his most respectable suffragans. Could nothing be done to remedy this evil? † Another member complained of some pamphlets which had lately appeared, and in which the Convocation was not treated with proper deference. The assembly took fire. Was it not monstrous that this heretical and schismatical trash should be cried by the hawkers about the streets, and should be exposed to sale in the booths of Westminster Hall, within a hundred yards of the Prolocutor's chair? The work of mutilating the Liturgy and of turning cathedrals into conventicles might surely be postponed till the Synod had taken measures to protect its own freedom and dignity. It was then debated how the printing of such scandalous books should be prevented. Some were for indictments, some for ecclesiastical censures.‡ In such deliberations as these week after week passed away. Not a single proposition tending to a Comprehension had been even discussed. Christmas was approaching. At Christmas there was to be a recess. The

* Historical Account of the Present Convocation; Burnet, ii. 58; Kennet's History of the Reign of William and Mary.
† Historical Account of the Present Convocation; Kennet's History.
‡ Historical Account of the Present Convocation; Kennet.

Bishops were desirous that, during the recess, a committee should sit to prepare business. The Lower House refused to consent.* That House, it was now evident, was fully determined not even to enter on the consideration of any part of the plan which had been framed by the Royal Commissioners. The proctors of the dioceses were in a worse humor than when they first came up to Westminster. Many of them had probably never before passed a week in the capital, and had not been aware how great the difference was betwen a town divine and a country divine. The sight of the luxuries and comforts enjoyed by the popular preachers of the city raised, not unnaturally, some sore feeling in a Lincolnshire or Caernarvonshire vicar who was accustomed to live as hardly as a small farmer. The very circumstance that the London clergy were generally for a comprehension made the representatives of the rural clergy obstinate on the other side.† The prelates were, as a body, sincerely desirous that some concession might be made to the nonconformists. But the prelates were utterly unable to curb the mutinous democracy. They were few in number. Some of them were objects of extreme dislike to the parochial clergy. The President had not the full authority of a primate; nor was he sorry to see those who had, as he conceived, used him ill, thwarted and mortified. It was necessary to yield. The Convocation was prorogued for six weeks. When those six weeks had expired, it was prorogued again; and many years elapsed before it was permitted to transact business.

So ended, and for ever, the hope that the Church of England might be induced to make some concession to the scruples of the nonconformists. A learned and respectable minority of the clerical order relinquished that hope with deep regret. Yet in a very short time even Burnet and Tillotson found reason to believe that their defeat was really an escape, and that victory would have been a disaster. A reform, such as, in the days of Elizabeth, would have united the great body of English Protestants, would, in the days of William, have alienated more hearts than it would have conciliated. The schism which the

---

* Historical Account of the Present Convocation.
† That there was such a jealousy as I have described is admitted in the pamphlet entitled Vox Cleri. "Some country ministers, now of the Convocation, do now see in what great ease and plenty the City ministers live, who have their readers and lecturers, and frequent supplies, and sometimes tarry in the vestry till prayers be ended, and have great dignities in the Church, beside their rich parishes in the City." The author of this tract, once widely celebrated, was Thomas Long, proctor for the clergy of the diocese of Exeter. In another pamphlet, published at this time, the rural clergymen are said to have seen with an evil eye their London brethren refreshing themselves with sack after preaching. Several satirical allusions to the fable of the Town Mouse and the Country Mouse will be found in the pamphlets of that winter.

oaths had produced was, as yet, insignificant. Innovations such as those proposed by the Royal Commissioners would have given it a terrible importance. As yet a layman, though he might think the proceedings of the Convention unjustifiable, and though he might applaud the virtue of the nonjuring clergy, still continued to sit under the accustomed pulpit, and to kneel at the accustomed altar. But if, just at this conjuncture, while his mind was irritated by what he thought the wrong done to his favorite divines, and while he was perhaps doubting whether he ought not to follow them, his ears and eyes had been shocked by changes in the worship to which he was fondly attached, if the compositions of the doctors of the Jerusalem Chamber had taken the place of the old collects, if he had seen clergymen without surplices carrying the chalice and the paten up and down the aisle to seated communicants, the tie which bound him to the Established Church would have been dissolved. He would have repaired to some nonjuring assembly, where the service which he loved was performed without mutilation. The new sect, which as yet consisted almost exclusively of priests, would soon have been swelled by numerous and large congregations: and in those congregations would have been found a much greater proportion of the opulent, of the highly descended, and of the highly educated, than any other body of dissenters could show. The episcopal schismatics, thus reinforced, would probably have been as formidable to the new King and his successors as ever the Puritan schismatics had been to the princes of the House of Stuart. It is an indisputable and a most instructive fact, that we are, in a great measure, indebted for the civil and religious liberty which we enjoy to the pertinacity with which the High Church party, in the Convocation of 1689, refused even to deliberate on any plan of Comprehension.*

---

* Burnet, ii. 33, 34. The best narratives of what passed in this Convocation are the Historical Account appended to the second edition of Vox Cleri ; and the passage in Kennet's History to which I have already referred the reader. The former narrative is by a very high churchman, the latter by a very low churchman. Those who are desirous of obtaining fuller information must consult the contemporary pamphlets. Among them are Vox Populi ; Vox Laici ; Vox Regis et Regni ; the Healing attempt ; the Letter to a Friend, by Dean Prideaux ; the Letter from a Minister in the Country to a Member of the Convocation ; the Answer to the Merry Answer to Vox Cleri ; the Remarks from the Country upon two Letters relating to the Convocation ; the Vindication of the Letters in answer to Vox Cleri ; the Answer to the Country Minister's Letter. All these tracts appeared late in 1689 or early in 1690.

CHAPTER XV.—(1689-1691).

WHILE the Convocation was wrangling on one side of Old Palace Yard, the Parliament was wrangling even more fiercely on the other. The Houses, which had separated on the twentieth of August, had met again on the nineteenth of October. On the day of meeting an important change struck every eye. Halifax was no longer on the woolsack. He had reason to expect that the persecution, from which he had narrowly escaped in the summer, would be renewed. The events which had taken place during the recess, and especially the disasters of the campaign in Ireland, had furnished his enemies with fresh means of annoyance. His administration had not been successful; and, though his failure was partly to be ascribed to causes against which no human wisdom could have contended, it was also partly to be ascribed to the peculiarities of his temper and his intellect. It was certain that a large party in the Commons would attempt to remove him; and he could no longer depend on the protection of his master. It was natural that a prince who was emphatically a man of action should become weary of a minister who was a man of speculation. Charles, who went to Council as he went to the play, solely to be amused, was delighted with an adviser who had a hundred pleasant and ingenious things to say on both sides of every question. But William had no taste for disquisitions and disputations, however lively and subtle, which occupied much time and led to no conclusion. It was reported, and is not improbable, that on one occasion he could not refrain from expressing in sharp terms at the council board his impatience at what seemed to him a morbid habit of indecision.* Halifax, mortified by his mischances in public life, dejected by domestic calamities, disturbed by apprehensions of an impeachment, and no longer supported by royal favor, became sick of public life, and began to pine for

---

* "Halifax a eu une réprimande sévère publiquement dans le conseil par le Prince d'Orange pour avoir trop balancé."—Avaux to De Croissy, Dublin, June 16-26, 1689. "His mercurial wit," says Burnet, ii. 4, "was not well suited with the King's phlegm."

the silence and solitude of his seat in Nottinghamshire, an old Cistersian Abbey buried deep among woods. Early in October it was known that he would no longer preside in the Upper House. It was at the same time whispered as a great secret that he meant to retire altogether from business, and that he retained the Privy seal only till a successor should be named. Chief Baron Atkyns was appointed Speaker of the Lords.*

On some important points there appeared to be no difference of opinion in the legislature. The Commons unanimously resolved that they would stand by the King in the work of reconquering Ireland, and that they would enable him to prosecute with vigor the war against France.† With equal unanimity they voted an extraordinary supply of two millions.‡ It was determined that the greater part of this sum should be levied by an assessment on real property. The rest was to be raised partly by a poll tax, and partly by new duties on tea, coffee, and chocolate. It was proposed that a hundred thousand pounds should be exacted from the Jews; and this proposition was at first favorably received by the house; but difficulties arose. The Jews presented a petition in which they declared that they could not afford to pay such a sum, and that they would rather leave the kingdom than stay there to be ruined. Enlightened politicians could not but perceive that special taxation, laid on a small class which happens to be rich, unpopular, and defenceless, is really confiscation, and must ultimately impoverish rather than enrich the State. After some discussion, the Jew tax was abandoned.§

The Bill of Rights, which, in the last Session, had, after causing much altercation between the Houses, been suffered to drop, was again introduced, and was speedily passed. The peers no longer insisted that any person should be designated by name as successor to the crown, if Mary, Anne, and William should all die without posterity. During eleven years nothing more was heard of the claims of the House of Brunswick.

The Bill of Rights contained some provisions which deserve special mention. The Convention had resolved that it was contrary to the interest of the kingdom to be governed by a Papist, but had prescribed no test which could ascertain

---

* Clarendon's Diary, Oct. 10, 1689; Lords' Journals, Oct. 19, 1689.
† Commons' Journals, Oct. 24, 1689.
‡ Commons' Journals, Nov. 2, 1689.
§ Commons' Journals, November 7, 19, Dec. 30, 1689. The rule of the House then was that no petition could be received against the imposition of a tax. This rule was, after a very hard fight, rescinded in 1842. The petition of the Jews was not received, and is not mentioned in the Journals. But something may be learned about it from Luttrell's Diary and from Grey's Debates, Nov. 19, 1689.

whether a prince was or was not a Papist. The defect was now supplied. It was enacted that every English Sovereign should, in full Parliament, and at the coronation, repeat and subscribe the Declaration against Transubstantiation.

It was also enacted that no person who should marry a Papist should be capable of reigning in England, and that, if the Sovereign should marry a Papist, the subject should be absolved from allegiance. Burnet boasts that this part of the Bill of Rights was his work. He had little reason to boast: for a more wretched specimen of legislative workmanship will not easily be found. In the first place, no test is prescribed. Whether the consort of a Sovereign has taken the oath of supremacy, has signed the declaration against transubstantiation, has communicated according to the ritual of the Church of England, are very simple issues of fact. But whether the consort of a Sovereign is or is not a Papist is a question about which people may argue for ever. What is a Papist? The word is not a word of definite signification either in law or in theology. It is merely a popular nickname, and means very different things in different mouths. Is every person a Papist who is willing to concede to the Bishop of Rome a primacy among Christian prelates? If so, James the First, Charles the First, Laud, Heylyn, were Papists.* Or is the appellation to be confined to persons who hold the ultramontane doctrines touching the authority of the Holy See? If so, neither Bossuet nor Pascal was a Papist.

What again is the legal effect of the words which absolve the subject from his allegiance? Is it meant that a person arraigned for high treason may tender evidence to prove that the Sovereign has married a Papist? Would Thistlewood, for example, have been entitled to an acquittal, if he could have proved that King George the Fourth had married Mrs. Fitzherbert, and that Mrs. Fitzherbert was a Papist? It is not easy to believe than any tribunal would have gone into such a question. Yet to what purpose is it to enact that, in a certain case, the subject shall be absolved from his allegiance, if the

---

* James, in the very treatise in which he tried to prove the Pope to be Anti-Christ, says: "For myself, if that were yet the question, I would with all my heart give my consent that the Bishop of Rome should have the first seat.' There is a remarkable letter on this subject written by James to Charles and Buckingham, when they were in Spain. Heylyn, speaking of Laud's negotiation with Rome, says: "So that upon the point the Pope was to content himself among us in England with a priority instead of a superiority over other Bishops, and with a primacy instead of a supremacy in these parts of Christendom, which I conceive no man of learning and sobriety would have grudged to grant him."

tribunal before which he is tried for a violation of his allegiance is not to go into the question whether that case has arisen?

The question of the dispensing power was treated in a very different manner, was fully considered, and was finally settled in the only way in which it could be settled. The Declaration of Right had gone no farther than to pronounce that the dispensing power, as of late exercised, was illegal. That a certain dispensing power belonged to the Crown was a proposition sanctioned by authorities and precedents of which even Whig lawyers could not speak without respect: but as to the precise extent of this power hardly any two jurists were agreed; and every attempt to frame a definition had failed. At length by the Bill of Rights the anomalous prerogative which had caused so many fierce disputes was absolutely and forever taken away.*

In the House of Commons there was, as might have been expected, a series of sharp debates on the misfortunes of the autumn. The negligence or corruption of the Navy Board, the frauds of the contractors, the rapacity of the captains of the King's ship, the losses of the London merchants, were themes for many keen speeches. There was indeed reason for anger. A severe inquiry, conducted by William in person at the Treasury, had just elicited the fact that much of the salt with which the meat furnished to the fleet had been cured had been by accident mixed with galls such as are used for the purpose of making ink. The victuallers threw the blame on the rats, and maintained that the provisions thus seasoned, though certainly disagreeable to the palate, were not injurious to health.† The Commons were in no temper to listen to such excuses. Several persons who had been concerned in cheating the government and poisoning the seamen were taken into custody by the Sergeant.‡ But no censure was passed on the chief offender, Torrington; nor does it appear that a single voice was raised against him. He had personal friends in both parties He had many popular qualities. Even his vices were not those which excite public hatred. The people readily forgave a courageous open-handed sailor for being too fond of his bottle, his boon companions, and his mistresses, and did not sufficiently consider how great must be the perils of a country of which the safety depends on a man sunk in indolence, stupefied by wine, enervated by licentiousness, ruined by prodigality, and enslaved by sycophants and harlots.

---

* Stat. 1 W & M. sess. 2, c. 2.
† Treasury Minute Book, Nov. 3, 1689.
‡ Commons' Journals and Grey's Debates, Nov. 12, 14, 18, 19, 23, 28, 1689.

The sufferings of the army in Ireland called forth strong expressions of sympathy and indignation. The Commons did justice to the firmness and wisdom with which Schomberg had conducted the most arduous of all campaigns. That he had not achieved more was attributed chiefly to the villainy of the Commissariat. The pestilence itself, it was said, would have been no serious calamity if it had not been aggravated by the wickedness of man. The disease had generally spared those who had warm garments and bedding, and had swept away by thousands those who were thinly clad and who slept on the wet ground. Immense sums had been drawn out of the Treasury; yet the pay of the troops was in arrear. Hundreds of horses, tens of thousands of shoes, had been paid for by the public: yet the baggage was left behind for want of beasts to draw it: and the soldiers were marching barefoot through the mire. Seventeen hundred pounds had been charged to the government for medicines; yet the common drugs with which every apothecary in the smallest market town was provided, were not to be found in the plague-stricken camp. The cry against Shales was loud. An address was carried to the throne, requesting that he might be sent for to England, and that his accounts and papers might be secured. With this request the King readily complied: but the Whig majority was not satisfied. By whom had Shales been recommended for so important a place as that of Commissary General? He had been a favorite at Whitehall in the worst times. He had been zealous for the Declaration of Indulgence. Why had this creature of James been entrusted with the business of catering for the army of William? It was proposed by some of those who were bent on driving all Tories and Trimmers from office to ask His Majesty by whose advice a man so undeserving of the royal confidence had been employed. The most moderate and judicious Whigs pointed out the indecency and impolicy of interrogating the King, and of forcing him either to accuse his ministers or to quarrel with the representatives of his people. "Advise His Majesty, if you will," said Somers, "to withdraw his confidence from the counsellors who recommended this unfortunate appointment. Such advice, given, as we should probably give it, unanimously, must have great weight with him. But do not put to him a question such as no private gentleman would willingly answer. Do not force him, in defence of his own personal dignity, to protect the very men whom you wish him to discard." After a hard fight of two days, and several divisions, the address was carried by a hundred and ninety five votes to a hundred and forty-six.* The King, as might have been foreseen, coldly refused to turn informer; and the House did not press him further.† To another address which requested that a Commission might he sent to examine into the state of things in Ireland, William returned a very gracious answer, and desired the Commons to name the Commissioners. The Commons, not to be outdone in courtesy, excused themselves, and left it to His Majesty's wisdom to select the fittest persons.‡

In the midst of the angry debates on the Irish war a pleasing incident produced for a moment good humor and unanimity. Walker had arrived in London, and had been received there with boundless enthusiasm. His face was in every print shop. Newsletters describing his person and his demeanor were sent to every corner of the kingdom. Broadsides of prose and verse written in his praise were cried in every street. The Companies of London feasted him splendidly in their halls. The common people crowded to gaze on him wherever he moved, and almost stifled him with rough caresses. Both the Universities offered him the degree of Doctor of Divinity. Some of his admirers advised him to present himself at the palace in that military garb in which he had repeatedly headed the sallies of his fellow-townsmen. But, with a better judgment than he sometimes showed, he made his appearance at Hampton Court in the peaceful robe of his profesion, was most graciously received, and was presented with an order for five thousand pounds. "And do not think, Doctor," William said, with great benignity, "that I offer you this sum as payment for your services. I assure you that I consider your claims on me as not at all diminished."§

It is true that amidst the general applause the voice of detraction made itself heard. The defenders of Londonderry were men of two nations and of two religions. During the siege, hatred of the Irishry had held together all Saxons; and hatred of Popery had held together all Protestants. But, when the danger was over, the Englishman and the Scotchman, the Episcopalian and the Presbyterian, began to wrangle about the distribution of praises and awards. The dissenting

---

* Commons' Journals and Grey's Debates, Nov. 26, and 27, 1689.
† Commons' Journals, November 28, December 2, 1689.
‡ Commons' Journals, and Grey's Debates, November 30, December 2, 1689.
§ London Gazette, September 2, 1689; Observations upon Mr. Walker's Account of the Siege of Londonderry, licensed October 4, 1689; Luttrell's Diary; Mr. J. Mackenzie's Narrative a False Libel, a Defence of Mr. G. Walker written by his Friend in his Absence, 1690.

preachers, who had zealously assisted Walker in the hour of peril, complained that, in the account which he had published of the siege, he had, though acknowledging that they had done good service, omitted to mention their names. The complaint was just, and, had it been made in a manner becoming Christians and gentlemen, would probably have produced a considerable effect on the public mind. But Walker's accusers in their resentment disregarded truth and decency, used scurrilous language, brought calumnious accusations which were triumphantly refuted, and thus threw away the advantage which they had possessed. Walker defended himself with moderation and candor. His friends fought his battle with vigor, and retaliated keenly on his assailants. At Edinburgh perhaps the public opinion might have been against him. But in London the controversy seems only to have raised his character. He was regarded as an Anglican divine of eminent merit, who, after having heroically defended his religion against an army of Irish Rapparees, was rabbled by a mob of Scotch Covenanters.*

He presented to the Commons a petition setting forth the destitute condition to which the widows and orphans of some brave men who had fallen during the siege were now reduced. The Commons instantly passed a vote of thanks to him, and resolved to present to the King an address requesting that ten thousands pounds might be distributed among the families whose sufferings had been so touchingly described. The next day it was rumored about the benches that Walker was in the lobby. He was called in. The Speaker, with great dignity and grace, informed him that the House had made haste to comply with his request, commended him in high terms for having taken on himself to govern and defend a city betrayed by its proper governors and defenders, and charged him to tell those who had fought under him that their fidelity and valor would always be held in grateful remembrance by the Commons of England.†

About the same time the course of parliamentary business was diversified by another curious and interesting episode,

---

* Walker's True Account, 1689; An Apology for the Failures charged on the True Account, 1689; Reflections on the Apology, 1689; A Vindication of the True Account by Walker, 1689; Mackenzie's Narrative, 1690; Mr. Mackenzie's Narrative a False Libel, 1690; Dr. Walker's Invisible Champion foyled by Mackenzie, 1690; Welwood's Mercurius Reformatus, Dec. 4, and 11, 1689. The Oxford editor of Burnet's History expresses his surprise at the silence which the Bishop observes about Walker. In the Burnet MS. Harl. 6584, there is an animated panegyric on Walker. Why that panegyric does not appear in the History I am at a loss to explain.

† Commons' Journals, November 18 and 19, 1689; and Grey's Debates.

which, like the former, sprang out of the events of the Irish war. In the preceding spring, when every messenger from Ireland brought evil tidings, and when the authority of James was acknowledged in every part of that kingdom, except behind the ramparts of Londonderry and on the banks of Lough Erne, it was natural that Englishmen should remember with how terrible an energy the great Puritan warriors of the preceding generation had crushed the insurrection of the Celtic race. The names of Cromwell, of Ireton, and of the other chiefs of the conquering army, were in many mouths. One of those chiefs, Edmund Ludlow, was still living At twenty-two he had served as a volunteer in the parliamentary army: at thirty he had risen to the rank of Lieutenant-General. He was now old : but the vigor of his mind was unimpaired. His courage was of the truest temper; his understanding strong, but narrow. What he saw he saw clearly: but he saw not much at a glance. In an age of perfidy and levity, he had, amidst manifold temptations and dangers, adhered firmly to the principles of his youth. His enemies could not deny that his life had been consistent, and that with the same spirit with which he had stood up against the Stuarts he had stood up against the Cromwells. There was but a single blemish on his fame. but that blemish, in the opinion of the great majority of his countrymen, was one for which no merit could compensate and which no time could efface. His name and seal were on the death warrant of Charles the First.

After the Restoration, Ludlow found a refuge on the shores of the Lake of Geneva. He was accompanied thither by another member of the High Court of Justice, John Lisle, the husband of that Alice Lisle whose death has left a lasting stain on the memory of James the Second. But even in Switzerland the regicides were not safe. A large price was set on their heads; and a succession of Irish adventurers, inflamed by national and religious animosity, attempted to earn the bribe. Lisle fell by the hand of one of these assassins. But Ludlow escaped unhurt from all the machinations of his enemies. A small knot of vehement and determined Whigs regarded him with a veneration, which increased as years rolled away, and left him almost the only survivor, certainly the most illustrious survivor, of a mighty race of men, the conquerors in a terrible civil war, the judges of a king, the founders of a republic. More than once he had been invited by the enemies of the House of Stuart to leave his asylum, to become their captain, and to give the signal for rebellion; but he had wisely refused to take any part in the desperate enterprises which the Wildmans and Fergusons were never weary of planning.*

The Revolution opened a new prospect to him. The right of the people to resist oppression, a right which, during many years, no man could assert without exposing himself to ecclesiastical anathemas and to civil penalties, had been solemnly recognized by the Estates of the realm, and had been proclaimed by Garter King at Arms on the very spot where the memorable scaffold had been set up forty years before. James had not, indeed, like Charles, died the death of a traitor. Yet the punishment of the son might seem to differ from the punishment of the father rather in degree than in principle. Those who had recently waged war on a tyrant, who had turned him out of his palace, who had frightened him out of his country, who had deprived him of his crown, might perhaps think that the crime of going one step further had been sufficiently expiated by thirty years of banishment. Ludlow's admirers, some of whom appear to have been in high public situations, assured him that he might safely venture over, nay, that he might expect to be sent in high command to Ireland, where his name was still cherished by his old soldiers and by their children. †
He came: and early in September it was known that he was in London.‡ But it soon appeared that he and his friends had misunderstood the temper of the English people. By all, except a small extreme section of the Whig party, the act, in which he had borne a part never to be forgotten, was regarded not merely with the disapprobation due to a great violation of law and justice, but with horror such as even the Gunpowder Plot had not excited. The absurd and almost impious service which is still read in our churches on the thirtieth of January had produced in the minds of the vulgar a strange association of ideas. The sufferings of Charles were confounded with the sufferings of the Redeemer of mankind; and every regicide was a Judas, a Caiaphas, or a Herod. It was true that, when Ludlow sate on the tribunal in Westminster Hall, he was an ardent enthusiast of twenty-eight, and that he now returned from exile a gray-headed and wrinkled man in his seventieth year. Perhaps, therefore, if he had been content to live in close retirement, and to shun places of public resort, even

* Wade's Confession, Harl. MS. 6845.
† See the Preface to the First Edition of his Memoirs, Vevay, 1698.
‡ "Colonel Ludlow, an old Oliverian, and one of King Charles the First his Judges,

zealous Royalists might not have grudged the Old Republican a grave in his native soil. But he had no thought of hiding himself. It was soon rumored that one of those murderers, who had brought on England guilt, for which she annually, in sackcloth and ashes, implored God not to enter into judgment with her, was strutting about the streets of her capital and boasting that he should ere long command her armies. His lodgings, it was said, were the headquarters of the most noted enemies of monarchy and episcopacy.* The subject was brought before the House of Commons. The Tory members called loudly for justice on the traitor. None of the Whigs ventured to say a word in his defence. One or two faintly expressed a doubt whether the fact of his return had been proved by evidence such as would warrant a parliamentary proceeding. This objection was disregarded. It was resolved, without a division, that the King should be requested to issue a proclamation for the apprehending of Ludlow. Seymour presented the address; and the King promised to do what was asked. Some days however elapsed before the proclamation appeared.† Ludlow had time to make his escape, and hid himself in his Alpine retreat, never again to emerge. English travellers are still taken to see his house close to the lake, and his tomb in a church among the vineyards which overlook the little town of Vevay. On the house was formerly legible an inscription purporting that to him to whom God is a father every land is a fatherland;‡ and the epitaph on the tomb still attests the feelings with which the stern old Puritan to the last regarded the people of Ireland and the House of Stuart.

Tories and Whigs had concurred, or had affected to concur, in paying honor to Walker and in putting a brand on Ludlow. But the feud between the two parties was more bitter than ever. The King had entertained a hope that, during the recess, the animosities which had in the preceding session prevented an Act of Indemnity from passing would have been mitigated. On the day on which the Houses reassembled, he had pressed them earnestly to put an end to the fear and discord which could never cease to exist, while great numbers held their property and their liberty, and not a few even their lives, by an uncertain tenure. His exhorta-

---

* Third Caveat against the Whigs, 1712.
† Commons' Journals, November 6 and 8, 1689; Grey's Debates; London Gazette, November 18.
‡ "Omne solum forti patria, quia patris." See Addison's Travels. It is a remarkable circumstance that Addison, though a Whig, speaks of Ludlow in language which would better have become a Tory, and sneers at the inscription as cant.

tion proved of no effect. October, November, December passed away; and nothing was done. An Indemnity Bill indeed had been brought in, and read once : but it had ever since lain neglected on the table of the House.* Vindictive as had been the mood in which the Whigs had left Westminster, the mood in which they returned was more vindictive still. Smarting from old sufferings, drunk with recent prosperity, burning with implacable resentment, confident of irresistible strength, they were not less rash and headstrong than in the days of the Exclusion Bill. Sixteen hundred and eighty was come again. Again all compromise was rejected. Again the voices of the wisest and most upright friends of liberty were drowned by the clamor of hotheaded and designing agitators. Again moderation was despised as cowardice, or execrated as treachery. All the lessons taught by a cruel experience were forgotten. The very same men who had expiated, by years of humiliation, of imprisonment, of penury, of exile, the folly with which they had misused the advantage given them by the Popish plot, now misused with equal folly the advantage given them by the Revolution. The second madness would in all probability, like the first, have ended in their proscription, dispersion, decimation, but for the magnanimity and wisdom of that great prince, who, bent on fulfilling his mission, and insensible alike to flattery and to outrage, coldly and inflexibly saved them in their own despite.

It seemed that nothing but blood would satisfy them. The aspect and the temper of the House of Commons reminded men of the time of the ascendency of Oates ; and that nothing might be wanting to the resemblance, Oates himself was there. As a witness, indeed, he could now render no service : but he had caught the scent of carnage, and came to gloat on the butchery in which he could no longer take an active part. His loathsome features were again daily seen, and his well known "Ah Laard, ah Laard!" was again daily heard in the lobbies and in the gallery.† The House fell first on the renegades of the late reign. Of those renegades the Earls of Peterborough and Salisbury were the highest in rank, but were also the lowest in intellect: for Salisbury had always been an idiot; and Peterborough had long been a dotard. It was however resolved by the Commons that both had, by joining the Church of Rome, committed high treason, and

* Commons' Journals, Nov. 1, 7, 1689.
† Roger North's Life of Dudley North.

that both should be impeached.* A message to that effect was sent to the Lords. Poor old Peterborough was instantly taken into custody and was sent tottering on a crutch, and wrapped up in woollen stuffs, to the Tower. The next day Salisbury was brought to the bar of his peers. He muttered something about his youth and his foreign education, and was then sent to bear Peterborough company.† The Commons had meanwhile passed on to offenders of humbler station and better understanding. Sir Edward Hales was brought before them. He had doubtless, by holding office in defiance of the Test Act, incurred heavy penalties. But these penalties fell far short of what the revengeful spirit of the victorious party demanded; and he was committed as a traitor.‡ Then Obadiah Walker was led in. He behaved with a pusillanimity and disingenuousness, which deprived him of all claim to respect or pity. He protested that he had never changed his religion, that his opinions had always been and still were those of some highly respectable divines of the Church of England, and that there were points on which he differed from the Papists. In spite of this quibbling, he was pronounced guilty of high treason, and sent to prison. § Then Castlemaine was put to the bar, interrogated, and committed under a warrant which charged him with the capital crime of trying to reconcile the kingdom to the Church of Rome.‖

In the meantime the Lords had appointed a Committee to inquire who were answerable for the deaths of Russell, of Sidney, and of some other eminent Whigs. Of this committee, which was popularly called the Murder Committee, the Earl of Stamford, a Whig who had been deeply concerned in the plots formed by his party against the Stuarts, was chairman.¶ The books of the Council were inspected: the clerks of the Council were examined: some facts disgraceful to the Judges, to the Solicitors of the Treasury, to the witnesses for the Crown, and to the keepers of the state prisons, were elicited: but about the packing of the juries no evidence could be obtained. The Sheriffs kept their own counsel. Sir Dudley North, in particular, underwent a most severe cross-examina-

---

* Commons' Journals, Oct. 26, 1689.
† Lords' Journals, October 26 and 27, 1689.
‡ Commons' Journals, Oct. 26, 1689.
§ Commons' Journals, Oct. 26 1689; Wood's Athenæ Oxonienses; Dod's Church History, VIII. ii. 3.
‖ Commons' Journals, October 28, 1689. The proceedings will be found in the collection of State Trials.
¶ Lords' Journals, Nov. 2 and 6, 1689.

tion with characteristic clearness of head and firmness of temper, and steadily asserted that he had never troubled himself about the political opinions of the persons whom he put on any panel, but had merely inquired whether they were substantial citizens. He was undoubtedly lying; and so some of the Whig peers told him in very plain words and in very loud tones: but, though they were morally certain of his guilt, they could find no proofs which would support a criminal charge against him. The indelible stain, however, remains on his memory, and is still a subject of lamentation to those who, while loathing his dishonesty and cruelty, cannot forget that he was one of the most original, profound, and accurate thinkers of his age.*

Halifax, more fortunate than Dudley North, was completely cleared, not only from legal, but also from moral guilt. He was the chief object of attack; and yet a severe examination brought nothing to light that was not to his honor. Tillotson was called as a witness. He swore that he had been the channel of communication between Halifax and Russell when Russell was a prisoner in the Tower. "My Lord Halifax," said the Doctor, "showed a very compassionate concern for my Lord Russell: and my Lord Russell charged me with his last thanks for my Lord Halifax's humanity and kindness." It was proved that the unfortunate Duke of Monmouth had borne similar testimony to Halifax's good nature. One hostile witness indeed was produced, John Hampden, whose mean supplications and enormous bribes had saved his neck from the halter. He was now a powerful and prosperous man: he was a leader of the dominant party in the House of Commons; and yet he was one of the most unhappy beings on the face of the earth. The recollection of the pitiable figure which he had made at the bar of the Old Bailey embittered his temper and impelled him to avenge himself without mercy on those who had directly or indirectly contributed to his humiliation. Of all the Whigs he was the most intolerant and the most obstinately hostile to all plans of amnesty. The consciousness that he had disgraced himself made him jealous of his dignity and quick to take offence. He constantly paraded his services and his sufferings, as if he hoped that this ostentatious display would hide from others the stain which nothing could hide from himself. Having during many months harangued vehemently against Halifax in the House of Commons, he now came to swear against Halifax

---

* Lords' Journals, Dec. 20, 1689; Life of Dudley North.

before the Lords. The scene was curious. The witness represented himself as having saved his country, as having planned the Revolution, as having placed Their Majesties on the throne. He then gave evidence intended to show that his life had been endangered by the machinations of the Lord Privy Seal: but that evidence missed the mark at which it was aimed, and recoiled on him from whom it proceeded. Hampden was forced to acknowledge that he had sent his wife to implore the intercession of the man whom he was now persecuting. "Is it not strange," asked Halifax, "that you should have requested the good offices of one whose arts had brought your head into peril?" "Not at all," said Hampden: "to whom was I to apply except to the men who were in power? I applied to Lord Jeffreys: I applied to Father Petre; and I paid them six thousand pounds for their services." "But did Lord Halifax take any money?" "No: I cannot say that he did." "And, Mr. Hampden, did not you afterwards send your wife to thank him for his kindness?" "Yes: I believe I did," answered Hampden; "but I know of no solid effects of that kindness. If there were any, I should be obliged to my Lord to tell me what they were." Disgraceful as had been the appearance which this degenerate heir of an illustrious name had made at the Old Bailey, the appearance which he made before the Committee of Murder was more disgraceful still.* It is pleasing to know that a person who had been far more cruelly wronged than he, but whose nature differed widely from his, the nobleminded Lady Russell, remonstrated against the injustice with which the extreme Whigs treated Halifax.†

The malice of John Hampden, however, was unwearied and unabashed. A few days later, in a committee of the whole House of Commons, on the state of the nation, he made a bitter speech, in which he ascribed all the disasters of the year to the influence of the men who had, in the day of the Exclusion Bill, been censured by Parliaments, of the men who had attempted to mediate between James and William. The King, he said, ought to dismiss from his counsels and presence all the three noblemen who had been sent to negotiate with him at Hungerford. He went on to speak of the danger of employing men of republican principles. He doubtless alluded to the chief object of his implacable malignity, For Halifax, though

---

* The report is in the Lords' Journals, Dec. 20, 1689. Hampden's examination was on the 18th of November.

† This, I think, is clear, from a letter of Lady Montague to Lady Russell, dated Dec. 23. 1680. three days after the Committee of Murder had reported.

from temper averse to violent changes, was well known to be in speculation a republican, and often talked, with much ingenuity and pleasantry, against hereditary monarchy. The only effect, however, of the reflection now thrown on him was to call forth a roar of derision. That a Hampden, that the grandson of the great leader of the Long Parliament, that a man who boasted of having conspired with Algernon Sidney against the royal House, should use the word republican as a term of reproach! When the storm of laughter had subsided, several members stood up to vindicate the accused statesman. Seymour declared that, much as he disapproved of the manner in which the administration had lately been conducted, he could not concur in the vote which John Hampden had proposed. "Look where you will," he said, "to Ireland, to Scotland, to the navy, to the army, you will find abundant proofs of mismanagement. If the war is still to be conducted by the same hands we can expect nothing but a recurrence of the same disasters. But I am not prepared to proscribe men for the best thing that they ever did in their lives, to proscribe men for attempting to avert a revolution by timely mediation." It was justly said by another speaker that Halifax and Nottingham had been sent to the Dutch camp because they possessed the confidence of the nation, because they were universally known to be hostile to the dispensing power, to the Popish religion, and to the French ascendency. It was at length resolved that the King should be requested in general terms to find out and remove the authors of the late miscarriages.* A committee was appointed to prepare an address. John Hampden was chairman, and drew up a representation in terms so bitter that, when it was reported to the House, his own father expressed disapprobation, and one member exclaimed: "This an address! It is a libel." After a sharp debate, the Address was recommitted, and was not again mentioned.†

Indeed, the animosity which a large part of the House had felt against Halifax was beginning to abate. It was known that, though he had not yet formally delivered up the Privy Seal, he had ceased to be a confidential adviser of the Crown. The power which he had enjoyed during the first months of the reign of William and Mary had passed to the more daring, more unscrupulous, and more practical Caermarthen, against whose influence Shrewsbury contended in vain. Personally Shrews-

---

* Commons' Journals, Dec. 14, 1689; Grey's Debates; Boyer's Life of William.
† Commons' Journals, Dec. 21; Grey's Debates; Oldmixon.

bury stood high in the royal favor : but he was a leader of the Whigs, and, like all leaders of parties, was frequently pushed forward against his will by those who seemed to follow him. He was himself inclined to a mild and moderate policy : but he had not sufficient firmness to withstand the clamorous importunity with which such politicians as John Howe and John Hampden demanded vengeance on their enemies. His advice had therefore, at this time, little weight with his master, who neither loved the Tories nor trusted them, but who was fully determined not to proscribe them.

Meanwhile the Whigs, conscious that they had lately sunk in the opinion both of the King and of the nation, resolved on making a bold and crafty attempt to become independent of both. A perfect account of that attempt cannot be constructed out of the scanty and widely dispersed materials which have come down to us. Yet the story, as it may still be put together, is both interesting and instructive.

A bill for restoring the rights of those corporations which had surrendered their charters to the Crown during the last two reigns had been brought into the House of Commons, had been received with general applause by men of all parties, had been read twice, and had been referred to a select committee, of which Somers was chairman. On the second of January Somers brought up the report. The attendance of Tories was scanty; for, as no important discussion was expected, many country gentlemen had left town, and were keeping a merry Christmas by the blazing chimneys of their manor house. The muster of zealous Whigs was strong. As soon as the bill had been reported, Sacheverell, renowned in the stormy Parliaments of the reign of Charles the Second as one of the ablest and keenest of the Exclusionists, stood up and moved to add a clause providing that every municipal functionary who had in any manner been a party to the surrendering of the franchises of a borough should be incapable for seven years of holding any office in that borough. The constitution of almost every corporate town in England had been remodelled during that hot fit of loyalty which followed the detection of the Rye House Plot; and, in almost every corporate town, the voice of the Tories had been for delivering up the charter, and for trusting everything to the paternal care of the Sovereign. The effect of Sacheverell's clause, therefore, was to make some thousands of the most opulent and highly considered men in the kingdom incapable, during seven years, of bearing any part in the government of the places in which they resided, and to secure to the

Whig party, during seven years, an overwhelming influence in borough elections.

The minority exclaimed against the gross injustice of passing rapidly, and by surprise, at a season when London was empty, a law of the highest importance, a law which retrospectively inflicted a severe penalty on many hundreds of respectable gentlemen, a law which would call forth the strongest passions in every town from Berwick to Saint Ives, a law which must have a serious effect on the composition of the House itself. Common decency required at least an adjournment. An adjournment was moved: but the motion was rejected by a hundred and twenty-seven votes to eighty-nine. The question was then put that Sacheverell's clause should stand part of the bill, and was carried by a hundred and thirty-three to sixty-eight. Sir Robert Howard immediately moved that every person who, being under Sacheverell's clause disqualified for municipal office, should presume to take any such office, should forfeit five hundred pounds, and should be for life incapable of holding any public employment whatever. The Tories did not venture to divide.* The rules of the House put it in the power of a minority to obstruct the progress of a bill; and this was assuredly one of the very rare occasions on which that power would have been with great propriety exerted. It does not appear however that the parliamentary tacticians of the seventeenth century were aware of the extent to which a small number of members can, without violating any form, retard the course of business.

It was immediately resolved that the bill, enlarged by Sacheverell's and Howard's clauses, should be engrossed. The most vehement Whigs were bent on finally passing it within forty-eight hours. The Lords, indeed, were not likely to regard it very favorably. But it should seem that some desperate men were prepared to withhold the supplies till it should pass, nay, even to tack it to the bill of supply, and thus to place the Upper House under the necessity of either consenting to a vast proscription of the Tories or refusing to the government the means of carrying on the war.† There were Whigs, however, honest enough to wish that fair play should be given to the hostile party, and prudent enough to know that an advantage obtained

---

* Commons' Journals, Jan. 2, 1689-90.

† Thus, I think, must be understood some remarkable words in a letter written by William to Portland, on the day after Sacheverell's bold and unexpected move. William calculates the amount of the supplies and then says: "S'ils n'y mettent des conditions que vous savez, c'est une bonne affaire: mais les Wigges sont si glorieux d'avoir vaincu qu'ils entreprendront tout."

by violence and cunning could not be permanent. These men insisted that at least a week should be suffered to elapse before the third reading, and carried their point. Their less scrupulous associates complained bitterly that the good cause was betrayed. What new laws of war were these? Why was chivalrous courtesy to be shown to foes who thought no stratagem immoral, and who had never given quarter? And what had been done that was not in strict accordance with the law of Parliament? That law knew nothing of short notices and long notices, of thin houses and full houses. It was the business of a representative of the people to be in his place. If he chose to shoot and guzzle at his country seat when important business was under consideration at Westminster, what right had he to murmur because more upright and laborious servants of the public passed, in his absence, a bill which appeared to them necessary to the public safety? As however a postponement of a few days appeared to be inevitable, those who had intended to gain the victory by stealing a march now disclamed that intention. They solemnly assured the King, who could not help showing some displeasure at their conduct, and who felt much more displeasure than he showed, that they had owed nothing to surprise, and that they were quite certain of a majority in the fullest house. Sacheverell is said to have declared with great warmth that he would stake his seat on the issue, and that if he found himself mistaken he would never show his face in Parliament again. Indeed, the general opinion at first was that the Whigs would win the day. But it soon became clear that the fight would be a hard one. The mails had carried out along all the high roads the tidings that, on the second of January, the Commons had agreed to a retrospective penal law against the whole Tory party, and that, on the tenth, that law would be considered for the last time. The whole kingdom was moved from Northumberland to Cornwall. A hundred knights and squires left their halls hung with mistletoe and holly, and their boards groaning with brawn and plum porridge, and rode up post to town, cursing the short days, the cold weather, the miry roads, and the villainous Whigs. The Whigs, too, brought up reinforcements, but not to the same extent; for the clauses were generally unpopular, and not without good cause. Assuredly no reasonable man of any party will deny that the Tories, in surrendering to the Crown all the municipal franchises of the realm, and, with those franchises, the power of altering the constitution of the House of Commons, committed a great fault. But in that fault the nation itself had been an accomplice. If the Mayors and Aldermen whom it was now proposed to punish had, when the tide of loyal enthusiasm ran high, sturdily refused to comply with the wish of their Sovereign, they would have been pointed at in the street as Roundhead knaves, preached at by the Rector, lampooned in ballads, and probably burned in effigy before their own doors. That a community should be hurried into errors alternately by fear of tyranny and by fear of anarchy is doubtless a great evil. But the remedy for that evil is not to punish for such errors some persons who have merely erred with the rest, and who have since repented with the rest. Nor ought it to have been forgotten that the offenders against whom Sacheverell's clause was directed had, in 1688, made large atonement for the misconduct of which they had been guilty in 1683. They had, as a class, stood up firmly against the dispensing power; and most of them had actually been turned out of their municipal offices by James for refusing to support his policy. It is not strange, therefore, that the attempt to inflict on all these men without exception a degrading punishment should have raised such a storm of public indignation as many Whig members of parliament were unwilling to face.

As the decisive conflict drew near, and as the muster of the Tories became hourly stronger and stronger, the uneasiness of Sacheverell and of his confederates increased. They found that they could hardly hope for a complete victory. They must propose to recommit the bill. They must declare themselves willing to consider whether any distinction could be made between the chief offenders and the multitudes who had been misled by evil example. But as the spirit of one party fell the spirit of the other rose. The Tories, glowing with resentment which was but too just, were resolved to listen to no terms of compromise.

The tenth of January came; and, before the late daybreak of that season, the House was crowded. More than a hundred and sixty members had come up to town within a week. From dawn till the candles had burned down to their sockets the ranks kept unbroken order; and few members left their seats except for a minute to take a crust of bread or a glass of claret. Messengers were in waiting to carry the result to Kensington, where William, though shaken by a violent cough, sate up till midnight, anxiously expecting the news, and writing to Portland, whom he had sent on an important mission to the Hague.

The only remaining account of the debate is defective and confused: but from that account it appears that the excitement was great. Sharp things were said. One young Whig member used language so hot that he was in danger of being called to the bar. Some reflections were thrown on the Speaker for allowing too much license to his own friends. But in truth it mattered little whether he called transgressors to order or not. The House had long been quite unmanageable: and veteran members bitterly regretted the old gravity of debate and the old authority of the chair.* That Somers disapproved of the violence of the party to which he belonged may be inferred, both from the whole course of his public life, and from the very significant fact that, though he had charge of the Corporation Bill, he did not move the penal clauses, but left that ungracious office to men more impetuous and less sagacious than himself. He did not however abandon his allies in this emergency, but spoke for them, and tried to make the best of a very bad case. The House divided several times. On the first division a hundred and seventy-four voted with Sacheverell, a hundred and seventy-nine against him. Still the battle was stubbornly kept up; but the majority increased from five to ten, from ten to twelve, and from twelve to eighteen. Then at length, after a stormy sitting of fourteen hours, the Whigs yielded. It was near midnight when, to the unspeakable joy and triumph of the Tories the clerk tore away from the parchment on which the bill had been engrossed the odious clauses of Sacheverell and Howard.†

Emboldened by this great victory, the Tories made an attempt to push forward the Indemnity Bill which had lain many

---

* "The authority of the chair, the awe and reverence to order, and the due method of debates being irrecoverably lost by the disorder and tumultuousness of the House."— Sir J. Trevor to the King, Appendix to Dalrymple's Memoirs, Part ii. Book 4.

† Commons' Journals, Jan. 10, 1689-90. I have done my best to frame an account of this contest out of very defective materials. Burnet's narrative contains more blunders than lines. He evidently trusted to his memory, and was completely deceived by it. My chief authorities are the Journals; Grey's Debates; William's Letters to Portland; the Despatches of Van Citters; a Letter concerning the Disabling Clauses, lately offered to the House of Commons, for regulating Corporations, 1690; The True Friends to Corporations vindicated, in an answer to a letter concerning the Disabling Clauses, 1690; and Some Queries concerning the Election of Members for the ensuing Parliament, 1690. To this last pamphlet is appended a list of those who voted for the Sacheverell clause. See also Clarendon's Diary, Jan. 10, 1689-90, and the Third Part of the Caveat against the Whigs, 1712. I will quote the last sentences of William's Letter of the 10th of January. The news of the first division only had reached Kensington. "Il est à présent onze eures de nuit, et à dix eures la Chambre Basse estoit encore ensemble. Ainsi je ne vous puis escrire par cette ordinaire l'issue de l'affaire. Les previos questions les Tories l'ont emporté de cinq vois. Ainsi vous pouvez voir que la chose est bien disputée. J'ay si grand somiel, et mon toux m'incomode que je ne vous en saurez dire d'avantage. Jusques à mourir à vous."

On the same night Van Citters wrote to the States General. The debate, he said, had been very sharp. The design of the Whigs, whom he calls the Presbyterians, had been nothing less than to exclude their opponents from all offices, and to obtain for themselves the exclusive possession of power.

weeks neglected on the table.* But the Whigs, notwithstanding their recent defeat, where still the majority of the House; and many members, who had shrunk from the unpopularity which they would have incurred by supporting the Sacheverell clause and the Howard clause, were perfectly willing to assist in retarding the general pardon. They still propounded their favorite dilemma. How, they asked, was it possible to defend this project of amnesty without condemning the Revolution? Could it be contended that crimes which had been grave enough to justify rebellion had not been grave enough to deserve punishment? And, if those crimes were of such magnitude that they could justly be visited on the Sovereign whom the Constitution had exempted from responsibility, on what principle was immunity to be granted to his advisers and tools, who were beyond all doubt responsible? One facetious member put this argument in a singular form. He contrived to place in the Speaker's chair a paper which, when examined, appeared to be a Bill of Indemnity for King James, with a sneering preamble about the mercy which had, since the Revolution, been extended to more heinous offenders, and about the Indulgence due to a King, who, in oppressing his people, had only acted after the fashion of all Kings.†

On the same day on which this mock Bill of Indemnity disturbed the gravity of the Commons, it was moved that the House should go into Committee on the real Bill. The Whigs threw the motion out by a hundred and ninety-three votes to a hundred and fifty-six. They then proceeded to resolve that a bill of pains and penalties against delinquents should be forthwith brought in, and engrafted on the Bill of Indemnity.‡

A few hours later a vote passed which showed more clearly than anything that had yet taken place how little chance there was that the public mind would be speedily quieted by an amnesty. Few persons stood higher in the estimation of the Tory party than Sir Robert Sawyer. He was a man of ample fortune and aristocratical connections, of orthodox opinions and regular life, an able and experienced lawyer, a well-read scholar, and, in spite of a little pomposity, a good speaker. He had been Attorney-General at the time of the detection of the Rye House Plot : had been employed for the Crown in the prosecutions which followed; and he had conducted those prosecutions with an eagerness which would, in our time, be called

---
* Commons' Journals, January 11, 1689-90.
† Luttrell's Diary, Jan. 16, 1690 ; Van Citters to the States General Jan. 21-31.
‡ Commons' Journals, Jan. 16, 1689-90.

cruelty by all parties, but which, in his own time, and to his own party, seemed to be merely laudable zeal. His friends indeed asserted that he was conscientious even to scrupulosity in matters of life and death: * but this is an eulogy which persons who bring the feelings of the nineteenth century to the study of the State Trials of the seventeenth century will have some difficulty in understanding. The best excuse which can be made for this part of his life is that the stain of innocent blood was common to him with almost all the eminent public men of those evil days. When we blame him for prosecuting Russell, we must not forget that Russell had prosecuted Stafford.

Great as Sawyer's offences were, he had made great atonement for them. He had stood up manfully against Popery and despotism: he had, in the very presence chamber, positively refused to draw warrants in contravention of Acts of Parliament: he had resigned his lucrative office rather than appear in Westminster Hall as the champion of the dispensing power: he had been the leading counsel for the seven Bishops; and he had on the day of their trial, done his duty ably, honestly, and fearlessly. He was therefore a favorite with High Churchmen, and might be thought to have fairly earned his pardon from the Whigs. But the Whigs were not in a pardoning mood; and Sawyer was now called to account for his conduct in the case of Sir Thomas Armstrong.

If Armstrong was not belied, he was deep in the worst secrets of the Rye House Plot, and was one of those who undertook to slay the two royal brothers. When the conspiracy was discovered, he fled to the Continent and was outlawed. The magistrates of Leyden were induced by a bribe to deliver him up. He was hurried on board of an English ship, carried to London, and brought before the King's Bench. Sawyer moved the Court to award execution on the outlawry. Armstrong represented that a year had not yet elapsed since he had been outlawed, and that, by an Act passed in the reign of Edward the Sixth, an outlaw who yielded himself within the year was entitled to plead Not Guilty, and to put himself on his country. To this it was answered that Armstrong had not yielded himself, that he had been dragged to the bar a prisoner, and that he had no right to claim a privilege which was evidently meant to be given only to persons who voluntarily rendered themselves up to public justice. Jeffreys and the other judges unanimously overruled Armstrong's objection.

---

* Roger North's Life of Guildford.

and granted the award of execution. Then followed one of the most terrible of the many terrible scenes which, in those times, disgraced our Courts. The daughter of the unhappy man was at his side. "My Lord," she cried out, "you will not murder my father. This is murdering a man." "How now?" roared the Chief Justice. "Who is this woman? Take her, Marshal. Take her away." She was forced out, crying as she went, "God Almighty's judgments light on you!" "God Almighty's judgments," said Jeffreys, "will light on traitors. Thank God, I am clamor proof." When she was gone, her father again insisted on what he conceived to be his right. "I ask," he said, "only the benefit of the law." "And, by the grace of God, you shall have it," said the judge. "Mr. Sheriff, see that execution be done on Friday next. There is the benefit of the law for you." On the following Friday, Armstrong was hanged, drawn and quartered; and his head was placed over Westminster Hall.*

The insolence and cruelty of Jeffreys excite, even at the distance of so many years, an indignation which makes it difficult to be just to him. Yet a perfectly dispassionate inquirer may perhaps think it by no means clear that the award of execution was illegal. There was no precedent; and the words of the Act of Edward the Sixth may, without any straining, be construed as the Court construed them. Indeed, had the penalty been only fine and imprisonment, nobody would have seen anything reprehensible in the proceeding. But to send a man to the gallows as a traitor, without confronting him with his accusers, without hearing his defence, solely because a timidity which s perfectly compatible with innocence has impelled him to hide himself, is surely a violation, if not of any written law, yet of those great principles to which all laws ought to conform. The case was brought before the House of Commons. The orphan daughter of Armstrong came to the bar to demand vengeance; and a warm debate followed. Sawyer was fiercely attacked, and strenuously defended. The Tories declared that he appeared to them to have done only what, as counsel for the Crown, he was bound to do, and to have discharged his duty to God, to the King, and to the prisoner. If the award was legal, nobody was to blame; and if the award was illegal, the blame lay, not with the Attorney-General, but with the Judges. There would be an end of all

---

* See the account of the proceedings in the collection of State Trials. It has been asserted that I have committed an error here, and that Armstrong's head was placed on Temple Bar. The truth is that one of his quarters was placed on Temple Bar. His head was on Westminster Hall. See Luttrell's Diary, June 1684.

liberty of speech at the bar, if an advocate was to be punished for making a strictly regular application to a Court, and for arguing that certain words in a statute were to be understood in a certain sense. The Whigs called Sawyer murderer, bloodhound, hangman. If the liberty of speech claimed by advocates meant the liberty of haranguing men to death, it was high time that the nation should rise up and exterminate the whole race of lawyers. "Things will never be well done," said one orator, "till some of that profession be made examples." "No crime to demand execution!" exclaimed John Hampden. "We shall be told next that it was no crime in the Jews to cry out, 'Crucify him.'" A wise and just man would probably have been of opinion that this was not a case for severity. Sawyer's conduct might have been, to a certain extent, culpable: but, if an Act of Indemnity was to be passed at all, it was to be passed for the benefit of persons whose conduct had been culpable. The question was not whether he was guiltless, but whether his guilt was of so peculiarly black a dye that he ought, notwithstanding all his sacrifices and services, to be excluded by name from the mercy which was to be granted to many thousands of offenders. This question calm and impartial judges would probably have decided in his favor. It was. however, resolved that he should be excepted from the Indemnity and expelled from the House.*

On the morrow the Bill of Indemnity, now transformed into a Bill of Pains and Penalties, was again discussed. The Whigs consented to refer it to a Committee of the whole House, but proposed to instruct the Committee to begin its labors by making out a list of the offenders who were to be proscribed. The Tories moved the previous question. The House divided: and the Whigs carried their point by a hundred and ninety votes to a hundred and seventy-three.†

The King watched these events with painful anxiety. He was weary of his crown. He had tried to do justice to both the contending parties; but justice would satisfy neither. The Tories hated him for protecting the Dissenters. The Whigs hated him for protecting the Tories. The amnesty seemed to

* Commons' Journals, Jan. 20, 1689-90; Grey's Debates, Jan. 18, and 20.
† Commons' Journals, Jan. 21, 1689-90. On the same day William wrote thus from Kensington to Portland: "C'est aujourd'hui le grand jour à l'éguard du Bill of Indemnité. Selon tout ce que je puis aprendre, il y aura beaucoup de chaleur, et rien déterminer; et de la manière que la chose est entourré, il n'y a point d'aparence que cette affaire viene à aucune conclusion. Et ainsi il se pouroit que la cession fust fort courte; n'ayant plus d'argent à espérer; et les esprits s'aigrissent l'un contre l'autre de plus en plus." Three days later Van Citters informed the States General that the excitement about the Bill of Indemnity was extreme.

be more remote than when, ten months before, he first recommended it from the throne. The last campaign in Ireland had been disastrous. It might well be that the next campaign would be more disastrous still. The malpractices, which had done more than the exhalations of the marshes of Dundalk to destroy the efficiency of the English troops were likely to be as monstrous as ever. Every part of the administration was thoroughly disorganized; and the people were surprised and angry because a foreigner, newly come among them, imperfectly acquainted with them, and constantly thwarted by them, had not, in a year, put the whole machine of government to rights. Most of his ministers, instead of assisting him, were trying to get up addresses and impeachments against each other. Yet if he employed his own countrymen, on whose fidelity and attachment he could rely, a general cry of rage was set up by all the English factions. The knavery of the English Commissariat had destroyed an army; yet a rumor that he intended to employ an able, experienced, and trusty Commissary from Holland had excited general discontent. The King felt that he could not, while thus situated, render any service to that great cause to which his whole soul was devoted. Already the glory which he had won by conducting to a successful issue the most important enterprise of that age was becoming dim. Even his friends had begun to doubt whether he really possessed all that sagacity and energy which had a few months before extorted the unwilling admiration of his enemies. But he would endure his splendid slavery no longer. He would return to his native country. He would content himself with being the first citizen of a commonwealth to which the name of Orange was dear. As such, he might still be foremost among those who were banded together in defence of the liberties of Europe. As for the turbulent and ungrateful islanders, who detested him because he would not let them tear each other in pieces, Mary must try what she could do with them. She was born on their soil. She spoke their language. She did not dislike some parts of their Liturgy, which they fancied to be essential, and which to him seemed at best harmless. If she had little knowledge of politics and war, she had what might be more useful, feminine grace and tact, a sweet temper, a smile and a kind word for everybody. She might be able to compose the disputes which distracted the State and the Church. Holland, under his government, and England under hers, might act cordially together against the common enemy.

He secretly ordered preparations to be made for his voyage. Having done this, he called together a few of his chief counsellors, and told them his purpose. A squadron, he said, was ready to convey him to his country. He had done with them. He hoped that the Queen would be more successful. The ministers were thunderstruck. For once all quarrels were suspended. The Tory Caermarthen on one side, the Whig Shrewsbury on the other, expostulated and implored with a pathetic vehemence rare in the conferences of statesmen. Many tears were shed. At length the King was induced to give up, at least for the present, his design of abdicating the government. But he announced another design which he was fully determined not to give up. Since he was still to remain at the head of the English administration, he would go himself to Ireland. He would try whether the whole royal authority, strenuously exerted on the spot where the fate of the empire was to be decided, would suffice to prevent peculation and to maintain discipline.*

That he had seriously meditated a retreat to Holland long continued to be a secret, not only to the multitude, but even to the Queen.† That he had resolved to take the command of his army in Ireland was soon rumored all over London. It was known that his camp furniture was making, and that Sir Christopher Wren was busied in constructing a house of wood which was to travel about, packed in two wagons, and to be set up wherever His Majesty might fix his quarters.‡ The Whigs raised a violent outcry against the whole scheme. Not knowing, or affecting not to know, that it had been formed by William, and by William alone, and that none of his ministers had dared to advise him to encounter the Irish swords and the Irish atmosphere, the whole party confidently affirmed that he had been misled by some traitor in the cabinet, by some Tory who hated the Revolution and all that had sprung from the Revolution. Would any true friend have advised His Majesty, infirm in health as he was, to expose himself, not only to the dangers of war, but to the malignity of a climate which had recently been fatal to thousands of men much stronger than himself? In private the King sneered bitterly at this anxiety for his safety. It was merely, in his judgment, the anxiety which a hard master feels lest his slaves should become unfit for their drudgery. The Whigs, he wrote to Portland, were afraid to lose their tool before they had done their work. "As to their

---

* Burnet, ii. 39 ; MS. Memoir written by the first Lord Lonsdale among the Mackintosh Papers.
† Burnet, ii. 40.   ‡ Luttrell's Diary, January and February.

friendship," he added, "you know what it is worth." His resolution, he told his friend, was unalterably fixed. Everything was at stake; and go he must even though the Parliament should present an address imploring him to stay.*

He soon learned that such an address would be immediately moved in both Houses and supported by the whole strength of the Whig party. This intelligence satisfied him that it was time to take a decisive step. He would not discard the Whigs; but he would give them a lesson of which they stood much in need. He would break the chain in which they imagined that they had him fast. He would not let them have the exclusive possession of power. He would not let them persecute the vanquished party. In their despite, he would grant an amnesty to his people. In their despite, he would take the command of his army in Ireland. He arranged his plan with characteristic prudence, firmness, and secrecy. A single Englishman it was necessary to trust: for William was not sufficiently master of our language to address the Houses from the throne in his own words; and on very important occasions, his practice was to write his speech in French, and to employ a translator. It is certain that to one person, and to one only, the King confided the momentous resolution which he had taken; and it can hardly be doubted that this person was Caermarthen.

On the twenty-seventh of January, Black Rod knocked at the door of the Commons. The Speaker and the members repaired to the House of Lords. The King was on the throne. He gave his assent to the Supply Bill, thanked the Houses for it, announced his intention of going to Ireland, and prorogued the Parliament. None could doubt that a dissolution would speedily follow. As the concluding words, "I have thought it convenient now to put an end to this session," were uttered, the Tories, both above and below the bar, broke forth into a shout of joy. The King meanwhile surveyed his audience from the throne with that bright eagle eye which nothing escaped. He might be pardoned if he felt some little vindictive pleasure

---

* William to Portland, Jan. 10-20, 1690. " Les Wiges ont peur de me perdre trop tost, avant qu'ils n'ayent fait avec moy ce qu'ils veulent : car, pour leur amitié, vous savez ce qu'il y a à compter làdessus en ce pays icy."

Jan. 14-24. " Me voilà le plus embarassé du monde, ne sachant quel parti prendre, estant toujours persuadé que, sans que j'aille en Irlande, l'on n'y faira rien qui vaille. Pour avoir du conseil en cette affaire, je n'en ay point à attendre, personne n'ausant dire ses sentimens. Et l'on commence déjà à dire ouvertement que ce sont des traitres qui m'ont conseillé de prendre cette résolution."

Jan. 21-31. " Je n'ay encore rien dit,"—he means to the Parliament,—" de mon voyage pour l'Irlande. Et je ne suis point encore déterminé si j'en parlerez : mais je crains que nonobstant j'aurez une adresse pour n'y point aller ; ce qui m'embarassera beaucoup, puis que c'est une nécessité absolue que j'y aille."

in annoying those who had cruelly annoyed him. "I saw," he wrote to Portland the next day, "faces an ell long. I saw some of those men change color twenty times while I was speaking."*

A few hours after the prorogation, a hundred and fifty Tory members of Parliament had a parting dinner together at the Apollo Tavern in Fleet Street, before they set out for their counties. They were in better temper with William than they had been since his father-in-law had been turned out of Whitehall. They had scarcely recovered from the joyful surprise with which they had heard it announced from the throne that the session was at an end. The recollection of their danger and the sense of their deliverance were still fresh. They talked of repairing to Court in a body to testify their gratitude; but they were induced to forego their intention; and not without cause; for a great crowd of squires, after a revel, at which doubtless neither October nor claret had been spared, might have caused some inconvenience in the presence chamber. Sir John Lowther, who in wealth and influence was inferior to no country gentleman of that age, was deputed to carry the thanks of the assembly to the palace. He spoke, he told the King, the sense of a great body of honest gentlemen. They begged His Majesty to be assured that they would in their counties do their best to serve him; and they cordially wished him a safe voyage to Ireland, a complete victory, a speedy return, and a long and happy reign. During the following week, many, who had never shown their faces in the circle at Saint James's since the Revolution, went to kiss the King's hand. So warmly indeed did those who had hitherto been regarded as half Jacobites express their approbation of the policy of the government, that the thorough-going Jacobites were much disgusted, and complained bitterly of the strange blindness which seemed to have come on the sons of the Church of England.†

All the acts of William, at this time, indicated his determination to restrain, steadily though gently, the violence of the Whigs, and to conciliate, if possible, the good will of the

---

* William to Portland, $\frac{\text{Jan. 28}}{\text{Feb. 7}}$ 1690; Van Citters to the States General, same date; Evelyn's Diary; Lords' Journals, Jan. 27. I will quote William's own words. "Vous vairez mon harangue imprimée: ainsi je ne vous en direz rien. Et pour les raisons qui m'y ont obligé, je les reserverez à vous les dire jusques à vostre retour. Il semble que les Toris en sont bien aise, mais point les Wiggs. Ils estoient tous fort surpris quand je leur parlois, n'ayant communiqué mon dessein qu'à une seule personne. Je vis des visages long comme un aune, changé de couleur vingt fois pendant que je parlois. Tous ces particularités jusques à vostre heureux retour."

† Evelyn's Diary; Clarendon's Diary, Feb. 9, 1690; Van Citters to the States General $\frac{\text{Jan. 31}}{\text{Feb. 10}}$; Lonsdale MS. quoted by Dalrymple.

Tories. Several persons whom the Commons had thrown into prison for treason were set at liberty on bail.* The prelates who held that their allegiance was still due to James were treated with a tenderness rare in the history of revolutions. Within a week after the prorogation, the first of February came, the day on which those ecclesiastics who refused to take the oaths were to be finally deprived. Several of the suspended clergy, after holding out till the last moment, swore just in time to save themselves from beggary. But the Primate and five of his suffragans were still inflexible. They consequently forfeited their bishoprics: but Sancroft was informed that the King had not yet relinquished the hope of being able to make some arrangement which might avert the necessity of appointing successors, and that the nonjuring prelates might continue for the present to reside in their palaces. Their receivers were appointed receivers for the Crown, and continued to collect the revenues of the vacant sees.† Similar indulgence was shown to some divines of lower rank. Sherlock, in particular, continued, after his deprivation, to live unmolested in his official mansion close to the Temple Church.

And now appeared a proclamation dissolving the Parliament. The writs for a general election went out; and soon every part of the kingdom was in a ferment. Van Citters, who had resided in England during many eventful years, declared that he had never seen London more violently agitated.‡ The excitement was kept up by compositions of all sorts, from sermons with sixteen heads down to jingling street ballads. Lists of divisions were, for the first time in our history, printed and dispersed for the information of constituent bodies. Two of these lists may still be seen in old libraries. One of the two, circulated by the Whigs, contained the names of those Tories who had voted against declaring the throne vacant. The other, circulated by the Tories, contained the names of those Whigs who had supported the Sacheverell clause.

It soon became clear that public feeling had undergone a great change during the year which had elapsed since the Convention had met: and it is impossible to deny that this change was, at least in part, the natural consequence and the just punishment of the intemperate and vindictive conduct of the Whigs. Of the City of London they thought themselves sure. The Livery had in the preceding year returned four

---

* Narcissus Luttrell's Diary.
† Clarendon's Diary, Feb. 11, 1690.
‡ Van Citters to the States General, February 14-24, 1690; Evelyn's Diary.

zealous Whigs without a contest. But all the four had voted for the Sacheverell clause; and by that clause many of the merchant princes of Lombard Street and Cornhill, men powerful in the twelve great companies, men whom the goldsmiths followed humbly, hat in hand, up and down the arcades of the Royal Exchange, would have been turned with all indignity out of the Court of Aldermen and out of the Common Council. The struggle was for life or death. No exertions, no artifices, were spared. William wrote to Portland that the Whigs of the City, in their despair, stuck at nothing, and that, as they went on, they would soon stand as much in need of an Act of Indemnity as the Tories Four Tories, however, were returned, and that by so decisive a majority that the Tory who stood lowest polled four hundred votes more than the Whig who stood highest.* The Sheriffs, desiring to defer as long as possible the triumph of their enemies, granted a scrutiny. But, though the majority was diminished, the result was not affected.† At Westminster, two opponents of the Sacheverell clause were elected without a contest.‡ But nothing indicated more strongly the disgust excited by the proceedings of the late House of Commons than what passed in the University of Cambridge. Newton retired to his quiet observatory over the gate of Trinity College. Two Tories were returned by an overwhelming majority. At the head of the poll was Sawyer, who had, but a few days before, been excepted from the Indemnity Bill and expelled from the House of Commons. The records of the University contain curious proofs that the unwise severity with which he had been treated had raised an enthusiastic feeling in his favor. Newton voted for Sawyer; and this remarkable fact justifies us in believing that the great philosopher, in whose genius and virtue the Whig party justly glories, had seen the headstrong and revengeful conduct of that party with concern and disapprobation.§

It was soon plain that the Tories would have a majority in the new House of Commons.‖ All the leading Whigs, however, obtained seats, with one exception. John Hampden was

---

* William to Portland, $\frac{\text{Feb. 28.}}{\text{March 10,}}$ 1690; Van Citters to the States General, March 4-14; Narcissus Luttrell's Diary.

† Van Citters, March 11-21, 1690; Narcissus Luttrell's Diary.

‡ Van Citters to the States General, March 11-21, 1690.

§ The votes were for Sawyer 165, for Finch 141, for Bennet, whom I suppose to have been a Whig, 87. At the University every voter delivers his vote in writing. One of the votes given on that occasion is in the following words, "Henricus Jenkes, ex amore justitiæ, aligit virum consultissimum Robertum Sawyer."

‖ Van Citters to the States General, March 18-28, 1690.

excluded, and was regretted only by the most intolerant and unreasonable members of his party.*

The King meanwhile was making, in almost every department of the executive government, a change corresponding to the change which the general election was making in the composition of the legislature. Still, however, he did not think of forming what is now called a ministry. He still reserved to himself more especially the direction of foreign affairs, and he superintended with minute attention all the preparations for the approaching campaign in Ireland. In his confidential letters he complained that he had to perform with little or no assistance, the task of organizing the disorganized military establishments of the kingdom. The work, he said, was heavy; but it must be done; for everything depended on it.† In general, the government was still a government by independent departments; and in almost every department Whigs and Tories were still mingled, though not exactly in the old proportions. The Whig element had decidedly predominated in 1689. The Tory element predominated, though not very decidedly, in 1690.

Halifax had laid down the Privy Seal. It was offered to Chesterfield, a Tory who had voted in the Convention for a Regency. But Chesterfield refused to quit his country house and gardens in Derbyshire for the Court and Council Chamber; and the Privy Seal was put into Commission.‡ Caermarthen was now the chief adviser of the crown on all matters relating to the internal administration and to the management of the two Houses of Parliament. The white staff, and the immense power which accompanied the white staff, William was still determined never to entrust to any subject. Caermarthen there-

---

* It is amusing to see how absurdly foreign pamphleteers, ignorant of the real state of things in England, exaggerated the importance of John Hampden, whose name they could not spell. In a French Dialogue between William and the Ghost of Monmouth, William says, "Entre ces membres de la Chambre Basse étoit un certain homme hardy, opiniâtre, et zélé à l'excès pour sa créance; on l'appelle Embden, également dangereux par son esprit et par son crédit. . . . . Je ne trouvay point de chemin plus court pour me délivrer de cette traverse que de casser le parlement, en convoquer un autre, et empescher que cet homme, qui me faisoit tant d'ombrages, ne fust nommé pour un des deputez au nouvel parlement." "Ainsi," says the Ghost, "cette cessation de parlement qui a fait tant de bruit, et a produit tant de raisonnements et de spéculations, n'estoit que pour exclure Embden. Mais s'il stoit si adroit et si zélé, comment as-tu pu trouver le moyen de la faire exclure du nombre les deputez?" To this sensible question the King replies, not very explicitly, "Il m'a allu faire d'étranges manœuvres pour en venir à bout."—L'Ombre de Monmouth, 1690.

† "A présent ut dépendra d'un bon succés en Irlande; et à quoy il faut que je m'aplique entiér ment pour régler le mieux que je puis toutte chose. . . . . . Je vous asseure que je n'ay pas peu sur les bras, estant aussi mal assisté que je suis."—William to Portland, $\frac{\text{Jan. 28,}}{\text{Feb. 7,}}$ 1690.

‡ Van Citters, Feb. 14-24, 1689-90, Memoir of the Earl of Chesterfield, by himself; Halifax to Chesterfield, Feb. 6; Chesterfield to Halifax, Feb. 8. The editor of the letters of the second Earl of Chesterfield, not allowing for the change of style, has misplaced this correspondence by a year.

fore continued to be Lord President; but he took possession of a suite of apartments in Saint James's Palace which was considered as peculiarly belonging to the Prime Minister.* He had, during the preceding year, pleaded ill health as an excuse for seldom appearing at the Council Board; and the plea was not without foundation: his digestive organs had some morbid peculiarities which puzzled the whole College of Physicians: his complexion was livid: his frame was meagre: and his face, handsome and intellectual as it was, had a haggard look which indicated the restlessness of pain as well as the restlessness of ambition.† As soon, however, as he was once more minister, he applied himself strenuously to business, and toiled every day, and all day long, with an energy which amazed everybody who saw his ghastly countenance and tottering gait.

Though he could not obtain for himself the office of Lord Treasurer, his influence at the Treasury was great. Monmouth, the First Commissioner, and Delamere, the Chancellor of the Exchequer, two of the most violent Whigs in England, quitted their seats. On this, as on many other occasions, it appeared that they had nothing but their Whiggism in common. The volatile Monmouth, sensible that he had none of the qualities of a financier, seems to have taken no personal offence at being removed from a place which he never ought to have occupied. He thankfully accepted a pension, which his profuse habits made necessary to him, and still continued to attend Councils, to frequent the Court, and to discharge the duties of a Lord of the Bedchamber.‡ He also tried to make himself useful in military business, which he understood, if not well, yet better than most of his brother nobles: and he professed, during a few months, a great regard for Caermarthen. Delamere was in a very different mood. It was in vain that his services were overpaid with honors and riches. He was created Earl of

* Van Citters to the States General, Feb. 11-21, 1690.

† A strange peculiarity of his constitution is mentioned in an account of him which was published a few months after his death. See the volume entitled "Lives and Characters of the most Illustrious Persons, British and Foreign, who died in the year 1712." So early as the days of Charles the Second, the leanness and ghastliness of Caermarthen were among the favorite topics of Whig satirists. In a ballad entitled the Chequer Inn are these lines.

> "He is as stiff as any stake,
> And leaner, Dick, than any rake:
> Envy is not so pale;
> And though, by selling of us all,
> He has wrought himself in to Whitehall,
> He looks like bird of gaol."

‡ Monmouth's pension and the good understanding between him and the Court are mentioned in a letter from a Jacobite agent in England, which is in the Archives of the French War Office. The date is April 8-18, 1690.

Warrington. He obtained a grant of all the lands that could be discovered belonging to Jesuits in five or six counties. A demand made by him on account of expenses incurred at the time of the Revolution was allowed; and he carried with him into retirement as the reward of his patriotic exertions a large sum which the State could ill spare. But his anger was not to be so appeased; and to the end of his life he continued to complain bitterly of the ingratitude with which he and his party had been treated.*

Sir John Lowther became first Lord of the Treasury, and was the person on whom Caermarthen chiefly relied for the conduct of the ostensible business of the House of Commons. Lowther was a man of ancient descent, ample estate, and great parliamentary interest. Though not an old man, he was an old senator: for he had, before he was of age, succeeded his father as knight of the shire for Westmoreland. In truth the representation of Westmoreland was almost as much one of the hereditaments of the Lowther family as Lowther Hall. Sir John's abilities were respectable; his manners, though sarcastically noticed in contemporary lampoons as too formal, were eminently courteous: his personal courage he was but too ready to prove: his morals were irreproachable: his time was divided between respectable labors and respectable pleasures: his chief business was to attend the House of Commons and to preside on the Bench of Justice: his favorite amusements were reading and gardening. In opinions he was a very moderate Tory. He was attached to hereditary monarchy and to the Established Church: but he had concurred in the Revolution; he had no misgivings touching the title of William and Mary; he had sworn allegiance to them without any mental reservation; and he appears to have strictly kept his oath. Between him and Caermarthen there was a close connection. They had acted together cordially in the Northern insurrection; and they agreed in their political views, as nearly as a very cunning statesman and a very honest country gentleman

---

* The grants of land obtained by Delamere are mentioned by Narcissus Luttrell. It appears from the Treasury Letter Book of 1690 that Delamere continued to dun the government for money after his retirement. As to his general character it would not be safe to trust the representations of his enemies. But his own writings, and the admissions of the divine who preached his funeral sermon, show that his temper was not the most gentle. Clarendon remarks (Dec. 17, 1688,) that a little thing sufficed to put Lord Delamere into a passion. In the poem entitled the King of Hearts, Delamere is described as—

"A restless malecontent even when preferred."

His countenance furnished a subject for satire:

"His boding looks a mind distracted show;
And envy sits engraved upon his brow."

could be expected to agree.* By Caermarthen's influence Lowther was now raised to one of the most important places in the kingdom. Unfortunately it was a place requiring qualities very different from those which suffice to make a valuable country member and chairman of quarter sessions. The tongue of the new First Lord of the Treasury was not sufficiently ready, nor was his temper sufficiently callous for his post. He had neither adroitness to parry, nor fortitude to endure, the gibes and reproaches to which, in his new character of courtier and placeman, he was exposed. There was also something to be done which he was too scrupulous to do; something which had never been done by Wolsey or Burleigh; something which has never been done by any English statesman of our generation; but which, from the time of Charles the Second to the time of George the Third, was one of the most important parts of the business of a minister.

The history of the rise, progress, and decline of parliamentary corruption in England still remains to be written. No subject has called forth a greater quantity of eloquent vituperation and stinging sarcasm. Three generations of serious and of sportive writers wept and laughed over the venality of the senate. That venality was denounced on the hustings, anathematized from the pulpit, and burlesqued on the stage; was attacked by Pope in brilliant verse, and by Bolingbroke in stately prose, by Swift with savage hatred, and by Gay with festive malice. The voices of Tories and Whigs, of Johnson and Akenside, of Smollett and Fielding, contributed to swell the cry. But none of those who railed or of those who jested took the trouble to verify the phenomena, or to trace them to the real causes.

Sometimes the evil was imputed to the depravity of a particular minister: but, when he had been driven from power, and when those who had most loudly accused him governed in his stead, it was found that the change of men had produced no change of system. Sometimes the evil was imputed to the degeneracy of the national character. Luxury and cupidity, it was said, had produced in our country the same effect which they had produced of old in the Roman republic. The modern Englishman was to the Englishman of the sixteenth

---

* My notion of Lowther's character has been chiefly formed from two papers written by himself, one of which has been printed, though I believe not published. A copy of the other is among the Mackintosh MSS. Something I have taken from contemporary satires That Lowther was too ready to expose his life in private encounters is sufficiently prove by the fact that, when he was First Lord of the Treasury, he accepted a challenge from a custom house officer whom he had dismissed. There was a duel; and Lowther was severely wounded. This event is mentioned in Luttrell's Diary, April 1690.

century what Verres and Curio were to Dentatus and Fabricius. Those who held this language were as ignorant and shallow as people generally are who extol the past at the expense of the present. A man of sense would have perceived that, if the English of the time of George the Second had really been more sordid and dishonest than their forefathers, the deterioration would not have shown itself in one place alone. The progress of judicial venality and of official venality would have kept pace with the progress of parliamentary venality. But nothing is more certain than that, while the legislature was becoming more and more venal, the courts of law and the public offices were becoming purer and purer. The representatives of the people were undoubtedly more mercenary in the days of Hardwicke and Pelham than in the days of the Tudors. But the Chancellors of the Tudors took plate, jewels, and purses of broad pieces, from suitors without scruple or shame; and Hardwicke would have committed for contempt any suitor who had dared to bring him a present. The Treasurers of the Tudors raised princely fortunes by the sale of places, titles, and pardons; and Pelham would have ordered his servants to turn out of his house any man who had offered him money for a peerage or a commissionership of customs. It is evident, therefore, that the prevalence of corruption in the parliament cannot be ascribed to a general depravation of morals. The taint was local: we must look for some local cause; and such a cause will without difficulty be found.

Under our ancient sovereigns the House of Commons rarely interfered with the executive administration. The Speaker was charged not to let the members meddle with matters of State. If any gentleman was very troublesome, he was cited before the Privy Council, interrogated, reprimanded, and sent to meditate on his undutiful conduct in the Tower. The Commons did their best to protect themselves by keeping their deliberations secret, by excluding strangers, by making it a crime to repeat out of doors what had passed within doors. But these precautions were of small avail. In so large an assembly there were always talebearers, ready to carry the evil report of their brethren to the palace. To oppose the Court was therefore a service of serious danger. In those days, of course, there was little or no buying of votes. For an honest man was not to be bought, and it was much cheaper to intimidate or to coerce a knave than to buy him.

For a very different reason there has been no direct buying of votes within the memory of the present generation. The

House of Commons is now supreme in the State, but is accountable to the nation. Even those members who are not chosen by large constituent bodies are kept in awe by public opinion. Everything is printed; everything is discussed; every material word uttered in debate is read by a million of people on the morrow. Within a few hours after an important division, the lists of the majority and the minority are scanned and analyzed in every town from Plymouth to Inverness. If a name be found where it ought not to be, the apostate is certain to be reminded in sharp language of the promises which he has broken, and of the professions which he has belied. At present, therefore, the best way in which a government can secure the support of a majority of the representative body is by gaining the confidence of the nation.

But between the time when our Parliaments ceased to be controlled by royal prerogative and the time when they began to be constantly and effectually controlled by public opinion there was a long interval. After the restoration, no government ventured to return to those methods by which, before the civil war, the freedom of deliberation had been restrained. A member could no longer be called to account for his harangues or his votes. He might obstruct the passing of bills of supply; he might arraign the whole foreign policy of the country; he might lay on the table articles of impeachment against all the chief ministers; and he ran not the smallest risk of being treated as Morrice had been treated by Elizabeth, or Eliot by Charles the First. The senator now stood in no awe of the Court. Nevertheless, all the defences behind which the feeble Parliaments of the sixteenth century had entrenched themselves against the attacks of prerogative were not only still kept up, but were extended and strengthened. No politician seems to have been aware that these defences were no longer needed for their original purpose, and had begun to serve a purpose very different. The rules which had been originally designed to secure faithful representatives against the displeasure of the Sovereign, now operated to secure unfaithful representatives against the displeasure of the people, and proved much more effectual for the latter end than they had ever been for the former. It was natural, it was inevitable, that, in a legislative body emancipated from the restraints of the sixteenth century, and not yet subjected to the restraints of the nineteenth century, in a legislative body which feared neither the King nor the public, there should be corruption.

The plague spot began to be visible and palpable in the

days of the Cabal. Clifford, the boldest and fiercest of the wicked Five, had the merit of discovering that a noisy patriot, whom it was no longer possible to send to prison, might be turned into a courtier by a goldsmith's note. Clifford's example was followed by his successors. It soon became a proverb that a Parliament resembled a pump. Often, the wits said, when a pump appears to be dry, if a very small quantity of water is poured in, a great quantity of water gushes out : and so, when a Parliament appears to be niggardly, ten thousand pounds judiciously given in bribes will often produce a million in supplies. The evil was not diminished, nay, it was aggravated, by that Revolution which freed our country from so many other evils. The House of Commons was now more powerful than ever as against the Crown, and yet was not more strictly responsible than formerly to the nation. The government had a new motive for buying the members; and the members had no new motive for refusing to sell themselves. William, indeed, had an aversion to bribery : he resolved to abstain from it; and during the first year of his reign, he kept his resolution. Unhappily the events of that year did not encourage him to persevere in his good intentions. As soon as Caermarthen was placed at the head of the internal administration of the realm, a complete change took place. He was in truth no novice in the art of purchasing votes. He had, sixteen years before, succeeded Clifford at the Treasury, had inherited Clifford's tactics, had improved upon them, and had employed them to an extent which would have amazed the inventor. From the day on which Caermarthen was called a second time to the chief direction of affairs, parliamentary corruption continued to be practised, with scarcely any intermission, by a long succession of statesmen, till the close of the American war. Neither of the great English parties can justly charge the other with any peculiar guilt on this account. The Tories were the first who introduced the system and the last who clung to it : but it attained its greatest vigor in the time of Whig ascendency. The extent to which parliamentary support was bartered for money cannot be with any precision ascertained. But it seems probable that the number of hirelings was greatly exaggerated by vulgar report, and was never large, though often sufficient to turn the scale on important divisions. An unprincipled minister eagerly accepted the services of these mercenaries. An honest minister reluctantly submitted, for the sake of the commonwealth, to what he considered as a shameful and odious extortion. But during many years every minister, whatever his personal character might be, consented, willingly or unwillingly, to manage the Parliament in the only way in which the Parliament could then be managed. It at length became as notorious that there was a market for votes at the Treasury as that there was a market for cattle in Smithfield. Numerous demagogues out of power declaimed against this vile traffic : but every one of those demagogues, as soon as he was in power, found himself driven by a kind of fatality to engage in that traffic, or at least to connive at it. Now and then perhaps a man who had romantic notions of public virtue refused to be himself the paymaster of the corrupt crew, and averted his eyes while his less scrupulous colleagues did that which he knew to be indispensable, and yet felt to be degrading. But the instances of this prudery were rare indeed. The doctrine generally received, even among upright and honorable politicians, was that it was shameful to receive bribes, but that it was necessary to distribute them. It is a remarkable fact that the evil reached the greatest height during the administration of Henry Pelham, a statesman of good intentions, of spotless morals in private life, and of exemplary disinterestedness. It is not difficult to guess by what arguments he and other well meaning men, who, like him, followed the fashion of their age, quieted their consciences. No casuist, however severe, has denied that it may be a duty to give what it is a crime to take. It was infamous in Jeffreys to demand money for the lives of the unhappy prisoners whom he tried at Dorchester and Taunton. But it was not infamous, nay, it was laudable, in the kinsmen and friends of a prisoner to contribute of their substance in order to make up a purse for Jeffreys. The Sallee rover, who threatened to bastinado a Christian captive to death unless a ransom was forthcoming, was an odious ruffian. But to ransom a Christian captive from a Sallee rover was, not merely an innocent, but a highly meritorious act. It is improper in such cases to use the word corruption. Those who receive the filthy lucre are corrupt already. He who bribes them does not make them wicked : he finds them so ; and he merely prevents their evil propensities from producing evil effects. And might not the same plea be urged in defence of a minister who, when no other expedient would avail, paid greedy and low-minded members of Parliament not to ruin their country?

It was by some such reasoning as this that the scruples of William were overcome. Honest Burnet, with the uncourtly courage which distinguished him, ventured to remonstrate with the King. "Nobody," William answered, "hates bribery more than I. But I have to do with a set of men who must be managed in this vile way or not at all. I must strain a point: or the country is lost."*

It was necessary for the Lord President to have in the House of Commons an agent for the purchase of members; and Lowther was both too awkward and too scrupulous to be such an agent. But a man in whom craft and profligacy were united in a high degree, was without difficulty found. This was the Master of the Rolls, Sir John Trevor, who had been Speaker in the single Parliament held by James. High as Trevor had risen in the world, there were people who could still remember him a strange looking clerk in the Inner Temple. Indeed, nobody who had ever seen him was likely to forget him. For his grotesque features and his hideous squint were far beyond the reach of caricature. His parts, which were quick and vigorous, had enabled him early to master the science of chicane. Gambling and betting were his amusements; and out of these amusements he contrived to extract much business in the way of his profession. For his opinion on a question arising out of a wager or a game at chance had as much authority as a judgment of any court in Westminster Hall. He soon rose to be one of the boon companions whom Jeffreys hugged in fits of maudlin friendship over the bottle at night, and cursed and reviled in court on the morrow. Under such a teacher, Trevor rapidly became a proficient in that peculiar kind of rhetoric which had enlivened the trials of Baxter and of Alice Lisle. Report indeed spoke of some scolding matches between the Chancellor and his friend, in which the disciple had been not less voluble and scurrilous than the master. These contests, however, did not take place till the younger adventurer had attained riches and dignities such that he no longer stood in need of the patronage which had raised him.†
Among High Churchmen Trevor, in spite of his notorious want of principle, had at this time a certain popularity, which he seems to have owed chiefly to their conviction that, however insincere he might be in general, his hatred of the dissenters was genuine and hearty. There was little doubt that, in a House of Commons in which the Tories had a majority, he might easily, with the support of the Court, be chosen Speaker. He was impatient to be again in his old post, which he well knew how to make one of the most lucrative in the kingdom;

---

* Burnet, ii. 76.   † Roger North's Life of Guildford.

and he willingly undertook that secret and shameful office for which Lowther was altogether unqualified.

Richard Hampden was appointed Chancellor of the Exchequer. This appointment was probably intended as a mark of royal gratitude for the moderation of his conduct, and for the attempts which he had made to curb the violence of his Whig friends, and especially of his son.

Godolphin voluntarily left the Treasury; why, we are not informed. We can scarcely doubt that the dissolution and the result of the general election must have given him pleasure. For his political opinions leaned towards Toryism; and he had, in the late reign, done some things which, though not very heinous, stood in need of an indemnity. It is probable that he did not think it compatible with his personal dignity to sit at the Board below Lowther, who was in rank his inferior.*

A new Commission of Admiralty was issued. At the head of the naval administration was placed Thomas Herbert, Earl of Pembroke, a high-born and high-bred man who had ranked among the Tories, who had voted for a Regency, and who had married the daughter of Sawyer. That Pembroke's Toryism, however, was not of a narrow and illiberal kind is sufficiently proved by the fact that, immediately after the Revolution, the Essay on the Human Understanding was dedicated to him by John Locke, in token of gratitude for kind offices done in evil times.†

Nothing was omitted which could reconcile Torrington to this change. For, though he had been found an incapable administrator, he still stood so high in general estimation as a seaman that the government was unwilling to lose his services. He was assured that no slight was intended to him. He could not serve his country at once on the ocean and at Westminster; and it had been thought less difficult to supply his place in his office than on the deck of his flagship. He was at first very angry, and actually laid down his commission: but some concessions were made to his pride: a pension of three thousand pounds a year and a grant of ten thousand acres of crown land in the Peterborough level were irresistible baits to his cupidity, and, in an evil hour for England, he consented to remain at the

---

* Till some years after this time the First Lord of the Treasury was always the man of highest rank at the Board. Thus Monmouth, Delamere, and Godolphin took their places according to the order of precedence in which they stood as peers.

† The dedication, however, was thought too laudatory. "The only thing, Mr. Pope used to say, he could never forgive his philosophic master was the dedication to the Essay."—Ruffhead's Life of Pope.

head of the naval force on which the safety of her coasts depended.*

While these changes were making in the offices round Whitehall, the Commissions of Lieutenancy all over the kingdom were revised. The Tories had, during twelve months, been complaining that their share in the government of the districts in which they lived bore no proportion to their number, to their wealth, and to the consideration which they enjoyed in society. They now regained with great delight their former position in their shires. The Whigs raised a cry that the King was foully betrayed, and that he had been induced by evil counsellors to put the sword into the hands of men who, as soon as a favorable opportunity offered, would turn the edge against himself. In a dialogue which was believed to have been written by the newly created Earl of Warrington, and which had a wide circulation at the time, but has long been forgotten, the Lord Lieutenant of a county was introduced expressing his apprehensions that the majority of his deputies were traitors at heart. †
But nowhere was the excitement produced by the new distribution of power so great as in the capital. By a Commission of Lieutenancy which had been issued immediately after the Revolution, the trainbands of London had been put under the command of stanch Whigs. Those powerful and opulent citizens whose names were omitted alleged that the list was filled with elders of Puritan congregations, with Shaftesbury's brisk boys, with Rye House plotters, and that it was scarcely possible to find, mingled with that multitude of fanatics and levellers, a single man sincerely attached to monarchy and to the Church. A new Commission now appeared framed by Caermarthen and Nottingham. They had taken counsel with Compton, the Bishop of the diocese; and Compton was not a very discreet adviser. He had originally been a High Churchman and a Tory. The severity with which he had been treated in the late reign had transformed him into a Latitudinarian and a rebel; and he had now, from jealousy of Tillotson, turned High Churchman and Tory again. The changes which were made by his recommendation raised a storm in the City. The Whigs complained that they were ungratefully proscribed by a government which owed its existence to them; that some of the best

---

* Van Citters to the States General, $\frac{\text{April 25,}}{\text{May 5,}}$ 1690; Narcissus Luttrell's Diary; Treasury Letter Book, Feb. 4, 1689-90.
† The Dialogue between a Lord Lieutenant and one of his Deputies will not be found in the collection of Warrington's writings which was published in 1694, under the sanction as it should seem, of his family.

friends of King William had been dismissed with contumely to make room for some of his worst enemies, for men who were as unworthy of trust as any Irish Rapparee, for men who had delivered up to a tyrant the charter and the immemorial privileges of London, for men who had made themselves notorious by the cruelty with which they had enforced the penal laws against Protestant dissenters, nay, for men who had sate on those juries which had found Russell and Cornish guilty.* The discontent was so great that it seemed, during a short time, likely to cause pecuniary embarrassment to the State. The supplies voted by the late Parliament came in slowly. The wants of the public service were pressing. In such circumstances it was to the citizens of the capital that the government always looked for help ; and the government of William had hitherto looked especially to those citizens who professed Whig opinions. Things were now changed. A few eminent Whigs, in their first anger, sullenly refused to advance money. Nay, one or two unexpectedly withdrew considerable sums from the Exchequer.† The financial difficulties might have been serious, had not some wealthy Tories, who, if Sacheverell's clause had become law, would have been excluded from all municipal honors, offered the Treasury a hundred thousand pounds down, and promised to raise a still larger sum.‡

While the City was thus agitated, came a day appointed by royal proclamation for a general fast. The reasons assigned for this solemn act of devotion were the lamentable state of Ireland and the approaching departure of the King. Prayers were offered up for the safety of His Majesty's person and for the success of his arms. The churches of London were crowded. The most eminent preachers of the capital, who were, with scarcely an exception, either moderate Tories or moderate Whigs, did their best to calm the public mind, and earnestly exhorted their flocks not to withhold, at this great conjuncture, a hearty support from the prince, with whose fate was bound up the fate of the whole nation. Burnet told a large congregation from the pulpit how the Greeks, when the great Turk was preparing to besiege Constantinople, could not be per-

---

* Van Citters to the States General, March 18-28, April 4-14, 1690; Narcissus Luttrell's Diary; Burnet, ii. 72. The Triennial Mayor, or the Rapparees, a Poem, 1691. The poet says of one of the new civil functionaries :

> "Soon his pretence to conscience we can rout,
> And in a bloody jury find him out,
> Where noble Publius worried was with rogues."

† Treasury Minute Book, Feb. 5, 1689-90.
‡ Van Citters, Feb. 11-21, Mar. 14-24, Mar. 14-28, 1690.

suaded to contribute any part of their wealth for the common defence, and how bitterly they repented of their avarice when they were compelled to deliver up to the victorious infidels the treasures which had been refused to the supplications of the last Christian emperor.*

The Whigs, however, as a party, did not stand in need of such an admonition. Grieved and angry as they were, they were perfectly sensible that on the stability of the throne of William depended all that they most highly prized. What some of them might, at this conjuncture, have been tempted to do if they could have found another leader, if, for example, their Protestant Duke, their King Monmouth, had still been living, may be doubted. But their only choice was between the Sovereign whom they had set up and the Sovereign whom they had pulled down. It would have been strange indeed if they had taken part with James in order to punish William, when the worst fault which they imputed to William was that he did not participate in the vindictive feeling with which they remembered the tyranny of James. Much as they disliked the Bill of Indemnity, they had not forgotten the Bloody Circuit. They therefore, even in their ill humor, continued true to their own King, and, while grumbling at him, were ready to stand by him against his adversary with their lives and fortunes.†

There were indeed exceptions: but they were very few; and they were to be found almost exclusively in two classes, which, though widely differing from each other in social position, closely resembled each other in laxity of principle. All the Whigs who are known to have trafficked with Saint Germains, belonged, not to the main body of the party, but either to the head or to the tail. They were either patricians high in rank and office, or caitiffs who had long been employed in the foulest drudgery of faction. To the former class belonged Shrewsbury. Of the latter class the most remarkable specimen was Robert Ferguson. From the day on which the Convention Parliament was dissolved, Shrewsbury began to waver in his allegiance: but that he had ever wavered was not, till long after, suspected by the public. That Ferguson had, a few months after the Revolution, become a furious Jacobite, was no secret to anybody, and ought not to have been matter of surprise to anybody. For his apostasy he could not plead even the miserable excuse that he had been neglected. The igno-

---

* Van Citters, March 14-26, 1690. But he is mistaken as to the preacher. The sermon is extant. It was preached at Bow Church before the Court of Aldermen.
† Welwood's Mercurius Reformatus, Feb. 12, 1690.

minious services which he had formerly rendered to his party as a spy, a raiser of riots, a dispenser of bribes, a writer of libels, a prompter of false witnesses, had been rewarded only too prodigally for the honor of the new government. That he should hold any high office was of course impossible. But a sinecure place of five hundred a year had been created for him in the department of the Excise. He now had what to him was opulence : but opulence did not satisfy him. For money indeed he had never scrupled to be guilty of fraud aggravated by hypocrisy : yet the love of money was not his strongest passion. Long habit had developed in him a moral disease from which people who have made political agitation their calling are seldom wholly free. He could not be quiet. Sedition, from being his business, had become his pleasure. It was as impossible for him to live without doing mischief as for an old dram drinker or an old opium eater to live without the daily dose of poison. The very discomforts and hazards of a lawless life had a strange attraction for him. He could no more be turned into a peaceable and loyal subject than the fox can be turned into a shepherd's dog, or than the kite can be taught the habits of the barn-door fowl. The Red Indian prefers his hunting ground to cultivated fields and stately cities : the gypsy, sheltered by a commodious root, and provided with meat in due season, still pines for the ragged tent on the moor and the chance meal of carrion ; and even so Ferguson became weary of plenty and security, of his salary, his house, his table, and his coach, and longed to be again the president of societies into which none could enter without a password, the director of secret presses, the distributor of inflammatory pamphlets ; to see the walls placarded with descriptions of his person and offers of reward for his apprehension ; to have six or seven names, with a different wig and cloak for each, and to change his lodgings thrice a week at dead of night. His hostility was not to Popery or to Protestantism, to monarchical government or to republican government, to the House of Stuart or to the House of Nassau, but to whatever was at the time established.

By the Jacobites this new ally was eagerly welcomed. They were at that moment busied with schemes in which the help of a veteran plotter was much needed. There had been a great stir among them from the day on which it had been announced that William had determined to take the command in Ireland ; and they were all looking forward with impatient hope to his departure. He was not one of those princes against whom men lightly venture to set up a standard of rebellion. His courage, his sagacity, the secrecy of his counsels, the success which had generally crowned his enterprises, overawed the vulgar. Even his most acrimonious enemies feared him at least as much as they hated him. While he was at Kensington, ready to take horse at a moment's notice, malecontents who prized their heads and their estates were generally content to vent their hatred by drinking confusion to his hooked nose, and by squeezing with significant energy the orange which was his emblem. But their courage rose when they reflected that the sea would soon roll between him and our island. In the military and political calculations of that age, thirty leagues of water were as important as three hundred leagues now are. The winds and waves frequently interrupted all communication between England and Ireland. It sometimes happened that, during a fortnight or three weeks, not a word of intelligence from London reached Dublin. Twenty English counties might be up in arms long before any rumor that an insurrection was even apprehended could reach Ulster. Early in the spring, therefore, the leading malecontents assembled in London for the purpose of concerting an extensive plan of action, and corresponded assiduously both with France and with Ireland.

Such was the temper of the English factions when, on the twentieth of March, the new Parliament met. The first duty which the Commons had to perform was that of choosing a Speaker. Trevor was proposed by Lowther, was elected without opposition, and was presented and approved with the ordinary ceremonial. The King then made a speech in which he especially recommended to the consideration of the Houses two important subjects, the settling of the revenue and the granting of an amnesty. He represented strongly the necessity of despatch. Every day was precious, the season for action was approaching. "Let not us," he said, "be engaged in debates while our enemies are in the field." *

The first subject which the Commons took into consideration was the state of the revenue. A great part of the taxes had, since the accession of William and Mary, been collected under the authority of Acts passed for short terms, and it was now time to determine on a permanent arrangement. A list of the salaries and pensions for which provision was to be made was laid before the House; and the amount of the sums thus expended called forth very just complaints from the indepen-

---

* Commons' Journals, March 20, 21, 22, 1689-90.

dent members, among whom Sir Charles Sedley distinguished himself by his sarcastic pleasantry. A clever speech which he made against the placemen stole into print and was widely circulated; it has since been often republished; and it proves, what his poems and plays might make us doubt, that his contemporaries were not mistaken in considering him as a man of parts and vivacity. Unfortunately the ill-humor which the sight of the Civil List caused evaporated in jests and invectives without producing any reform.

The ordinary revenue by which the government had been supported before the Revolution had been partly hereditary, and had been partly drawn from taxes granted to each sovereign for life. The hereditary revenue had passed, with the crown, to William and Mary. It was derived from the rents of the royal domains, from fees, from fines, from wine licenses, from the first fruits and tenths of benefices, from the receipts of the Post Office, and from that part of the excise which had, immediately after the Restoration, been granted to Charles the Second and to his successors for ever in lieu of the feudal services due to our ancient kings. The income from all these sources was estimated at between four and five hundred thousand pounds.*

Those duties of excise and customs which had been granted to James for life had, at the close of his reign, yielded about nine hundred thousand pounds annually. William naturally wished to have this income on the same terms on which his uncle had enjoyed it; and his ministers did their best to gratify his wishes. Lowther moved that the grant should be to the King and Queen for their joint and separate lives, and spoke repeatedly and earnestly in defence of this motion. He set forth William's claims to public gratitude and confidence; the nation rescued from Popery and arbitrary power; the Church delivered from persecution; the constitution established on a firm basis. Would the Commons deal grudgingly with a prince who had done more for England than had ever been done for her by any of his predecessors in so short a time, with a prince who was now about to expose himself to hostile weapons and pestilential air in order to preserve the English colony in Ireland, with a prince who was prayed for in every corner of the world where a congregation of Protestants could meet for the worship of God? † But on this subject Lowther harangued in

---

* Commons' Journals, March 28, 1690, and March 1, and March 20, 1688-9.
† Grey's Debates, March 27, and 28, 1690.

vain. Whigs and Tories were equally fixed in the opinion that the liberality of Parliaments had been the chief cause of the disasters of the last thirty years; that to the liberality of the Parliament of 1660 was to be ascribed the misgovernment of the Cabal, that to the liberality of the Parliament of 1685 was to be abscribed the Declaration of Indulgence, and that the Parliament of 1690 would be inexcusable if it did not profit by experience. After much dispute a compromise was made. That portion of the excise which had been settled for life on James, and which was estimated at three hundred thousand pounds a year, was settled on William and Mary for their joint and separate lives. It was supposed that with the hereditary revenue, and with three hundred thousand a year more from the excise, Their Majesties would have, independent of parliamentary control, between seven and eight hundred thousand a year. Out of this income was to be defrayed the charge both of the royal household and of those civil offices of which a list had been laid before the House. This income was, therefore, called the Civil List. The expenses of the royal household are now entirely separated from the expenses of the civil government; but, by a whimsical perversion, the name of Civil List has remained attached to that portion of the revenue which is appropriated to the expenses of the royal household. It is still more strange that several neighboring nations should have thought this most unmeaning of all names worth borrowing. Those duties of customs which had been settled for life on Charles and James successively, and which, in the year before the Revolution, had yielded six hundred thousand pounds, were granted to the Crown for a term of only four years.*

William was by no means well pleased with this arrangement. He thought it unjust and ungrateful in a people whose liberties he had saved to bind him over to his good behavior. "The gentlemen of England," he said to Burnet, "trusted King James, who was an enemy of their religion and of their laws; and they will not trust me by whom their religion and their laws have been preserved." Burnet answered very properly that there was no mark of personal confidence which His Majesty was not entitled to demand, but that this question was not a question of personal confidence. The Estates of the Realm wished to establish a general principle. They wished to set a precedent which might secure a remote posterity against

* Commons' Journals, Mar. 28, 1690. A very clear and exact account of the way in which the revenue was settled was sent by Van Citters to the States General, April 7-17, 1690.

evils such as the indiscreet liberality of former parliaments had produced. "From those evils Your Majesty has delivered this generation. By accepting the gift of the Commons on the terms on which it is offered, Your Majesty will be also a deliverer of future generations." William was not convinced: but he had too much wisdom and self-command to give way to his ill humor, and he accepted graciously what he could not but consider as ungraciously given.*

The Civil List was charged with an annuity of twenty thousand pounds to the Princess of Denmark, in addition to an annuity of thirty thousand pounds which had been settled on her at the time of her marriage. This arrangement was the result of a compromise which had been effected with much difficulty and after many irritating disputes. The King and Queen had never, since the commencement of their reign, been on very good terms with their sister. That William should have been disliked by a woman who had just sense enough to perceive that his temper was sour and his manners repulsive, and who was utterly incapable of appreciating his higher qualities, is not extraordinary. But Mary was made to be loved. So lively and intelligent a woman could not indeed derive much pleasure from the society of Anne, who, when in good humor, was meekly stupid, and, when in bad humor, was sulkily stupid. Yet the Queen, whose kindness had endeared her to her humblest attendants, would hardly have made an enemy of one whom it was her duty and her interest to make a friend, had not an interest strangely potent and strangely malignant been incessantly at work to divide the Royal House against itself. The fondness of the Princess for Lady Marlborough was such as, in a superstitious age, would have been ascribed to some talisman or potion. Not only had the friends, in their confidential intercourse with each other, dropped all ceremony and all titles, and become plain Mrs. Morley and plain Mrs. Freeman; but even Prince George, who cared as much for the dignity of his birth as he was capable of caring for anything but claret and calvered salmon, submitted to be Mr. Morley. The countess boasted that she had selected the name of Freeman because it was peculiarly suited to the frankness and boldness of her character; and, to do her justice, it was not by the ordinary arts of courtiers that she established and long maintained her despotic empire over the feeblest of minds. She had little of that tact which is the characteristic talent of her sex: she was

---

* Burnet, ii. 43.

far too violent to flatter or to dissemble : but, by a rare chance, she had fallen in with a nature on which dictation and contradiction acted as philters. In this grotesque friendship all the loyalty, the patience, the self-devotion, was on the side of the mistress. The whims, the haughty airs, the fits of ill temper, were on the side of the waiting woman.

Nothing is more curious than the relation in which the two ladies stood to Mr. Freeman, as they called Marlborough. In foreign countries people knew in general that Anne was governed by the Churchills. They knew also that the man who appeared to enjoy so large a share of her favor was not only a great soldier and politician, but also one of the finest gentlemen of his time, that his face and figure were eminently handsome, his temper at once bland and resolute, his manners at once engaging and noble. Nothing could be more natural than that graces and accomplishments like his should win a female heart. On the Continent therefore many persons imagined that he was Anne's favored lover ; and he was so described in contemporary French libels which have long been forgotten. In England this calumny never gained credit even with the vulgar, and is nowhere to be found even in the most ribald doggrel that was sung about our streets. In truth the Princess seems never to have been guilty of a thought inconsistent with her conjugal vows. To her, Marlborough, with all his genius and his valor, his beauty and his grace, was nothing but the husband of her friend. Direct power over Her Royal Highness he had none. He could influence her only by the instrumentality of his wife ; and his wife was no passive instrument. Though it is impossible to discover, in anything that she ever did, said, or wrote, any indication of superior understanding, her fierce passions and strong will enabled her often to rule a husband who was born to rule grave senates and mighty armies. His courage, that courage which the most perilous emergencies of war only made cooler and more steady, failed him when he had to encounter his Sarah's ready tears and voluble reproaches, the poutings of her lip and the tossings of her head. History exhibits to us few spectacles more remarkable than that of a great and wise man, who, when he had contrived vast and profound schemes of policy, could carry them into effect only by inducing one foolish woman, who was often unmanageable, to manage another woman who was more foolish still.

In one point the Earl and the Countess were perfectly agreed. They were equally bent on getting money ; though, when it was got, he loved to hoard it, and she was not unwilling to spend it.* The favor of the Princess they both regarded as a valuable estate. In her father's reign they had begun to grow rich by means of her bounty. She was naturally inclined to parsimony, and even when she was on the throne, her equipages and tables were by no means sumptuous.† It might have been thought, therefore, that, while she was a subject, thirty thousand a year, with a residence in the palace, would have been more than sufficient for all her wants. There were probably not in the kingdom two noblemen possessed of such an income. But no income would satisfy the greediness of those who governed her. She repeatedly contracted debts which James repeatedly discharged, not without expressing much surprise and displeasure.

The Revolution opened to the Churchills a new and boundless prospect of gain. The whole conduct of their mistress at the great crisis had proved that she had no will, no judgment, no conscience, but theirs. To them she had sacrificed affections, prejudices, habits, interests. In obedience to them, she had joined in the conspiracy against her father; she had fled from Whitehall in the depth of winter, through ice and mire, to a hackney coach : she had taken refuge in the rebel camp: she had consented to yield her place in the order of succession to the Prince of Orange. They saw with pleasure that she, over whom they possessed such boundless influence, possessed no common influence over others. Scarcely had the Revolution been accomplished when many Tories, disliking both the King who had been driven out and the King who had come in, and doubting whether their religion had more to fear from Jesuits or from Latitudinarians, showed a strong disposition to rally round Anne. Nature had made her a bigot. Such was the constitution of her mind that to the religion of her nursery she could not but adhere, without examination and without doubt, till she was laid in her coffin. In the court of her father she had been deaf to all that could be urged in favor of transubstantiation and auricular confession. In the court of her brother-in-law she was equally deaf to all that could be urged in favor of a general union among Protestants. This slowness and obstinacy made her important. It

---

* In a contemporary lampoon are these lines :
 "Oh, happy couple ! In their life
  There does appear no sign of strife ;
  They do agree so in the main,
  To sacrifice their souls for gain."—The Female Nine, 1690.

† Swift mentions the deficiency of hospitality and magnificence in her household. Journal to Stella, August 8, 1711.

was a great thing to be the only member of the Royal Family
who regarded Papists and Presbyterians with impartial aversion.
While a large party was disposed to make her an idol, she was
regarded by her two artful servants merely as a puppet. They
knew that she had it in her power to give serious annoyance to
the government; and they determined to use this power in
order to extort money, nominally for her, but really for themselves.
While Marlborough was commanding the English
forces in the Low Countries, the execution of the plan was
necessarily left to his wife; and she acted, not as he would
doubtless have acted, with prudence and temper, but, as is plain
even from her own narrative, with odious violence and insolence.
Indeed she had passions to gratify from which he was altogether
free. He, though one of the most covetous, was one of the least
acrimonious of mankind: but malignity was in her a stronger
passion than avarice. She hated easily: she hated heartily: and
she hated implacably. Among the objects of her hatred were
all who were related to her mistress either on the paternal or on
the maternal side. No person who had a natural interest in the
Princess could observe without uneasiness the strange infatuation
which made her the slave of an imperious and reckless
termagant. This the Countess well knew. In her view the
Royal Family and the family of Hyde, however they might differ
as to other matters, were leagued against her; and she detested
them all, James and James's Queen, William and Mary, Clarendon
and Rochester. Now was the time to wreak the accumulated
spite of years. It was not enough to obtain a great, a
regal, revenue for Anne. That revenue must be obtained by
means which would wound and humble those whom the favorite
abhorred. It must not be asked, it must not be accepted, as a
mark of fraternal kindness, but demanded in hostile tones, and
wrung by force from reluctant hands. No application was
made to the King and Queen. But they learned with astonishment
that Lady Marlborough was indefatigable in canvassing
the Tory members of Parliament, that a Princess's party was
forming, that the House of Commons would be moved to settle
on Her Royal Highness a vast income independent of the
Crown. Mary asked her sister what these proceedings meant.
"I hear," said Anne, "that my friends have a mind to make
me some settlement." It is said that the Queen, greatly hurt
by an expression which seemed to imply that she and her husband
were not among her sister's friends, replied with unwonted
sharpness. "Of what friends do you speak? What

friends have you except the King and me?"* The subject was never again mentioned between the sisters. Mary was probably sensible that she had made a mistake, in addressing herself to one who was merely a passive instrument in the hands of others. An attempt was made to open a negotiation with the Countess. After some inferior agents had expostulated with her in vain, Shrewsbury waited on her. It might have been expected that his intervention would have been successful: for, if the scandalous chronicle of those times could be trusted, he had stood high, too high, in her favor.† He was authorized by the King to promise that, if the Princess would desist from soliciting the members of the House of Commons to support her cause, the income of Her Royal Highness should be increased from thirty thousand pounds to fifty thousand. The Countess flatly rejected this offer. The King's word, she had the insolence to hint, was not a sufficient security. "I am confident," said Shrewsbury, "that His Majesty will strictly fulfil his engagements. If he breaks them I will not serve him an hour longer." "That may be very honorable in you," answered the pertinacious vixen: "but it will be very poor comfort to the Princess." Shrewsbury after vainly attempting to move the servant, was at length admitted to an audience of the mistress. Anne, in language doubtless dictated by her friend Sarah, told him that the business had gone too far to be stopped, and must be left to the decision of the Commons. ‡

The truth was that the Princess's prompters hoped to obtain from Parliament a much larger sum than was offered by the King. Nothing less than seventy thousand a year would content them. But their cupidity overreached itself. The House of Commons showed a great disposition to gratify Her Royal Highness. But, when at length her too eager adherents ventured to name the sum which they wished to grant, the murmurs were loud. Seventy thousand a year at a time when the necessary expenses of the State were daily increasing, when the receipt of the customs was daily diminishing, when trade was low, when every gentleman, every merchant, was retrenching something from the charge of his table and his cellar! The general opinion was that the sum which the King was under

---

* Duchess of Marlborough's Vindication. But the Duchess was so abandoned a liar that it is impossible to believe a word that she says, except when she accuses herself.

† See the Female Nine.

‡ The Duchess of Marlborough's Vindication. With that habitual inaccuracy, which, even when she has no motive for lying, makes it necessary to read every word written or dictated by her with suspicion, she creates Shrewsbury a Duke, and represents herself as calling him "Your Grace." He was not made a Duke till 1694.

stood to be willing to give would be amply sufficient.* At last something was conceded on both sides. The Princess was forced to content herself with fifty thousand a year; and William agreed that this sum should be settled on her by Act of Parliament. She rewarded the services of Lady Marlborough with a pension of a thousand a year;† but this was in all probability a very small part of what the Churchills gained by the arrangement.

After these transactions the two royal sisters continued during many months to live on terms of civility and even of apparent friendship. But Mary, though she seems to have borne no malice to Anne, undoubtedly felt against Lady Marlborough as much resentment as a very gentle heart is capable of feeling. Marlborough had been out of England during a great part of the time which his wife had spent in canvassing among the Tories, and, though he had undoubtedly acted in concert with her, had acted, as usual, with temper and decorum. He therefore continued to receive from William many marks of favor which were unaccompanied by any indication of displeasure.

In the debates on the settling of the revenue, the distinction between Whigs and Tories does not appear to have been very clearly marked. In truth, if there was anything about which the two parties were agreed, it was the expediency of granting the customs to the Crown for a time not exceeding four years. But there were other questions which called forth the old animosity in all its strength. The Whigs were now a minority, but a minority formidable in numbers, and more formidable in ability. They carried on the parliamentary war, not less acrimoniously than when they were a majority, but somewhat more artfully. They brought forward several motions, such as no High Churchman could well support, yet such as no servant of William and Mary could well oppose. The Tory who voted for those motions would run a great risk of being pointed at as a turncoat by the sturdy Cavaliers of his country. The Tory who voted against those motions would run a great risk of being frowned upon at Kensington.

It was apparently in pursuance of this policy that the Whigs laid on the table of the House of Lords a bill declaring all the laws passed by the Parliament to be valid laws. No sooner had this bill been read than the controversy of the preceding spring was renewed. The Whigs were joined on this occasion by almost all those noblemen who were connected with the

---

* Commons' Journals, December 17 and 18, 1689.
† Vindication of the Duchess of Marlborough.

government. The rigid Tories, with Nottingham at their head, professed themselves willing to enact that every statute passed in 1689 should have the same force that it would have had if it had been passed by a parliament convoked in a regular manner: but nothing would induce them to acknowledge that an assembly of lords and gentlemen, who had come together without authority from the Great Seal, was constitutionally a Parliament. Few questions seem to have excited stronger passions than the question, practically altogether unimportant, whether the bill should or should not be declaratory. Nottingham, always upright and honorable, but a bigot and a formalist, was on this subject singularly obstinate and unreasonable. In one debate he lost his temper, forgot the decorum which in general he strictly observed, and narrowly escaped being committed to the custody of the Black Rod.* After much wrangling, the Whigs carried their point by a majority of seven.† Many peers signed a strong protest written by Nottingham. In this protest the bill, which was indeed open to verbal criticism, was contemptuously described as being neither good English nor good sense. The majority passed a resolution that the protest should be expunged; and against this resolution Nottingham and his followers again protested.‡ The King was displeased by the pertinacity of his Secretary of State; so much displeased indeed that Nottingham declared his intention of resigning the Seals: but the dispute was soon accommodated. William was too wise not to know the value of an honest man in a dishonest age. The very scrupulosity which made Nottingham a mutineer was a security that he would never be a traitor.§

The Bill went down to the Lower House; and it was fully expected that the contest there would be long and fierce; but a single speech settled the question. Somers, with a force and eloquence which surprised even an audience accustomed to hear him with pleasure, exposed the absurdity of the doctrine held by the High Tories. "If the Convention,"—it was thus that he argued,—" was not a Parliament, how can we be a Parliament? An Act of Elizabeth provides that no person shall sit or vote in this House till he has taken the old oath of supremacy. Not one of us has taken that oath. Instead of it, we have all taken the new oath of supremacy which the late

---

* Van Citters, April 8-18, 1690.
† Van Citters, April 8-18; Luttrell's Diary.
‡ Lords' Journals, April 8 and 10, 1690; Burnet, ii. 42.
§ Van Citters, April 25/May 5, 1690.

Parliament substituted for the old oath. It is, therefore, a contradiction to say that the Acts of the late Parliament are not now valid, and yet to ask us to enact that they shall henceforth be valid. For either they already are so, or we never can make them so." This reasoning, which was in truth as unanswerable as that of Euclid, brought the debate to a speedy close. The bill passed the Commons within forty-eight hours after it had been read the first time.*

This was the only victory won by the Whigs during the whole session. They complained loudly in the Lower House of the change which had been made in the military government of the City of London. The Tories, conscious of their strength, and heated by resentment, not only refused to censure what had been done, but determined to express publicly and formally their gratitude to the King for having brought in so many churchmen and turned out so many schismatics. An address of thanks was moved by Clarges, member for Westminster, who was known to be attached to Caermarthen. "The alterations which have been made in the City," said Clarges, "show that His Majesty has a tender care of us. I hope that he will make similar alterations in every county of the realm." The minority struggled hard. "Will you thank the King," they said, "for putting the sword into the hands of his most dangerous enemies? Some of those whom he had been advised to entrust with military command had not yet been able to bring themselves to take the oath of allegiance to him. Others were well known, in the evil days, as stanch jurymen, who were sure to find an Exclusionist guilty on any evidence or no evidence." Nor did the Whig orators refrain from using those topics on which all factions are eloquent in the hour of distress, and which all factions are but too ready to treat lightly in the hour of prosperity. "Let us not," they said, "pass a vote which conveys a reflection on a large body of our countrymen, good subjects, good Protestants. The King ought to be the head of his whole people. Let us not make him the head of a party." This was excellent doctrine: but it scarcely became the lips of men who, a few weeks before, had opposed the Indemnity Bill and voted for the Sacheverell clause. The address was carried by a hundred and eighty-five votes to a hundred and thirty-six.†

As soon as the numbers had been announced, the minority

---

* Commons' Journals, April 8 and 9, 1690; Grey's Debates; Burnet, ii. 42. Van Citters, writing on the 8th, mentions that a great struggle in the Lower House was expected.

† Commons' Journals, April 24, 1690; Grey's Debates.

smarting from their defeat, brought forward a motion which caused no little embarrassment to the Tory placemen. The oath of allegiance, the Whigs said, was drawn in terms far too lax. It might exclude from public employment a few honest Jacobites who were generally too dull to be mischievous: but it was altogether inefficient as a means of binding the supple and slippery consciences of cunning priests, who, while affecting to hold the Jesuits in abhorrence, were proficients in that immoral casuistry which was the worst part of Jesuitism. Some grave divines had openly said, others had even dared to write, that they had sworn fealty to William in a sense altogether different from that in which they had sworn fealty to James. To James they had plighted the entire faith which a loyal subject owes to a rightful sovereign: but, when they promised to bear true allegiance to William, they meant only that they would not, whilst he was able to hang them for rebelling or conspiring against him, run any risk of being hanged. None could wonder that the precepts and example of the malecontent clergy should have corrupted the malecontent laity. When Prebendaries and Rectors were not ashamed to avow that they had equivocated in the very act of kissing the Gospels, it was hardly to be expected that attorneys and tax-gatherers would be more scrupulous. The consequence was that every department swarmed with traitors; that men who ate the King's bread, men who were entrusted with the duty of collecting and disbursing his revenues, of victualling his ships, of clothing his soldiers, of making his artillery ready for the field, were in the habit of calling him an usurper, and of drinking to his speedy downfall. Could any government be safe which was hated and betrayed by its own servants? And was not the English government exposed to dangers which even if all its servants were true, might well excite serious apprehensions? A disputed succession, war with France, war in Scotland, war in Ireland, was not all this enough without treachery in every arsenal and in every custom-house? There must be an oath drawn in language too precise to be explained away, in language which no Jacobite could repeat without the consciousness that he was perjuring himself. Though the zealots of indefeasible hereditary right had in general no objection to swear allegiance to William, they would probably not choose to abjure James. On such grounds as these, an Abjuration Bill of extreme severity was brought into the House of Commons. It was proposed to enact that every person who held any office, civil, military, or spiritual, should, on pain of deprivation, solemnly abjure the exiled King; that the oath of abjuration might be tendered by any justice of the peace to any subject of Their Majesties; and that, if it were refused, the recusant should be sent to prison, and should lie there as long as he continued obstinate.

The severity of this last provision was generally and most justly blamed. To turn every ignorant meddling magistrate into a state inquisitor, to insist that a plain man, who lived peaceably, who obeyed the laws, who paid his taxes, who had never held and who did not expect ever to hold any office, and who had never troubled his head about problems of political philosophy, should declare, under the sanction of an oath, a decided opinion on a point about which the most learned doctors of the age had written whole libraries of controversial books, and to send him to rot in a jail if he could not bring himself to swear, would surely have been the height of tyranny. The clause, which required public functionaries, on pain of a deprivation, to abjure the deposed King, was not open to the same objection. Yet even against this clause some weighty arguments were urged. A man, it was said, who has an honest heart and a sound understanding, is sufficiently bound by the present oath. Every such man when he swears to be faithful and to bear true allegiance to King William, does, by necessary implication, abjure King James. There may doubtless be among the servants of the State, and even among the ministers of the Church, some persons who have no sense of honor or religion, and who are ready to forswear themselves for lucre. There may be others who have contracted the pernicious habit of quibbling away the most sacred obligations, and who have convinced themselves that they can innocently make, with a mental reservation, a promise which it would be sinful to make without such a reservation. Against these two classes of Jacobites it is true that the present test affords no security. But will the new test, will any test, be more efficacious? Will a person who has no conscience, or a person whose conscience can be set at rest by immoral sophistry, hesitate to repeat any phrase you can dictate? The former will kiss the book without any scruple at all. The scruples of the latter will be very easily removed. He now swears allegiance to one King with a mental reservation. He will then abjure the other King with a mental reservation. Do not flatter yourselves that the ingenuity of lawgivers will ever devise an oath which the ingenuity of casuists will not evade. What indeed is the value of any oath in such a matter? Among the many lessons which the troubles of the last generation have left us none is more plain than this, that no form of words, however precise, no imprecation, however awful, ever saved, or ever will save, a government from destruction. Was not the Solemn League and Covenant burned by the common hangman amidst the huzzas of tens of thousands who had themselves subscribed it? Among the statesmen and warriors who bore the chief part in restoring Charles the Second, how many were there who had not repeatedly abjured him? Nay, is it not well known that some of those persons boastfully declared that, if they had not abjured him, they never could have restored him?

The debates were sharp; and the issue during a short time seemed doubtful: for some of the Tories who were in office were unwilling to give a vote which might be thought to indicate that they were lukewarm in the cause of the King whom they served. William, however, took care to let it be understood that he had no wish to impose a new test on his subjects. A few words from him decided the event of the conflict. The bill was rejected thirty-six hours after it had been brought in by a hundred and ninety-two votes to a hundred and sixty-five.*

Even after this defeat the Whigs pertinaciously returned to the attack. Having failed in one House they renewed the battle in the other. Five days after the Abjuration Bill had been thrown out in the Commons, another Abjuration Bill, somewhat milder, but still very severe, was laid on the table of the Lords.† What was now proposed was that no person should sit in either House of Parliament or hold any office, civil, military, or judicial, without making a declaration that he would stand by William and Mary against James and James's adherents. Every male in the kingdom who had attained the age of sixteen was to make the same declaration before a certain day. If he failed to do so he was to pay double taxes and to be incapable of exercising the elective franchise.

On the day fixed for the second reading, the King came down to the House of Peers. He gave his assent in form to several laws, unrobed, took his seat on a chair of state which had been placed for him, and listened with much interest to the debate. To the general surprise, two noblemen who had been

---

* Commons' Journals, April 24, 25, and 26; Grey's Debates; Narcissus Luttrell's Diary. Narcissus is unusually angry. He calls the bill " a perfect trick of the fanatics to turn out the Bishops and most of the Church of England Clergy." In a Whig pasquinade entitled, " A Speech intended to have been spoken on the Triennial Bill, on Jan. 28,' 1692-3, the King is said to have " browbeaten the Abjuration Bill."

† Lords' Journals, May 1, 1690. This Bill is among the Archives of the House of Lords. Burnet confounds it with the bill which the Commons had rejected in the preceding week. Ralph, who saw that Burnet had committed a blunder, but did not see what the blunder was, has, in trying to correct it, added several blunders of his own; and the Oxford editor of Burnet has been misled by Ralph.

eminently zealous for the Revolution spoke against the proposed test. Lord Wharton, a Puritan who had fought for the Long Parliament, said, with amusing simplicity, that he was a very old man, that he had lived through troubled times, that he had taken a great many oaths in his day, and that he was afraid that he had not kept them all. He prayed that the sin might not be laid to his charge; and he declared that he could not consent to lay any more snares for his own soul and for the souls of his neighbors. The Earl of Macclesfield, the captain of the English volunteers who had accompanied William from Helvoetsluys to Torbay, declared that he was much in the same case with Lord Wharton. Marlborough supported the bill. He wondered, he said, that it should be opposed by Macclesfield, who had borne so prominent a part in the Revolution. Macclesfield, irritated by the charge of inconsistency, retorted with terrible severity: "The noble Earl," he said, "exaggerates the share which I had in the deliverance of our country. I was ready, indeed, and always shall be ready, to venture my life in defence of her laws and liberties. But there are lengths to which, even for the sake of her laws and liberties, I could never go. I only rebelled against a bad King; there were those who did much more." Marlborough, though not easily discomposed, could not but feel the edge of this sarcasm: William looked displeased; and the aspect of the whole House was troubled and gloomy. It was resolved by fifty-one votes to forty that the bill should be committed; and it was committed, but never reported. After many hard struggles between the Whigs headed by Shrewsbury and the Tories headed by Caermarthen, it was so much mutilated that it retained little more than its name, and did not seem to those who had introduced it to be worth any further contest.*

The discomfiture of the Whigs was completed by a communication from the King. Caermarthen appeared in the House of Lords bearing in his hand a parchment signed by William. It was an Act of Grace for political offences.

Between an Act of Grace originating with the Sovereign and an Act of Indemnity originating with the Estates of the Realm there are some remarkable distinctions. An Act of Indemnity passes through all the stages through which other laws pass, and may, during its progress, be amended by either House. An Act of Grace is received with peculiar marks of respect, is read only

* Lords' Journals. May, 2 and 3, 1690; Van Citters, May 2; Narcissus Luttrell's Diary; Burnet, ii, 44; and Lord Dartmouth's note. The changes made by the Committee may be seen on the bill in the archives of the House of Lords.

once by the Lords and once by the Commons, and must be either rejected altogether or accepted as it stands.* William had not ventured to submit such an Act to the preceding Parliament. But in the new Parliament he was certain of a majority. The minority gave no trouble. The stubborn spirit which had, during two sessions, obstructed the progress of the Bill of Indemnity had been at length broken by defeats and humiliations. Both Houses stood up uncovered while the Act of Grace was read, and gave their sanction to it without one dissentient voice.

There would not have been this unanimity had not a few great criminals been excluded from the benefits of the amnesty. Foremost among them stood the surviving members of the High Court of Justice which had sate on Charles the First. With these ancient men were joined the two nameless executioners who had done their office, with masked faces, on the scaffold before the Banqueting House. None knew who they were, or of what rank. It was probable that they had been long dead. Yet it was thought necessary to declare that, if even now, after the lapse of forty-one years, they should be discovered, they would still be liable to the punishment of their great crime. Perhaps it would hardly have been thought necessary to mention these men, if the animosities of the preceding generation had not been rekindled by the recent appearance of Ludlow in England. About thirty of the agents of the tyranny of James were left to the law. With these exceptions, all political offences, committed before the day on which the royal signature was affixed to the Act, were covered with a general oblivion.† Even the criminals who were by name excluded had little to fear. Many of them were in foreign countries; and those who were in England were well assured that, unless they committed some new fault, they would not be molested.

The Act of Grace the nation owed to William alone; and it is one of his noblest and purest titles to renown. From the commencement of the civil troubles of the seventeenth century down to the Revolution, every victory gained by either party had been followed by a sanguinary proscription. When the Roundheads triumphed over the Cavaliers, when the Cavaliers triumphed over the Roundheads, when the fable of the Popish plot gave the ascendency to the Whigs, when the detection of the Rye House Plot transferred the ascendancy to the Tories, blood, and more blood, and still more blood, had flowed. Every

---

* These distinctions were much discussed at the time. Van Citters, May 20-30, 1690.
† Stat. 2 W. & M. sess. 1, c. 10.

great explosion and every great recoil of public feeling had been accompanied by severities which, at the time, the predominant faction loudly applauded, but which on a calm review, history and posterity have condemned. No wise and humane man, whatever may be his political opinions, now mentions without reprehension the death either of Laud or of Anne, either of Stafford or of Russell. Of the alternate butcheries the last and the worst is that which is inseparably associated with the name of James and Jeffreys. But it assuredly would not have been the last, perhaps it might not have been the worst, if William had not had the virtue and the firmness resolutely to withstand the importunity of his most zealous adherents. These men were bent on exacting a terrible retribution for all they had undergone during seven disastrous years. The scaffold of Sidney, the gibbet of Cornish, the stake at which Elizabeth Gaunt had perished in the flames for the crime of harboring a fugitive, the porches of the Somersetshire churches surmounted by the skulls and quarters of murdered peasants, the holds of those Jamaica ships from which every day the carcass of some prisoner dead of thirst and foul air had been flung to the sharks, all these things were fresh in the memory of the party which the Revolution had made, for a time, dominant in the State. Some chiefs of that party had redeemed their necks by paying heavy ransom. Others had languished long in Newgate. Others had starved and shivered, winter after winter, in the garrets of Amsterdam. It was natural that in the day of their power and prosperity they should wish to inflict some part of what they had suffered. During a whole year they pursued their scheme of revenge. They succeeded in defeating Indemnity Bill after Indemnity Bill. Nothing stood between them and their victims, but William's immutable resolution that the glory of the great deliverance which he had wrought should not be sullied by cruelty. His clemency was peculiar to himself. It was not the clemency of an ostentatious man, or of a sentimental man, or of an easy tempered man. It was cold, unconciliating, inflexible. It produced no fine stage effects. It drew on him the savage invectives of those whose malevolent passions he refused to satisfy. It won for him no gratitude from those who owed to him fortune, liberty, and life. While the violent Whigs railed at his lenity, the agents of the fallen tyranny, as soon as they found themselves safe, instead of acknowledging their obligations to him, reproached him in insulting language with the mercy which he had extended to them. His Act of Grace, they said, had completely refuted his Declaration. Was it possible to believe that, if there had been any truth in the charges which he had brought against the late government, he would have granted impunity to the guilty? It was now acknowledged by himself, under his own hand, that the stories by which he and his friends had deluded the nation and driven away the royal family were mere calumnies devised to serve a turn. The turn had been served; and the accusations by which he had inflamed the public mind to madness were coolly withdrawn.* But none of these things moved him. He had done well. He had risked his popularity with men who had been his warmest admirers, in order to give repose and security to men by whom his name was never mentioned without a curse. Nor had he conferred a less benefit on those whom he had disappointed of their revenge than on those whom he had protected. If he had saved one faction from a proscription, he had saved the other from the reaction which such a proscription would inevitably have produced. If his people did not justly appreciate his policy, so much the worse for them. He had discharged his duty by them. He feared no obloquy; and he wanted no thanks.

On the twentieth of May the Act of Grace was passed. The King then informed the Houses that his visit to Ireland could no longer be delayed, that he had therefore determined to prorogue them, and that, unless some unexpected emergency made their advice and assistance necessary to him, he should not call them again from their homes till the next winter. "Then," he said, "I hope, by the blessing of God, we shall have a happy meeting."

The Parliament had passed an Act providing that, whenever he should go out of England, it should be lawful for Mary to administer the government of the kingdom in his name and her own. It was added that he should, nevertheless, during his absence, retain all of his authority. Some objections were made to this arrangement. Here, it was said, were two supreme powers in one State. A public functionary might receive diametrically opposite orders from the King and the Queen, and might not know which to obey. The objection was, beyond all doubt, speculatively just; but there was such perfect confidence and affection between the royal pair that no practical inconvenience was to be apprehended.†

As far as Ireland was concerned, the prospects of William

---

* Roger North was one of the many malecontents who were never tired of harping on this string.
† 2 W. & M. ses. i. c. 6; Grey's Debates. April 29, May 1, 5, 6, 7, 1690.

were much more cheering than they had been a few months earlier. The activity with which he had personally urged forward the preparations for the next campaign had produced an extraordinary effect. The nerves of the government were new strung. In every department of the military administration the influence of a vigorous mind was perceptible. Abundant supplies of food, clothing, and medicine, very different in quality from those which Shales had furnished, were sent across Saint George's Channel. A thousand baggage wagons had been made or collected with great expedition; and, during some weeks, the road between London and Chester was covered with them. Great numbers of recruits were sent to fill the chasms which pestilence had made in the English ranks. Fresh regiments from Scotland, Cheshire, Lancashire, and Cumberland had landed in the Bay of Belfast. The uniforms and arms of the new comers clearly indicated the potent influence of the master's eye. With the British battalions were interspersed several hardy bands of German and Scandinavian mercenaries. Before the end of May the English force in Ulster amounted to thirty thousand fighting men. A few more troops and an immense quantity of military stores were on board of a fleet which lay in the estuary of the Dee, and which was ready to weigh anchor as soon as the King was on board.*

James ought to have made an equally good use of the time during which his army had been in winter quarters. Strict discipline and regular drilling might, in the interval between November and May, have turned the athletic and enthusiastic peasants who were assembled under his standard into good soldiers. But the opportunity was lost. The Court of Dublin was, during that season of inaction, busied with dice and claret, love letters and challenges. The aspect of the capital was indeed not very brilliant. The whole number of coaches which could be mustered there, those of the King and of the French legation included, did not amount to forty.† But though there was little splendor there was much dissoluteness. Grave Roman Catholics shook their heads and said that the Castle did not look like the palace of a King who gloried in being the champion of the Church.‡ The military administration was as deplorable as

---

* Story's Impartial History; Narcissus Luttrell's Diary. † Avaux, Jan. 15-25. 1690.
‡ Macariæ Excidium This most curious work has been recently edited with great care and diligence by Mr. O'Callaghan. I owe so much to his learning and industry that I must readily excuse the national partialty which sometimes, I cannot but think, perverts his judgment. When I quote the Macariæ Excidium, I alway quote the Latin text. The English version is, I am convinced, merely a translation from the Latin, and a very careless and imperfect translation.

ever. The cavalry indeed was, by the exertions of some gallant officers, kept in a high state of efficiency. But a regiment of infantry differed in nothing but name from a large gang of Rapparees. Indeed a gang of Rapparees gave less annoyance to peaceable citizens, and more annoyance to the enemy, than a regiment of infantry. Avaux strongly represented, in a memorial which he delivered to James, the abuses which made the Irish foot a curse and a scandal to Ireland. Whole companies, said the ambassador, quit their colors on the line of march and wander to right and left pillaging and destroying: the soldier takes no care of his arms: the captain never troubles himself to ascertain whether the arms are in good order: the consequence is that one man in every three has lost his musket, and that another man in every three has a musket that will not go off. Avaux adjured the King to prohibit marauding, to give orders that the troops should be regularly exercised, and to punish every officer who suffered his men to neglect their weapons and accoutrements. If these things were done, His Majesty might hope to have, in the approaching spring, an army with which the enemy would be unable to contend. This was good advice: but James was so far from taking it that he would hardly listen to it with patience. Before he heard eight lines read he flew into a passion and accused the ambassador of exaggeration. "This paper, Sir," said Avaux, "is not written to be published. It is meant solely for Your Majesty's information; and, in a paper meant solely for Your Majesty's information, flattery and disguise would be out of place: but I will not persist in reading what is so disagreeable." "Go on," said James very angrily; "I will hear the whole." He gradually became calmer, took the memorial, and promised to adopt some of the suggestions which it contained. But his promise was soon forgotten.*

His financial administration was of a piece with his military administration. His one fiscal resource was robbery, direct or indirect. Every Protestant who had remained in any part of the three southern provinces of Ireland was robbed directly, by the simple process of taking money out of his strong box, drink out of his cellars, fuel from his turf stack, and clothes from his wardrobe. He was robbed indirectly by a new issue of counters, smaller in size and baser in material than any which had yet borne the image and superscription of James. Even brass had begun to be scarce at Dublin; and it was

---

* Avaux. Nov. 14-24, 1689.

necessary to ask assistance from Lewis, who charitably bestowed on his ally an old cracked piece of cannon, to be coined into crowns and shillings.*

But the French king had determined to send over succors of a very different kind. He proposed to take into his own service, and to form by the best discipline then known in the world, four Irish regiments. They were to be commanded by Macarthy, who had been severely wounded and taken prisoner at Newton Butler. His wounds had been healed; and he had regained his liberty by violating his parole. This disgraceful breach of faith he had made more disgraceful by paltry tricks and sophistical excuses which would have become a Jesuit better than a gentleman and a soldier. Lewis was willing that the Irish regiments should be sent to him in rags and unarmed, and insisted only that the men should be stout, and that the officers should not be bankrupt traders, and discarded lacqueys, but, if possible, men of good family, who had seen service. In return for these troops, who were in number not quite four thousand, he undertook to send to Ireland between seven and eight thousand excellent French infantry, who were likely in a day of battle to be of more use than all the kernes of Leinster, Munster, and Connaught together.†

One great error he committed. The army which he was sending to assist James, though small indeed when compared with the army of Flanders or with the army of the Rhine, was destined for a service on which the fate of Europe might depend, and ought therefore to have been commanded by a general of eminent abilities. There was no want of such generals in the French service. But James and his Queen begged hard for Lauzun, and carried this point against the strong representations of Avaux, against the advice of Louvois, and against the judgment of Lewis himself.

When Lauzun went to the cabinet of Louvois to receive in-

---

* Louvois writes to Avaux, $\frac{\text{Dec. 26}}{\text{Jan. 5}}$ 1689-90; "Comme le Roy a veu par vos lettres que le Roy d'Angleterre craignoit de manquer de cuivre pour faire de la monnoye, Sa Majesté a donné ordre que l'on mist sur lee bastiment que portera cette lettre une pièce de canon du calibre de deux qui est eventée, de laquelle ceux qui travaillent à la monnoye du Roy d'Angleterre pourront se servir pour continuer à faire de la monnoye."

Louvois to Avaux, Nov. 1-11, 1689. The force sent by Lewis to Ireland appears by the lists at the French War Office to have amounted to seven thousand two hundred and ninety-one men of all ranks. At the French War Office is a letter from Marshal d'Estrées who saw the four Irish regiments soon after they had landed at Brest. He describes them as "mal chaussés, mal vêtus, et n'ayant point d'uniforme dans leurs habits, si ce n'es q'uils sont tous fort mauvais." A very exact account of Macarthy's breach of parole will be found in Mr. O'Callaghan's History of the Irish Brigades. I am sorry that a writer to whom I owe so much should try to vindicate conduct which, as described by himself, was in the highest degree dishonorable.

structions, the wise minister held language which showed how little confidence he felt in the vain and eccentric knight errant. "Do not, for God's sake, suffer yourself to be hurried away by your desire of fighting. Put all your glory in tiring the English out; and, above all things, maintain strict discipline."*

Not only was the appointment of Lauzun in itself a bad appointment; but, in order that one man might fill a post for which he was unfit, it was necessary to remove two men from posts for which they were eminently fit. Immoral and hardhearted as Rosen and Avaux were, Rosen was a skilful captain, and Avaux was a skilful politician. Though it is not probable that they would have been able to avert the doom of Ireland, it is probable that they might have been able to protract the contest; and it was evidently for the interest of France that the contest should be protracted. But it would have been an affront to the old general to put him under the orders of Lauzun; and between the ambassador and Lauzun there was such an enmity that they could not be expected to act cordially together. Both Rosen and Avaux, therefore, were, with many soothing assurances of royal approbation and favor, recalled to France. They sailed from Cork early in the spring by the fleet which had conveyed Lauzun thither.† Lauzun had so sooner landed than he found that, though he had been long expected, nothing had been prepared for his reception. No lodgings had been provided for his men, no place of security for his stores, no horses, no carriages.‡ His troops had to undergo the hardships of a long march through a desert before they arrived at Dublin. At Dublin, indeed, they found tolerable accommodation. They were billeted on Protestants, lived at free quarters, had plenty of bread, and threepence a day. Lauzun was appointed Commander-in-Chief of the Irish army and took up his residence in the Castle.§ His salary was the same with that of the Lord Lieutenant, eight thousand Jacobuses, equivalent to ten thousand pounds sterling a year. This sum James offered to pay, not in the brass which bore his own effigy, but in French gold. But Lauzun, among whose faults avarice had no place, refused to fill his own coffers from an almost empty treasury. ‖

---

* Lauzun to Louvois, $\frac{\text{May 28,}}{\text{June 7,}}$ and June 16-26, 1690, at the French War Office.
† See the later letters of Avaux.
‡ Avaux to Louvois, March 14-24, 1690; Lauzun to Louvois, $\frac{\text{March 23,}}{\text{April 2.}}$
§ Story's Impartial History; Lauzun to Louvois, May 20-30, 1690.
‖ Lauzun to Louvois, $\frac{\text{May 28,}}{\text{June 7,}}$ 1690.

On him and on the Frenchmen who accompanied him the misery of the Irish people and the imbecility of the Irish administration produced an effect which they found it difficult to describe. Lauzun wrote to Louvois that the Court and the whole kingdom were in a state not to be imagined by a person who had always lived in happier countries. It was, he said, a chaos, such as he had read of in the book of Genesis. The whole business of all the public functionaries was to quarrel with each other, and to plunder the government and the people. After he had been about a month at the Castle, he declared that he would not go through such another month for all the world. His ablest officers confirmed his testimony.* One of them, indeed, was so unjust as to represent the people of Ireland, not merely as ignorant and idle, which they were, but as hopelessly stupid and unfeeling, which they assuredly were not. The English policy, he said, had so completely brutalized them that they could hardly be called human beings. They were insensible to praise and blame, to promises and threats. And yet it was pity of them; for they were physically the finest race of men in the world.†

By this time Schomberg had opened the campaign auspiciously. He had with little difficulty taken Charlemont, the last important fastness which the Irish occupied in Ulster. But the great work of reconquering the three southern provinces of the island he deferred till William should arrive. William meanwhile was busied in making arrangements for the government and defence of England during his absence. He well knew that the Jacobites were on the alert. They had not till very lately been an united and organized faction. There had been, to use Melfort's phrase, numerous gangs, which were all in communication with James at Dublin Castle, or with Mary of Modena at Saint Germains, but which had no connection with each other and were unwilling to trust each other.‡ But since it had been known that the usurper was about to cross the sea, and that his scepter would be left in a female hand, these gangs had been drawing close together, and had begun to

---

* Lauzun to Louvois, April 2-12, May 10-20, 1690. La Hoguette, who held the rank of Maréchal de Camp, wrote to Louvois to the same effect about the same time.

† "La politique des Anglois a été de tenir ces peuples cy comme des esclaves, et si bas qu'il ne leur estoit pas permis d'apprendre à lire et à écrire. Cela les a rendu si bestes qu'ils n'ont presque point d'humanité. Rien ne les esmeut. Ils sont peu sensibles à l'honneur; et les menaces ne les estonnent point. L'interest même ne les peut engager au travail. Ce sont pourtant les gens du monde les mieux faits."—Desgrigny to Louvois, $\frac{\text{May 27,}}{\text{June 6,}}$ 1690.

‡ See Melfort's Letters to James written in October 1689. They are among the Nairne Papers, and were printed by Macpherson.

form one extensive confederacy. Clarendon, who had refused
the oaths, and Aylesbury, who had dishonestly taken them, were
among the chief traitors. Dartmouth, though he had sworn
allegiance to the sovereigns who were in possession, was one of
their most active enemies, and undertook what may be called
the maritime department of the plot. His mind was constantly
occupied by schemes, disgraceful to an English seaman, for the
destruction of the English fleets and arsenals. He was in close
communication with some naval officers, who, though they served
the new government, served it sullenly and with half a heart;
and he flattered himself that by promising these men ample
rewards, and by artfully inflaming the jealous animosity with
which they regarded the Dutch flag, he should prevail on them
to desert and to carry their ships into some French or Irish
port.*

The conduct of Penn was scarcely less scandalous. He was
a zealous and busy Jacobite; and his new way of life was even
more unfavorable than his late way of life had been to moral
purity. It was hardly possible to be at once a consistent Quaker
and a courtier: but it was utterly impossible to be at once a
consistent Quaker and a conspirator. It is melancholy to
relate that Penn, while professing to consider even defensive
war as sinful, did everything in his power to bring a foreign
army into the heart of his own country. He wrote to inform
James that the adherents of the Prince of Orange dreaded nothing so much as an appeal to the sword, and that, if England
were now invaded from France or from Ireland, the number of
Royalists would appear to be greater than ever. Avaux thought
this letter so important, that he sent a translation of it to Lewis.†
A good effect, the shrewd ambassador wrote, had been produced,
by this and similar communications, on the mind of King James.
His Majesty was at last convinced that he could recover his
dominions only sword in hand. It is a curious fact that it
should have been reserved for the great preacher of peace to

---

* Life of James, ii. 443, 450; and Trials of Ashton and Preston.
† Avaux wrote thus to Lewis on the 5th of June 1689: "Il nous est venu des nouvelles assez considérables d'Angleterre et d'Ecosse. Je me donne l'honneur d'en envoyer des mémoires à vostre Majesté, tels que je les ay receus du Roy de la Grande Bretagne. Le commencement des nouvelles dattées d'Angleterre est la copie d'une lettre de M. Pen, que j'ay veue en original." The Mémoire des Nouvelles d'Angleterre et d'Ecosse, which was sent with this despatch, begins with the following sentences, which must therefore have been part of Penn's letter: "Le Prince d'Orange commence d'estre fort dégoutté de l'humeur des Anglois; et la face des choses change bien viste, selon la nature des insulaires; et sa santé est fort mauvaise. Il y a un nuage qui commence à se former au nord des deux royaumes, où le Roy a beaucoup d'amis, ce qui donne beaucoup d'inquiétude aux principaux amis du Prince d'Orange, qui, estant riches, commencent à estre persuadez que ce sera l'espée qui décidera de leur sort, ce qu'ils ont tant taché d'éviter. Ils appréhendent une invasion d'Irlande et de France; et en ce cas le Roy aura plus d'amis que jamais."

produce this conviction in the mind of the old tyrant.* Penn's proceedings had not escaped the observation of the government. Warrants had been out against him; and he had been taken into custody; but the evidence against him had not been such as would support a charge of high treason: he had, as, with all his faults, he deserved to have, many friends in every party: he therefore soon regained his liberty, and returned to his plots.†

But the chief conspirator was Richard Graham, Viscount Preston, who had, in the late reign, been Secretary of State. Though a peer in Scotland, he was only a baronet in England. He had, indeed, received from Saint Germains an English patent of nobility, but the patent bore a date posterior to that flight which the Convention had pronounced an abdication. The Lords had, therefore, not only refused to admit him to a share of their privileges, but had sent him to prison for presuming to c ll himself one of their order. He had, however, by humbling himself and by withdrawing his claim, obtained his liberty.‡ Though the submissive language which he had condescended to use on this occasion did not indicate a spirit prepared for martyrdom, he was regarded by his party, and by the world in general, as a man of courage and honor. He still retained the seals of his office, and was still considered by the adherents of indefeasible hereditary right as the real Secretary of State. He was in high favor with Lewis, at whose court he had formerly resided, and had, since the Revolution, been entrusted by the French Government with considerable sums of money for political purposes.§

While Preston was consulting in the capital with the other heads of the faction, the rustic Jacobites were laying in arms, holding musters, and forming themselves into companies, troops, and regiments. There were alarming symptoms in Worcestershire. In Lancashire many gentlemen had received commissions signed by James, called themselves colonels and captains, and made out long lists of non-commissioned officers and privates. Letters from Yorkshire brought news that large bodies of men, who seemed to have met for no good purpose,

---

* "Le bon effet, Sire, que ces lettres d'Escosse et d'Angleterre ont produit, est qu'elles ont enfin persuadé le Roy d'Angleterre qu'il ne recouvrera ses estats que les armes à la main; et ce n'est pas peu de l'en avoir convaincu."

† Van Citters to the States General, March 1-11, 1689. Van Citters calls Penn "den bekenden Archquaker."

‡ See his trial in the Collection of State Trials, and the Lords' Journals of Nov. 11, 12 and 27, 1689.

§ One remittance of two thousand pistoles is mentioned in a letter of Croissy to Avaux, Feb. 16-26, 1689. James, in a letter dated Jan. 26, 1689, directs Preston to consider himself as still Secretary, notwithstanding Melfort's appointment.

had been seen on the moors near Knaresborough. Letters from Newcastle gave an account of a great match at football which had been played in Northumberland, and was suspected to have been a pretext for a gathering of the disaffected. In the crowd, it was said, were a hundred and fifty horsemen well mounted and armed, of whom many were Paptists.*

Meantime packets of letters full of treason were constantly passing and repassing between Kent and Picardy, and between Wales and Ireland. Some of the messengers were honest fanatics: but others were mere mercenaries, and trafficked in the secrets of which they were the bearers.

Of these double traitors the most remarkable was William Fuller. This man has himself told us that, when he was very young, he fell in with a pamphlet which contained an account of the flagitious life and horrible death of Dangerfield. The boy's imagination was set on fire: he devoured the book: he almost got it by heart; and he was soon seized, and ever after haunted, by a strange presentiment that his fate would resemble that of the wretched adventurer whose history he had so eagerly read.† It might have been supposed that the prospect of dying in Newgate, with a back flayed and an eye knocked out, would not have seemed very attractive. But experience proves that there are some distempered minds for which notoriety, even when accompanied with pain and shame, has an irresistible fascination. Animated by this loathsome ambition, Fuller equalled, and perhaps surpassed, his model. He was bred a Roman Catholic, and was page to Lady Melfort, when lady Melfort shone at Whitehall as one of the loveliest women in the train of Mary of Modena. After the Revolution, he followed his mistress to France, was repeatedly employed in delicate and perilous commissions, and was thought at Saint Germains to be a devoted servant of the House of Stuart. In truth, however, he had, in the course of one of his expeditions to London, sold himself to the new government, and had abjured the faith in which he had been brought up. The honor, if it is to be so called, of turning him from a worthless Papist into a worthless Protestant, he ascribed, with

---

* Narcissus Luttrell's Diary; Commons' Journals, May 14, 15, 20, 1690; Kingston's True History, 1697.

† The Whole Life of Mr. William Fuller, being an Impartial Account of his Birth, Education, Relations, and Introduction into the service of the late King James and his Queen, together with a True Discovery of the Intrigues for which he lies now confined; as also of the Persons that employed and assisted him therein, with his Hearty Repentance for the Misdemeanors he did in the late Reign, and all others whom he hath injured; impartially writ by Himself during his Confinement in the Queen's Bench, 1703. Of course I shall use this narrative with caution.

characteristic impudence, to the lucid reasoning and blameless life of Tillotson.

In the spring of 1690, Mary of Modena wished to send to her correspondents in London some highly important despatches. As these despatches were too bulky to be concealed in the clothes of a single messenger, it was necessary to employ two confidential persons. Fuller was one. The other was a zealous young Jacobite named Crone. Before they set out, they received full instructions from the Queen herself. Not a scrap of paper was to be detected about them by an ordinary search; but their buttons contained letters written in invisible ink.

The pair proceeded to Calais. The governor of that town furnished them with a boat, which, under cover of the night, set them on the low marshy coast of Kent, near the lighthouse of Dungeness. They walked to a farmhouse, procured horses, and took different roads to London. Fuller hastened to the palace at Kensington, and delivered the documents with which he was charged into the King's hand. The first letter which William unrolled seemed to contain only florid compliments: but a pan of charocal was lighted: a liquor well known to the diplomatists of that age was applied to the paper: an unsavory steam filled the closet; and lines full of grave meaning began to appear.

The first thing to be done was to secure Crone. He had unfortunately had time to deliver his letters before he was caught; but a snare was laid for him into which he easily fell. In truth, the sincere Jacobites were generally wretched plotters. There was among them an unusually large proportion of sots, braggarts, and babblers; and Crone was one of these. Had he been wise, he would have shunned places of public resort, kept strict guard over his tongue, and stinted himself to one bottle at a meal. He was found by the messengers of the government at a tavern table in Grace-church Street, swallowing bumpers the health of King James, and ranting about the coming restoration, the French fleet, and the thousands of honest Englishmen who were awaiting the signal to rise in arms for their rightful Sovereign. He was carried to the Secretary's office at Whitehall. He at first seemed to be confident and at his ease; but when, among the bystanders, Fuller appeared at liberty, and in a fashionable garb, with a sword, the prisoner's courage fell; and he was scarcely able to articulate.*

---

* Fuller's Life of himself.

The news that Fuller had turned king's evidence, that Crone had been arrested, and that important letters from Saint Germains were in the hands of William, flew fast through London, and spread dismay among all who were conscious of guilt.* It was true that the testimony of one witness, even if that witness had been more respectable than Fuller, was not legally sufficient to convict any person of high treason. But Fuller had so managed matters that several witnesses could be produced to corroborate his evidence against Crone; and, if Crone, under the strong terror of death, should imitate Fuller's example, the heads of all the chiefs of the conspiracy would be at the mercy of the government. The spirits of the Jacobites rose, however, when it was known that Crone, though repeatedly interrogated by those who had him in their power, and though assured that nothing but a frank confession could save his life, had resolutely continued silent. What effect a verdict of Guilty and the near prospect of the gallows might produce on him remained to be seen. His accomplices were by no means willing that his fortitude should be tried by so severe a test. They therefore employed numerous artifices, legal and illegal, to avert a conviction. A woman named Clifford, with whom he had lodged, and who was one of the most active and cunning agents of the Jacobite faction, was entrusted with the duty of keeping him steady to the cause, and of rendering to him services from which scrupulous or timid agents might have shrunk. When the dreaded day came, Fuller was too ill to appear in the witness box, and the trial was consequently postponed. He asserted that his malady was not natural, that a noxious drug had been administered to him in a dish of porridge, that his nails were discolored, that his hair came off, and that able physicians pronounced him poisoned. But such stories, even when they rest on authority much better than his, ought to be received with very great distrust.

While Crone was awaiting his trial, another agent of the Court of Saint Germains, named Tempest, was seized on the road between Dover and London, and was found to be the bearer of numerous letters addressed to malecontents in England.† Every day it became more plain that the State was surrounded by dangers; and yet it was absolutely necessary that at this conjuncture, the Chief of the State should quit his post.

---

* Clarendon's Diary, March 9, 1690; Narcissus Luttrell's Diary.
† Clarendon's Diary, May 10, 1690.

William, with painful anxiety, such as he alone was able to conceal under an appearance of stoical serenity, prepared to take his departure. Mary was in agonies of grief; and her distress affected him more than was imagined by those who judged of his heart by his demeanor.* He knew too that he was about to leave her surrounded by difficulties with which her habits had not qualified her to contend. She would be in constant need of wise and upright counsel; and where was such counsel to be found? There were indeed among his servants many able men, and a few virtuous men. But, even when he was present, their political and personal animosities had too often made both their abilities and their virtues useless to him. What chance was there that the gentle Mary would be able to restrain that party spirit and that emulation which had been but very imperfectly kept in order by her resolute and politic husband? If the interior cabinet which was to assist the Queen were composed exclusively either of Whigs or of Tories, half the nation would be disgusted. Yet, if Whigs and Tories were mixed, it was certain that there would be constant dissension. Such was William's situation that he had only a choice of evils.

All these difficulties were increased by the conduct of Shrewsbury. The character of this man is a curious study. He seemed to be the petted favorite both of nature and of fortune. Illustrious birth, exalted rank, ample possessions, fine parts, extensive acquirements, an agreeable person, manners singularly graceful and engaging, combined to make him an object of admiration and envy. But, with all these advantages, he had some moral and intellectual peculiarities which made him a torment to himself and to all connected with him. His conduct at the time of the Revolution had given the world a high opinion, not merely of his patriotism, but of his courage, energy, and decision. It should seem, however, that youthful enthusiasm and the exhilaration produced by public sympathy and applause had, on that occasion, raised him above himself. Scarcely any other part of his life was of a piece with that splendid commencement. He had hardly become Secretary of State when it appeared that his nerves were too weak for such a post. The daily toil, the heavy responsibility, the failures, the mortifications, the obloquy, which are inseparable from power, broke his spirit, soured his temper, and impaired his health. To such natures as his the sustaining power of high

---

* He wrote to Portland, "Je plains la povre reine, qui est en des terribles afflictions."

religious principle seems to be peculiarly necessary; and unfortunately Shrewsbury had, in the act of shaking off the yoke of that superstition in which he had been brought up, liberated himself also from more salutary bands which might perhaps have braced his too delicately constituted mind into steadfastness and uprightness. Destitute of such support, he was, with great abilities, a weak man, and though endowed with many amiable and attractive qualities, could not be called an honest man. For his own happiness, he should either have been much better or much worse. As it was, he never knew either that noble peace of mind which is the reward of rectitude, or that abject peace of mind which springs from impudence and insensibility. Few people who have had so little power to resist temptation have suffered so cruelly from remorse and shame.

To a man of this temper the situation of a minister of state during the year which followed the Revolution must have been constant torture. The difficulties by which the government was beset on all sides, the malignity of its enemies, the unreasonableness of its friends, the virulence with which the hostile factions fell on each other and on every mediator who attempted to part them, might indeed have discouraged a more resolute spirit. Before Shrewsbury had been six months in office, he had completely lost heart and head. He began to address to William letters which it is difficult to imagine that a prince so strong-minded can have read without mingled compassion and contempt. "I am sensible,"—such was the constant burden of these epistles,—"that I am unfit for my place. I cannot exert myself. I am not the same man that I was half a year ago. My health is giving way. My mind is on the rack. My memory is failing. Nothing but quiet and retirement can restore me." William returned friendly and soothing answers; and for a time these answers calmed the troubled mind of his minister.* But at length the dissolution, the general election, the change in the Commissions of Peace and Lieutenancy, and finally the debates on the two Abjuration Bills, threw Shrewsbury into a state bordering on distraction. He was angry with the Whigs for using the King ill, and still more angry with the King for showing favor to the Tories. At what moment and by what influence the unhappy man was induced to commit a treason, the consciousness of which threw a dark shade over all his remaining years, is not accurately known. But it is highly probable that his mother, who, though the most abandoned of women, had

---

* See the Letters of Shrewsbury in Coxe's Correspondence, Part I, chap. i.

great power over him, took a fatal advantage of some unguarded hour, when he was irritated by finding his advice slighted, and that of Danby and Nottingham preferred. She was still a member of that church which her son had quitted, and may have thought that, by reclaiming him from rebellion, she might make some atonement for the violation of her marraige vow and the murder of her lord.* What is certain is that, before the end of the spring of 1690, Shrewsbury had offered his services to James, and that James had accepted them. One proof of the sincerity of the convert was demanded. He must resign the seals which he had taken from the hand of the usurper.† It is probable that Shrewsbury had scarcely committed his fault when he began to repent of it. But he had not strength of mind to stop short in the path of evil. Loathing his own baseness, dreading a detection which must be fatal to his honor, afraid to go forward, afraid to go back, he underwent tortures of which it is impossible to think without commiseration. The true cause of his distress was as yet a profound secret: but his mental struggles and changes of purpose were generally known, and furnished the town, during some weeks, with topics of conversation. One night, when he was actually setting out in a state of great excitement for the palace, with the seals in his hand, he was induced by Burnet to defer his resignation for a few hours. Some days later the eloquence of Tillotson was employed for the same purpose.‡ Three or four times the Earl laid the ensigns of his office on the table of the royal closet, and was three or four times induced, by the kind expostulations of the master whom he was conscious of having wronged, to take them up and carry them away. Thus the resignation was deferred till the eve of the King's departure. By that time agitation had thrown Shrewsbury into a low fever. Bentinck, who made a last effort to persuade him to retain office, found him in bed and too ill for conversation.§ The resignation so often tendered was at last accepted, and during some months Nottingham was the only Secretary of State.

It was no small addition to William's trouble that, at such a moment, his government should be weakened by this defec-

---

* That Lady Shrewsbury was a Jacobite, and did her best to make her son so, is certain from Lloyd's Paper of May 1694, which is among the Nairne MSS., and was printed by Macpherson.

† This is proved by a few words in a paper which James, in November 1692, laid before the French government. "Il y a," says he, "le Comte de Shrusbery, qui, étant Secrétaire d'Etat du Prince d'Orange, s'est défait de sa charge par mon ordre." One copy of this most valuable paper is in the Archives of the French Foreign Office. Another is among the Nairne MSS. in the Bodleian Library. A translation into English will be found in Macpherson's collection.

‡ Burnet, ii. 45.   § Shrewsbury to Somers, Sept 22, 1697.

tion. He tried, however, to do his best with the materials which remained to him, and finally selected nine privy councillors, by whose advice he enjoined Mary to be guided. Four of these, Devonshire, Dorset, Monmouth, and Edward Russell, were Whigs. The other five, Caermarthen, Pembroke, Nottingham, Marlborough, and Lowther, were Tories.*

William ordered the nine to attend him at the office of the Secretary of State. When they were assembled, he came leading in the Queen, desired them to be seated, and addressed to them a few earnest and weighty words. "She wants experience," he said: "but I hope that, by choosing you to be her counsellors, I have supplied that defect. I put my kingdom into your hands. Nothing foreign or domestic shall be kept secret from you. I implore you to be diligent and to be united."† In private he told his wife what he thought of the characters of the Nine; and it should seem, from her letters to him, that there were few of the number for whom he expressed any high esteem. Marlborough was to be her guide in military affairs, and was to command the troops in England. Russell, who was Admiral of the Blue, and had been rewarded for the service which he had done at the time of the Revolution with the lucrative place of Treasurer of the Navy, was well fitted to be her adviser on all questions relating to the fleet. But Caermarthen was designated as the person on whom, in case of any difference of opinion in the council, she ought chiefly to rely. Caermarthen's sagacity and experience were unquestionable: his principles, indeed, were lax: but if there was any person in existence to whom he was likely to be true, that person was Mary. He had long been in a peculiar manner her friend and servant: he had gained a high place in her favor by bringing about her marriage; and he had, in the Convention, carried his zeal for her interest to a length which she had herself blamed as excessive. There was, therefore, every reason to hope that he would serve her at this critical conjuncture with sincere good will.‡

One of her nearest kinsmen, on the other hand, was one of her bitterest enemies. The evidence which was in the possession of the government proved beyond dispute that Clarendon

---

* Among the State Poems (vol. ii. p. 211) will be found a piece which some ignorant editor has entitled, "A Satyr written when the K—— went to Flanders and left nine Lords Justices." I have a manuscript copy of this satire, evidently contemporary, and bearing the date 1690. It is indeed evident at a glance that the nine persons satirized are the nine members of the interior council which William appointed to assist Mary when he went to Ireland. Some of them never were Lords Justices.

† From a narrative written by Lowther, which is among the Mackintosh MSS.

‡ See Mary's Letters to William, published by Dalrymple.

was deeply concerned in the Jacobite scheme of insurrection,
But the Queen was most unwilling that her kindred should be
harshly treated; and William, remembering through what ties
she had broken, and what reproaches she had incurred, for his
sake, readily gave her uncle's life and liberty to her intercession. But before the King set out for Ireland, he spoke seriously to Rochester. "Your brother has been plotting against
me. I am sure of it. I have the proofs under his own hand.
I was urged to leave him out of the Act of Grace ; but I would
not do what would have given so much pain to the Queen. For
her sake I forgive the past: but my Lord Clarendon will do
well to be cautious for the future. If not, he will find that
these are no jesting matters." Rochester communicated the
admonition to Clarendon. Clarendon, who was in constant
correspondence with Dublin and Saint Germains, protested
that his only wish was to be quiet, and that, though he felt a
scruple about the oaths, the existing government had not a
more obedient subject than he purposed to be.*

Among the letters which the government had intercepted
was one from James to Penn. That letter, indeed, was not
legal evidence to prove that the person to whom it was addressed had been guilty of high treason : but it raised suspi-
cions which are now known to have been well founded. Penn
was brought before the Privy Council, and interrogated. He
said very truly that he could not prevent people from writing
to him, and that he was not accountable for what they might
write him. He acknowledged that he was bound to the late
King by ties of gratitude and affection which no change of fortune could dissolve " I should be glad to do him any service
in his private affairs : but I owe a sacred duty to my country ;
and therefore I was never so wicked as even to think of endeavoring to bring him back." This was a falsehood; and
William was probably aware that it was so. He was unwilling
however to deal harshly with a man who had many titles to
respect, and who was not likely to be a very formidable plotter.
He therefore declared himself satisfied, and proposed to discharge the prisoner. Some of the Privy Councillors, however,
remonstrated; and Penn was required to give bail.†

On the day before William's departure, he called Burnet
into his closet, and, in firm but mournful language, spoke of
the dangers which on every side menaced the realm, of the
fury of the contending factions, and of the evil spirit which

---

* Clarendon's Diary, May 30, 1690. † Gerard Crosse.

seemed to possess too many of the clergy. "But my trust is in God. I will go through with my work or perish in it. Only I cannot help feeling for the poor Queen; and twice he repeated with unwonted tenderness, "the poor Queen." "If you love me," he added, "wait on her often, and give her what help you can. As for me, but for one thing, I should enjoy the prospect of being on horseback and under canva again. For I am sure that I am fitter to direct a campaign than to manage your Houses of Lords and Commons. But though I know that I am in the path of duty, it is hard on my wife that her father and I must be opposed to each other in the field. God send that no harm may happen to him. Let me have your prayers, Doctor." Burnet retired greatly moved, and doubtless put up, with no common fervor, those prayers for which his master had asked.*

On the following day, the fourth of June, the King set out for Ireland. Prince George had offered his services, had equipped himself at great charge, and fully expected to be complimented with a seat in the royal coach. But William, who promised himself little pleasure or advantage from His Royal Highness's conversation, and who seldom stood on ceremony, took Portland for a travelling companion, and never once, during the whole of that eventful campaign, seemed to be aware of the Prince's existence.† George, if left to himself, would hardly have noticed the affront. But, though he was too dull to feel, his wife felt for him; and her resentment was studiously kept alive by mischief-makers of no common dexterity. On this, as on many other occasions, the infirmities of William's temper proved seriously detrimental to the great interests of which he was the guardian. His reign would have been far more prosperous if, with his own courage, capacity, and elevation of mind, he had had a little of the easy good humor and politeness of his uncle Charles.

In four days the King arrived at Chester, where a fleet of transports was awaiting the signal for sailing. He embarked on the eleventh of June, and was conveyed across Saint George's Channel by a squadron of men of war under the command of Sir Cloudesley Shovel. ‡

The month which followed William's departure from London was one of the most eventful and anxious months in the

---

* Burnet, ii. 46. † The Duchess of Marlborough's Vindication.
‡ London Gazettes, June, 5, 12, 16, 1690; Hop to the States General from Chester. June 9, 1; Hop attended William to Ireland as envoy from the States.

whole history of England. A few hours after he had set out, Crone was brought to the bar of the Old Bailey. A great array of judges was on the bench. Fuller had recovered sufficiently to make his appearance in court; and the trial proceeded. The Jacobites had been indefatigable in their efforts to ascertain the political opinions of the persons whose names were on the jury list. So many were challenged that there was some difficulty in making up the number of twelve; and among the twelve was one on whom the malecontents thought that they could depend. Nor were they altogether mistaken; for this man held out against his eleven companions all night and half the next day; and he would probably have starved them into submission had not Mrs. Clifford, who was in league with him, been caught throwing sweetmeats to him through the window. His supplies having been cut off, he yielded; and a verdict of Guilty, which, it was said, cost two of the jurymen their lives, was returned. A motion in arrest of judgment was instantly made, on the ground that a Latin word endorsed on the back of the indictment was incorrectly spelt. The objection was undoubtedly frivolous. Jeffreys would have at once overruled it with a torrent of curses, and would have proceeded to the most agreeable part of his duty, that of describing to the prisoner the whole process of half-hanging, disembowelling, mutilating, and quartering. But Holt and his brethren remembered that they were now for the first time since the Revolution trying a culprit on a charge of high treason. It was, therefore, desirable to show, in a manner not to be misunderstood, that a new era had commenced, and that the tribunals would in future rather err on the side of humanity than imitate the cruel haste and levity with which Cornish had, when pleading for his life, been silenced by servile judges. The passing of the sentence was, therefore, deferred: a day was appointed for considering the point raised by Crone; and counsel were assigned to argue in his behalf. "This would not have been done, Mr. Crone," said the Lord Chief Justice significantly, "in either of the last two reigns." After a full hearing, the Bench unanimously pronounced the error to be immaterial; and the prisoner was condemned to death. He owned that his trial had been fair, thanked the judges for their patience, and besought them to intercede for him with the Queen.*

He was soon informed that his fate was in his own hands.

* Clarendon's Diary, June 7 and 12, 1690; Narcissus Luttrell's Diary; Baden, the Dutch Secretary of Legation, to Van Citters. June 10-20: Fuller's Life of himself; Welwood's Mercurius Reformatus, June 11, 1690.

The government was willing to spare him if he would earn his pardon by a full confession. The struggle in his mind was terrible and doubtful. At one time Mrs. Clifford, who had access to his cell, reported to the Jacobite chiefs that he was in a great agony. He could not die, he said: he was too young to be a martyr.* The next morning she found him cheerful and resolute.† He held out till the eve of the day fixed for his execution. Then he sent to ask for an interview with the Secretary of State. Nottingham went to Newgate: but, before he arrived, Crone had changed his mind, and was determined to say nothing. "Then," said Nottingham, "I shall see you no more: for to-morrow will assuredly be your last day." But, after Nottingham had departed, Monmouth repaired to the jail, and flattered himself that he had shaken the prisoner's resolution. At a very late hour that night came a respite for a week.‡ The week however passed away without any disclosure: the gallows and quartering block were ready at Tyburn: the sledge and axe were at the door of Newgate: the crowd was thick all up Holborn Hill and along the Oxford road; when a messenger brought another respite, and Crone, instead of being dragged to the place of execution, was conducted to the Council chamber at Whitehall. His fortitude had been at last overcome by the near prospect of death; and on this occasion he gave important information.§

Such information as he had it in his power to give was indeed at that moment much needed. Both an invasion and an insurrection were hourly expected.‖ Scarcely had William set out from London when a great French fleet commanded by the Count of Tourville left the port of Brest and entered the British Channel. Tourville was the ablest maritime commander that his country then possessed. He had studied every part of his profession. It was said of him that he was competent to fill any place on shipboard from that of carpenter up to that of Admiral. It was said of him, also, that to the dauntless courage of a seaman he united the suavity and urbanity of an accomplished gentleman.¶ He now stood over to the English shore, and approached it so near that his ships could be plainly descried from the ramparts of Plymouth. From Plymouth he proceeded slowly along the coast of Devonshire and Dorset-

---

* Clarendon's Diary, June 8, 1690. † Clarendon's Diary, June 10.
‡ Baden to Van Citters, June 20-30, 1690: Clarendon's Diary, June 19; Luttrell's Diary.
§ Clarendon's Diary, June 25.
‖ Luttrell's Diary.
¶ Memoirs of Saint Simon.

shire. There was great reason to apprehend that his movements had been concerted with the English malecontents.*

The Queen and her Council hastened to take measures for the defence of the country against both foreign and domestic enemies. Torrington took the command of the English fleet which lay in the Downs, and sailed to Saint Helens'. He was there joined by a Dutch squadron under the command of Evertsen. It seemed that the cliffs of the Isle of Wight would witness one of the greatest naval conflicts recorded in history. A hundred and fifty ships of the line could be counted at once from the watchtower of Saint Catharine. On the east of the huge precipice of Black Gang Chine, and in full view of the richly wooded rocks of Saint Lawrence and Ventnor, were collected the maritime forces of England and Holland. On the west, stretching to that white cape where the waves roar among the Needles, lay the armament of France.

It was on the twenty-sixth of June, less than a fortnight after William had sailed for Ireland, that the hostile fleets took up these positions. A few hours earlier, there had been an important and anxious sitting of the Privy Council at Whitehall. The malecontents who were leagued with France were alert and full of hope. Mary had remarked, while taking her airing, that Hyde Park was swarming with them. The whole board was of opinion that it was necessary to arrest some persons of whose guilt the government had proofs. When Clarendon was named, something was said in his behalf by his friend and relation Sir Henry Capel. The other councillors stared, but remained silent. It was no pleasant task to accuse the Queen's kinsman in the Queen's presence. Mary had scarcely ever opened her lips at Council : but now, being possessed of clear proofs of her uncle's treason in his own handwriting, and knowing that respect for her prevented her advisers from proposing what the public safety required, she broke silence. " Sir Henry," she said, " I know, and everybody here knows as well as I, that there is too much against my Lord Clarendon to leave him out." The warrant was drawn up; and Capel signed it with the rest. " I am more sorry for Lord Clarendon," Mary wrote to her husband, " than, may be, will be believed." That evening, Clarendon and several other noted Jacobites, were lodged in the Tower.†

---

* London Gazette, June 26, 1690; Baden to Van Citters, $\frac{\text{June 24,}}{\text{July 4.}}$

† Mary to William, June 26, 1690; Clarendon's Diary of the same date ; Narcissus Luttrell's Diary.

When the Privy Council had risen, the Queen and the interior Council of Nine had to consider a question of the gravest importance. What orders were to be sent to Torrington? The safety of the State might depend on his judgment and presence of mind; and some of Mary's advisers apprehended that he would not be found equal to the occasion. Their anxiety increased when news came that he had abandoned the coast of the Isle of Wight to the French, and was retreating before them towards the Straits of Dover. The sagacious Caermarthen and the enterprising Monmouth agreed in blaming these cautious tactics. It was true that Torrington had not so many vessels as Tourville, but Caermarthen thought that, at such a time, it was advisable to fight, although against odds; and Monmouth was, through life, for fighting at all times and against all odds. Russell, who was indisputably one of the best seamen of the age, held that the disparity of numbers was not such as ought to cause any uneasiness to an officer who commanded English and Dutch sailors. He therefore proposed to send to the Admiral a reprimand couched in terms so severe that the Queen did not like to sign it. The language was much softened: but, in the main, Russell's advice was followed. Torrington was positively ordered to retreat no further, and to give battle immediately. Devonshire, however, was still unsatisfied. "It is my duty, Madam," he said, "to tell Your Majesty exactly what I think on a matter of this importance; and I think that my Lord Torrington is not a man to be trusted with the fate of three kingdoms." Devonshire was right: but his colleagues were unanimously of opinion that to supersede a commander in sight of the enemy, and on the eve of a general action, would be a course full of danger; and it is difficult to say that they were wrong. "You must either," said Russell, "leave him where he is, or send for him as a prisoner." Several expedients were suggested. Caermarthen proposed that Russell should be sent to assist Torrington. Monmouth passionately implored permission to join the fleet in any capacity, as a captain, or as a volunteer. "Only let me be once on board; and I pledge my life that there shall be a battle. After much discussion and hesitation, it was resolved that both Russell and Monmouth should go down to the coast.* They set out, but too late. The despatch which ordered Torrington to fight had preceded them. It reached him when he was off Beachy Head. He read it, and was in a great strait. Not to

---

* Mary to William, June 28 and July 2, 1690.

give battle was to be guilty of direct disobedience. To give battle was, in his judgment, to incur serious risk of defeat. He probably suspected,—for he was of a captious and jealous temper,—that the instructions which placed him in so painful a dilemma had been framed by enemies and rivals with a design unfriendly to his fortune and his fame. He was exasperated by the thought that he was ordered about and overruled by Russell, who, though his inferior in professional rank, exercised, as one of the Council of Nine, a supreme control over all the departments of the public service. There seems to be no sufficient ground for charging Torrington with disaffection. Still less can it be suspected that an officer, whose whole life had been passed in confronting danger, and who had always borne himself bravely, wanted the personal courage which hundreds of sailors on board of every ship under his command possessed. But there is a higher courage of which Torrington was wholly destitute. He shrank from all responsibility, from the responsibility of fighting, and from the responsibility of not fighting; and he succeeded in finding out a middle way which united all the inconveniences which he wished to avoid. He would conform to the letter of his instructions: yet he would not put everything to hazard. Some of his ships should skirmish with the enemy: but the great body of his fleet should not be risked. It was evident that the vessels which engaged the French would be placed in a most dangerous situation, and would suffer much loss; and there is but too good reason to believe that Torrington was base enough to lay his plans in such a manner that the danger and loss might fall almost exclusively to the share of the Dutch. He bore them no love; and in England they were so unpopular that the destruction of their whole squadron was likely to cause fewer murmurs than the capture of one of our own frigates.

It was on the twenty-ninth of June that the Admiral received the orders to fight. The next day, at four in the morning, he bore down on the French fleet and formed his vessels in order of battle. He had not sixty sail of the line, and the French had at least eighty; but his ships were more strongly manned than those of the enemy. He placed the Dutch in the van and gave them the signal to engage. That signal was promptly obeyed. Evertsen and his countrymen fought with a courage to which both their English allies and their French enemies, in spite of national prejudices, did full justice. In none of Van Tromp's or DeRuyter's battles had the honor of the Batavian flag been more gallantly upheld. During many hours the van maintained the unequal contest with very little assistance from any other part of the fleet. At length the Dutch Admiral drew off, leaving one shattered and dismasted hull to the enemy. His second in command and several officers of high rank had fallen. To keep the sea against the French after this disastrous and ignominious action was impossible. The Dutch ships which had come out of the fight were in a lamentable condition. Torrington ordered some of them to be destroyed: the rest he took in tow: he then fled along the coast of Kent, and sought a refuge in the Thames. As soon as he was in the river, he ordered all the buoys to be pulled up, and thus made the navigation so dangerous, that the pursuers could not venture to follow him.*

It was, however, thought by many, and especially by the French ministers, that, if Tourville had been more enterprising, the allied fleet might have been destroyed. He seems to have borne, in one respect, too much resemblance to his vanquished opponent. Though a brave man, he was a timid commander. His life he exposed with careless gayety; but it was said that he was nervously anxious and pusillanimously cautious when his professional reputation was in danger. He was so much annoyed by these censures that he soon became, unfortunately for his country, bold even to temerity.†

There has scarcely ever been so sad a day in London as that on which the news of the Battle of Beachy Head arrived. The shame was insupportable: the peril was imminent. What if the victorious enemy should do what De Ruyter had done? What if the dockyards of Chatham should again be destroyed? What if the Tower itself should be bombarded? What if the vast wood of masts and yardarms below London Bridge should be in a blaze? Nor was this all. Evil tidings had just arrived from the Low Countries. The allied forces under Waldeck had, in the neighborhood of Fleurus, encountered the French commanded by the Duke of Luxemburg. The day

---

* Report of the Commissioners of the Admiralty to the Queen, dated Sheerness, July 18, 1690; Evidence of Captains Cornwall, Jones, Martin and Hubbard, and of Vice Admiral Delaval; Burnet, ii. 52, and Speaker Onslow's note; Mémoires du Maréchal de Tourville; Memoirs of Transactions at Sea by Josiah Burchett, Esq., Secretary to the Admiralty, 1703; London Gazette, July 3; Historical and Political Mercury for July 1690; Mary to William, July 2; Torrington to Caermarthen, July 1. The account of the battle in the Paris Gazette of July 15, 1690, is not to be read without shame. "On a sçeu que les Hollandois s'estoient très bien battus, et qu'ils s'estoient comportez en cette occasion en braves gens, mais que les Anglois n'en avoient pas agi de même." In the French official relation of the battle of Cape Bevézier,—an odd corruption of Pevensey,—are some passages to the same effect: "Les Hollandois combattirent avec beaucoup de courage et de fermeté; mais ils ne furent pas bien secondez par les Anglois." "Les Anglois se distinguèrent des vaisseaux de Hollande par le peu de valeur qu'ils montrèrent dans le combat."

† Life of James, ii. 409; Burnet, ii. 5.

had been long and fiercely disputed. At length the skill of
the French general and the impetuous valor of the French
cavalry had prevailed.* Thus at the same moment the army
of Lewis was victorious in Flanders, and his navy was in undisputed possession of the Channel. Marshal Humieres with
a considerable force lay not far from the Straits of Dover. It
had been given out that he was about to join Luxemburg. But
the information which the English government received from
able military men in the Netherlands and from spies who mixed
with the Jacobites, and which to so great a master of the art
of war as Marlborough seemed to deserve serious attention,
was, that the army of Humieres would instantly march to Dun-
kirk and would there be taken on board of the fleet of Tourville.† Between the coast of Artois and the Nore not a single
ship bearing the red cross of Saint George could venture to
show herself. The embarkation would be the business of a
few hours. A few hours more might suffice for the voyage.
At any moment London might be appalled by the news that
twenty thousand French veterans were in Kent. It was notorious that, in every part of the kingdom, the Jacobites had been,
during some months, making preparations for a rising. All
the regular troops who could be assembled for the defence of
the island did not amount to more than ten thousand men. It
may be doubted whether our country has ever passed through
a more alarming crisis than that of the first week of July, 1690.

But the evil brought with it its own remedy. Those little
knew England who imagined that she could be in danger at
once of rebellion and invasion: for in truth the danger of invasion was the best security against the danger of rebellion.
The cause of James was the cause of France; and though, to
superficial observers, the French alliance seemed to be his chief
support, it really was the obstacle which made his restoration
impossible. In the patriotism, the too often unamiable and
unsocial patriotism of our forefathers, lay the secret at once of
William's weakness and of his strength. They were jealous
of his love for Holland: but they cordially sympathized with
his hatred of Lewis. To their strong sentiment of nationality
are to be ascribed almost all those petty annoyances which
made the throne of the Deliverer, from his accession to his death,
so uneasy a seat. But to the same sentiment it is to be ascribed
that his throne, constantly menaced and frequently shaken, was
never subverted. For, much as his people detested his foreign

---

* London Gazette, June 30, 1690; Historical and Political Mercury for July 1690.
† Nottingham to William, July 15, 1690.

favorites, they detested his foreign adversaries still more. The Dutch were Protestants; the French were Papists. The Dutch were regarded as self-seeking, grasping, overreaching allies. The French were mortal enemies. The worst that could be apprehended from the Dutch was that they might obtain too large a share of the patronage of the crown, that they might throw on us too large a part of the burdens of the war, that they might obtain commercial advantages at our expense. But the French would conquer us; the French would enslave us, the French would inflict on us calamities such as those which had turned the fair fields and cities of the Palatinate into a desert. The hop-grounds of Kent would be as the vineyards of the Neckar. The High Street of Oxford and the close of Salisbury would be piled with ruins such as those which covered the spots where the palaces and churches of Heidelberg and Manheim had once stood. The parsonage overshadowed by the old steeple, the farm-house peeping from among beehives and apple-blossoms, the manorial hall embosomed in elms, would be given up to a soldiery which knew not what it was to pity old men, or delicate women, or sucking children. The words, "the French are coming," like a spell, quelled at once all murmurs about taxes and abuses, about William's ungracious manners and Portland's lucrative places, and raised a spirit as high and unconquerable as had pervaded, a hundred years before, the ranks which Elizabeth reviewed at Tilbury. Had the army of Humieres landed, it would assuredly have been withstood by almost every male capable of bearing arms. Not only the muskets and pikes, but the scythes and pitchforks, would have been too few for the hundreds of thousands who, forgetting all distinction of sect or faction, would have risen up like one man to defend the English soil.

The immediate effect, therefore, of the disasters in the Channel and in Flanders was to unite for a moment the great body of the people. The national antipathy to the Dutch seemed to be suspended. Their gallant conduct in the fight at Beachy Head was loudly applauded. The inaction of Torrington was loudly condemned. London set the example of concert and of exertion. The irritation produced by the late election at once subsided. All distinctions of party disappeared. The lord-mayor was summoned to attend the queen. She requested him to ascertain as soon as possible what the capital would undertake to do if the enemy should venture to make a descent. He called together the representatives of the wards, conferred with them, and returned to Whitehall to report that they had unanimously bound themselves to stand by the government with life and fortune; that a hundred thousand pounds were ready to be paid into the Exchequer; that ten thousand Londoners, well armed and appointed, were prepared to march at an hour's notice, and that an additional force, consisting of six regiments of foot, a strong regiment of horse, and a thousand dragoons, should be instantly raised without costing the crown a farthing. Of her majesty the city had nothing to ask but that she would be pleased to set over these troops officers in whom she could confide. The same spirit was shown in every part of the country. Though in the southern counties the harvest was at hand, the rustics repaired with unusual cheerfulness to the muster of the militia. The Jacobite country gentlemen, who had during several months, been making preparations for the general rising which was to take place as soon as William was gone, and as help arrived from France, now that William was gone, now that a French invasion was hourly expected, burned their commissions signed by James, and hid their arms behind wainscots or in haystacks. The Jacobites in the towns were insulted wherever they appeared, and were forced to shut themselves up in their houses from the exasperated populace.*

Nothing is more interesting to those who love to study the intricacies of the human heart than the effect which the public danger produced on Shrewsbury. For a moment he was again the Shrewsbury of 1688. His nature, lamentably unstable, was not ignoble; and the thought that, by standing foremost in the defence of his country at so perilous a crisis, he might repair his great fault and regain his own esteem, gave new energy to his body and his mind. He had retired to Epsom in the hope that quiet and pure air would produce a salutary effect on his shattered frame and wounded spirit. But a few hours after the news of the battle of Beachy Head had arrived, he was at Whitehall, and had offered his purse and sword to the queen. It had been in contemplation to put the fleet under the command of some great nobleman, with two experienced naval officers to advise him. Shrewsbury begged that, if such an arrangement were made, he might be appointed. It concerned, he said, the interest and the honor of every man in the kingdom not to let the enemy ride victorious in the Channel, and he would gladly risk his life to retrieve the lost fame of the English flag.†

---

* Burnet, ii., 53, 54; Narcissus Luttrell's Diary, July 7th, 11th, 1690; London Gazette, July 14th, 1690.
† Mary to William, July 3, 10, 1690; Shrewsbury to Caermarthen, July 15.

His offer was not accepted. Indeed, the plan of dividing the naval command between a man of quality who did not know the points of the compass, and two weather-beaten old seamen who had risen from being cabin-boys to be admirals, was very wisely laid aside. Active exertions were made to prepare the allied squadrons for service. Nothing was omitted which could assuage the natural resentment of the Dutch. The queen sent a privy councillor charged with a special mission to the States General. He was the bearer of a letter to them, in which she extolled the valor of Evertsen's gallant squadron. She assured them that their ships should be repaired in the English dock-yards, and that the wounded Dutchmen should be as carefully tended as wounded Englishmen. It was announced that a strict inquiry would be instituted into the causes of the late disaster; and Torrington, who, indeed, could not at that moment have appeared in public without risk of being torn in pieces, was sent to the Tower.*

During the three days which followed the arrival of the disastrous tidings from Beachy Head, the aspect of London was gloomy and agitated. But on the fourth day all was changed. Bells were pealing: flags were flying; candles were arranged in the windows for an illumination; men were eagerly shaking hands with each other in the streets. A courier had that morning arrived at Whitehall with great news from Ireland.

---

* Mary to the States General, July 12; Burchett's Memoirs; An important Account of some remarkable Passages in the Life of Arthur, Earl of Torrington, 1691.